SSAT* & ISEE* Prep

For P   endent

ns

KAPLAN

PUBLISHING

New York

© 2018 by Kaplan, Inc.

Published by Kaplan Publishing, a division of Kaplan, Inc.
750 Third Avenue
New York, NY 10017

Printed in the United States of America

10 9 8 7 6 5 4 3 2 1

ISBN: 978-1-5062-4258-3

Kaplan Publishing print books are available at special quantity discounts to use for sales promotions, employee premiums, or educational purposes. For more information or to purchase books, please call the Simon & Schuster special sales department at 866-506-1949.

TABLE OF CONTENTS

Part 1: SSAT Workshop

Chapter 1: Inside the SSAT 3

Chapter 2: SSAT Analogies 11

Part 2: ISEE Workshop

Chapter 3: Inside the ISEE 45

Chapter 4: ISEE Sentence Completions.. 51

Chapter 5: ISEE Quantitative Comparisons 81

Part 3: Common Content for the SSAT and ISEE

Chapter 6: SSAT and ISEE Mastery 101

Chapter 7: Synonyms... 109

Chapter 8: Reading Comprehension 127

Chapter 9: The Essay 191

Chapter 10: Introduction to SSAT and ISEE Math 215

Chapter 11: Word Problems... 229

Chapter 12: Arithmetic.. 245

Chapter 13: Algebra 275

Chapter 14: Geometry and Measurement 293

Chapter 15: Data Analysis and Probability 321

Part 4: Learning Resources

Chapter 16: Study Planning. 341

Chapter 17: Managing Your Stress 355

Chapter 18: Verbal Wrap-Up 361

Chapter 19: Verbal Reference 373

Chapter 20: Math Wrap-Up 425

Chapter 21: 100 Essential Math Concepts. 435

Chapter 22: Writing Wrap-Up 463

Part 5: SSAT Practice Tests and Explanations

Chapter 23: SSAT Upper/Middle Level Practice Test 1 475

Chapter 24: SSAT Upper/Middle Level Practice Test 2 547

Chapter 25: Scoring Your SSAT Practice Test. 617

Part 6: ISEE Practice Tests and Explanations

Chapter 26: ISEE Upper/Middle Level Practice Test 1 623

Chapter 27: ISEE Upper/Middle Level Practice Test 2 685

Chapter 28: Scoring Your ISEE Practice Test 747

A NOTE TO STUDENTS: GETTING STARTED

Kaplan's experience shows that the best SSAT and ISEE scores result from active and thorough preparation. We'll give you direction and focus for your training. We'll teach you the specific skills that the test demands and the most effective strategies to help you improve your score. However, your effort is crucial to your success. The more time and effort you spend in preparing for the test, the higher the score you'll earn. In your hands, you have the best test prep available for the SSAT and ISEE, admissions tests for private and independent schools.

This book covers **the Middle and Upper Levels** of the SSAT and ISEE.

This book is for:

SSAT

- Upper Level (for students currently in grades 8–11)

- Middle Level (for students currently in grades 5–7)

ISEE

- Upper Level (for students currently in grades 8–11)

- Middle Level (for students currently in grades 6 and 7)

This book is not for:

SSAT

- Elementary Level (for students currently in grades 3 and 4)

ISEE

- Lower Level (for students currently in grades 4 and 5)

- Primary Level (for students currently in grades 1–3)

This book covers both the Middle and Upper Levels of the SSAT and ISEE—that means these two test levels span six grades! Depending on your current progress in school, you might find some questions too difficult. You should try your best to solve all of the questions, but do not be discouraged if you cannot. Other students in your age group will find these questions hard to solve as well. Keep in mind that your test will be scored in relation to other students your age; this should help relieve some pressure.

Not every topic covered in this book applies equally to the test you will take. At the beginning of each chapter, there is a note indicating what test applies to each topic. Keep an eye out for these notes to guide you in your preparation, and skip those chapters that are not relevant.

Ideally, you should take a couple of months to work through this book. That gives you enough time before Test Day to absorb the strategies thoroughly so that they become second nature during practice and on Test Day. Do just two or three chapters a week and let the material sink in slowly. If you have more than two months, plan to cover some chapters more than once.

If you have less than two months to prepare, however, don't freak out: by working through a chapter or two every day, you can finish this book in a couple of weeks. If you don't have enough time for that, prioritize the chapters that will help you improve your score as much as possible. Use our SmartPoints system and practice tests to determine which topics to study.

Here's how you should approach your preparation:

- Read through each chapter completely, learning from the examples and trying the practice questions. Don't just read passively, however. Work through the passages and questions as much as you can before reading the explanation. The sooner you learn the test's structure, content, and question types, and master Kaplan's strategies, the sooner you can work on your speed.

- Read Chapters 16 and 17 to learn more about stress management and setting the stage for your studying and testing success.

- Take the practice tests under strictly-timed conditions. Score your tests, find out where you need help, and then review the appropriate chapters.

- Create an initial plan for your prep using Chapter 16: Study Planning and revisit this plan each week.

Don't hesitate to take some time off from your SSAT/ISEE preparation when you need to.

Q. It's two days before the SSAT/ISEE and I'm clueless. What should I do?

A. First of all, don't panic. If you have only a day or two to prepare, then you must accept that you won't be able to prepare thoroughly. That doesn't mean you should give up, though, because there are still steps you can take in your final days. First and foremost, get familiar with the test. Then, if you don't have time to do anything else, take a full-length practice test under reasonably test-like conditions. When you have finished that, check your answers to see what you got incorrect and review your results using the explanations.

Q. The test is tomorrow. Should I stay up all night studying geometry formulas or memorizing vocabulary words?

A. The best thing to do now is to keep calm. Read Chapter 17 to find out the best way to survive—and thrive—on Test Day.

Q. I don't feel confident. Should I just guess?

A. That depends on whether you're taking the SSAT or the ISEE. The SSAT penalizes you for incorrect answers (one-quarter of a point), so you want to be careful, but that doesn't mean you should never guess. If you can rule out at least one answer choice, preferably two, you should guess because you have statistically better odds of guessing correctly. If you're taking the ISEE, you should ALWAYS guess because there's no incorrect answer penalty.

Q. What's the most important thing I can do to get ready as quickly as possible?

A. In addition to assessing basic math and verbal skills, the SSAT/ISEE tests your ability to take the test. This means that the most important thing you can do in a short period of time is to familiarize yourself with the directions, the question types, the answer grid, and the overall structure of the test. Read everything carefully; many mistakes are the result of simply not reading thoroughly enough. If you have additional time, visit Chapter 16 to review the Kaplan Methods Cheat Sheet for either the SSAT or the ISEE.

Q. So it's okay to panic, right?

A. No! No matter how prepared you are for the test, stress will hurt your performance, and it's really no fun. Stay confident and don't cram. So…breathe, stay calm, and remember: it's just a test. It does NOT define you!

A NOTE TO PARENTS: GETTING STARTED

Congratulations! By purchasing this book, you have taken the first step toward helping your son or daughter prepare for the SSAT or ISEE, the required admissions tests for independent schools. Each school has a different requirement policy for admissions exams, so check with your schools of interest to find out which test your child should take. These days, many schools accept either test.

How can I help my child prepare for the exam?

This book covers only the Middle and Upper Levels of the SSAT and ISEE. After purchasing this book, sit down with your student and write out a study plan.

If your son or daughter is applying to private high school, chances are that he or she already studies well alone. Check on progress regularly by proctoring practice tests as the test date nears. If your child is at the Middle Level, you may need to be more involved or consider enlisting a tutor for extra support. Regardless of whether your student is preparing for the Upper or Middle Level test, the first step of SSAT/ISEE prep should include taking a practice exam under timed conditions. This will establish a baseline and help the student identify specific areas of opportunity.

What do the scores mean?

Scores are designed to measure a student's potential performance in private school—NOT to measure intelligence. Each level of the SSAT or ISEE encompasses more than one grade level, but students are graded only against others in their own grade.

What should I know about Test Day?

There are a few things you will want to know about Test Day:

- On the SSAT, students must mark their current grade levels on the answer sheet, not the grades they will be entering in the following year. On the ISEE, students must mark the Exam Level. Students entering grade 7 or 8 will take the Middle Level test, while students entering grades 9 through 12 will take the Upper Level test.

- No calculators, cell phones, electronic alarm watches, fitness trackers, or books will be permitted in the test room. You should visit the test maker's website to confirm the exact list of prohibited materials before Test Day.

- For the SSAT, testing often begins at 9:00 a.m., so students should arrive at the test center by 8:15–8:30 a.m. The ISEE start times can vary, so students should confirm their start time using their Verification Letters.

- It is possible to get a good score even if students do not spend time on every question. It's common for students to leave a few questions unanswered on the SSAT because this exam includes a penalty for incorrect answers. Students should never leave questions blank on the ISEE, however, because this exam only considers correct answers when calculating the raw score.

HOW TO USE THIS BOOK

SSAT	ISEE
• Chapters 1–2	• Chapters 3–22
• Chapters 6–22	• Chapter 26: Practice Test 1
• Chapter 23: Practice Test 1	• Chapter 27: Practice Test 2
• Chapter 24: Practice Test 2	• Chapter 28: Scoring Your ISEE Practice Tests
• Chapter 25: Scoring Your SSAT Practice Tests	

FOR ANY TEST CHANGES OR LATE-BREAKING DEVELOPMENTS

The material in this book is up-to-date at the time of publication. However, the test makers may have instituted changes in the test after this book was published. Be sure to carefully read the materials you receive when you register for the test.

For customer service, please contact us at **book.support@kaplan.com**.

PART 1

SSAT Workshop

CHAPTER 1

Inside the SSAT

CHAPTER OBJECTIVES

With practice, this chapter will help you:

1. Describe the structure of the SSAT and the timing of each section

2. Summarize SSAT scoring

THE SSAT EXAM

The SSAT (Secondary School Admission Test) is a required entrance exam at many private and independent schools throughout the United States. The test, created and administered by the Secondary School Admission Test Board in Princeton, New Jersey, is a multiple-choice exam that consists of Verbal, Reading Comprehension, and Quantitative (Math) sections. In addition, there is a writing sample in which you respond to a prompt. This writing sample is not graded, but it is submitted along with your multiple-choice score report to the schools to which you have applied. For the writing sample on the Upper and Middle Levels of the SSAT, students have the option to respond to either of two written prompts. On the Elementary Level of the exam, students will write a short story responding to a picture prompt. The SSAT also includes an unscored experimental section at the end of the exam, which consists of a mix of content questions (Verbal, Reading, and Quantitative). This experimental section provides the exam creators an opportunity to try out new questions that may inform content for future tests.

The SSAT is administered at three different levels:

- Upper Level (for students currently in grades 8–11)
- Middle Level (for students currently in grades 5–7)
- Elementary Level (for students currently in grades 3–4)

Though information is provided below for each level, this book is designed specifically for students who will be taking the Upper Level or Middle Level exam.

Following is a breakdown of the tests.

SSAT Elementary Level		
Section	**Questions**	**Time Allowed**
Quantitative (Math)	30 questions	30 minutes
Verbal	30 questions	20 minutes
Break		15 minutes
Reading	28 questions	30 minutes
Writing Sample	1 picture prompt	15 minutes
Experimental*	15–17 questions	15 minutes
Total	**104–106 questions**	**2 hours, 5 minutes**
*Of the 104–106 items including the writing sample, only 89 questions are scored.		

SSAT Upper and Middle Levels		
Section	**Questions**	**Time Allowed**
Writing Sample	1 prompt	25 minutes
Break		5 minutes
Quantitative (Math)	25 questions	30 minutes
Reading	40 questions	40 minutes
Break		10 minutes
Verbal	60 questions	30 minutes
Quantitative (Math)	25 questions	30 minutes
Experimental*	16 questions	15 minutes
Total	**167 questions**	**3 hours, 5 minutes**
*Of the 167 items including the writing sample, only 150 questions are scored.		

Some things to note for Test Day:

- All questions have five answer choices: A, B, C, D, and E.

- You are not permitted to use calculators, dictionaries, tablets, or rulers. Cell phones and electronic watches, including fitness trackers, are not allowed.

- Bring at least two #2 pencils with erasers; they will not be provided. Neither mechanical pencils nor pens will be allowed.

SCORING

The first thing you might notice with respect to grades is that students in other grade levels are taking the same level test as you. Not to worry! You are graded on the SSAT according to your grade level. In other words, if you're in 9th grade, you aren't expected to get as many questions correct as someone in 11th grade, even though you're taking the same test.

Be careful: you are scored according to the grade level you report on the answer sheet on Test Day. For the SSAT, you must indicate your *current* grade level, not the grade to which you are applying. Given this fact, you can expect to see questions on the test that may be too hard for you. Just remember, you don't need to get every question correct to get a great score.

Keep moving. Timing is extremely tight on the SSAT, so it's critical that you spend your time working on questions that you know you can solve without too much difficulty. Give yourself a time limit for each question, and move on once you reach that limit, even if you haven't answered the question.

Be flexible. You don't have to answer the questions in the order they're presented on the test. If a particular question type is your strength, get points under your belt by tackling those questions first. For the same reason, don't panic when you encounter a tough question. If it's too hard, skip it. You can always return to it later if you reach the end of the section before time is called.

Be careful how you bubble. Don't lose points on Test Day by bubbling in your correct answers in the incorrect place! Here are some tips:

- Circle your chosen answers in the test booklet.

- Enter your answers on the grid five at a time.

- At the end of each section, check your gridded answers against the circled answers in your test booklet.

Your official exam score report will include the following:

A test question breakdown, which is the number of Right, Wrong, and Not Answered questions for each section. Remember, each correct answer increases your raw score by one point, while each incorrect answer decreases your raw score by a quarter of a point (incorrect answer penalty). Omitted questions are not factored into your raw score because you neither gain nor lose points for questions you omit. This raw scored is then turned into your scaled score.

It can be helpful to remind yourself that no matter how difficult the question may be, all questions are worth the same: one point each. Don't waste precious test time agonizing over a difficult question (that you may still not get correct) when you could be answering five easier questions correctly.

Depending on the test you take, the same raw score from one test administration can be converted to different scaled scores and different corresponding percentiles.

Scaled scores are provided for the three subject areas: Verbal, Quantitative (Math), and Reading. Each level of the test has a slightly different scaled score range:

Upper Level Score Range: 500–800

Middle Level Score Range: 440–710

Elementary Level Score Range: 300–600

In addition to scaled scores for Verbal, Quantitative/Math, and Reading, there is a total scaled score for the test as a whole.

Scaled scores on the SSAT are converted to **percentile ranks** to show how you compare to other students in your *norm group*. Percentile ranks describe the percentage of test takers who scored equal to or less than your scaled score. The SSAT score report actually includes two norm groups to produce two sets of percentile ranks. The first set of percentile ranks compares your scores with those of all other students—not just test takers!—of the same grade, regardless of gender. The second set compares your scores with those of other students of the same grade and gender. Both percentile ranks are comparisons with first-time scores from students who have taken the SSAT in the past three years. (For students who have taken the SSAT more than once, only their first set of scores is included in the comparisons.)

Your score report will also contain **scaled score ranges** for each section, which provide a spectrum of scores for your estimated proficiency in each subject area. Your particular score for each subject area is usually located within the center of this range.

How the Incorrect Answer Penalty Works

1. ● ⓑ ⓒ ⓓ ⓔ X $-\frac{1}{4}$
2. ● ⓑ ⓒ ⓓ ⓔ X $-\frac{1}{4}$
3. ● ⓑ ⓒ ⓓ ⓔ X $-\frac{1}{4}$
4. ● ⓑ ⓒ ⓓ ⓔ X $-\frac{1}{4}$
5. ● ⓑ ⓒ ⓓ ⓔ ✓ $+1$
$$= 0$$

As previously explained, there is an incorrect answer penalty on the Upper and Middle Levels of the SSAT. This means that you lose a quarter point for answering a question incorrectly. If you decide to guess on a question, you should try to eliminate incorrect answers to increase the likelihood of picking the correct answer. If you were to guess randomly throughout the exam without strategically eliminating certain choices, the points you lose for incorrect answers would likely cancel out the points you gain for correct answers. However, if you can eliminate at least one incorrect answer, your odds of guessing the correct answer statistically increases to overcome the incorrect answer penalty.

Bottom line: If you can eliminate at least one answer choice, it is in your best interest to guess.

When should you guess? Guess when (and only when) you can eliminate at least one of the incorrect answer choices. Random guessing won't increase your score, but strategic guessing by eliminating incorrect answer choices can be very helpful.

Scores are mailed to you and your school approximately two to three weeks after you take the exam. Make sure you test early enough in the year so schools will receive your scores by application deadlines. If you feel that you have not tested well after you leave the exam, you have the option of canceling your score. To do so, you must send your request to SSAT by mail, fax, or email. This request must be received no later than the Tuesday after Test Day. If you cancel them, your canceled scores will not be sent to any of your designated score recipients.

SMARTPOINTS™

On most standardized tests, certain types of questions are more common than others. For example, on the SSAT, there are more questions that test Algebra than Geometry. The exact number of Algebra and Geometry questions may change from test to test, but the proportion of total questions represented by each category remains relatively constant. Therefore, to get the most points on Test Day, it makes sense to focus the majority of your attention on the areas of the test that are the most common and will provide you the most opportunities to earn more points.

To represent this relative frequency of question types on different tests, Kaplan created SmartPoints. The table below shows a breakdown of SSAT SmartPoints. By studying the information released by the test maker, Kaplan has been able to determine how often certain topics are likely to show up on the test, and, therefore, how many points these topics are worth on Test Day. If you master a given topic, you can expect to earn the corresponding number of SmartPoints on Test Day. The breakdown of SmartPoints for Verbal, Reading Comprehension, and Math are summarized in the following table.

As you work through the chapters in this book, use Kaplan SmartPoints to guide you in your at-home studies. Learn topics that are new to you and review topics with which you are familiar, but always spend more time on topics with the highest number of SmartPoints.

SSAT SmartPoints Categories and Values

	SSAT Upper Level Test Point Values	SSAT Middle Level Test Point Values
Verbal		
Synonyms	150	135
Analogies	150	135
Total Earnable Points	**300**	**270**
Reading Comprehension		
Main Idea	20	15
Supporting Ideas	60	55
Inference	70	65
Vocab-in-Context	20	15
Tone/Style/Figurative Language	60	55
Author's Purpose/Arguments	70	65
Total Earnable Points	**300***	**270****
Quantitative (Math)		
Arithmetic	75	80
Algebra	100	90
Geometry and Measurement	55	50
Data Analysis and Probability	70	50
Total Earnable Points	**300**	**270**

*For Upper Level students, the minimum score is 500 and the maximum score is 800 per section; the difference is 300 earnable points on Test Day.

**For Middle Level students, the minimum score is 440 and the maximum score is 710 per section; the difference is 270 earnable points on Test Day.

HOW TO REGISTER

There are two different types of administration of the SSAT: Standard and Flex. Flex Tests are proctored by educational consultants or schools at times that can be more convenient for busy students' schedules and are subject to an administration fee. The Upper and Middle Level Standard Tests are administered on eight designated Saturdays, one Saturday per month, during the following months: October, November, December, January, February, March, April, and June. (The Elementary Level SSAT is administered on six designated Saturdays, starting in December.) Students may also take the test on a Sunday during the academic year but only with official approval for accommodations due to religious observance.

While most students choose a Standard test option, a Flex test is helpful for students who are unable to meet the eight scheduled Standard times. However, a student can only take one Flex test between August and July. You must register online at the official test website, **http://ssat.org**, to apply for accommodations or Sunday testing, choose a test date and site, pay or apply for a fee waiver, and more.

Phone:	609-683-4440
Email:	info@ssat.org
Fax:	(609) 683-4507
Mail:	SSATB
	CN 5339
	Princeton, NJ 08543

HOW THE SSAT DIFFERS FROM THE ISEE

There are a few main differences between the SSAT and the ISEE:

- On the SSAT, the Verbal section contains Synonym and Analogy questions. On the ISEE, the Verbal section contains Synonym and Sentence Completion questions.

- On the SSAT, there are no Quantitative Comparisons.

- On the SSAT, there is a penalty for an incorrect answer. That means you should only guess if you can eliminate at least one answer choice.

- On the SSAT, there are five answer choices: A, B, C, D, and E. On the ISEE, there are only four answer choices: A, B, C, and D.

CHAPTER 2

SSAT Analogies

CHAPTER OBJECTIVES

With practice, this chapter will help you:

1. Explain the concept of analogy and the format of SSAT Analogy questions

2. Use the Kaplan 3-Step Method for Analogy Questions to answer Analogy questions accurately and efficiently

3. Use Backsolving and educated guessing to answer Analogy questions

Analogies appear **only on the SSAT**. If you are not taking the SSAT, you should skip this section.

THE FORMAT

The SSAT Verbal section has 30 Synonym questions and 30 Analogy questions. The instructions for an Analogy question will tell you to select the pair of words that are *related in the same way* as the two words in the beginning of the question. Those two words are called the *stem words*.

Analogies may seem frightening because they look pretty weird at first glance. You'll feel better about them as soon as you realize that you speak and think in analogies all the time. Anytime you say, "My sister is like a slug," you're drawing an analogy between your sister and slugs—perhaps your sister is as gross as a slug, or maybe she's as slow as a slug getting out of bed in the morning. That may not be the kind of relationship that will appear on your test, but the thinking is the same.

Once you become familiar with their format, you'll find that Analogy questions are pretty straightforward and very predictable. In fact, prepping often gains you more points on Analogies than on any other Verbal question type. With practice, you can learn to get them correct even when you don't know all of the vocabulary words involved.

BRIDGES

SSAT Analogies test your ability to determine relationships between words. These relationships are called *bridges*. There are many possible bridges that could be used in an analogy, but the SSAT tests certain specific relationships time and time again. These are called *classic bridges*.

Learning how to identify the bridge quickly will help you save yourself a lot of time as you go through Analogy questions on Test Day. Six of the most common bridges are listed below in alphabetical order.

Bridge Type 1: Degree

One word is a greater or lesser degree of the other word.

Deafening is to loud could be a Degree Bridge: something deafening is extremely loud.

Bridge Type 2: Function

One word names an object; the other word defines its purpose.

Scissors is to cut could be a Function Bridge: scissors are used to cut.

Bridge Type 3: Part/Whole

One word is a part of the other word.

Arm is to wrist could be a Whole/Part Bridge: a wrist is a part of an arm.

Bridge Type 4: Synonyms/Antonyms

One word has the same or the opposite meaning of the other word.

Fascinating is to engrossing could be a Synonym Bridge: fascinating and engrossing have the same meaning.

Bridge Type 5: Type/Kind

One word is a type or kind of the other.

Cat is to feline could be a Type Bridge: a cat is a type of feline.

Bridge Type 6: Word/Grammar

Both words are related in some language or grammatical way.

Sitting is to sat could be a Grammar Bridge: sitting is present tense and sat is past tense.

Other Bridge Types

In addition to these six classic bridges, there are other classic bridge types you might see on Test Day:

- Association
- Cause-and-Effect
- Definition
- Example
- Individual/Object
- Lack
- Purpose

KAPLAN 3-STEP METHOD FOR ANALOGIES

Putting the relationship in an Analogy question into your own words is a crucial skill to help you handle any question you might see on Test Day. By determining the bridge used in a question, you can approach that question systematically, rather than just using instinct to guess or wasting time trying to find a connection between two things that seem unrelated. Use Kaplan's 3-Step Method for Analogies to answer any Analogy efficiently and effectively:

Step 1. Build a bridge

Step 2. Plug in the answer choices

Step 3. Adjust your bridge if necessary

Take a closer look to see how it works.

Step 1. Build a Bridge

In every Analogy question, there's a strong, definite connection between the two stem words. Your task is to identify this relationship and then look for a similar relationship among the answer pairs. Remember, this relationship is called a bridge.

So, what is a strong, definite relationship?

- The words *flake* and *snow* have a strong, definite connection. A small unit of *snow* is called a *flake*. *Flake is to snow as* could be a question stem.

- The words *flake* and *winter* do not have a strong, definite connection. A flake may or may not have anything to do with winter, and vice versa. *Flake is to winter as* would never be a question stem.

On Test Day, think of your bridge as a short sentence that relates the two words in the stem. Every pair of stem words will have a strong bridge that links them. If you have trouble quickly identifying the bridge for any question, just skip it and come back if you have time.

Step 2. Plug In the Answer Choices

You figured out how the words *flake* and *snow* are related using a Degree Bridge. Now, you need to determine which answer choice relates words in the same way. Don't just rely on your feeling about the words unless you don't know the vocabulary (more on that later). Go through the choices systematically, building bridges between each word pair. Here's how it would work:

Flake is to snow as

(A) storm is to hail

(B) drop is to rain

(C) field is to wheat

(D) stack is to hay

(E) cloud is to fog

When you plug in the answer choices, only one of them makes sense:

Flake is *a small unit of* snow

(A) Is a storm *a small unit of* hail? No.

(B) Is a drop *a small unit of* rain? Yes.

(C) Is a field *a small unit of* wheat? No.

(D) Is a stack *a small unit of* hay? No.

(E) Is a cloud *a small unit of* fog? No.

Since only choice (B) fits the bridge you created, you would be done. Answer the question and move on.

Step 3: Adjust Your Bridge If Necessary

If your bridge is very specific, you won't need to go to step 3, but sometimes you will. For example, consider the following question:

Fish is to gill as

(A) oyster is to shell

(B) penguin is to wing

(C) whale is to tail

(D) mammal is to lung

(E) dolphin is to flipper

Say you made a Whole/Part Bridge: "A fish has a gill." Then, you went to the choices and plugged in that bridge:

A fish *has* a gill.

(A) Does an oyster *have* a shell? Yes.

(B) Does a penguin *have* a wing? Yes.

(C) Does a whale *have* a tail? Yes.

(D) Does a mammal *have* a lung? Yes.

(E) Does a dolphin *have* a flipper? Yes.

Every choice fits! In this case, the bridge was too general, so you'll need to adjust your bridge.

What would a good adjustment be? Try to articulate to yourself the most specific relationship between the words, because the more specific your bridge is, the fewer choices will match it. A good bridge for this pair might be a Purpose Bridge: "A fish uses a gill to breathe." Now try plugging the bridge into the answer choices:

A fish *uses* a gill *to breathe.*

(A) Does an oyster *use* a shell *to breathe*? No.

(B) Does a penguin use a wing *to breathe*? No.

(C) Does a whale use a tail *to breathe*? No.

(D) Does a mammal use a lung *to breathe*? Yes.

(E) Does a dolphin use a flipper *to breathe*? No.

It should now be easier to see the correct answer, choice (D): a mammal *uses* a lung *to breathe*, just like a fish *uses* a gill *to breathe.*

PRACTICE

> Just to make sure you have your strong and weak bridges straight, try the following exercise. For each phrase, decide whether there is a strong relationship or a weak one.

Dog is to canine is a _____ relationship.

Dog is to friendly is a _____ relationship.

Dog is to kennel is a _____ relationship.

Dog is to mammal is a _____ relationship.

Dog is to cat is a _____ relationship.

Dog is to paw is a _____ relationship.

Dog is to puppy is a _____ relationship.

Dog is to hound is a _____ relationship.

Dog is to bark is a _____ relationship.

Dog is to biscuit is a _____ relationship.

ANSWERS AND EXPLANATIONS

Dog is to canine is a _____*strong*_____ relationship.

Dog is to friendly is a _____*weak*_____ relationship.

Dog is to kennel is a _____*strong*_____ relationship.

Dog is to mammal is a _____*strong*_____ relationship.

Dog is to cat is a _____*weak*_____ relationship.

Dog is to paw is a _____*strong*_____ relationship.

Dog is to puppy is a _____*strong*_____ relationship.

Dog is to hound is a _____*strong*_____ relationship.

Dog is to bark is a _____*strong*_____ relationship.

Dog is to biscuit is a _____*weak*_____ relationship.

PREDICTING ON THREE-TERM ANALOGIES

Some Analogies will have three terms in the stem and only one word in each answer choice. For example:

> Delight is to grin as dismay is to
>
> **(A)** frown
>
> **(B)** smile
>
> **(C)** shrug
>
> **(D)** stare
>
> **(E)** giggle

Three-term Analogies aren't very different from two-term Analogies. The key difference is that you need to predict your answer *before* you look at the answer choices. Otherwise, the choices won't make much sense to you. Here's how it works.

First, make your bridge:

> A grin shows delight and a ------- shows dismay.

Now predict your answer. What might show *dismay? Tears,* perhaps, or a *frown.* Look at the answer choices. At this point, the question should be easier than a two-term Analogy, because you already have one of the two words in the answer:

Does a *frown* show dismay? Yes.

Does a *smile* show dismay? No.

Does a *shrug* show dismay? No.

Does a *stare* show dismay? No.

Does a *giggle* show dismay? No.

As you'll see, choice (A) is the answer: a frown shows dismay. That makes a lot of sense. Can you see how much harder this would have been if you hadn't gone through the steps of building a bridge and predicting the answer? You might end up staring blankly at all five words, thinking about all of the reasons why one or the other might work. Always predict your answer on three-term Analogies, and you'll whiz through them in no time.

Practice your skills of prediction on these three stems:

1. Thicket is to bush as grove is to -------.

2. Mason is to brick as carpenter is to -------.

3. Enthusiast is to apathy as miser is to -------.

Now see how well you did on predicting:

1. Thicket is to bush as grove is to *tree*.

2. Mason is to brick as carpenter is to *wood*.

3. Enthusiast is to apathy as miser is to *generosity*.

WHEN YOU GET STUCK

Even with your arsenal of tools, you may run into Analogy questions where you don't know what to do. Perhaps you won't know what a word in the question stem means or how the words relate to one another. What should you do? There are a few strategies that will really increase your chances of getting the question correct, even if you're stuck.

Backsolving

What is Backsolving? It may sound like an obscure form of chiropractic medicine, but it's actually just a nifty way of approaching Analogies when you can't answer them directly. So how does it work?

Backsolving is what you might know as "guess and check." Basically, you skip right past the question stem and head straight for the answer choices so you can plug them into the question. You may be wondering, "How can I figure out the answer without knowing what the question is asking?" Well, you can't necessarily figure out the answer right away, but you can start to eliminate *clearly* incorrect answer choices, leaving fewer options. When you rule out choices that you know can't be correct, the odds are better that you'll pick the correct choice from what's left. For example:

Screwdriver is to tool as

(A) animal is to plant

(B) garden is to bed

(C) banana is to bread

(D) tree is to leaf

(E) rose is to flower

Even if you didn't know that a screwdriver is a type of tool, what could you rule out? Well, in choice A, there's no logical connection between animal and plant, except that they're both living things. Choice B, "garden is to bed," also sounds somewhat off. You could make the argument that a garden has a bed, but does it have to? What about a hanging garden or a rock garden? You can rule out choice B because it has a weak bridge.

BOTH ARE...INCORRECT!

Watch out for the "both are…" trap, shown in choice A in the screwdriver example: Both *animal* and *plant* are part of a larger group, but there's no connection, by definition, between the words themselves. Bread and bananas are both types of food, but what exactly is their relationship? Bananas aren't a type of bread, a lack of bread, or a function of bread. Watch out for this trap, particularly on the more difficult Analogy questions.

Educated Guessing

What if you reach the point where you can't figure out the bridge for the stem words, you can't rule out incorrect answer choices, and you want to cry? Well, first of all, don't cry. It's a waste of time and it makes it difficult to read the questions. You have a few options.

Technique 1: Use Word Parts

You know that the classic bridges discussed earlier in this chapter often show up on SSAT Analogy questions. So, even if you don't know the exact definition of one (or both!) words, you can still make an educated guess about the bridge using your knowledge of language. For example, say you saw this stem:

Word is to philologist as

What might the bridge be? Well, a *philologist* sounds like a type of person who is some sort of scientist (since it ends in *-ologist*), and a *word* is a thing, so maybe a philologist does something with words. Philologist is a tricky word, but you could make a great guess by saying that a philologist studies words…which is exactly right!

Technique 2: Remember the Context

Sometimes a word sounds familiar, but you can't remember why. If that happens, try to think of a place where you may have heard it before. Putting words into context makes it easier to determine their meaning. For example:

Vote is to suffrage as

What does *suffrage* mean? Have you heard of the suffrage movement? Or the suffragists? Think about the word *suffrage* in the context of *voting*. What could the words have to do with each other? Well, suffrage is the right to vote, and the movement to give women the right to vote at the beginning of the 20th century was commonly known as the Suffrage Movement. Just looking at the word *suffrage* in isolation might have left you scratching your head, but putting it in context with the concept of voting could get you back on track and help you home in on the correct answer.

Technique 3: Use Word Charge

Some words give you the feeling that they're either positive or negative. Use this sense to help you figure out the bridge between words in the stem when you don't actually know what one—or both!—of them means!. For example:

Decide whether the following words are positive or negative:

1. *Cruel (+, −) is to clemency (+, −) as*
2. *Boorish (+, −) is to polite (+, −) as*
3. *Animated (+, −) is to ecstatic (+, −) as*
4. *Annoyed (+, −) is to enraged (+, −) as*

So how does word charge help you find the correct answer? Once you determine the charge of the words in the stem pair, you can look for words in the answer choices that have the same charge relationship. If both words in the stem are either positive or negative, both words in the correct answer choice will have the same charge, too, although that charge may be the opposite charge from the pair of words in the question stem. If one stem word is positive and the other is negative, chances are that the correct answer will have the same relationship.

So what charge does each word above have?

1. Cruel: −, clemency: +
2. Boorish: −, polite: +
3. Animated: +, ecstatic: +
4. Annoyed: −, enraged: −

By eliminating even one illogical answer choice, you'll narrow down your choices and have a better chance of getting the question correct. Always keep your eye out for "both are" traps and weak bridges as you work through the Analogy section, and you'll rack up lots of points on even the toughest questions.

PRACTICE QUESTIONS

1. Circumference is to circle as

   (A) diameter is to sphere

   (B) height is to width

   (C) side is to hexagon

   (D) perimeter is to square

   (E) round is to oval

2. Write is to paper as paint is to

   (A) board

   (B) canvas

   (C) brush

   (D) palette

   (E) can

3. Collar is to shirt as

   (A) toe is to shoe

   (B) cuff is to trousers

   (C) waist is to belt

   (D) hat is to head

   (E) zipper is to button

4. Hysteric is to control as

   (A) joke is to laughter

   (B) feeling is to emotion

   (C) absurd is to sense

   (D) calm is to serenity

   (E) passion is to insanity

5. Square is to cube as

   (A) dot is to point

   (B) angle is to triangle

   (C) rectangle is to parallelogram

   (D) hexagon is to octagon

   (E) circle is to sphere

6. Shark is to aquatic as

   (A) world is to hungry

   (B) camel is to terrestrial

   (C) bird is to winged

   (D) bat is to blind

   (E) pig is to hairless

7. Chide is to mild as castigate is to

   (A) tepid

   (B) sweet

   (C) unbeatable

   (D) uncertain

   (E) harsh

8. Abrupt is to gradual as

   (A) corrupt is to virtuous

   (B) stirring is to sudden

   (C) sneaky is to criminal

   (D) remarkable is to alarming

   (E) conspicuous is to extreme

9. Stanza is to poem as

   (A) rhythm is to beat

   (B) verse is to word

   (C) movement is to symphony

   (D) play is to theater

   (E) column is to journal

10. Violin is to string as

    (A) harp is to angelic

    (B) drum is to stick

    (C) score is to music

    (D) oboe is to reed

    (E) bass is to large

11. Canter is to horse as

   (A) hop is to rabbit

   (B) halt is to pony

   (C) hunt is to lion

   (D) beg is to dog

   (E) chew is to cow

12. Baseball is to game as

   (A) hurricane is to storm

   (B) overcast is to cloud

   (C) stadium is to sport

   (D) wind is to tornado

   (E) conflict is to violence

13. Rigid is to bend as

   (A) tremulous is to sway

   (B) incomprehensible is to think

   (C) immortal is to die

   (D) lazy is to perspire

   (E) stiff is to divide

14. Canine is to wolf as feline is to

   (A) panther

   (B) pig

   (C) monkey

   (D) rat

   (E) vulture

15. Rind is to melon as

   (A) skin is to mammal

   (B) armor is to shield

   (C) shell is to claw

   (D) peel is to core

   (E) pod is to vine

16. Mile is to length as

   (A) acre is to land

   (B) inch is to foot

   (C) kilometer is to race

   (D) yard is to fabric

   (E) fathom is to depth

17. Truthful is to dishonest as arid is to

   (A) sublime

   (B) aloof

   (C) innocent

   (D) moist

   (E) clear

18. Tarnish is to silver as

   (A) break is to glass

   (B) dirt is to car

   (C) rust is to iron

   (D) dull is to wax

   (E) dust is to wood

19. Delay is to hasten as

   (A) misunderstand is to dislike

   (B) undermine is to improve

   (C) sink is to descend

   (D) remove is to indict

   (E) facilitate is to impede

20. Think is to daydream as walk is to

   (A) stagger

   (B) crawl

   (C) meander

   (D) run

   (E) prance

21. Gram is to ounce as

    (A) Celsius is to temperature
    (B) minute is to year
    (C) meter is to yard
    (D) ton is to pound
    (E) dollar is to cent

22. Veil is to bride as

    (A) hat is to pitcher
    (B) helmet is to soldier
    (C) crown is to monarch
    (D) apron is to gourmet
    (E) goggles is to scientist

23. Anomalous is to standard as

    (A) rude is to kind
    (B) demonstrative is to impassive
    (C) profound is to brief
    (D) taxing is to exhausting
    (E) stoic is to urbane

24. Wing is to bird as

    (A) scale is to fish
    (B) rudder is to canoe
    (C) foot is to human
    (D) talon is to raptor
    (E) shell is to tortoise

25. Fight is to surrender as resist is to

    (A) affect
    (B) triumph
    (C) evade
    (D) submit
    (E) deny

26. Defilement is to shrine as

    (A) disrespect is to fool
    (B) vilification is to traitor
    (C) execution is to dungeon
    (D) breach is to contract
    (E) ostracism is to politician

27. Restaurant is to pasture as

    (A) fountain is to trough
    (B) meal is to feed
    (C) cafeteria is to lavatory
    (D) kitchen is to dining room
    (E) stable is to barracks

28. Necessity is to luxury as water is to

    (A) oxygen
    (B) food
    (C) sleep
    (D) shelter
    (E) soda

29. Idealistic is to quixotic as

    (A) crazy is to insane
    (B) smart is to intelligent
    (C) jaded is to cynical
    (D) resolute is to stubborn
    (E) weak is to forceful

30. Soap is to bubbles as

    (A) broth is to vegetables
    (B) shower is to steam
    (C) juice is to blender
    (D) oil is to gasoline
    (E) cream is to butter

31. Fish is to school as

   (A) cow is to cattle

   (B) crop is to farm

   (C) gaggle is to geese

   (D) lion is to pride

   (E) general is to army

32. Silo is to grain as

   (A) ramp is to boat

   (B) arsenal is to munitions

   (C) gate is to horse

   (D) student is to school

   (E) meat is to ice

33. Aquarium is to fish as arboretum is to

   (A) elephant

   (B) horse

   (C) flower

   (D) tree

   (E) dog

34. Cadet is to soldier as

   (A) apprentice is to craftsman

   (B) private is to army

   (C) yeoman is to sailor

   (D) rookie is to athlete

   (E) lawyer is to judge

35. Passive is to aggressive as

   (A) simple is to complex

   (B) meek is to overbearing

   (C) shy is to garrulous

   (D) bellicose is to amiable

   (E) terrified is to composed

36. Dime is to coin as almond is to

   (A) fruit

   (B) delicacy

   (C) food

   (D) bush

   (E) nut

37. Ice is to skating as

   (A) highway is to driving

   (B) ballroom is to dancing

   (C) ring is to boxing

   (D) felt is to billiards

   (E) water is to diving

38. Paranoid is to suspicious as

   (A) distraught is to perturbed

   (B) urban is to rural

   (C) wealthy is to affluent

   (D) jubilant is to irate

   (E) despair is to aloof

39. Fireman is to extinguish as

   (A) principal is to teach

   (B) vendor is to sell

   (C) policeman is to warn

   (D) worker is to retire

   (E) accountant is to save

40. Pearl is to oyster as

   (A) silk is to thread

   (B) marble is to statue

   (C) web is to spider

   (D) ivory is to elephant

   (E) calcium is to bone

41. Chandler is to wax as

    (A) cooper is to barrel

    (B) wheelwright is to wheel

    (C) baker is to bread

    (D) carpenter is to wood

    (E) blacksmith is to horseshoe

42. Gathering is to mob as

    (A) frenzy is to shark

    (B) stray is to cat

    (C) fire is to inferno

    (D) storm is to tempest

    (E) filibuster is to speech

43. Acre is to land as

    (A) luminosity is to space

    (B) piquant is to dish

    (C) fathom is to water

    (D) millimeter is to fluid

    (E) second is to velocity

44. Bison is to plains as kangaroo is to

    (A) savanna

    (B) desert

    (C) tundra

    (D) outback

    (E) forest

45. Grape is to vineyard as

    (A) pumpkin is to patch

    (B) cherry is to blossom

    (C) cabbage is to vine

    (D) milk is to dairy

    (E) potato is to orchard

46. Head is to neck as

    (A) arm is to leg

    (B) hand is to glove

    (C) foot is to ankle

    (D) finger is to toe

    (E) ear is to eye

47. Liquid is to gas as condensation is to

    (A) precipitation

    (B) evaporation

    (C) sublimation

    (D) freezing

    (E) crystallization

48. Authenticity is to verify as

    (A) skill is to jump

    (B) competence is to test

    (C) science is to reason

    (D) soundtrack is to compose

    (E) bliss is to uphold

49. Gap is to continuity as

    (A) intermission is to film

    (B) prosperity is to happiness

    (C) native is to tribal

    (D) mannequin is to display

    (E) destruction is to design

50. Wrist is to watch as

    (A) remote control is to button

    (B) wallet is to money

    (C) camper is to tent

    (D) skin is to muscle

    (E) torso is to shirt

51. Watt is to energy as

   (A) joule is to distance
   (P) crime is to civil unrest
   (C) string is to guitar
   (D) grade is to quality
   (E) stock market is to money

52. Mongoose is to mammal as

   (A) bush is to crustacean
   (B) sycamore is to tree
   (C) reptile is to flora
   (D) venom is to snake
   (E) fool is to human

53. Vassal is to king as

   (A) employee is to manager
   (B) financier is to accountant
   (C) stranger is to outsider
   (D) journeyman is to neophyte
   (E) infielder is to outfielder

54. Turtle is to shell as

   (A) lion is to roar
   (B) human is to house
   (C) letter is to mailbox
   (D) cola is to bottle
   (E) disk is to computer

55. Gondola is to Ferris wheel as

   (A) Sun is to galaxy
   (B) wheel is to car
   (C) glove is to boot
   (D) fire is to inferno
   (E) Moon is to Earth

56. Knife is to dull as

   (A) conceptualization is to execution
   (B) tire is to flat
   (C) hammer is to weak
   (D) torch is to burn
   (E) microphone is to static

57. Time is to control as

   (A) tiger is to cage
   (B) strength is to increase
   (C) falsehood is to substantiate
   (D) product is to import
   (E) fool is to follow

58. Shadow is to substantial as

   (A) book is to clever
   (B) forest is to wild
   (C) fire is to raging
   (D) machine is to alive
   (E) currency is to wealth

59. Fervent is to nonchalant as

   (A) stalwart is to timid
   (B) furnace is to heat
   (C) anger is to aggression
   (D) balmy is to torpid
   (E) rancid is to spoiled

60. Ship is to port as

   (A) card is to deck
   (B) leviathan is to ocean
   (C) turn is to game
   (D) flight is to destination
   (E) traveler is to hotel

61. Sketch is to painting as

    (A) dream is to reality
    (B) note is to symphony
    (C) design is to prototype
    (D) amoeba is to dog
    (E) birth is to death

62. Ornamented is to plain as

    (A) shovel is to spade
    (B) conceal is to reveal
    (C) philosophy is to questions
    (D) automobile is to bicycle
    (E) strong is to simple

63. Iron is to steel as

    (A) apathy is to interest
    (B) love is to silence
    (C) wheat is to bread
    (D) structure is to high-rise
    (E) truck is to van

64. Medicine is to illness as

    (A) might is to weakness
    (B) affliction is to malady
    (C) evidence is to vindication
    (D) food is to hunger
    (E) sail is to wind

65. Hope is to optimism as melancholy is to

    (A) sadness
    (B) pessimism
    (C) desolation
    (D) skepticism
    (E) ostracism

66. Fireman is to fire as editor is to

    (A) newspaper
    (B) style
    (C) error
    (D) story
    (E) book

67. Accolade is to accomplishment as disappoint-
    ment is to

    (A) underachievement
    (B) pain
    (C) confusion
    (D) misanthropy
    (E) happiness

68. Conflict is to peace as

    (A) calm is to quiet
    (B) mobile is to stationary
    (C) chaos is to order
    (D) wave is to ripple
    (E) hurricane is to storm

69. Piano is to pianist as

    (A) flute is to flautist
    (B) piccolo is to percussionist
    (C) harpsichord is to harpist
    (D) rhythm is to guitarist
    (E) tenor is to vocalist

70. Punchline is to joke as

    (A) bookend is to shelf
    (B) word is to dictionary
    (C) moral is to fable
    (D) line is to play
    (E) equation is to math

71. Quartz is to mineral as

    (A) grape is to vine
    (B) quadruped is to mammal
    (C) player is to team
    (D) squash is to vegetable
    (E) heat is to fire

72. Cleat is to soccer as skate is to

    (A) tennis
    (B) hockey
    (C) baseball
    (D) skiing
    (E) squash

73. Perimeter is to square as

    (A) chord is to cylinder
    (B) side is to polygon
    (C) degree is to angle
    (D) height is to pyramid
    (E) circumference is to circle

74. Brick is to wall as

    (A) house is to roof
    (B) mortar is to stone
    (C) pixel is to picture
    (D) car is to road
    (E) sand is to beach

75. Incensed is to calm as

    (A) hasty is to lenient
    (B) enraged is to sedate
    (C) tragic is to relaxed
    (D) fussy is to picky
    (E) furious is to angry

76. Speaker is to sound as

    (A) ocean is to water
    (B) projector is to light
    (C) speech is to voice
    (D) orator is to volume
    (E) spray is to geyser

77. Cheese is to milk as

    (A) churn is to butter
    (B) juice is to squeeze
    (C) bread is to grain
    (D) bake is to oven
    (E) apple is to pie

78. City is to Chicago as sport is to

    (A) game
    (B) exercise
    (C) ball
    (D) athlete
    (E) tennis

79. Flower is to sour as

    (A) fable is to table
    (B) morrow is to sorrow
    (C) anemone is to lemony
    (D) flavor is to quaver
    (E) rose is to sweet

80. Raise is to lower as

    (A) port is to starboard
    (B) upward is to onward
    (C) sprint is to dash
    (D) advance is to retreat
    (E) ascend is to descend

81. Year is to month as

  (A) foot is to inch
  (B) cloth is to thread
  (C) yard is to foot
  (D) juror is to jury
  (E) hour is to minute

82. Stately is to undignified as

  (A) noble is to gas
  (B) metal is to base
  (C) capable is to cruel
  (D) august is to ignoble
  (E) condition is to intend

83. Script is to movie as blueprint is to

  (A) building
  (B) carpenter
  (C) plan
  (D) city
  (E) actor

84. Drizzle is to downpour as breeze is to

  (A) hail
  (B) torrent
  (C) gust
  (D) thunder
  (E) flood

85. Spray is to skunk as

  (A) beaver is to dam
  (B) quill is to porcupine
  (C) wool is to sheep
  (D) bee is to sting
  (E) aerie is to eagle

86. Flock is to sheep as

  (A) ship is to fleet
  (B) lion is to pride
  (C) herd is to cattle
  (D) fork is to road
  (E) jam is to traffic

87. Dehydrate is to water as

  (A) drought is to dry
  (B) dark is to shine
  (C) draft is to fan
  (D) smother is to air
  (E) heat is to sun

88. Experience is to naive as

  (A) obedience is to order
  (B) expose is to mask
  (C) width is to depth
  (D) field is to stream
  (E) caution is to reckless

89. Cow is to milk as bee is to

  (A) comb
  (B) queen
  (C) hive
  (D) sting
  (E) honey

90. Miller is to flour as

  (A) connoisseur is to wine
  (B) librarian is to newspaper
  (C) soldier is to firearm
  (D) baker is to bread
  (E) spectator is to binoculars

91. Conductor is to symphony as foreman is to

    (A) client
    (B) worker
    (C) welder
    (D) architect
    (E) project

92. Helicopter is to aircraft as

    (A) hammer is to tool
    (B) jet is to blimp
    (C) blimp is to glider
    (D) plier is to wrench
    (E) blowtorch is to fire

93. Oak is to maple as

    (A) poplar is to tree
    (B) moss is to fern
    (C) hedge is to vine
    (D) dandelion is to mushroom
    (E) daffodil is to violet

94. Ounce is to gram as

    (A) scale is to kilogram
    (B) acre is to fathom
    (C) inch is to centimeter
    (D) millimeter is to mile
    (E) Celsius is to degree

95. Dash is to race as

    (A) marathon is to triathlon
    (B) skirmish is to battle
    (C) sprint is to hurdle
    (D) hour is to day
    (E) set is to match

96. Balloon is to inflate as tank is to

    (A) fill
    (B) drive
    (C) ignite
    (D) gasoline
    (E) hold

97. Telegraph is to communication as abacus is to

    (A) decoration
    (B) arrangement
    (C) navigation
    (D) calculation
    (E) design

98. Piercing is to sound as

    (A) illusory is to sight
    (B) lukewarm is sensation
    (C) piquant is to flavor
    (D) shocking is to sight
    (E) odorless is to smell

99. Cafeteria is to students as

    (A) trough is to horses
    (B) feed is to livestock
    (C) kitchen is to families
    (D) mess hall is to soldiers
    (E) restaurant is to waiters

100. Ungulate is to donkey as amphibian is to

    (A) alligator
    (B) frog
    (C) reptile
    (D) turtle
    (E) fish

101. Lace is to shoe as

(A) cuff is to pants

(B) hand is to watch

(C) bridge is to spectacles

(D) brim is to hat

(E) catch is to necklace

102. Strait is to sea as

(A) exit is to roadway

(B) isthmus is to landmass

(C) island is to archipelago

(D) ridge is to mountain

(E) port is to harbor

103. Conscription is to enlistment as tax is to

(A) payment

(B) collection

(C) adherence

(D) refund

(E) revenue

104. Stoic is to reaction as spontaneous is to

(A) randomness

(B) intelligence

(C) remorse

(D) forethought

(E) shallowness

105. Crow is to murder as

(A) dog is to kennel

(B) whale is to pod

(C) bird is to nest

(D) elephant is to gaggle

(E) lion is to pack

106. Arc is to circumference as

(A) radius is to circle

(B) speed is to distance

(C) segment is to line

(D) diagonal is to square

(E) degree is to triangle

107. Tool is to shed as

(A) money is to vault

(B) car is to road

(C) water is to faucet

(D) chemical is to test tube

(E) guard is to prison

108. Pasture is to pastor as

(A) sensor is to censor

(B) creature is to censor

(C) censure is to censor

(D) cinch is to censor

(E) simple is to censor

109. Equivocal is to ambivalent as boorish is to

(A) cruel

(B) rude

(C) inept

(D) stubborn

(E) rash

110. Scalding is to tepid as

(A) hot is to boiling

(B) frigid is to freezing

(C) ecstatic is to indifferent

(D) demure is to piqued

(E) loud is to deafening

111. Helpful is to patronizing as witty is to

    (A) humorous
    (B) condescending
    (C) vulgar
    (D) fake
    (E) smug

112. Adore is to loathe as

    (A) honor is to defame
    (B) worship is to revere
    (C) cherish is to salvage
    (D) encourage is to coach
    (E) despise is to condemn

113. Arm is to shoulder as leg is to

    (A) knee
    (B) joint
    (C) foot
    (D) hip
    (E) neck

114. Thrifty is to miser as

    (A) charitable is to benefactor
    (B) cheap is to pauper
    (C) frugal is to accountant
    (D) frivolous is to youth
    (E) violent is to convict

115. Delectable is to dish as

    (A) prosaic is to artwork
    (B) simple is to costume
    (C) eloquent is to speech
    (D) phlegmatic is to match
    (E) luscious is to novel

116. Needle is to sewing as

    (A) memories is to scrapbook
    (B) hammer is to nail
    (C) pen is to calligraphy
    (D) bat is to hitter
    (E) flash is to photograph

117. Erratic is to consistency as

    (A) absurd is to foolishness
    (B) unique is to commonness
    (C) runner is to track
    (D) appropriate is to choice
    (E) unusual is to helpfulness

118. Former is to previous as imminent is to

    (A) prior
    (B) present
    (C) bygone
    (D) next
    (E) current

119. Belief is to discredited as

    (A) authority is to obeyed
    (B) task is to completed
    (C) responsibility is to denied
    (D) claim is to challenged
    (E) personality is to assuaged

120. Rose is to poppy as

    (A) granite is to slate
    (B) oat is to corn
    (C) bread is to sandwich
    (D) calorie is to nutrient
    (E) miller is to farmer

121. Inevitable is to possible as will is to

    (A) must
    (B) won't
    (C) do
    (D) shall
    (E) might

122. Wheat is to flour as

    (A) barley is to hops
    (B) leaves are to root
    (C) coarse is to smooth
    (D) acorns are to sapling
    (E) apples are to cider

123. Arboretum is to fruit as greenhouse is to

    (A) seed
    (B) bud
    (C) dirt
    (D) flower
    (E) sapling

124. Amateur is to champion as

    (A) matriculant is to graduate
    (B) intern is to volunteer
    (C) teacher is to principal
    (D) prodigy is to professional
    (E) student is to subject

125. Active is to passive as

    (A) joyful is to pleasant
    (B) tranquil is to bored
    (C) placid is to pleased
    (D) sorrowful is to cry
    (E) frenetic is to apathetic

126. Concerned is to apprehensive as

    (A) appealing is to attractive
    (B) objective is to subjective
    (C) untenable is to intrigued
    (D) dissuaded is to convinced
    (E) interested is to eager

127. Meteorologist is to forecast as

    (A) zoologist is to animal
    (B) scientist is to hypothesis
    (C) psychologist is to disease
    (D) internist is to nurse
    (E) obstetrician is to maternity

128. Steep is to tea as

    (A) percolate is to coffee
    (B) stir is to ingredients
    (C) steam is to broil
    (D) baste is to gravy
    (E) simmer is to broth

129. Cartographer is to map as

    (A) photographer is to camera
    (B) biographer is to author
    (C) navigator is to ship
    (D) stenographer is to transcription
    (E) sculptor is to chisel

130. Frond is to palm as

    (A) petal is to daisy
    (B) leaf is to branch
    (C) school is to fish
    (D) coach is to team
    (E) letter is to vowel

131. Midpoint is to line as

    (A) hypotenuse is to triangle
    (B) volume is to solid
    (C) diameter is to circle
    (D) gallon is to milk
    (E) length is to depth

132. Bison is to plain as cougar is to

    (A) desert
    (B) valley
    (C) crest
    (D) mountain
    (E) bay

133. Finale is to musical as

    (A) intermission is to play
    (B) stanza is to poem
    (C) epilogue is to novel
    (D) lyric is to sing
    (E) overture is to orchestra

PRACTICE QUESTIONS ANSWERS AND EXPLANATIONS

1. D
Choice (D) is the correct answer. This is a Definition Bridge. By definition, circumference is the distance around a circle. By definition, perimeter is the distance around a square.

2. B
Choice (B) is correct. This is a Word (specifically verb-noun) Bridge. Paper can be used, along with a writing utensil, to write. Canvas can be used, along with a paintbrush, to paint.

3. B
Choice (B) is correct. This is a Part/Whole Bridge. A collar is part of a shirt. A cuff is part of a pair of trousers.

4. C
Choice (C) is correct. This is a Lack Bridge. Someone who is hysteric will often lack control. Someone who is absurd will often lack sense.

5. E
Choice (E) is correct. This is a Definition Bridge. Several instances of a square form a cube. Several instances of a circle form a sphere.

6. B
Choice (B) is correct. This is an Association Bridge. A shark is associated with living in an aquatic environment. A camel is associated with living in terrestrial environment.

7. E
Choice (E) is correct. This is a Definition Bridge. By definition, chide is a mild reprimand. By definition, castigate is a harsh reprimand.

8. A
Choice (A) is correct. This is an Antonym Bridge. Abrupt is the opposite of gradual. Corrupt is the opposite of virtuous.

9. C
Choice (C) is correct. This is a Part/Whole Bridge. A stanza is a part of a poem. A movement is part of a symphony.

10. D
Choice (D) is correct. This is a Part/Whole Bridge. A string is a part of a violin. A reed is a part of an oboe.

11. A
Choice (A) is correct. This is an Association Bridge. Canter describes the movement of a horse. Hop describes the movement of a rabbit.

12. A
Choice (A) is correct. This is a Type/Kind Bridge. Baseball is a type of a game. A hurricane is a type of a storm.

13. C
Choice (C) is correct. This is a Lack Bridge. If something is rigid, then it lacks the ability to bend. If something is immortal, then it lacks the ability to die.

14. A
Choice (A) is correct. This is a Type/Kind Bridge. A wolf is a type of a canine. A panther is a type of a feline.

15. A
Choice (A) is correct. This is a Part/Whole Bridge. Rind is the protective outer covering of a melon. Skin is the protective outer covering of a mammal.

16. E
Choice (E) is correct. This is a Function Bridge. The function of a mile is to measure length. The function of a fathom is to measure depth.

17. D
Choice (D) is correct. This is a Lack Bridge. Something that is truthful is not dishonest. Something that is arid is not moist.

18. C
Choice (C) is correct. This is a Cause-and-Effect Bridge. Tarnish is what happens to silver when exposed to moisture. Rust is what happens to iron when exposed to moisture.

19. E

Choice (E) is correct. This is an Antonym Bridge. Delaying is the opposite of hastening. Facilitating is the opposite of impeding.

20. C

Choice (C) is correct. This is an Antonym Bridge. Thinking is a focused action, but daydreaming is not. Walking is a focused action, but meandering is not.

21. C

Choice (C) is correct. This is an Association Bridge. A gram is associated with a metric measure of weight and an ounce is a associated with the imperial measure of weight. A meter is associated with a metric measure of length and a yard is associated with an imperial measure of length.

22. C

Choice (C) is correct. This is an Association Bridge. A veil is the headwear of a bride. A crown is the headwear of a monarch.

23. B

Choice (B) is correct. This is an Antonym Bridge. Something that is anomalous is the opposite of standard. Something that is demonstrative is the opposite of impassive.

24. C

Choice (C) is correct. This is a Purpose Bridge. A wing is used by a bird to move. A foot is used by a human to move.

25. D

Choice (D) is correct. This is an Antonym Bridge. Fighting is the opposite of surrendering. Resisting is the opposite of submitting.

26. D

Choice (D) is correct. This is an Association Bridge. Defilement describes the ruining of a sacred object, such as a shrine. Breach describes the ruining—breaking—a contract.

27. A

Choice (A) is correct. This is an Association Bridge. A restaurant is a place where people go to eat and a pasture is a place where animals go to eat. A fountain is a place where people go to drink and a trough is a place where animals go to drink.

28. E

Choice (E) is correct. This is an Association Bridge. A necessity is a need and a luxury is a want. Water is a need and soda is a want.

29. D

Choice (D) is correct. This is a Degree Bridge. To be extremely idealistic is to be quixotic. To be extremely resolute is to be stubborn.

30. E

Choice (E) is correct. This is an Association Bridge. Soap is associated with producing bubbles. Cream is associated with producing butter.

31. D

Choice (D) is correct. This is a Part/Whole Bridge. A fish is part of a school. A lion is part of a pride.

32. B

Choice (B) is correct. This is a Purpose Bridge. A silo is used to store grain. An arsenal is used to store munitions.

33. D

Choice (D) is correct. This is a Purpose Bridge. An aquarium is used to house a fish collection. An arboretum is used to house a tree collection.

34. A

Choice (A) is correct. This is a Degree Bridge. A trained cadet is a solider. A trained apprentice is a craftsman.

35. B

Choice (B) is correct. This is an Antonym Bridge. A person who is passive is not aggressive. A person who is meek is not overbearing.

36. E

Choice (E) is correct. This is a Type/Kind Bridge. A dime is a type of coin. An almond is a type of nut.

37. D

Choice (D) is correct. This is a Purpose Bridge. Ice is used as a a surface for skating. Felt is used as a surface for billiards.

38. A

Choice (A) is correct. This is a Degree Bridge. A person who is paranoid is extremely suspicious. A person who is distraught is extremely perturbed.

39. B

Choice (B) is correct. This is a Function Bridge. The function of a fireman is to extinguish fires. The function of a vendor is to sell merchandise.

40. D

Choice (D) is correct. This is a Part/Whole Bridge. A pearl is a part of the shell of an oyster. Ivory is a part of the head of an elephant.

41. D

Choice (D) is correct. This is an Association Bridge. A chandler is someone who makes or sells wax products. A carpenter is someone who makes or sells wood products.

42. C

Choice (C) is correct. This is a Degree Bridge. A gathering that is out of control is a mob. A fire that is out of control is an inferno.

43. C

Choice (C) is correct. This is a Function Bridge. The function of an acre is to measure land size. The function of a fathom is to measure water depth.

44. D

Choice (D) is correct. This is an Association Bridge. A bison roams the plains. A kangaroo roams the outback.

45. A

Choice (A) is correct. This is an Association Bridge. A grape is grown at a vineyard. A pumpkin is grown at a patch.

46. C

Choice (C) is correct. This is an Association Bridge. The head is attached to the neck. The foot is attached to the ankle.

47. B

Choice (B) is correct. This is an Association Bridge. Liquid transitions to gas when heated. Condensation transitions to evaporation when heated.

48. B

Choice (B) is correct. This is a Word/Grammar Bridge. You verify authenticity, and you test competence.

49. A

Choice (A) is correct. This is a Purpose Bridge. A gap is used to create a break in continuity. An intermission is used to create a break in a film.

50. E

Choice (E) is correct. This is a Purpose Bridge. A wrist is used to wear a watch. A torso is used to wear a shirt.

51. D

Choice (D) is correct. This is a Function Bridge. The function of a watt is to measure energy. The function of a grade is to measure quality.

52. B

Choice (B) is correct. This is a Type/Kind Bridge. A mongoose is a type of mammal. A sycamore is a type of tree.

53. A

Choice (A) is correct. This is an Association Bridge. A vassal is subordinate to a king. An employee is subordinate to a manager.

54. B

Choice (B) is correct. This is a Purpose Bridge. A turtle uses a shell for protection. A human uses a house for protection.

55. E

Choice (E) is correct. This is an Association Bridge. A gondola revolves around a Ferris wheel. The Moon revolves around Earth.

56. B

Choice (B) is correct. This is an Association Bridge. A knife is only useful if it is not dull. A tire is only useful if it is not flat.

57. C

Choice (C) is correct. This is a Lack Bridge. Time lacks the possibility of being controlled. Falsehoods lack the possibility of being substantiated.

58. D

Choice (D) is correct. This is a Lack Bridge. Something that is a shadow is not substantial. Something that is a machine is not alive.

59. A

Choice (A) is correct. This is an Antonym Bridge. Someone who is fervent is not nonchalant. Someone who is stalwart is not timid.

60. E

Choice (E) is correct. This is an Association Bridge. A ship takes refuge at a port. A traveler takes refuge at a hotel.

61. C

Choice (C) is correct. This is a Degree Bridge. A sketch is the draft of a painting. A design is the draft of a prototype.

62. B

Choice (B) is correct. This is an Antonym Bridge. Something that is ornamented is the opposite of plain. Something that is concealed is the opposite of revealed.

63. C

Choice (C) is correct. This is a Purpose Bridge. Iron is used to make steel. Wheat is used to make bread.

64. D

Choice (D) is correct. This is a Function Bridge. The function of medicine is to cure illness. The function of food is to cure hunger.

65. B

Choice (B) is correct. This is a Degree Bridge. Hope is a less extreme form of optimism. Melancholy is a less extreme form of pessimism.

66. C

Choice (C) is correct. This is an Association Bridge. A fireman helps "fix" a fire by putting it out. An editor fixes an error by correcting it.

67. A

Choice (A) is correct. This is a Cause-and-Effect Bridge. An accolade, or an award, is a result of accomplishment. Disappointment is a result of underachievement.

68. C

Choice (C) is correct. This is a Lack Bridge. Conflict lacks peace. Chaos lacks order.

69. A

Choice (A) is correct. This is a Defining Bridge. A piano is played by a pianist. A flute is played by a flautist.

70. C

Choice (C) is correct. This is a Function Bridge. A punchline functions as the final phrase of a joke. A moral functions as the final phrase of a fable.

71. D

Choice (D) is correct. This is a Type/Kind Bridge. Quartz is a type of mineral. A squash is a type of vegetable.

72. B

Choice (B) is correct. This is a Function Bridge. A function of a cleat is as footwear for soccer. A function of a skate is as footwear for hockey.

73. E

Choice (E) is correct. This is an Association Bridge. Perimeter is the distance around a square. Circumference is the distance around a circle.

74. C

Choice (C) is correct. This is a Function Bridge. A brick functions as one piece of a wall. A pixel functions as one piece of a picture.

75. B

Choice (B) is correct. This is an Antonym Bridge. Someone who is incensed is the opposite of calm. Someone who is enraged is the opposite of sedate.

76. B

Choice (B) is correct. This is a Function Bridge. The function of a speaker is to project sound. The function of a projector is to project light.

77. C

Choice (C) is correct. This is an Association Bridge. Cheese is made from milk. Bread is made from grain.

78. E

Choice (E) is correct. This is an Association Bridge. An example of a city is Chicago. An example of a sport is tennis.

79. C

Choice (C) is correct. This is a Word/Grammar Bridge. Flower rhymes with sour, and anemone rhymes with lemony.

80. E

Choice (E) is correct. This is a Word/Grammar Bridge. Raise is the opposite of lower, and ascend is the opposite of descend. Raise and ascend have similar meanings. Lower and descend have similar meanings.

81. A

Choice (A) is correct. This is a Whole/Part Bridge. A year can be divided into 12 parts, and each one is called a month. A foot can be divided into 12 parts, and each one is called an inch.

82. D

Choice (D) is correct. This is an Antonym Bridge. Someone who is stately is the opposite of undignified. Someone who is august is the opposite of ignoble.

83. A

Choice (A) is correct. This is a Function Bridge. A script functions as the basis for a movie. A blueprint functions as the basis for a building.

84. C

Choice (C) is correct. This is a Degree Bridge. An extreme drizzle is a downpour. An extreme breeze is a gust.

85. B

Choice (B) is correct. This is a Function Bridge. Spray functions as a defensive mechanism by a skunk. A quill functions as a defensive mechanism by a porcupine.

86. C

Choice (C) is correct. This is a Whole/Part Bridge. A flock is a whole group of sheep. A herd is a whole group of cattle.

87. D

Choice (D) is correct. This is a Lack Bridge. Dehydrated fruit or animals lack water, and a smothered animal lacks air.

88. E

Choice (E) is correct. This is a Lack Bridge. To lack experience is to be naive. To lack caution is to be reckless.

89. E

Choice (E) is correct. This is an Association Bridge. A cow produces the edible product milk. A bee produces the edible product honey.

90. D

Choice (D) is correct. This is a Defining Bridge. A miller produces flour. A baker produces bread.

91. E

Choice (E) is correct. This is an Association Bridge. A conductor directs a symphony. A foreman directs a project.

92. A

Choice (A) is correct. This is a Type/Kind Bridge. A helicopter is a type of an aircraft. A hammer is a type of a tool.

93. E

Choice (E) is correct. This is an Association Bridge. Oaks and maples are both trees. Daffodils and violets are both flowering plants.

94. C

Choice (C) is correct. This is an Association Bridge. An ounce is associated with an imperial measure of weight and a gram is a associated with a metric measure of weight. An inch is associated with an imperial measure of length and a centimeter is associated with a metric measure of length.

95. B

Choice (B) is correct. This is a Degree Bridge. A dash is a short race. A skirmish is a short battle.

96. A

Choice (A) is correct. This is a Word/Grammar Bridge. A balloon can be inflated. A tank can be filled.

97. D

Choice (D) is correct. This is a Purpose Bridge. A telegraph is used for communication. An abacus is used for calculation.

98. C

Choice (C) is correct. This is a Type/Kind Bridge. Piercing is a type of sound. Piquant is a type of flavor.

99. D

Choice (D) is correct. This is an Association Bridge. A cafeteria is a building where groups of students eat together. A mess hall is a building where groups of soldiers eat together.

100. B

Choice (B) is correct. This is a Type/Kind Bridge. A type of an ungulate is a donkey. A type of an amphibian is a frog.

101. E

Choice (E) is correct. This is a Purpose Bridge. A lace fastens a shoe. A catch fastens a necklace.

102. B

Choice (B) is correct. This is an Association Bridge. A strait is a narrow passage connecting two sections of sea. An isthmus is a narrow passage connecting two sections of landmass.

103. A

Choice (A) is correct. This is a Degree Bridge. Conscription is a government based form of enlistment. A tax is a government-based form of payment.

104. D

Choice (D) is correct. This is a Lack Bridge. Someone who is stoic lacks reaction. Someone who is spontaneous lacks forethought.

105. B

Choice (B) is correct. This is a Part/Whole Bridge. A group of crows is a murder. A group of whales is a pod.

106. C

Choice (C) is correct. This is a Part/Whole Bridge. An arc is a part of the length of a circumference. A segment is a part of the length of a line.

107. A

Choice (A) is correct. This is an Association Bridge. Tools are stored in a shed. Money is stored in a vault.

108. C

Choice (C) is correct. This is a Word/Grammar Bridge. Pasture is a word ending in the letters *r* and *e* that is similar sounding to the word pastor ending in the letters *o* and *r*. Censure is a word ending in the letters *r* and *e* that is similar sounding to the word censor ending in the letters *o* and *r*.

109. B

Choice (B) is correct. This is a Synonym Bridge. To be equivocal is to be ambivalent. To be boorish is to be rude.

110. C

Choice (C) is correct. This is an Antonym Bridge. Something scalding is the opposite of tepid. Someone ecstatic is the opposite of indifferent.

111. E

Choice (E) is correct. This is a Degree Bridge. To be excessively and offensively helpful is to be patronizing. To be excessively and offensively witty is to be smug.

112. A

Choice (A) is correct. This is an Antonym Bridge. The opposite of adore is loathe. The opposite of honor is defame.

113. D

Choice (D) is correct. This is a Whole/Part Bridge. The arm is a whole that includes a part called the shoulder. The leg is a whole that includes a part called the hip.

114. A

Choice (A) is correct. This is an Association Bridge. Someone who is thrifty is often referred to as a miser. Someone who is charitable is often referred to as a benefactor.

115. C

Choice (C) is correct. This is an Association Bridge. Delectable can describe an extremely tasty dish. Eloquent can describe an extremely well-written speech.

116. C

Choice (C) is correct. This is a Purpose Bridge. A needle is a tool used as an implement for sewing. A pen is a tool used as an implement for calligraphy.

117. B

Choice (B) is correct. This is a Lack Bridge. Something erratic lacks consistency. Something unique lacks commonness.

118. D

Choice (D) is correct. This is a Word/Grammar Bridge. Former is a formal word for previous. Imminent is a formal word for next.

119. D

Choice (D) is correct. This is a Lack Bridge. A belief that lacks reliability is discredited. A claim that lacks reliability is challenged.

120. A

Choice (A) is correct. This is an Association Bridge. A poppy shares the same color as a rose. Granite shares the same color as slate.

121. E

Choice (E) is correct. This is a Degree Bridge. Something that is inevitable will happen, but something that is possible might not happen. Something that will happen is a guarantee, but something that might happen actually might not happen.

122. E

Choice (E) is correct. This is a Purpose Bridge. Wheat is used to produce flour and apples are used to produce cider.

123. D

Choice (D) is correct. This is an Association Bridge. An arboretum can include mature trees with fruit. A greenhouse can include mature plants with flowers.

124. A

Choice (A) is correct. This is a Degree Bridge. An amateur aspires to become a champion. A matriculant aspires to become a a graduate.

125. E

Choice (E) is correct. This is an Antonym Bridge. Someone who is active is the opposite of passive. Someone who is frenetic is the opposite of apathetic.

126. E

Choice (E) is correct. This is a Degree Bridge. A person who is extremely concerned can be described as apprehensive. A person who is extremely interested can be described as eager.

127. B

Choice (B) is correct. This is a Function Bridge. The function of a meteorologist is to generate a forecast. The function of a scientist is to generate a hypothesis.

128. A

Choice (A) is correct. This is a Cause-and-Effect Bridge. Steeping a tea bag in water will result in tea. Percolating water through coffee grounds will result in coffee.

129. D

Choice (D) is correct. This is an Individual-to-Object Bridge. A cartographer produces a map. A stenographer produces a transcription.

130. A

Choice (A) is correct. This is a Part/Whole Bridge. A frond is a part of the palm. A petal is a part of a daisy.

131. C

Choice (C) is correct. This is a Purpose Bridge. A midpoint is used to divide a line into two equal halves. A diameter is used to divide a circle into two equal halves.

132. D

Choice (D) is correct. This is an Association Bridge. A bison roams the plain. A cougar roams the mountain.

133. C

Choice (C) is correct. This is a Function Bridge. The function of a finale is to signal the end of a musical. The function of an epilogue is to signal the end of a novel.

PART 2

ISEE Workshop

CHAPTER 3

Inside the ISEE

CHAPTER OBJECTIVES

With practice, this chapter will help you:

1. Describe the structure of the ISEE and the timing of each section

2. Summarize ISEE scoring

THE ISEE EXAM

The ISEE (Independent School Entrance Exam) is an admissions test used for private and independent schools. The ISEE is administered at four different levels:

- Upper Level (for students currently in grades 8–11)

- Middle Level (for students currently in grades 6 or 7)

- Lower Level (for students currently in grades 4 or 5)

- Primary Level (for students currently in grades 1–3)

Though information is provided below for each level, this book is designed specifically for students who will be taking the Upper or Middle Level exam.

The ISEE Primary Level exam is an online test that itself is administered at three different levels: Primary Level 2 for students currently in 1st grade, Primary Level 3 for students currently in 2nd grade, and Primary Level 4 for students currently in 3rd grade. Each Primary Level exam contains a Mathematics section, a Reading section, and a Writing Sample.

There are some differences between each of the Primary Level exams. For example, both the Primary Level 2 and 3 exams contain a picture prompt, which offers students the opportunity to be creative and self-expressive with their individual writing styles. Also, in the Primary Level 2 exam, there is a short Auditory Comprehension section that tests how students listen to a passage with no written text. After finishing the passage, students answer questions that are related.

The ISEE Primary Level exams are only available at select schools. For all Primary Level tests, the Writing Sample is untimed, allowing all students to type at their own pace. The following table is a breakdown of the digital Primary Level tests.

ISEE Primary Levels			
Section	Primary 2 (for current 1st grade students)	Primary 3 (for current 2nd grade students)	Primary 4 (for current 3rd grade students)
Auditory Comprehension	6 questions (7 minutes)	N/A	N/A
Reading	18 questions (20 minutes)	24 questions (28 minutes)	28 questions (30 minutes)
One short break			
Mathematics	24 questions (26 minutes)	24 questions (26 minutes)	28 questions (30 minutes)
Writing Sample	1 picture prompt (untimed)	1 picture prompt (untimed)	1 writing prompt (untimed)
Total Time	**53 minutes** **(+ break & writing time)**	**54 minutes** **(+ break & writing time)**	**1 hour** **(+ break & writing time)**

*The writing sample will neither be scored nor included with your home report, but it will be sent to the schools to which you are applying.

The following table is a breakdown of the paper-based Upper, Middle, and Lower Level tests.

ISEE Upper, Middle, & Lower Levels		
Section	**Lower Level**	**Upper & Middle Levels**
Verbal Reasoning	34 questions (20 minutes)	40 questions (20 minutes)
Quantitative Reasoning	38 questions (35 minutes)	37 questions (35 minutes)
Break (5–10 minutes)		
Reading Comprehension	25 questions (25 minutes)	36 questions (35 minutes)
Mathematics Achievement	30 questions (30 minutes)	47 questions (40 minutes)
Break (5–10 minutes)		
Essay*	1 writing prompt (30 minutes)	1 writing prompt (30 minutes)
Total Time	**2 hours, 30 minutes–2 hours, 40 minutes**	**2 hours, 50 minutes–3 hours**

* The essay will neither be scored nor included with your home report, but it will be sent to the schools to which you are applying.

Some things to note for Test Day:

- All questions have four answer choices: A, B, C, and D.

- You are not permitted to use calculators, dictionaries, or rulers.

- You must bring your own #2 pencils and erasers and black or blue pens for your essay.

SCORING

Scores on the ISEE are calculated somewhat similarly as those on the SSAT, though there are a few differences. First, there is no incorrect answer penalty for incorrect responses, so the raw score is just the sum of all correct answers. Given that this is the case, you should never leave an answer blank for an ISEE question, even though there may be some questions that are more difficult or cover material you're unfamiliar with.

The raw scores, based on the number of questions you answer correctly, are converted to scaled scores. The Upper, Middle, and Lower Levels of the exam are all reported on the same scale: 760–940. Scaled scores on the Primary Levels of the exam range as follows:

- Primary 2 scaled score range: 200–299

- Primary 3 scaled score range: 300–399

- Primary 4 scaled score range: 400–499

Scaled scores are then converted to percentile ranks to show how you compare to your norm group. For Upper, Middle, and Lower Level students, your ISEE norm group is the group of all students of the same grade who have taken the ISEE in the past three years. Primary Level students' scores are also compared to scores of other students of the same grade.

ISEE scores are reported through the **Individual Score Report** (ISR). The ISR will include the scaled score for each multiple-choice section of the test, the percentile rank 1st–99th for each section, and the stanine score 1–9 for each section. Think of stanines in groups of three: a stanine of 1–3 is below average, a stanine of 4–6 is an average score, and a stanine of 7–9 indicates an above average performance.

Percentile	Stanine
1–3	1
4–10	2
11–22	3
23–39	4
40–59	5
60–76	6
77–88	7
89–95	8
96–99	9

The ISR also includes an analysis of the question types within each section of the exam. This analysis will show you the number of questions you answered correctly, incorrectly, or skipped. It may even help you notice the questions that you may not have been able to get to before time was up.

SMARTPOINTS™

On most standardized tests, certain types of questions are more common than others. For example, on the ISEE, there are more questions on Arithmetic than on Data Analysis and Probability. The exact number of Arithmetic and Data Analysis and Probability questions may change from test to test, but the proportion of total questions represented by each category remains relatively constant. Therefore, to get the most points on Test Day, it makes sense to focus the majority of your attention on the areas of the test that are the most common and will provide you the most opportunities to earn more points.

To represent this relative frequency of question types on different tests, Kaplan created SmartPoints. The table below shows a breakdown of ISEE SmartPoints. By studying the information released by the test maker, Kaplan has been able to determine how often certain topics are likely to show up on the test, and, therefore, how many points these topics are worth on Test Day. If you master a given topic, you can expect to earn the corresponding number of SmartPoints on Test Day. The breakdown of SmartPoints for Verbal Reasoning, Reading Comprehension, and Math are summarized in the following table.

As you work through the chapters in this book, use Kaplan SmartPoints to guide you in your at-home studies. Learn topics that are new to you and review topics with which you are familiar, but always spend more time on topics with the highest number of SmartPoints.

ISEE SmartPoints Categories and Values

	ISEE Middle Level Test Point Values	ISEE Upper Level Test Point Values
Verbal Reasoning		
Synonyms	90	90
Sentence Completions	90	90
Total earnable points	**180**	**180**
Reading Comprehension		
Main Idea	20	30
Supporting Ideas	65	35
Inference	25	40
Vocab-in-Context	20	20
Tone/Style/Figurative Language	20	20
Organization/Logic Questions	30	35
Total earnable points	**180**	**180**
Quantitative Reasoning and Math Achievement Combined		
Arithmetic	95	75
Algebra	60	110
Geometry and Measurement	95	90
Data Analysis and Probability	110	85
Total earnable points	**360**	**360**

HOW TO REGISTER

ISEE accepts registration online. For more information, go to the official website at **www.erblearn. org/services/isee-overview**.

Phone:	800-446-0320
Mail:	ISEE Operations
	423 Morris Street
	Durham, NC 27701
Email:	iseeoperations@erblearn.org

HOW THE ISEE DIFFERS FROM THE SSAT

There are a few main differences between the SSAT and the ISEE:

- On the ISEE, the Verbal section contains Synonym and Sentence Completion questions. On the SSAT, the Verbal section contains Synonym and Analogy questions.

- On the ISEE, there are Quantitative Comparisons in the Quantitative Reasoning section (Upper and Middle Levels only).

- On the ISEE, there is no penalty for an incorrect answer. That means it is always in your favor to guess if you're not sure of the answer.

- On the ISEE, there are four answer choices: A, B, C, and D. On the SSAT, there are five answer choices: A, B, C, D, and E.

CHAPTER 4

ISEE Sentence Completions

CHAPTER OBJECTIVES

With practice, this chapter will help you:

1. Explain the concept of a sentence completion and the format of ISEE Sentence Completion questions

2. Use the Kaplan 4-Step Method for Sentence Completions to answer Verbal Reasoning questions accurately and efficiently

3. Determine the meaning of an unfamiliar word or phrase through context

4. Identify clues related to contrast, cause-and-effect, and definition relationships

Sentence Completions appear **only on the ISEE**. If you are not taking the ISEE, you should skip this section.

THE FORMAT

Of all the questions in the Verbal Reasoning section, approximately half are Sentence Completions. They're arranged in order of increasing difficulty.

Sentence Completions are fill-in-the-blank questions. Each question will have one or two blanks, and you must select the best fit from the four choices provided.

These are probably the simplest of all the Verbal Reasoning question types. Unlike Analogies on the SSAT, Sentence Completions give you some context in which to think about vocabulary words, and unlike Reading Comprehension questions, they require you to focus on only a single sentence at a time.

Sentence Completions are about the sentence much more than they are about the answer choices. To answer these questions correctly on Test Day, look for clues in each sentence and predict the answer before approaching the choices. This way, you will answer Sentence Completions more quickly, reliably, and accurately than you would by rushing to the answer choices.

First, familiarize yourself with the directions before you take the official test:

Select the word(s) that best fits the meaning of each sentence.

Now, review this example of a test-like question:

> Although the tomato looked sweet and -------, it tasted more like a very sour, dried-out old sponge.
>
> **(A)** arid
>
> **(B)** juicy
>
> **(C)** enormous
>
> **(D)** cloying

A contrast is presented between the way the tomato looked and the way it tasted. It tasted sour and had the texture of a dry sponge. Because you were previously told that it looked *sweet* (the opposite of *sour*), you can infer that you need to find the opposite of *dry*. Therefore, the tomato must have looked juicy, so choice (B) is the correct answer.

KAPLAN 4-STEP METHOD FOR SENTENCE COMPLETIONS

Step 1. Read the sentence, marking clues

Step 2. Predict the answer

Step 3. Find the fit

Step 4. Plug in your selection

To check your answers, always read the selected choice back into the sentence. Sometimes, a selected choice may feel correct at first, but does not actually make sense in the context of the sentence. Take a closer look at each step.

> **EXPERT TIP**
>
> The meaning of each missing word in a Sentence Completion question is provided by the clues in the sentence.

Step 1. Read the Sentence, Marking Clues

Think carefully about the sentence before looking at the answer choices. What does the sentence mean? Are there any clue words?

Step 2. Predict the Answer

Take a look at the following examples:

"They say that M&M's do not melt in your hands, but last summer…"

"Despite the fact that it was 50 degrees below zero, we were…"

"I am so hungry I could…"

You could probably fill in the rest of these sentences using words similar to the speaker's own. It's often easy to see the direction in which a sentence is going; that's because the structure and the tone of a sentence can clue you in to its meaning.

Your job for the ISEE Sentence Completion questions is to fill in the missing piece. One way to do this is to anticipate the answer before looking at the answer choices. Clue words and sentence structure (construction and punctuation) can help you determine where a sentence is headed.

Making an exact prediction isn't necessary. If you can even identify the missing word as being positive or negative, that will often be sufficient.

Step 3. Find the Fit

Make sure to scan every choice before deciding. Find the answer choice that is the best fit for the blank.

Step 4. Plug In Your Selection

Only one of the four possible answer choices will make sense. However, if you've gone through the four steps and more than one choice still seems possible, don't dwell on it. Try to eliminate at least one choice, guess, and move on. Remember, on the ISEE, an incorrect answer will not affect your score.

Using some examples, see how Kaplan's 4-Step Method works:

> The ------- pace of life in the crowded city became so upsetting to Amy that she decided to move to the country.
>
> (A) hectic
>
> (B) agreeable
>
> (C) accidental
>
> (D) confused

Step 1. Read the sentence, marking clues. What kind of "pace of life" would be "upsetting"?

Step 2. Predict an answer.

PREDICTION: *frantic, hectic*

Step 3. Find the fit—select the answer choice that best fits your prediction. Which choice is the best match?

Step 4. Plug in your selection—read your answer choice back into the sentence to check it.

Choice (A) is the correct answer.

Most North American marsupials are -------; at night they forage for food and during the day they sleep.

(A) fastidious

(B) amiable

(C) monolithic

(D) nocturnal

Read the sentence carefully, looking for clues. The semicolon (;) is a big clue. It tells you that what comes after the semicolon follows the direction of what comes before it. In other words, you're looking for a word that means nighttime activity and daytime rest.

Predict which word should go into the blank.

Compare the answer choices with your prediction. Pick the best match. Choice A, *fastidious*, has nothing to do with being active at night. Neither does choice B, *amiable*, or for that matter choice C, *monolithic*. Choice (D), *nocturnal*, however, means to be active at night, so that seems correct.

Check your choice by plugging it into the sentence. "Most North American marsupials are nocturnal; at night they forage for food and during the day they sleep." Sounds pretty good. Finally, scan the other choices to make sure that choice (D) is indeed the best choice. No other choice works in the sentence, so choice (D) is correct.

Juniper skated with such ------- that no one could ------- her talent any longer.

(A) speed...ascertain

(B) melancholy...deny

(C) agility...question

(D) grace...affirm

Read the sentence carefully, looking for clue words. A major clue here is *such...that*. You know that Juniper's skating ability, whether good or bad, has led to everybody agreeing about her talent. So whichever words go into the two blanks, they must agree.

Predict the words that go into the blanks, making sure that whatever goes in the second blank supports the meaning of the first. If Juniper skated well, no one would deny that she had a lot of talent. If she skated terribly, everyone would agree that she had no talent. Don't let the negative structure of the second part of the sentence fool you: it's written as "no one could -------" as opposed to "everyone could -------." Make some predictions about the two missing pieces.

Compare your predictions with each answer choice and pick the best fit. Which two words, when in context, will agree and support each other?

In choice A, *speed* and *ascertain* don't make sense together. In choice B, *melancholy* and *deny* don't support one another. It doesn't make sense that "no one could *deny* her talent" because she skated sadly, or with *melancholy*. In choice (C), *agility* and *question* do fit together well. Juniper skates with *agility*, so who could *question* her ability? In choice D, *grace* and *affirm* initially seem to support one another. But remember the negative in the second part of the sentence: "…*no one* could ------- her talent." It's illogical to say that she skated with such *grace* that "no one could *affirm* her talent." Choice (C) must be the answer.

PICKING UP ON CLUES

In order to do well on Sentence Completions, you need to show how a sentence fits together. Clue words will help you do that. The more clues you can find, the clearer the sentence will become. The clearer the sentence, the better your prediction.

What are clue words? There are a variety of clue words. Some will indicate **cause and effect** and others a **contrast**, and some others will **define the missing word**. For example:

- Clues that indicate cause and effect:

  <u>Because</u> he was so scared of the dark, we were ------- to find him sleeping without a night light.

  As a result of her constant lying, Amaya was ------- to trust anyone else.

- Clues that indicate contrast:

  Rita is funny and lighthearted; her twin, Shama, <u>however</u>, is ------- and -------.

  <u>Following</u> the wonderful news, Alejandro's visage changed <u>from</u> an expression of ------- to one of -------.

- Clues that define the missing word:

  A <u>loud and tiresome child</u>, he acted particularly ------- during the long car trip.

  <u>Smart and witty</u>, Xavier was the most ------- student in the class.

> **EXPERT TIP**
>
> Clue words such as *and, but, such as, however,* and *although* can indicate where a sentence is heading. Keep your eyes open for these kinds of helpful words.

Fiona's bedroom still looks like -------, despite her efforts to keep it tidy.

In this example, whatever goes into the blank must complete the contrast implied by the word *despite*. You know then that it must describe the *opposite of tidy*. *Messy* or *disorganized* would be good predictions.

> **EXPERT TIP**
>
> A single word can change the meaning of the entire sentence, so make sure to read the sentence carefully.

PRACTICE

> Practice making predictions on the following examples. Begin by circling the clue words in each sentence, then fill in your prediction.

I like baseball and other -------.

With clothes and empty soda cans all over the floor, Sam's apartment was very -------.

Selah's ------- expression was a clear indication that something great had happened.

She was very ------- and had never hesitated to say what she thought.

The sergeant used ------- language to show his contempt for the recruits.

Even more ------- in person than in her photos, the actress dazzled us.

The violin is a ------- instrument that many people find hard to play.

Some problems are unexpected, but others are -------.

Turning the corner, the car ------- on the slippery road.

Even the musician's critics ------- his fundraising efforts.

> **EXPERT TIP**
>
> Concentrate on making a good prediction first. If you look at the answer choices before you make your prediction, you are much more likely to fall for distracting incorrect answers.

ANSWERS AND EXPLANATIONS

I like baseball (and other) _____sports_____ .

(With) clothes and empty soda cans all over the floor, Sam's apartment was very _____messy_____ .

Selah's _____joyous_____ expression (was a clear indication) that something great had happened.

She was very _____outspoken_____ (and) had never hesitated to say what she thought.

The sergeant used _____condescending_____ language (to show) his contempt for the recruits.

(Even more) _____beautiful_____ in person than in her photos, the actress dazzled us.

The violin (is) a _____difficult_____ instrument (that) many people find hard to play.

Some problems are unexpected, (but others) are _____foreseeable_____ .

Turning the corner, the car _____skidded_____ on the slippery road.

(Even) the musician's critics _____applauded_____ his fundraising efforts.

TACKLING HARD QUESTIONS

Sentence Completions will get more difficult as you go through them, so the last few will be the most difficult. If you get stuck, here are a few tips to help you through:

- Avoid tricky incorrecct answers.

- Take apart tough sentences.

- Work around tough vocabulary.

Avoid Tricky Incorrecct Answers

Toward the end of a set, keep your eyes open for tricky answer choices. Do your best to avoid the most common distractors:

- Opposites of the correct answer

- Words that may sound correct because they are tough

- Questions with two missing pieces, where one word sounds correct but the other doesn't. Note: Lower Level ISEE Sentence Completion questions will have only one blank.

The following example would likely be the twelfth question in a 15-question set:

> At first, the house seemed frightening with all its cobwebs and creaking shutters, but we soon realized that it was quite -------.
>
> **(A)** benign
>
> **(B)** deceptive
>
> **(C)** affluent
>
> **(D)** haunted

Read this sentence carefully. If you read it too quickly, it may sound like, "The house was really scary with all of those cobwebs and creaking shutters, and we soon realized…it was!" So you would pick choice D, *haunted*, or maybe choice B, *deceptive*, when in fact the correct answer is choice (A), *benign*.

Pick Up the Clues

There are two major clues here, and you should have picked them up right away. The first one, *At first*, indicates that the author perceived something to be one way in the beginning—but after taking a second look realized it was different. That leads you to the second clue word, *but*. Just as predicted, the author thought the house was creepy at first *but* then felt differently. You know, therefore, that the word in the blank must be the *opposite* of *creepy* or *haunted*.

Affluent, choice C in the previous example, means wealthy. You might have been tempted to choose it if you were clueless because it looks or sounds impressive. However, it's thrown in there just to tempt you and doesn't make sense in this context. Don't choose a word without good reason.

Take Apart Tough Sentences

Sometimes, it is helpful to break apart tough sentences to decide whether to keep or eliminate an answer choice. Look at the following example, which would likely be the last question in a 15-question set:

> The ------- agreement had never been written down but was understood and upheld by the governments of both countries.
>
> **(A)** tacit
>
> **(B)** public
>
> **(C)** distinguished
>
> **(D)** illegal

What if you were stumped? What if you had no idea which word to pick? Try taking apart the sentence:

Tacit—Hmm, sounds familiar, but no idea what it means. Keep it for now.

Public—Nope. It doesn't sound correct in this context.

Distinguished—If it was so distinguished, why was it never written down?

Illegal—Nope. Do governments uphold illegal agreements? That doesn't sound correct.

Choice (A) sounds the best. As it turns out, it's also correct. *Tacit* agreements are unspoken or silent ones; they're not expressed or declared openly but instead are implied.

TWO-BLANK SENTENCES

Sentences with two blanks can be easier than those with one blank. The best approach is to follow these two rules:

1. Try the easier blank first.

2. Save time by eliminating all choices that won't work for that blank.

Work Around Tough Vocabulary

Don't Pick an Answer Just Because It Sounds Hard

You will almost certainly see unfamiliar words on the ISEE. You should not choose an answer choice just because it sounds hard. Look at a two-blank sentence. The following example would likely be the fifteenth question in a 15-question set:

Screaming and laughing, the students were ------- by their ------- experience on the white-water raft.

(A) amused…tepid

(B) irritated…continued

(C) exhilarated…first

(D) frightened…secure

An unprepared test taker may choose choice A simply because "tepid" sounds like a hard word. That test taker would get this question incorrect. Instead, use the other strategies described in this chapter to avoid tricky incorrect answers and efficiently identify the correct ones.

Look at All the Choices

Check out the first blank first. Sometimes you can eliminate one or more answer choices right away if some possibilities don't fit. *Irritated* and/or *frightened* students do not scream and laugh, so eliminate choices B and D.

Now check the second blank. A *tepid* (or half-hearted) experience wouldn't make a bunch of students scream and laugh, either, so choice A is out. Only choice (C) fits both of the blanks: the students would laugh and scream due to *exhilaration* on their *first* white-water rafting experience.

Try a complex sentence with two blanks. Remember the two rules:

1. Try the easier blank first.

2. Save time by eliminating all choices that won't work for that blank.

    The old ------- hated parties and refused to ------- in the festivities.

    (A) actor...direct

    (B) curmudgeon...partake

    (C) mediator...take

    (D) surgeon...place

For the first blank, it's impossible to rule out any choices because an actor, a curmudgeon (especially), a mediator, and a surgeon all have the potential to be old and to hate parties.

Try the second blank and see what can be ruled out. Choice A doesn't make any sense; what does *direct in the festivities* mean? It's nonsensical. Choice (B), *partake* makes sense. Choice C, *take* in the festivities, doesn't sound correct, and neither does choice D, *place* in the festivities. That leaves (B) as the best and only fit. A *curmudgeon* is, by definition, an ornery or grumpy person, so it makes sense that he wouldn't want to *partake* in the festivities.

Here are some final strategies to help you on Test Day:

- On tough Sentence Completions, remember that you can eliminate answer choices that you know are incorrect. Make an educated guess among the remaining answer choices.

- When eliminating, look for a word charge—is your prediction strongly positive or negative? Eliminate any choices with an opposite or neutral charge.

- Trust your ear! Sometimes the correct answer sounds like it fits the situation. Many phrases on the ISEE will be familiar terms you have heard or seen before.

- Finally, remember to use structural clues in the sentence to predict the missing word(s).

PRACTICE QUESTIONS

1. The funds projected for next year's budget are so ------- that the library will barely be able to maintain its regular hours.

   (A) generous
   (B) meager
   (C) expansive
   (D) extravagant

2. Despite a stern and forbidding demeanor in class, the professor was ------- to students who approached him in his office.

   (A) insensitive
   (B) inhospitable
   (C) remote
   (D) receptive

3. Certain types of spiders are poisonous, while others are relatively -------.

   (A) social
   (B) adventurous
   (C) harmless
   (D) energetic

4. Because of ------- in the temperature of the region, it is difficult to know whether to dress for hot weather or cold.

   (A) rainfalls
   (B) changes
   (C) heat waves
   (D) cold snaps

5. The two houses do not ------- each other; there is a narrow alleyway ------- them.

   (A) neighbor...separating
   (B) resemble...under
   (C) face...above
   (D) touch...between

6. The athlete was so ------- by the heat that he could barely walk.

   (A) annoyed
   (B) strengthened
   (C) pleased
   (D) exhausted

7. Only the most ------- soldiers volunteered to be in the platoon, because that was where they were in greatest danger of being wounded or -------.

   (A) cheerful...promoted
   (B) clever...scratched
   (C) polite...maimed
   (D) courageous...killed

8. The new senator was -------, so he only proposed legislation that stood a reasonable chance of passing.

   (A) confident
   (B) realistic
   (C) ambitious
   (D) inexperienced

9. She didn't like her birthday present, but she ------- to like it to avoid ------- her grandfather's feelings.

   (A) hid...showing
   (B) suppressed...displaying
   (C) pretended...hurting
   (D) felt...creating

10. Rats mature very quickly and ------- prolifically, facilitating the ------- of disease.

    (A) run...control
    (B) hide...prevention
    (C) breed...spread
    (D) mutate...obstruction

11. A public official who accepts ------- is guilty of -------.

   (A) aid...abuse
   (B) awards...dishonesty
   (C) bribes...corruption
   (D) advice...misbehavior

12. Though Elena had received the company's ------- possible service award, her supervisor felt it necessary to ------- her for arriving ten minutes late.

   (A) highest...admonish
   (B) poorest...vex
   (C) best...commend
   (D) finest...extol

13. As the supply of fresh water -------, the castaways were forced to ------- the remainder.

   (A) dwindled...ration
   (B) stabilized...waste
   (C) grew...preserve
   (D) drained...distribute

14. He was an ------- art collector and had ------- several fine paintings by such artists as Picasso and Matisse.

   (A) unsuccessful...bought
   (B) active...released
   (C) avid...acquired
   (D) enthusiastic...destroyed

15. Most of those polled seemed ------- a change and ------- that they would vote to reelect the mayor.

   (A) wary of...stated
   (B) cautious about...denied
   (C) afraid of...disputed
   (D) open to...asserted

16. Before rolling out the pie crust, the chef ------- the counter with flour to ------- the dough from sticking.

   (A) drenched...halt
   (B) baked...banish
   (C) kneaded...alleviate
   (D) dusted...prevent

17. Despite the ------- price of the car, Jose's parents were ------- to permit him to buy it.

   (A) affordable...willing
   (B) outrageous...hesitant
   (C) usual...afraid
   (D) reasonable...reluctant

18. The speaker ------- on for hours, repeating herself at length and ------- her audience to tears.

   (A) prated...frightening
   (B) simpered...forcing
   (C) whined...provoking
   (D) droned...boring

19. He was ------- enough by the affront to ------- the person who had insulted him.

   (A) incensed...strike
   (B) sad...congratulate
   (C) glad...thank
   (D) scared...frighten

20. Although they were intelligent people, they were ------- by the advertiser's false -------.

   (A) addressed...messages
   (B) displeased...speech
   (C) amused...budget
   (D) deceived...claims

21. Newcastle in northern England is an important source of coal, so "carrying coals to Newcastle" means doing something -------.

    (A) appropriate
    (B) normal
    (C) unnecessary
    (D) dirty

22. Isaiah concealed his true ------- under a guise of -------.

    (A) passions...instability
    (B) humility...modesty
    (C) concern...indifference
    (D) generosity...altruism

23. Though normally quite -------, the grizzly can become ------- when disturbed by a human.

    (A) enormous...frightened
    (B) affectionate...happy
    (C) harmless...ferocious
    (D) voracious...appeased

24. Many people ------- that owls are intelligent, but this claim is nothing more than a -------.

    (A) assume...fact
    (B) agree...rebuttal
    (C) refute...tale
    (D) believe...myth

25. Roberta was ------- for cheating, though she believed that her ------- use of encyclopedia entries was not deceitful.

    (A) censured...fraudulent
    (B) reprimanded...paltry
    (C) honored...primitive
    (D) chastised...treacherous

26. The newspaper editorial argued that allowing violence to pass without ------- gives the appearance of ------- it.

    (A) comment...condoning
    (B) incident...provoking
    (C) activity...soothing
    (D) agitation...pacifying

27. Investigators believe that the rash of fires was not the work of ------- but a ------- of unfortunate accidents.

    (A) a pyromaniac...factor
    (B) an accomplice...consequence
    (C) a criminal...premonition
    (D) an arsonist...series

28. Archaeologists ------- the documents while ------- the remains of a 1,000-year-old Roman fort in what is now northern England.

    (A) attached...marring
    (B) unearthed...excavating
    (C) diverted...mourning
    (D) construed...surmising

29. At his concert debut, the young violinist tossed off the most difficult passages without any apparent effort, ------- the audience with his -------.

    (A) enraging...timorousness
    (B) impressing...prestige
    (C) enthralling...stolidity
    (D) dazzling...virtuosity

30. Except for a few ------- shrubs, the frozen, windswept tundra provides little ------- for the herds of caribou that migrate across it seasonally.

    (A) stunted...nourishment
    (B) harmful...credit
    (C) formless...refuge
    (D) premature...privacy

31. The writing process is ------- for most, but she is able to compose poems without much -------.

    (A) repugnant...skill

    (B) amusing...pain

    (C) tedious...excitement

    (D) arduous...effort

32. Despite the ------- predictions of noted meteorologists, the damage caused by the storm was -------.

    (A) accurate...foreseen

    (B) ominous...minimal

    (C) dire...terrible

    (D) encouraging...slight

33. Tony and Marcia spent an ------- afternoon ------- hand in hand through the sun-dappled park.

    (A) untimely...traipsing

    (B) ebullient...recurring

    (C) exhaustive...persevering

    (D) idyllic...strolling

34. Because Ricky's college interview had gone well, his counselor was ------- to learn that he was ------- about applying for college.

    (A) relieved...ambivalent

    (B) troubled...decisive

    (C) disappointed...unenthusiastic

    (D) delighted...aghast

35. Deirdre was ------- as a leader in student government, even though she would have been just as happy to play a(n) ------- role.

    (A) questioned...minor

    (B) applauded...pivotal

    (C) hailed...integral

    (D) recognized...supporting

36. Later that evening, the snow ------- in huge drifts, making driving ------- difficult and finally impossible.

    (A) melted...continually

    (B) accumulated...increasingly

    (C) amassed...conversely

    (D) evaporated...starkly

37. Because the astronomy textbook was so difficult to -------, she had to rely on the physics professor's lectures to explain the more ------- concepts.

    (A) consider...intricate

    (B) orbit...essential

    (C) repudiate...basic

    (D) follow...complicated

38. The 16th century chateau is ------- decorated with delicately wrought tapestries, hand-crafted -------, and leaded stained glass windows.

    (A) sumptuously...furnishings

    (B) artistically...accompaniments

    (C) concisely...cadences

    (D) imprudently...trappings

39. At the mercy of his ------- appetite, Jaiden was ------- to stay on his diet.

    (A) light...unwilling

    (B) moderate...free

    (C) massive...sure

    (D) healthy...unable

40. Weighted down with heavy armor, medieval knights ------- their broadswords too ------- to fight for more than a few minutes at a time.

    (A) wielded...awkwardly

    (B) parried...perversely

    (C) hoisted...obdurately

    (D) swung...actively

41. To his admirers, the Prime Minister was -------; to his -------, merely stubborn.

    (A) eminent...imitators
    (B) remarkable...adherents
    (C) tenacious...detractors
    (D) complimentary...endorsers

42. In his ------- to eliminate clutter, Terry discarded old files and documents -------, heedless of their potential future importance.

    (A) zeal...indiscriminately
    (B) agitation...persuasively
    (C) bravado...competitively
    (D) insomnia...tactfully

43. The author's first novel was critically acclaimed for its originality and -------, but its ------- appeal was limited.

    (A) repartee...individual
    (B) suspensefulness...vital
    (C) obscurity...lasting
    (D) sophistication...popular

44. Given the ------- in today's market, our sale predictions may have been a little -------.

    (A) upturn...inexact
    (B) boom...audacious
    (C) instability...reckless
    (D) stagnation...optimistic

45. Tory painted a(n) ------- view of the city, starting at the lakefront and ------- inland for several miles.

    (A) panoramic...ranging
    (B) impressionistic...burnishing
    (C) ascetic...eddying
    (D) intrinsic...embellishing

46. The film has a ------- effect on viewers, leaving them emotionally ------- and physically spent.

    (A) flippant...relaxed
    (B) cathartic...drained
    (C) normal...intact
    (D) stern...laconic

47. She was a(n) -------, living by herself and avoiding other people.

    (A) adventurer
    (B) socialite
    (C) hermit
    (D) fool

48. As a strict vegetarian, she ------- meat, eggs, and dairy products.

    (A) sells
    (B) ignores
    (C) avoids
    (D) grades

49. The professor's students ------- him so much that they would ------- his mannerisms and style of dress.

    (A) admired...imitate
    (B) feared...plan
    (C) ignored...notice
    (D) fought...see

50. The utter failure in which the project ended is evidence of the ------- of the people who planned it.

    (A) lack of ability
    (B) strength of character
    (C) careful planning
    (D) wild imagination

51. The hummingbird is a voracious eater, ------- many times its own weight in food each day.

    (A) finding

    (B) rejecting

    (C) making

    (D) consuming

52. The witness had always shown great ------- in the past, so it seemed reasonable to believe her account now.

    (A) honesty

    (B) kindness

    (C) cowardice

    (D) care

53. Some animals will ------- themselves when presented with a(n) ------- amount of food.

    (A) control...absent

    (B) deceive...plentiful

    (C) starve...eaten

    (D) gorge...unlimited

54. He was too ------- to compromise even with people whose views were relatively close to his own.

    (A) loyal to his friends

    (B) strongly opinionated

    (C) quick to action

    (D) friendly to strangers

55. The child was obedient and well-behaved at home, but at school her teachers found her -------.

    (A) small and weak

    (B) hard to control

    (C) eager to learn

    (D) slow and careful

56. The theory of evolution is probably true, because scientists have found a lot of ------- for it.

    (A) supporting evidence

    (B) other names

    (C) public scorn

    (D) popular support

57. Because the instructor was so -------, the explanation took much longer than necessary.

    (A) serious

    (B) intelligent

    (C) wordy

    (D) experienced

58. On an assembly line, each step in the production process is ------- in exactly the same way every time, ensuring that the finished items are -------.

    (A) costly...cheap

    (B) repeated...identical

    (C) complicated...efficient

    (D) strange...unique

59. It was once common for younger people to show ------- by standing up when an elder entered the room.

    (A) respect

    (B) bravery

    (C) fear

    (D) intelligence

60. Because leather is so -------, it is used in clothing to ------- fabric from cuts and scrapes.

    (A) tough...protect

    (B) warm...cool

    (C) smelly...prevent

    (D) attractive...design

61. Widely reported incidents of crime in a city tend to ------- fear and suspicion among the residents.

(A) create

(B) reduce

(C) confuse

(D) condemn

62. In the film *Citizen Kane*, a reporter tries and fails to make sense of the title character's ------- last word, "Rosebud."

(A) clever

(B) mysterious

(C) sarcastic

(D) dying

63. The governor's opponents looked for evidence of past wrongdoing on her part, but her record was -------.

(A) unbroken

(B) conclusive

(C) popular

(D) spotless

64. The teacher tried to ------- the student's ------- use of grammar and vocabulary.

(A) replace...remarkable

(B) distort...uncomplimentary

(C) approve...perfect

(D) correct...faulty

65. After its engine -------, the boat drifted ------- for days.

(A) started...swiftly

(B) raced...slowly

(C) died...aimlessly

(D) broke...briefly

66. Cowbirds ------- their eggs in the nests of other birds, who ------- raise the chicks as their own.

(A) deposit...unwittingly

(B) steal...enthusiastically

(C) exchange...debatably

(D) ignore...unanimously

67. The politician's thoughtful ------- helped to ------- the skeptical public.

(A) beliefs...warn

(B) service...justify

(C) presence...betray

(D) argument...convince

68. The lake was in serious jeopardy; it was being contaminated and ------- by human beings faster than nature could ------- and replenish it.

(A) endangered...flow

(B) drained...purify

(C) modified...improve

(D) impelled...filter

69. Because it features many ------- actors, the new film is ------- to be a major box office success.

(A) important...doomed

(B) prominent...expected

(C) unknown...certain

(D) talented...unlikely

70. The shrewd private investigator noticed several ------- clues that the police had failed to -------.

(A) significant...detect

(B) irrelevant...pursue

(C) crucial...scan

(D) spurious...find

71. After being unfairly ------- by the chairperson, Luis ------- out of the meeting room.

    (A) upbraided...stormed

    (B) burdened...sauntered

    (C) scrutinized...strolled

    (D) heckled...strutted

72. Through years of -------, the once ------- cathedral was allowed to become shabby, dirty, and increasingly unappealing.

    (A) renovation...impressive

    (B) adornment...decrepit

    (C) neglect...majestic

    (D) improvement...towering

73. Although the game was ------- in its early stages, it later turned into a -------.

    (A) unfair   debacle

    (B) close...rout

    (C) uneven...trouncing

    (D) uncontested...stalemate

74. The news wire service ------- information so ------- that events are reported all over the world shortly after they happen.

    (A) records...precisely

    (B) falsifies...deliberately

    (C) verifies...painstakingly

    (D) disseminates...rapidly

75. Nearly everyone has seen photographs of the Grand Canyon, but its ------- topography cannot be fully ------- through two-dimensional images.

    (A) spectacular...appreciated

    (B) copious...decorated

    (C) dingy...screened

    (D) peripheral...saturated

76. The farmers continued to work long hours throughout the fall and winter, ------- their ------- and repairing buildings and equipment.

    (A) clearing...crop

    (B) reaping...fauna

    (C) securing...debris

    (D) tending...livestock

77. The ancient stone carvings are wonderfully -------, depicting in intricate detail the ------- in battle of thousands of soldiers.

    (A) fragmentary...succumbing

    (B) beautiful...lunging

    (C) worn...enacting

    (D) ornate...clashing

78. Faced with such a paucity of ------- information about the millionaire's new husband, the newspaper has ------- printing unsubstantiated rumors.

    (A) paramount...balked at

    (B) reliable...resorted to

    (C) wealthy...refrained from

    (D) immediate...wavered about

79. Once ------- across the continent, wolves had been ------- almost to extinction by the 1950s.

    (A) nonexistent...propelled

    (B) numerous...hunted

    (C) garrulous...abducted

    (D) captive...secured

80. The hostess invited relatively ------- guests, making the party seem less ------- than it had last year.

    (A) eccentric...unique

    (B) talkative...lengthy

    (C) ordinary...banal

    (D) undistinguished...exclusive

81. The best archaeological evidence ------- that the gigantic structures were ------- by an extinct aboriginal people.

    (A) indicates...erected
    (B) specifies...registered
    (C) replies...built
    (D) imagines...drafted

82. Cockroaches are one of the most ------- of all creatures because they can ------- in almost any situation.

    (A) adaptable...thrive
    (B) disgusting...reside
    (C) frail...survive
    (D) versatile...die

83. The violinist gave an ------- performance in the final movement and left the audience -------.

    (A) extended...early
    (B) accomplished...astounded
    (C) exquisite...afflicted
    (D) absorbing...distracted

84. Somehow, in spite of her ------- study habits, Mary always received ------- grades on her history exams.

    (A) atrocious...failing
    (B) lackadaisical...mediocre
    (C) careful...outstanding
    (D) excellent...poor

85. Having seen the film before, Caleb was ------- to be as ------- as we who were viewing it for the first time.

    (A) prone...bewildered
    (B) predicted...critical
    (C) flagrant...blissful
    (D) unlikely...shocked

86. A born pessimist, Kylie was ------- when her favorite team ------- in the final quarter of the last regular season game.

    (A) impartial...tied
    (B) forgiven...forfeited
    (C) depressed...conceded
    (D) stunned...triumphed

87. Having procrastinated far too long, he attacked the project so ------- that he made many ------- errors.

    (A) hastily...inadvertent
    (B) learnedly...noticeable
    (C) methodically...fundamental
    (D) weakly...trivial

88. Most of the opinions expressed in her book are -------, but it does contain a few ------- insights.

    (A) sensible...intelligent
    (B) absurd...brilliant
    (C) useless...ambitious
    (D) sound...practical

89. The politician ------- his position and ------- a proposal he had previously opposed.

    (A) changed...criticized
    (B) reversed...supported
    (C) modified...blocked
    (D) upheld...defended

90. Moviegoers were thrilled by the hero's daring ------- and amused by his sidekick's madcap -------.

    (A) feats...tribulations
    (B) escapades...ordeals
    (C) tedium...zaniness
    (D) exploits...antics

91. Some claim that the new educational project ------- to gifted pupils while ------- the needs of average students, who constitute a clear majority.

    (A) adapts...emulating
    (B) salutes...effecting
    (C) objects...implying
    (D) caters...ignoring

92. The bears that frequent the campground are bold and occasionally ------- in their ------- for food.

    (A) abundant...capacity
    (B) emphatic...inclination
    (C) aggressive...quest
    (D) unbalanced...pressure

93. Sai brought Gabby's horse back to the stable by improvising a harness that ------- the mare to his own -------.

    (A) hitched...zenith
    (B) motivated...goal
    (C) spurred...steed
    (D) yoked...mount

94. The whale shark is ------- encountered by divers because of its low numbers and ------- habits.

    (A) successfully...congenial
    (B) anxiously...unfortunate
    (C) constantly....indifferent
    (D) rarely...solitary

95. The ------- deposited tons of mineral-rich volcanic ash, restoring to the soil nutrients ------- decades of farming.

    (A) eruption...depleted by
    (B) abyss...harvested during
    (C) tumult...alien to
    (D) barrier...entrenched in

96. Members of the sect ------- from before sun up until long after dusk, ------- the sin of sloth.

    (A) fasted...savoring
    (B) sanctified...tainting
    (C) concealed...deploring
    (D) toiled...avoiding

97. Meteorologists ------- storm systems in order to give shoreline residents adequate ------- of hurricanes, floods, and other disasters.

    (A) track...forewarning
    (B) study...almanacs
    (C) record...barometers
    (D) design...pretense

98. The firm employed many lackadaisical employees, who had a(n) ------- approach to their work.

    (A) creative
    (B) independent
    (C) unproductive
    (D) discontented

99. Due to ------- weather, the school ------- all classes.

    (A) cold...continued
    (B) severe...canceled
    (C) humid...relieved
    (D) frosty...alleviated

100. Many paleontologists believe that modern birds and crocodiles are the ------- of the ancient dinosaurs.

    (A) descendants
    (B) ancestors
    (C) neologisms
    (D) reptiles

101. Her eyes were wide with ------- as the ship, ------- with gold, jewels, and precious metals, sailed into port.

    (A) amazement...arrived
    (B) reason...purged
    (C) wonder...laden
    (D) purpose...meandered

102. It was Mount Vesuvius that erupted and ------- the city of Pompeii in the year 79 C.E.

    (A) desiccated
    (B) decimated
    (C) erected
    (D) detected

103. The determined young cadet ------- every character trait that the ideal soldier should have.

    (A) embodied
    (B) created
    (C) secluded
    (D) vaporized

PRACTICE QUESTIONS ANSWERS AND EXPLANATIONS

1. B

Choice (B) is the correct answer choice. If the library will barely be able to maintain its regular hours, there must be *limited* funds. "Meager" means lacking in quality or quantity, which is a perfect match.

2. D

Choice (D) is the correct answer choice. The word "despite" is a clue that this Sentence Completion question involves a contrast. Although the professor seems stern and forbidding, he must be different in his office, so the best answer will be similar to *friendly*, and "receptive" is closest in meaning.

3. C

Choice (C) is the correct answer choice. The word "while" creates a contrast between spiders that are "poisonous," or dangerous, and those that are *not dangerous, or* "harmless."

4. B

Choice (B) is the correct answer choice. The clue word "because" indicates cause and effect, and the key phrase "difficult to know whether to dress for hot or cold" indicates contrast. "Changes" in temperature would make it difficult to know how to dress. "Heat waves" and "cold snaps" may be tempting, but the sentence requires an answer that addresses both hot and cold weather.

5. D

Choice (D) is the correct answer choice. The first part of the sentence indicates that the houses do not do something to each other. The key phase in the second half of the sentence, "narrow alleyway" indicates that the buildings are separate. Predict that the houses do not *connect* to each other because there is an alleyway *between* them. Only "touch" has a similar meaning to your prediction, and "between" is a perfect match.

6. D

Choice (D) is the correct answer choice. Heat left the athlete in a state where he could barely walk, so the blank must be a choice close to *weakened*. The word "exhausted" is correct.

7. D

Choice (D) is the correct answer choice. The first part of the sentence describes the nature of the solders. Note the cause-and-effect word, "because" and the key phrase "greatest danger of being wounded." This would indicate that fist blank would be a word like "brave," so "courageous" fits. The second blank is preceded by the word "or," which is used to link alternatives, so "killed" is correct here.

8. B

Choice (B) is the correct answer choice. The clue word "so" indicates cause and effect. The key phrase here is "stood a reasonable chance of passing," so "realistic" is the most consistent adjective to describe the senator.

9. C

Choice (C) is the correct answer choice. The clue word is "but," which indicates contrast. The first part of the sentence indicates she didn't like her present, and therefore the correct word choices have to be words that provide that contrast and sense.

10. C

Choice (C) is the correct answer choice. The word "and" suggests that this is description clue. "Mature very quickly and breed prolifically" (meaning a lot) describes why rats contribute to the "spread" of disease.

11. C

Choice (C) is the correct answer choice. This is a cause-and-effect statement. You can rephase this as an "if…then" clue. If a public official accepts "bribes," then he or she is guilty of "corruption."

12. A

Choice (A) is the correct answer choice. The clue word "though" indicates contrast. Elena was "ten minutes late," so you can assume her supervisor would "admonish," or scold, her. This stands in direct contrast to the fact that she received the "highest" service award.

13. A

Choice (A) is the correct answer choice. The clue word "as" indicates cause and effect. You are looking for words that provide a logical description of the water supply. Only "dwindled" and "rationed" make sense.

14. C

Choice (C) is the correct answer choice. Look carefully for the clues in this sentence. What kind of an art collector would have paintings by Picasso and Matisse? Someone either (C), "avid," or D, "enthusiastic." However, only the second part of (C), "acquired," makes any sense in the second blank.

15. A

Choice (A) is the correct answer choice. Voters who say they would "vote to reelect the mayor" are either *not in favor of* change or "wary of" change, and this is what they "stated."

16. D

Choice (D) is the correct answer choice. What would the chef do to the counter? Would he want the pie crust to stick? He'd probably want to "prevent" it from sticking, and he'd do this by making sure that he'd "dusted" the counter with flour.

17. D

Choice (D) is the correct answer choice. The contrast clue word "Despite" tells you that the cost of the car and Jose's parents response to his buying it were in opposition to each other. While the cost was "reasonable," his parents were "reluctant."

18. D

Choice (D) is the correct answer choice. The speaker repeated herself at length—in other words, she "droned" on for hours, consequently "boring" her audience to tears.

19. A

Choice (A) is the correct answer choice. The clue word here is "affront," which is an action or remark that causes outrage or offense. This would cause a negative reaction, which is only offered by choice (A).

20. D

Choice (D) is the correct answer choice. The clue word "Although" indicates a contrast between the intelligence of the people described and their behavior. Choice (D) supplies the correct contrast—they were "deceived" by false "claims."

21. C

Choice (C) is the correct answer choice. The cause-and-effect clue word is "so". If there is coal in Newcastle, then bringing more is "unnecessary."

22. C

Choice (C) is the correct answer choice. The clue words "true" and "guise" indicate a contrast between the two words. Isaiah concealed his "concern" under a guise of "indifference."

23. C

Choice (C) is the correct answer choice. The clue word "though" indicates a contrast. The grizzly is normally "harmless" but can become "ferocious."

24. D

Choice (D) is the correct answer choice. The clue word "but" indicates contrast. "But this claim" suggests that what people "believe" about owls is false—"believe" and "myth" fit the assumption-reality structure here.

25. A

Choice (A) is the correct answer choice. The second blank, preceded by the clue word "though" indicating contrast, suggests cheating. It is Roberta's "fraudulent" use of encyclopedia entries that gets her in trouble. "Censured" means scolded or reprimanded.

26. A

Choice (A) is the correct answer choice. "Condoning" means approving, so if a newspaper editorial does not offer any "comment" on a violent incident, it may appear they are "condoning" violence.

27. D

Choice (D) is the correct answer choice. "Arsonist" and "pyromaniac" are both words for people who start fires but "series" is the only word that fits the second blank in the sentence.

28. B

Choice (B) is the correct answer choice. Archaeologists "unearth" or find something in the ground by digging things up. While doing so, they may also "excavate," or remove, earth carefully and systematically in order to find buried remains.

29. D

Choice (D) is the correct answer choice. The initial part of the sentence describes an extremely impressive performance by the violinist who displayed great musical skill. "Dazzling" and "virtuosity" match that description.

30. A

Choice (A) is the correct answer choice. The clue phase "except for" indicates a contrast. Except for "stunted" shrubs, the tundra provides little "nourishment" for the caribou.

31. D

Choice (D) is the correct answer choice. The clue word "but" indicates a contrast between the two parts of the sentence. The sentence is a comparison between most people's experience and that of the poet. Most people find writing "arduous" (hard work), but she does it without "effort."

32. B

Choice (B) is the correct answer choice. "Despite" indicates that the predictions of the meteorologists were the opposite of the damage the storm actually caused. "Ominous" and "minimal" are the contrasting words that work in this sentence.

33. D

Choice (D) is the correct answer choice. The phrases "hand in hand" and "sun-dappled" suggest that Tony and Marcia's walk was pleasant or "idyllic." Only "strolling" for the second word is in keeping with the tone of the sentence.

34. C

Choice (C) is the correct answer choice. There are two clue words in this sentence. "Because" indicates cause and effect. Ricky's interview went well, "but" (the second clue word) his counselor was "disappointed" to learn Ricky was "unenthusiastic" about going to college would correctly fit the sentence.

35. D

Choice (D) is the correct answer choice. "Even though" tells you that you have a contrast. While Deidre was a leader, or "recognized" as a leader, she was just as happy to play a secondary, or "supporting," role.

36. B

Choice (B) is the correct answer choice. Driving must go from one state of difficulty to being "finally impossible." Logically, only "increasingly" difficult fits here. Also, the fact that the snow "accumulated" in big drifts accounts for the worsening driving conditions.

37. D

Choice (D) is the correct answer choice. The textbook was difficult, so it logically follows that the professor's lectures would have to help her with the more "intricate," choice A, or "complicated," choice (D), concepts. However, only "follow" logically fits in the first blank.

38. A

Choice (A) is the correct answer choice. What would be hand-crafted? A strong case can be made for "furnishings," and a weaker case made for "trappings." Looking at the first blank, however, only "sumptuously," choice (A), makes sense.

39. D

Choice (D) is the correct answer choice. "At the mercy of" is the clue here. Jaiden has a "healthy" appetite, which renders him "unable" to stay on his diet.

40. A

Choice (A) is the correct answer choice. The knights are "Weighted down with heavy armor." It follows logically that "wielding" a sword with all that armor would be very uncomfortably, or "awkwardly," performed.

41. C

Choice (C) is the correct answer choice. The semicolon and the key word "merely" indicate that you need words that are opposites. His admirers found the Prime Minister tough, or "tenacious," but his enemies, or "detractors," found him merely stubborn.

42. A

Choice (A) is the correct answer choice. "Heedless" tells you that Terry was a little careless and overeager to clean up his mess. In other words, he had too much "zeal" and carelessly, or "indiscriminately," discarded the files.

43. D

Choice (D) is the correct answer choice. The first blank calls for a positive word to go with "originality," so "sophistication" works. For the second blank, the clue word "but" indicates contrast. Limited in "popular" appeal is another way of saying the book did not appeal to a broad range of people.

44. D

Choice (D) is the correct answer choice. "Given" and "may have been" tell you that whatever the market is doing, the "predictions" were the opposite. Given the "stagnation," or slowness, of the market, predictions were too "optimistic," or positive.

45. A

Choice (A) is the correct answer choice. Tory's painting depicts the "lakefront" and "inland." Such a broad view is summed up in the word "panoramic" for the first blank. "Ranging" is also the only word to fit logically into the second blank.

46. B

Choice (B) is the correct answer choice. The phrase "And physically spent" is a clue that the viewers were also emotionally spent, or "drained." Something "cathartic" would accomplish this.

47. C

Choice (C) is the correct answer choice. The key phrase here is "living by herself," which tells you that the woman may be reclusive and "a hermit."

48. C

Choice (C) is the correct answer choice. This is a Sentence Completion question that heavily relies on logic: If she is a vegetarian, she must not eat meat. In other words, she "avoids" it.

49. A

Choice (A) is the correct answer choice. This two-blank cause-and-effect Sentence Completion question must have a second blank that logically follows the implication of the first blank. Using word charge, you'll find that "admired...imitate" is the only positive-positive pair.

50. A

Choice (A) is the correct answer choice. "Utter failure" is the strong clue phrase here—these words show that the project planners had a "lack of ability." Choices B, C, and D are too positive.

51. D

Choice (D) is the correct answer choice. "Voracious eater" is the key phrase here. You're looking for a word that means eating; "consuming" fits the bill.

52. A

Choice (A) is the correct answer choice. "Reasonable to believe her" is the key phrase in this question, indicating that "honesty" is the word you're looking for.

53. D

Choice (D) is the correct answer choice. There's a strong connection between the two blanks here, so plug each choice in to see which one fits. "Gorge...unlimited" has the most logical connection.

54. B

Choice (B) is the correct answer choice. "Too ------- to compromise" is the key phrase in this question, indicating that "strongly opinionated" is the phrase you're looking for.

55. B

Choice (B) is the correct answer choice. In this sentence, the clue word "but" indicates a contrast. If the child is "obedient and well behaved at home," then you are looking for an answer that means the opposite. The only answer that fits this is (B), "hard to control."

56. A

Choice (A) is the correct answer choice. To answer this question, ask yourself: what phrase supports the assertion that a theory was "probably true"? "Supporting evidence" is the best answer.

57. C

Choice (C) is the correct answer choice. If the "explanations took longer than necessary," then this instructor must use *too many words*. This prediction is an easy match to the correct answer, "wordy."

58. B

Choice (B) is the correct answer choice. The key phrase is "exactly the same way," which tells you to look for a word that means the same in the second blank. When steps are "repeated," they do not change; they are "identical" each time. Eliminate A because "costly" and "cheap" have opposite meanings. Choices C and D do not make sense in context.

59. A

Choice (A) is the correct answer choice. By "standing up when an elder [enters]," a person shows "respect."

60. A

Choice (A) is the correct answer choice. The key phrase is "from cuts and scrapes," which tells you that the second blank should indicate that leather "protects" against cuts and scrapes. Only the pair in choice (A) fits both blanks.

61. A

Choice (A) is the correct answer choice. Increases in crime reports often lead to fear, so "create" is the most logical choice.

62. B

Choice (B) is the correct answer choice. The key phrase is "make sense of," which leads you to "mysterious," or hard to explain.

63. D

Choice (D) is the correct answer choice. The structural clue word "but" tells you that if opponents searched for wrongdoing, the blank should indicate that they didn't find any. "Spotless" is correct.

64. D

Choice (D) is the correct answer choice. What's a likely scenario between a teacher and student here? "Correct" and "faulty" make the best sense in this sentence.

65. C

Choice (C) is the correct answer choice. "Drifted" is the clue word here—a boat would drift "aimlessly" if its engine "died."

66. A

Choice (A) is the correct answer choice. Here, it's hard to predict the blanks; you have to plug in each answer choice. Only "deposit…unwittingly" makes sense—other birds would "unwittingly" (without realizing it) raise cowbird chicks as their own if the eggs were "deposited" in their nests.

67. D

Choice (D) is the correct answer choice. The clue words "thoughtful" and "helped" indicate positive words for both blanks here. With a thoughtful "argument," a politician might "convince" a skeptical public.

68. B

Choice (B) is the correct answer choice. Only "purify" fits the second blank here; "purify" describes the natural process by which a lake replenishes itself.

69. B

Choice (B) is the correct answer choice. This is a typical cause-and-effect sentence: because *x*, *y*. Predict that a movie with *famous actors* would be *predicted* to be a success. "Prominent…expected" fits the structure of the sentence; a film with "prominent," or *famous*, actors would be "expected" to be successful.

70. A

Choice (A) is the correct answer choice. The first blank could work with either choice (A), "significant," or C, "crucial." Only "detect" fits the second blank, however.

71. A

Choice (A) is the correct answer choice. "After" indicates cause and effect, and "unfairly" tells you that Luis was not treated kindly. This means that he was either "upbraided" or "heckled." Only "stormed" shows the effect of this treatment, as it is unlikely that someone who was being treated unfairly would have "strutted out of the meeting room."

72. C

Choice (C) is the correct answer choice. This is a cause-and-effect Sentence Completion question. The cathedral has become "shabby, dirty, and increasingly unappealing," so the cathedral was once either "impressive" or "majestic." The first blank describes the poor—or lack of any—care the cathedral received, so only "neglect…majestic" works in this sentence.

73. B

Choice (B) is the correct answer choice. This Sentence Completion question includes opposites. The game was "close" but became a "rout."

74. D

Choice (D) is the correct answer choice. The news wire service is able to *spread*, or "disseminate," information *quickly*, or "rapidly", after events happen.

75. A

Choice (A) is the correct answer choice. "But" tells you that "photographs" and "two-dimensional images" don't give the full impact of the real Grand Canyon. Its "spectacular" topography cannot be fully "appreciated" through pictures alone.

76. D

Choice (D) is the correct answer choice. Only "tending…livestock" makes sense here. While "repairing buildings and equipment," farmers are also *taking care of* their *animals*; in other words, they are "tending" their "livestock."

77. D

Choice (D) is the correct answer choice. The stone carvings depict a battle scene "in intricate detail." While both "beautiful" and "ornate" are possibilities for the first blank, the correct answer is "ornate…clashing" because "clashing" is the only appropriate word to describe the battle scene described in the second part of the sentence.

78. B

Choice (B) is the correct answer choice. "Paucity" means scarcity. "Unsubstantiated" means unproven. This means that you can assume that the newspaper has very little *proven*, or "reliable," information and has *relied on*, or "resorted to," rumors.

79. B

Choice (B) is the correct answer choice. The word "Once" tells you that while wolves are now extinct, they were "numerous" at one point. The only word to logically fit into the second blank is "hunted."

80. D

Choice (D) is the correct answer choice. The hostess has done something to make this year's party less ------- than last year's. In other words, the correct answer choices will be opposites. "Undistinguished" and "exclusive" fit the bill.

81. A

Choice (A) is the correct answer choice. What would "an extinct aboriginal people" have done with a "gigantic structure"? Either they "erected" it or "built" it. However, there are no clues to support the idea that the best evidence "replies," so only "indicates…erected" fits the sentence in this question.

82. A

Choice (A) is the correct answer choice. The two words should relate closely to each other. The first word will describe cockroaches, and the second work will describe what the cockroaches can do in relation to that description. "Adaptable" and "thrive" are the only words that relate to each other in this way.

83. B

Choice (B) is the correct answer choice. The audience reacted in a particular way as a direct result of how the violinist played. This means that the correct answer will include a pair of words that relate to each other strongly. Only "accomplished" and "astounded" fit the bill.

84. D

Choice (D) is the correct answer choice. "In spite of" tells you that Mary's study habits and grades are in opposition to each other. The correct answer must be a pair of opposites, and only "excellent…poor" fit the sentence.

85. D

Choice (D) is the correct answer choice. Caleb has already seen the film, while everyone else is seeing it for the first time. Both parties' reactions will be opposite each other. Caleb is "unlikely" to be as "shocked" as everyone else.

86. D

Choice (D) is the correct answer choice. This question starts by describing Kylie as "a born pessimist," or someone who focuses on the negative side of things. This means that she would have been either *surprised* if her team *did do well* or *not surprised* if her team *did not do well*. Only "stunned…triumphed" fits one of these two predictions.

87. A

Choice (A) is the correct answer choice. He "procrastinated," or waited until the last minute to do his work. This makes it likely that he would have to attack the project *in a hurry*, or "hastily." As a result of this haste, it follows that he would make *careless*, or "inadvertent," errors.

88. B

Choice (B) is the correct answer choice. "But" indicates a contrast, so you know you are looking for a pair of opposites. If her opinions are "absurd," then "brilliant" insights would stand in contrast. "Absurd" and "brilliant" oppose each other in the way you are looking for.

89. B

Choice (B) is the correct answer choice. "Previously" tells you that what the politician is now doing with the proposal stands in opposition to what he did formerly. In other words, he "reversed" his position on a proposal that he had "supported" earlier.

90. D

Choice (D) is the correct answer choice. A hero would perform either daring "escapades" or "exploits." However, only "antics" would amuse an audience; it's unlikely that anyone would find "ordeals" amusing.

91. D

Choice (D) is the correct answer choice. "While" tells you that the "new educational project" appears one way to some and another way to others. In other words, it "caters" to some people while "ignoring" others.

92. C

Choice (C) is the correct answer choice. If the bears are "bold," it follows logically that they would be "aggressive" in their *search*, or "quest," for food.

93. D

Choice (D) is the correct answer choice. If Sai "improvised" a harness, he had to make one up. "Hitched" and "yoked" both make sense for the first blank, but only "mount" fits the second blank.

94. D

Choice (D) is the correct answer choice. "Low numbers" tells you that there aren't many sharks. In other words, they are "rarely" encountered by divers due to their *lonely*, or "solitary," habits.

95. A

Choice (A) is the correct answer choice. You know that soil nutrients were restored. This must mean that the soil nutrients were at one time *taken away*, or "depleted," from the Earth. Volcanic ash is deposited by a volcano's "eruption."

96. D

Choice (D) is the correct answer choice. What would a sect do from "sun up until long after dark"? Logically, they would *work*, or "toil," thus "avoiding" laziness, a trait that sloths are known for. This can be referred to as "sin of sloth."

97. A

Choice (A) is the correct answer choice. Meteorologists would either "track" or "study" storm systems. However, only "forewarning" fits logically into the second blank.

98. C

Choice (C) is the correct answer choice. "Lackadaisical" means showing a lack of interest or spirit, being listless or languid. If the firm employed lackadaisical workers, these workers probably had an "unproductive" approach to their work.

99. B

Choice (B) is the correct answer choice. If you tried each of the first blank answer choices, you'd see that they all fit. This means you must use the second blank to choose the correct answer; only one of them will make sense. Plugging these four words back into the sentence, only chcoice (B) makes sense: "Due to severe weather, the school canceled all classes."

100. A

Choice (A) is the correct answer choice. This question is filled with elements to make it more complicated. Both the answer choices and the question stem contain difficult vocabulary, such as "neologisms" and "paleontologists," and the antonyms "modern" and "ancient" are mentioned to present an additional contrast. However, the only answer choice that makes sense is "descendants." Modern creatures cannot be the ancestors of ancient creatures. You may not recognize the word "neologisms," but your knowledge of word parts will help you deduce that this word likely involves the study of something new, which doesn't fit this sentence. Finally, the statement that modern creatures are "the reptiles of the ancient dinosaurs" just doesn't make sense.

101. C

Choice (C) is the correct answer choice. Her eyes could well have been wide with any of the four answer choices for the first blank—"amazement," "reason," "wonder," or "purpose"—as the ship sailed in. However, the only choice that makes sense for the second blank is that "the ship, laden with gold, jewels, and precious metals, sailed into port." The other combinations just don't make sense.

102. B

Choice (B) is the correct answer choice. It's possible to infer from the information in the sentence that Mount Vesuvius is a volcano. Regular hills and mountains don't erupt; only volcanoes do. Volcanoes don't "erect" cities, nor do they "detect" or "desiccate" them. Indeed, volcanoes are very dangerous exactly because they have the potential to *destroy*, or "decimate," human lives and homes.

103. A

Choice (A) is the correct answer choice. To "embody" means to personify. The cadet doesn't "create" the characters of an ideal soldier, nor does he "seclude" or for that matter "vaporize" those character traits.

CHAPTER 5

ISEE Quantitative Comparisons

CHAPTER OBJECTIVES

With practice, this chapter will help you:

1. Explain the concept of a quantitative comparison and the format of ISEE Quantitative Comparison questions

2. Use Kaplan's Strategies for Quantitative Comparisons to answer Quantitative Comparison questions accurately and efficiently

3. Compare quantities to decide whether their relationship can be determine

Quantitative Comparisons appear **only on the ISEE**. If you are not taking the ISEE, you may skip this section.

THE FORMAT

Of the approximately 37 math questions in the Quantitative Reasoning section, about 15 will be Quantitative Comparisons. In a Quantitative Comparison question, you must compare two quantities instead of solving for one particular value. You will see two mathematical expressions: one in Column A and the other in Column B. Your job is to compare them and draw a conclusion about their values.

Some questions include additional information about one or both quantities. This information is centered and unboxed above the two quantities, and it is essential to making the comparison.

The directions will look something like this:

Using the information given in each question, compare the quantity in Column A to the quantity in Column B. All questions in Part Two have these answer choices:

(A)   The quantity in Column A is greater.

(B)   The quantity in Column B is greater.

(C)   The two quantities are equal.

(D)   The relationship cannot be determined from the information given.

Three Rules for Choice D

Choice D is the only choice that represents a relationship that cannot be determined. Choices A, B, and C all mean that a definite relationship can be found between the quantities in Columns A and B.

There are three things to remember about choice D:

1.   Choice D is rarely correct for the first few Quantitative Comparison questions.

2.   Choice D is never correct if the two columns contain only numbers.

3.   Choice D is correct if there's more than one possible relationship between the two columns.

Now, review this example of a test-like question:

(A) The quantity in Column A is greater.

(B) The quantity in Column B is greater.

(C) The two quantities are equal.

(D) The relationship cannot be determined from the information given.c

Column A	Column B
$3x$	$2x$

If x is a positive number, then Column A is larger. If x is equal to zero, then the quantities in Columns A and B are equal. If x is a negative number, then Column B is larger.

There is more than one possible relationship between Columns A and B here, so according to rule 3, choice (D) is the correct answer choice. As soon as you realize that there is more than one possible relationship, choose choice (D) and move on.

KAPLAN'S STRATEGIES FOR QUANTITATIVE COMPARISONS

The following strategies will help you to make quick comparisons. The key is to *compare* the values rather than *calculate* them.

- Compare piece by piece

- Make one column look like the other

- Do the same thing to both columns

- Pick Numbers

- Avoid Quantitative Comparison distractors

EXPERT TIP

Compare, don't calculate. There's usually an easier way to solve a Quantitative Comparison question than to calculate the value of a complex expression.

Look at each strategy in detail.

Compare Piece by Piece

This applies to Quantitative Comparison questions that compare two sums or two products. For example:

$$a > b > c > d$$

Column A	Column B
$a + c$	$b + d$

You are given four variables, or "pieces," in the above example, as well as the relationship between these pieces. You're told that a is greater than all of the other pieces, while c is greater than only d, etc. The next step is to compare the value of each piece in each column. If every piece in one column is greater than the corresponding piece in the other column, and if addition is the only mathematical operation involved, the column with the greater individual values ($a > b$ and $c > d$) will have the greater total value ($a + c > b + d$).

In other words, you know from the information given that $a > b$, and $c > d$. Therefore, the first term in Column A, a, is greater than its corresponding term in Column B, b. Following similar logic, the second term in Column A, c, is greater than d, its corresponding term in Column B. Because each individual "piece" in Column A is greater than its corresponding "piece" in Column B, the total value of Column A must be greater. The answer is choice (A).

Make One Column Look Like the Other

Use this strategy when the quantities in the two columns look so different that a direct comparison would be impossible.

If the quantities in Columns A and B are expressed differently or if one looks more complicated than the other, try to make a direct comparison easier by changing one column to look more like the other.

Try an example in which the quantities in Column A and Column B are expressed differently:

Column A	Column B
$2(x + 1)$	$2x + 2$

In the example above, it's difficult to make a direct comparison as the quantities are written. If you get rid of the parentheses in Column A, however, so that the quantity more closely resembles that in Column B, you might have seen the relationship right away. When you multiply to get rid of the parentheses in Column A, you end up with $2x + 2$ in both columns. Therefore, the columns are equal in value, so the answer is choice (C).

This strategy is also useful when one column looks more complicated than the other. For example:

Column A	Column B
$\dfrac{2\sqrt{3}}{\sqrt{6}}$	$\sqrt{2}$

Try simplifying Column A, because it is the more complicated-looking quantity. To simplify this fraction, follow these steps:

Step 1. $\quad \dfrac{2\sqrt{3}}{\sqrt{6}} = \dfrac{2\sqrt{3}}{\sqrt{2}\sqrt{3}}$

Step 2. $\quad \dfrac{2\sqrt{3}}{\sqrt{2}\sqrt{3}} = \dfrac{2}{\sqrt{2}}$

Step 3. $\quad \dfrac{2}{\sqrt{2}} = \dfrac{2}{\sqrt{2}} \times \dfrac{\sqrt{2}}{\sqrt{2}} = \dfrac{2\sqrt{2}}{2}$

Step 4. $\quad \dfrac{2\sqrt{2}}{2} = \sqrt{2}$

By simplifying Column A, you are able to make a direct and easy comparison between the two columns. Column A, when simplified, is equivalent to $\sqrt{2}$, which is the quantity in Column B. Therefore, choice (C) is the correct answer.

Do the Same Thing to Both Columns

By adding or subtracting the same amount from both columns, you can often declutter a comparison and make the relationship more apparent. You can also multiply or divide both columns by the same positive number. This keeps the relationship between the columns the same. If the quantities in both columns are positive, you can square both columns. This also keeps the relationship between the columns the same.

Changing the values, and not just the appearances of the quantities in both columns, is often helpful in tackling Quantitative Comparison questions. Set up the problem as an inequality with the two columns as opposing sides of the inequality.

To change the values of the columns, add or subtract the same amount from both columns and multiply or divide by a positive number without changing the absolute relationship. However, be careful: remember that the direction of an inequality sign will be reversed if you multiply or divide by a negative number. Because this reversal will alter the relationship between the two columns, avoid multiplying or dividing by a negative number.

You can also square the quantities in both columns when both columns are positive. However, be careful: do not square both columns unless you know for certain that both columns are positive. Remember these two things when squaring the quantities in both columns: (1) the direction of an inequality sign can be reversed if one or both quantities are negative, and (2) the inequality sign can be changed to an equals sign if one quantity is positive and the other quantity is negative, with one quantity being the negative of the other. For example: $4 > -5$, yet $4^2 < (-5)^2$, because $16 < 25$. Likewise, $2 > -2$, yet $2^2 = (-2)^2$, because $2^2 = (-2)^2 = 4$.

In the Quantitative Comparison question below, what could you do to both columns?

$$x > y > 0$$

Column A	Column B
$\dfrac{2y + x}{2}$	$y + x$

Start by multiplying both columns by 2 to get rid of that fraction in Column A. You're left with $2y + x$ in Column A and $2y + 2x$ in Column B. You know that $2y = 2y$. But what about the relationship between x and $2x$? The centered information tells you that $x > 0$. Therefore, $2x > x$, so Column B is greater than Column A. Choice (B) is the correct answer.

> **EXPERT TIP**
>
> When you plug in negative numbers and fractions, remember the following:
>
> - When you square a positive fraction less than 1, the result is a smaller positive fraction than the original.
>
> - When you square a negative number, the result is a positive number.
>
> - When you square 0 and 1, these numbers remain the same.

In the next Quantitative Comparison question, what could you do to both columns?

Column A	Column B
$\dfrac{1}{4} + \dfrac{1}{5} - \dfrac{1}{3}$	$\dfrac{1}{2} - \dfrac{1}{3} + \dfrac{1}{20}$

Try adding $\dfrac{1}{3}$ to both sides.

If you do this, you'll be left with $\dfrac{1}{4} + \dfrac{1}{5}$ in Column A and $\dfrac{1}{2} + \dfrac{1}{20}$ in Column B. Now, treat this Quantitative Comparison question like a standard fraction problem. To find the sums in each column, you must find the lowest common denominator. Upon adding, you get $\dfrac{9}{20}$ in Column A and $\dfrac{11}{20}$ in Column B. Column B is greater than Column A, so the answer is choice (B).

Pick Numbers

Substitute numbers into those abstract algebra Quantitative Comparison questions. Try using a positive, a negative, and zero. A fraction can also be a handy choice for high difficulty problems.

If a Quantitative Comparison question involves variables, Pick Numbers to clarify the relationship. Follow these three steps:

1. Pick numbers that are easy to work with: positive, negative, zero, and fraction.

2. Plug in the numbers and calculate the values. What's the relationship between the columns?

3. Pick a different number for each variable and recalculate. See if you get a different relationship.

EXPERT TIP

Try setting up a chart when you Pick Numbers to keep your scratchwork organized and efficient. When in doubt, sketch it out!

$$x > 0$$

Column A	Column B
x	$\dfrac{1}{x}$

This example has a restriction: $x > 0$. This means that the number you pick should be positive. Try to pick different types of numbers: 1, 100, and $\dfrac{1}{2}$. Notice that these numbers are examples of a wide spectrum of positive numbers.

Number	Column A	Column B	Answer Choice
1	1	$\dfrac{1}{1} = 1$	C
100	100	$\dfrac{1}{100} = 0.01$	A
$\dfrac{1}{2}$	$\dfrac{1}{2}$	2	B

You might have selected choice (D) immediately after trying 1 and 100. At that point, you have identified situations where the values in both columns are the same and where the value in Column A is greater than the value in Column B. If you do try a third number, such as $\dfrac{1}{2}$, then the value of Column B will be greater than the value of Column A. This gives you three different possible answers, and on the ISEE, only one answer choice is correct; the relationship cannot be determined from the information given, so choice (D) is the correct answer.

Pick Different Kinds of Numbers

Never assume that all variables represent positive integers. Unless you're told otherwise, as in the example above, variables can be positive or negative, and they can be zero or fractions. Because different kinds of numbers behave differently, you should always choose a different kind of number the second time around. In the previous example, you knew that *x* wasn't a negative number, and it wasn't zero, so you tried a fraction and discovered that the relationship between the columns did not remain the same.

> **EXPERT TIP**
>
> Not all numbers are positive. Not all numbers are integers. When you have to pick more than one number, be intentional about the second, third, or fourth numbers you pick. If you pick an odd number to start, try an even number. If you've tried several composite numbers, try a prime number. Remember to focus on how the values of the columns change.

PRACTICE

In the next three examples, practice Strategy 4 by choosing different kinds of numbers and observing the results. For each comparison, start by picking a number. Determine what the correct answer (A–D) would be based on only that number. Do this for a total of at least five numbers per comparison. Finally, use the answers in the fourth column to determine the correct answer to the Quantitative Comparison question. If the fourth column has only one letter after you've tried several numbers, pick it! However, if the fourth column includes more than one letter, then choice (D) must be correct.

> All Quantitative Comparison questions have these answer choices:
>
> (A)   The quantity in Column A is greater.
>
> (B)   The quantity in Column B is greater.
>
> (C)   The two quantities are equal.
>
> (D)   The relationship cannot be determined from the information given.

1.

Column A	Column B
$-b$	b

Number	Column A	Column B	Answer Choice

2.

$$m > 2$$

Column A	Column B
$m + \dfrac{1}{m}$	2

Number	Column A	Column B	Answer Choice

3.

Column A	Column B
$\dfrac{xy^2}{x^3 y^5}$	$x^{-2} y^{-3}$

Number	Column A	Column B	Answer Choice

ANSWERS AND EXPLANATIONS

1.

Column A	Column B
$-b$	b

Selected numbers were 0, 2, -2, and $\dfrac{1}{2}$.

Number	Column A	Column B	Answer Choice
0	0	0	C
2	-2	2	B
-2	2	-2	A
$\dfrac{1}{2}$	$-\dfrac{1}{2}$	$\dfrac{1}{2}$	B

Because there is more than one possible answer choice, choice (D) is the correct choice.

2.

$$m \geq 2$$

Column A	Column B
$m + \dfrac{1}{m}$	2

Selected numbers were 2, 3, and 100.

Number	Column A	Column B	Answer Choice
2	$2\dfrac{1}{2}$	2	A
3	$3\dfrac{1}{3}$	2	A
100	$100\dfrac{1}{100}$	2	A

Choice A is always greater than Choice B. Choice (A) is the correct choice.

3.

Column A	Column B
$\dfrac{xy^2}{x^3 y^5}$	$x^{-2} y^{-3}$

Selected number sets were both x and y equal -1, either number equals 0, and $x = 3$, $y = 2$.

Number	Column A	Column B	Answer Choice
$x = -1$ $y = -1$	-1	-1	C
If either number is 0	0	0	C
$x = 3$ $y = 2$	$\dfrac{1}{72}$	$\dfrac{1}{72}$	C

For all three situations, both columns are equal. Choice (C) is the correct choice.

Avoid Quantitative Comparison Distractors

Keep your eyes open for those trick questions designed to fool you into the obvious but incorrect answer. Questions are arranged in order of increasing difficulty, so chances are you'll see traps toward the end of the set.

To avoid these nasty traps, always be on your toes. Never assume anything. Be particularly careful toward the end of a Quantitative Comparison set.

Don't Be Tricked by Misleading Information

Read this example carefully:

Frank weighs more than Hector.

Column A	Column B
Frank's height in meters	Hector's height in meters

The test makers are hoping that you'll follow some faulty logic and think, "If Frank is heavier, he must be taller," but that's not necessarily so. There is a correlation between height and weight, but you cannot determine someone's height using only their weight! The answer to this question would be choice (D). If you keep your eyes open for Quantitative Comparison questions with unrelated or misleading information, then you're more likely to answer them correctly.

> **EXPERT TIP**
>
> Don't be afraid to choose answer choice D. The test maker ensures that all answer choices are equally likely, and there will be Quantitative Comparison questions where the relationship cannot be determined. Use Kaplan's Strategies for Quantitative Comparison questions to be prepared for the Quantitative Comparison questions you will see on Test Day.

Don't Assume

Consider the assumptions you might make if you read this question too quickly:

$$1 + x^2 = 10$$

Column A	Column B
x	3

A common mistake on Quantitative Comparison questions is to assume that variables represent positive integers. You already dealt with these kinds of problems when you used the Picking Numbers strategy. Remember that positive and negative numbers, as well as fractions and zeros, behave differently.

In the previous example, the test makers are hoping you'll assume that $x = 3$, because the square of $3 = 9$. But x could also be equal to -3. Because x could be 3 or -3, choice (D) is the correct answer.

Don't Fall for Look-Alikes

Be on the lookout for columns that look alike:

Column A	Column B
$\sqrt{4} + \sqrt{4}$	$\sqrt{8}$

Now, $4 + 4 = 8$, *but* $\sqrt{4} + \sqrt{4} > \sqrt{8}$! Don't forget the rules of radicals. The test makers are counting on you to rush and look for the obvious choice, (C), that the two quantities are equal. Don't let them fool you. If $a > 0$ and $b > 0$, then $\sqrt{a+b} \neq \sqrt{a} + \sqrt{b}$.

Remember the convention that if x is positive, $\sqrt{x}$ means the positive square root. So $\sqrt{4} + \sqrt{4} = 2 + 2 = 4$. Now you have 4 in Column A and $\sqrt{8}$ in Column B. Because $\sqrt{8} < \sqrt{9}$ and $\sqrt{9} = 3$, $\sqrt{8} < 3 < 4$. Thus, $4 > \sqrt{8}$, so Column A is greater. Because 4 and $\sqrt{8}$ are both positive, you could also show that $4 > \sqrt{8}$ by squaring both 4 and $\sqrt{8} : 4^2 = 16$ and $\left(\sqrt{8}\right)^2 = 8$; $16 > 8$, so $4 > \sqrt{8}$. Choice (A) is correct.

PRACTICE QUESTIONS

Directions

All questions in Part Two of the ISEE Upper Level Quantitative Reasoning section are quantitative comparisons between the quantities shown in Column A and Column B. Using the information given in each question, compare the quantity in Column A to the quantity in Column B, and choose one of these four answer choices:

(A) The quantity in Column A is greater.

(B) The quantity in Column B is greater.

(C) The two quantities are equal.

(D) The relationship cannot be determined from the information given.

$$x < 0$$

	Column A	Column B
1.	x	x^2

$$a > b > c > 0$$

	Column A	Column B
2.	$a - c$	$b - c$

	Column A	Column B
3.	$4x + 5$	$5x$

	Column A	Column B
4.	$\sqrt{10} + \sqrt{65}$	$3 + 8$

	Column A	Column B
5.	52% of 34	17

	Column A	Column B
6.	0.76	$\dfrac{3}{4}$

$$0 < x < 1$$

	Column A	Column B
7.	$3x$	$2x$

	Column A	Column B
8.	x	$x - 1$

	Column A	Column B
9.	x	$-x$

	Column A	Column B
10.	$\dfrac{1}{8} + \dfrac{1}{10}$	$\dfrac{1}{9} + \dfrac{1}{11}$

	Column A	Column B
11.	50×8.01	$\dfrac{801}{2}$

	Column A	Column B
12.	$\dfrac{(-2)(-4)}{(-6)(-8)}$	$\dfrac{(-6)(-8)}{(-4)(-12)(-12)}$

$$a \neq 0$$

	Column A	Column B
13.	$-a^2$	$(-a)^2$

$$14 < x < 16$$
$$18 < y < 20$$

	Column A	Column B
14.	34	$x + y$

	Column A	Column B
15.	$748 + 749 +$ $750 + 751 + 752$	$5(750)$

$x > 0$

	Column A	Column B
16.	$\dfrac{99x}{100}$	$\dfrac{100}{99x}$

The product of two integers is 10.

	Column A	Column B
17.	6	The sum of the integers

	Column A	Column B
18.	$19(56) + 44(19)$	$1,901$

$AC = BD$

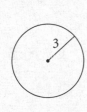

$A \quad B \quad C \quad D$

	Column A	Column B
19.	AB	BC

	Column A	Column B

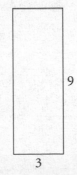

	Column A	Column B
20.	The area of the circle	The area of the rectangle

	Column A	Column B
21.	The average of 106, 117, 123, and 195	The average of 110, 118, 124, and 196

$2x - 6 = 2x + 3x$

	Column A	Column B
22.	x^2	4

$x > 0$
$y > 0$

	Column A	Column B
23.	$x - y$	$y - x$

$x \neq 0$

	Column A	Column B
24.	$\dfrac{x + 2}{3}$	$x + 5$

x is an even integer.

	Column A	Column B
25.	x^2	x^3

	Column A	Column B
26.	$\dfrac{6 + \sqrt{3}}{2}$	$\dfrac{3 + \sqrt{6}}{\sqrt{4}}$

	Column A	Column B
27.	$6 + 10$	$\sqrt{16} + \sqrt{36}$

	Column A	Column B
28.	25% of 65	$65 \times \sqrt{\dfrac{1}{4}}$

$a > b > c > d$

	Column A	Column B
29.	$a^2 + c$	$b^2 + d$

PRACTICE QUESTIONS ANSWERS AND EXPLANATIONS

1. B

Because *x* is negative, Column A will always be negative. However, a negative number that is squared will become positive, so Column B will always be positive. Therefore, Column B is greater than Column A and answer choice (B) is correct.

2. A

If you add *c* to both columns, then you end up comparing *a* and *b*. The centered information tells you straight out that *a* is greater than *b*, so answer choice (A) is correct.

3. D

If you tried to do this one using the Picking Numbers strategy and all you picked were small integers like 1, 2, or 3, you'd be convinced that Column A is greater. However, you should always pick varying numbers, especially to try to find multiple relationships in Quantitative Comparisons. Because Column B has 5*x*, try out an *x* that's greater than 5. When *x* = 6, Column A is 29 and Column B is 30, and now Column B is greater than Column A. Because more than one relationship is possible, the answer is choice (D).

4. A

Compare piece by piece. You know that $\sqrt{9}$ is 3, so $\sqrt{10}$ is more than 3. By similar reasoning, you know that $\sqrt{65}$ is more than 8. Each piece of Column A is greater than the corresponding piece of Column B, so the sum of the pieces in Column A will be greater than the sum of the pieces in Column B. Choice (A) is correct.

5. A

Don't calculate the exact value of 52% of 34; instead, look for a percent of 34 that's easy to determine without a calculator. It's easy to find 50% of a value; it's half, so 50% of 34 is 17. Looking back at Column A, 52% of 34 will be just a bit more than 50% of 34, so Column A is a little bit greater than 17 and must be greater than Column B. Answer choice (A) is correct.

6. A

If you know your standard fraction-decimal equivalents, you know that $\frac{3}{4}$ is the same as 0.75. This will always be less than 0.76, so answer choice (A) is correct.

7. A

Be careful with questions like these! Tripling *x* doesn't necessarily give you more than doubling *x*; if *x* is a negative number, then Column B would end up being greater than Column A. Careful test takers, however, will notice the common information above the columns stating that *x* is a positive fraction. In that case, multiplying that positive fraction by three will make it greater than multiplying it by two, so Column A will always be greater than Column B, and choice (A) is correct.

8. A

Without any limits for *x*, this question is straightforward. The value of Column B will always be one less than the value of Column A, so Column A is greater than Column B and choice (A) is correct.

9. D

At first glance, you might think that *x* is greater than −*x* because a positive is greater than a negative; this would make Column A greater than Column B. However, nothing says that *x* has to be positive or that −*x* has to be negative. If *x* is negative to start with, then −*x* is positive, so Column B is greater than Column A. If *x* = 0, the columns are equal. Because more than one relationship is possible, the correct answer is choice (D).

10. A

Don't calculate; compare piece by piece. The first fraction in Column A is greater than the first fraction in Column B, and the second fraction in Column A is greater than the second fraction in Column B. Therefore, the sum in Column A is also greater, so choice (A) is correct.

11. C

Start by multiplying both columns by 2 to make them easier to compare. You end up with 100 × 8.01 = 801 in Column A and 801 in Column B. These values are the same, so choice (C) is correct.

12. A

You can avoid evaluating these expressions if you use your arithmetic knowledge to figure out whether Column A and Column B are positive or negative. A negative multiplied by a negative results in a positive. This means that Column A has positives in both the numerator and the denominator, which will ultimately yield a positive number. Column B, however, will have a positive divided by a negative, which is negative. There's no need to calculate to see that Column A is greater. Choice (A) is correct.

13. B

Both positive and negative numbers become positive when they are squared. Remember, in the order of operations, you must calculate exponents before multiplying. That means Column A will always be negative because the negative will be applied after the number has been squared. Column B will always be positive, whether the value inside the parentheses is negative or positive. Positive numbers are always greater than negative numbers, so choice (B) is correct.

14. D

Use what you know about x and y to figure out the greatest and least possible values of $x + y$. If you start with the integer possibilities, you would make $x = 15$ and $y = 19$, and then the columns would be equal. Don't assume they have to be integers, though! The value for x might be less than 15, such as 14.5, and y might be less than 19, such as 18.5. In that case, Column A would be greater. (It's also possible for $x + y$ to be *greater* than 34.) More than one relationship is possible, so the correct answer is choice (D).

15. C

There's no need to calculate. The sum of the five consecutive integers in Column A will be simply 5 times the middle number, exactly what you have in Column B. If you didn't know this, you could use logic to "balance" the addition on the left:

$$748 + 749 + 750 + 751 + 752$$

$$(748 + 2) + (749 + 1) + 750 + (751 - 1) + (752 - 2)$$

$$750 + 750 + 750 + 750 + 750$$

$$5(750)$$

Answer choice (C) is correct.

16. D

These two quantities are reciprocals, so when Column A is greater than 1, Column B is less than 1, and vice versa. Column A will be greater than 1, and consequently greater than Column B, when $99x$ is greater than 100—in other words, when x is greater than $\frac{100}{99}$. On the other hand, Column A will be less than 1, and consequently less than Column B, when x is *less* than $\frac{100}{99}$. And, of course, the columns will be equal when $x = \frac{100}{99}$. More than one relationship is possible, so the correct answer is choice (D).

17. D

There are several pairs of integers that have a product of 10. You don't need to find every pair. Just try to find a pair that has a sum greater than 6 (like 5 and 2) and another pair that has a sum less than 6 (like −5 and −2). Because more than one relationship is possible, the correct answer is choice (D).

18. B

Note that if you factor 19 out of the expression in Column A, you end up with $19 \times (56 + 44) = 19(100) = 1,900$. This is one less than 1,901. Column B is greater than Column A, so choice (B) is correct.

19. D

At first glance, it looks like B and C divide the segment into three equal pieces. But check the mathematics of the situation to be sure. You're given that $AC = BD$:

What can you deduce from that? You can subtract BC from both equal lengths, and you'll end up with another equality: $AB = CD$. But what about BC? Does it have to be the same as AB and CD? No. The diagram could also be sketched like this:

Now you can see that it's possible for *AC* and *BD* to be equal but for *BC* to be longer than *AB*. It's also possible for *BC* to be shorter:

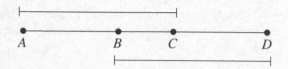

More than one relationship is possible, so the answer is choice (D).

20. A

The area of the circle is $\pi r^2 = \pi(3)^2 = 9\pi$. The area of the rectangle is 9×3. Don't just work out the math without thinking; it's easier to compare Column B in the form 9×3 instead of in the form 27. Both columns include 9 multiplied by something, and that something in Column A (π), is greater than that something in Column B (3), so Column A is greater than Column B. Choice (A) is correct.

21. B

Answer this question most effectively by comparing the two pieces. The corresponding numbers in Column B are greater than those in Column A (110 is greater than 106, 118 is greater than 117, 124 is greater than 123, and 196 is greater than 195). Therefore, the average of the numbers in Column B must be greater than the average of the numbers in Column A. Choice (B) is correct.

22. C

Solve for *x* in the centered equation. First, subtract $2x$ from both sides. This will leave you with $-6 = 3x$. Now, divide both sides by 3. This tells you that $x = -2$. Plug in -2 for *x* to find the value of x^2 in Column A: $x^2 = (-2)^2 = 4$. The quantities in both columns are equal. Choice (C) is correct.

23. D

From the centered information, you know that the variables *x* and *y* must be positive. To figure out the relationship between the columns, Pick Numbers, starting with some positive integers. If $x = 5$ and $y = 3$, then Column A is $x - y = 5 - 3 = 2$ and Column B is $y - x = 3 - 5 = -2$. In this case, Column A is greater. Now, plug in some different numbers. You can pick new numbers or just switch the values that you used on the first try. Now,

$x = 3$ and $y = 5$, which means that Column A is $x - y = 3 - 5 = -2$ and Column B is $y - x = 5 - 3 = 2$. In this case, Column B is greater. Because more than one relationship between the columns is possible, choice (D) is correct.

24. D

This question appears to be an obvious candidate for the Picking Numbers strategy, but be careful with the numbers you choose. For example, plug in 2 for *x*. Column A is $\frac{2+2}{3} = \frac{4}{3}$, and Column B is $2 + 5 = 7$. This makes Column B greater. Your next likely step would be to switch your chosen number from a positive to a negative, but be careful! When $x = -2$, you find that Column A is $\frac{-2+2}{3} = 0$ and Column B is $-2 + 5 = 3$. Once again, Column B is greater. Try something different: what happens if you plug in a negative number considerably farther away from 0? If $x = -100$, then Column A is $\frac{-100+2}{3} = \frac{-98}{3}$ and Column B is $-100 + 5 = -95$. In this case, the value in Column A is greater than the value in Column B. More than one relationship between the columns is possible, so choice (D) is correct.

25. D

This is another Picking Numbers type of question. Begin by plugging in a positive value for *x* that is consistent with the centered information. Let $x = 2$. So Column A is $2^2 = 2 \times 2$, or 4, and Column B is $2^3 = 2 \times 2 \times 2$, or 8. In this case, Column B is greater. Now, try out a negative value for *x* that is consistent with the centered information. Let $x = -2$. Now Column A is $(-2)^2 = (-2) \times (-2) = 4$ and Column B is $(-2)^3 = (-2) \times (-2) \times (-2) = -8$. Column A is greater. Because more than one relationship between the columns is possible, choice (D) is correct.

26. A

Finding the square root of a perfect square, such as 4, is easy to do without a calculator, so start there. Because both sides now have 2 in the denominator, compare the numerators. Your scratchwork should include $6 + \sqrt{3}$ for Column A and $3 + \sqrt{6}$ for Column B. If you subtract 3 from both columns, you have $3 + \sqrt{3}$ for Column A and $\sqrt{6}$ for Column B.

You might be feeling stuck, but don't give up yet! Try to manipulate the expression In Column A to make it easier to compare. If you change 3 into radical form $\left(3 = \sqrt{9}\right)$, you can see that $\sqrt{9}$ is greater than $\sqrt{6}$. This means that Column A is greater than Column B, and choice (A) is correct.

27. A

In Column A, $6 + 10 = 16$. In Column B, you have $\sqrt{16} + \sqrt{36}$. Use your knowledge of perfect squares to determine that $\sqrt{16} = 4$ and $\sqrt{36} = 6$. Because $4 + 6 = 10$, Column A is greater than Column B. Choice (A) is correct.

28. B

Change one of the columns to put the numbers in the same form so you can make a direct comparison. You can convert among percentages, fractions, and decimals, so when you're working with more than one form, pick one and convert numbers as needed. It's useful to work with fractions, so convert 25% in Column A to a fraction. You convert a percent to a fraction (or decimal) by dividing the percent by 100%, so $25\% = \frac{25\%}{100\%} = \frac{25}{100} = \frac{1}{4}$. The fractional equivalent of 25% is $\frac{1}{4}$.

Convert Column A into an expression $\left(\frac{1}{4} \times 65\right)$, and compare $\frac{1}{4} \times 65$ to $65 \times \sqrt{\frac{1}{4}}$. Simplify $\sqrt{\frac{1}{4}}$ to $\frac{\sqrt{1}}{\sqrt{4}} = \frac{1}{2}$.

Column A divides 65 into fourths, and Column B divides 65 in half, so even without knowing the exact values, you can determine that Column B is greater. Choice (B) is correct.

29. D

Because the variables can be positive or negative, pick different kinds of numbers for the variables to see if different relationships between the columns are possible. Remember that the values you pick must be consistent with the centered information, which is that $a > b > c > d$.

If $a = 4$, $b = 3$, $c = 2$, and $d = 1$, then the value of Column A is $a^2 + c = 4^2 + 2 = 16 + 2 = 18$, and the value of Column B is $b^2 + d = 3^2 + 1 = 9 + 1 = 10$. Column A is greater. If you pick only positive numbers, then it will always be true that $a^2 + c$ is greater than $b^2 + d$, and you might incorrectly choose choice A. Remember to test a variety of numbers; let some or all of the variables be negative. Let $a = -1$, $b = -2$, $c = -3$, and $d = -4$. These values follow the rules of the centered information. This time, the value of Column A is $a^2 + c = (-1)^2 + (-3) = 1 - 3 = -2$, and the value of Column B is $b^2 + d = (-2)^2 + (-4) = 4 - 4 = 0$. With this second set of numbers, Column B is greater. More than one relationship between the columns is possible, so choice (D) is correct.

PART 3

Common Content for the SSAT and ISEE

CHAPTER 6

SSAT and ISEE Mastery

CHAPTER OBJECTIVES

With practice, this chapter will help you:

1. Answer common questions about the SSAT and ISEE

2. Take advantage of the test's structure

3. Approach the questions strategically to better manage Test Day stress

TEST-TAKING SKILLS

Every year, around 100,000 students take either the SSAT or ISEE for admission to independent and private schools around the world. Although the components of the two tests are remarkably similar, there are some critical differences.

To get a great score on an admissions test, you need to master some key things beyond just knowing certain vocabulary words or the length of sides of an isosceles triangle. Namely, you need to know how to be a good test taker, and this requires the following:

- You need to have a basic understanding of the nature of the test.

- You need to hone your math and verbal skills.

- You need to develop test-taking strategies and techniques.

Having a solid grasp of the content on the test is obviously important. You can't do well if you don't know the material. However, getting the score you want also requires you to know how the test is set up, what kinds of questions it has, and what kinds of distractor answers you can expect to see. If you don't know these things, you will be at a disadvantage on Test Day.

USING THE TEST STRUCTURE TO YOUR ADVANTAGE

Whether you're taking the SSAT (Secondary School Admission Test) or the ISEE (Independent School Entrance Exam), you'll notice pretty quickly that it is very different from the tests you're used to taking in school. On a school test, you're often told to show your work, spend more time on tough questions (given that they are often worth more points), and work thoroughly, even if it means taking extra time.

None of these things apply in the world of standardized testing. On your private school admissions test, it won't matter how you solve a question; it only matters what your final answer is. Also, all questions are worth the same number of points, so it's always to your advantage to answer easier questions first to get them out of the way and to answer as many question as possible in the limited time you're given.

The SSAT and ISEE are each given to students in a range of grades. Luckily, if you're in 9th grade, for example, you're not expected to get as many questions correct on the Upper Level test as someone in 11th grade. Keep that in mind as you take the test so you don't get discouraged if you find a lot of questions that you can't answer!

To succeed in this unique testing environment, you need to know some fundamentals. The SSAT and ISEE have differences, so be sure to prep carefully.

Because the format and directions of the SSAT and ISEE remain relatively unchanged from year to year, you can learn the setup in advance. Then, on Test Day, all you'll have to worry about will be answering each question, not learning how a Synonym question works.

One of the easiest and most useful things you can do to boost your performance is to learn and understand the directions before Test Day. Because the instructions are always exactly the same, you should review an official practice test, from the test maker, before taking the test. Learn them beforehand, while you go through this book, and you'll be able to skip them during the test.

Skipping Around

You're allowed to skip around as much as you'd like within each section of the SSAT or ISEE. Strong test takers know this and use it to their advantage. They move through the test efficiently, quickly marking and leaving questions they can't answer immediately, racking up points on questions they do know, then coming back to the tough ones later. They don't dwell on any question, even a hard one, until they've tried every question at least once.

When you see questions that look tough, circle them in your test booklet and skip them for later. Gather points on easy questions first. On a second look, some tricky-looking questions can turn out to be much easier than they initially seemed. Remember, if you're on the younger side of the testing group within your level, expect to see several questions that you won't be able to answer. The test is intentionally set up this way, so don't let it discourage you.

Guessing—Know Your Test

When should you guess? That's a common question. The answer, however, depends on which test you're taking. Guessing is one of the few areas in which the SSAT and ISEE operate differently, so read carefully and follow the instructions for the test you will be taking.

SSAT: There *is* an **incorrect answer penalty**. For each answer you get correct, you get one point. For each answer you get incorrect, one-quarter of a point is deducted from your total score. Does this mean you shouldn't guess? Not at all! It just means that you need to be smart about it. Essentially, if you can eliminate at least one—preferably two—answer choice, it's to your advantage to guess because you've tipped the odds of guessing correctly in your favor. If you can't eliminate anything, however, you're better off leaving the question blank.

ISEE: There is *not* an incorrect answer penalty. This means that you should answer every single question on the test, even if you have no idea what it's asking you. The ISEE calculates your score simply by adding up your correct answers, so you might as well fill in all those ovals completely. You never know what you might answer correctly by guessing!

EXPERT TIP

On the SSAT, guess only if you can eliminate at least one or two answer choices. On the ISEE, always guess, even if you can't eliminate *anything*.

Gridding—The Answer Grid Has No Heart

Misgridding—it sounds so basic, but it happens all the time. When time is short, it's easy to get confused going back and forth between your test booklet and your answer grid. If you know the answer but grid the answer booklet incorrectly, you'll lose those points, so be careful! Don't let it happen to you; read on for some tips to help you avoid making mistakes on the answer grid.

Circle the Questions You Skip

Put a big circle in your test booklet around any question numbers you skip. When you go back, these questions will be easy to locate. Also, if you accidentally skip a box on the grid, you can check your grid against your booklet to see where you went wrong.

Always Circle the Answers You Choose

Circling your answers in the test booklet, as well as clearly marking your answers in the answer grid as you work on each question, makes it easier to check your grid against your booklet.

Grid Five or More Answers at Once

Don't worry about transferring your answers to the grid after every question. Instead, think about doing it after every five questions or at the end of each reading passage. That way, you won't keep breaking your concentration, you'll save time, and you'll gain accuracy.

Be careful at the end of a section, when time may be running out. You don't want to have your answers in the test booklet and not be able to transfer them to your answer grid because you ran out of time. Make sure to transfer your answers after every five questions or so, and pay special attention to the five-minute warning.

CIRCLE BEFORE YOU SKIP

One common test disaster is filling in all of the questions with the correct answers…in the incorrect spots. Every time you skip a question, *circle it* in your test book and pay close attention to make sure that you skip it on the answer grid, too.

APPROACHING SSAT OR ISEE QUESTIONS

Apart from knowing the setup of the SSAT or ISEE, you need to have a system for attacking the questions. You wouldn't travel around a foreign city without a map, and you shouldn't approach your private school admissions test without a plan, either. Once you know the basics about how each test is set up, you can approach each section more strategically. We recommend the following method for approaching test questions systematically:

- Think about the question looking at the answer

- Use Backdoor strategies when necessary

- Pace yourself

- Locate quick points when running out of time

Think About the Question Before Looking at the Answer

The people who make the tests love to put distractors among the answer choices. Distractors are answer choices that look like the correct answer, but aren't. If you jump right into the answer choices without thinking first about what you're looking for, you're more likely to fall for one of these traps.

Use Backdoor Strategies When Necessary

There are usually a number of ways to get to the correct answer on an SSAT or ISEE question. Most of the questions are multiple-choice. That means the answer is right in front of you—you just have to find it. If you can't figure out the answer in a straightforward way, however, be flexible and try other techniques. We'll talk about specific Kaplan strategies, such as Backsolving, Picking Numbers, and eliminating incorrect answers throughout the book.

Pace Yourself

The SSAT and ISEE give you a lot of questions in a short period of time. In order to get through an entire section, you can't spend too much time on any one question. Keep moving through the test at a good speed; if you run into a hard question, circle it, skip it, and go back to it later if there's time. If it's the SSAT and you run out of time, leave it blank. If it's the ISEE and you run out of time, make sure you guess before time is up.

Typically, the questions get harder as you move through a problem set. Ideally, you can work through the easy problems at a brisk, steady clip and use a little more of your time for the harder ones that come at the end of the set.

One caution: don't completely rush through the easy problems just to save time for the harder ones. These early problems are points in your pocket, and you don't want to work through them with such haste that you end up making careless mistakes.

Locate Quick Points When Running Out of Time

Some questions can be done quickly; for instance, some reading questions will ask you to identify the meaning of a particular word in the passage. These can be done at the last minute, even if you haven't read the passage. When you start to run out of time, locate and answer any of the quick points that remain.

When you take the SSAT or ISEE, you have one clear objective in mind: to score as many points as you can. It's that simple. The rest of this book will help you do that.

MANAGING STRESS

The countdown has begun. Your date with the test is looming on the horizon. Anxiety is on the rise. The butterflies in your stomach have gone ballistic. Your thinking is getting cloudy. You might be worried that you won't be ready. You might already know your stuff, but it doesn't matter; you're going into panic mode anyway.

Stop and take three deep breaths. Don't freak out! It's possible to tame that anxiety and stress— before, during, and after the test. Read on for more tips about taking control and mastering your physical well-being.

As you wrap up your prep, remember: a little stress can be good for you. Anxiety can be a motivation to study, and the adrenaline that gets pumped into your bloodstream when you're stressed helps you stay alert and think more clearly. However, if you feel that the tension is so great that it's preventing you from using your study time effectively, there are some things you can do to get it under control.

Make a Plan

A lack of control can be a prime cause of stress. Research shows that if you don't have a sense of control over what's happening in your life, you can easily end up feeling helpless and hopeless. Try to identify the sources of the stress you feel. Which sources can you do something about? Can you find ways to reduce the stress you're feeling about any of these sources? Write down the answers to these questions to keep you focused over the next few weeks.

Focus on Your Strengths

Make a list of strengths you have that will help you to do well on the test. We all have strengths, and recognizing your own is like finding money in your pocket when you put on your favorite pair of pants. You'll be able to draw on your reserves when you need them, helping you solve difficult questions, maintain confidence, and keep test stress and anxiety at a distance. Every time you recognize a new area of strength, solve a challenging problem, or score well on a Practice Test, you'll increase your reserves and add to your list of strengths.

Imagine Yourself Succeeding

Close your eyes and imagine yourself in a relaxing situation. Breathe easily and naturally. Think of a real-life situation in which you scored well on a test or did well on an assignment. Focus on this success.

Now, turn your thoughts to the SSAT or ISEE, and keep your thoughts and feelings in line with that successful experience. Don't make comparisons between them. Instead, imagine yourself taking the upcoming test with the same feelings of confidence and relaxed control.

Set Realistic Goals

Facing your problem areas gives you some distinct advantages. What can you accomplish in the time you have remaining before Test Day? Make a list of realistic goals. You can't help but feel more confident when you know you're actively improving your chances of earning a higher test score.

Master Your Physical Well-Being

How well you do on Test Day doesn't only have to do with how prepared you are. It also has to do with what kind of condition you are in physically.

Exercise Your Frustrations Away

Whether it's jogging, spinning, weights, or a pickup basketball game, physical exercise will stimulate your mind and body and improve your ability to think and concentrate. A surprising number of students fall out of the habit of regular exercise; ironically, this tends to happen because they're spending so much time prepping for exams. A little physical exertion will help to keep your mind and body in sync and help you sleep better at night.

Eat Well

Good nutrition will help you focus and think clearly. Eat plenty of fruits and vegetables; low-fat protein such as fish, skinless poultry, beans, and legumes; and whole grains such as brown rice, whole-wheat bread, and pastas. Don't eat a lot of sugar and high-fat snacks or salty foods.

Keep Breathing

Conscious attention to breathing is an excellent way to manage stress while you're taking the test. Most of the people who get into trouble during tests take shallow breaths: they breathe using only their upper chests and shoulder muscles, and they may even hold their breath for long periods of time. Conversely, those test takers who breathe deeply in a slow, relaxed manner are likely to be in better control during the session.

Stretch

If you find yourself getting spaced out or burned out as you study or take the test, stop for a brief moment and stretch. Flex your feet and arms. Even though you'll be pausing on the test for a moment, it's a moment well spent. Stretching will help to refresh you and refocus your thoughts.

CHAPTER 7

Synonyms

CHAPTER OBJECTIVES

With practice, this chapter will help you:

1. Explain the concept of a synonym and the format of SSAT and ISEE Synonym questions

2. Explain the steps of the Kaplan 3-Step Method for Synonyms

3. Determine the synonym for a given word

4. List clues for determining a word's equivalent meaning

THE FORMAT

Synonyms appear on all levels of the SSAT and ISEE. At its most basic level, a synonym is a word that is similar in meaning to another defined word. *Fast* is a synonym for *quick*. Okay, that makes sense. Unfortunately, if synonyms were that easy on the SSAT or ISEE, the tests wouldn't tell admissions officers very much.

The synonyms you'll see on your actual test will be much more challenging than the previous example, but all Synonym questions follow the same logic. You'll see a word in capital letters (we call this the *stem word*) with a colon followed by five other words on the SSAT or four on the ISEE. One of the answer choices will be the synonym of the given word, and the others will not. For example:

AUTHENTIC:

- **(A)** genuine
- **(B)** valuable
- **(C)** ancient
- **(D)** damaged
- **(E)** historical

Which of these words means authentic? Maybe you "just knew" that the answer was (A), *genuine*, or maybe you didn't. Either way, you need a method that will work for you on all Synonym questions, no matter the difficulty. What you need is the...

KAPLAN 3-STEP METHOD FOR SYNONYMS

Step 1. Define the stem word

Step 2. Find the answer choice that best fits your definition

Step 3. If no choice fits, think of other definitions for the stem word and go through the choices again

Now, take another look at the previous example, this time using the Kaplan 3-Step Method for Synonyms.

WALK THE WALK

What if WAVE is the stem word? Ask yourself the following question: What part of speech is it? For an SSAT or ISEE question, WAVE could be the *act of waving* (a verb) or *an ocean wave* (a noun). To answer this question, just look at the answer choices. They'll always be the same part of speech as the stem word. So you'll always know whether to WAVE to your friend or ride the WAVE!

Step 1. Define the Stem Word

What does *authentic* mean? Something authentic is something *real,* such as an authentic signature, rather than a forgery. Your definition might look like this: something authentic can be *proven* to be what it *claims* to be.

Step 2. Find the Answer Choice That Best Fits Your Definition

Go through the answer choices one by one to see which one fits best. Your options are *genuine, valuable, ancient, damaged,* and *historical.* Something authentic could be worth a lot or not much at all, old or new, in good shape or bad, or even recent or historical. The only word that really means the same thing as authentic is choice (A), genuine.

Step 3. If No Choice Fits, Think of Other Definitions for the Stem Word and Go Through the Choices Again

In the previous example, the first choice fit. Now, take a look at an example where the first choice does not fit.

GRAVE:

(A) regrettable

(B) unpleasant

(C) serious

(D) careful

(E) lengthy

You might start by defining *grave* as *a* burial location. You look at the choices and don't see any words like *tomb* or *coffin.* What do you do? Move to Step 3 and go back to the stem word, thinking about other definitions. Have you ever heard of a "grave situation"? *Grave* can also mean serious or solemn, and you can see that choice (C), *serious,* now fits the bill perfectly. If at first none of the answer choices seem to work with your definition, there may be a secondary definition you haven't yet considered.

AVOIDING PITFALLS

The Kaplan 3-Step Method for Synonyms should always be your basis for tackling Synonym questions, but there are still a few other things you need to know to perform your best on this question type. There are two main pitfalls to watch out for:

Pitfall 1: Running Out of Time

Pitfall 2: Choosing Tempting Incorrect Answers

Pitfall 1: Running Out of Time

Pace yourself. You have a limited amount of time, so make sure you use it wisely. Never waste time on a question you don't know—circle it and come back to it later. Synonym questions get more difficult as they go, so move through the early questions quickly, leaving more time for the tougher ones at the end.

Pitfall 2: Choosing Tempting Incorrect Answers

The test makers choose their incorrect answer choices very carefully. In fact, these incorrect answer choices actually have a name: distractors. Distractors are answer choices that are designed to tempt you but are not correct.

DIFFICULT OR JUST INTIMIDATING?

Sometimes incorrect answer choices simply sound intimidating. In particular, if the stem word sounds complicated, you will likely be tempted to pick an answer choice that sounds similarly complicated. Often, the correct answer is straightforward. When you see a difficult word, keep calm and ask yourself: is this difficult or does it just sound scary?

What kinds of distractors are we talking about specifically? There are two types to watch out for: answers that are *almost correct* and answers that *sound like the stem word*. For example:

1. REPUTE:

    (A) renewal

    (B) renown

    (C) priority

    (D) mutability

    (E) reaction

2. FAVOR:

    (A) award

    (B) recognize

    (C) respect

    (D) improve

    (E) prefer

1. Choices A, B, and E might be tempting because they all start with the prefix *re-*, just like the stem word, *repute*. It's important that you examine all the answer choices, because otherwise you might choose choice A and never get to the correct answer, choice (B).

2. You might look at the word *favor* and think, "oh, that's something positive." It's something you do for someone else. It sounds a lot like choice A, *award*. Some students might choose *award* and move on, but if you do that, you would have chosen the incorrect answer. The correct answer is choice (E), *prefer*, because *favor* is being used as a verb, and to favor someone or something is to like it better than something else, in other words, to prefer it. As in the first example, if you don't read through all of the choices, you might be tempted into choosing an incorrect answer.

At this point, you have a great set of tools for answering most Synonym questions. You know how to approach this question type, and you know some common types of distractors to avoid. However, what should you do if you look at the stem word and don't know what it means?

VOCABULARY TECHNIQUES

There are several things you can do to figure out the meaning of a tough vocabulary word and, thus, to answer a hard Synonym question. Here are four techniques that will help you when you don't know a stem word:

> **Technique 1.** Look for familiar roots and prefixes
>
> **Technique 2.** Use your knowledge of foreign languages
>
> **Technique 3.** Remember the context
>
> **Technique 4.** Use word charge

Examine each technique more closely.

Technique 1. Look for Familiar Roots and Prefixes

Remember how we told you in Chapter 6 to start working on your vocabulary skills? Well, having a good grasp of how words are put together will help you tremendously on Synonyms, especially when you don't know a difficult word. If you can break a word into pieces that you *do* understand, you'll be able to answer questions that you might have thought too difficult to tackle.

Examine at the words below. Write down any prefixes or roots that you recognize, even if you cannot explain the exact meaning of the word part.

- BENEVOLENCE
- INSOMNIA
- INSCRIBE
- CONSPIRE
- VERITY

Bene means good; *somn* has to do with sleep; *scrib* has to do with writing; *con* means doing something together; and *ver* has to do with truth. As you continue to prepare for the SSAT or the ISEE, keep track of word parts you recognize in both questions and explanations.

Technique 2. Use Your Knowledge of Foreign Languages

Do you study a foreign language? If so, it can help you decode lots of vocabulary words on the SSAT or ISEE, especially if it's Latin, a Romance language (such as French, Spanish, Italian, or Portuguese), or a Germanic language (such as German or Dutch). Look at the list of words below. Do you recognize any foreign language words in them?

- FACILITATE
- DORMANT
- EXPLICATE

Facile means "easy" in French and Italian; *dormir* means "to sleep" in French and Spanish; and *expliquer* (French) and *explique* (Spanish) mean "to explain."

Technique 3. Remember the Context

Sometimes a word might look strange sitting on the page by itself, but if you think about it, you realize you've heard it before in other situations. If you can put the word into context, such as in a cliché or a book, you're well on your way to deciphering its meaning. For example:

1. GNARLED:
   - **(A)** fruitful
   - **(B)** dead
   - **(C)** twisted
   - **(D)** flowering
   - **(E)** drooping

What kind of plant have you heard described as *gnarled*? Trees, particularly old ones, are often described as gnarled in fairy tales. They are knotty and twisted, the kind you think would appear in fairy tales. The answer is (C).

2. ALLEGATION:

   (A) evidence

   (B) accusation

   (C) conservation

   (D) foundation

   (E) fabrication

What does "making an allegation" mean? "Making an allegation" is accusing someone of committing a crime, a phrase you might have seen on the news or a TV show. The correct answer is choice (B).

3. LAURELS:

   (A) vines

   (B) acclaim

   (C) lavender

   (D) cushions

   (E) struggles

Have you heard the expression, "don't rest on your laurels"? What do you think it might mean? Even if you wouldn't feel comfortable explaining the meaning to someone else, you likely associate someone "resting on their laurels" with someone who relies on their past achievements to show how great they are. The phrase "don't rest on your laurels" originated in ancient Greece, where heroes were given wreaths of laurel branches to signify their accomplishments. Saying you shouldn't "rest on your laurels" is the same thing as saying you shouldn't get too comfortable or smug, enjoying your accomplishment rather than striving for improvement. "Acclaim" is enthusiastic praise, which fits the idea that you are comfortable enjoying your accomplishment instead of striving for improvement. Choice (B) is correct.

Technique 4. Use Word Charge

Even when you know nothing about a word, have never seen it before, don't recognize any prefixes or roots, and can't think of any word it resembles in another language, you can still make a final effort at answering a Synonym question as accurately as possible. One useful strategy when you're stumped is Word Charge.

What do we mean by word charge? Are some words electric, or do they spend too much money on credit cards? No to both. Word charge refers to the *feeling* that a word gives you as to whether it's a positive word or a negative one. For example:

VILIFY: This sounds like *villain*, a word most people would say is bad.

GLORIFY: This sounds like *glorious*, a word most people would say is good.

Say that *vilify* has a negative charge (−) and *glorify* has a positive charge (+). On all Synonym questions, the correct answer will have *the same charge as the stem word*, so use your instincts about word charge to help you when you're stuck on a tough word.

PRACTICE

Decide whether each of the following words has a positive (+) or negative (−) charge.

1. AUSPICIOUS   _____

2. MALADY   _____

3. NOXIOUS   _____

4. AMIABLE   _____

5. BOORISH   _____

6. MELANCHOLY   _____

7. HUMANE   _____

Often words that sound harsh have a negative meaning, while smooth-sounding words tend to have positive meanings. If *cantankerous* sounds negative to you, you would be correct. It means difficult to handle.

You can also use prefixes and roots to help determine a word's charge. *Mal, de, dis, un, in, im, a,* and *mis* often indicate a negative, while *pro, ben,* and *magn* are often positives.

Not all words sound positive; some sound neutral. But if you can define the charge, you can probably eliminate some answer choices on that basis alone.

Now, check and see how you did on identifying the charge of the words listed above.

ANSWERS AND EXPLANATIONS

1. negative (−)

2. negative (−)

3. negative (−)

4. positive (+)

5. negative (−)

6. negative (−)

7. positive (+)

Auspicious (+) means favorable; a *malady* (−) means an illness; *noxious* (−) means harmful; *amiable* (+) means agreeable; *boorish* (−) means rude; *melancholy* (−) means sadness; and *humane* (+) means kind.

Practice Makes Permanent

Now that you've been through all of the techniques to succeed on Synonym questions, it's time for some practice. Work through the following questions using the Kaplan 3-Step Method, avoiding pitfalls and employing vocabulary techniques when you get stuck.

PRACTICE QUESTIONS

1. DISMAL:

   (A) bleak

   (B) crowded

   (C) comfortable

   (D) temporary

   (E) typical

2. HUMID:

   (A) damp

   (B) windy

   (C) hot

   (D) stormy

   (E) hazy

3. DEPORT:

   (A) punish

   (B) banish

   (C) censor

   (D) jail

   (E) praise

4. PEDDLE:

   (A) assemble

   (B) steal

   (C) edit

   (D) deliver

   (E) sell

5. TERMINATE:

   (A) extend

   (B) renew

   (C) end

   (D) sell

   (E) finalize

6. DEARTH:

   (A) explosion

   (B) increase

   (C) shortage

   (D) change

   (E) surplus

7. OBSCURE:

   (A) tragic

   (B) enigmatic

   (C) obligatory

   (D) ignored

   (E) legendary

8. MOURN:

   (A) inaugurate

   (B) celebrate

   (C) greet

   (D) oppose

   (E) grieve

9. RECLUSE:

   (A) artist

   (B) beggar

   (C) lunatic

   (D) scavenger

   (E) hermit

10. HOMAGE:

   (A) youth

   (B) wreath

   (C) respect

   (D) affection

   (E) household

11. HERBIVOROUS:

    (A) huge

    (B) warm-blooded

    (C) endangered

    (D) plant-eating

    (E) intelligent

12. SYNOPSIS:

    (A) summary

    (B) satire

    (C) paragraph

    (D) update

    (E) rebuttal

13. IMPERIOUS:

    (A) royal

    (B) friendly

    (C) gusty

    (D) arrogant

    (E) insightful

14. HALLOW:

    (A) revere

    (B) dig

    (C) inhabit

    (D) discover

    (E) release

15. BLISS:

    (A) ecstasy

    (B) escape

    (C) prayer

    (D) terror

    (E) fun

16. TANGIBLE:

    (A) unrelated

    (B) glib

    (C) touchable

    (D) tanned

    (E) incapable

17. FEROCITY:

    (A) hardness

    (B) humility

    (C) narrowness

    (D) scarcity

    (E) fierceness

18. TENACIOUS:

    (A) tender

    (B) determined

    (C) temporary

    (D) talkative

    (E) discouraged

19. PROFOUND:

    (A) weighty

    (B) large

    (C) historical

    (D) argumenative

    (E) commonly held

20. PERSPECTIVE:

    (A) vacation

    (B) frame

    (C) context

    (D) motion

    (E) attitude

21. CONVERGENCE:

    (A) protection

    (B) blessing

    (C) oblivion

    (D) convolution

    (E) junction

22. ELECTIVE:

    (A) hamstring

    (B) creation

    (C) voting

    (D) discretionary

    (E) facile

23. BENEVOLENT:

    (A) cooked

    (B) charitable

    (C) caustic

    (D) passionate

    (E) musical

24. REMOTE:

    (A) infrared

    (B) aerial

    (C) outlying

    (D) computerized

    (E) reliable

25. VERITY:

    (A) truth

    (B) contagion

    (C) similarity

    (D) militarization

    (E) edifice

26. INQUIRE:

    (A) exact

    (B) silent

    (C) detain

    (D) question

    (E) withhold

27. CONCILIATE:

    (A) advise

    (B) unpleasant

    (C) separate

    (D) conceptual

    (E) appease

28. SECURE:

    (A) fasten

    (B) decree

    (C) impair

    (D) save

    (E) explore

29. ENTERPRISE:

    (A) want

    (B) venture

    (C) offer

    (D) shorten

    (E) disaster

30. ABYSMAL:

    (A) horrible

    (B) sharp

    (C) great

    (D) submerged

    (E) canyon

31. AMBIGUOUS:

   (A) simple

   (B) curious

   (C) double

   (D) hazy

   (E) hidden

32. PROSCRIBE:

   (A) write

   (B) order

   (C) outlaw

   (D) advise

   (E) legislate

33. ACQUIESCENCE:

   (A) immersion

   (B) condescension

   (C) reticence

   (D) permission

   (E) silence

34. DELVE:

   (A) invent

   (B) explore

   (C) dive

   (D) divide

   (E) cut

35. DILIGENCE:

   (A) surveillance

   (B) eavesdropping

   (C) serenity

   (D) attentiveness

   (E) caress

36. LEVY:

   (A) balustrade

   (B) assess

   (C) summon

   (D) conspire

   (E) loan

37. CRITERION:

   (A) perception

   (B) classification

   (C) credential

   (D) benchmark

   (E) experience

38. FORLORN:

   (A) forgotten

   (B) exonerated

   (C) dejected

   (D) rotten

   (E) mistaken

39. BASTION:

   (A) fortress

   (B) beachhead

   (C) tower

   (D) arsenal

   (E) station

40. FRONTIER:

   (A) thickness

   (B) adversity

   (C) surge

   (D) refuge

   (E) border

41. HABITUAL:

   (A) regular
   (B) permitted
   (C) towering
   (D) oppressive
   (E) shared

42. PROFESS:

   (A) repel
   (B) predict
   (C) declare
   (D) upset
   (E) instigate

43. INGENUOUS:

   (A) inventive
   (B) addictive
   (C) imaginative
   (D) artless
   (E) dependent

44. PROPEL:

   (A) disobey
   (B) push
   (C) notify
   (D) acquit
   (E) conjoin

45. AGITATION:

   (A) likeness
   (B) advantage
   (C) disturbance
   (D) deftness
   (E) inexperience

46. WREST:

   (A) glide
   (B) elevate
   (C) smash
   (D) seize
   (E) shove

47. AFFINITY:

   (A) dispatch
   (B) connection
   (C) hoax
   (D) conviction
   (E) abuse

PRACTICE QUESTIONS ANSWERS AND EXPLANATIONS

1. A

Choice (A) is the correct answer choice. *Dismal* means depressing or causing gloom, misery, or bad feelings. *Bleak* means harsh and not cheerful.

2. A

Choice (A) is the correct answer choice. *Humid* means damp or muggy. *Damp,* which means slightly wet, is a perfect match.

3. B

Choice (B) is the correct answer choice. *Deport* means remove someone (a foreigner) from a country. *Banish* means send someone away from a place.

4. E

Choice (E) is the correct answer choice. *Peddle* means try to sell something, especially small goods, by going from place to place. *Sell* means give or hand over something in exchange for money.

5. C

Choice (C) is the correct answer choice. *Terminate* means bring to an end. This is a perfect match for *end*.

6. C

Choice (C) is the correct answer choice. *Dearth* means a scarcity or lack of something. *Shortage* means being in short supply.

7. B

Choice (B) is the correct answer choice. *Obscure* means unclear or difficult to see or understand. *Enigmatic* means puzzling or mysterious.

8. E

Choice (E) is the correct answer choice. *Mourn* means feel or show deep sorrow or regret for someone or their death. *Grieve* means to suffer deep sorrow, especially sorrow caused by someone's death.

9. E

Choice (E) is the correct answer choice. *Recluse* means a person who tends to avoid leaving home or socializing with others. *Hermit* means a person living in solitude.

10. C

Choice (C) is the correct answer choice. *Homage* means special honor or respect shown publicly. *Respect* means the state of being admired or respected.

11. D

Choice (D) is the correct answer choice. *Herbivorous* describes an animal that eats plants, which is an exact match for *plant-eating*.

12. A

Choice (A) is the correct answer choice. *Synopsis* means a brief summary or general survey of something. *Summary* means a brief statement or account of the main points of something.

13. D

Choice (D) is the correct answer choice. *Imperious* means arrogant and domineering. *Arrogant* means having or revealing an exaggerated sense of one's own importance or abilities.

14. A

Choice (A) is the correct answer choice. *Hallow* means make sacred. *Revere* means feel deep respect or admiration for something.

15. A

Choice (A) is the correct answer choice. *Bliss* means pure happiness. *Ecstasy* means an overwhelming feeling of joyful excitement.

16. C

Choice (C) is the correct answer choice. *Tangible* means having a physical existence. *Touchable* means exactly what it sounds like: capable of being touched.

17. E

Choice (E) is the correct answer choice. *Ferocity* means the state of being savagely fierce, cruel, or violent. *Fierceness* means the state of having or displaying an intense or ferocious aggressiveness.

18. B

Choice (B) is the correct answer choice. *Tenacious* means stubborn or having a strong hold. *Determined* means having made a firm decision and being resolved not to change it.

19. A

Choice (A) is the correct answer choice. *Profound* means very great or intense. *Weighty* means of great seriousness and importance.

20. C

Choice (C) is the correct answer choice. *Perspective* means a point of view. *Context* means the parts of something written or spoken that clarify its meaning.

21. E

Choice (E) is the correct answer choice. *Convergence* means the state of several people or things coming together from different directions so as eventually to meet. *Junction* means a point where two or more things are joined.

22. D

Choice (D) is the correct answer choice. *Elective* means permitting a choice. *Discretionary* means left to individual choice or judgment.

23. B

Choice (B) is the correct answer choice. *Benevolent* means marked by or disposed to doing good. *Charitable* means full of love for and goodwill toward others.

24. C

Choice (C) is the correct answer choice. *Remote* means far removed in space, time, or relation. *Outlying* means remote from a center or main body.

25. A

Choice (A) is the correct answer choice. *Verity* means the quality or state of being truthful or honest. *Truth* is an exact match for this.

26. D

Choice (D) is the correct answer choice. *Inquire* means to ask about. *Question* means an act or instance of asking.

27. E

Choice (E) is the correct answer choice. *Conciliate* means to gain something, such as goodwill, by pleasing acts. *Appease* means to bring to a state of peace or quiet.

28. A

Choice (A) is the correct answer choice. *Secure* means attach in a strong or firm way. *Fasten* means fix or hold in place.

29. B

Choice (B) is the correct answer choice. *Enterprise* means a business or company. *Venture* means a risky job or effort.

30. A

Choice (A) is the correct answer choice. *Abysmal* means extremely bad. *Horrible* means extremely bad or shocking.

31. D

Choice (D) is the correct answer choice. *Ambiguous* means unclear or up to interpretation. *Hazy* means vague or difficult to see.

32. C

Choice (C) is the correct answer choice. *Proscribe* means forbid or prohibit something, especially by law. *Outlaw* means ban or make illegal.

33. D

Choice (D) is the correct answer choice. *Acquiescence* means the reluctant acceptance of something without protest. *Permission* means consent or authorization.

34. B

Choice (B) is the correct answer choice. *Delve* means research or make painstaking inquiries into something. *Explore* means inquire into or discuss a subject or issue in detail.

35. D

Choice (D) is the correct answer choice. *Diligence* means careful and persistent work or effort. *Attentiveness* means the action of paying close attention to something.

36. B

Choice (B) is the correct answer choice. *Levy* means impose a tax, fee, or fine on. *Assess* means determine the value of a tax, fine, or other rate for a person or property.

37. D

Choice (D) is the correct answer choice. *Criterion* means standard of judgment or criticism. *Benchmark* means expected level of achievement.

38. C

Choice (C) is the correct answer choice. *Forlorn* means hopeless or brokenhearted. *Dejected* means sad, depressed, or dispirited.

39. A

Choice (A) is the correct answer choice. *Bastion* means a fortified area or position. *Fortress* means a heavily protected and impenetrable building.

40. E

Choice (E) is the correct answer choice. *Frontier* means the edges of a place or depth of knowledge. *Border* means a line separating two political or geographical areas, especially countries.

41. A

Choice (A) is the correct answer choice. *Habitual* means commonly used or done. *Regular* means done or happening frequently.

42. C

Choice (C) is the correct answer choice. *Profess* means to declare or admit openly or freely. *Declare* means to make known formally, officially, or explicitly.

43. D

Choice (D) is the correct answer choice. *Ingenuous* means candid or sincere. *Artless* means without guile or deception.

44. B

Choice (B) is the correct answer choice. *Propel* means to drive forward or onward. *Push* means to thrust forward, downward, or outward.

45. C

Choice (C) is the correct answer choice. *Agitation* means to excite and often trouble the mind or feelings of. *Disturbance* means to throw into disorder.

46. D

Choice (D) is the correct answer choice. *Wrest* means to gain with difficulty by or as if by force, violence, or determined labor. *Seize* means to possess or take by force.

47. B

Choice (B) is the correct answer choice. *Affinity* means a spontaneous or natural liking or sympathy for someone or something. *Connection* means a relationship in which a person, thing, or idea is linked or associated with something else.

CHAPTER 8

Reading Comprehension

CHAPTER OBJECTIVES

With practice, this chapter will help you:

1. Use the Kaplan 4-Step Method for Reading Comprehension to answer Reading questions accurately and efficiently

2. Create Passage Maps for passages using Kaplan Reading strategies

3. Identify Reading Comprehension question types

4. Predict answers and find matches among the answer choices using Passage Map notes

READING ON THE SSAT AND ISEE

Reading Comprehension questions appear on both the Upper and Middle Levels of the SSAT and ISEE. The Reading section presents you with five to seven passages (depending on the test and level) with questions that follow. The passages will generally cover topics such as history, science, or literature. For each passage, you'll be asked about the main idea and supporting ideas presented. You'll only get points for answering questions correctly, not for reading the text with deep comprehension, so keep your attention on reading as quickly as possible and answering as many questions as you can.

If you are in the lower grade within your level, you *do not* need to answer all of the questions—in fact, you don't often even need to read all of the passages. You can get a great score even if you don't answer all the questions, so don't sweat it.

READ, DON'T LEARN

On the SSAT or ISEE, you'll have to read quickly and efficiently. Your goal is not to learn the information presented or even to think about it very much. Rather, you need to figure out the main point and where to look for any details you might be asked about.

KAPLAN 4-STEP METHOD FOR READING COMPREHENSION

Step 1. Read the passage and take notes

Step 2. Decode the question stem

Step 3. Research the details

Step 4. Predict the answer and check the choices

Like the other multistep methods, the Kaplan 4-Step Method for Reading Comprehension requires you to do most of your work before you attempt to answer the questions. It's very tempting to read the questions and immediately jump to the answer choices. Don't do this. The work you do up front will not only save you time in the long run but also increase your chances of avoiding the tempting incorrect answers.

Step 1. Read the Passage and Take Notes

The first thing to do is to read the passage. This shouldn't come as a big surprise. Although you don't need to memorize or dissect the passage, you *do* need to read it. If you try to answer the questions without doing so, you're likely to make mistakes. Although you'll learn more about *how* to read the passages later, keep in mind that the main things you want to look for are the main idea and the focus of each paragraph. Additionally, you'll want to consider what the passage might discuss next.

For example, if you saw the following passage (which, admittedly, is a little shorter than the average SSAT or ISEE passage), here some of the things you might want to note:

> The first detective stories, written by Edgar Allan Poe and Sir Arthur Conan Doyle, emerged in the mid-nineteenth century, at a time when there was an enormous public interest in scientific progress. The newspapers of the day continually publicized the
>
> Line 5   latest scientific discoveries, and scientists were acclaimed as the heroes of the age.
>
> Poe and Conan Doyle shared this fascination with the step-by-step, logical approach used by scientists in their experiments, and instilled in their detective heroes outstanding powers of scientific
>
> 10   reasoning.
>
> The character of Sherlock Holmes, for example, illustrates Conan Doyle's admiration for the scientific mind. In each case that Holmes investigates, he is able to use the most insubstantial evidence to track down his opponent. Using only his restless eye
>
> 15   and ingenious reasoning powers, Holmes pieces together the identity of the villain from such unremarkable details as the type of cigar ashes left at the crime scene or the kind of ink used in a handwritten letter.
>
> In fact, Holmes's painstaking attention to detail often reminds
>
> 20   the reader of Charles Darwin's *On the Origin of Species*, published some twenty years earlier.

This passage is basically about detective stories...and science.

Poe and Conan Doyle seem to be important.

Holmes is an example *of a detective hero with a brilliant scientific mind*

This is a comparison between Holmes and Darwin.

Again, you'll spend more time later learning how to read the passage. The point here is that the first thing you want to do is read through the entire passage noting the major themes and a few details.

Step 2. Decode the Question Stem

Several questions will follow the passage. *Before* you can answer each question, you'll have to figure out exactly what is being asked. You need to make the question make sense to you. Check out the following question:

Which of the following is implied by the statement that Holmes was able to identify the villain based on "unremarkable details" (line 16)?

(A) Holmes's enemies left no traces at the crime scene.

(B) The character of Holmes was based on Charles Darwin.

(C) Few real detectives would have been capable of solving Holmes's cases.

(D) Holmes was particularly brilliant in powers of detection.

(E) Criminal investigation often involves tedious, time-consuming tasks.

Remember, you should predict before you peek at the answer choices. First, determine what the question is asking. The word "implied" means that you need to understand how the phrase "unremarkable details" relates to Holmes's ability to identify the villain.

Step 3. Research the Details

This does *not* mean that you should start rereading the entire passage from the beginning to find the location of "unremarkable details." Focus your research using the notes you took. Where does the author mention Holmes? You should have noted when you read the passage that the author discusses Holmes in the second paragraph. Scan that paragraph for the reference to "unremarkable details." (Hint: The reference can be found in line 16.)

Additionally, don't answer questions based on your memory. Go back and do the research. In other words, if you can answer questions based on your memory, you have spent too much time on the passage.

EXPERT TIP

Don't try to answer questions just from your memory.

Step 4: Predict the Answer and Check the Choices

When you find the detail in the passage, think about the *purpose* that it serves. Why does the author mention the "unremarkable details"? If you read the lines surrounding the phrase, you'll see that the author talks about how amazing it is that Holmes can solve mysteries based on such little evidence. Therefore, the *reason* the author mentions "unremarkable details" is to show how impressive Holmes is. Now, scan your answer choices:

(A) Holmes's enemies left no traces at the crime scene.

(B) The character of Holmes was based on Charles Darwin.

(C) Few real detectives would have been capable of solving Holmes's cases.

(D) Holmes was particularly brilliant in powers of detection.

(E) Criminal investigation often involves tedious, time-consuming tasks.

Lines 11–18 focus on Holmes's ability to solve a crime using the smallest details. Answer choice (D) should stand out to you based on this prediction. If not, you can eliminate the other choices using evidence from throughout the rest of the passage. Choice A is incorrect because this sentence mentions the "cigar ashes left at the crime scene." Choice B is incorrect because these lines focus on Holmes's ability to solve crimes, not the origin of his character. Choice C is incorrect because this part of the passage focuses exclusively on Holmes, not other detectives. Finally, choice E is incorrect because this part of the passage does not discuss the speed with which Holmes can solve crimes.

PASSAGE TYPES

You will always see the same types of passages on the SSAT or ISEE. The table below summarizes their major features.

Passage Type	Description
Science	Describes or offers a perspective on a scientific theory or phenomenon
History	Describes or offers a perspective on an historical event
Literature	Extracted from novels or poetry
Contemporary Life	Short essays on emerging careers or topics of general interest in the 21st century

READING QUESTION TYPES

The SSAT and ISEE Reading section always asks the same type of questions. Knowing what to expect can give you a huge advantage.

Question Type	Description
Main Idea	Asks about the passage's overall message or theme
Supporting Ideas	Asks about points that reinforce the author's main idea
Inference	Asks you to deduce what must be true based on the evidence in the passage
Vocab-in-Context	Asks about the meaning of a specific word or phrase in context
Tone/Style/Figurative Language	Asks how the author employs rhetorical elements to support her main idea
Organization/Logic (ISEE only)	Asks about how the author structures the passage or the function of a specific sentence or paragraph
Author's Purpose and Arguments (SSAT only)	Asks about the author's purpose for writing and the arguments and claims

COMMON INCORRECT ANSWER CHOICES

Knowing what common incorrect answer choices the test makers will write for Test Day can help you avoid them. Study the table below and be on the look out for these common distractor answer choices.

Trap	Description
Out of Scope	Introduces something that was never mentioned in the passage
Distortion	Distorts the logical relationship between two ideas in the passage
Opposite	Is the reverse of what the passage actually says
Extreme	Has the correct idea but goes too far; includes words like "always," "never," and "every"
Misused Detail	Cites a true detail from the passage that has no relevance to the question at hand

READING STRATEGIES

On the one hand, it's a good thing that you're inherently prepared for this section because you already know how to read. On the other hand, your previous reading experience has the potential to get you into a bit of trouble on this section of the test. Traditional reading habits that serve you well in school can get in the way on the test.

There are three mistakes that students commonly make when taking the test:

Mistake 1: Reading too slowly.

Mistake 2: Continually rereading things you do not understand.

Mistake 3: Spending more time on the passages than on the questions.

In general, it is a mistake to approach the reading passages with the intention of understanding them thoroughly. Make sure the notes you are taking will help you answer the questions, not teach someone else the topic.

Passage Mapping

Learn how to passage map! Passage mapping is the process of taking notes as you read to help you quickly locate the evidence you need to answer questions.

When passage mapping nonfiction passages, consider the following:

- Locate the central idea in the first paragraph.
- Note how each paragraph relates to the central idea. Does the paragraph…
  - Explain?
  - Support?
  - Refute?
  - Summarize?
- Don't be distracted by jargon or antiquated and technical terms.
  - Unfamiliar terms will generally be defined within the passage or in a footnote.

When passage mapping fiction passages, consider the following:

- Identify the characters and evaluate how the author describes them.
  - What do the characters want?
  - What are the characters doing?
  - What adjectives describe each character?
- Assess the characters' opinions of each other and themselves.
  - Do they like each other? Dislike each other?
  - Why does each character make a particular decision or take a particular course of action?
  - What do these decisions or actions tell you about a character?
- Identify the themes of the story.
  - What are the "turning points" in the passage?
  - Is there a moral to the story?

Remember, the SSAT and ISEE Reading sections are open-book tests. The answer is always in the passage.

SSAT and ISEE Reading Is Different from Everyday Reading

This is an important point. You already know how to read, but the way that you read normally may not help you maximize your points on the test. There are three main skills you'll need to employ to ace the Reading Comprehension section:

1. **Summarize:** You'll need to be able to sum up what the passage is all about.

2. **Research:** You'll need to be able to find facts, figures, and names in the passage.

3. **Make inferences:** You'll need to be able to figure out information that isn't directly stated.

How can you make sure you do all of these very official-sounding things? Here are six solid strategies.

1. Look for the Big Idea

Don't read as if you're memorizing everything. Aim to pick up just the gist of the passage—the author's main idea.

2. Pay Attention to Language

The author's choice of words can tell you everything about his or her point of view, attitude, and style.

3. Be a Critical Reader

As you read, ask yourself critical questions: "What's the author's main idea? What supporting ideas is the author trying to get across?"

4. Make It Simple

Despite the complicated language, Reading passages are usually about pretty simple topics. Don't get bogged down by technical language; instead, translate the author's ideas into your *own words*.

5. Keep Moving

Try not to spend more than one minute reading each passage; remember, just reading the passage won't score you points.

6. Don't Sweat the Details

Don't waste time reading and rereading parts you don't understand. Move swiftly through the passage to answer the questions, which is what really counts.

You've probably realized by now that Kaplan has a multistep method for all the question types on the SSAT and ISEE. It's in your best interest to approach the test as a whole and the individual sections systematically. If you approach every passage the same way, you'll work your way through the Reading Comprehension section efficiently.

READING SKILLS IN ACTION

Remember the three key reading skills: summarizing, researching, and making inferences. Look at how these skills can help you not only to read the passage but also to answer the questions.

Summarizing

For the purposes of the SSAT and ISEE, *summarizing* means capturing in a single phrase what the *entire* passage is about. Most passages will be followed by a question that deals with the passage as a whole. Incorrect answers will include choices that cover only one paragraph or some other subset of the passage. You'll need to recognize the answer choice that deals with the passage as a whole. If you've thought about the Main Idea ahead of time, you're more likely to determine the correct answer. For example:

> The four brightest moons of Jupiter were the first objects in the solar system discovered with the use of the telescope. Their proven existence played a central role in Galileo's famous argument in support of the Copernican model of the solar system, in which the planets are described as revolving around the Sun.
>
> *Line 5*   For several hundred years after their discovery by Galileo in 1610, scientific understanding of these moons increased fairly slowly. Scientists on Earth succeeded in measuring their approximate diameters, their relative densities, and, eventually, some of their light-reflecting characteristics. However, the spectacular close-up photographs sent back by the 1979 *Voyager* missions forever changed our impressions of these bodies.

Which of the following best explains what this passage is about?

(A) Galileo's invention of the telescope

(B) The discovery of the Galilean moons

(C) Scientific knowledge about Jupiter's four brightest moons

(D) The Copernican model of the solar system

(E) The early history of astronomy

Decode the question first. This question is a Main Idea question; it focuses on the main idea of the entire passage. Try to summarize the paragraphs as one whole entity.

Only answer choice (C) here sums up the contents of both paragraphs. Choice B is just a detail. Choice A cannot be correct because Galileo's telescope is not even mentioned. Choice D is mentioned only in the first paragraph and is a distortion of the author's point. Choice E is too broad in scope.

Choice (C) summarizes the entire passage. The passage deals with scientific knowledge about Jupiter's four brightest moons. The four moons are the first things mentioned in the first paragraph, and the rest of the first paragraph discusses the role they played for Galileo. The second paragraph deals with how the moons were perceived by scientists throughout history. In sum, both paragraphs deal with scientific knowledge about these moons.

Researching

Researching essentially means knowing *where* to look for the details. Generally, if you note your paragraph topics, you should be in pretty good shape to find the details. Once you know where to look, just scan for key phrases found in the question. For example:

> A human body can survive without water for several days and without food for as much as several weeks. If breathing stops for as little as three to six minutes, however, death is likely. All animals require a constant supply of oxygen to the body tissues,
>
> *Line 5* and especially, to the heart or brain. In the human body, the respiratory system performs this function by delivering air containing oxygen to the blood.
>
> Respiration in large animals possessing lungs involves more than just breathing, however. It is a complex process that delivers
> 10 oxygen to internal tissues while eliminating waste carbon dioxide produced by cells. More specifically, respiration involves two processes known as bulk flow and diffusion. Oxygen and carbon dioxide are moved in bulk through the respiratory and circulatory systems; gaseous diffusion occurs at different points
> 15 across thin tissue membranes.

Breathing is the most urgent human bodily function.

Respiration in large animals is a complex process.

Take a look at the previous passage and paragraph topics. The paragraph topics are very general; they just note the gist of the paragraphs. If you saw the following questions, would you know where to find the answers?

Which bodily function, according to the passage, is least essential to the survival of the average human being?

The first paragraph deals with bodily functions. Lines 1–2 note that food is most expendable.

(A) Eating

(B) Drinking

(C) Breathing

(D) Blood circulation

(E) The oxygen supply

Now that you have researched the passage in the correct location, find the choice that has the correct answer. Because food is most expendable, it is therefore least essential. The correct answer is choice (A).

Which part of an animal's body is responsible for producing waste carbon dioxide?

The second paragraph deals with the complex details of respiration. Carbon dioxide is mentioned in lines 9–11.

(A) The internal tissues

(B) The circulatory systems

(C) The tissue membranes

(D) The bloodstream

(E) The cells

According to lines 10–11, waste carbon dioxide is "produced by cells." Therefore, choice (E) is correct.

Making Inferences

Making an inference means looking for something that is strongly implied but not stated explicitly. In other words, making an inference means *reading between the lines*. What did the author *almost* say (but not say exactly)?

Inferences will not stray too far from the language of the text. Incorrect answers on Inference questions will often fall beyond the subject matter of the passage. For example:

> Children have an amazing talent for learning vocabulary. Between the ages of one and
> seventeen, the average person learns the meaning of about 80,000 words—about 14 per day.
> Dictionaries and traditional classroom vocabulary lessons only account for part of this
> spectacular knowledge growth. More influential are individuals' reading habits and their
>
> *Line 5*   interaction with people whose vocabularies are larger than their own. Reading shows
> students how words are used in sentences. Conversation offers several extra benefits that
> make vocabulary learning engaging—it supplies visual information, offers frequent
> repetition of new words, and gives students the chance to ask questions.

The author of the passage most likely believes that a child is most receptive to learning the meaning of new words at which time?

(A) When the child reaches high school age

(B) When the child is talking to other students

(C) When the child is assigned vocabulary exercises

(D) When the child is regularly told that he or she needs to improve

(E) When vocabulary learning is made interesting

This short passage discusses how children learn vocabulary. The question asks when children are *most* receptive to learning new words. No sentence in the passage states that "children are *most* receptive to learning new words…." In lines 4–5, however, the author mentions that reading and conversation are particularly helpful. Lines 6–7 note how conversation makes vocabulary engaging. This is consistent with choice (E). Nothing in the passage suggests that children learn more at high school age, choice A. Choice B might be tempting, but it is too specific: there's no reason to believe that talking to students is more helpful than talking to anyone else. Choice C contradicts the passage, and choice D is never mentioned at all.

At this point, you have a lot of tools to help you read passages and approach questions. It's a good idea to have a solid understanding of what the questions are, what types of questions you'll see, and how to best approach each one. There are three common question types in the Reading Comprehension section: Main Idea, Supporting Ideas, and Inference questions.

Since you can't exactly deal with questions unless you have an accompanying passage, take one or two minutes to read the following passage. As usual, mark it up. Read it with the goal of answering questions afterwards.

The first truly American art movement was formed by a group of landscape painters that emerged in the early nineteenth century called the Hudson River School. The first works in this style were created by Thomas Cole, Thomas Doughty, and Asher Durand, a trio of painters who worked during the 1820s in the Hudson River Valley and surrounding

Line 5 locations. Heavily influenced by European Romanticism, these painters set out to convey the remoteness and splendor of the American wilderness. The strongly nationalistic tone of their paintings caught the spirit of the times, and within a generation the movement had mushroomed to include landscape painters from all over the United States. Canvases celebrating such typically American scenes as Niagara Falls, Boston Harbor, and the

10 expansion of the railroad into rural Pennsylvania were greeted with enormous popular acclaim.

One factor contributing to the success of the Hudson River School was the rapid growth of American nationalism in the early nineteenth century. The War of 1812 had given the United States a new sense of pride in its identity, and as the nation continued to grow, there

15 was a desire to compete with Europe on both economic and cultural grounds. The vast panoramas of the Hudson River School fit the bill perfectly by providing a new movement in art that was unmistakably American in origin. The Hudson River School also arrived at a time when writers in the United States were turning their attention to the wilderness as a unique aspect of their nationality. The Hudson River School profited from this nostalgia

20 because they effectively represented the continent the way it used to be. The view that the American character was formed by the frontier experience was widely held, and many writers were concerned about the future of a country that was becoming increasingly urbanized.

In keeping with this nationalistic spirit, even the painting style of the Hudson River

25 School exhibited a strong sense of American identity. Although many of the artists studied in Europe, their paintings show a desire to be free of European artistic rules. Regarding the natural landscape as a direct manifestation of God, the Hudson River School painters attempted to record what they saw as accurately as possible. Unlike European painters who brought to their canvases the styles and techniques of centuries, they sought neither to

30 embellish nor to idealize their scenes, portraying nature with the care and attention to detail of naturalists.

Hopefully, you understood that this passage was about why the Hudson River School became so successful. You should have also noted that the second paragraph addresses how American nationalism contributed to the success of the Hudson River School and the third paragraph discusses how nationalist sentiment was evident in the Hudson River School painting style.

Main Idea Questions

A Main Idea question asks you to summarize the topic of the passage.

Which of the following best explains what this passage is about?

(A) The history of American landscape painting

(B) Why an art movement caught the public imagination

(C) How European painters influenced the Hudson River School

(D) Why writers began to romanticize the American wilderness

(E) The origins of nationalism in the United States

Main Idea questions are pretty easy to recognize. They will always ask something general about the passage.

Look for the answer choice that summarizes the entire passage. Rule out choices that are too broad or too narrow.

Do you see which one of these answers describes the entire passage without being too broad or too narrow?

Choice A is too broad, as is choice E. The passage is not about all American landscape painting; it's about the Hudson River School. Nationalism in the United States is much larger than the role of nationalism in a particular art movement. Choices C and D are too narrow. European painters did influence the Hudson River School painters, but that wasn't the point of the whole passage. Similarly, writers are mentioned in paragraph 2, but the passage is about an art movement. Only choice (B) captures the essence of the passage—it's about an art movement that caught the public imagination.

Supporting Ideas Questions

Supporting Ideas questions are straightforward—all you've got to do is locate the relevant information in the passage. The key strategy is to research the details by relating facts, figures, and names in the question to a *specific* paragraph.

Which of the following is not mentioned as one of the reasons for the success of the Hudson River School?

(A) American nationalism increased after the War of 1812.

(B) Americans were nostalgic about the frontier.

(C) Writers began to focus on the wilderness.

(D) The United States wanted to compete with Europe.

(E) City dwellers became concerned about environmental pollution.

Note how the Supporting Ideas question asks about what is specifically mentioned—or not mentioned.

Scan the passage words or phrases in the answer choices. When you find the references, cross out the answer choices that do appear in the passage. The one left over will be the correct answer.

Four of the five answer choices are mentioned explicitly in the passage. Choice A is mentioned in lines 11–15. Choice B appears in lines 20–21. Choice C shows up in lines 17–20. Choice D is mentioned in line 15. Only choice (E) does not appear in the passage.

Inference Questions

An **Inference** question, like a Supporting Ideas question, asks you to find relevant information in the passage. But once you've located the details, you have to go one step farther: you have to figure out the underlying point of a particular phrase or example. Use your inference skills to figure out the author's point. The answer will not be stated, but it will be *strongly implied.*

Which of the following best describes what is suggested by the statement that the Hudson River School paintings "fit the bill perfectly" (line 16)?

(A) The paintings depicted famous battle scenes.

(B) The paintings were very successful commercially.

(C) The paintings reflected a new pride in the United States.

(D) The paintings were favorably received in Europe.

(E) The paintings were accurate in their portrayal of nature.

"Suggested" is a classic Inference clue. If something is "suggested," it is not stated outright.

Read the lines surrounding the quote. Summarize the author's point in your mind before you check the answer choices.

First, read the lines surrounding the quote to put the quote in context. Paragraph 2 talks about American pride; that's why Hudson River School paintings "fit the bill." Hudson River School paintings were about America. Choice (C) summarizes the point nicely. Note how this question revolves around the interplay between main idea and details. This detail strengthens the topic of the paragraph, the growing sense of nationalism in America. Choice A superficially relates to the War of 1812 but doesn't answer the question. Choices B, D, and E are way off base.

A Reminder about Timing

Plan to spend approximately one minute reading the passage and roughly a minute to a minute and a half on each question. When you first start practicing, you'll probably find yourself spending more time than that on the passages. That's okay. You need to pay attention to your timing, however, and cut the time down to around a minute. If you don't, it will hurt you in the long run.

A WORD ABOUT SCIENCE PASSAGES

At least one Reading passage may deal with a scientific or technical topic. You will NOT be tested on any outside science knowledge, so do not answer the questions based on anything other than the information contained in the passage.

PRACTICE QUESTIONS

This is an SSAT-style passage.

> The environment of the coral reef is formed over thousands of years by the life cycle of vast numbers of coral animals. The main architect of the reef is the stony coral, a relative of the sea anemone that lives in tropical climates and secretes a skeleton of almost pure calcium carbonate. Its partner is the green alga, a tiny unicellular plant, which lives within the tissues of the coral. The two
> Line 5   organisms coexist in a mutually beneficial relationship, with the algae consuming carbon dioxide given off by the corals and the corals thriving in the abundant oxygen produced photosynthetically by the algae. When the coral dies, its skeleton is left, and other organisms grow on top of it. Over the years, the sheer mass of coral skeletons, together with those of associated organisms, combine to form the petrified underwater forest that divers find so fascinating.

1. According to the passage, the skeleton of the stony coral is mostly composed of

   (A) cartilage
   (B) stone
   (C) calcium carbonate
   (D) carbon dioxide
   (E) sediment

2. This passage primarily deals with

   (A) different forms of marine life
   (B) the contribution of the stony coral to reef formation
   (C) the interaction between two inhabitants of coral reefs
   (D) the physical beauty of coral reefs
   (E) the geological origins of reef islands

3. It can be inferred from the passage that divers are primarily interested in which aspect of reefs?

   (A) the biological cycles of reef animals
   (B) the visual appeal of a mass of coral skeletons
   (C) the fertile growing environment that reefs provide
   (D) the historical implications of reef development
   (E) the actual number of dead animals required to form a reef

4. The relationship between the coral and the algae is best described as

   (A) inhospitable
   (B) competitive
   (C) predatory
   (D) collaborative
   (E) mysterious

5. All of the following are mentioned in the passage as part of the life cycle of reef organisms EXCEPT

   (A) corals live within the tissues of the algae
   (B) algae consume carbon dioxide emitted by corals
   (C) the skeleton of the coral provides an environment for other organisms
   (D) corals secrete a calcium carbonate skeleton
   (E) corals consume oxygen produced by algae

GO ON TO THE NEXT PAGE. ▶ ▶ ▶

This is an SSAT-style passage.

> Tunnel construction is costly and dangerous, but new technologies are allowing tunnelers to work more quickly and safely than ever before. Today's rock tunnels are being drilled by modern full-face tunnel-boring machines (TBMs). The drilling end of a TBM consists of a rotating cutterhead whose diameter covers the entire face of a tunnel. As the cutterhead turns, hard-steel blades cut steadily
> Line 5 through the rock. The first successful hard-rock TBM was built in 1957, and many improvements have been made in TBM design in subsequent years.
>
> Developments in TBM technology have helped spur ambitious new projects. Most notable is the 50-kilometer Eurotunnel (also known as the Chunnel), which was bored by modern TBMs beneath the English Channel. The tunneling was done by British and French teams that started on opposite
> 10 sides of the Channel and eventually met underground, in the middle. Thus, TBMs have contributed to building a technological and cultural milestone. Trains can now travel between England and France in less than an hour, and, for the first time, Britain and continental Europe are linked by land.

6. The passage suggests that, despite three decades' worth of technological improvement, tunnel construction is

   (A) rarely worth the risks involved

   (B) still expensive

   (C) possible only with international cooperation

   (D) heavily reliant on geological guesswork

   (E) not as efficient as possible

7. The author's main purpose for writing the passage is most likely to

   (A) explain why tunnel construction is expensive and dangerous

   (B) compare past and present methods of tunnel construction

   (C) inform the reader how TBMs operate

   (D) describe the impact of TBMs on tunnel construction

   (E) dispel myths about why the Eurotunnel was difficult to dig

8. As it is used in line 7, the word "notable" most nearly means

   (A) popular

   (B) legendary

   (C) remarkable

   (D) weighty

   (E) memorable

9. The author most likely describes the Eurotunnel as a "cultural milestone" (line 11) because it

   (A) lifts travel restrictions among all European countries

   (B) connects Europe and Britain by land for the first time

   (C) harms the relationship between Britain and France

   (D) affects the way all future tunnels will be dug

   (E) changes the political climate in Europe

10. The attitude of the writer towards the subject is best described as

    (A) enthusiastic

    (B) uncertain

    (C) cautious

    (D) bitter

    (E) euphoric

GO ON TO THE NEXT PAGE. ▶ ▶ ▶

This is an SSAT-style passage.

Usually regarded as pests, the termites of South Florida provide an excellent illustration of nature of nature at work. In the natural world, when two or more different organisms coexist to each other's benefit, it's called a symbiotic relationship. The dominant member of the symbiotic pair or group is known as the "host," while the smaller, less dominant member is the "parasite." A
Line 5 classic symbiotic relationship of this kind takes place in the digestive tract of Florida wood-eating termites. We think of a termite as being able to digest wood, but it really cannot. The termite plays host to parasitic protozoans, single-celled organisms that live in the termite's gut. The protozoans provide the termite with a service necessary to its survival: they digest the cellulose in the wood that it consumes.

11. Which of the following is suggested in the passage about the protozoans?

(A) They are essential to the continued existence of termites.

(B) They are both a parasitic and a host organism.

(C) They are roughly equal in size to bacteria.

(D) They attach themselves to the membranes of termites.

(E) They can survive on their own when necessary.

12. Which of the following titles best describes the content of the passage?

(A) Practical Parasites

(B) How Termites Eat Wood

(C) Pests in Florida

(D) The Evolution of Symbiotic Relationships

(E) Cooperating to Survive

13. According to the passage, a "host" (line 4) organism is generally

(A) found only in South Florida

(B) the dominant partner in a symbiotic relationship

(C) unable to digest cellulose without assistance

(D) able to survive on its own, without a parasite

(E) associated with single-celled organisms

14. With which of the following statements about a symbiotic relationship would the author most likely agree?

(A) It involves organisms that are alike.

(B) It often involves harmful parasites.

(C) It mostly involves tiny organisms.

(D) It usually involves organisms that are different.

(E) It may be beneficial to both organisms.

15. The author's tone can best be described as

(A) bored

(B) enthusiastic

(C) annoyed

(D) informed

(E) humorous

GO ON TO THE NEXT PAGE. ▶ ▶ ▶

This is an ISEE-style passage.

1   The ozone layer of the atmosphere protects
2   Earth from harmful solar radiation. However, the
3   atmosphere is fragile, and evidence indicates that
4   it has thinned. In 1989, the Montreal Protocol was
5   put into effect to counter human damage to the
6   ozone layer, and there have been signs of progress
7   since then. Despite these efforts, the amount of solar
8   radiation reaching Earth has increased steadily.
9   The implications of this are not good. Solar
10 radiation causes cancer and contributes to other
11 serious illnesses. Also, as radiation increases, more
12 and more warm air gets trapped near Earth, and
13 hot, humid conditions like those in a greenhouse
14 begin to prevail. The average global temperature
15 has increased about 1.4 degrees Fahrenheit since

16 about 1880, and two-thirds of that warming has
17 occurred since about 1975. Global temperature
18 changes drastically affect Earth's climate, so
19 people can expect increasingly frequent extreme
20 weather events and higher sea levels to occur as
21 the global temperature continues to rise.
22   While some measures of ozone in our atmosphere
23 have shown signs of improvement, more work is
24 needed to prevent further temperature increases.
25 The greenhouse gases that have contributed to
26 the increase in radiation take time to leave our
27 atmosphere, so total ozone recovery and the
28 stabilization of Earth's temperature is predicted to
29 take a century or more.

16. This passage deals primarily with

(A) the reasons why solar radiation is damaging.

(B) the ozone in the atmosphere over Antarctica.

(C) the discovery of the hole in the ozone layer.

(D) the loss of ozone from the ozone layer.

17. In line 3, "fragile" most nearly means

(A) vulnerable.

(B) weak.

(C) breakable.

(D) brittle.

18. Which of the following is directly mentioned as evidence of ozone depletion?

(A) A decrease in the amount of sunlight reaching the Earth

(B) A decline in skin cancers among people

(C) An increase in solar radiation reaching the Earth's surface

(D) Gaps in the atmosphere over North America

19. Which of the following explains why ozone depletion has occurred?

(A) Oxygen is disappearing from the atmosphere.

(B) The ozone layer is being broken down by pollutants.

(C) The sun's rays are becoming stronger.

(D) Sea levels are falling and temperatures are rising.

GO ON TO THE NEXT PAGE. ▶ ▶ ▶

20. The author most likely mentions "a greenhouse" (line 13) in order to

(A) suggest a way to protect plants from harmful radiation.

(B) describe an effect of increasing solar radiation.

(C) explain how ozone forms in the atmosphere.

(D) explain that heat and humidity are destroying the atmosphere.

21. The passage suggests that a full restoration of the atmosphere

(A) is the only way to save Antarctica from destruction.

(B) depends on the frequency of future volcanic eruptions.

(C) remains an impossibility despite international efforts.

(D) is highly unlikely in the near future.

This is an SSAT-style passage.

For thousands of years, smallpox was one of the world's most dreaded diseases. An acutely infectious disease spread by a virus, smallpox was the scourge of medieval Europe, where it was known by its symptoms of extreme fever and disfiguring rash as "the invisible fire." In many outbreaks, mortality rates were higher than 25 percent. Ancient Chinese medical texts show that the disease was known as long
Line 5 ago as 1122 b.c.e. But as recently as 1967, more than 2 million people died from the disease annually.

A method of conferring immunity from smallpox was discovered in 1796 by an English doctor named Edward Jenner. It was not until 1966, however, that the World Health Organization was able to marshal the resources to launch a worldwide campaign to wipe out the disease. In an immense project involving thousands of health workers, WHO teams moved from country to country,
10 locating every case of active smallpox and vaccinating all potential contacts. In 1977, the last active case of smallpox was found and eliminated. Since there are no animal carriers of smallpox, the WHO was able to declare in 1980 that the dreaded killer had been conquered. For the first time in the history of medicine, a disease had been completely destroyed.

22. Which of the following best tells what this passage is about?

(A) how to treat viral diseases

(B) the purpose of the World Health Organization

(C) the tragic symptoms of smallpox

(D) the history of the fight against smallpox

(E) early efforts at controlling infectious diseases

23. In line 1, the word "acutely" most nearly means

(A) painfully

(B) extremely

(C) unnaturally

(D) sensitively

(E) partly

GO ON TO THE NEXT PAGE. ▶ ▶ ▶

24. It can be inferred from the passage that the earliest recorded cases of smallpox were located in

(A) China

(B) Europe

(C) the Middle East

(D) North America

(E) Africa

25. The passage implies that smallpox was not eliminated before 1966 because

(A) vaccination did not prevent all forms of the disease

(B) not enough was known about immunity to disease

(C) there was no effective protection against animal carriers

(D) there had never been a coordinated worldwide vaccination campaign

(E) the disease would lie dormant for many years and then reappear

26. According to the passage, the WHO's fight against smallpox was a unique event because

(A) it involved a worldwide campaign of vaccination

(B) a disease had never before been utterly wiped out

(C) animal carriers had to be isolated and vaccinated

(D) doctors were uncertain as to whether Jenner's methods would work

(E) it was more expensive than any other single vaccination campaign

This is an ISEE-style passage.

1   Almost everyone enjoys hearing some kind of live
2   music. However, few of us realize the complex process
3   that goes into designing the acoustics of concert and
4   lecture halls. In the design of any building where
5   audibility of sound is a major consideration, architects
6   have to carefully match the space and materials they
7   use to the intended purpose of the venue.
8   One problem is that the intensity of sound may build
9   too quickly in an enclosed space. Another problem is
10 that only part of the sound we hear in any large room
11 or auditorium comes directly from the source.
12 Much of it reaches us a fraction of a second later after
13 it has been reflected off the walls, ceiling, and floor
14 as reverberated sound. How much each room
15 reverberates depends upon both its size and the ability
16 of its contents to absorb sound. Too little reverberation
17 can make music sound thin and weak; too much can
18 blur the listener's sense of where one note stops and
19 the next begins. Consequently, the most important
20 factor in acoustic design is the time it takes for these
21 reverberations to die down altogether, called the
22 reverberation time.

GO ON TO THE NEXT PAGE. ▶ ▶ ▶

27. Which best expresses the main idea of the passage?

    (A) the challenges of an architect's job

    (B) the differences between speech and music

    (C) the experience of hearing live music

    (D) the role of reverberation in acoustic design

28. The passage suggests that the "complex process" of acoustic design (line 2) is

    (A) not widely appreciated by the public.

    (B) really a matter of listener sensitivity.

    (C) wholly dependent on the choice of construction materials.

    (D) an engineer's problem, not an architect's.

29. According to the passage, audibility of sound is influenced by which of the following factors?

    I.   The type of materials used to construct a building

    II. The reflection of sound off a room's ceiling or walls

    III. The size and purpose of a particular room or space

    (A) I only

    (B) II only

    (C) I and II only

    (D) I, II, and III

30. According to the passage, too little reverberation in a concert hall can result in

    (A) a rapid increase in the volume of sound.

    (B) the blurring of details in a piece of music.

    (C) a quiet and insubstantial quality of sound.

    (D) confusion among a listening audience.

31. Which of the following does the author regard as the most significant consideration in the design of a concert hall?

    (A) an appreciation for music

    (B) an understanding of reverberation time

    (C) the choice of building materials

    (D) the purpose of the venue

32. The author most likely mentions the problems encountered in designing concert and lecture halls in order to

    (A) convince audiences to appreciate the design of concert halls.

    (B) emphasize the challenges faced by architects.

    (C) argue for the need to increase ticket prices.

    (D) explain why reverberation is important.

GO ON TO THE NEXT PAGE. ▶ ▶ ▶

This is an SSAT-style passage.

The American Revolution is more notable for the absence of major American victories in set-piece battles than for their occurrence. While it is widely known that George Washington was an American hero in the nascent United States' successful bid to win independence, a cursory examination reveals that Washington was soundly defeated in almost every pitched battle he fought

Line 5 against the British. Two principal American cities, New York and Philadelphia, were captured by the British, and Washington could do nothing to prevent their capture or to take back either city. In a classic example of Colonial military futility, Washington deployed his troops on Brooklyn Heights to repel the British invasion of New York. After his troops were thoroughly routed, Washington regrouped in Manhattan, only to be chased from the island with the humiliating sound of foxhunt

10 bugles in his ears. The retreat would not stop until he and his troops safely crossed the Delaware River into Pennsylvania.

Unfortunately for the British, however, America was not a land of Old World conventions. The Colonial soldier did not fight for wealth, for territory, or out of service to a nobleman. He fought for his home, and his war required a different level of commitment. George Washington is remembered

15 as an American hero not because he was able to win battles against the British by their own rules of engagement but because he was able to outlast their resolve, defiantly keep an army in the field, and await foreign aid. While Washington had little to do with the long awaited set-piece victory at Saratoga*, his principal success was in his tenacity and daring to keep fighting. Washington's victories at Trenton and Princeton were over minuscule forces, but they kept his army together and resurrected

20 the American cause in the minds of his countrymen at an hour when the Colonies seemed certain of its failure. It is only fitting that when the final vise grip was applied to Cornwallis at Yorktown, George Washington was there to preside over the culmination of his uniquely American war.

*Major Colonial win in upstate New York in 1777 that earned the Colonies the recognition and aid of the French

33. According to the passage, George Washington is regarded as successful because

   (A) he waged war according to unconventional rules.

   (B) he triumphed over the British at Saratoga.

   (C) he was able to defend American cities.

   (D) he was able to find a way to win pitched battles.

   (E) he was able to cross the Delaware into Pennsylvania.

34. The author mentions which of the following about the victories at Trenton and Princeton?

   (A) They had a significant impact on Colonial morale.

   (B) They were achieved over sizeable forces.

   (C) They earned French aid in the Revolution.

   (D) They lasted longer than any other battle.

   (E) They assured the defeat of the Colonists.

GO ON TO THE NEXT PAGE. ▶ ▶ ▶

35. According to the passage, which of the following was a "classic example of Colonial military futility" (lines 6–7)?

    (A) Washington's failure to win a pitched battle

    (B) Washington's inability to keep an army in the field

    (C) the American failure to attract foreign aid

    (D) Washington's inability to repel the attack on New York

    (E) the deployment of Washington's troops on Brooklyn Heights

36. Why does the author state in line 12 that "America was not a land of Old World conventions"?

    (A) to indicate why the Colonial troops were unable to imitate British victories in pitched battle

    (B) to illustrate how Washington's successes did not follow the British model for victory

    (C) to praise Washington's indifference to failure in pitched battle

    (D) to give the Americans credit for their defiance of British customs

    (E) to excuse the Colonial defeats at New York and Philadelphia

37. Which of the following does the author suggest is the reason for the American triumph in the Revolution?

    (A) the American victory in a pitched battle at Saratoga

    (B) the lack of British commitment to winning as compared to the Americans

    (C) the better morale and supplies of the American troops

    (D) the inherent superiority of George Washington's military strategy

    (E) the American victories at Trenton and Princeton

GO ON TO THE NEXT PAGE. ▶ ▶ ▶

This is an SSAT-style passage.

> On one of the ridges of that wintry waste stood the low log house in which John Bergson was dying. The Bergson homestead was easier to find than many others because it overlooked Norway Creek—a shallow, muddy stream that sometimes flowed and sometimes stood still—at the bottom of a winding ravine with steep, shelving sides that were overgrown with brush and cottonwoods and dwarf ash. This
> Line 5 creek gave a sort of identity to the farms that bordered it. Of all the bewildering things about a new country, the absence of human landmarks was one of the most depressing and disheartening. The houses on the Divide were small and usually tucked away in low places; you did not see them until you came directly upon them. Most of them were built of the sod itself and were simply the inescapable ground in another form. The roads were but faint tracks in the grass, and the fields were scarcely noticeable. The record of
> 10 the plow was insignificant, like the feeble scratches on stone left by prehistoric races, so indeterminate that they may, after all, be only the markings of glaciers, and not a record of human strivings.
>
> After eleven long years, John Bergson had made little impression upon the wild land he had come to tame. It was still a wild thing that had its ugly moods; and no one knew when they were likely to come, or why. Mischance hung over it. Its genius was unfriendly to man. The sick man was feeling
> 15 this as he lay looking out of the window, after the doctor had left him, on the day following Alexandra's trip to town. There it lay outside his door, the same land, the same lead-colored miles. He knew every ridge and draw and gully between him and the horizon. To the south, his plowed fields; to the east, the sod stables, the cattle corral, the pond—and then the grass.
>
> (Adapted from Willa Cather's *O Pioneers!,* 1913)

38. According to the passage, most houses on the Divide were made of

    (A) earth
    (B) planks
    (C) bricks
    (D) stone
    (E) logs

39. The Bergson homestead was more distinctive than others because it was

    (A) a large farmstead
    (B) on Norway Creek
    (C) in the new country
    (D) surrounded by plowed fields
    (E) easy to see from afar

40. According to the author, the settler's plowed fields were

    (A) carved out by glaciers
    (B) bordered by cottonwood trees
    (C) planted with corn
    (D) slight compared to the plains
    (E) west of Norway Creek

GO ON TO THE NEXT PAGE. ▶ ▶ ▶

41. According to the passage, John Bergson's life on the frontier has

(A) not given him freedom to express his genius

(B) been characterized by illness

(C) transformed the town of Norway Creek

(D) had little impact on the plains

(E) required very little effort or struggle

42. The author's tone is best be described as

(A) bleak

(B) informative

(C) objective

(D) sunny

(E) comic

This is an ISEE-style passage.

1　The Trans-Alaska Pipeline System is a 799-mile
2　long pipe that carries oil from the Arctic Ocean to a
3　port in Valdez, on the southern coast of Alaska.
4　Before construction of the pipeline began in 1975,
5　scientists undertook environmental impact studies to
6　predict how the pipeline might affect the migration of
7　Alaska's North Slope caribou. These caribou travel
8　hundreds of miles between their winter feeding
9　grounds and their spring calving grounds, and there
10　was concern that the four-foot-diameter elevated
11　pipeline might hamper this migration. Scientists
12　worried that any delays might cause caribou cows to
13　give birth in transit and abandon their newborn
14　calves as they instinctively continued north. To avoid
15　this, special pipeline crossings were built, including
16　sections of buried pipe and sections that were
17　elevated so high that caribou could pass underneath
18　without being aware of the pipe overhead. After the
19　completion of the pipeline, however, scientists found
20　that caribou would cross it at any point, not just at
21　the crossings. While the design precautions were
22　ultimately unnecessary, the pipeline planners were
23　wise not to run risks that could have harmed the
24　region's wildlife.

43. Which answer choice best expresses the main idea of the passage?

(A) Human development has harmed northern caribou populations.

(B) Planners took steps to protect caribou along the pipeline.

(C) Scientists have mapped caribou migration routes.

(D) Most Alaskans are concerned about the ecosystem.

44. What did scientists worry might happen if caribou migrations were disrupted?

(A) Migrating herds would interfere with oil production.

(B) Caribou would not be able to feed in the winter.

(C) Births during migration would cause caribou to orphan their calves.

(D) The caribou would find a route farther away from humans.

GO ON TO THE NEXT PAGE. ▶ ▶ ▶

45. The author of the passage appears to think that the special pipeline crossings

    (A) were a waste of state resources.

    (B) were essential to protecting the caribou.

    (C) were worthwhile, though ultimately unnecessary.

    (D) were not well designed to do the job.

46. Why did planners expect the pipeline might disrupt migrations?

    (A) Construction was planned during the migration season.

    (B) Frequent oil spills created a toxic environment.

    (C) Caribou avoid objects that bear human scent.

    (D) The pipe was physically bulky and built aboveground.

47. In line 11, "hamper" most nearly means

    (A) accelerate.

    (B) obstruct.

    (C) contain.

    (D) direct.

48. The passage answers which of the following questions?

    (A) Exactly how high is the pipeline elevated above the ground?

    (B) How many caribou live on Alaska's North Slope?

    (C) Migration disruptions cause how many caribou deaths per year?

    (D) What is the purpose of the Trans-Alaska Pipeline?

GO ON TO THE NEXT PAGE. ▶ ▶ ▶

This is an SSAT-style passage.

> Five months ago the stream did flow,
> The lilies bloomed within the sedge,
> And we were lingering to and fro
> Where none will track thee in this snow,
> *Line 5* Along the stream, beside the hedge.
> Ah, sweet, be free to love and go!
> For, if I do not hear thy foot,
> The frozen river is as mute,
> The flowers have dried down to the root:
> 10 And why, since these be changed since May,
> Shouldst *thou* change less than *they*?
> And slow, slow as the winter snow,
> The tears have drifted to mine eyes;
> And my poor cheeks, five months ago
> 15 Set blushing at thy praises so,
> Put paleness on for a disguise.
> Ah, sweet, be free to praise and go!
> For, if my face is turned too pale,
> It was thine oath that first did fail;
> 20 It was thy love proved false and frail:
> And why, since these be changed enow,
> Should *I* change less than *thou*?
>
> (From "Change upon Change," Elizabeth Barrett Browning, 1846)

49. In this poem, the changing emotions of the writer's beloved are compared to which of the following?

    (A) flowers that have died and shriveled

    (B) the drifting winter snow

    (C) lilies blooming along a stream

    (D) the ebb and flow of a stream

    (E) the tears flowing from the author's eyes

50. The writer's lament that she "put paleness on for a disguise" (line 16) suggests that

    (A) she powdered her face

    (B) the falling snow covered her face

    (C) she put on a mask to hide her unhappiness

    (D) her sadness has changed how her face looks.

    (E) winter made her cheeks cold

GO ON TO THE NEXT PAGE. ▶ ▶ ▶

51. The flowing stream and the frozen river most likely represent

    (A) the passing of time

    (B) warmth and cold

    (C) love and hate

    (D) the writer's attitude toward nature

    (E) waning love

52. The writer would most likely agree with which of the following statements about love?

    (A) Love is immutable and everlasting, just like a river.

    (B) Changes in emotion are unusual and unexpected when you're in love.

    (C) People may not always feel as strongly about their beloved as they do at the beginning of a relationship.

    (D) People in love are seldom affected by any emotional changes in their beloved.

    (E) Love is full of difficult obstacles and should be avoided.

GO ON TO THE NEXT PAGE. ▶ ▶ ▶

This is an ISEE-style passage.

1   Over the past two decades, the field of information
2   technology has become one of the most popular
3   career destinations for new graduates in the
4   United States. High pay, strong benefits, and the
5   allure of working in a cutting-edge field have made
6   IT* the most explosive industry in the world. Despite
7   the much-publicized failed investments that have
8   hurt the tech sector's "Wall Street Cred," the IT
9   industry continues to grow at a staggering pace.
10 In 2004, the U.S. Department of Labor reported
11 that more than 2.5 million Americans worked in
12 a "computer occupation." Considering that the
13 Department of Labor did not even have a "computer
14 occupation" category in the 1970s, that number is
15 astounding. It only continues to increase with the
16 proliferation of (and dependence on) computer
17 technology in twenty-first century America.
18   The independence of the computer industry from
19 outside influences makes it unique among historical
20 "boom industries." Unlike wartime manufacturing or
21 disaster reconstruction, for example, the computer
22 industry is mostly free from political and
23 environmental constraints. Because of the industry's
24 independence and steady growth, a new graduate
25 with a computer degree should have strong earning
26 potential until retirement. This long-term career
27 track remains attractive to young professionals
28 willing to look past the media hype regarding the
29 "collapse of the dot-com bubble," especially
30 considering the high median salary and strong benefits
31 common in the field. Health and dental plans are
32 expected in the industry, as are the enticing
33 investment opportunities that have created so many
34 thirty-year-old millionaires.
35   The considerable advantages that come with a job in
36 information technology are not without costs to the
37 worker, however. Frequent training and retraining is
38 necessary due to the ever-changing and highly technical
39 nature of the field. Computer programmers must
40 occasionally learn newer, more robust programming
41 languages, in addition to conforming to the style
42 guidelines of each individual workplace. Network
43 technicians must continuously adapt their highly
44 technical work to a field that sees new systems and
45 technology introduced every four to six months. In
46 addition to the perpetual training, many in the IT field,
47 particularly programmers, complain of long hours
48 during the "crunch time" required when a deadline
49 is looming.
50   On the whole, though, tech workers are generally
51 more pleased with their jobs than are other laborers. A
52 recent study conducted by the Department of Labor
53 found that the majority of IT professionals described
54 themselves as "satisfied" to "very satisfied" with their
55 employment. This trend has contributed to the unusually
56 high workforce retention in the tech sector and is one
57 of many factors that combine to project steady growth
58 for IT in the future. As one analyst for Merrill-Lynch
59 commented, "The more complex the machines get, the
60 more of these guys are needed to fix them."

*A common abbreviation for information technology

53. The primary purpose of the passage is to

(A) discuss the popularity and long-term
    potential of "computer occupations."

(B) encourage university freshmen to major
    in computer science.

(C) weigh the financial benefits of
    information technology against other
    careers.

(D) point out the disparity between working
    in the computer field and investing in it.

54. In line 9, "staggering" most nearly means

(A) unsteady.

(B) astonishing.

(C) tottering.

(D) wavering.

GO ON TO THE NEXT PAGE. ▶ ▶ ▶

55. Information technology can best be described as

    (A) a relatively new industry populated by skilled computer workers.

    (B) a consortium of major tech-sector employers.

    (C) a field with limited investment opportunities.

    (D) a new workforce for the twenty-first century.

56. The author of the passage appears to care most deeply about the fact that

    (A) a career in information technology is a hassle due to the frequent training.

    (B) careers in the information technology industry are essentially the same as careers in other industries.

    (C) tomorrow's workplace will not include computers.

    (D) there is a direct relationship between salary and job satisfaction.

57. The author implies that

    (A) the market for IT workers will never collapse.

    (B) the Department of Labor considers "computer occupations" the best new career track for university graduates.

    (C) information technology is usually chosen as a career because of the strong financial benefits.

    (D) investment firms (such as Merrill-Lynch) believe that computers are a great investment opportunity.

58. The author's tone when discussing information technology is best described as

    (A) promotional.

    (B) critical.

    (C) informative.

    (D) caustic.

GO ON TO THE NEXT PAGE. ▶ ▶ ▶

This is an SSAT-style passage.

> Life is a stream
> On which we strew
> Petal by petal the flower of our heart;
> The end lost in dream,
> Line 5   They float past our view,
> We only watch their glad, early start.
> Freighted with hope,
> Crimsoned with joy,
> We scatter the leaves of our opening rose;
> 10   Their widening scope,
> Their distant employ,
> We never shall know. And the stream as it flows
> Sweeps them away,
> Each one is gone
> 15   Ever beyond into infinite ways.
> We alone stay
> While years hurry on,
> The flower fared forth, though its fragrance still stays.
>
> (From "Petals," Amy Lowell, 1916)

59. In the poem, our lives are compared with which of the following?

(A) a stream

(B) a ship

(C) a perfume

(D) a dream

(E) a heart

60. "The end lost in dream" (line 4) suggests that

(A) the flower petals sink after some distance

(B) the flower petals become trapped in eddy currents

(C) the flower petals do not lose their red color

(D) the destination of the flower petals can only be imagined

(E) the narrator is asleep

61. In this poem, the rose most probably represents

(A) employment opportunities

(B) love

(C) death

(D) happiness

(E) life

62. With which of the following statements about life is the speaker most likely to agree?

(A) The future can be determined through careful planning.

(B) The course of life is determined equally in old age as in youth.

(C) Follow your heart and have few regrets.

(D) Nothing lasts from life's early experiences.

(E) There are only a few true friends but many acquaintances.

GO ON TO THE NEXT PAGE. ▶ ▶ ▶

This is an SSAT-style passage.

> In Central Europe, the confluence of nations and cultures can be staggering. Vienna, the city of Mozart, Beethoven, and Freud, the seat of the former Austro-Hungarian Empire and Habsburg dynasties, lies on the Danube River, called the *Donau* in German. This grand city lies a scant 30 miles from Bratislava, the capital of Slovakia, whose inhabitants refer to the river in the Slavic
>
> Line 5 tongue as the *Dunaj*. Ninety miles further up the river lies the magnificent city of Budapest, where Hungarians call the river the *Duna*. The rising spires of her parliament and august grandeur of the Chain Bridge present Hungary's proudest and most exquisite face. The three languages spoken in this short stretch of the broad Danube are most striking in their total dissimilarity to one another. Their cultures likewise could not be more disparate, and yet throughout a long, volatile history, they have
>
> 10 been unified under common empires, fought common enemies, and suffered common privations.

63. The passage is mainly focused on

    (A) the difficulty of navigating a river that lies in so many different countries

    (B) the grandeur of Central European cities

    (C) the juxtaposition of different cultures in Central Europe

    (D) the difficult history endured by the people of Vienna, Bratislava, and Budapest

    (E) the notable challenges for linguists who study Central European languages

64. Which of the following is true, according to the passage?

    (A) The people of Bratislava call the Danube a different name in Slavic.

    (B) The Chain Bridge and Parliament can be found in Austria.

    (C) The people of Vienna, Bratislava, and Budapest have a common ancestry.

    (D) The three cities mentioned in the passage are unified in their reliance on the Danube.

    (E) The people of Vienna, Bratislava, and Budapest cannot understand one another.

65. The author of this passage implies which of the following?

    (A) The people of Vienna, Bratislava, and Budapest share common history, cultures, and languages.

    (B) The city of Budapest is more exquisite than either Bratislava or Vienna.

    (C) The disparity between the three cultures in such a small area is overwhelming to outsiders.

    (D) The history of the people of Vienna, Bratislava, and Budapest is marked by an absence of privation and strife.

    (E) All three cities have at one time or another been under the possession of foreign powers.

GO ON TO THE NEXT PAGE. ▶ ▶ ▶

66. The author most likely mentions the different words for the Danube River in order to

(A) emphasize the river's length

(B) illustrate specific linguistic differences in the three cities

(C) highlight the differences in language and culture in such a small area

(D) demonstrate the need for a unified translation of the word

(E) discuss the differences created by repeated wars in Central Europe

67. The passage suggests which of the following about languages in the three cities?

(A) They are difficult for visitors to the region to master.

(B) They have significant differences between them, which is one of their most notable characteristics.

(C) They are exquisite sounding to anyone who hears them.

(D) They have taken on many similarities because of the unification of the region under past empires.

(E) They represent a cultural distinctness found nowhere else in the world.

GO ON TO THE NEXT PAGE. ▶ ▶ ▶

This is an ISEE-style passage.

1　　During peak travel hours, as many as 5,000
2　airplanes fly in the continental United States. How
3　can each airplane be sure to take off and land safely,
4　avoiding the others? Air traffic control coordinates all
5　air travel, directing takeoffs and landings, ensuring
6　safe distances between airplanes, and keeping routes
7　away from bad weather. The air traffic control system
8　forms a seamless web across all private commercial
9　airline flight. As an airplane travels, a well-defined
10　authority, or responsibility for the flight, is passed
11　from one air traffic controller to the next. Smooth
12　transfer of authority ensures safe travel; this authority
13　passes from the most local level, at airport control
14　towers, to the most national level, at centralized
15　national facilities, and back again during flight.
16　　Prior to takeoff, the airplane's path is guided by local
17　air traffic controllers located in towers near the airport.
18　These controllers make a record of each departing
19　flight, direct all ground traffic on the airport runways,
20　and determine when it is safe for airplanes to take off.
21　Once an airplane is cleared for takeoff, the pilot is in
22　control, but authority for the flight is transferred to the
23　TRACON facility nearby. After this transfer, the pilot
24　of the flight speaks with a newly assigned controller.
25　　The TRACON (Terminal Radar Approach
26　CONtrol) area covers a fifty-mile radius around a
27　control tower. This area may include several airports.
28　A controller in this facility dictates to the pilot what
29　path to follow on ascent, making sure that the
30　corridor is clear and a safe distance is maintained
31　between this and other departing aircraft.
32　　When the flight departs TRACON airspace,
33　authority is transferred to an Air Route Traffic Control
34　Center (ARTCC). These regional control centers, of
35　which 21 exist in the continental US, cover zones
36　roughly equal in area and centered around major
37　airports. ARTCC controllers communicate with
38　national level controllers, who direct flights around
39　bad weather, turbulence, and inactive runways.
40　　Given the enormous volume of air travel and its
41　ongoing growth, improved information systems are
42　needed to assist air traffic controllers. TRACON
43　controllers direct an aircraft's final approach, before
44　transferring authority back to local airport air traffic
45　controllers. They coordinate several planes
46　approaching from different directions into a closely
47　spaced, single-file line. This task, like much of
48　air-traffic control, requires superb three-dimensional
49　visualization skills and split-second decision-making
50　abilities. Only computer-controlled direction
51　systems can help lighten the difficult burden placed
52　on the TRACON staff.

68. The primary purpose of the passage is to

(A) describe the air traffic control system and its needs as the volume of air traffic increases.

(B) argue against the system of transfer of authority.

(C) compare and contrast airplane travel with other modes of transportation.

(D) add to the long-running debate between ARTCC and TRACON authority systems.

69. In air traffic control, the purpose of transfer of authority for a flight is to

(A) delegate powers in the event of an emergency.

(B) designate a control center that can direct the pilot at a given time.

(C) allow computer control.

(D) complete the sale of excess seating.

GO ON TO THE NEXT PAGE. ▶ ▶ ▶

70. According to the passage, all are true about TRACON areas EXCEPT

    (A) TRACON areas must include only one or two airports.

    (B) TRACON controllers direct takeoff and landing.

    (C) TRACON areas are smaller than ARTCC areas.

    (D) TRACON controls flights in airspace near airports.

71. The author appears to believe that

    (A) ARTCC control rooms are generously staffed.

    (B) improved computer systems cannot aid air traffic control.

    (C) air traffic controllers must be highly capable to handle the demands of routing air traffic.

    (D) air traffic controllers do not have an important role in air travel.

72. The author's tone when discussing air traffic controllers is best described as

    (A) worried.

    (B) critical.

    (C) humorous.

    (D) admiring.

73. In line 51, "lighten" most nearly means

    (A) brighten.

    (B) reduce.

    (C) calcify.

    (D) compound.

This is an ISEE-style passage.

1   The quest for glory consumed Howard Hughes,
2 who was interested in aircraft and flying for most of his
3 life. He set many world records and initiated the
4 construction of custom aircraft. In 1935, he set the
5 landplane airspeed record of 352 mph. Hughes's record
6 was the last time in history a private individual would
7 build an aircraft that set the world airspeed record.
8   Howard Hughes also survived four airplane
9 accidents during the 1930s and 1940s. One accident
10 occurred while he was filming a movie, one at Lake
11 Mead, and another while he was setting the airspeed
12 record. In July of 1946, his test flight of a prototype
13 XF-11 spy plane over Los Angeles ended in disaster.
14 Hughes, the self-proclaimed "fastest man in the world,"

15 was forced to crash land in Beverly Hills. After
16 tearing the roofs from three houses, the plane
17 smashed into the ground, leaving Hughes all but
18 dead. His brush with death changed him, speeding
19 him into the madness that would consume the
20 twilight of his life.
21   In the decades that followed the crash, Hughes
22 gradually became more myth than man, the subject
23 of a thousand folk tales and outrageous stories. The
24 eccentric entrepreneur and adventurer became a
25 recluse. His death in 1976 became public spectacle;
26 even after two decades of complete isolation, he was
27 still perhaps the most popular, romanticized, and
28 genuinely interesting celebrity of the twentieth century.

GO ON TO THE NEXT PAGE. ▶ ▶ ▶

74. The passage was most likely written as part of

    (A) an argument detailing the psychological causes of Hughes's madness.

    (B) a drastic reinterpretation of the life of a famous individual.

    (C) a clinical study of mental illness in America.

    (D) a discussion about the most prominent figures of the modern era.

75. The passage deals primarily with the subject of

    (A) fame.

    (B) aviation.

    (C) isolation.

    (D) madness.

76. As a result of his crash landing in Beverly Hills, Howard Hughes

    (A) paid damages to the three homeowners who suffered property damage.

    (B) was romanticized in modern myth.

    (C) began to behave in an even more eccentric manner.

    (D) had to abandon the XF-11 project.

77. The author would most likely describe Howard Hughes as

    (A) arrogant and ambitious.

    (B) both tragic and intriguing.

    (C) completely insane.

    (D) underappreciated in his time.

78. The author's attitude toward Howard Hughes can best be described as

    (A) condescending.

    (B) sympathetic.

    (C) spiteful.

    (D) awestruck.

79. In line 20, "twilight" most nearly means

    (A) gloom.

    (B) evening.

    (C) dusk.

    (D) final years.

GO ON TO THE NEXT PAGE. ▶ ▶ ▶

This is an ISEE-style passage.

1 Samuel Morse, born in 1791, was an American
2 painter and inventor. Morse supported himself
3 while in college by painting. After graduating, he
4 continued painting. In 1825, New York City
5 commissioned Morse to paint a portrait of
6 someone in another city. While he was away, his
7 wife became ill. Unfortunately, Morse did not
8 receive the message with enough time to return
9 home before her death. He became interested in
10 electricity, and in 1932, after overhearing a
11 conversation on a ship, a seed was planted. In
12 1832, he made the decision to give up his
13 profession as an artist, and twelve years later, on
14 May 24, 1844, Samuel Morse sent the first
15 telegram from Baltimore to Washington, D.C. His
16 simple message "What hath God wrought?" marked
17 the beginning of modern telecommunications.

18 Within two decades, telegraph cables crisscrossed
19 the United States. The telegraph allowed real-time
20 communication between troops during the American
21 Civil War. After the laying of the transatlantic cable in
22 1866, such communication became possible the world
23 over. For the first time, the instantaneous transmission
24 of information around the globe was possible.

25 More than a century and a half after Morse's coded
26 message, the telegraph has been rendered completely
27 obsolete, first by the telephone, then by the fax
28 machine and Internet. In January 2006, Western
29 Union brought the telegraph era to a close by
30 discontinuing their telegraph service. Even though
31 the dots and dashes of Morse code are now a thing of
32 the past, the telecommunications industry and,
33 indeed, modern journalism owe a considerable
34 amount of their development to the telegraph.

80. Which of the following best describes the author's main idea in this passage?

(A) the development of modern telecommunications

(B) the disappearance of the telegram as a form of communication

(C) the invention, use, and obsolescence of telegraph technology

(D) the story of the last telegram transmitted by Western Union

81. The author's tone when discussing Samuel Morse and Morse code is best described as

(A) discouraged.

(B) respectful.

(C) descriptive.

(D) nostalgic.

82. According to the passage, all of the following are true of the telegraph EXCEPT that

(A) Samuel Morse sent the first telegram from Baltimore to Washington, D.C.

(B) The invention of the telegraph was made possible by the laying of the transatlantic cable.

(C) Journalism benefited greatly from the telecommunications possibilities offered by the telegraph.

(D) The subsequent development of other telecommunications systems rendered the telegraph obsolete.

83. In line 11, "seed" most nearly means

(A) core.

(B) idea.

(C) beginning.

(D) young.

GO ON TO THE NEXT PAGE. ▶ ▶ ▶

84. The passage suggests which of the following?

(A) The development of the telegraph system was slowed by the American Civil War.

(B) Western Union stopped telegraph service because of the Internet.

(C) The difficulty of Morse code prevented most people from learning how to use the telegraph.

(D) Gathering and reporting the news before the invention of the telegraph was more difficult.

85. All of the following are listed as causes of the telegraph becoming obsolete EXCEPT

(A) the fax machine.

(B) the telephone.

(C) the cell phone.

(D) the Internet.

This is an ISEE-style passage.

1　On April 12 at 4:30 a.m. in Charleston Harbor,
2　the strongest blow against the institution of slavery
3　was struck—by its very defenders. After U.S. Army
4　Major Robert Anderson gallantly refused the rebel
5　General Beauregard's demands to surrender the
6　fortress, Beauregard gave the order to open fire.
7　Despite President Lincoln's best efforts to assure the
8　suspicious Southerners of his and the Federal
9　government's desire for peace, the secessionists have
10　brought civil war upon themselves. Reportedly,
11　Secretary of State Robert Toombs of the newly
12　formed Confederate States of America has himself
13　decried the attack, stating "[it] will lose us every
14　friend at the North. You will wantonly strike a hornet's
15　nest…. Legions now quiet will swarm out and sting
16　us to death. It is unnecessary; it puts us in the wrong;
17　it is fatal."
18　　In accordance with Secretary Toombs's prophetic
19　words, President Lincoln, upon hearing of the
20　surrender of Fort Sumter, has called for 75,000
21　volunteers to recapture all Federal forts ceded to the
22　Confederacy and to preserve the Union by any and
23　all means necessary. The response to the President's
24　call has been overwhelming throughout states still
25　loyal to the Union. Throughout the North, the strains
26　of the *Star Spangled Banner* can be heard as an
27　unparalleled surge of patriotism sweeps the nation.
28　With the advantages of men and material that the
29　North possesses and this newly galvanized
30　determination, it should be a short war indeed!

86. The primary purpose of the passage is to

(A) chronicle a major historic event.

(B) justify a particular side in a conflict.

(C) call for volunteers in a military struggle.

(D) ensure a Confederate victory.

87. The author suggests that the coming civil war

(A) was spurred by the words of Secretary of State Robert Toombs.

(B) was initiated against President Abraham Lincoln's explicit orders.

(C) was begun to end slavery in the Confederate States of America.

(D) was not the aim of the Federal government before the attack.

GO ON TO THE NEXT PAGE. ▶ ▶ ▶

88. In line 2, "strongest blow" most probably refers to

(A) the author's belief that, by starting a war that they will most likely lose, the Southerners have ensured slavery's destruction.

(B) Robert Toombs's statement that the attack on Fort Sumter alienated all Northern supporters of slavery.

(C) the fact that the Southerners had finally found the means to bring slavery to an end.

(D) the strength of the attack ordered by General Beauregard against the garrison at Fort Sumter.

89. The author would most likely characterize the Southerners as

(A) treacherous.

(B) distrustful.

(C) belligerent.

(D) patriotic.

90. In line 25, "strains" most nearly means

(A) difficulties.

(B) sounds.

(C) exclamations.

(D) outbursts.

91. Each of the following is mentioned as a response to the attack on Fort Sumter EXCEPT

(A) the fall of the fort's garrison.

(B) the raising of volunteer troops.

(C) a changing of federal policy.

(D) an incredible decline in patriotism.

This is an SSAT-style passage.

"I stand before you today not to voice a complaint, but to plead for justice. I implore the council to reconsider the recent decision to rebuild my neighborhood, the area surrounding the North Freeway.

In recent legislation, our friends on the city council described this area as dilapidated and, therefore, a threat to the local economy. Council members determined that these homes should be replaced with

Line 5 newer construction simply because the area is unattractive to tourists. In response to this decision, I would like to point out that the houses in this neighborhood are homes to several families. These families—these citizens—do not wish to leave the homes they cherish. Though one house may be more attractive than another, no home that houses a comfortable, tax-paying family should be deemed a threat to the economy. This is not *Animal Farm*, in which George Orwell wrote 'all animals are equal, but some animals are more

10 equal than others.' I remind the council that the citizens of this neighborhood are already equal. Replacing older houses with newer ones will not make the area 'more equal' than it currently is.

Today, I request that the council reconsider the justification of rebuilding the North Freeway community. This project will prove a great injustice to the citizens of this neighborhood. The families who live in these homes have the same rights as other citizens in this city and do not deserve to be

15 forced out of their homes."

GO ON TO THE NEXT PAGE. ▶ ▶ ▶

92. In paragraph 2, the speaker's reference to "our friends" is ironic because

    (A) the council members were opposed to the speaker's neighborhood

    (B) the speaker did not personally know the members of the council

    (C) most of the audience knew him very well

    (D) those in the audience who were his friends were not city council members

    (E) the speaker did not have permission to speak on this topic

93. This speech mentions an idea presented in the novel *Animal Farm* in order to show that

    (A) no neighborhood or group of citizens is more important than another

    (B) educated people can solve the construction problems in the city

    (C) certain citizens can only have a small interest in city government

    (D) the speaker was violating his rights as a citizen

    (E) any action that violates the U.S. Constitution will not be voted into action

94. Why does the speaker claim that the reconstruction project would be "a great injustice" (line 13)?

    (A) The U.S. Constitution explicitly prohibits the city's actions.

    (B) The city is blessed by beautiful neighborhoods.

    (C) The people of this neighborhood would be happy to leave the dilapidated area.

    (D) Tourists only want to see the most attractive neighborhoods.

    (E) The people in this neighborhood are equal to other citizens and do not deserve to lose their homes.

95. Which of the following is the purpose of this speech?

    (A) to influence the citizens of a particular area

    (B) to prove that the city council promotes tourism

    (C) to convince the audience that a project is unfair

    (D) to present a new plan to the city council

    (E) to convince people of the need for social justice

GO ON TO THE NEXT PAGE. ▶ ▶ ▶

This is an ISEE-style passage.

1   She trudged through the remnants of the once
2 swirling storm. Her only landmarks were the colored
3 plastic stakes and occasional cairn the others had left
4 behind. Every so often, through the haze, the
5 amorphous shape of a snow-covered boulder rose
6 into sight. The trees were gone. She had left those
7 behind long ago. Though she knew this to be true,
8 she thought she caught a glimpse of the tree line from
9 the corner of her eye. At times, severe bursts of wind
10 penetrated her specialized, technical coverings and
11 made her feel as if she were fighting to take each step
12 forward as she continued to traverse the landscape.
13   As she began to ascend the final peak, she witnessed
14 what appeared to be a glittering ice wall. When at last
15 the sun retreated behind the occasional cloud she
16 realized the vision had been an illusion. Her limbs felt
17 numb, though she was, in fact, stronger than ever. She
18 had been climbing for two days now, but time had
19 succumbed to force of will. Suddenly she heard a
20 distant rumble.
21   She feared the worst. An avalanche now would be
22 the end. Sweating with fear and anticipation despite
23 the frigid cold, she had no choice but to continue her
24 trek, so on she ventured, into the blank landscape.
25 She relied on her vast well of experience, her senses,
26 and the aura of footsteps that had come before to lead
27 the way. Finally, she started to make out the vague
28 outline of a structure. First, a mere dot, then, quickly
29 the cottage came into view. She pounded on the door.
30 "It's me, I found you!" the desperate relief spilled
31 from her mouth. The door opened to a warm,
32 familiar scene. She was gratefully welcomed.

96. The protagonist must battle

    (A) an active avalanche.

    (B) severe wind.

    (C) thick cloud cover.

    (D) an ice wall.

97. It can be inferred that the story takes place

    (A) on the beach.

    (B) in a swampy area.

    (C) on a mountaintop.

    (D) in the desert.

98. According to the passage, the main character relies on all of the following to persevere EXCEPT

    (A) physical strength.

    (B) her senses.

    (C) prior knowledge.

    (D) navigational instruments.

99. As used in line 5, the word "amorphous" most nearly means

    (A) distinct.

    (B) rugged.

    (C) triangular.

    (D) formless.

GO ON TO THE NEXT PAGE. ▶ ▶ ▶

This is an ISEE-style passage.

1   Nuclear fallout, radioactive material left behind
2 after a nuclear explosion, is known to be hazardous
3 to humans. While many people realize that direct
4 contact with contaminated objects is harmful to the
5 human body, many do not realize that the fallout
6 can enter the human body in a variety of other
7 ways. Years after a nuclear incident, various carriers
8 can deliver fallout material to humans.
9   When radioactive material enters the atmosphere
10 of an explosion site, it becomes a danger to plants.
11 Just as the air is immediately affected, the soil
12 absorbs the material. Unfortunately, the radioactive
13 material dusted across the soil remains toxic and
14 eventually poisons local plant life. Plants absorbing
15 radioactive materials present in the soil can be
16 detrimental to the health of humans, because the
17 human diet often consists of vegetables and fruits
18 produced by these plants.
19   Just as the radioactive material can affect the plants
20 eaten by humans, it can contaminate animals and
21 milk. As cows eat grass from a contaminated site, the
22 milk and beef become poisonous as well. Then, when
23 humans drink the milk or eat the beef, they absorb
24 the same harmful material that the cows ingested.

100. Which of the following states the main purpose of the passage?

(A) to report the effects of nuclear fallout on cows

(B) to discuss the changes an environment may experience after a nuclear explosion

(C) to show that radioactive material can enter humans in various ways

(D) to examine the effect of nuclear fallout on the environment

101. According to the passage, nuclear fallout enters plants primarily through

(A) contaminated soil.

(B) contaminated cow's milk.

(C) contaminated air.

(D) contaminated fertilizer.

102. The tone of the passage is best described as

(A) excited.

(B) fearful.

(C) informative.

(D) argumentative.

103. The author would most likely follow this passage with a paragraph that includes which of the following?

(A) a detailed list of plants most susceptible to nuclear contamination

(B) more details about the many ways humans can be contaminated

(C) a comparison of different fallout scenes across the world

(D) a list of the various causes of nuclear explosions

104. The author most likely mentions contaminated cow's milk in order to show

(A) the potential harm to certain animal species.

(B) the food chain of an explosion site.

(C) how nuclear fallout affects plants and animals.

(D) the role of animals in the human contamination process.

105. The passage mentions the contamination of each of the following EXCEPT

(A) cows.

(B) humans.

(C) plants.

(D) dust.

GO ON TO THE NEXT PAGE. ▶ ▶ ▶

This is an SSAT-style passage.

> Wintry boughs against a wintry sky;
> Yet the sky is partly blue
> And the clouds are partly bright—
> Who can tell but sap is mounting high
> *Line 5*   Out of sight,
> Ready to burst through?
>
> Winter is the mother-nurse of Spring,
> Lovely for her daughter's sake,
> 10 Not unlovely for her own:
> For a future buds in everything;
> Grown, or blown,
> Or about to break.

(From "There Is a Budding Morrow in Midnight," Christina Rossetti, 1888)

106. In this poem, which of the following is presented to symbolize a distinct season?

- **(A)** buds about to bloom
- **(B)** bare branches on the trees
- **(C)** mothers and their children
- **(D)** sap production across the world
- **(E)** broken branches and buds

107. "Who can tell but sap is mounting high" (line 4) suggests that

- **(A)** sap from the trees is ready to collect
- **(B)** winter trees don't produce any sap
- **(C)** the cloudy sky doesn't prevent the trees from producing sap
- **(D)** sap is produced only in the warmer weather
- **(E)** some natural cycles may not be visible in winter

108. In this poem, the wintry sky and the partly blue sky most likely represent

- **(A)** different weather conditions
- **(B)** an approaching snow storm
- **(C)** sorrow and joy
- **(D)** present and future
- **(E)** winter and spring

109. The author would most likely agree with which of the following statements about the seasons?

- **(A)** Spring doesn't last long enough.
- **(B)** People should prefer spring to winter.
- **(C)** Winter is enjoyable even if it seems bleak.
- **(D)** People only enjoy winter because they know it leads to spring.
- **(E)** Broken branches in winter turn into new growth in spring.

GO ON TO THE NEXT PAGE. ▶ ▶ ▶

This is an SSAT-style passage.

> Much attention and envy is always directed toward the unusual genius. Countless biographies and biographical films chronicle a modern world shaped by the blinding innovations of restless mavericks. For example, Alexander Fleming discovered the antibacterial agent in penicillin by accidentally allowing a culture plate to be contaminated by mold, but he is hailed for his insight and originality.
>
> Line 5 For every Fleming, however, there is always a Jonas Salk. Salk was ridiculed by much of the scientific community for his use of other scientists' research and mundane scientific procedure in his successful quest to cure polio. Nevertheless, Salk did develop the cure for a twentieth-century plague. While the restless genius may sometimes catch lightning in a bottle, it is the unheralded and methodical scholar who often carries the bulk of the scientific workload.

110. According to the passage, what is the principal reason Salk's discovery was ridiculed by other scientists?

(A) Salk borrowed heavily from the work of Alexander Fleming.

(B) Salk was unable to master mundane scientific procedure.

(C) The cure for polio was found to be the work of other scientists.

(D) Salk's work did not rely principally on independent innovation.

(E) Salk was incapable of blinding innovation.

111. The author discusses biographies and biographical films in the second sentence in order to

(A) demonstrate the layperson's total lack of interest in scientific discovery.

(B) illustrate the degree to which people are curious about individualistic thinkers.

(C) describe the controversy surrounding the discovery of penicillin.

(D) demonstrate the need for a biography detailing the life and discoveries of Jonas Salk.

(E) emphasize a need for greater research into the lives of modern innovators.

112. The author suggests that other scientists initially viewed Salk's work as

(A) brilliant

(B) innovative

(C) prosaic

(D) complex

(E) minor

113. Which of the following best describes the author's main purpose in writing this passage?

(A) to show that not all scientific discovery is made by unconventional geniuses

(B) to relate the superiority of one method of scientific discovery over another

(C) to describe the dramatic discovery of penicillin by Alexander Fleming

(D) to give examples of discoveries that were not made by maverick innovators

(E) to recommend greater scientific funding for scientists whose work mirrors Salk's

PRACTICE QUESTIONS ANSWERS AND EXPLANATIONS

1. C

The stony coral secretes a skeleton of calcium carbonate, as stated in line 3. Choices A, B, D, and E do not match this information from the passage. Choice (C) is correct.

2. C

The passage describes how coral reefs are formed by both green algae and stony coral. This is a match for answer choice (C). Choice A is too broad; it needs to mention algae and coral specifically. Choice B may look tempting but it's too narrow—the passage is about how *both* the stony coral and the green algae interact to help form coral reefs. Finally, choices D and E are out of scope; the passage is not concerned with reefs' beauty or how they form islands.

3. B

You can infer from the final sentence that divers are primarily interested in the visual appeal of the coral reef. This makes answer choice (B) correct. Answer choices A, C, D, and E are all out of scope; the passage does not mention how these topics relate to divers.

4. D

Choice (D) is correct because the passage states in line 5 that the coral and the algae have a "mutually beneficial relationship." This means that choices A, B, and C are all opposites. Finally, choice E is out of scope; nothing in the passage suggests that this relationship is obscure or hard to understand.

5. A

Read the question carefully. The correct answer will *NOT* be mentioned in the passage. Choice (A) has things backwards; the algae live within the tissues of corals. Since choice (A) is the opposite of what's in the passage, it is the correct answer. All of the other choices are mentioned in the passage. Choice B is mentioned in lines 5–6. Choice C is mentioned in line 7. Choice D is mentioned in line 3. Finally, choice E is mentioned in lines 6–7.

6. B

In the very first sentence, the author says that tunnel construction is costly and dangerous, and he does not say that TBMs have made tunnel construction less expensive. This makes choice (B) correct. Choices A, C, D, and E are all out of scope; the passage provides no support for them.

7. D

This passage is concerned with tunnel construction and how tunnel boring machines (TBMs) can aid this endeavor. This is a match for choice (D). Choice A is out of scope; the passage does not state why tunnel construction is expensive or dangerous. Choice B is tempting, but the author never discusses past methods of tunnel construction, so it is incorrect. Choice C is too narrow; the details of TBM operation are discussed only in the first paragraph. Finally, choice E is out of scope; the passage gives no information about why the Eurotunnel was difficult to dig or related myths.

8. C

"Notable" is used to describe the Eurotunnel, a project the author clearly views positively. You therefore need a word that matches this positive attitude. Choice (C) is correct. While choices A and B are also positive, they do not make sense in the context of the sentence. Choices D and E are incorrect because they are neutral words; something "weighty" or "memorable" could be this way for either good or bad reasons. The question requires something strictly positive.

9. B

In the final sentence of the passage, the author describes how Britain and mainland Europe are now linked for the first time in history. This matches answer choice (B). All other answer choices are out of scope; the passage does not discuss travel restrictions (choice A), the relationship between the two countries (choice C), the Eurotunnel's impact on the way future tunnels will be dug (choice D), or the political climate in Europe (choice E).

10. A

The author clearly thinks positively about TBMs, so choice (A) is correct. Answer choices B, C, and D are all opposite. Be careful with choice E. Although "euphoric" is a positive word (meaning intensely happy), it is too extreme to match the tone of this passage.

11. A

The last sentence of the passage says that the protozoans provide the termite with a service necessary to its survival, so choice (A) is correct. Choice B is a distortion; according to lines 6–7, protozoans are parasites. Choices C, D, and E are out of scope. The author only compares the sizes of the host and the parasite, not those of the parasite and the bacteria. The author only states that the parasite is in the gut of the termite, not how they are attached. Finally, the author does not mention what would happen to the protozoans without the termite, and based on the author's definition of these symbiotic relationships, it's unlikely the protozoan would be able to survive on its own.

12. E

The passage is about the symbiotic relationship between termites and protozoans, two organisms that cooperate to survive. This makes choice (E) the correct answer. Choice A is out of scope; this passage is focused on the relationship between parasites and their hosts, not the practicality of parasites. Choice B is also out of scope; the passage says that the termite cannot digest wood, but it does not focus on the physical process. Choice C is a distortion; although this paragraph focuses on one pest in Florida, the passage does not discuss parasites in Florida generally. Finally, choice D is out of scope; the passage says that symbiotic relationships exist but doesn't discuss their development over time.

13. B

According to lines 3–4, the host organism is the dominant member of the symbiotic pair or group. This matches choice (B). Choice A is a distortion; termites are found in South Florida, but host organisms in general might not be. Choice C is also a distortion; again, being unable to digest cellulose is something that termites, not host organisms in general, are unable to do. Choices D and E are out of scope; the passage does not state whether hosts can survive on their own or whether they are usually associated with single-celled organisms.

14. E

The author defines a symbiotic relationship as one in which two organisms coexist to each other's benefit, so choice (E) is correct. All other answer choices go beyond what the passage actually states. The author does not provide any information about how similar or different the two organisms might be, so choices A and D are incorrect. While it is possible for the parasite to be harmful, Choice B is incorrect because this author does not provide any support for the idea that this is often the case. Choice C might be tempting since the author mentions the comparative sizes of hosts and parasites, but there is no discussion of the actual size of either.

15. D

This passage is written using mostly neutral words and describes a scientific concept from a third-person point-of-view. Choice (D) is the best match, as the author is informed about this topic and example. While you may not personally be interested in the topic of this passage, the author's descriptions show interest in the topic, so choice A is incorrect. An enthusiastic or annoyed tone would be reflected in language that's strongly positive or negative, but this author uses mostly neutral language throughout, so choices B and C are both incorrect. While a neutral tone can also be humorous, this author does not use humor to convey information about symbiotic relationships, so choice E is incorrect.

16. D

The passage discusses the depletion of the ozone layer and its potential effects on the environment and human health. This is a perfect match for choice (D). Choice A is too narrow; the passage discusses the effects of solar radiation only in the second paragraph. Choices B and C are out of scope; Antarctica and holes in the ozone layer are never mentioned in the passage.

17. A

Remember, answering Vocab-in-Context questions requires you to determine the meaning of the word in the context of the passage. While something that is fragile can be weak (choice B), breakable (choice C), or brittle (choice D), the passage is focused on how easily the atmosphere can be changed. Choice (A) is correct.

18. C

Supporting Ideas questions like this require you to look for specific support in the passage. Choice A is a distortion; the amount of sunlight reaching Earth is not increasing. Instead, as lines 7–8 describe, solar radiation is increasing. This means that choice (C) is the correct answer. On Test Day, stop here and move on to the next question. For those tempted: choice B is the opposite of what's in the passage; skin cancer rates are increasing. Finally, choice D is out of scope; ozone gaps are never mentioned.

19. B

The passage states that the international community responded to the ozone problem by banning CFCs and other pollutants; this was supposed to stop ozone loss by the year 2000. From this, you can infer that ozone loss was due to pollutants. Choice (B) is correct. Choices A and C are out of scope; the passage never states these things. Choice D is opposite; sea levels are rising, not falling.

20. B

The author uses the greenhouse image to describe the effect of increased radiation on the climate of the Earth. This makes answer choice (B) correct. Choice A is a distortion; the passage is concerned with human health, not plant health. Choice C is out of scope; the passage never discusses how ozone forms. Finally, choice D is also a distortion; pollutants are destroying the atmosphere. Heat and humidity are a *result* of this destruction.

21. D

The author ends the passage on a pessimistic note, saying that "total ozone recovery" will not occur for more than 100 years. This makes choice (D) correct. Choices A and B are out of scope; Antarctica and volcanic eruptions are never mentioned in the passage. Choice C is extreme and out of scope; the passage never states whether or not the full restoration of the atmosphere is "impossible."

22. D

The passage describes the deadly disease smallpox and the efforts to eradicate it. This is a perfect match for answer choice (D). Choice A is out of scope; the passage is concerned only with smallpox, not viral diseases in general. Choice B is also out of scope; the passage never mentions this information. Choice C is mentioned in the passage, but only in the first paragraph. The correct answer to a Main Idea question must encompass all parts of the passage. Finally, choice (E) is out of scope; only the fight against smallpox is mentioned.

23. B

For Vocab-in-Context questions, always go back to the passage and research the context. Then plug each answer choice into the original sentence and see which one makes the most sense. In the context of the second sentence, an "acutely infectious disease" means an "extremely infectious disease." Choice (B) is correct. None of the other answer choices make sense when plugged back into the original sentence.

24. A

The first paragraph describes how the first cases of smallpox were recorded in China in 1122 B.C.E. This makes choice (A) correct. Choice B is a distortion; smallpox ravaged Europe in the Middle Ages, but the disease was not first recorded there. Choices C, D, and E are all out of scope; none of these landmasses are mentioned in the passage.

25. D

The passage states that the smallpox immunization was created in 1796. This implies that the problem was not a lack of medical knowledge, but a lack of coordination. Smallpox could be stamped out in one area, only to reappear again in another and spread again. This situation matches answer choice (D). Choice A is opposite; vaccinations were indeed effective against smallpox. Choice B is also opposite; as described above, the smallpox vaccine had been around since 1796. Choice C is irrelevant; smallpox is not carried by animals. Finally, choice E is out of scope; nothing in the passage suggests this kind of behavior.

26. B

The last sentence of the passage describes the eradication of smallpox as a "first" in the history of medicine. This makes choice (B) correct. Choice A is close, but not exactly correct. There could have been other worldwide vaccination campaigns, but the smallpox campaign was the first successful elimination of a dreaded disease. Choice C is irrelevant; smallpox is not carried by animals. Choice D is out of scope; the passage does not state other doctors' opinions. Choice E is also out of scope; the passage gives no information about expenses.

27. D

Main Idea questions can best be solved with a prediction based on your passage map. For this passage, you might predict something like *factors to consider in acoustic design*. Lines 12–22 focus on reverberation, which the author describes as the "most important factor in acoustic design" at the end of the passage. Together with your prediction, this is a good match for answer choice (D). Answer choice A is a distortion; while the passage mentions some problems that must be overcome in design concert space, it does not speak about the entirety of the architect's job. Answer choice B is out of scope; the differences between speech and music are never mentioned. Answer choice C is also out of scope; live music is only mentioned in the first sentence and the passage does not elaborate on "the experience."

28. A

Inference questions ask you to draw conclusions based on evidence in the passage. In line 2, the author states that "few of us realize the complex process involved." The fact that few people realize the complexity of the process indicates that the complex process of acoustic design is not widely appreciated by the public; this matches answer choice (A). Answer choice B is incorrect because the passage does not discuss individual listeners. Answer choice C is extreme; the passage mentions that architects must consider choice of materials, but not that it is entirely dependent upon that one factor. Answer choice D is out of scope; engineers are never mentioned in the passage.

29. D

When you see the phase "according to the passage" go back to the text to locate the answer for this Supporting Ideas question. Statement I is mentioned in line 6; Statement II is mentioned in lines 12–13; and Statement III is mentioned in lines 15–16. All three options are mentioned in the passage as factors that affect the acoustics of a building, so answer choice (D) is the correct answer.

30. C

When answering a Supporting Ideas question, always go back to the text. Too little reverberation is mentioned in lines 16–17: "too little reverberation can make music

sound thin and weak." This matches answer choice (C). Answer choice A is out of scope because the passage does not mention sound volume. Answer choice B is a distortion; too much reverberation can cause the blurring of details, not to little. Answer choice D is also a distortion; too much—not too little—reverberation would cause the listening audience to not know when one note ends and another begins but wouldn't necessarily cause them to be "confused."

31. B

The final sentence of the passage says that the most important factor in acoustic design is the reverberation time, which makes answer choice (B) correct. Answer choice A is irrelevant to the passage. Answer choice C is a misused detail; choice of building materials is a factor, but not the most important. Answer choice D is a distortion; the purpose of the building is a major consideration when selecting building materials.

32. B

This Inference question asks you to think about why the author wrote a particular part of the passage. Identify what function those lines served in the overall purpose of text. In this passage, the author describes the acoustic design as a "complex process" (line 2) and then proceeds to describe various difficulties that architects face. This prediction matches choice (B). Answer choice A is a distortion of what's in the passage; the author mentions that few people realize the process, but the tone of the piece is not trying to sway or convince the reader otherwise. Answer choice C is out of scope; the author does not mention ticket prices anywhere in the passage. Answer choice D is a misused detail; elsewhere in the passage the author discusses the importance of reverberation, but that is not the reason the author lists the problems architects encounter.

33. A

Supporting Ideas questions are a great place to rack up points. Make sure that you read the question carefully so that you don't miss the opportunity. The passage discusses the fact that George Washington was a hero not because he was able to win major battles over the British, but because he was able to keep the Colonial war effort together. The passage credits Washington with choice (A), winning a "uniquely American war" (line 22).

Choice B is opposite; line 17 states that Washington had "little to do" with the victory at Saratoga. Choice C is also opposite; line 6 states that Washington could not protect or take back New York or Philadelphia. Choice D is out of scope; the passage never states that Washington was able to find a way to win pitched battles. Finally, choice E is a misused detail; the passage does state that Washington crossed the Delaware, but it does not give this as a reason for Washington's success.

34. A

The victories at Trenton and Princeton "kept [Washington's] army together and resurrected the American cause in the minds of his countrymen" (lines 19–20). Choice (A) is correct. Choice B is the opposite of what's in the passage. Line 19 states that the victories at Trenton and Princeton "were over minuscule forces." Choices C and D are out of scope; the author never mentions French aid or the length of these battles. Choice E is the opposite of what's stated; while "the Colonies seemed certain of its failure" (lines 20–21), the two battles at Trenton and Princeton were seen as overcoming this mindset, not ensuring their failure.

35. D

Watch out for certain verbal cues that indicate what question type you are reading. The words "according to the passage" indicate a Supporting Ideas question. Lines 6–11 discuss Washington's defeats in both Brooklyn Heights and Manhattan, as well as the retreat across the Delaware, as details of the British invasion of New York. Choice (D) matches this prediction.

Choice A is a misused detail; while the passage does cite this failure, it is not the "classic example" referred to by the question. Choice B is opposite; the passage states that Washington was able to keep an army in the field. Choice C is also opposite; the passage does state that the Colonies were able to secure the aid of the French. Finally, choice E is a misused detail; while Washington's deployment of troops on Brooklyn Heights did result in defeat, the futility referred to is ultimately the total failure to defend New York.

36. B

When it comes to Tone questions, you need to consider how the details or cited lines support the author's overall point. The cited lines serve as an introduction to the second paragraph, which shows that Washington was not a conventional hero. Line 12, beginning "Unfortunately for the British," indicates that their strategy for success was different from Washington's and ultimately foreshadows Washington's victory. Choice (B) matches this prediction.

Choice A is a distortion; while the passage does state that Washington was unable to win pitched battles, the cited lines refer to Washington's unconventional battle tactics, not his inability to imitate the British. Choice C is extreme; the passage does not state that Washington was indifferent to his losses. Choice D is out of scope; the passage never discusses the American defiance of British customs. Choice E is extreme; the author never attempts to excuse the defeats at New York and Philadelphia.

37. B

When a question asks what the author "suggests," the answer must be supported by information in the passage. Paragraph 2 discusses the reasons for Washington's reputation as a hero and the American success in the Revolution; the passage states that Washington was able to "outlast" the British "resolve." In addition, lines 12–14 state that the level of commitment was different for the American soldier. Choice (B) agrees with this information.

Choice A is a misused detail; the passage does cite Saratoga as an important victory, but Saratoga is not credited with the ultimate triumph in the war. Choice C is out of scope; the passage does not compare the morale or supplies of the American and British troops. Choice D is extreme; the passage does not state that Washington's strategy was inherently superior, only that it worked. Choice E is a misused detail; the passage does not state that Trenton and Princeton were responsible for American victory.

38. A

Supporting Ideas questions occasionally test your ability to define a word. When you research "houses" or "Divide" in the passage, you'll find that they were "built of the sod itself" (line 8). If you identify "sod" as blocks of dirt with grass on top, you can choose answer choice (A). There are also context clues that connect "sod" to the "inescapable ground." Answer choices B, C, and D are incorrect because these details do not appear in the passage. Choice E is incorrect because although the Bergson house was made of logs, the other houses were predominantly sod.

39. B

Don't rely on your memory to eliminate incorrect answer choices; go back to the passage and find evidence for the correct answer. Research will tell you that the Bergson homestead was easier to find than others "because it overlooked Norway Creek" (line 2). This is an almost perfect match for answer choice (B). Answer choice A is incorrect because the passage suggests the opposite; it mentions how little impression John Bergson had made on the land. Answer choice C is a misused detail; the Bergson house was in the new country, but so were all of the other houses on the Divide. Answer choice D is also a misused detail, as the ground was plowed only to the south. Choice C is a distortion; while the passage does state that the homestead was easier to find than many others, there is no evidence to support the idea that it could be seen from far away.

40. D

Your understanding of the scope and tone of a passage can often give you extra insight into Supporting Ideas questions. The passage mentions plowed earth twice: first noting that the marks of the plow were insignificant, then mentioning the fields south of Bergson's house. Of these, "insignificant," or *not very important*, is a good match for choice (D). You can also get a clue from the fact that the passage stresses the insignificance of people on the Great Plains, or you can use elimination strategies to get rid of the incorrect answers. Answer choice A is a misused detail; glaciers are mentioned only as a metaphor, to show how little impact people have had on the land. Answer choice B is also a misused detail; cottonwood trees are mentioned, but they surround the ravine, not the field. Answer choice C is a detail that does not appear in the passage. Answer choice E is also a misused detail; the placement of the fields is given in relation to the house, not the creek.

41. D

You will frequently see incorrect answer choices that misuse details from the passage. Line 12 states that "Bergson had made little impression upon the wild land," so use this as your prediction to choose the correct answer, choice (D). It is also possible to eliminate your way to the correct answer, but remember that you shouldn't rely on elimination for every question because it is a time consuming strategy. Answer choice A is incorrect because the "genius" mentioned in the passage is a reference to nature's indifference to man, not Bergson

himself. Answer choice B is extreme; while Bergson is ill in the passage, there is no reason to suspect his entire life has been defined by illness. Answer choice C is a misused detail; Norway Creek is a waterway, not a town. Choice E is opposite; the references to previously plowed fields and attempts at taming the land counter the idea that Bergson did not have to put forth effort or struggle during his time on the frontier.

42. A

When you read the passage, your passage map should form a broad picture of both the content and the tone. The passage repeats the idea that human strivings are insignificant compared to nature. The author credits the environment with "ugly moods" (line 13) and unfriendly genius and describes it as "lead-colored" (line 16). This is a *grim and gloomy* tone, which matches answer choice (A). Answer choice B is incorrect because, although this passage contains information, an informative tone is neutral, like the voice of a textbook writer or a journalist. Answer choice C is incorrect for similar reasons; an objective tone conveys information without bias or opinion, but this writer clearly has a point of view. Answer choices D and E are the opposite of your prediction; "sunny" and "comic" are bright and cheery words, whereas this passage is more dark and gloomy.

43. B

For questions like this one, think about which choice would make the best headline for the passage. Main Idea questions can best be solved with a prediction based on your critical read. For this passage, you might predict something like *scientists tried to protect migrating caribou in various ways*, which is a good match for answer choice (B). Answer choice A is the opposite of what's needed; the passage claims that the pipeline has NOT disrupted caribou migrations. Answer choice C is a distortion; migration routes appear in the passage, but they are not the main idea. Answer choice D is incorrect because the passage does not speak on behalf of "most Alaskans."

44. C

Supporting Ideas questions will often test your vocabulary as well as your critical reading skills. The evidence in the passage may not be written word for word, so you may need to look for synonyms when you predict the answer to a Supporting Ideas question. When you look for evidence, you will notice words like "affect," "hamper," and "worried." The passage states in lines 11–14 that "scientists worried that…caribou…might abandon their newborn calves." This is a good match for answer choice (C). Answer choice A is incorrect because the passage says nothing about how the migration would affect oil production. Answer choice B is a misused detail; while the passage mentions winter feeding grounds, it does so in another context. Answer choice D is incorrect because the passage does not discuss how the migration would be disrupted.

45. C

One careful read with written notes that summarize the key points will prepare you for broad Inference questions. Use these notes to think about the paragraph or passage as a whole as you research the passage for evidence. In this case, the last line calls the crossing planners "wise" for avoiding risks. While the crossings were ultimately unnecessary, they were still a good idea; this idea best matches answer choice (C). Answer choice A is incorrect because the passage does not discuss the cost of the crossings. Answer choice B is a misused detail; while the crossings were not needed to protect the caribou, this was not known before construction began. Answer choice D is a distortion; the passage says the crossings were not needed, not that they were badly designed.

46. D

Remember to eliminate answer choices that don't appear within the passage to improve your odds if your prediction doesn't immediately lead you to the correct answer.

The sentence that mentions how the migration might be hampered also includes a discussion of the dimensions of the pipe and the fact that it is elevated. This matches answer choice (D). Answer choice A is incorrect because although seasons are mentioned, the precise timing of the construction is not. Answer choice B is incorrect because the passage discusses the possible impact of the pipeline, not the oil that it carries. The passage does not discuss how caribou react to people, so answer choice C is also incorrect.

47. B

Some words have multiple definitions. Always read for context clues. The sentences around the word "hamper" contain words like "delay" and a discussion of the size of the pipe. These clues might lead you to predict a synonym

like *block*, *impede*, or *interfere with*. Answer choice (B) matches all three of these predictions. Answer choice A is incorrect because "accelerate" means to speed up, which is the opposite of "hamper." A hamper is one word for a type of basket or container, but, in this context, that meaning does not fit, so answer choice C is incorrect. Answer choice D is incorrect because, while the pipeline might cause caribou to redirect their migration, the passage only explicitly states that scientists were concerned about blocking the migration.

48. D

Never rely on memory to answer a Supporting Ideas question. Always refer directly to the passage. A question like this must be handled by process of elimination. As you test each choice, you'll find that only answer choice (D) appears in the passage—specifically, in the first sentence. The passage tells you the pipe is elevated, but never exactly how high, so answer choice A is incorrect. The passage discusses North Slope caribou, but never gives their number, so answer choice B is incorrect. The passage speculates that migration disruption could orphan calves, but it never provides a number of deaths, so answer choice C is incorrect.

49. A

Use your notes to evaluate one statement at a time. Line 9, "the flowers have dried down to the root," provides a paraphrase for choice (A) and is therefore correct. The drifting snow is referenced in line 12, but this is compared to the way the author's tears are falling, so both choices B and E are incorrect. Line 2, "the lilies bloomed within the sedge," is the only line that refers to lilies, but the first half of this stanza does not refer to any changes in the beloved's emotions, so choice C is incorrect. The flow of the stream is introduced in line 1, but this is only to present a contrast between the stream five months ago and at present, "the frozen river" (line 8).

50. D

Many Supporting Ideas questions on poetry passages require you to use some of your critical thinking skills, just like Inference questions do, because you need to be able to interpret language that doesn't explicitly say what it means. If you reread line 16, you can see from the period at the end that this line forms the final part of an idea that begins two lines earlier. Reread lines 14–15 ("And my poor cheeks, five months ago / Set blushing at thy praises so") to understand the context of the line quoted in the question stem. You can then understand that the writer has become sad because of some change in her beloved, and this sadness has caused her face to turn pale, which matches answer choice (D).

Choice A is out of scope; nothing in the poem suggests that the writer actively tried to make her face white or paler by putting on makeup. Choice B is a distortion; the beginning of the second stanza refers to snow in the context of how long it took the writer to become sad, so the comparison to snow is not directly related to the writer's face. Choice C is out of scope; the writer never mentions or suggests that she has physically put on a mask to hide herself. Choice E is a distortion; the writer doesn't blame winter for her paleness, and, as the explanation for choice B points out, the comparison to snow and winter is not directly related to the appearance of the writer's face.

51. E

Sometimes you'll need to reread several lines of a poem to fully understand the meaning of a specific detail. Do so if the question stems direct you to particularly difficult lines. The first stanza contains the references in the question stem. Line 1 ("Five months ago the stream did flow") and line 8 ("The frozen river is as mute") demonstrate the contrast and change that have occurred in the writer's beloved as the latter begins to lose interest. Answer choice (E) is correct.

Choice A is a misused detail; although the poem does refer to passing time ("Five months ago"), the references to the stream are used figuratively to represent changing emotions rather than as proof of the changing seasons. Choice B is a distortion; again, the change in the river reflects the emotional change in the writer's beloved and doesn't refer to the tangible sensations of warmth and cold. Choice C is extreme; nothing in the poem suggests that the writer's beloved has changed so drastically as to hate her. Choice D is a distortion; the writer doesn't express her feelings about nature but rather uses examples from nature to illustrate the changing emotions of her beloved.

52. C

Sometimes you can use your understanding of the writer's tone and attitude to answer an Inference question, just like you would a Main Idea question. Remember to always look for familiar themes in poetry passages to help you stay focused on the writer's central idea. The overall theme of this poem is that the emotions of the writer's beloved have changed as some time has passed. The writer compares these changes to the changes that occur in nature with the passing of the seasons and concludes that it's equally natural for people to change as well (lines 10–11, "And why, since these be changed since May, / Shouldst *thou* change less than *they*?" and lines 21–22, "And why, since these be changed now, / Should I change less than *thou*?"). Although the writer is sad that her beloved has changed, she implies through these lines that she can understand this as a natural part of the relationship, which matches choice (C).

Choice A is opposite; the entire poem focuses on changes in love. Choice B is also opposite; the writer suggests that changes are common and can be expected. Choice D is yet another opposite; the writer describes her sadness at the change in her beloved's emotions. Choice E is a distortion; although the writer acknowledges that love may be difficult if one person starts to lost interest, she never recommends avoiding love entirely.

53. A

To answer Main Idea questions, look at the passage as a whole, rather than focusing on specific details. The author makes his purpose clear at the start of the passage. He gives us reasons why IT is a popular field and also discusses long-term career potential, which matches answer choice (A). Answer choice B is out of scope; majoring in computer science is never discussed and the tone of the passage is not encouraging. Answer choice C is a misused detail; although it is noted that information technology pays well, this is not the focus of the passage. Answer choice D is also a misused detail; the author does mention that investing in the field has not been as attractive as working in it, but this is not the primary intent of the passage.

54. B

To answer Vocab-in-Context questions, focus on the cited text and how the word is used in that sentence and in the larger context of the passage. The word "staggering" is describing the growth of the "explosive" IT industry. Predict that the large growth was *extreme*. Answer choice (B) fits this. Answer choice A is the opposite of what's in the passage; the IT industry is booming despite recent fluctuations. Answer choices C and D are distortions; the IT industry's growth is sustained, not intermittent.

55. A

To answer a Supporting Ideas question effectively, look for more information on the detail being presented. Information technology is a *field* or *sector*. Choice (A) best matches this prediction. Answer choice B is out of scope; IT employers are never discussed directly in the passage. Answer choice C is a misused detail; the industry's "Wall Street Cred" (line 8) is not applicable here. Answer choice D is also a misused detail; this is a projection regarding the industry, not a definition of it.

56. D

The answer to an Inference question always follows from what is in the passage. Don't stray too far from what is on the page. Since this question stem does not include a lot of information to help you make a prediction, examine each answer choice carefully and find evidence to support the correct answer. Although the author does mention frequent training, he does not imply that it is bothersome, so you can eliminate answer choice A. The author is focused on the ways that the field of information technology is different from other industries, so answer choice B is the opposite of what the author states and is therefore incorrect. The author refers to the "escalation of (and dependence on) computer technology," so he would not agree that "tomorrow's workplace will not include computers," and answer choice C is incorrect. The author discusses both the fact that technology jobs have a higher salary and the fact that IT workers are more satisfied with their jobs, so answer choice (D) is a logical conclusion.

57. C

Inference questions will always be related to an idea within the passage. The author states that the career is attractive because of a "high median salary and strong benefits" (line 30), which matches answer choice (C). Answer choice A is a distortion; the author states that it is only *unlikely* that the market will collapse, not that it will *never* happen. Answer choice B is also a distortion; this opinion is implied by the author, not by the Department of Labor. Answer choice D is the opposite; the passage indicates that the computer industry provides good careers for workers but questionable investment opportunities.

58. C

Answer Tone questions by getting a feel for the entirety of the passage. Don't focus on small details. The author notes that the IT industry is booming and then touches on some of the pros and cons of the field. He explains both the positive and negative aspects of a career in information technology, and then lists reasons why it is likely to remain a strong industry in the future. This best matches answer choice (C). Answer choice A is a distortion; the author discusses the benefits of a career in IT but devotes just as much time to explaining the drawbacks. Answer choice B is also a distortion; the author does point out some of the common problems with information technology but also states that it is a strong career option. Answer choice D is a third distortion; the author is not overly critical of IT careers, nor is the commentary vicious.

59. A

Remember to look for relevant details directly in the text. "Life is a stream" is the opening line of the poem, therefore, choice (A) is correct. Choices B–E are incorrect because they do not match the comparison that is explicitly stated by the author.

60. D

Inferences need to be supported by the text. In the poem, the writer stands on the bank of a stream (of life) and tosses flower petals in, after which they drift out of view: "Their distant employ / we shall never know" (lines 11–12). Choice (D) describes the writer's comfortable uncertainty regarding the path of the rose petals. Choices A and B are out of scope; sinking and eddy currents are not mentioned in the poem. Choice C is a misused detail; the rose's color is not relevant. Choice E is a distortion; the narrator is not asleep.

61. B

This question asks about the broader sense of the poem. Look carefully for specific words in the poem to support a particular interpretation. In the symbolism of the poem, the rose ("flower of our heart," line 3) is tossed petal by petal into the stream of life; the petals "widening scope…we never shall know" (lines 10–12). The emphasis on the heart and the lingering fragrance of the flower suggests that love is symbolized in the poem. Choice (B) is correct. Choice A is a misused detail; "employ" is not the same as employment. Choice C is out of scope; death is not a subject of the poem. Choice D is a misused detail;

"joy" does not describe the petals at all points on their drift. Choice E is opposite; life is symbolized by the stream; the petals are carried on by life.

62. C

Poetry questions requiring Inferences need to be answered carefully, finding specific words to support each claim. The representation of life as a stream, unknowable in destination, communicates unpredictability. The author comfortably states that once petals are launched, "each one is gone" (line 14). Choice (C) is correct.

Choice A is the opposite; life as a stream does not allow for predicted consequences. Choice B is extreme; Line 6, "We only watch their glad, early start," communicates greater influence over the beginning of life experiences. Choice D is also extreme; the last line, "its fragrance still stays," means something remains of early experiences. Finally, choice E is out of scope; the poem does not address friendship.

63. C

The correct answer to a Main Idea question must take into account information found throughout the passage. The author focuses on how very different cultures live in close proximity in Central Europe. Answer choice (C) is correct.

Choice A is out of scope; the author never discusses the difficulty of navigating the Danube. Choice B is a misused detail; while the grandeur of these cities is certainly described, this is not the focus of the passage. Choice D is a misused detail; the history endured by Central European people is only mentioned at the end of the passage. Choice E is out of scope; the challenges to linguists are not discussed in this passage.

64. A

The key to correctly answering Supporting Ideas questions is to research the passage carefully. The passage mentions people from each of three cities calling the Danube a different name. Choice (A) is correct.

Choice B is opposite; these landmarks can be found in Budapest, not Vienna. Choice C is out of scope; while the passage does state that these three peoples have common history, the passage never states that they have a common origin. Choice D is out of scope; reliance on the river is never discussed in the passage. Choice E is

extreme; the passage states that the languages are dissimilar, not necessarily that the people cannot understand each other.

65. E

When a Supporting Ideas question does not offer specific line references, you must research each answer choice to find evidence to support or eliminate it. The passage, in the discussion of history found at the end, mentions that the three cities have been united under common empires, which means that they had been the territories of other powers. Answer choice (E) is correct.

Choice A is opposite; the passage clearly states that their cultures and languages are very different. Choice B is extreme; the passage never states which city is the most beautiful. Choice C is also extreme; the passage does not state that it is overwhelming, merely that the disparity can be staggering. Choice D is opposite; the passage states that the people of the three cities have privation and strife in common.

66. C

The answer to an Inference question will not be stated in the passage, but it will be supported by the text. The passage is most concerned with the differences in culture in cities that are in close proximity to each other. Mentioning different words for the Danube emphasizes this. Answer choice (C) is correct.

Choice A is out of scope; the passage never discusses the length of the river. Choice B is a misused detail; the author is not focused on the differences between the three languages, but rather on how many linguistic and cultural differences there are in such a small geographic area. Choice D is out of scope; the need for a unified translation is never discussed. Choice E is a distortion; the difference between the languages is never linked to the wars in this passage.

67. B

Incorrect answers will often employ language from the passage. Forming a good prediction will help you avoid confusion. The passage discusses languages in the Danube region to emphasize their dissimilarity. This matches answer choice (B).

Choice A is out of scope; the passage never states how difficult these languages are to master. Choice C is out of scope; the passage never mentions how these languages sound to observers. Choice D is a distortion; the passage does not state that the languages of the three cities have taken on any similarities because of forced unification. Choice E is extreme; the passage does not state that such distinctness cannot be found elsewhere.

68. A

This Main Idea question tests your overall comprehension of the passage. Several tempting answers are given, but answer choice (A) is the only choice that describes the real sense of the section, which presents no debate and has no broader content. Answer choice B is the opposite of what is in the passage; the author presents no such argument. Answer choice C is a distortion; the author does not compare airplane travel with other modes of transportation. Answer choice D is out of scope; the author presents no conflict between the two control centers, which are part of the same system.

69. B

Supporting Ideas questions ask for you to find specific information in the text. Supporting details can be found only in the text; do not use your prior knowledge or jump to conclusions. Only answer choice (B) explains the purpose of the transfer of authority. Answer choice A is out of scope because the author does not mention emergencies. Answer choice C is a misused detail; while computer assistance may be helpful for controllers, according to the author, it is not enabled by transfer of authority. Answer choice D is out of scope; the author does not mention excess seating.

70. A

Supporting Ideas questions ask you to find specific details in the text. This is an EXCEPT question, so you are looking for the supporting idea that is not in the passage; this is answer choice (A). Answer choice B is mentioned in paragraph 2. Answer choice C is mentioned in paragraph 4. Answer choice D is mentioned in paragraph 3.

71. C

This Author's Purpose and Arguments question is worded in such a way that it is difficult to predict the correct answer. Instead, use evidence from the passage to prove each answer choice correct or incorrect.

Though the author does state that TRACON centers have a heavy burden, no mention is made of staffing needs at ARTCC, so answer choice A is incorrect.

Answer choice B is incorrect because the author spends the entire final paragraph discussing the ways that improved computer systems can aid air traffic control.

In lines 4–7, the author states that, "Air traffic control coordinates all air travel, directing takeoffs and landings, ensuring safe distances between airplanes, and keeping routes away from bad weather." In lines 47–50, the author mentions that "[Coordinating several planes], like much of air-traffic control, requires superb three-dimensional visualization skills and split-second decision-making abilities." Both of these pieces of evidence support the idea that "air traffic controllers must be highly capable to handle the demands of routing air traffic," so answer choice (C) is correct.

Once you prove answer choice (C) correct, there is no need to check answer choice D. That said, answer choice D is incorrect because the author states, in lines 4–5, "Air traffic control coordinates all air travel." Therefore, the author must believe that air traffic controllers have an important role in air travel.

72. D

Tone questions concern the point of view of the author. Key words and phrases like "a seamless web" and "superb" indicate the author's positive opinion of the air traffic controllers. This matches answer choice (D), "admiring." There is nothing to suggest that the author is "worried" about or "critical" of the air traffic controller, so choices A and B are incorrect. Although answer choice C, "humorous," is usually used in a positive way, it does not the fit the mostly informative tone of this passage.

73. B

Remember that context is key on Vocab-in-Context questions that ask for the meaning of a specific word. Several words that are similar at first glance will not fit when considered carefully. Only "reduced," answer choice (B), fits the sentence by describing the reduction of a burden. Answer choice A is a distortion; "brighten" sounds similar to the chosen word but does not have a similar meaning in the context of the sentence. Answer choice C is also a distortion; it is placed here to tempt you, since it's spelled similarly to "clarify." Answer choice D is the opposite of what is in the passage; "compound" would imply a desire to make the situation yet more difficult, which is the opposite of "lighten."

74. D

Even though the passage doesn't tell you the source of the text, you can—and must!—use evidence from the passage to determine which answer choice is correct. The passage discusses Howard Hughes and how his life changed after a plane crash. The author seems particularly interested in Hughes's fame and legacy and how his behavior affected public perception of him. Predict that the passage source would be concerned mostly with famous people, answer choice (D). Answer choice A is a distortion; although the passage indicates that Hughes's madness was worsened by the crash, this is not the focal point of the passage. Answer choice B is out of scope; there is nothing in the passage to suggest that this is a new or revolutionary analysis of Hughes's life. Answer choice C is a distortion; Hughes's mental illness is discussed, but the tone and scope of the passage are not at all indicative of a clinical study.

75. A

To answer Main Idea questions, focus on the author's main theme and predict carefully. The passage deals with Howard Hughes, his "quest for glory" (line 1), his eventual madness, and his public legacy. The best prediction here is that the passage deals with celebrity, (A). Answer choice B is a misused detail; Hughes was a pilot and aircraft designer, but this is not the focus of the passage. The plane crash is a detail used to explain his worsening mental condition. Answer choice C is another misused detail; Hughes was a recluse later in his life, but this is mostly mentioned to show how his ambition affected his life and his reputation. Answer choice D is a distortion; although Hughes's ambition and eccentricities contributed to his fame, it is his fame that is the focus of the passage.

76. C

Answers to Supporting Ideas questions will always be found in the passage. The passage states that the crash nearly killed Hughes and that the "brush with death" (line 18) changed the man. Predict that after the crash, Hughes's behavior was different, which matches answer choice (C). Answer choice A is out of scope; although Hughes probably did compensate the homeowners, this is never stated in the passage. Answer choice B is a misused detail; although the passage states that Hughes was romanticized,

this is not necessarily linked to the crash. Answer choice D is out of scope; the continuation of the XF-11 project is not mentioned.

77. B

Make sure to keep the author's tone and overall point in mind when answering a Tone / Style / Figurative Language question. The author uses the words "interesting" (line 28) and "adventurer" (line 24) to describe Hughes, who became increasingly disturbed after a major flying accident. Predict that *Hughes is not only an interesting figure but also a tragic one*, which matches answer choice (B). Answer choice A is a distortion; although his "quest for glory" (line 1) indicates that Hughes was ambitious, there is no evidence to support the assertion that he was arrogant. Answer choice C is extreme; although the passage deals with Hughes's madness in his later years, the author counters this by mentioning his other qualities as well. Answer choice D is the opposite of what's in the passage; Hughes was quite a celebrity in his time.

78. B

Tone, Style, and Figurative Language questions require an understanding of the author's position. The author states that, despite the way Hughes lived out his later years, he remained "genuinely interesting" (line 28). Predict that *the author viewed Hughes as a compelling and tragic figure, rather than a larger-than-life hero or a tyrant*. Answer choice (B) matches this idea the best. Answer choice A is a distortion; the author states that Hughes was a mad recluse but does not ridicule or attempt to debase him. Answer choice C is out of scope; the author never displays any anger or hostility toward Hughes or his legacy. Answer choice D is a distortion; the author does not gush over Hughes or seem intimidated by him.

79. D

When answering a Vocab-in-Context question, be wary of the most common definition of the cited word; a secondary definition is more likely to be correct on Test Day. In line 20, "twilight" refers to a particular time of Hughes's life. In this case, you might predict *later years* or *end*. Answer choice (D) is close to your prediction. Answer choice A neither fits your definition nor makes sense in the sentence. Answer choice B is a literal definition of twilight, but this does not make sense in context. Answer choice C is again too close to the literal definition and does not fit in the context of the passage.

80. C

When answering a Main Idea question, you must consider the passage as a whole, not merely isolated ideas or details. The passage focuses in paragraph 1 on the invention of the telegraph and the growth of its use. Paragraph 2 discusses how the telegraph became obsolete. The correct answer will encompass this information. Answer choice (C) does so and is thus correct. Answer choice A is out of scope; the passage is not focused on telecommunications in general but specifically on the telegraph. Answer choice B is a misused detail; the disappearance of the telegraph is solely the focus of paragraph 2. Answer choice D is another misused detail; while this fact is mentioned, the passage is not focused on it.

81. C

Tone questions ask you to assess the overall feel of the passage. The passage discusses the telegraph in fairly neutral to positive terms. The author's purpose is to describe, not to make recommendations or warnings, answer choice (C). Answer choice A is the opposite of what's in the passage; the author is never negative in his description. Answer choice B is extreme; while there is a positive tone in the passage, the author never focuses his effort on specifically praising the telegraph. Answer choice D is also extreme; while the author does state that the telegraph is obsolete, the passage never focuses negatively or positively on this.

82. B

Pay close attention to the exact wording of questions. Reading too quickly can result in missing critical words like EXCEPT or NOT. The author states that the transatlantic cable was laid because of the telegraph's invention, not the other way around, so answer choice (B) is NOT true and is therefore correct. Answer choice A is mentioned in lines 14–15 and is therefore incorrect. Answer choice C is mentioned in lines 33–34 and is thus incorrect. Answer choice D is incorrect because it is mentioned in paragraph 3; telephone, fax, and email have rendered the telegraph "completely obsolete" (lines 26–27).

83. B

To answer this Vocab-in-Context question, go back to the passage to find context to help you predict a synonym for the word in the question stem. The passage states that, after overhearing a conversation on a ship, "a seed was planted," and soon, Morse invented the telegraph. It can be inferred that the seed that was planted was the idea of a way to communicate over large distances quickly and easily. Choice (B) is correct. Choices A and D do not make sense in context. Choice C is tempting, but it is an idea, not the beginning of the invention, that was "planted" on a ship.

84. D

Remember, the correct answer to an Inference question MUST be true based on evidence from the passage. This question is too open-ended to predict, so evaluate each answer choice in turn; the passage suggests that the telegraph was a major innovation that improved communications. Answer choice (D) follows logically. Answer choice A is a distortion; the passage never discusses how the telegraph was affected by the war. Answer choice B is also a distortion; despite the Internet, Western Union probably would have continued service had there been a demand for it. Answer choice C is out of scope; the difficulty of Morse code is never discussed in the passage.

85. C

Don't rely on your memory to eliminate incorrect answer choices; go back to the passage and find proof for the correct answer. In lines 26–28, the passage indicates that "the telegraph has been rendered completely obsolete, first by the telephone, then by the fax machine and Internet." Answer choice (C) includes the only item not mentioned as a cause of the telegraph becoming obsolete and is therefore correct. Answer choices A, B, and D are all causes of the telegraph becoming obsolete and are therefore incorrect.

86. B

Questions that ask about the author's purpose for writing a passage are concerned with the passage as a whole. You should consider the author's tone throughout the passage as well as what the author is trying to accomplish. There are several instances in which the author praises the Northern cause in this passage. While the author does describe the events of Fort Sumter's surrender, there is a distinct indication of support toward the Northern cause. This partiality is best reflected in answer choice (B). Answer choice A is a distortion; the writer doesn't know at the point he writes how significant this act will be. Answer choice C is a misused detail; the passage discusses Lincoln's call to arms, but that is not the purpose of the passage. Answer choice D is opposite; the last sentence of the passage indicates that the North, not the Confederacy, possesses the advantage in the coming war.

87. D

The correct answer to an Inference question must be supported by information in the passage. The passage states in lines 7–9 that both the Federal government and President Lincoln desired peace, answer choice (D). Answer choice A is opposite; lines 11–13 make it clear that Toombs did not support the attack. Answer choice B is out of scope; the passage never discusses Lincoln's explicit orders. Answer choice C is a distortion; the passage does mention slavery but states that the Southerners, described as defenders of slavery in lines 2–3, brought the war on themselves.

88. A

The correct answer to an Inference question must follow logically from the passage. This is a tricky question, but as always, the answer will use evidence directly from the passage. After researching the citation, it is clear that the Southerners are the defenders of slavery, and they started the war by attacking Fort Sumter. The author further suggests in lines 27–30 that, because of its advantages, the North will win the war. From this information, you can infer that, because they started the war and will probably lose, the Southerners have doomed slavery; this matches answer choice (A). Answer choice B is out of scope; the author does not mention any Northern supporters of slavery. Answer choice C is opposite; the first sentence of the passage states that the Southerners were defenders of slavery. Answer choice D is a misused detail; the "blow" mentioned refers to a threat to slavery, not the strength of Beauregard's attack.

89. B

Be on the lookout for clues that reveal the author's views. The author states in line 8 that the Southerners are "suspicious," which best matches answer choice (B). Answer choice A is extreme; while the author does state that the Northerners are loyal, the Southerners are never explicitly referred to as traitors. Answer choice C is a distortion; while the Southerners do attack the fort, the author never explicitly states that they are "belligerent." Answer choice D is opposite; the author states that it is the Northerners who are patriotic.

90. B

When answering a Vocab-in-Context question, beware of the most common definition of the cited word. A secondary definition will likely be correct on Test Day since these questions are testing the meaning of the vocabulary word or phrase within the context of the passage. In line 25, "strains" refers to the playing of the *Star Spangled Banner* So, in this sentence, "strains" can be predicted to mean *tones* or *playing*. Answer choice (B) is closest to this prediction. Answer choice A is the primary definition of "strains" and does not fit your prediction. Answer choice C, "exclamations," is close to the correct meaning but still too literal. Answer choice D is, again, close, but "outbursts" is too literal an answer choice.

91. D

Always be sure to read each question stem and answer choice carefully! There is no need to lose points on Supporting Ideas questions from careless errors. The response to the attack is discussed in paragraph 2. The author states that there was an intense upsurge of patriotism, not a "decline," choice (D). Answer choice A is located in line 20, which states that Fort Sumter was surrendered. Answer B is located in lines 20–21, which state that Lincoln called for 75,000 volunteers. Answer C is located in lines 21–23, which state that Lincoln called for troops and authorization of any means to preserve the Union, which is a change from his desire for peace.

92. A

Consider the context of this quote. The speaker does not use this term in its literal sense. He refers to the council as "friends" to show the unfriendliness or injustice of their actions. Choice (A) shows this contrast between the designation of "friends" and the actions of the city council and is therefore correct. Choices B and C misuse the meaning of the word in context. Choice D is incorrect because this speech solely addresses the city council and makes no mention of the speaker's actual friends. Choice E is incorrect because the passage does not state whether the speaker received any sort of permission to address the council.

93. A

You will need to determine the content of the quotation. By using this quotation, the speaker sets up a comparison. He shows that the people in his neighborhood are already "equal." The council's plan is a flawed attempt to make it "more equal." Choice (A) is correct. Choices B and C are the opposite; this quote reminds the council that citizens are equal; it doesn't claim that educated people have more rights to the government. Choice D is a distortion; the speaker was not in violation. In fact, he claims that the city's actions were a violation of equality. Finally, choice E is out of scope. The passage does not discuss the Constitution or voting.

94. E

Answers to Author's Purpose and Arguments questions are always found in the passage. The author mentions several facts and opinions about the North Freeway neighborhood, so be careful as you sort through the answers to determine which piece of evidence is presented to support his opinion: the people of the neighborhood have equal right to their homes. Choice (E) is correct. Choices A and B are out of scope; the passage does not discuss the Constitution or the other beautiful neighborhoods in the city. Choice C is the opposite; the speech makes clear that the citizens should *not* be forced to leave the area. Choice D is a misused detail; while the area is described as "unattractive to tourists" (line 5), this statement is not used to support the speaker's claim that the project is an injustice.

95. C

Take the entire passage into consideration when answering Main Idea questions. The speaker is concerned with the reconstruction project. His speech is meant to point out the injustice of this venture. Choice (C) is correct. Choice A is a distortion; the speaker wants to influence the city council members, not "citizens of a particular area." Choice B is a misused detail; the speaker does mention tourism in his speech. However, this reference is only a detail; his purpose is to discuss the reconstruction project, not tourism. Choice D is out of scope; the speaker argues that one plan is unjust, but he does not present an alternative plan. Choice E is a misused detail; the speaker uses a reference to social justice and equality. However, this reference is only a detail; his purpose is more focused on the reconstruction project.

96. B

Remember to look for details directly in the passage. The answer to this Supporting Ideas question is in the final sentence of paragraph 1: "At times, severe bursts of wind penetrated her specialized, technical coverings and made her feel as if she were fighting to take each step forward." Choice (B) is correct.

Choice A is a misused detail; the climber worries about the possibility of an avalanche, but it does not occur. Choice C is opposite; paragraph 1 mentions only an occasional cloud. Choice D is a misused detail; the ice wall is a hallucination.

97. C

Look for supporting details when making an inference. The passage mentions several details describing a mountain setting: tree line, final peak, avalanche. Choice (C) is correct. Choices A, B, and D are all opposites; the setting describes cold, snow, and wind, rather than warmth, sand, sun, heat, or the humid or dry atmospheres of a swamp or desert.

98. D

Look for specific information in the text to help answer Inference questions. For NOT or EXCEPT questions, eliminate one choice at a time. Line 17 mentions her physical strength, and line 25 describes "her vast well of experience [and] her senses," so choices A, B, and C are all incorrect. Navigational instruments are not described in the text, so choice (D) is correct.

99. D

Use context to determine the meaning of an unknown word. A snow-covered boulder would just look like a big pile of snow. This pile of snow would most likely be pretty "formless," so choice (D) is correct.

Choice A is the opposite; "amorphous" shapes are not distinct shapes by definition. Choice B is a distortion; something can be "amorphous" and not "rugged." Choice C is another opposite; something that is "triangular" has a very definite shape, but something that is "amorphous" does not.

100. C

Many Main Idea questions will ask you to identify the purpose of the passage. To answer this type of question, ask yourself why the author presented this information and what the author wanted the reader to learn from this passage. This passage talks about nuclear fallout and its dangers and effects. Paragraph 1 reveals the purpose by stating that nuclear fallout may contaminate humans in many ways. The next paragraphs then show ways in which humans come into contact with the toxic material. You can predict that the author is primarily concerned with human contamination. Choice (C) is correct.

Choice A is a misused detail that focuses on only the last paragraph. Choices B and D are distortions; the passage is primarily concerned with how humans absorb nuclear material. The environmental changes are only details used in support of this purpose. Choice D is also a misused detail; this answer focuses on one sentence in paragraph 1. You need an answer that takes into account the entire passage.

101. A

This is a Supporting Ideas question, so you only need to look at a small portion of the information given. Paragraph 2 discusses how plants become toxic. The author writes, "The soil remains toxic and eventually poisons local plant life," so you'll need an answer that states that the soil contaminates the plants. Choice (A) is correct. Choices B and C are misused details; the author states that both the air and cow's meat and milk are contaminated, but it is only the soil that directly affects the plants. Choice D is out of scope; the passage does not mention fertilizer.

102. C

On Test Day, you will be asked to identify the tone of some passages. To answer these questions, think about the author's purpose. The author writes in third person with a very straightforward tone and does not use persuasive or emotional language. You can predict that the passage is simply meant to present information, choice (C). Choice A is out of scope; there is no emotional language to show excitement in this passage. Choices B and D are both distortions; the passage presents the information in an objective manner and does not offer any feelings of fear or attempt to persuade the reader in any way.

103. B

To predict what the author would write about next, you must consider the outline of the passage so far. First, the

author presents the claim that nuclear fallout is dangerous. The first supporting paragraph describes the danger to plants and the effect of plant changes on humans. The second supporting paragraph describes the danger to animals and the effect of animal changes on humans. Logically, the next paragraph would discuss more about the effects on humans, which matches choice (B).

Choice A is a distortion; the contamination of plants is discussed in paragraph 2, so the logical placement for a paragraph like this would be after paragraph 2. Choices C and D are out of scope; the passage never discusses any particular fallout scenes or the causes of explosions; the author is only concerned with how humans are exposed to fallout through various carriers.

104. D

Answers to Inference questions will follow logically from the text. Paragraph 3 uses cow's milk as an example of animal products passing radioactive contamination to humans. Look for an answer that uses the cows as an illustration of the main point. Choice (D) is correct.

Choice A is a distortion; the example is used to show how cows help to contaminate humans, not to show the effect on the cows themselves. Choice B is out of scope; while the author does show the cows being part of the food chain, this is not the purpose of this detail. The contaminated cows are examples of how nuclear fallout is passed on through affected milk. Choice C is a misused detail; the plants are discussed in paragraph 2.

105. D

When dealing with an EXCEPT question, you must rule out the incorrect answers. Each of these items is mentioned in the passage. The key here is identifying which one is not a contamination source. While paragraph 2 does use the word "dust," the author is not using the word to show that the dust is contaminated. Choice (D) is correct.

Choice A is incorrect because the last paragraph discusses the milk and meat of cows being contaminated. Choice B is incorrect because the entire passage focuses on how humans are contaminated through plant and animal sources. Choice C is incorrect because paragraph 2 discusses plants absorbing nuclear fallout through the soil.

106. B

You can eliminate choice A because the second stanza includes the line "For a future buds in everything," which symbolizes the future of all beings, not a particular season. The first line of the poem mentions "Wintry boughs against a wintry sky." Since most trees lose their leaves in winter, this statement paraphrases that line, and represents that season. Choice (B) is correct. If needed, you can eliminate choice C because this is a distortion of lines 7–8 and doesn't describe a seasonal symbol. Sap is mentioned in line 4, but sap production as a whole is out of scope, so choice D is incorrect. Broken branches are not mentioned, and buds that are about to break are only mentioned in line 12 in relation to the analogy about the future, so choice E is incorrect.

107. E

When you see a line reference in a question stem, that's a strong indication that you're looking at a Supporting Ideas question, which will ask about a specific piece of information in the passage. Read a line or two before and after the quoted phrase to understand the context of the detail, especially in a poetry passage. Here, the clues come in lines 5–6: "Out of sight, / Ready to burst through?" Based on these lines, you can predict that the quoted line refers to some sort of natural activity that isn't visible to human eyes, which matches choice (E).

Choice A is a distortion; nothing in the poem suggests that the sap is ready for harvest. Choice B is extreme; the poem suggests that the trees may actually be producing sap even if the end product is not yet visible. Choice C is out of scope; the poem doesn't try to create any direct link between the sky and the trees. Finally, choice D is extreme; line 4 suggests that the production of sap begins during the colder weather.

108. D

Even if the question stem doesn't give you a line reference, you can scan the passage to find clues and then reread the relevant lines. The first two lines of the poem describe different aspects of the sky. "Wintry" sky suggests cold and bleak conditions, but the "partly blue" sky suggests that some warmth may be coming soon. For these reasons, the "wintry" sky refers to the present conditions, and the "partly blue" sky refers to the near future, which matches choice (D).

Choices A and B are too literal, since the poem uses weather to figuratively represent the seasons. Choice C is incorrect because the poem doesn't mention feelings associated with each type of sky. Finally, choice E is incorrect because the second stanza personifies winter and spring by comparing them to a mother and daughter, so the references to the sky in the first stanza are not directly related to this symbolism.

109. C

The phrase "would most likely agree" in a question stem indicates an Inference question. Predicting answers for Inference questions can be challenging, so go directly to the answer choices and determine whether each is true or false, based on the passage. The writer of this poem has an overall positive tone toward both seasons. She doesn't state a strong preference or suggest that either season is better than the other, rather that both have positive characteristics, including winter, as suggested in lines 7–9: "Winter is the mother-nurse of Spring, / Lovely for her daughter's sake, / Not unlovely for her own." Answer choice (C) expresses this idea.

Answer choice A is out of scope; the poem doesn't discuss the duration of spring. Choice B is a distortion; the author doesn't make any recommendations. Choice D is opposite; lines 7–9 suggest that the author enjoys winter for its own sake, not simply because it leads to spring. Finally, choice E is a distortion; no connection is made between the "wintry boughs" in the first stanza and the "future buds" in the second stanza.

110. D

For a Supporting Ideas question, always refer directly back to the passage. The author uses the work of Jonas Salk to contrast the work of innovative geniuses such as Fleming. The author states that Salk's work was based on the work of others and scientific principle, rather than on independent innovation, choice (D).

Choice A is a distortion; the passage states that Salk borrowed from other scientists but does not specifically state that he borrowed from Fleming. Choice B is opposite; the passage states that Salk based his work on mundane procedure. Choice C is extreme; while the passage states that Salk did base much of his work on that of others, the author never gives credit to other scientists for curing polio. Choice E is also extreme; the passage states that Salk did not rely on innovation, not that he was incapable of such discoveries.

111. B

This Author's Purpose and Arguments question requires you to draw a conclusion based on facts, just like Inference questions. This means that you should be able to support your answer with facts from the passage. The passage is focused on the disproportionate credit given to maverick innovators for scientific discovery. The author mentions biographies and biographical films in order to illustrate this tendency, choice (B).

Choice A is opposite; the passage states that people are interested. Choice C is out of scope; the passage never discusses a controversy surrounding penicillin. Choice D is a misused detail; the passage does not discuss the need for biographies of Salk. Choice E is extreme; the passage is describing the curiosity of others, not a need for more information.

112. C

The word "suggests" should be your clue that this is an Inference question. The correct answer will be something not directly stated but clearly implied. The passage discusses Salk's work in comparison with the highly respected, unorthodox techniques of Alexander Fleming. The passage states that other scientists ridiculed Salk's work as "mundane" because it was based on other people's work and basic scientific procedure rather than dramatic innovation, choice (C).

Choice A is opposite; while the author gives credit to Salk, other scientists ridiculed his work. Choice B is also opposite; again the author states this, but other scientists do not. Choice D is out of scope; the passage does not discuss the complexity of Salk's work. Choice E is opposite; the passage states that Salk discovered a major cure.

113. A

The correct answer to a Main Idea question will reference the entire passage, not just isolated details. The author argues in this passage that discoveries are made not only by maverick geniuses, but also by methodical workers like Jonas Salk, choice (A).

Choice B is extreme; the author never recommends a particular method. Choice C is a misused detail; the passage does not focus on Fleming. Choice D is a misused detail; while Salk is a nondramatic example, this is not the author's overall purpose. Choice E is out of scope; the author never makes funding recommendations.

CHAPTER 9

The Essay

CHAPTER OBJECTIVES

With practice, this chapter will help you:

1. Recall the format and timing of the ISEE Essay and the SSAT Writing Sample

2. Explain the steps of the Kaplan 4-Step Method for Writing

INTRODUCTION TO THE ESSAY

Both the SSAT and ISEE—all levels—require an essay, but these written responses are not scored. So…if this section isn't scored, why should you put any effort into writing it on Test Day? Well, the written response is sent directly to schools, so it's a great way for them to see how you express yourself. The rest of the test tells them how well you perform on a series of standard tasks, but the written response is the one part of the exam where you get to shine as an individual. Schools look closely at your written response, so think of it as part of your application and take it seriously.

> **EXPERT TIP**
>
> The ISEE Middle and Upper Levels include an Essay as the fifth section of the test. There is only one prompt, and it requires an essay-style response. The SSAT Middle and Upper Levels include a Writing Sample as the first section of the test. There are two prompts to choose from, and these prompts might require either an essay- or a story-style response. You will learn more about the differences between these two sections later in this chapter.

What do you need to know to write a written response that will stand out? There are a few key things you should remember to do well on any writing task:

1. Most importantly, stick to the topic. For the ISEE, you have to write the prompt in the box at the top of the page, so use this as a reference to keep yourself focused as you write. If you're taking the SSAT, be careful not to get the two prompts mixed up at any point.

2. Write clearly and logically. Creating a plan before you start will ensure your written response makes sense. Be as concise as possible without leaving out important ideas. A shorter response that is more clear and makes logical sense is better than a long response that drifts off topic and leaves the reader confused.

3. Finally, be sure to save time to proofread your response before you finish. Even if you think you have been very careful, you'll always find at least one small thing that you'll want to fix or change. It's very easy to misuse punctuation, make a capitalization error, or even forget an entire word or phrase when you're busy trying to record the ideas in your head. You should save time to proofread any meaningful writing you do.

There are several specific details you should know before taking an official ISEE or SSAT:

1. You'll need to organize your thoughts for the essay quickly. You only have 25 minutes for the SSAT Writing Sample and 30 minutes for the ISEE Essay, and this time limit includes planning, writing, and proofreading your entire response.

2. Your essay is limited to the two pages in the answer grid booklet. This page limit includes the space on the ISEE answer grid where you write the essay prompt or the space on the SSAT answer grid that includes the directions and the two prompts.

3. The topics will be easy to grasp and relate to students your age.

4. The content of your response is more important than the presence of perfect grammar and vocabulary or the length of your essay or story.

5. Remember, your response will not be scored. Instead, it is sent directly to secondary/independent schools.

DIFFERENCES BETWEEN THE ESSAYS ON THE SSAT AND ISEE

The written responses on both the SSAT and ISEE are fairly comparable, though there are a few differences worth noting.

The SSAT Writing Sample

The SSAT Writing Sample is a 25-minute section (for the Upper and Middle Levels) that provides two distinct prompts.

On the Upper Level of the exam, you have a choice between responding to a creative writing prompt (which requires you to write a story based on the topic presented) or a traditional essay prompt (which requires you to write an explanatory or persuasive essay, providing reasoning and/or examples to support your perspective).

For Middle Level students, you may only choose between two creative writing (story) prompts. Regardless of which prompt you choose, the Kaplan 4-Step Method for Writing will help you master this part of the SSAT.

The ISEE Essay

The ISEE Essay is a 30-minute section (for the Upper and Middle Levels) that provides one prompt. There are over 100 prompts that have been developed for ISEE test takers of all levels, but it is predictable that this prompt will either ask you for your opinion or to share a personal experience through a descriptive, explanatory, or persuasive essay. Be sure to provide details or reasoning to tell your story or help support your perspective. Whatever the prompt may be, the Kaplan 4-Step Method for Writing will help you master this part of the ISEE.

One important thing to keep in mind for the ISEE essay only: even though there is only one prompt, you must rewrite it at the top of the first page of your essay.

KAPLAN 4-STEP METHOD FOR WRITING

Step 1. Prompt (brainstorm the topic)

Step 2. Plan your response

Step 3. Produce your writing

Step 4. Proofread

This Kaplan Method might sound pretty general and a lot like the process you've followed for essays for school. In fact, the essay is the part of the test that most closely resembles the work you do in school. Unlike the essays you do for school, however, the SSAT writing sample and the ISEE essay are standardized and follow a much more specific format than you might be used to. In addition, you just don't have a lot of time to get it done. What does all of this mean? It's very important that you have a plan to work as efficiently as possible, and the best way to do this is to follow all four steps of the Kaplan Method as you work. Break them down.

Step 1. Prompt (Brainstorm the Topic)

Read the prompt(s). When you start to brainstorm for ideas, first think about the topic. If you're taking the SSAT, you may want to brainstorm ideas for both topics before you make your choice, giving you time to decide which prompt you can answer better. If you're writing an essay, ask yourself: what examples can I use to support this point of view? If you're writing a story, ask yourself: in one or two sentences, what do the beginning, middle, and end of my story look like?

It's important that you're clear in your head about your point of view or overall story *before* you start to organize your essay. Once you start to put your examples together, you don't want to have to go back and figure out what you're trying to show.

Step 2. Plan Your Response

Once you've decided on your topic, opinion, or story, the next step is to write an outline. Come up with three examples to support your points or opinion or summarize the beginning, middle, and end of your story.

If you're writing an essay, decide the best order in which to present your examples. What is the most logical way to lay out your ideas? How do you want to start your essay? How do you want to end it? What is your strongest example? If you're writing a story, you should outline the plot, setting, and characters before you start writing. You don't need to outline every paragraph, but you should have a general idea of how you will group your events or sets of dialogue and write a complete story in the given space. Remember, you have limited time and space!

No matter what type of essay you write, make some notes on your scratch paper so when you start to write, you can glance at them to keep you on track and moving quickly.

Step 3. Produce Your Writing

Now, you have to write the essay. Follow your outline carefully, but be flexible. You might think of another great idea midway through your writing; should you ignore it or should you substitute it for the third example you had planned to include? If you think it's better than what you originally came up with and fits well with what you've already written, go ahead and write about it instead. Just make sure that any deviation you make from your outline is in fact an improvement over the original idea.

Step 4. Proofread

Wrap up your writing five minutes before the end of your allotted time. Give your essay a good read-through, making sure you haven't made any spelling mistakes, written any run-on sentences, or forgotten to capitalize a proper name. You won't be able to make any huge changes at this point—after all, you only have a few minutes left—but you do want to make sure that you haven't made any obvious or extreme errors.

PACING

How much time should you spend on each step? Use the clock and these guidelines as you write. You want to give yourself sufficient time for each step because planning and proofreading will make your essay much stronger.

	SSAT	ISEE
Brainstorming/Planning	5 minutes	5 minutes
Writing	15 minutes	20 minutes
Proofreading	5 minutes	5 minutes
Total Time	**25 minutes**	**30 minutes**

BRAINSTORMING IN ACTION

When you get to the essay section, the last thing you want to happen is a *brain freeze*. You know the feeling: you look at the page, you see the words, your brain doesn't register, you stare into space...but you can't think of a thing to write about.

How do you avoid such a situation? One of the best ways to make sure your brain is in gear and ready to brainstorm on the spot is to practice doing it. Take a look at the following statements. If it is an "agree or disagree" prompt, decide what position you would take and think of three examples you would present in support of your opinion. If it is a "describe" or "explain" prompt, pick your topic and think of three examples you would use to explain or describe your topic. Give yourself about five minutes to do each one.

Sample Topic 1: Should free speech on the Internet be protected? Why or why not?

_____

_____

_____

_____

_____

_____

_____

Sample Topic 2: Do we learn more from our mistakes than our successes? Why?

_____

_____

_____

_____

_____

_____

_____

Sample Topic 3: What is your fondest memory? Why?

_____

_____

_____

_____

_____

_____

_____

SHOW, DON'T TELL

You've probably heard the saying that good writing *shows* rather than *tells*. What does that mean, and what do examples have to do with it?

Think about the saying, "You can't teach an old dog new tricks." If you wanted to disagree with it, you could explain why you believe the statement isn't true, what you think about teaching and age, and so forth. On the other hand, you could use examples that *show* the same ideas. You could discuss the fact that retired people now use the Internet on a regular basis. The fact that people generally considered *old* by society are adapting to a *new* technology in large numbers serves to show that you can, in fact, teach an old dog new tricks.

What makes a good example? A good example illustrates the point you want to make. In addition, it comes from the world at large rather than from your personal life. While it may be true that your grandmother emails you, it's more powerful to say that many retirees use the Internet every day.

If you're not doing so already, try reading news articles, blogs, and other lengthy pieces of writing on a regular basis. Not only will you know more about what's going on in the world and be ready with great examples for your essays, but also you'll improve your vocabulary and stamina, which will improve your performance on the Verbal section of your test.

> **EXPERT TIP**
>
> When you read a newspaper (whether paper or digital), make sure you look at the editorial page. You'll see how writers argue their opinions on a variety of topics and what kinds of examples they use. You might even learn something interesting in the process!

JUST THE FACTS

What do you need to do as you write your essay?

- Develop and organize your ideas.

- Use 3–5 paragraphs for essay-style responses.

- Use appropriate examples.

- Write in English, using an academic style.

- Stick to the topic.

- Use proper spelling, grammar, and punctuation.

What's Wrong with This Picture?

Take a look at the following paragraph and think about what's wrong with it. Use the space that follows to jot down the errors you notice.

Sample Topic: Do you agree that no good deed goes unpunished?

It always bothers me when people talk about punishment. It's not fair. I mean, there are some kids out there who do really good things, even though people don't notice them. In my opinion, everyone spends too much time talking about whether or not there is enough punishment in the world. We should really be talking about more important things like the environment...

_____

_____

_____

_____

_____

_____

_____

Common Pitfalls in Essay Writing

What's wrong with the paragraph you just read? The biggest problem is that it goes off topic. Granted, you're only seeing the beginning of the essay, but you can tell from the way it ends that the author is about to go off on a tangent about the environment instead of discussing the topic. Remember, *always* stay on topic.

What else is wrong with the sample paragraph? You might have noticed that it sounds very casual, almost like a conversation. Phrases such as "I mean" and "In my opinion" give the essay a tone that's too familiar and too emotional. While you want to present your opinion, you should try to do it in a detached, formal way, as if writing a newspaper article. While you will be talking about yourself in every ISEE essay and in response to an SSAT essay-style prompt, you should avoid using "I" or "me" in every sentence. If removing the reference to yourself does not affect the meaning of the sentence, get rid of it!

How can you avoid making these types of mistakes? How can you make sure you don't get sidetracked while you write or repeat yourself? Following the Kaplan 4-Step Method for Writing when you write your essay will ensure that you create an organized, clear response.

EXPERT TIP

The golden rule of writing is to stick to the topic. Whether a prompt requires an essay (ISEE or SSAT) or a story (SSAT only), there should always be a beginning or introduction, a middle (body paragraphs), and a conclusion. If you're writing an essay, use examples to support your ideas. If you're writing a story, use your outline to stay on track with pacing, space, and level of detail.

PRACTICE ESSAYS

> Work through these topics as though they are the real thing. Brainstorm your ideas, make an outline, write, and proofread. Time yourself (25 minutes for the SSAT or 30 minutes for the ISEE).

1. **Prompt:** If you could read only one book for the rest of your life, what would it be and why?

   Step 1. Brainstorm

   Brainstorm in the space provided below. Do you agree or disagree? What examples might you use to support your argument? (Remember, give yourself only a few minutes to do this!)

   _____

   _____

   _____

   _____

   _____

   Step 2. Make an outline

   Write your outline here. Aim to write an essay that is three to five paragraphs. Paragraph 1 is your introduction. Paragraphs 2, 3, and 4 include examples, and paragraph 5 is your conclusion. If you run out of time or space to write five total paragraphs, leave out paragraphs 3 and 4 as needed. Always save time for a conclusion!

   Introduction

   _____

   _____

   Support

   _____

   _____

   Conclusion

   _____

   _____

Step 3. Write your essay

Write your essay below. Give yourself 15 minutes if you're taking the SSAT and 20 minutes if you're taking the ISEE.

_____

_____

_____

_____

_____

_____

_____

_____

_____

_____

_____

_____

_____

_____

_____

_____

_____

_____

_____

_____

_____

_____

_____

_____

_____

_____

_____

_____

_____

_____

_____

_____

_____

_____

_____

_____

_____

_____

_____

_____

Step 4. Proofread

Go back to your essay and read through it again. Does it make sense? Have you made any spelling or grammar errors? Fix them. Get used to making corrections clearly on your page, because that's what you will do the day of the test.

2. **Prompt (SSAT only):** The pigeon flapped its wings weakly.

Step 1. Brainstorm

Brainstorm in the space provided below. What happens next? In one or two sentences, describe the beginning, middle, and end. Who will be the character(s)? Where will the story take place? Is there anything else you want to be sure to include? (Remember, you have 5 minutes to brainstorm AND make your outline, so don't spend too much time on Step 1!)

_____

_____

_____

_____

_____

_____

Step 2. Make an outline

Write your outline here. Aim to write a story that has a clear plot, strong details, and logical structure. Use this outline to think through your story and mentally plan out your writing time. If you run out of time or space to write everything you planned, leave out detail from the middle of your story as needed. Always save time for a conclusion!

Beginning

_____

_____

Middle

_____

_____

End

_____

_____

Step 3. Write your essay

Write your essay below. Give yourself 15 minutes.

_____

_____

_____

_____

_____

_____

_____

_____

_____

_____

_____

_____

_____

_____

_____

_____

_____

_____

_____

Step 4. Proofread

Go back to your essay and read through it again. Does it make sense? Have you made any spelling or grammar errors? Fix them. Get used to making corrections clearly on your page, because that's what you will do the day of the test.

3. **Prompt:** If you could have a superpower, what would it be and why?

Step 1. Brainstorm

Brainstorm in the space provided below. Do you agree or disagree? What examples might you use to support your argument? (Remember, give yourself only a few minutes to do this!)

_____

_____

_____

_____

_____

_____

_____

Step 2. Make an outline

Write your outline here. Aim to write an essay that is three to five paragraphs. Paragraph 1 is your introduction. Paragraphs 2, 3, and 4 include examples, and paragraph 5 is your conclusion. If you run out of time or space to write five total paragraphs, leave out paragraphs 3 and 4 as needed. Always save time for a conclusion!

Introduction

_____

_____

Support

_____

_____

Conclusion

_____

_____

Step 3. Write your essay

Write your essay below. Give yourself 15 minutes if you're taking the SSAT and 20 minutes if you're taking the ISEE.

_____

_____

_____

_____

_____

_____

_____

_____

_____

_____

_____

_____

_____

_____

_____

_____

_____

_____

_____

_____

_____

_____

_____

_____

_____

_____

_____

_____

_____

_____

_____

_____

_____

_____

_____

_____

_____

_____

_____

Step 4. Proofread

Go back to your essay and read through it again. Does it make sense? Have you made any spelling or grammar errors? Fix them. Get used to making corrections clearly on your page, because that's what you will do the day of the test.

4. **Prompt (SSAT only):** The moon rose blood red over the prairie.

Step 1. Brainstorm

Brainstorm in the space provided below. What happens next? In one or two sentences, describe the beginning, middle, and end. Who will be the character(s)? Where will the story take place? Is there anything else you want to be sure to include? (Remember, you have 5 minutes to brainstorm AND make your outline, so don't spend too much time on Step 1!)

_____

_____

_____

_____

_____

_____

_____

Step 2. Make an outline

Write your outline here. Aim to write a story that has a clear plot, strong details, and logical structure. Use this outline to think through your story and mentally plan out your writing time. If you run out of time or space to write everything you planned, leave out detail from the middle of your story as needed. Always save time for a conclusion!

Beginning

_____

_____

Middle

_____

_____

End

_____

_____

Step 3. Write your essay

Write your essay below. Give yourself 15 minutes if you're taking the SSAT and 20 minutes if you're taking the ISEE.

_____

_____

_____

_____

_____

_____

_____

_____

_____

_____

_____

_____

_____

_____

_____

_____

_____

_____

_____

_____

_____

_____

_____

_____

_____

_____

_____

_____

_____

_____

_____

_____

_____

_____

_____

_____

_____

_____

_____

Step 4. Proofread

Go back to your essay and read through it again. Does it make sense? Have you made any spelling or grammar errors? Fix them. Get used to making corrections clearly on your page, because that's what you will do the day of the test.

PRACTICE ESSAYS ANSWERS AND EXPLANATIONS

Prompt 1 Sample Response: *If I could read only one book for the rest of my life, I would choose The Golden Compass by Philip Pullman. Although there are many incredible books in this world, none are as engaging or detailed as his.*

The Golden Compass focuses on a girl and her daemon, an animal representing the "other part" of herself. Throughout The Golden Compass and the two sequels, Pullman creates a world that feels real. He describes the characters so well that you care about them and become emotionally attached. The writing is so good that it's almost impossible to put the book down.

Pullman also uses a lot of details to make his books interesting. Instead of just telling the reader the color of someone's daemon, he describes it as "autumn-colored." His descriptions of the daemons' different forms help you really understand how those forms reflect their peoples' characters. Throughout the book, he describes the characters so well that you feel like they are your own friends or family members. Because of these details, every minute of the story is fascinating.

When you finish The Golden Compass, you won't be able to wait to read The Subtle Knife. Pullman's writing is so interesting and descriptive that it's impossible to put down. Even if I read this book for the rest of my life, I would continue to find new things to love about it!

Prompt 2 Sample Response: *The pigeon flapped its wings weakly. "Calm down, Chester. You've flown a long way, and you need to rest." I took Chester in my arms and set him in his cage. As I fed and watered the tired bird, my thoughts drifted to the great battles in faraway Normandy.*

I was only 10 years old, so I couldn't join in the efforts to free France from the Germans. I had begged and pleaded with my father, but his answer was always the same—I was needed at home, to watch out for my mother and sisters. Britain had plenty of full grown men ready and willing to fight. I would be needed to help rebuild the country after the war.

Although I understood this in my head, my heart couldn't accept it. It felt so wrong to sit here safe and sound while so many brave men were out there risking their lives. When I told my mother of my feelings, she suggested another way that I could help.

"Pigeons are very special birds. They can fly hundreds of miles and always find their ways back home. In ancient times, they were used to carry messages between cities. You're too young to fight, but you can do your part to bring up troop morale by sending messages on the pigeon post. Getting a message from a citizen like you reminds these soldiers why they're fighting. It will help more than you can understand."

I was skeptical at first, but sending that first note over the English Channel and getting my first response from a real, live hero fighting to protect me changed my mind. I grew to love my birds and helping in my own small way.

Prompt 3 Sample Response: *If could have a superpower, I would choose flight. Having the ability to fly would improve my life in so many ways.*

For one thing, I could stop driving places. Why go through the hassle of fighting traffic or taking long, sometimes indirect routes to my destination? This would save my family a lot of money and also allow me to get to places more quickly. Imagine the look on my friends' faces when I FLY to our next party!

Flying would also be the ultimate escape. Have you ever looked out the window at a bird and imagined what it would be like if you could simply fly away too? From up in the sky, all of my problems would seem small and insignificant. It's very easy to get caught up in the humdrum of everyday life. Flying would help me clear my mind and put things in perspective.

Finally, flying would also give me a deeper appreciation of nature. I love to hike and explore different landscapes on foot. It's great to be able to examine things up close, but it would also be awesome to be able to "zoom out" and take in everything from a distance.

Flying may not be as flashy as super strength or heat vision, but these powers are so limited. You can do only a couple of special things with them. Flying, on the other hand, opens up entirely new worlds.

Prompt 4 Sample Response: *The moon rose blood red over the prairie. It was the middle of April, but still there was a chill in the air. The night, usually full of the chitter-chatter of insects and the coyotes the gentle lowing of cows, was eerily silent. Maybe the animals knew something I didn't. Maybe they knew it was better to stay at home tonight.*

I took a step forward, destroying the perfect silence. My destination was clear: California. The pictures of its sun-drenched beaches and palm trees were in stark contrast to the cold, barren prairie I trudged through.

I had left my home in West Virginia two months earlier. I just couldn't stand to be there anymore. Ever since I was a little kid, I had known that I wanted to be a movie star. "A movie star from West Virginia; right." That's what all my friends—and even my family—said to me. "Forget it, Dave. You have to be born into that kind of life. You don't have a chance. Just get a job here in town like everybody else and be happy."

Well, that just wasn't good enough for me. I wanted more. After years and years of being mocked for my dreams, I couldn't take it anymore. I ran away with no money in my pocket and only the clothes on my back. I figured I'd hitchhike my way out West, maybe hop a train, something— anything—to bring me closer to Hollywood.

Taking this detour through a deserted farm in Nebraska wasn't exactly part of this plan, but I took a deep breath, steadied my nerves, and kept plodding on. Every step brought me closer to California.

CHAPTER 10

Introduction to SSAT and ISEE Math

CHAPTER OBJECTIVES

With practice, this chapter will help you:

1. Apply the Kaplan 3-Step Method for Math

2. Pick Numbers and Backsolve when efficient to determine missing quantities

HOW TO APPROACH SSAT OR ISEE MATH QUESTIONS

Before we dive into the actual math on the SSAT/ISEE, take a step back and think about how to approach math problems in general. You've done math in school already. In all likelihood, you've already been exposed to most of the math concepts you'll see on your private school admissions test. So why do you need to approach SSAT or ISEE math differently than you approach any other math?

The answer is, it's not that you have to do the math *differently*; it's just that you have to do it *deliberately* and *efficiently*. You'll be under a lot of time pressure when you take your test, so you need to use your time well.

Ultimately, the best way to take control of your testing experience is to approach every math question the same way. This doesn't mean that the *strategies* or *math skills* you will use to answer SSAT or ISEE math questions will never change. Rather, it means that you'll use the same *process* to decide how to answer—or even whether to answer—each question.

Note that this chapter will focus on non-Quantitative Comparison math questions. For more information about ISEE Quantitative Comparisons, refer to Chapter 5.

Some people intuitively understand algebra. Others have a harder time with it. The same is true for geometry, word problems, etc. There's often more than one way to solve a question. The *best* method is the method that will get you the correct answer accurately and quickly. Focus on what works for you, not others.

If you're taking the SSAT, you should only guess if you can eliminate at least one answer choice. If you're taking the ISEE, however, then you should not leave any answers blank. There's no penalty for incorrect answers on the ISEE, so there is no harm in guessing.

When you do guess, be strategic about it. Eliminate as many answer choices as you can. Then, either make your best guess from the remaining choices or use a Letter of the Day—because all answer choices are equally likely, you should choose one of the four ISEE options or five SSAT options and use that letter any time you are unable to make a more educated guess. If you eliminate your Letter of the Day before you're ready to guess, just pick one of the remaining choices and move on. For example:

What is the greatest common factor of 95 and 114?

(A) 1

(B) 5

(C) 6

(D) 19

(E) 38

If you couldn't remember how to find the greatest common factor or were running out of time and wanted to save your time for other questions, you should be able to eliminate at least one answer choice pretty easily. Do you see which one?

Because all multiples of 5 end in 5 or 0, 5 cannot be a factor of 114. Therefore, choice B must be incorrect. Eliminate it and then guess, starting with the largest answer choice. For example, 38 divides evenly into 114, but $95 \div 38 = 2.5$. This means that you can eliminate choice E. Next, try 19, which divides evenly into both numbers, so it must be correct. Therefore, choice (D) is the correct answer.

KAPLAN 3-STEP METHOD FOR MATH

Step 1. Read through the question and decide when to answer it

Step 2. Answer the question by:

    a. Using math skills

    b. Backsolving

    c. Picking Numbers

    d. Guessing strategically

Step 3. Check that you answered the question

Step 1. Read through the question and decide when to answer it

Step 1 has two parts. Look at each one.

Read Through the Question

Okay, this may seem a little too obvious. Of course you're going to read the question; how else can you answer the question? In reality, however, this step isn't quite as obvious as it seems. The point here is that you need to read the entire question and figure out the goal before you start doing math. When you don't read carefully, it's incredibly easy to make careless mistakes. Consider the following question:

For what positive value of x does $\frac{4}{3} = \frac{x^2}{27}$?

(A) 3

(B) 6

(C) 12

(D) 18

(E) 36

It's crucial that you pay close attention to precisely what the question is asking. The question contains a classic trap that's very easy to fall into if you don't read it carefully. Did you notice how easy it would be to solve for x^2 instead of x? Yes, it would be careless, but it's easy to be careless when you're working quickly. Students who aren't reading through the question will incorrectly choose choice E, but the correct answer is choice (B).

There are other reasons to read the whole question before you start answering the question. One is that you may save yourself some work. If you start to answer too quickly, you may assume that a question is more difficult than it actually is. On the other hand, you might assume that it is *less* difficult than it actually is and skip a necessary step or two.

Another reason to read carefully before answering is that you most likely shouldn't answer every question on your first pass. Taking control of your test experience means deciding which questions to answer, which to save for later, and which to skip completely (unless you're taking the ISEE, in which case you should NEVER skip a question).

Decide When to Answer It

Each time you approach a new math question, you have the option of answering it immediately or putting it aside. You have to make a decision each time about how best to use your time. You have three options:

1. **If you can answer the question relatively quickly and efficiently, do it!** This is the best option.

2. **If you think you can answer it but that it will take you a long time, circle the number in your test booklet and go back to it later.** Remember that when you go back to the questions you have skipped the first time, you'll want to try your best to fill in an answer. Don't underestimate your ability to eliminate incorrect answers even when you don't know the correct one. Every time you rule out a incorrect answer choice, you increase your chances of guessing correctly.

3. **If you have no idea what to do, skip the question and circle it.** Save your time for the questions you *can* do. If you're taking the SSAT, make sure you leave these questions blank. If you're taking the ISEE, guess.

> **EXPERT TIP**
>
> When you skip a question, circle it in your test booklet so that it will be easy to spot if you have time to go back. At the five-minute warning, stop and make sure you haven't left any questions blank that you think you can answer.

Consider another question:

> Tamika, Becky, and Kym were investors in a new restaurant. Tamika and Becky each invested one-half as much as Kym invested. If the total investment made was $5,200, how much did Kym invest?

(A) $900

(B) $1,300

(C) $1,800

(D) $2,100

(E) $2,600

Different test takers will have different reactions to this question. Some students may quickly see the algebra—or the backdoor method for answering this question—and do the math. Others may see a word problem and want to run screaming from the room. This approach is not recommended. However, if you know that you habitually have difficulty with word problems that involve algebra, you may choose to save this question for later or make an educated guess.

Step 2. Answer the Question

You have four options when answering an ISEE or SSAT Math question. One option is to use straightforward math skills. For the above example, that means using algebra. Kym, Tamika, and Becky contributed a total of $5,200. You can represent this algebraically as $K + T + B = \$5,200$. Because Tamika and Becky each contributed half as much as Kym, you can represent these relationships as follows:

$$T = \frac{1}{2}K$$

$$B = \frac{1}{2}K$$

Now, substitute variables to solve the equation:

$$K + T + B = 5,200$$

$$K + \frac{1}{2}K + \frac{1}{2}K = 5,200$$

$$2K = 5,200$$

$$K = 2,600, \text{ choice (E)}$$

Check out the section on Backsolving for a look at answering this question using that strategy. This question was not a good candidate for Picking Numbers because it did not use variables and had simple numbers as the answer choices. Unlike the other three options for answering Math questions, however, knowing when to guess strategically depends on you. If you had no idea what to do to answer this question, consider guessing on the ISEE or leaving it blank on the SSAT. If you think you can answer it but need more time than you might have, circle it and save it for later. No matter what, when you choose to answer a question and work through Step 2, always look for the most efficient strategy.

Step 3. Check That You Answered the Question

Before you move on to the next question, make sure you answered the question you were asked. This question wants to know how much Kym invested. If you answer how much Tamika or Becky invested, you would choose the incorrect answer choice. Likewise, if you found the difference between two amounts or did any other unnecessary calculations, you might waste time or select the incorrect choice.

PICKING NUMBERS

Sometimes a Math question can appear more difficult than it actually is because it's general or abstract. You can make it more concrete—and easier—by temporarily substituting numbers for the variables. Picking Numbers can be extremely helpful when the answer choices to a Word Problem contain variables.

What is the value of $3a(2b + 2)$?

(A) $2b + 3a$

(B) $5ab + 2b$

(C) $5ab + 2a + 1$

(D) $6ab + 2a$

(E) $6ab + 6a$

You might find it easy to answer this question by working with algebraic expressions. The algebra in this question is pretty straightforward if you have experience with this level of math. According to the distributive property, $3a(2b + 2) = (3a)(2b) + (3a)(2) = 6ab + 6a$, which matches choice (E). However, if you struggle with algebra, encounter a more difficult Algebra question, or simply find that the algebraic method takes you a long time, you can approach these questions in another way.

To answer this question using Picking Numbers, pick simple numbers for a and b and plug them into the expression $3a(2b + 2)$. If $a = 2$ and $b = 3$, then $3a(2b + 2) = (3)(2)[2(3) + 2] = 6(6 + 2) = 48$. Now you know that if $a = 2$ and $b = 3$, you can determine that the expression equals 48.

Once you know this, you can substitute 2 for a and 3 for b in each of the answer choices and eliminate any answer choice that does not equal 48:

(A) $2b + 3a = 2(3) + 3(2) = 12$

(B) $5ab + 2b = 5(2)(3) + 2(3) = 36$

(C) $5ab + 2a + 1 = 5(2)(3) + 2(2) + 1 = 35$

(D) $6ab + 2a = 6(2)(3) + 2(2) = 40$

(E) $6ab + 6a = 6(2)(3) + 6(2) = 48$

Only choice (E) equals 48, so it is the correct answer.

If two or more answer choices had come out to 48, you would need to do a little more work. When more than one answer choice is left, you will pick new numbers for the variables (a and b), come up with a new value for the expression in the question stem, and then plug those numbers into the answer choices that came out the same the first time.

For practice, think about what you would do if both choices B and (E) had equaled 48: start by picking new numbers, such as $a = 3$ and $b = 4$. Using these values for a and b, you will find that the original expression $3a(2b + 2)$ would equal 90. When you plug in $a = 3$ and $b = 4$ into only choices B and (E), you will find that choice B would equal 68, while choice (E) would equal 90. Picking a second set of numbers will usually help you quickly choose between two or three remaining choices.

EXPERT TIP

When you use this strategy, be sure to pick small numbers that are easy to use, but you will usually want to avoid 0 or 1. Even though they might seem like small, easy to use numbers, they often give several "possibly correct" answers or act in unusual ways. On the other hand, if you're Picking Numbers and find yourself stuck between two or three choices, you might be able to use one of these "unusual numbers" to try to eliminate an incorrect choice.

Jenna is now x years old, and Amy is 3 years younger than Jenna. In terms of x, how old will Amy be in 4 years?

(A) $x - 1$

(B) x

(C) $x + 1$

(D) $x + 4$

(E) $2x + 1$

First, the algebraic solution: If Jenna is x years old, then Amy is $x - 3$ years old, because Amy is 3 years younger than Jenna. So, in 4 years, Amy will be $(x - 3) + 4$, or $x + 1$. The correct answer is choice (C).

Now, look at the Picking Numbers solution. Suppose that $x = 10$. This means Jenna is now 10 years old. Amy is now 7 years old because Amy is 3 years younger than Jenna. In 4 years, Amy will be 11. Once you have figured out how old Amy will be in 4 years based on the question stem, plug $x = 10$ into all of the answer choices and see which one(s) also equals 11. If an answer choice does not equal 11, eliminate it.

(A) $10 - 1 = 9$

(B) 10

(C) $10 + 1 = 11$

(D) $10 + 4 = 14$

(E) $2(10) + 1 = 21$

Only choice (C), $x + 1$, equals 11, so that is the correct answer choice.

The most important takeaway here is that you have to know your own strengths. Sometimes, you might be more efficient Picking Numbers than doing the straightforward math, even though another student you know is faster doing the straightforward math than Picking Numbers. In other cases, you might prefer Backsolving when another student uses strategic guessing. Nobody is checking your work; remember, the important part is choosing the correct answer as quickly and effectively as *you* can!

Picking Numbers with Percents

If you see a question that deals with percents, picking 100 is the easiest and quickest way to solve.

If the price of a share of stock decreases by 20 percent, and then by an additional 25 percent, by what percent has the price decreased from its original value?

(A) 40%

(B) 45%

(C) 50%

(D) 55%

(E) 60%

To efficiently Pick Numbers for this question, make the original price of the stock $100. The initial 20 percent decrease brings the price down to $80 (20 percent of 100 is 20). Twenty-five percent of 80, or one-quarter of $80, is $20, so the stock price is decreased by an additional $20, bringing the final price down to $60. Because the price dropped from $100 to $60, the total decrease is $40, or 40 percent of the original price. Choice (A) is the correct answer.

You may have been able to answer this question by setting up algebraic equations, but picking 100 is easier and faster here.

EXPERT TIP

Always pick the number 100 for percent questions. It will help you find the answer *quickly* and *accurately*.

BACKSOLVING

Backsolving is another tool to help you determine a math answer more quickly. What this means is that you can work backward from the answer choices. Backsolving will work only if your answer choices are all numbers (and they don't include variables).

Here's how it works. When answer choices are numbers—that is, not variables or words—you can expect them to be arranged from *small to large* or *large to small*. The test maker does not get creative with the order of the answer choices. Always start with the *middle* answer choice and plug it directly into the question. If it works, you're set. If it doesn't, you can usually determine whether to try a larger or smaller answer choice. Look at the following question and explanation.

Think back to the original example from this chapter and your options for Step 2.

> Tamika, Becky, and Kym were investors in a new restaurant. Tamika and Becky each invested one-half as much as Kym invested. If the total investment made was $5,200, how much did Kym invest?
>
> **(A)** $900
>
> **(B)** $1,300
>
> **(C)** $1,800
>
> **(D)** $2,100
>
> **(E)** $2,600

This question uses simple dollar amounts as the answer choices, so you can avoid the algebra using Backsolving. Start with choice C: If Kym invested $1,800 and Tamika and Becky each invested half of that ($900 each), then the total investment would have been $1,800 + $900 + $900 = $3,600. However, the question stem tells you that the total investment was $5,200, so the answer you came up with using choice C isn't large enough, and you can eliminate this choice. But wait—because choice C isn't large enough, that means that choices A and B will not be large enough either, so you can eliminate those as well.

Next, try either of the remaining choices to find the correct answer. To answer this question, use choice D: $2,100 + $1,050 + $1,050 = $4,200. This is still not enough money, which means that the answer must be choice (E). Think about it: if the numbers are arranged from small to large and the second-largest number gives you an answer that is too small, you know that the largest number must be correct; any of the other choices would be too small.

If you want to confirm this answer, simply substitute choice (E): $2,600 + $1,300 + $1,300 = $5,200, which is the correct total investment. Choice (E) is the correct answer.

Three consecutive multiples of 20 have a sum of 300. What is the middle of these numbers?

(A) 60

(B) 80

(C) 100

(D) 120

(E) 140

Begin with the middle answer choice. If 100 is the middle of the three numbers, the three numbers must be 120, 100, and 80, and 120 + 100 + 80 = 300. Choice (C) is correct.

LOGIC AND SSAT MATH

The SSAT includes some unique math question types that can require a combination of math and logic skills. While these questions can still fit into one of the main math content categories, answering these questions will require you to use both your math skills and logic.

One type of SSAT Math question that will require logic could appear as a vertical addition or subtraction question using letters instead of numbers. To answer these questions, you should look for repeating letters and think flexibly. Don't just think about the ones digits. Instead, move between the ones, tens, and hundreds (or more, depending on the question) and the three pieces of the equation. Look at a sample question.

In the addition of the three-digit numbers shown, the letters K, L, M, and N each represent a unique single digit. Which of the following could be the sum of $K + L + M + N$?

$$
\begin{array}{cccc}
 & M & L & N \\
+ & K & L & N \\
\hline
1 & 5 & 6 & 2 \\
\end{array}
$$

(A) 10

(B) 14

(C) 23

(D) 25

(E) 37

This is a question that can be solved with a little bit of arithmetic knowledge and a lot of logic. If you start by thinking about $N + N$, you know that N can either equal 1 ($1 + 1 = 2$) or 6 ($6 + 6 = 12$). N can only be a single digit, so $11 + 11 = 22$ would not work.

Next, think about $L + L$, which can either equal 6 or 16 (there's no way for $L + L$ to equal anything greater than 18 because L represents only one digit). If $N + N$ equals 12, then the tens digit would give us $L + L + 1 = 16$, which simplifies into $2L = 15$. Because L wouldn't be a whole number, we know that N must equal 1. Just like N, L can only be a single digit, so $L + L$ cannot equal 26, so we know that L must either equal 3 or 8.

Next, consider M, K, and 15. Either $L + L = 16$ and $M + K + 1 = 15$ or $L + L = 6$ and $M + K = 15$. If $L = 3$, then adding the four letters together will give you either $1 + 3 + 14$ or $1 + 3 + 15$ for a total of either 18 or 19. Because this doesn't match any of the answer choices, check $L = 8$. In this case, you have either $1 + 8 + 14$ or $1 + 8 + 15$ for a total of either 23 or 24. Because only 23 is an answer choice, you know that answer choice (C) is correct.

Another type of SSAT Math question that will require logic involves visualization. These questions might include tasks like tracing shapes or manipulating objects. Use any drawings provided by the test maker and create additional drawings whenever needed to eliminate incorrect choices and identify the correct answer as quickly as possible. Look at another sample question.

The figure below shows a P pentomino. Which rectangle can be completely covered by placing P pentominoes on the rectangle without overlapping?

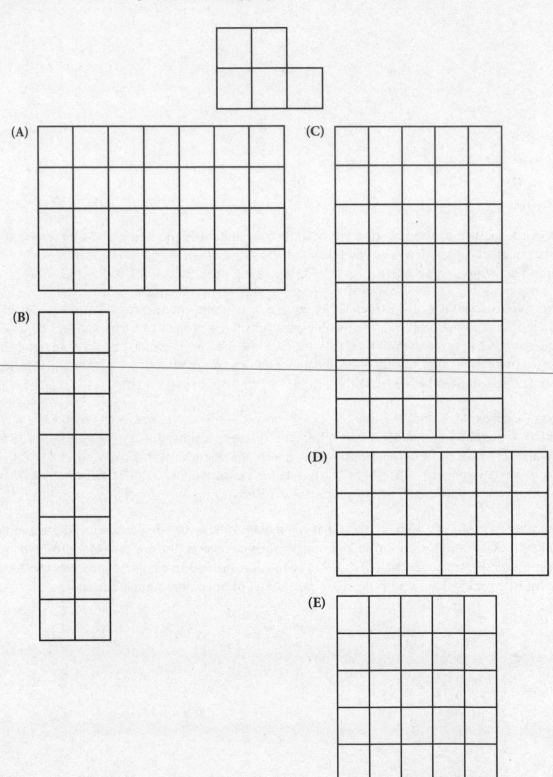

To answer these types of logic questions, draw your scratchwork directly in the test booklet.

(A)

(C)

(B)

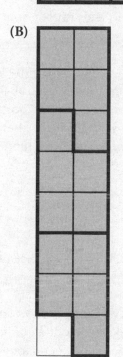

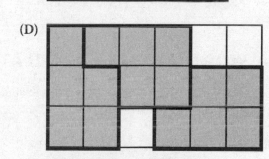

(D)

(E)

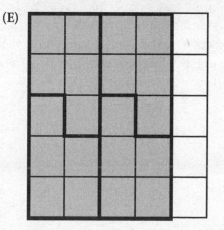

A third common question type includes drawings that can be made with a pencil. Some Geometry questions ask you to determine whether a figure can be drawn without lifting the pencil or retracing any part. There's a simple rule for determining this: in any given figure, if exactly zero or two points have an odd number of intersecting line segments and/or curves, it can be drawn without lifting the pencil or retracing.

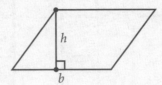

The figure above has two points that have an odd number of intersecting lines (three), so it can be drawn without lifting your pencil.

You probably noticed that these questions can be really time intensive to think through the logic and determine the correct answer. Rather than worrying about answering every one of these questions correctly, focus on getting the most SSAT Math questions correct as quickly as possible. As you work through the Kaplan 3-Step Method for Math, remember to skip questions that you either don't know how to solve or know will take you a long time to solve. If you have time, you can always go back.

A WORD ABOUT CALCULATORS

This is an easy one. You *cannot* use a calculator on either the SSAT or the ISEE. Leave your calculator home.

The rest of the Math chapters in this book deal with Math content review. Some of this content might be familiar; other parts may be less familiar or completely new. Take a look at all of it, but spend more time with the subjects that aren't as familiar to you. Whether or not you need to review a particular subject, make sure you complete a practice set for each chapter. There's no harm in extra practice, and answering questions related to your areas of strengths can help increase your confidence on Test Day.

CHAPTER 11

Word Problems

CHAPTER OBJECTIVES

With practice, this chapter will help you:

1. Translate word problems into mathematical terms

2. Describe strategies, such as Picking Numbers and Backsolving, for attacking word problems

3. Identify relevant information within a question with symbolism, formulas, or Roman numerals

INTRODUCTION TO WORD PROBLEMS

Word problems: two simple words that often evoke more fear and loathing than most other math concepts and question types combined. When the subject of word problems arises, you might envision the following nightmare:

> Two trains are loaded with equal amounts of rock salt and ball bearings. Train A leaves Frogboro at 10:00 a.m. carrying 62 passengers. Train B leaves Toadville at 11:30 a.m. carrying 104 passengers. If Train A is traveling at a speed of 85 mph and makes four stops, and Train B is traveling at an average speed of 86 mph and makes three stops, and the trains both arrive at Lizard Hollow at 4:30 p.m., what is the average weight of the passengers on Train B?

The good news is that you won't see anything this ugly. SSAT and ISEE word problems are pretty straightforward, and generally, all you have to do is translate the English to math and solve.

The bad news is that you can expect to see a lot of word problems on your test. Keep in mind that, while word problems are generally Algebra problems, they can contain other math concepts.

TRANSLATION

Many word problems seem tricky because it's hard to figure out what they're asking. It can be difficult to translate English into math. The following table lists some common words and phrases that turn up in word problems, along with their mathematical translations.

When you see:	Think:
sum, plus, more than, added to, combined total	+
minus, less than, difference between, decreased by	−
is, was, equals, is equivalent to, is the same as, adds up to	=
times, product, multiplied by, of, twice, double, triple	×
divided by, over, quotient, per, out of, into	÷
what, how much, how many, a number	x, n, etc.

Now, try translating the following five phrases from English to math.

English   **Math**

1. y is 5 more than x.   _____

2. r equals half of s.   _____

3. x is twice as great as y.   _____

4. 2 less than m is equal to n.   _____

5. The product of a and b is 3 more than their sum.   _____

Now, look at the correct answers below and determine how you did:

1. $y = x + 5$

2. $r = \dfrac{1}{2}s$ or $2r = s$

3. $x = 2y$

4. $n = m - 2$

5. $ab = (a + b) + 3$

EXPERT TIP

In some questions, the translation will be embedded within a "story." Don't be put off by the details of the scenario—it's the numbers that matter. Focus on the math and translate.

BACKDOOR STRATEGIES

Word problems are extraordinarily susceptible to backdoor strategies. Here's a quick recap of Kaplan's Picking Numbers and Backsolving strategies.

Picking Numbers

Step 1. Pick simple, easy-to-use numbers for each variable.

Step 2. Solve the problem using the numbers you pick.

Step 3. Substitute your numbers into each answer choice. The choice that gives you the same numerical solution you arrived at in step 2 is correct.

When using this strategy, here are a few things to remember:

- You can Pick Numbers when the answer choices contain variables.

- Pick easy numbers rather than realistic ones. Keep the numbers small and manageable.

- You must try all the answer choices. If more than one works, pick another set of numbers.

- Don't pick the same number for more than one variable.

- When picking a number for a remainder problem, add the remainder to the number you're dividing by.

- Always pick 100 for percent questions.

Review this example:

The average of four numbers is n. If three of the numbers are $n + 3$, $n + 5$, and $n - 2$, what is the value of the fourth number?

(A) $n - 6$

(B) $n - 4$

(C) n

(D) $n + 2$

(E) $n + 4$

Pick an easy number for n, such as 10. If the average of four numbers is 10, the sum of the four numbers is 40 ($4 \times 10 = 40$). If three of the numbers are $n + 3$, $n + 5$, and $n - 2$, then those three numbers are $10 + 3$, $10 + 5$, and $10 - 2$—13, 15, and 8. Then $13 + 15 + 8 = 36$. The sum of the four numbers must equal 40, so the remaining number is 4. If you substitute 10 for n in each of the answer choices, only choice (A) gives you 4.

Backsolving

When using the Backsolving strategy, keep in mind the following:

- You can Backsolve when the answer choices are only numbers.

- Always start with the middle answer choice, answer choice C.

- If the middle answer choice is not correct, you can usually eliminate two more choices simply by determining whether the value you're looking for must be higher or lower.

For example:

> Mike has n Hawaiian shirts, and Adam has three times as many Hawaiian shirts. If Adam gives Mike six Hawaiian shirts, both boys would have an equal number of Hawaiian shirts. How many Hawaiian shirts does Mike have?
>
> **(A)** 3
>
> **(B)** 6
>
> **(C)** 9
>
> **(D)** 15
>
> **(E)** 18

Start with the middle answer choice, 9. If Mike has 9 shirts, then Adam has three times as many, or 27. If Adam gives Mike 6 shirts, Adam now has 21 and Mike has 15. This is not equal, so choice C is not correct. Since Adam was left with too many shirts when Mike had 9, Mike must have fewer than 9, so choices C, D, and E are all incorrect. Next, try choice (B). If Mike has 6 shirts, then Adam has 18. If Adam gives Mike 6, then they both have 12 shirts. Bingo, choice (B) is correct.

SYMBOLISM WORD PROBLEMS

Word problems, by definition, require you to translate English to math. While some word problems contain an extra level of translation, *symbolism* word problems are like just any other word problem. First, translate the English and the symbols into math. Then, find the missing value. For example:

> Assume that the notation $\square(w, x, y, z)$ means "Divide the sum of w and x by y and multiply the result by z." What is the value of $\square(10, 4, 7, 8) + \square(2, 6, 4, 5)$?

EXPERT TIP
If you see a symbol you've never seen before, it's usually a safe bet that the test maker just made it up.

First, translate the English/symbols into math:

$$\square(w, x, y, z) \text{ means } \frac{w + x}{y} \times z$$

Next, substitute the given values into the expression:

$$\square(10, 4, 7, 8) + \square(2, 6, 4, 5) = \frac{10 + 4}{7} \times 8 + \frac{2 + 6}{4} \times 5$$

$$= 16 + 10$$

$$= 26$$

WORD PROBLEMS WITH FORMULAS

Some of the more difficult word problems may involve translations into mathematical formulas. For example, you might see questions dealing with averages, rates, or areas of geometric figures. Since the SSAT and ISEE does *not* provide formulas for you, you'll have to know these going in.

> If a truck travels at 50 miles per hour for $6\frac{1}{2}$ hours, how far will the truck travel?
>
> **(A)** 600 miles
>
> **(B)** 500 miles
>
> **(C)** 425 miles
>
> **(D)** 325 miles
>
> **(E)** 300 miles

To answer this question, you need to remember that distance = rate × time. Once you note the formula, you can just plug in the numbers:

$D = 50 \times 6.5$

$D = 325$ miles, choice (D)

Choice (D) is correct.

ROMAN NUMERAL WORD PROBLEMS

You might see a Roman numeral problem on your test. If you do, keep a few things in mind. In keeping with the problem style, lay them out using Roman numerals:

I. You don't have to work with the statements in the order they are given. Deal with them in whatever order is easiest for you.

II. If you find a statement that is true, eliminate all of the choices that *do NOT* include it.

III. If you find a statement that is false, eliminate all of the choices that *do* include it.

If the product of the positive numbers x and y is 20 and x is less than 4, which of the following must be true?

I. y is greater than 5.

II. The sum of x and y is greater than 10.

III. Twice the product of x and y is equal to 40.

(A) I only

(B) II only

(C) I and III only

(D) II and III only

(E) I, II, and III

You're told that $xy = 20$ and $x < 4$. Now, look at the statements. Statement I says that $y > 5$. Because $xy = 20$, $y = \frac{20}{x}$. When $x = 4$, $y = 5$. If you replace x with a smaller number than 4 in $\frac{20}{x}$, then $\frac{20}{x}$ which is y, will be greater than 5. Statement I is true, so it must be part of the correct answer. Eliminate choices B and D. Statement II says that $x + y > 10$. Try picking some values such that $xy = 20$ and $x < 4$. If $x = 3$, then $\frac{20}{x} = \frac{20}{3} = 6\frac{2}{3}$. The sum of x and y is not greater than 10. Statement II does not have to be true. It will not be part of the correct answer. Eliminate choice E. Statement III says that $2(xy) = 40$, or $2xy = 40$. The question stem says that $xy = 20$. Multiplying both sides of the equation $xy = 20$ by 2, you have that $2(xy) = 2(20)$, or $2xy = 40$. Statement III must be true. Choice (C) is correct.

Now, it's time to put all of your skills into play with some practice questions. Remember to translate English into math, consider the most efficient path, and keep your cool. Good luck!

PRACTICE QUESTIONS

1. During a sale, a bookstore sold $\frac{1}{2}$ of all its books in stock. On the following day, the bookstore sold 4,000 more books. Now, only $\frac{1}{10}$ of the books in stock before the sale are remaining in the store. How many books were in stock before the sale?

   (A) 8,000
   (B) 10,000
   (C) 12,000
   (D) 15,000
   (E) 20,000

2. Brad bought an MP3 player on sale at a 20% discount from its regular price of $120. If there is a 5% sales tax that is calculated on the sale price, how much did Brad pay?

   (A) $24.00
   (B) $91.20
   (C) $96.00
   (D) $100.80
   (E) $134.80

3. Sheila charges $25 per haircut during the week and $35 during the weekend. If Sheila usually schedules six haircuts per day and takes Sundays and Mondays off, how much money does she collect from clients in an average week excluding tips?

   (A) $150
   (B) $210
   (C) $600
   (D) $810
   (E) $960

4. The original price of a television decreases by 20 percent. By what percent must the discounted price increase to reach its original value?

   (A) 15%
   (B) 20%
   (C) 25%
   (D) 30%
   (E) 40%

5. Ed has $100 more than Robert. After Ed spends $20 on groceries, Ed has five times as much money as Robert. How much money does Robert have?

   (A) $20
   (B) $30
   (C) $40
   (D) $50
   (E) $120

6. A worker earns $15 per hour for the first 40 hours she works each week and one and a half times as much for every hour over 40 hours. If she earned $710 for one week's work, how many hours did she work?

   (A) 40
   (B) 42
   (C) 44
   (D) 45
   (E) 46

7. Liza has 40 less than three times the number of books that Janice has. If B is equal to the number of books that Janice has, which of the following expressions shows the total number of books that Liza and Janice have together?

    (A) $3B - 40$

    (B) $3B + 40$

    (C) $4B - 40$

    (D) $4B$

    (E) $4B + 40$

8. If $a @ b = \dfrac{ab}{a-b}$, which of the following does $3 @ 2$ equal?

    (A) $2 @ 3$

    (B) $6 @ 1$

    (C) $6 @ 2$

    (D) $6 @ 3$

    (E) $8 @ 4$

9. If William divides the amount of money he has by 5 and then adds \$8, the result will be \$20. If d is equal to the number of dollars that William has, which of the following equations shows this relationship?

    (A) $(d \div 8) + 5 = 20$

    (B) $(d \div 5) + 8 = 20$

    (C) $(d + 8) \div 5 = 20$

    (D) $(d + 5) \div 8 = 20$

    (E) $8(d + 5) = 20$

10. If a six-sided pencil with a trademark on one of its sides is rolled on a table, what is the probability that the side with the trademark is not touching the surface of the table when the pencil stops?

    (A) $\dfrac{1}{6}$

    (B) $\dfrac{1}{3}$

    (C) $\dfrac{1}{2}$

    (D) $\dfrac{2}{3}$

    (E) $\dfrac{5}{6}$

11. Yesterday, a store sold 8 times as many hats as it sold coats. It also sold 3 times as many sweaters as it sold coats. What could be the total number of hats, sweaters, and coats that were sold?

    (A) 16

    (B) 21

    (C) 25

    (D) 36

    (E) 54

12. Four hundred eighty-seven people are traveling by bus for a field trip. If each bus seats 48 people and all the buses are filled to capacity except one, how many people sit in the unfilled bus?

    (A) 37

    (B) 36

    (C) 12

    (D) 11

    (E) 7

13. Rose has finished $\frac{5}{6}$ of her novel after one week of reading. If she reads an additional tenth of the novel during the next two days, what part of the novel will she have read?

    (A) $\frac{1}{10}$

    (B) $\frac{7}{15}$

    (C) $\frac{4}{5}$

    (D) $\frac{14}{15}$

    (E) $\frac{29}{30}$

14. A farmer has $4\frac{2}{3}$ acres of land for growing corn and $2\frac{1}{2}$ times as many acres for growing wheat. How many acres does she have for wheat?

    (A) $2\frac{2}{3}$

    (B) $4\frac{1}{2}$

    (C) $8\frac{1}{6}$

    (D) $10\frac{1}{2}$

    (E) $11\frac{2}{3}$

15. Joyce baked 42 biscuits for her 12 guests. If 6 biscuits remain uneaten, what is the average number of biscuits that the guests ate?

    (A) 2

    (B) 3

    (C) 4

    (D) 6

    (E) 12

16. The average weight of Jake, Ken, and Larry is 60 kilograms. If Jake and Ken both weigh 50 kilograms, how much, in kilograms, does Larry weigh?

    (A) 40

    (B) 50

    (C) 60

    (D) 70

    (E) 80

17. If 3 added to 4 times a number is 11, then what is the number?

    (A) 1

    (B) 2

    (C) 3

    (D) 4

    (E) 5

18. The sum of 8 and a certain number is equal to 20 minus the same number. What is the number?

    (A) 2

    (B) 4

    (C) 6

    (D) 10

    (E) 14

19. Liz worked 3 hours less than twice as many hours as Rachel did. If R is the number of hours Rachel worked, which of the following expressions shows the total number of hours worked by Liz and Rachel together?

    (A) $2R - 3$

    (B) $2R + 3$

    (C) $3R - 3$

    (D) $3R + 3$

    (E) $4R - 2$

20. If the circumference of circle A is $h\pi$ units, what is the area of the circle in terms of h?

    (A) $h^2 r^2$

    (B) $\dfrac{\pi h^2}{4}$

    (C) $\dfrac{\pi h^2}{2}$

    (D) πh^2

    (E) $4\pi h^2$

21. If m does not equal 0 or 1 and $m\ddagger = \dfrac{m}{m^2 - m}$, what is the value of $(6\ddagger) - (-5\ddagger)$?

    (A) $\dfrac{1}{30}$

    (B) $\dfrac{1}{20}$

    (C) $\dfrac{1}{4}$

    (D) $\dfrac{11}{30}$

    (E) $\dfrac{9}{20}$

22. Five less than 3 times a certain number is equal to twice the original number plus 7. What is the original number?

    (A) 2

    (B) $2\dfrac{2}{5}$

    (C) 6

    (D) 11

    (E) 12

23. The volume of a sphere is $\dfrac{4}{3}\pi r^3$, where r is the radius. What is the volume of a sphere with a radius of 3?

    (A) 4π

    (B) 8π

    (C) 16π

    (D) 36π

    (E) 72π

PRACTICE QUESTIONS ANSWERS AND EXPLANATIONS

1. B

You can create an equation and solve for a variable to answer this question. Alternatively, you can Backsolve.

If choice C is correct, the bookstore had 12,000 books before the sale. They would have sold 6,000 the first day and 4,00 the second day. When you subtract $12,000 - 6,000 - 4,000$, you find that the bookstore would have 2,000 books left. Since $\frac{1}{10}$ of 12,000 is 1,200, choice C is too large. You can eliminate choices C, D, and E.

Try choice (B). If the bookstore started with 10,000 books, then they sold 5,000 the first day and 4,000 the second day. Therefore, $10,000 - 5,000 - 4,000 = 1,000$, so the bookstore would have 1,000 books left after the sale. Because $\frac{1}{10}$ of 10,000 is 1,000, choice (B) is correct.

2. D

This problem needs to be done in several steps. First, find out the sale price of the MP3 player. The discount was 20%, so the sale price is 80% of the original price:

$$\text{percent} \times \text{whole} = \text{part}$$

$$80\% \times \$120 = \text{sale price}$$

$$0.80 \times \$120 = \text{sale price}$$

$$\$96 = \text{sale price}$$

Now, figure out how much tax Brad paid. The tax was 5% of the sale price:

$$\text{percent} \times \text{whole} = \text{part}$$

$$5\% \times \$96 = \text{tax}$$

$$0.05 \times \$96 = \text{tax}$$

$$\$4.80 = \text{tax}$$

Don't forget to add the tax to the sale price:

$$\$96.00 + \$4.80 = \$100.80$$

Answer choice (D) is correct.

3. D

Each weekday, Sheila earns $\$25 \times 6$ haircuts $= \$150$. Each Saturday, Sheila earns $\$35 \times 6$ haircuts $= \$210$. In four weekdays, she earns $4 \times \$150 = \$600$. In one Saturday, she earns $\$210$. So in four weekdays plus one Saturday, she earns $\$600 + \$210$, or $\$810$. Choice (D) is correct.

4. C

It is important to note that while the value of the television decreases and increases by the same dollar amount, it doesn't increase and decrease by the same percent. Pick $100 for the price of the television. If the price decreases by 20%, and since 20% of $100 is $20, the price decreases by $20. The new price is $100 − $20, or $80. For the new price to reach the original price ($100), it must be increased by $20. Twenty dollars is $\frac{1}{4}$ of 80, or 25% of $80. The new price must be increased by 25%, choice (C).

5. A

Translate the English in this question into two math equations. Let E be the amount Ed has and R be the amount Robert has. "Ed has $100 more than Robert" becomes $E = R + 100$. "Ed spends $20" means he'll have $20 less, or $E - 20$. "Five times as much as Robert" becomes $5R$. Therefore, $E - 20 = 5R$. Substitute $R + 100$ for E in the second equation and solve for R:

$$(R + 100) - 20 = 5R$$

$$R + 80 = 5R$$

$$80 = 4R$$

$$20 = R$$

Robert has $20, so choice (A) is correct.

6. E

Use Backsolving to see which answer choice gives you a total of $710. Keep in mind that the worker will make $\frac{3}{2}$ times $15 = \$22.50$ per hour for any hours worked over 40.

As usual, the answer choices are in numerical order, start with choice C. If she works for 44 hours, she earns $15 per hour for the first 40 hours, or $600, and $22.50 per hour for the extra 4, or $90. If choice C is correct, she earned $600 + \$90 = \$690$. This isn't enough, so you can eliminate choices C, B, and A.

Try out choice D. The worker still earns $600 for the first 40 hours, but now she earns one extra hour of overtime. Because $690 + \$22.50 = \$712.50$, choice D is also too small, so choice (E) must be correct.

7. C

This is a straightforward translation problem. You're told that Janice has B books. Liza has 40 less than three times the number of books Janice has, which you can translate as $L = 3B - 40$. The total number they have together equals $B + (3B - 40)$, which simplifies to $4B - 40$.

8. D

Substitute the given values. Then, try the values in each answer choice until you find the one that produces the same result. Substituting 3 and 2 yields $\frac{(3)(2)}{3-2} = \frac{6}{1} = 6$. This means you're looking for the answer choice that produces a result of 6. Try each one:

Choice A: $2 @ 3 = \frac{(2)(3)}{2-3} = \frac{6}{-1} = -6$

Choice B: $6 @ 1 = \frac{(6)(1)}{6-1} = \frac{6}{5}$

Choice C: $6 @ 2 = \frac{(6)(2)}{6-2} = \frac{12}{4} = 3$

Choice (D): $6 @ 3 = \frac{(6)(3)}{6-3} = \frac{18}{3} = 6$

If you try Choice E: $8 @ 4 = \frac{(8)(4)}{8-4} = \frac{32}{4} = 8$

Only choice (D) equals the value of 3 @ 2 and is therefore correct.

9. B

This problem asks you to translate English sentences into math. Use the variable from the answer choices to represent William's amount of money: d. This amount is divided by 5: $(d \div 5)$. Add 8 dollars: $(d \div 5) + 8$. This will all equal the result: $20.

When you put it all together, the final equation is $(d \div 5) + 8 = 20$. This matches choice (B). You may have noted that since division comes before addition in the order of operations, the parentheses aren't really necessary, but ultimately, you must choose from one of the answer choices provided.

10. E

The probability of an event happening is the ratio of the number of desired outcomes to the number of possible outcomes, or:

$$\text{probability} = \frac{\text{number of desirable outcomes}}{\text{number of possble outcomes}}$$

One side of the pencil has the trademark on it, and the other five sides are blank. When any one of the five blank sides is touching the surface of the table, the marked side cannot be touching the table. So there are five different ways for the pencil to lie on the table without the marked side touching the surface. The total number of possible sides for the pencil to lie on is six. The probability that the trademark will not be touching the surface of the table when the pencil stops rolling is $\frac{5}{6}$, choice (E).

11. D

Let c be the number of coats that the store sold yesterday. Keep in mind that c must be an integer. The store sold 8 times the number of hats as coats yesterday. So the store sold $8c$ hats. The store sold 3 times the number of sweaters as coats yesterday. So the store sold $3c$ sweaters. The total number of hats, sweaters, and coats that the store sold was $8c + 3c + c = 12c$. Because c is an integer, $12c$ must be a multiple of 12. Only choice (D), 36, is a multiple of 12 ($36 = 3 \times 12$).

12. E

There are 487 people traveling, and each bus holds 48 people. Therefore, $487 \div 48 = 10$ with a remainder of 7. This means that 10 buses are full and 7 people remain to ride in the unfilled bus. Choice (E) is correct.

13. D

Rose read $\frac{5}{6}$ of the novel and plans to read another $\frac{1}{10}$, which will result in her having read $\frac{5}{6} + \frac{1}{10}$ of the novel. Add these two fractions using 30 as the common denominator: $\frac{5}{6} + \frac{1}{10} = \frac{25}{30} + \frac{3}{30} = \frac{28}{30} = \frac{14}{15}$. Choice (D) is correct.

14. E

The farmer has $2\frac{1}{2} \times 4\frac{2}{3}$ acres for growing wheat. Change these mixed numbers to improper fractions in order to multiply:

$$\frac{5}{\overset{}{\underset{1}{2}}} \times \frac{\overset{7}{14}}{3} = \frac{35}{3} = 11\frac{2}{3} \text{ acres}$$

Choice (E) is correct.

15. B

If 6 biscuits remain, $42 - 6 = 36$ were eaten by the 12 guests. Substitute this into the average formula:

$$\text{average} = \frac{\text{sum of the terms}}{\text{number of the terms}}$$

Therefore, the average number of biscuits eaten by the guests is $\frac{36}{12} = 3$. Choice (B) is correct.

16. E

Use the average formula to figure out Larry's weight. The average weight is 60 and there are three people altogether.

$$\text{average} = \frac{\text{sum of the terms}}{\text{number of the terms}}$$
$$60 = \frac{\text{total weight}}{3}$$
$$60 \times 3 = \text{total weight}$$
$$180 = \text{total weight}$$

Jake and Ken each weigh 50 kilograms, so $50 + 50 +$ Larry's weight $= 180$ kilograms. Larry must weigh 80 kilograms, so choice (E) is correct.

17. B

Let the number be n. Translating gives you $3 + 4n = 11$. Therefore, $4n = 8$ and $n = 2$. Choice (B) is correct.

18. C

Translate from English to math. The sum of 8 and b is $8 + b$. The question states that this is equal to 20 minus the same number, or $20 - b$. So your equation is $8 + b = 20 - b$, and you can solve for b:

$$8 + b = 20 - b$$
$$8 + 2b = 20$$
$$2b = 12$$
$$b = 6$$

Choice (C) is correct.

19. C

Rachel worked R hours, and Liz worked 3 hours less than twice as many hours as Rachel, or $2R - 3$. Add these expressions to find the total number of hours worked by Liz and Rachel together:

$$R + 2R - 3 = 3R - 3$$

Choice (C) is correct.

20. B

The circumference of a circle is π times diameter, so a circumference of $h\pi$ means the diameter is equal to h. The area of a circle is πr^2, so find the the radius by dividing the diameter by 2: $\frac{h}{2}$. Substitute $\frac{h}{2}$ into the area formula:

$$\pi\left(\frac{h}{2}\right)^2 = \pi\left(\frac{h^2}{4}\right) = \frac{h^2\pi}{4}$$

Choice (B) is correct.

21. D

Substitute $(6‡) - (-5‡)$ into the expression that defines the symbol ‡:

$$(6‡) - (-5)‡ = \frac{6}{6^2 - 6} - \frac{-5}{(-5)^2 - (-5)}$$
$$= \frac{6}{36 - 6} - \frac{-5}{25 + 5}$$
$$= \frac{6}{30} - \frac{-5}{30}$$
$$= \frac{6}{30} + \frac{5}{30}$$
$$= \frac{11}{30}$$

At two points in your calculation, it is crucial to remember that subtracting a negative is the same as adding a positive. Choice (D) is correct.

22. E

Call the unknown number x. Five less than 3 times the number, or $3x - 5$, equals twice the original number plus 7, or $2x + 7$. Write the equation $3x - 5 = 2x + 7$. Solve for x:

$$3x - 5 = 2x + 7$$
$$x - 5 = 7$$
$$x = 12$$

Choice (E) is correct.

23. D

Substitute the value of $r = 3$ into the formula and simplify:

$$\text{volume} = \frac{4}{3}\pi(3)^3$$
$$= \frac{4}{3}\pi(27)$$
$$= 36\pi$$

Choice (D) is correct.

CHAPTER 12

Arithmetic

CHAPTER OBJECTIVES

With practice, this chapter will help you:

1. Define arithmetic terms that may appear on the SSAT or ISEE

2. Demonstrate the order of operations

3. Add and subtract fractions and decimals

4. Apply rules of exponents to simplify expressions and to manipulate numbers written in scientific notation

5. Simplify numerical expressions that contain square roots and cube roots

DEFINITIONS

On the SSAT and ISEE, **arithmetic** means more than addition and subtraction. Arithmetic is the umbrella term for a wide range of math concepts, including **number properties, factors, divisibility, fractions, decimals, exponents**, and **radicals**. These concepts are summarized in your Math Reference at the end of the book. This section will go over these important concepts and give you a chance to practice questions dealing with these subjects.

Number Type	Definition	Examples
Integers	**Integers** are whole numbers including 0 and their opposites (negative whole numbers).	$-900, -3, 0, 1, 54$
Fractions	A **fraction** is a number that is written in the form $\frac{A}{B}$ where A is the numerator and B is the denominator.	$-\frac{5}{6}, -\frac{3}{17}, \frac{1}{2}, \frac{899}{901}$
Improper fractions	An **improper fraction** is a fraction whose value is greater than 1 (or less than -1).	$-\frac{65}{64}, \frac{9}{8}, \frac{57}{10}$
Mixed numbers	An improper fraction can be converted into a **mixed number**. A mixed number has an integer part and a fraction part.	$-1\frac{1}{64}, 1\frac{1}{8}, 5\frac{7}{10}$
Positive/Negative	Numbers greater than 0 are **positive numbers**; numbers less than 0 are **negative**. 0 is neither positive nor negative.	Positive: $\frac{7}{8}, 1, 5, 900$ Negative: $-64, -40, -11, -\frac{6}{13}$
Even/Odd	An **even number** is an integer that is a multiple of 2. Even numbers end in 0, 2, 4, 6, or 8. An **odd number** is an integer that is not a multiple of 2. Odd numbers end in 1, 3, 5, 7, or 9.	Even numbers: $-8, -2, 0, 4, 12, 188$ Odd numbers: $-17, -1, 3, 9, 457$
Prime numbers	A **prime number** is an integer greater than 1 that has exactly two factors: 1 and itself. 2 is the only even prime number.	2, 3, 5, 7, 11, 59, 83
Composite numbers	A **composite number** is an integer greater than 1 that has more than two factors.	12, 35, 84
Consecutive numbers	**Consecutive numbers** are numbers that follow one after another, in order, without skipping any.	Consecutive integers: 3, 4, 5, 6 Consecutive even integers: 2, 4, 6, 8, 10 Consecutive multiples of 9: 9, 18, 27, 36
Factors	A **factor** is a positive integer that divides evenly into a given number with no remainder.	The complete list of factors of 12: 1, 2, 3, 4, 6, 12
Multiples	A **multiple** is a number that a given number will divide into with no remainder.	Some multiples of 12: 0, 12, 24, 60

Odds and Evens

There are a few things to remember when you're dealing with odd and even numbers:

Even $\pm$ Even = Even

Even $\pm$ Odd = Odd

Odd $\pm$ Odd = Even

Even $\times$ Even = Even

Even $\times$ Odd = Even

Odd $\times$ Odd = Odd

Positives and Negatives

You may not see many problems that focus specifically on positives and negatives, but you must know the basics because these concepts will show up as part of harder problems.

Positives/Negatives Facts

Negative $\times$ Negative $-$ Positive

Negative $\div$ Negative = Positive

Positive $\times$ Negative = Negative

Positive $\div$ Negative = Negative

Positive $\times$ Positive = Positive

Positive $\div$ Positive = Positive

To **add** any two integers with the **same sign**, keep the sign and add the integers. Here are two examples:

$$(-3) + (-8) = -11$$

$$9 + 12 = 21$$

To **add** any two integers with **opposite signs**, keep the sign of the integer farther from zero, then subtract the integers, ignoring the signs. Here are two examples:

$$3 + (-8) = -(8 - 3) = -5$$

$$-9 + 12 = +(12 - 9) = 3$$

To **subtract** two integers, change the subtraction sign to addition, then change the sign of the number being subtracted to its opposite. Here are two examples:

$$(3) - (-8) = 3 + (+8) = 11$$

$$-9 - 12 = -9 + (-12) = -21$$

Multiplying and **dividing** positives and negatives is like all other multiplication and division, with one catch. To figure out whether your answer is positive or negative, count the number of negatives you had to start. If you had an odd number of negatives, the answer is negative. If you had an even number of negatives, the answer is positive. For example:

$$6 \times (-4) = -24 \text{ (1 negative} \rightarrow \text{negative product)}$$

$$(-6) \times (-4) = 24 \text{ (2 negatives} \rightarrow \text{positive product)}$$

$$(-1) \times (-6) \times (-4) = -24 \text{ (3 negatives} \rightarrow \text{negative product)}$$

Similarly:

$$-24 \div 6 = -4 \text{ (1 negative} \rightarrow \text{negative quotient)}$$

$$-24 \div (-4) = 6 \text{ (2 negatives} \rightarrow \text{positive quotient)}$$

Absolute Value

To find the **absolute value** of a number, simply find the number's distance from zero on a number line. Because distance cannot be negative, the absolute value of a number will always be greater than or equal to zero. For example:

$$|4| = 4 \text{ (because 4 is four units from zero)}$$

$$|-4| = 4 \text{ (because } -4 \text{ is four units from zero)}$$

When absolute value expressions contain different arithmetic operations, perform the operation inside the bars first and then find the absolute value of the result. For example:

$$|-6 + 4| = |-2| = 2$$

$$|(-6) \times 4| = |-24| = 24$$

Factors and Multiples

To find the **prime factorization** of a number, keep factoring it until you are left with only prime numbers. Here is one way to find the prime factorization of 168:

$$168 = 4 \times 42$$
$$= 4 \times 6 \times 7$$
$$= 2 \times 2 \times 2 \times 3 \times 7$$

To find the **greatest common factor (GCF)** of two integers, break each integer into its prime factorization and multiply all prime factors they have in common. If you're looking for the GCF of 40 and 140, first identify the prime factors of each integer:

$$40 = 4 \times 10$$
$$= 2 \times 2 \times 2 \times 5$$

$$140 = 10 \times 14$$
$$= 2 \times 5 \times 2 \times 7$$
$$= 2 \times 2 \times 5 \times 7$$

Next, see what prime factors the two numbers have in common and then multiply these common factors. Both integers share two 2s and one 5, so the GCF is $2 \times 2 \times 5$, or 20.

If you need to find a **common multiple** of two integers, you can always multiply them. However, you can use prime factors to find the **least common multiple (LCM)**. To do this, multiply all of the prime factors of each integer the most amount of times as they appear. This may sound confusing, but it's easier in practice. Take a look at the example to see how it works:

Find a common multiple of 20 and 16: $20 \times 16 = 320$

Although 320 is a common multiple of 20 and 16, it is not the least common multiple.

Find the LCM of 20 and 16: $20 = 2 \times 2 \times 5$

$$16 = 2 \times 2 \times 2 \times 2$$
$$= 2 \times 2 \times 2 \times 2 \times 5 = 80$$

Note that there are four factors of 2 in the LCM because there were four factors of 2 in 16, and that's the largest number of 2s present in either number. The lowest common multiple of 20 and 16 is 80.

THE ORDER OF OPERATIONS

There is a specific order in which arithmetic operations must be performed:

1. **Parentheses:** Simplify all operations inside parentheses first.

2. **Exponents:** Simplify any exponential expressions.

3. **Multiplication and Division:** Perform all multiplications and divisions as they occur in the problem from left to right.

4. **Addition and Subtraction:** Perform all additions and subtractions as they occur in the problem from left to right.

An easy way to help you remember this order is to use the mnemonic "Please Excuse My Dear Aunt Sally" (or **PEMDAS**). This phrase uses the first letter of each operation in the order in which it is to be performed. For example:

$$(3 + 5)^2 - 7 + 4 = (8)^2 - 7 + 4$$
$$= 64 - 7 + 4$$
$$= 57 + 4$$
$$= 61$$

RULES FOR DIVISIBILITY

If you've forgotten—or never learned—divisibility rules, spend a little time with this chart. Even if you remember the rules, take a moment to refresh your memory. Remember, there are no easy divisibility rules for 7 and 8.

Divisible by	The Rule	Example: 558...
2	The last digit is even.	IS a multiple of 2 because 8 is even.
3	The sum of the digits is a multiple of 3.	IS a multiple of 3 because $5 + 5 + 8 = 18$, which is a multiple of 3.
4	The last two digits comprise a two-digit multiple of 4.	is NOT a multiple of 4 because 58 is not a multiple of 4.
5	The last digit is 5 or 0.	is NOT a multiple of 5 because it doesn't end in 5 or 0.
6	The number is a multiple of both 2 and 3.	IS a multiple of 6 because it's an even number and a multiple of 3 ($5 + 5 + 8 = 18$ and 18 is a multiple of 3, so 558 is, too).
9	The sum of the digits is a multiple of 9.	IS a multiple of 9 because $5 + 5 + 8 = 18$, which is a multiple of 9.
10	The last digit is 0.	is NOT a multiple of 10 because it doesn't end in 0.

Hint: To test for 2, 4, 5, or 10, look at the last digit or two. To test for 3, 6, or 9, add all the digits.

FRACTIONS AND DECIMALS

Generally, there are eight operations you should feel comfortable performing with fractions:

1. Simplifying fractions

2. Converting a fraction to one with a different denominator

3. Adding fractions

4. Subtracting fractions

5. Multiplying fractions

6. Dividing fractions

7. Comparing fractions

8. Converting fractions to decimals and vice versa

To **simplify a fraction**, find the GCF of the numerator and denominator of the fraction, then divide both numerator and denominator by this quantity.

Simplify $\frac{18}{30}$.

The GCF of 18 and 30 is 6, so divide both 18 and 30 by 6:

$$\frac{18}{30} = \frac{18 \div 6}{30 \div 6} = \frac{3}{5}$$

To **convert a fraction to one with a different denominator**, multiply both numerator and denominator by the same quantity.

Convert $\frac{3}{7}$ into a fraction with a denominator of 28.

The math fact $7 \times 4 = 28$ means you can multiply the 3 and the 7 each by 4 to find an equivalent fraction with a denominator of 28:

$$\frac{3}{7} = \frac{3 \times 4}{7 \times 4} = \frac{12}{28}$$

To **add and subtract fractions with the same denominator**, keep the denominator the same and add or subtract the numerators. Simplify the result if possible.

Add.

$$\frac{1}{8} + \frac{3}{8} = \frac{4}{8} = \frac{1}{2}$$

To **add and subtract fractions with the different denominators**, find the LCM of the denominators, convert the fractions so they have this denominator, and then add or subtract and simplify.

Subtract:

$$\frac{7}{8} - \frac{5}{12} = \frac{21}{24} - \frac{10}{24} = \frac{11}{24}$$

To **multiply fractions**, multiply the numerators and multiply the denominators, then simplify the result. It is also possible to simplify the fractions before multiplying by canceling like factors from the numerators and denominators of the fractions.

Multiply:

$$\frac{11}{12} \times \frac{9}{22} = \frac{99}{264} \text{ OR } \times = \frac{\cancel{11}^1 \ \cancel{9}^3}{\cancel{12}_4 \ \cancel{22}_2} \frac{3}{8}$$

$$= \frac{99 \div 3}{264 \div 3}$$

$$= \frac{33 \div 11}{88 \div 11}$$

$$= \frac{3}{8}$$

To **divide fractions**, multiply the dividend (the first fraction) by the reciprocal of the divisor (the second fraction).

Divide:

$$\frac{8}{15} \div \frac{2}{3} = \frac{\cancel{8}^4}{\cancel{15}_5} \times \frac{\cancel{3}^1}{\cancel{2}_1} = \frac{4}{5}$$

To **compare fractions**, convert both fractions to the same denominator and compare the numerators or find the cross-products and compare:

Which is larger, $\frac{3}{4}$ or $\frac{10}{13}$?

Find the cross-products by multiplying the numerator of the first fraction by the denominator of the second, then multiplying the denominator of the first by the numerator of the second:

$$3 \times 13 \qquad 4 \times 10$$

$$39 \qquad\qquad 40$$

Because 39 is less than 40, the first fraction is less than the second. The second fraction is the larger fraction.

EXPERT TIP

Dividing by a fraction is the same as multiplying by its reciprocal.

To **convert a fraction to a decimal**, divide the denominator into the numerator.

To convert $\frac{8}{25}$ to a decimal, divide 25 into 8.00.

$$
\begin{array}{r}
.32 \\
25\overline{)8.00} \\
-75 \\
\hline
50 \\
-50 \\
\hline
0
\end{array}
$$

To **convert a decimal to a fraction**, use the place value of the digits in the decimal. Recall that beginning at the decimal point, the first place to the right is the tenths place, followed by the hundredths place, the thousandths place, the ten-thousandths place, the hundred-thousandths place, etc. For example:

Convert the decimal 0.4 into a fraction.

Because the last decimal place is the tenths place, the decimal is four-tenths, so the fraction is as well:

$$0.4 = \frac{4}{10} = \frac{2}{5}$$

Convert the decimal 0.825 into a fraction.

Because the last decimal place is the thousandths place, the decimal is eight hundred twenty-five thousandths, so the fraction is as well:

$$0.825 = \frac{825}{1,000}$$
$$= \frac{165}{200}$$
$$= \frac{33}{40}$$

EXPONENTS AND ROOTS

Exponents are the small raised numbers written to the upper right of a variable or number. They indicate the number of times that variable or number is to be used as a factor. On the SSAT or ISEE, you'll usually deal with numbers or variables that are squared, but you could see a few other concepts involving exponents. Here are some examples:

$$2^3 = 2 \times 2 \times 2 = 8$$

$$-(3^2) = -(3 \times 3) = -9$$

$$3(-2)^2 = 3[(-2)(-2)]$$
$$= 3(4)$$
$$= 12$$

A **square root** of a non-negative number is a number that, when multiplied by itself, produces the given quantity. The radical sign $\sqrt{}$ is used to represent the positive square root of a number, so $\sqrt{25} = 5$ because $5 \times 5 = 25$.

To **add** or **subtract** radicals, make sure the numbers under the radical sign are the same. If they are, you can add or subtract the coefficients outside the radical signs:

$$2\sqrt{2} + 3\sqrt{2} = 5\sqrt{2}$$

However, $\sqrt{2} + \sqrt{3}$ cannot be combined because the quantities inside the radical signs are not the same.

To **simplify** a radical, factor out the perfect square factor(s) from under the radical, simplify them, and put the result in front of the radical sign:

$$\sqrt{32} = \sqrt{16 \times 2} = \sqrt{16}\sqrt{2} = 4\sqrt{2}$$

To **multiply** or **divide** radicals, multiply (or divide) the coefficients outside the radical. Then, multiply (or divide) the numbers inside the radicals:

$$\sqrt{x} \times \sqrt{y} = \sqrt{xy}$$

$$3\sqrt{2} \times 4\sqrt{5} = 12\sqrt{10}$$

$$\frac{\sqrt{x}}{\sqrt{y}} = \sqrt{\frac{x}{y}}$$

$$\frac{12\sqrt{10}}{3\sqrt{2}} = 4\sqrt{5}$$

To **take the square root of a fraction**, break the fraction into two separate roots and take the square root of the numerator and the denominator:

$$\sqrt{\frac{16}{25}} = \frac{\sqrt{16}}{\sqrt{25}} = \frac{4}{5}$$

POWERS OF 10 AND SCIENTIFIC NOTATION

The exponent of a power of 10 indicates how many zeros the number would contain if it were written out. For example, $10^4 = 10,000$ (four zeros) because the product of four factors of 10 is equal to 10,000.

When multiplying a number by a power of 10, move the decimal point to the right the same number of places as the number of zeros in that power of 10:

$0.0123 \times 10^4 = 123$ The decimal point is moved to the right four places.

When dividing by a power of 10, move the decimal point to the left:

$43.21 \div 10^3 = 0.04321$ The decimal point is moved to the left three places.

Multiplying by a power with a negative exponent is the same as dividing by a power with a positive exponent. Therefore, when you multiply by a number with a positive exponent, move the decimal to the right. When you multiply by a number with a negative exponent, move the decimal to the left:

$$28.5 \times 10^{-2} = 28.5 \div 10^2$$
$$= 0.285$$
$$0.36 \div 10^{-4} = 0.36 \times 10^4$$
$$= 3,600$$

Scientific notation is commonly used in science and mathematics as a shorthand method for writing very large or very small numbers. A number is in scientific notation if it is in the form $a \times 10^n$, where $1 \leq |a| < 10$ and n is an integer.

To convert a number from **standard notation to scientific notation**, simply move the decimal point in the number to the right if the exponent on 10 is a positive number and to the left if the exponent is negative:

$4.23 \times 10^6 = 4,230,000$ The decimal point is moved to the right six places.

$9.6 \times 10^{-2} = 0.096$ The decimal point is moved to the left two places.

To convert a number from **scientific notation to standard notation**, find the decimal point in the number. If there is no decimal point, put one at the end of the number. Now move the decimal point to the right or to the left until the resulting quantity is a number whose absolute value is greater than or equal to 1, but less than 10. The number of places the decimal point moved indicates the exponent to be placed on the 10. The direction indicates the sign of the exponent; if the decimal point was moved to the left, the exponent will be positive, if the decimal point was moved to the right, the exponent will be negative.

$82,000,000,000 = 8.2 \times 10^{10}$ The decimal point moved from the end of 82,000,000,000 to the left 10 places.

$0.00004138 = 4.138 \times 10^{-5}$ The decimal point moved from the front of 0.00004138 to the right 5 places.

STRANGE SYMBOLISM AND TERMINOLOGY

Some questions will be confusing because you're unfamiliar with the math concept being tested. Others will seem confusing because the math has literally been made up just for the purposes of the test. The test makers make up math symbols and terminology to test your ability to deal with unfamiliar concepts.

These problems aren't as hard as they seem. When you see a strange symbol, the question stem will *always* indicate what the symbol means. And if you see strange terminology, it will *always* be defined. The problems are essentially about following directions, so don't panic when you see them. All you have to do is slow down, read the problem, and follow the directions. For example:

If $x <<>> y = \sqrt{x + y}$, what is $9 <<>> 16$?

All you have to do here is to substitute 9 and 16 for x and y into the defining equation:

$$9 <<>> 16 = \sqrt{9 + 16} = \sqrt{25} = 5$$

PRACTICE QUESTIONS

1. Which of the following integers is not even?

    (A) 330

    (B) 436

    (C) 752

    (D) 861

    (E) 974

2. What is the least prime number greater than 50?

    (A) 51

    (B) 53

    (C) 55

    (D) 57

    (E) 59

3. Which of the following integers is a multiple of 2?

    (A) 271

    (B) 357

    (C) 463

    (D) 599

    (E) 756

4. $\dfrac{15 \times 7 \times 3}{9 \times 5 \times 2} =$

    (A) $\dfrac{2}{7}$

    (B) $\dfrac{3}{5}$

    (C) $3\dfrac{1}{2}$

    (D) 7

    (E) $7\dfrac{1}{2}$

5. What is the least common multiple of 18 and 24?

    (A) 6

    (B) 54

    (C) 72

    (D) 96

    (E) 432

6. Which of the following numbers is a multiple of 3?

    (A) 115

    (B) 370

    (C) 465

    (D) 589

    (E) 890

7. $-6(3 - 4 \times 3) =$

    (A) -66

    (B) -54

    (C) -12

    (D) 18

    (E) 54

8. Which of the following numbers is a multiple of 10?

    (A) 10,005

    (B) 10,030

    (C) 10,101

    (D) 100,005

    (E) 101,101

9. Which of the following numbers is a multiple of both 5 and 2?

    (A) 1,005

    (B) 2,203

    (C) 2,342

    (D) 7,790

    (E) 9,821

10. Which of the following numbers is a multiple of both 3 and 10?

    (A) 103

    (B) 130

    (C) 210

    (D) 310

    (E) 460

11. Which of the following numbers is a multiple of 2, 3, and 5?

    (A) 165
    (B) 235
    (C) 350
    (D) 420
    (E) 532

12. Which of the following numbers is an even multiple of both 3 and 5?

    (A) 132
    (B) 160
    (C) 255
    (D) 358
    (E) 390

13. Professor Jones bought a large box of books. She gave 3 books to each student in her class, and there were no books left over. Which of the following could be the number of books she distributed?

    (A) 133
    (B) 143
    (C) 252
    (D) 271
    (E) 332

14. Two teams are having a contest. The prize is a box of candy that the members of the winning team will divide evenly. If team A wins, each player will get exactly 3 pieces of candy, and if team B wins, each player will get exactly 5 pieces. Which of the following could be the number of pieces of candy in the box?

    (A) 153
    (B) 325
    (C) 333
    (D) 425
    (E) 555

15. Three consecutive multiples of 4 have a sum of 60. What is the greatest of these numbers?

    (A) 8
    (B) 12
    (C) 16
    (D) 20
    (E) 24

16. Sheila cuts a 60-foot wire cable into equal strips of $\frac{4}{5}$ of a foot each. How many strips does she make?

    (A) 48
    (B) 51
    (C) 60
    (D) 70
    (E) 75

17. Which of the following numbers is NOT odd?

    (A) 349
    (B) 537
    (C) 735
    (D) 841
    (E) 918

18. Which of the following numbers could be the sum of two negative numbers?

    (A) 4
    (B) 2
    (C) 1
    (D) 0
    (E) −1

19. Which of the following is NOT a prime number?

    (A) 2
    (B) 7
    (C) 17
    (D) 87
    (E) 101

20. All of the following numbers could be the product of a negative integer and positive integer EXCEPT

   (A) 1
   (B) −1
   (C) −2
   (D) −4
   (E) −6

21. Susie and Dennis are training for a marathon. On Monday, they both run 3.2 miles. On Tuesday, Susie runs $5\frac{1}{5}$ miles and Dennis runs 3.6 miles. On Wednesday, Susie runs 4.8 miles and Dennis runs $2\frac{2}{5}$ miles. During those 3 days, how many more miles does Susie run than Dennis?

   (A) 4.8
   (B) 4
   (C) 3.2
   (D) 3
   (E) 2.4

22. Which of the following numbers is a multiple of 60?

   (A) 213
   (B) 350
   (C) 540
   (D) 666
   (E) 1,060

23. Two odd integers and one even integer are multiplied together. Which of the following numbers could be their product?

   (A) 1.5
   (B) 3
   (C) 6
   (D) 7.2
   (E) 15

24. If the number 9,899,399 is increased by 2,082, the result will be

   (A) 9,902,481
   (B) 9,901,481
   (C) 9,901,471
   (D) 9,900,481
   (E) 9,900,471

25. What is the sum of five consecutive integers if the middle integer is 13?

   (A) 55
   (B) 60
   (C) 65
   (D) 70
   (E) 75

26. $\dfrac{4x^5}{2x^2} =$

   (A) $2x^2$
   (B) $2x^3$
   (C) $2x^4$
   (D) $4x^2$
   (E) $4x^3$

27. $-2^3(1-2)^3 + (-2)^3 =$

   (A) −12
   (B) −4
   (C) 0
   (D) 4
   (E) 12

28. $a \triangle b = \dfrac{3a}{b}$. What is $\dfrac{14}{32} \triangle 1\frac{3}{4}$?

   (A) $\dfrac{1}{4}$
   (B) $\dfrac{1}{3}$
   (C) $\dfrac{1}{2}$
   (D) $\dfrac{3}{4}$
   (E) $\dfrac{49}{64}$

29. $\sqrt{1,500} =$

    (A) $10 + \sqrt{15}$

    (B) $10\sqrt{15}$

    (C) 25

    (D) $100 + \sqrt{15}$

    (E) $10\sqrt{150}$

30. $2(3 \times 2)^2 - 27(6 \div 2) + 3^2 =$

    (A) 72

    (B) 9

    (C) 3

    (D) 0

    (E) -24

31. Which of the following numbers is closest to the product of 48.9 × 21.2?

    (A) 10,000

    (B) 8,000

    (C) 1,000

    (D) 100

    (E) 70

32. $|16 - 25| + \sqrt{25 - 16} =$

    (A) -12

    (B) -6

    (C) 0

    (D) 6

    (E) 12

33. Which of the following numbers is 81,455 rounded to the nearest 100?

    (A) 81,000

    (B) 81,400

    (C) 81,450

    (D) 81,500

    (E) 82,000

34. A number is considered "blue" if the sum of its digits is equal to the product of its digits. Which of the following numbers is "blue"?

    (A) 111

    (B) 220

    (C) 321

    (D) 422

    (E) 521

35. To "fix" a number, you must perform the following four steps:

    Step 1: Raise the number to the third power.

    Step 2: Divide the result by 2.

    Step 3: Take the absolute value of the result of Step 2.

    Step 4: Round off this result to the nearest whole number.

    When you "fix" -3, you get

    (A) -13

    (B) 4

    (C) 5

    (D) 13

    (E) 14

36. When D is divided by 15, the result is 6 with a remainder of 2. What is the remainder when D is divided by 6?

    (A) 0

    (B) 1

    (C) 2

    (D) 3

    (E) 4

37. For any two numbers a and b, $a \, ? \, b = (a + b)$ $(a - b)$. For example, $10 \, ? \, 5 = (10 + 5)(10 - 5) = (15)(5) = 75$. The value of $7 \, ? \, 5$ is

(A) 2

(B) 12

(C) 24

(D) 36

(E) 48

38. What is the greatest integer less than $\frac{71}{6}$?

(A) 9

(B) 10

(C) 11

(D) 12

(E) 13

39. Which of the following fractions is NOT less than 0.25?

(A) $\frac{2}{9}$

(B) $\frac{3}{14}$

(C) $\frac{16}{64}$

(D) $\frac{19}{80}$

(E) $\frac{4}{17}$

40. $2,600 - 402 =$

(A) 2,208

(B) 2,202

(C) 2,198

(D) 2,192

(E) 2,098

41. All of the following products are equal EXCEPT

(A) $3 \times \frac{4}{6}$

(B) $6 \times \frac{4}{12}$

(C) $9 \times \frac{4}{18}$

(D) $12 \times \frac{4}{24}$

(E) $15 \times \frac{40}{30}$

42. Jim's fruit stand had 13 boxes of fruit, each a different kind. Yvonne bought 4 boxes and Jim's father gave him 9 more boxes of fruit to sell. Of these 9, three were kinds of fruit that the fruit stand now has. How many kinds of fruit does Jim now have at his fruit stand?

(A) 13

(B) 15

(C) 16

(D) 17

(E) 22

43. A piece of carpet is $18\frac{2}{3}$ yards long. The carpet needs to be cut into strips that are four feet long. How many strips can be cut from this one piece?

(A) 4

(B) 14

(C) 15

(D) 19

(E) 28

44. $0.0075 \times 200.00 =$

    (A) 0.015

    (B) 0.15

    (C) 1.5

    (D) 15

    (E) 150

45. Grace had 18 kinds of flowers in her garden. She planted 7 new flowers. Of these, 5 were kinds already growing in her garden. How many kinds of flowers are now growing in Grace's garden?

    (A) 16

    (B) 18

    (C) 20

    (D) 25

    (E) 30

46. $\frac{1}{9} \times 53 \times 18 \times \frac{1}{2} =$

    (A) 2

    (B) 9

    (C) 18

    (D) 53

    (E) 106

47. $0.005 \times 1.200 =$

    (A) 0.0006

    (B) 0.006

    (C) 0.06

    (D) 0.6

    (E) 6.0

48. A hiker started her hike in a valley that measured 6 meters below sea level. If three hours later she had climbed up 13 meters from her starting point, then she had climbed to

    (A) 19 meters below sea level.

    (B) 13 meters below sea level.

    (C) 6 meters below sea level.

    (D) 7 meters above sea level.

    (E) 19 meters above sea level.

49. $6\overline{)654} =$

    (A) $\frac{600}{6} + \frac{54}{6}$

    (B) $\frac{60}{6} + \frac{50}{6} + \frac{4}{6}$

    (C) $\frac{60}{6} + \frac{54}{6}$

    (D) $\frac{600}{6} + \frac{9}{6}$

    (E) $\frac{600}{6} \times \frac{50}{6} \times \frac{4}{6}$

50. Miss Tony wants balloons to decorate her kindergarten classroom for a party. Each package contains 12 balloons. If she wants 5 balloons at each of the 10 tables, how many packages should she buy?

    (A) 2

    (B) 3

    (C) 5

    (D) 8

    (E) 10

51. Molly had 30 different comic books. She lost 7 of them at a party and her friend gave her 12 new ones. Of these 12, 4 were copies of comic books that she already had. How many different comic books does Molly have now?

(A) 26

(B) 28

(C) 31

(D) 33

(E) 35

52. $75 - 16\frac{5}{21} =$

(A) $59\frac{16}{21}$

(B) $58\frac{3}{7}$

(C) $58\frac{16}{21}$

(D) $57\frac{3}{7}$

(E) $56\frac{16}{21}$

53. Sari has a strip of ribbon $2\frac{2}{5}$ inches long that she wants to cut into 6 equal-length pieces. How long will each piece be in inches?

(A) 0.20 inches

(B) 0.25 inches

(C) 0.30 inches

(D) 0.40 inches

(E) 0.50 inches

54. $0.004 \times 0.3 =$

(A) 12

(B) 1.2

(C) 0.12

(D) 0.012

(E) 0.0012

55. $2\frac{1}{5} + 8\frac{2}{5} + 3\frac{4}{5} =$

(A) 13.4

(B) 14.2

(C) 14.4

(D) 14.8

(E) 15.2

56. Which of the following products are equivalent?

I. $6 \times \frac{1}{2}$

II. $12 \times \frac{1}{4}$

III. $24 \times \frac{1}{6}$

(A) None

(B) I and II only

(C) I and III only

(D) II and III only

(E) I, II, and III

57. Julia bought four dozen marbles on sale for $1.44. What was the cost per marble?

(A) $0.01

(B) $0.02

(C) $0.03

(D) $0.04

(E) $0.05

58. $6\overline{)1,236} =$

(A) $\frac{1}{6} + \frac{2}{6} + \frac{3}{6} + \frac{6}{6}$

(B) $\frac{1,200}{6} + \frac{360}{6}$

(C) $\frac{12}{6} + \frac{36}{6}$

(D) $\frac{1,200}{6} + \frac{30}{6} + \frac{6}{6}$

(E) $\frac{1,200}{6} \times \frac{30}{6} \times \frac{6}{6}$

59. If $\frac{1}{2}$ the weight of a male elephant is about 6,000 pounds, the weight of three males in a herd that have the same weight can be found by multiplying 6,000 pounds by

    (A) $\frac{1}{3}$

    (B) $1\frac{1}{3}$

    (C) 2

    (D) 3

    (E) 6

60. If n is an odd number, which of the following expressions is always odd?

    (A) $2n + 4$

    (B) $3n + 2$

    (C) $3n + 5$

    (D) $5n + 5$

    (E) $5n + 7$

61. If x and y are integers, in which equation must x be negative?

    (A) $xy = -1$

    (B) $xy^2 = -1$

    (C) $x^2y = -1$

    (D) $x^2y^2 = 1$

    (E) $xy^2 = 1$

62. If x is an odd integer and y is an even integer, which of the following expressions MUST be odd?

    (A) $2x + y$

    (B) $2(x + y)$

    (C) $x^2 + y^2$

    (D) $xy + y$

    (E) $2x + y^2$

PRACTICE QUESTIONS ANSWERS AND EXPLANATIONS

1. D

The way to tell if an integer is even is to look at the last digit to the right (the ones digit). If that digit is 0 or divisible by 2, the number is even. Looking at the choices, only choice (D) ends in a number that isn't divisible by 2, so it is not even.

2. B

A prime number is an integer greater than 1 that is divisible only by itself and 1. Of the choices, only choices (B) and E are prime. You want the least prime number greater than 50, which makes choice (B) is correct. Using the divisibility rules would quickly show you that 51 and 57 are divisible by 3, while 55 is divisible by 5.

3. E

If the ones digit of a number is even (0, 2, 4, 6, or 8), the number is even. The only choice whose last digit is even is choice (E), 756.

4. C

Before you do the multiplication, see which common factors in the numerator and denominator can be canceled. Canceling a 3 from the 3 in the numerator and the 9 in the denominator leaves $\frac{15 \times 7 \times 1}{3 \times 5 \times 2}$. Canceling a 5 from the 15 in the numerator and the 5 in the denominator leaves $\frac{3 \times 7 \times 1}{3 \times 1 \times 2}$. Canceling the 3 in the numerator and the 3 in the denominator leaves $\frac{7 \times 1}{1 \times 2} = \frac{7}{2} = 3\frac{1}{2}$, choice (C).

5. C

The LCM of two integers is the product of their prime factors, each raised to the highest power with which it appears. The prime factorization of 18 is 2×3^2 and that of 24 is $2^3 \times 3$. So their LCM is $2^3 \times 3^2 = 8 \times 9 = 72$. You could also find their LCM by checking out the multiples of the larger integer until you find the one that's also a multiple of the smaller. Try the multiples of 24: 24? No. 48? No. 72? Yes, $72 = 4 \times 18$. Choice (C) is correct.

6. C

If a number is divisible by 3, the sum of its digits will be divisible by 3. Checking the answer choices, only choice (C), 465, works because $4 + 6 + 5 = 15$, which is divisible by 3.

7. E

According to PEMDAS, start in the parentheses. Perform multiplication before subtraction: $-6(3 - 12)$. When you simplify it further, you're left with -6×-9. Because a negative times a negative is a positive, the answer is 54, choice (E).

8. B

If a number is divisible by 10, its last digit will be a 0. Only choice (B) fits this criterion.

9. D

If a number is divisible by both 5 and 2, then it must also be divisible by 5×2, or 10. Because a number divisible by 10 must have a 0 as its last digit, choice (D) is correct.

10. C

For a number to be divisible by 3 and 10, it must satisfy the divisibility rules of both: its last digit must be 0, which automatically eliminates choice A, and the sum of its digits must be divisible by 3. Checking the rest of the answer choices, only choice (C) is also divisible by 3, because $2 + 1 + 0 = 3$.

11. D

For a number to be a multiple of both 2 and 5, it must also be a multiple of $2 \times 5 = 10$. This means it must have a 0 as its last digit, which eliminates all but choices C and (D). To be a multiple of 3, the number's digits must sum to a multiple of 3. Choice (D) is the only remaining choice that fits this requirement, because $4 + 2 + 0 = 6$.

12. E

Eliminate choice C because it is odd. If the number is divisible by 5, its last digit must be 5 or 0, so you can eliminate choices A and D. To be a multiple of 3, its digits must sum to a multiple of 3. When you check choice B, the digits add to $1 + 6 + 0 = 7$, and because 7 is not a multiple of 3, 160 is also not a multiple of 3. This leaves only 390, which is even, a multiple of 5, and a multiple of 3 ($3 + 9 + 0 = 12$, which is a multiple of 3). Choice (E) is correct.

13. C

If Professor Jones was able to distribute all the books in groups of 3 without any left over, the number of books she started with was divisible by 3. Whichever choice is divisible by 3 must therefore be correct. For a number to be divisible by 3, the sum of its digits must also be divisible by 3. Only choice (C) fits this requirement: $2 + 5 + 2 = 9$.

14. E

The question tells you that the number of pieces of candy in the box can be evenly divided by 3 and 5. So the correct answer has a 0 or 5 as its last digit, and the sum of its digits is divisible by 3. Eliminate choices A and C because they don't end in either 0 or 5. Of the remaining choices, only choice (E) is also divisible by 3, because $5 + 5 + 5 = 15$.

15. E

Use the answer choices to help find the solution. When Backsolving, start with the middle choice, because it will help you determine if the correct answer needs to be greater than or less than it. In this case, the middle choice is 16. The sum of 16 and two numbers that are each smaller than 16 has to be less than 3×16, or 48, so it is obviously too small. Choices A and B must also be too small, so you can eliminate all three. Try choice D. Again, 20 plus two numbers smaller than 20 will be less than 3×20, or 60, so choice D is not large enough. The only choice remaining is choice (E), 24, so it must be correct. To prove it, 24 plus the two preceding consecutive multiples of 4, which are 16 and 20, do indeed sum to 60: $16 + 20 + 24 = 60$.

16. E

When you're asked how many strips $\frac{4}{5}$ of a foot long can be cut from a 60-foot piece of wire, you're being asked how many times $\frac{4}{5}$ goes into 60, or what is $60 \div \frac{4}{5}$. Before you do the division, you can eliminate some unreasonable answer choices. Because $\frac{4}{5}$ is less than 1, $\frac{4}{5}$ must go into 60 more than 60 times. Eliminate choices A, B, and C because they're all less than or equal to 60. Dividing by a fraction is the same as multiplying by its reciprocal, so $60 \div \frac{4}{5} = 60 \times \frac{5}{4} = 75$. Choice (E) is correct.

17. E

If a number is odd, its last digit must be odd. Choice (E) ends in an even digit, so it is not odd.

18. E

The sum of two negative numbers is always negative. Choice (E) is the only negative choice, so it must be correct. If you're wondering how two negative numbers can add up to -1, remember that "number" doesn't necessarily mean "integer." It can also mean "fraction." For example, $\left(-\frac{1}{4}\right) + \left(-\frac{3}{4}\right) = -1$.

Always read the questions carefully to see what types of numbers are involved.

19. D

A prime number has only two different positive factors, 1 and itself. The numbers 2, 7, and 17 are easily identified as prime, so eliminate them. Use the divisibility rules to check out the two remaining choices. Both end in an odd number, so neither is divisible by 2. However, the digits of 87 sum to 15, which is a multiple of 3, so 87 is divisible by 3 and is therefore not prime. Choice (D) is correct.

20. A

The product of a positive integer and a negative integer is always negative. Choice (A) is positive, so it couldn't be the product of a negative and a positive.

21. B

The simplest way to answer this question is to convert the numbers so that they're all decimals or all fractions:

$$5\frac{1}{5} = 5\frac{2}{10} = 5.2$$

$$2\frac{2}{5} = 2\frac{4}{10} = 2.4$$

Now you can more easily compare the distances. On Monday, they ran the same number of miles. On Tuesday, Susie ran 5.2 miles and Dennis ran 3.6 miles. The difference between the two amounts is $5.2 - 3.6$, or 1.6, so on Tuesday Susie ran 1.6 more miles than Dennis did. On Wednesday, Susie ran 4.8 miles and Dennis ran 2.4. Then $4.8 - 2.4 = 2.4$, so on Wednesday Susie ran 2.4 miles more than Dennis. The total difference for the three days is $1.6 + 2.4 = 4.0$ more miles. Choice (B) is correct.

22. C

A number that is a multiple of 60 must also be a multiple of every factor of 60. The factors of 60 are 1, 2, 3, 4, 5, 6, 10, 12, 15, 20, 30, and 60. Choices A and D are not multiples of 10, so eliminate them. Choices B and E are not multiples of 3. The answer is 540, choice (C).

23. C

The product of three integers must be an integer, so eliminate choices A and D. A product of integers that has at least one even factor is even, so the product of two odd integers and one even integer must be even. The only even choice is 6, choice (C).

24. B

This question is simply asking for the sum of 9,899,399 and 2,082, which is 9,901,481, choice (B).

25. C

If the middle of five consecutive integers is 13, the first two are 11 and 12 and the last two are 14 and 15. You can find the sum by adding $11 + 12 + 13 + 14 + 15 = 65$. However, you could get to this answer more quickly if you knew that the middle term in a group of consecutive numbers is equal to the average of the group of numbers. In other words, the average of these five integers is 13, so their sum would be $13 \times 5 = 65$. Choice (C) is correct.

26. B

Simplify the expression by first simplifying the fraction $\frac{4}{2}$, which equals 2. Then, to divide the exponential expressions with the same base, subtract the exponents:

$$\frac{x^5}{x^2} = x^{5-2}$$

$$= x^3$$

$$\text{So } \frac{4x^5}{2x^2} = 2x^3$$

Choice (B) is correct.

27. C

A negative number raised to an odd power is negative. Using PEMDAS:

$$-2^3 (1-2)^3 + (-2)^3 = -8(-1)^3 + (-8)$$

$$= -8(-1) - 8$$

$$= 8 - 8$$

$$= 0$$

Choice (C) is correct.

28. D

Substitute the number on the left for a and the number on the right for b in the formula given for the strange symbol. First, convert b to an improper fraction: $\frac{7}{4}$. So the numerator is 3 times $\frac{14}{32}$, or (simplifying the fraction) 3 times $\frac{7}{16}$, or $\frac{21}{16}$. Dividing by $\frac{7}{4}$ is the same as multiplying by $\frac{4}{7}$. So you have $\frac{21}{16} \times \frac{4}{7} = \frac{3}{4} \times \frac{1}{1} = \frac{3}{4}$. Choice (D) is correct.

29. B

To simplify the square root of a large number, break the number down into two or more factors and write the number as the product of the square roots of those factors. This is especially useful when one of the factors is a perfect square. In this case, break 1,500 down into two factors: $1,500 = 15 \times 100$, and 100 is a perfect square. So $1,500 = \sqrt{100 \times 15} = \sqrt{100} \times \sqrt{15} = 10\sqrt{15}$. Choice (B) is correct.

30. D

This is a basic arithmetic question, and if you remember PEMDAS, it will be a breeze. PEMDAS tells you the order in which you need to do the different calculations: parentheses, exponents, multiplication and division, addition and subtraction. Take the expression and simplify the parts in that order:

$$2(3 \times 2)^2 - 27(6 \div 2) + 3^2$$

$$= 2(6)^2 - 27(3) + 3^2$$

$$= 2(36) - 27(3) + 9$$

$$= 72 - 81 + 9$$

$$= -9 + 9$$

$$= 0$$

Choice (D) is correct.

31. C

One way to answer this one would be to do the calculation. But this is really a test to see if you understand how to approximate a calculation by rounding off numbers. You could round off both numbers to the nearest whole number, but that wouldn't make the calculation much easier. Additionally, the answer choices you're choosing between are pretty far apart, so you can probably round both numbers to the nearest ten. Then 48.9 is close to 50, so round it up to 50. And 21.2 is close to 20, so round it down to 20. Now the multiplication is 50 × 20, or 1,000, which matches choice (C).

32. E

In terms of order of operations, treat absolute value bars and roots just like parentheses: simplify them first. In this case, first find the value of 16 − 25: 16 − 25 = −9. The absolute value of a number is its distance from zero on the number line. Now −9 is 9 units from zero, so:

$$|16 - 25| = |-9|$$
$$-9$$

Now, simplify $\sqrt{25 - 16}$. You have 25 − 16 = 9, so $\sqrt{25 - 16} = \sqrt{9}$. Because the radical sign is being used, simplify $\sqrt{9}$ by finding only the positive square root of 9, which is 3. The question becomes 9 + 3, which is 12, choice (E).

33. D

You're being asked whether 81,455 is closer to 81,400 or 81,500. Logically, because 81,455 is greater than 81,450 (the halfway point between 81,400 and 81,500), it is closer to 81,500. Formally, to round a number to the nearest hundred, consider the tens digit. If the tens digit is 5 or greater, round the hundreds digit up 1. If the tens digit is 4 or smaller, keep the same hundreds digit. Here the tens digit is 5, so round the hundreds digit up 1 from 4 to 5. To the nearest 100, 81,455 is rounded up to 81,500, choice (C).

34. C

In this type of question, you're given a rule or definition you've never heard before and then asked a question involving that new rule. In this example, you're given a definition of the term "blue": a number is "blue" if the sum of its digits is equal to the product of its digits. To find the answer, simply try each answer until you find the one that fits the definition of "blue." Only choice (C) is blue, because 3 + 2 + 1 = 3 × 2 × 1 = 6.

35. E

This is another invented rule question. This time all you have to do is follow directions. To "fix" −3, you first raise it to the third power: $(-3)^3 = -27$. Then divide this result by 2: −27 ÷ 2 = −13.5. Next, take the absolute value of −13.5, which is just 13.5. Finally, round off this result to the nearest integer: 13.5 rounds up to 14, choice (E).

36. C

One way to do this question is to realize that the remainder would have to be the same whether D were divided by 15 or by 6, because $D = 15 \times 6 + 2$. In other words, D is 2 more than a multiple of both 15 and 6. Therefore, the remainder is 2 regardless of whether D is divided by 15 or 6.

You can find the actual value of D by calculating:

$$D = 15 \times 6 + 2$$
$$= 90 + 2$$
$$= 92$$

Now, divide D by 6 to find the remainder: 92 ÷ 6 = 15, with a remainder of 2. Choice (C) is correct.

37. C

This is another Function question. The question stem defines the function [a and b, a ? $b = (a + b)(a − b)$], and you just need to substitute 7 for a and 5 for b. So 7 ? 5 = (7 + 5)(7 − 5) = (12)(2) = 24, choice (C).

38. C

Start by converting the improper fraction to a mixed number: $\frac{71}{6} = 11\frac{5}{6}$. Therefore, the greatest integer less than $\frac{71}{6}$ is 11. Choice (C) is correct.

39. C

The decimal 0.25 is equal to the fraction $\frac{1}{4}$, so the correct answer will be the only fraction that is NOT less than $\frac{1}{4}$. You can start with whatever fraction stands out to you, but choice (C) has even numbers in the numerator and denominator, so it will likely be the easiest to compare. When you simplify it, $\frac{16}{64}$ reduces to $\frac{1}{4}$; this is equal to, not less than, 0.25, so choice (C) is correct.

40. C

Don't try to save time by doing Arithmetic questions in your head. You'll avoid mistakes by taking the extra time to work them out on paper:

$$2,60\overset{9\ \ \cancel{10}}{\cancel{0}}\cancel{0}$$
$$\underline{-40\ 2}$$
$$2,19\ 8$$

Answer choice (C) is correct.

41. E

When a question uses the phrase "all of the following," you will have to evaluate each answer choice to find the correct answer. In other words, Backsolving is the only way to answer such a question. Be extremely careful with your arithmetic to avoid selecting the incorrect answer choice.

Take the product of all five answer choices and see which one is different:

Choice A: $3 \times \dfrac{4}{6} = \dfrac{4}{2} = 2$

Choice B: $6 \times \dfrac{4}{12} = \dfrac{4}{2} = 2$

Choice C: $9 \times \dfrac{4}{18} = \dfrac{4}{2} = 2$

Choice D: $12 \times \dfrac{4}{24} = \dfrac{4}{2} = 2$

Choice (E): $15 \times \dfrac{40}{30} = \dfrac{40}{2} = 20$

Choice (E) is the only one that doesn't match the other four answer choices, so it is the correct answer.

There is a quicker way to see the answer without having to go through all the calculation if you notice that the numerators of the fractions in A, B, C, and D are 4. Because the denominator is twice the whole number that is multiplied to the fraction, you can cross-reduce the fraction to $\dfrac{1}{2}$. Choice (E) has 40 in the numerator instead of 4, so it must be the only number that is not equal to the other answer choices.

42. B

While the math isn't difficult, be careful not to get the numbers mixed up. Jim started with 13 kinds of fruit. Yvonne bought 4, leaving him with $13 - 4 = 9$. Jim's

father adds 9 boxes to the stand for a total of $9 + 9 = 18$ boxes. However, three of these were kinds of fruit that Jim already had, so the fruit stand has a total of $18 - 3 = 15$ different kinds of fruit. Choice (B) is correct.

43. B

Always pay attention to the units of the numbers given in word problems; they are not always the same. You must put all values given in the question in the same units before proceeding.

One yard is equal to three feet. Start using straightforward math by converting the length of the carpet from yards to feet:

$$18\tfrac{2}{3} \text{ yards} = 18\tfrac{2}{3} \times 3 = 54 + \tfrac{6}{3} = 54 + 2 = 56 \text{ feet}$$

Now, find the number of times that 4 feet goes evenly into 56 feet:

$$\frac{56}{4} = 14$$

To Backsolve this question, you still have to get all units in terms of feet first. Once you've done that, you can multiply the answer choices by 4 feet to see which one gives you 56 feet:

If choice C is correct, then you can cut 15 strips that are 4 feet each: $15 \times 4 = 60$, which is too large. This means you can eliminate choices C, D, and E.

Now, try either choice A or (B). You might quickly notice that $4 \times 4 = 16$, which is definitely not enough. If you do multiply 14×4, you'll find that this equals 56 and makes choice (B) the correct answer.

44. C

Be careful with your decimal places whenever you multiply or divide decimal expressions. Multiplying decimal numbers less than 1 always means moving decimal places to the left. Multiply the non-zero numbers after the decimal place first, and then move the appropriate number of decimal places to the left:

$$0.0075 \times 200.00 = 1.5$$

Choice (C) is correct.

45. C

Some questions will sound confusing when you first read them. Don't be intimidated, and take them one step at a time. If Grace planted 7 flowers, and 5 of these were kinds that were already growing in her garden, then she planted $7 - 5 = 2$ new kinds of flowers. She had 18 kinds of flowers growing, so the 2 new kinds gave her $18 + 2 = 20$ kinds of flowers. Choice (C) is correct.

46. D

When a multiplication question includes fractions, see if you can simplify anything before doing the math:

$$\frac{1}{9} \times 53 \times 18 \times \frac{1}{2} = 53 \times 18 \times \frac{1}{18}$$

$$= 53 \times \frac{18}{18}$$

$$= 53 \times 1$$

Answer choice (D) is correct.

47. B

Use estimation to eliminate trap answer choices. When multiplying decimals, the number of significant digits (anything other than a trailing 0) after the decimal point before multiplying is the same as the number of digits after the decimal point in the product. For example:

$$5 \times 12 = 60$$

There are no significant digits after the decimal points before multiplying, so the decimal point falls after both digits in the product. However:

$$5 \times 1.2 = 6.0$$

Here, there is one significant digit after the decimal point before multiplying, so the product contains one digit after the decimal point. For this question:

$$0.005 \times 1.2 = 0.0060$$

There are four digits after the decimal before multiplying, so the product contains four digits after the decimal point. Choice (B) is correct.

48. D

This question requires you to use your knowledge of positive and negative numbers. The hiker started out 6 meters below sea level and hiked up 13 meters from

there. Don't fall into the trap of adding the two numbers together—6 meters below sea level is negative 6. Add 13 to -6 to get the hiker's final distance:

$$-6 + 13 = 7$$

Because 7 is positive, the hiker was 7 meters above sea level, choice (D).

49. A

Mastering less difficult concepts will allow you to maximize your score by giving you more time to answer difficult questions on Test Day.

$6\overline{)654}$ can also be written as $\frac{654}{6}$. As long as the denominator is the same, the numerator can be broken into any number of pieces:

$$\frac{654}{6} = \frac{600 + 54}{6} = \frac{600}{6} + \frac{54}{6}$$

Choice (A) is correct.

50. C

Use the white space in your test booklet on Test Day to minimize mistakes. Start by asking how many balloons Miss Tony needs. There are to be 5 balloons at each of the 10 tables, so she needs $5 \times 10 = 50$ total balloons. Divide this number by 12 to find the number of packages:

$$\frac{50}{12} = 4.\overline{16}$$

Because Miss Tony needs a little more than 4 packages, she will need to buy 5 packages of balloons. Choice (C) is correct.

51. C

When an Arithmetic question has multiple steps, do them one at a time. Molly started with 30 different comic books. She lost 7, leaving her with $30 - 7 = 23$. Her friend gave her 12, but 4 of them were copies of comic books she had, so she got $12 - 4 = 8$ new comic books from her friend. Therefore, Molly now has $23 + 8 = 31$ different comic books. Choice (C) is correct.

52. C

Remember the rules for working with fractions: to add or subtract, the fractions must have a common denominator.

First, make the mixed number an improper fraction:

$$16\frac{5}{21} = \frac{(16 \times 21) + 5}{21} = \frac{341}{21}$$

To subtract fractions, both fractions need to have the same denominator. Multiply the first value by $\frac{21}{21}$:

$$\frac{75}{1} \times \frac{21}{21} = \frac{1,575}{21}$$

Now, subtract:

$$\frac{1,575}{21} - \frac{341}{21} = \frac{1,234}{21}$$

Because the answer is in mixed number form, simplify the fraction:

$$\frac{1,234}{21} = 58\frac{16}{21}$$

There is another way to approach this question that might not take as long. Because you need common denominators in order to subtract fractions, think of a logical way to convert 75 into a mixed number with 21 as its denominator: 75 is the same as $74\frac{21}{21}$. Therefore, 74 and one whole is the same as 75. Subtraction should now be simple:

$$74\frac{21}{21} - 16\frac{5}{21} = 58\frac{16}{21}$$

Choice (C) is correct.

53. D

Some questions require you to convert between fractions and decimals to select the correct answer. First, convert the mixed fraction into an improper fraction:

$$2\frac{2}{5} \text{ inches} = \frac{(2 \times 5) + 2}{5} = \frac{12}{5}$$

Now, divide the fraction by 6:

$$\frac{\left(\frac{12}{5}\right) \text{ inches}}{6} = \frac{12}{30} = \frac{2}{5} \text{ inches}$$

$$\frac{2}{5} = \frac{4}{10} = 0.4 \text{ inches}$$

Choice (D) is the correct answer.

54. E

Converting from decimals to fractions can often make multiplying easier. Convert the decimals to fractions first:

$$0.004 = \frac{4}{1,000}$$

$$0.03 = \frac{3}{10}$$

Then multiply:

$$\frac{4}{1,000} \times \frac{3}{10} = \frac{12}{10,000} = 0.0012$$

Choice (E) is the correct answer.

55. C

To add or subtract fractions, you must find a common denominator. First, convert all the mixed fractions to complex fractions. Then add:

$$\frac{11}{5} + \frac{42}{5} + \frac{19}{5} = \frac{72}{5}$$

Look for ways to turn your final answer into a value that matches one of the answer choices.

$$\begin{array}{r} 14.4 \\ 5\overline{)72.0} \\ \underline{5} \\ 22 \\ \underline{20} \\ 20 \\ \underline{20} \end{array}$$

Choice (C) is correct.

56. B

On Roman numeral questions, predicting an answer before you look at the choices is a good way to avoid falling into answer traps. Multiply out each Roman numeral to determine which numbers equal the same product:

   I. $6 \times \frac{1}{2} = 3$

   II. $12 \times \frac{1}{4} = 3$

   III. $24 \times \frac{1}{6} = 4$

Only I and II are the same. Choice (B) is correct.

57. C

Make sure you read the question carefully and take your time with simple calculations to earn easy points on Test Day.

$$\frac{1.44}{(12)(4)} = \cos t \text{ per marble}$$

$$\frac{1.44}{48} = 0.03$$

Choice (C) is correct.

58. D

Mastering less difficult concepts will allow you to spend more time answering more difficult questions on Test Day. The division question in the stem can be arranged as a fraction (remember, a fraction line is the same as the division sign!). Therefore, the correct answer choice should match the fraction $\frac{1,236}{6}$, or 206:

Choice A: Adding these fractions together produces a combined fraction of $\frac{12}{6}$ or 2, which is incorrect.

Choice B: This fraction yields $\frac{1,560}{6}$ or 260, also incorrect.

Choice C: $\frac{48}{6} = 8$. This is incorrect.

Choice (D): The digits in these fractions' numerators sum to 1,236. This is correct!

Choice E: Multiplying the numerators yields $\frac{216,560}{216}$ or 1,000. This is incorrect.

Only choice (D) yields a correct answer.

59. E

Reading the question carefully is the first step to successfully translating from English to math. If 6,000 pounds is $\frac{1}{2}$ the weight of a male elephant, then the total weight must be 12,000 pounds. The weight of three males is $12,000 \times 3 = 36,000$. Because $6 \times 6 = 36$, it is also true that 36,000 is 6 times greater than 6,000, making choice (E) the correct answer.

60. B

You're told that n is odd, so you don't have to check to see what happens if n is even. You do have to try each answer to see which one represents an odd number. Suppose that $n = 3$ and replace all the n's with 3's:

Choice A: $2n + 4 = 2(3) + 4 = 6 + 4 = 10$. 10 is even.

Choice (B): $3n + 2 = 3(3) + 2 = 9 + 2 = 11$. 11 is odd, so choice (B) is the correct answer.

61. B

Try each answer choice until you find the correct one:

Choice A: If the product of two integers is negative, then one of the two integers must be negative. In this case, x could be negative, but it's possible that y is negative and x is positive. You are looking for an equation where x will always have to be negative.

Choice (B): The exponent here applies only to the y, not to the x. The square of any non-zero number is positive, so whatever y is, y^2 must be positive. (y is not zero; if it were, then the product xy^2 would also be zero.) Since y^2 is positive and the product of y^2 and x is negative, x must be negative. Choice (B) is the correct answer.

62. C

This is another "try each answer" question. You know that x is odd and y is even. Pick numbers to make each answer choice easier to think about. Suppose that $x = 3$ and $y = 4$:

Choice A: $2x + y = 2(3) + 4 = 6 + 4 = 10$. 10 is even, so this isn't correct.

Choice B: $2(x + y) = 2(3 + 4) = 2(3 + 4) = 2(7) = 14$. 14 is even, so this isn't correct.

Choice (C): $x^2 + y^2 = 3^2 + 4^2 = 9 + 16 = 25$. 25 is odd, so answer choice (C) is correct.

CHAPTER 13

Algebra

CHAPTER OBJECTIVES

With practice, this chapter will help you:

1. Define algebra terms that may appear on the SSAT or ISEE

2. Evaluate algebraic expressions and solve algebraic equations and inequalities

3. Identify and represent patterns and functions

ALGEBRA CONCEPTS

Algebra problems will appear in two forms on the SSAT or ISEE: as straightforward math problems and as word problems. Word problems are the focus of Chapter 11. This chapter will give you a chance to review the basic algebra concepts that you'll see on the test.

Vocabulary

Algebra consists of the same basic operations as arithmetic, so in a sense, it can best be defined as abstract arithmetic. The difference is that letters, called *variables*, are often substituted for numbers. Before you practice algebraic topics, review some important definitions.

A **variable** is a letter (usually lowercase) used to represent a numerical value that is unknown. The value of the variable may differ in any particular problem.

A **constant** is a value that does not change its value regardless of the problem. Constants are typically numbers.

A **term** is a variable, a constant, or the product of a constant and one or more variables. The variables may be raised to exponents. A term containing only a number is called a *constant term* because it contains no variable factors.

The **coefficient** of a term is understood to be the numerical factor of that term. If no numerical factor is present, the coefficient is understood to be 1 (or −1).

Look at how the parts of these example terms can be named:

Term	Variable	Coefficient	Constant
12			12
x	x	1	
$5t$	t	5	
$-3yz$	y, z	-3	-3

Like terms are terms that contain exactly the same variables raised to exactly the same exponents. Like terms can be added and subtracted by combining the numerical coefficients and keeping the variable portion of the terms.

Example	Can be simplified to:
$7x + 5x$	$12x$
$3xy - 2 - xy$	$2xy - 2$
$8a^2b + 5ab^2 - 4a^2b$	$4a^2b + 5ab^2$ (This expression cannot be simplified further because the exponents on the variables a and b are not the same.)

In algebra, you work with expressions and equations. An algebraic **expression** contains one or more terms separated by addition and subtraction signs:

$$4x^3 + 12x^2 + 7x + 8$$

$$18a^3b^4 + 14a^2b^5 + 12a + 56$$

An algebraic **equation** is a statement that two expressions are equal. An equal sign, $=$, is used to indicate that the two expressions are equal:

$$5a + 10 = 4a + 26$$

$$x^2 + 7x + 12 = 3(x + 4)$$

A **polynomial** is an algebraic expression that is the sum of two or more terms. If a polynomial has two terms, it is called a **binomial**. If it has three terms, it is called a **trinomial**. If an expression only has one term, it is called a **monomial**. For example, the following expressions can be named in one or more ways:

$16x^3 - 10x^2$	binomial, polynomial
$-3a^3b^4 + 4a + 6$	trinomial, polynomial
$13p^6k^9$	monomial

REMEMBER

Make sure you combine only like terms. Unlike terms must be added or subtracted separately.

Substitution

If a problem gives you the value for a variable, you can substitute the value into the expression and solve. Make sure that you follow the correct order of operations and are careful with your calculations. Try an example:

If $x = 15$ and $y = 10$, what is the value of $4x(x - y)$?

Substitute 15 for x and 10 for y:

$$4(15)(15 - 10) =$$

Then evaluate:

$$(60)(5) = 300$$

Simplifying Polynomial Expressions

To simplify a polynomial expression, remove all grouping symbols (parentheses) using distribution, simplify each term so that each variable appears no more than once in any one term, and then combine like terms. Review these examples:

$$6(3b - 4) = 18b - 24$$

$$-3(4x + 1) + 2 = -12x - 3 + 2$$
$$= -12x - 1$$

$$(2b)^3 - 5b^2(3b) = 8b^3 - 15b^3$$
$$= -7b^3$$

$$3a + 2b - 8a = 3a - 8a + 2b$$
$$= -5a + 2b \text{ or } 2b - 5a$$

$$(4w + 9h) - (3w - 4h) = 4w + 9h - 3w + 4h$$
$$= 4w - 3w + 9h + 4h$$
$$= w + 13h$$

Factoring Polynomial Expressions

The main factoring method you need to master for the test is factoring using the **greatest common factor (GCF)** of an algebraic expression. The GCF of an expression consists of the largest numerical factor and the largest number of variable factors that can be factored out of all terms in the expression.

To find the GCF of an expression, first make sure that the expression is simplified. Second, find the largest factor common to all coefficients in the expression (it is possible to have a numerical GCF of 1). Finally, identify the variable factors common to all terms in the expression. The GCF will contain these factors raised to the lowest exponent given on the variable in any one term.

To write an expression in factored form, use the distributive property to write the GCF followed by the polynomial factor in parentheses:

$$7y^3 + 14y^2 - 21y = 7y(y^2 + 2y - 3)$$

$$12ab^3 - 15a^2b^2 = 3ab^2(4b - 5a)$$

In the first example, $7y$ is the GCF of the expression. In the second example, $3ab^2$ is the GCF of the expression.

Multiplying and Dividing Monomials and Binomials

To **add** or **subtract** terms consisting of a coefficient (the number in front of the variable) multiplied by a power (a power is a base raised to an exponent), both the base and the exponent *must* be the same. As long as the bases and the exponents are the same, you can add the coefficients:

$$x^2 + x^2 = 2x^2$$

$$3x^4 - 2x^4 = x^4$$

$x^2 + x^3$ cannot be combined.

$x^2 + y^2$ cannot be combined.

To **multiply** terms consisting of coefficients multiplied by powers having the same base, multiply the coefficients and add the exponents:

$$2x^5 \times 8x^7 = (2 \times 8)(x^{5+7}) = 16x^{12}$$

To **divide** terms consisting of coefficients multiplied by powers having the same base, divide the coefficients and subtract the exponents:

$$6x^7 \div 2x^5 = (6 \div 2)(x^{7-5}) = 3x^2$$

To **raise a power to an exponent**, multiply the exponents:

$$(x^2)^4 = x^{2 \times 4} = x^8$$

When you multiply monomials, multiply the coefficients of each term. (In other words, multiply the numbers that come before the variables.) Then, multiply the variables. Exponents of like variables should be added. For example:

$$(6a)(4b) = (6 \times 4)(a \times b) = 24ab$$

$$(2m)(5mn) = (2 \times 5)(m \times m \times n) =$$
$$= (2 \times 5)(m^{1+1} \times n)$$
$$= 10m^2n$$

When you divide monomials, divide the coefficient of the numerator by the coefficient of the denominator. When the same variable appears in both the numerator and the denominator, subtract the exponent of that variable in the denominator from the exponent of that variable in the numerator:

$$24a \div 3b = \frac{24a}{3b} = \frac{8a}{b}$$

$$40x^2y^5 \div 5xy^2z^4 = \frac{40x^2y^5}{5xy^2z^4} = \frac{8x^{2-1}y^{5-2}}{z^4} = \frac{8x^1y^3}{z^4} = \frac{8xy^3}{z^4}$$

Remember that $x^1 = x$.

Sometimes, you will use the FOIL method to **multiply binomials**. FOIL stands for **F**irst + **O**uter + **I**nner + **L**ast. Add these terms together for the most reduced equation, a *trinomial*. For example:

$$(y + 1)(y + 2) = (y \times y) + (y \times 2) + (1 \times y) + (1 \times 2)$$
$$= y^2 + 2y + y + 2$$
$$= y^2 + 3y + 2$$

WORKING WITH EQUATIONS

The key to **solving equations** is to do the same thing to both sides of the equation until you have the variable isolated on one side of the equation and all of the numbers on the other side. Try an example:

$$12a + 8 = 23 - 3a$$

First, subtract 8 from each side so that the left side of the equation has only a variable term:

$$12u + 8 - 8 = 23 - 3a - 8$$
$$12a = 15 - 3a$$

Then, add $3a$ to each side so that the right side of the equation has only numbers:

$$12a + 3a = 15 - 3a + 3a$$
$$15a = 15$$

Finally, divide both sides by 15 to isolate the variable:

$$\frac{15a}{15} = \frac{15}{15}$$
$$a = 1$$

Sometimes you're given an equation with two variables and asked to **solve for one variable in terms of the other**. This means that you must isolate the variable for which you are solving on one side of the equation and put everything else on the other side. In other words, when you're done, you'll have x (or whatever the variable is) on one side of the equation and an expression on the other side. Try an example:

Solve $7x + 2y = 3x + 10y - 16$ for x in terms of y.

Since you want to isolate x on one side of the equation, begin by subtracting $2y$ from both sides:

$$7x + 2y - 2y = 3x + 10y - 16 - 2y$$
$$7x = 3x + 8y - 16$$

Then, subtract $3x$ from both sides to get all the x's on one side of the equation:

$$7x - 3x = 3x + 8y - 16 - 3x$$
$$4x = 8y - 16$$

Finally, divide both sides by 4 to isolate x:

$$\frac{4x}{4} = \frac{8y - 16}{4}$$
$$x = 2y - 4$$

WORKING WITH INEQUALITIES

Solving inequalities is very similar to solving equations, but there are two important differences:

1. When multiplying or dividing both sides of an inequality by a negative number, the direction of the inequality must change.

2. The solution of an inequality will be a range of values for the variable, rather than just one value.

When solving the inequality $-5a < 10$, for example, it is correct to divide both sides of the inequality by -5. Because -5 is a negative number, the solution, after simplifying, would be $a > -2$, not $a < -2$.

If this is confusing, consider the rules for multiplying signed numbers. If -5 multiplied by some value must be less than 10, any positive number will do. That's because -5 multiplied by a positive number yields a negative number, and ALL negative numbers are less than 10. In addition, some negative numbers like -1 and $-\frac{1}{2}$ will also work; though when multiplied by -5, they yield positive results, and the positive product is less than 10. If -5 is multiplied by -2 or smaller numbers, however, the product becomes too large. Review these examples:

$$4a + 6 > 2a + 10$$
$$4a - 2a > 10 - 6$$
$$2a > 4$$
$$a > 2$$

$$5(g - 6) \leq 6g + 18$$
$$5g - 30 \leq 6g + 18$$
$$5g - 6g \leq 18 + 30$$
$$-g \leq 48$$
$$g \geq -48$$

PRACTICE QUESTIONS

1. What is the value of $a(b-1) + \frac{bc}{2}$ if $a = 3$, $b = 6$, and $c = 5$?

   (A) 0

   (B) 15

   (C) 30

   (D) 45

   (E) 60

2. If $\frac{c}{d} = 3$ and $d = 1$, then $3c + d =$

   (A) 3

   (B) 4

   (C) 6

   (D) 7

   (E) 10

3. What is the value of x in the equation $5x - 7 - y$, if $y = 8$?

   (A) -1

   (B) 1

   (C) 2

   (D) 3

   (E) 70

4. What is the value of $x(y - 2) + xz$, if $x = 2$, $y = 5$, and $z = 7$?

   (A) 12

   (B) 20

   (C) 22

   (D) 28

   (E) 32

5. If $x = \sqrt{3}$, $y = 2$, and $z = \frac{1}{2}$, then $x^2 - 5yz + y^2 =$

   (A) 1

   (B) 2

   (C) 4

   (D) 7

   (E) 8

6. If $x + y = 7$, what is the value of $2x + 2y - 2$?

   (A) 5

   (B) 9

   (C) 12

   (D) 14

   (E) 16

7. What is the value of a in the equation $3a - 6 = b$ if $b = 18$?

   (A) 4

   (B) 6

   (C) 8

   (D) 10

   (E) 18

8. If $\frac{x}{y} = \frac{2}{5}$ and $x = 10$, $y =$

   (A) 4

   (B) 10

   (C) 15

   (D) 20

   (E) 25

9. $-5n(3m - 2) =$

   (A) $-15mn + 10n$

   (B) $15mn - 10n$

   (C) $-8mn + 7n$

   (D) $8mn + 7n$

   (E) $-2mn - 7n$

10. What is the value of $(a + b)^2$, when $a = -1$ and $b = 3$?

    (A) 2

    (B) 4

    (C) 8

    (D) 10

    (E) 16

11. If $s - t = 5$, what is the value of $3s - 3t + 3$?

    (A) 2

    (B) 8

    (C) 11

    (D) 12

    (E) 18

12. $(3d - 7) - (5 - 2d) =$

    (A) $d - 12$

    (B) $5d - 2$

    (C) $5d + 12$

    (D) $5d - 12$

    (E) $8d + 5$

13. What is the value of $xyz + y(z - x) + 2x$ if $x = -2$, $y = 3$, and $z = 1$?

    (A) -13

    (B) -7

    (C) -1

    (D) 7

    (E) 19

14. If $3x + 7 = 14$, then $x =$

    (A) -14

    (B) 0

    (C) $\dfrac{7}{3}$

    (D) 3

    (E) 7

15. If x is an integer, which of the following expressions is always even?

    (A) $2x + 1$

    (B) $3x + 2$

    (C) $4x + 3$

    (D) $5x + 4$

    (E) $6x + 2$

16. If $4z - 3 = -19$, then $z =$

    (A) -16

    (B) $-5\dfrac{1}{2}$

    (C) -4

    (D) 0

    (E) 4

17. If $3ab = 6$, what is the value of a in terms of b?

    (A) 2

    (B) $\dfrac{2}{b}$

    (C) $\dfrac{2}{b^2}$

    (D) $2b$

    (E) $2b^2$

18. If $5p + 12 = 17 - 4\left(\dfrac{p}{2} + 1\right)$, what is the value of p?

    (A) $\dfrac{1}{7}$

    (B) $\dfrac{1}{3}$

    (C) $\dfrac{6}{7}$

    (D) $1\dfrac{2}{7}$

    (E) 2

19. If $\dfrac{2x}{5y} = 6$, what is the value of y, in terms of x?

    (A) $\dfrac{x}{15}$

    (B) $\dfrac{x}{2}$

    (C) $\dfrac{8}{2}$

    (D) $15x$

    (E) $\dfrac{30}{x}$

20. If $100 \div x = 10n$, then which of the following is equal to nx?

    (A) 10
    (B) $10x$
    (C) 100
    (D) $10xn$
    (E) 1,000

21. For what value of y is $4(y-1) = 2(y+2)$?

    (A) 0
    (B) 2
    (C) 4
    (D) 6
    (E) 8

22. $\frac{3}{4} + x = 8.3$

    What is the value of x in the equation above?

    (A) 4.9
    (B) 6.75
    (C) 7.55
    (D) 8
    (E) 9.05

23. If $2(a + m) = 5m - 3 + a$, what is the value of a, in terms of m?

    (A) $\frac{3m}{2}$
    (B) 3
    (C) $5m$
    (D) $4m + 33$
    (E) $3m - 3$

24. For what range of values of x is $11 < -x < 5$?

    (A) $x < -16$
    (B) $x < -6$
    (C) $x < 0$
    (D) $x > 6$
    (E) $x > 16$

25. If $x < 0$, which of the following has the least value?

    (A) $3x - 1$
    (B) x
    (C) $x + 1$
    (D) $\frac{x}{x + 3}$
    (E) $\frac{x + 3}{x}$

26. If the value of x is an integer and $x < 2$, then $3x + 6$ could NOT be

    (A) 12
    (B) 9
    (C) 6
    (D) 3
    (E) -3

27. If b is an integer and $b > 12$, which of the following has the least value?

    (A) $\frac{b + 6}{b}$
    (B) $\frac{6}{b + 6}$
    (C) b^2
    (D) $\sqrt{b}$
    (E) $b\sqrt{81}$

28. When $x = 2$, which is the value of
    $(|x^2 - 2x| - 3)^2 - 4x$?

    (A) 1

    (B) 5

    (C) 9

    (D) 17

29. If $x = -2$, then $14 - 3(x + 3) =$

    (A) −1

    (B) 11

    (C) 14

    (D) 17

    (E) 29

30. If paintbrushes cost $1.50 each and canvases cost 6 times that much, which of the following represents the cost, in dollars, of p paintbrushes and c canvases?

    (A) $7.5pc$

    (B) $10.5pc$

    (C) $9c + 1.5p$

    (D) $7.5(p + c)$

    (E) $10.5(p + c)$

PRACTICE QUESTIONS ANSWERS AND EXPLANATIONS

1. C

Substitute $a = 3$, $b = 6$, and $c = 5$.

$$3(6-1) + \frac{6 \times 5}{2} = 3(5) + \frac{30}{2}$$
$$= 15 + 15$$
$$= 30$$

The correct answer is choice (C).

2. E

Since you're told the value of d, you can substitute it into the equation $\frac{c}{d} = 3$ to find the value of c. You are told that $d = 1$, so $\frac{c}{d} = 3$ can be rewritten as $\frac{c}{1} = 3$. Since $\frac{c}{1}$ is the same as c, you can rewrite the equation again as $c = 3$. Don't stop yet! Make sure you substitute the values of c and d into the expression $3c + d$ to get $3(3) + 1 = 10$. This matches answer choice (E).

3. D

You are told that $y = 8$, so substitute 8 for y. Then, solve for x:

$$5x - 7 = y$$
$$5x - 7 = 8$$

Now, add 7 to both sides:

$$5x - 7 + 7 = 8 + 7$$
$$5x = 15$$

Next, divide both sides by 5:

$$\frac{5x}{5} = \frac{15}{5}$$
$$x = 3$$

This matches answer choice (D).

4. B

There are three values to substitute. Remember, xz means x times z. After you substitute the values of x, y, and z, you will do the operations in PEMDAS order—parentheses, exponents, multiplication and division, addition and subtraction:

$$x(y-2) + xz = 2(5-2) + 2 \times 7$$
$$= 2(3) + 2 \times 7$$
$$= 6 + 14$$
$$= 20$$

Answer choice (B) is correct.

5. B

This is another "plug-in" question. Remember, $5yz$ means $5 \times y \times z$. First, replace x, y, and z with the values given. Next, carry out the indicated operations using PEMDAS:

$$x^2 - 5yz + y^2 = \left(\sqrt{3}\right)^2 - 5 \times 2 \times \frac{1}{2} + 2^2$$
$$= 3 - 5 \times 2 \times \frac{1}{2} + 4$$
$$= 3 - 5 + 4$$
$$= -2 + 4$$
$$= 2$$

Answer choice (B) is correct.

6. C

If you look carefully at the expression $2x + 2y - 2$, you should see some similarity to $x + y = 7$. If you ignore the -2 for a moment, $2x + 2y$ is really just twice $x + y$. If it helps to make it clearer, you can factor out the 2, making $2x + 2y$ into $2(x + y)$. Since $x + y = 7$, $2(x + y)$ must equal $2(7)$, or 14. If you replace $2x + 2y$ with 14, the expression $2x + 2y - 2$ becomes $14 - 2$, which equals 12. This makes choice (C) correct.

7.   C

Plug in 18 for *b* in the equation:

$$3a - 6 = 18$$

Isolate *a* on one side of the equation:

$$3a = 18 + 6$$
$$3a = 24$$

Divide both sides by 3 to find that $a = 8$. Choice (C) is correct.

8.   E

Substitute 10 for *x* in the equation:

$$\frac{10}{y} = \frac{2}{5}$$

Cross multiply:

$$(10)(5) = (2)(y)$$
$$50 = 2y$$

Divide both sides by 2 to find the value of *y*:

$$\frac{50}{2} = \frac{2y}{2}$$
$$25 = y$$

This matches choice (E).

9.   A

Distribute $-5n$ to each term within the parentheses:

$$-5n(3m - 2) = (-5n)(3m) + (-5n)(-2)$$

Multiply:

$$= -15mn + 10n$$

Note that $(-5n)(-2) = +10n$ since a negative times a negative yields a positive. Choice (A) is correct.

10.   B

Substitute -1 for *a* and 3 for *b* into the expression, then simplify:

$$(-1 + 3)^2$$
$$= (2)^2$$
$$= 4$$

This matches choice (B).

11.   E

The expression can be rewritten as $3(s - t) + 3$.

Plug in 5 for $s - t$:

$$3(5) + 3 = 15 + 3$$
$$= 18$$

Answer choice (E) is correct.

12.   D

Distribute the minus sign and combine like terms:

$$3d - 7 - 5 - (-2d)$$
$$3d - (-2d) - 7 - 5$$
$$5d - 12$$

Answer choice (D) is correct.

13.   C

Substitute the values $x = -2$, $y = 3$, and $z = 1$, and simplify:

$$(-2)(3)(1) + 3[1 - (-2)] + 2(-2)$$
$$= -6 + 3(3) - 4$$
$$= -6 + 9 - 4$$
$$= 3 - 4$$
$$= -1$$

This matches answer choice (C).

14.   C

Rearrange the equation until the *x* is alone on one side of the equal sign. You must always do the same thing to both sides of the equation.

$$3x + 7 = 14$$
$$3x + 7 - 7 = 14 - 7$$
$$3x = 7$$
$$\frac{3x}{3} = \frac{7}{3}$$
$$x = \frac{7}{3}$$

Answer choice (C) is correct.

15. E

Notice that the question asks which expression is always even. Choices A and C are always odd regardless of what integer is substituted for x. Choices B and D are even only when x is even. Answer choice (E) is correct because the product of an even number and any integer is even, so $6x$ is always even. Then, when two even numbers are added together, their sum is also even. Therefore, $6x + 2$ is even.

16. C

Rearrange the equation until z is alone on one side of the equal sign. Anything done to one side of the equation must also be done to the other side. First, add 3 to both sides:

$$4z - 3 = -19$$
$$4z - 3 + 3 = -19 + 3$$
$$4z = -16$$

Then, divide both sides by 4:

$$\frac{4z}{4} = -\frac{16}{4}$$
$$z = -4$$

Answer choice (C) is correct.

17. B

Rearrange the equation until the variable a is alone on one side of the equal sign:

$$3ab = 6$$
$$\frac{3ab}{3} = \frac{6}{3}$$
$$ab = 2$$
$$\frac{ab}{b} = \frac{2}{b}$$
$$a = \frac{2}{b}$$

This matches answer choice (B).

18. A

This equation takes a few more steps to solve than the previous ones, but it follows the same rules.

First, apply the distributive law:

$$5p + 12 = 17 - 4\left(\frac{p}{2} + 1\right)$$
$$5p + 12 = 17 + (-4)\left(\frac{p}{2}\right) + (-4)(1)$$
$$5p + 12 = 17 + \left(-\frac{4p}{2}\right) + (-4)$$

$+\left(-\frac{4p}{2}\right)$ is equal to $-2p$, so $5p + 12 = 17 - 2p - 4$

Combine the integers on the right side:

$$5p + 12 = 13 - 2p$$

Add $2p$ to each side to get all the p's on one side:

$$5p + 2p + 12 = 13 - 2p + 2p$$
$$7p + 12 = 13$$

Now, subtract 12 from both sides:

$$7p + 12 - 12 = 13 - 12$$
$$7p = 1$$

Lastly, divide both sides by 7.

$$\frac{7p}{7} = \frac{1}{7}$$
$$p = \frac{1}{7}$$

This matches choice (A).

19. A

Rearrange the equation until y is alone on one side of the equal sign:

$$\frac{2x}{5y} = 6$$
$$(5y)\frac{2x}{5y} = 6(5y)$$
$$2x = 30y$$
$$\frac{2x}{30} = y$$
$$\frac{x}{15} = y$$

Answer choice (A) is correct.

20. A

This question looks harder than it really is. Isolate nx the same way you would a single variable:

$$\frac{100}{x} = 10n$$

$$100 = 10nx$$

$$10 = nx$$

Answer choice (A) is correct.

21. C

Distribute and solve for y by isolating it on one side of the equation:

$$4(y - 1) = 2(y + 2)$$

$$4y - 4 = 2y + 4$$

$$2y - 4 = 4$$

$$2y = 8$$

$$\frac{2y}{2} = \frac{8}{2}$$

$$y = 4$$

This matches answer choice (C).

22. C

Remembering common fraction to decimal equivalents makes this question a snap:

$$\frac{3}{4} + x = 8.3$$

$$.75 + x = 8.3$$

$$x = 7.55$$

Answer choice (C) is correct.

23. E

Find a in terms of m by isolating a on one side of the equation:

$$2(a + m) = 5m - 3 + a$$

$$2a + 2m = 5m - 3 + a$$

$$2a = 3m - 3 + a$$

$$a = 3m - 3$$

Answer choice (E) is correct.

24. D

Remember that you must change the direction of the inequality sign if you multiply or divide by a negative number:

$$11 - x < 5$$

$$11 < 5 + x$$

$$6 < x$$

or

$$11 - x < 5$$

$$-x < -6$$

$$x > 6$$

Answer choice (D) is correct.

25. A

Picking Numbers is a great way to solve questions that involve number properties and variables in the answer choices. Be sure to select numbers that are easy to work with and fit the information in the question stem.

Since the question states $x < 0$, select an easy negative integer to work with, like -1. Substitute -1 for x in each of the 5 answer choices to find the correct answer:

Choice (A): $3(-1) - 1 = -3 - 1 = -4$

Choice B: -1

Choice C: $-1 + 1 = 0$

Choice D: $\frac{-1}{-1 + 3} = -\frac{1}{2}$

Choice E: $\frac{-1 + 3}{-1} = \frac{2}{-1} = -2$

Answer choice (A) is the least of these, making it the correct answer. Remember that the least among negative numbers will have the greatest absolute value; in other words, remember that $-10 < -9$. Forgetting this property is the easiest way to miss this question.

26. A

Picking Numbers works well on Inequalities questions.

The greatest possible integer value of x for $x < 2$ is $x = 1$. Substiute that into the given expression:

$$3(1) + 6 = 9$$

The greatest possible value of $3x + 6$ is 9, so choice (A) is the correct answer.

27. B

Picking Numbers makes questions about number properties much more concrete and easy to evaluate.

Pick a number for b. Say $b = 13$. Now, substitute that value into the answer choices and find the least result:

Choice A: $\dfrac{(13 + 6)}{13} \approx 1.5$

Choice (B): $\dfrac{13}{(13 + 6)} \approx \dfrac{6}{20} = \dfrac{30}{100} = 0.3$

Choice C: $(13)^2 = 169$

Choice D: $\sqrt{3} \approx 3.6$

Choice E: $13\sqrt{18} = (13 \times 9) = 117$

As the value of b increases, all of the results will increase except for answer choice (B), which will become smaller. This means that choice (B) is correct.

28. A

Plug in the value for x and simplify:

$$\left(|x^2 - 2x| - 3\right)^2 - 4x = \left(|4 - 4| - 3\right)^2 - 8$$
$$= 9 - 8$$
$$= 1$$

Choice (A) is correct.

29. B

Substitute -2 for x in the given expression. Be careful with the negatives and remember to follow the order of operations:

$$14 - 3(x + 3) \rightarrow 14 - 3[(-2) + 3]$$
$$= 14 - 3(1)$$
$$= 11$$

This means choice (B) is correct.

30. C

The total cost of the two kinds of items is the cost of the paintbrushes multiplied by the number purchased plus the cost of the canvases multiplied by the number purchased. Because a canvas costs "6 times" the cost of a paintbrush, a canvas costs $6(\$1.50) = \$9$:

Total cost of paintbrushes: $1.50 \times p$ or $1.5p$

Total cost of canvases: $9 \times c$ or $9c$

Sum of both: $9c + 1.5p$

Therefore, choice (C) is correct.

CHAPTER 14

Geometry and Measurement

CHAPTER OBJECTIVES

With practice, this chapter will help you:

1. Solve Geometry questions involving lines, angles, triangles, and other complex shapes

2. Apply the Pythagorean theorem and basic trigonometric ratios to right triangles

3. Solve for unknown parts of a circle

4. Find points on and measure figures in the coordinate grid

INTRODUCTION TO GEOMETRY AND MEASUREMENT

Like the rest of the math you'll see on your admissions test, the Geometry and Measurement questions will range from straightforward to difficult. You can count on seeing questions that test your knowledge of lines and angles, triangles, circles, and other assorted geometric figures. You will also see a little coordinate geometry. You will also see Geometry questions without diagrams that show up in the form of word problems. When a Geometry question doesn't include a diagram, it is often helpful to draw your own.

The most helpful thing you can do is review geometry content and practice. If you're concerned about your math readiness, spend more time with the subjects that are less familiar to you. Make certain that you do all of the problems in the practice set even if you feel comfortable with the example questions presented.

It's important to know that on both the SSAT and the ISEE, *figures are drawn to scale* unless otherwise indicated. That means you can usually eyeball the measurements of a figure.

LINES AND ANGLES

Line Segments

Some of the most basic Geometry questions deal with line segments. A **line segment** is a piece of a line, and it has an exact measurable length. A question might give you a segment divided into several pieces, provide the measurements of some of these pieces, and ask you for the measurement of a remaining piece. For example:

$$P \qquad Q \quad R$$

If $PR = 12$ and $QR = 4$, $PQ =$

$PQ = PR - QR$

$PQ = 12 - 4$

$PQ = 8$

The point exactly in the middle of a line segment, halfway between the endpoints, is called the **midpoint** of the line segment. To **bisect** means to cut in half, so the midpoint of a line segment bisects that line segment as shown here:

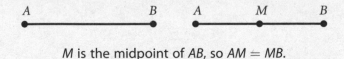

M is the midpoint of *AB*, so *AM* = *MB*.

Angles

A **right angle** measures 90 degrees and is usually indicated in a diagram by a little box. The figure is a right angle. Lines that intersect to form right angles are said to be **perpendicular**:

Angles that form **a straight line add up to 180 degrees**. In the figure, $a + b = 180$:

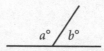

> **REMEMBER**
>
> A straight angle contains 180°. Complementary angles add to 90°, and supplementary angles add to 180°. Adjacent angles are angles that are next to each other; they have a common vertex and a common side.

When two lines intersect, **adjacent angles are supplementary**, meaning they add up to 180 degrees. In the following figure, $a + b = 180$. Note that angles can be adjacent without being supplementary, so be careful to only apply this relationship when the adjacent angles are the result of two, and only two, intersecting lines:

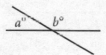

Angles around a point add up to 360 degrees. In the figure, $a + b + c + d + e = 360$:

When lines intersect, angles across the vertex from each other are called **vertical angles** and **are equal to each other**:

$a = c$ and $b = d$

Parallel Lines

There are a few basic rules that are good to know when parallel lines are crossed by a transversal:

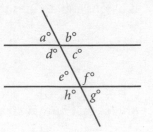

- Corresponding angles are equal (for example, $a = e$).

- Alternate interior angles are equal ($d = f$).

- Same-side interior angles are supplementary ($c + f = 180$).

- All four acute angles are equal, as are all four obtuse angles.

TRIANGLES

There are a few basic rules that apply to triangles in general.

The three interior angles of any triangle add up to 180°. In the figure, $x + 50 + 100 = 180$, so $x = 30$.

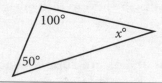

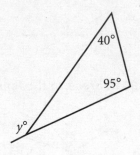

An exterior angle equals the sum of the remote interior angles. In the figure, the exterior angle labeled $y°$ equals the sum of the remote interior angles: $y° = 40 + 95 = 135$ degrees.

The length of one side of a triangle must be greater than the positive difference and less than the sum of the lengths of the other two sides. If it is given that the length of one side is 3 and the length of another side is 4, then the length of the third side must be greater than $4 - 3 = 1$ and less than $4 + 3 = 7$.

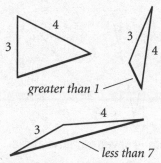

Triangles—Perimeter and Area

The **perimeter** of a triangle is the sum of the lengths of its sides.

The perimeter of the triangle in the figure is $3 + 4 + 6 = 13$.

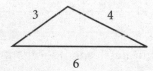

The **area** of a triangle is one-half base times height. The height is the perpendicular distance between the side that's chosen as the base and the opposite vertex. In this triangle, 4 is the height when the 7 is chosen as the base.

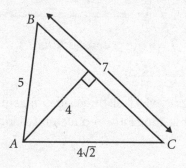

$$\text{area} = \frac{1}{2}bh = \frac{1}{2}(7)(4) = 14$$

Be careful! Many students assume that the height and base are 5 and $4\sqrt{2}$. However, notice that there is no symbol indicating that those two sides are perpendicular. Look for the 90° sign in a figure to isolate the base and height.

Similar Triangles

Similar triangles have the same shape: **corresponding angles are equal, and corresponding sides are proportional**.

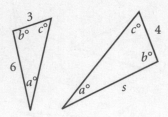

These triangles are similar because they have the same angles. The 3 corresponds to the 4, and the 6 corresponds to the *s*.

$$\frac{3}{4} = \frac{6}{s}$$

$$3s = 24$$

$$s = 8$$

Special Triangles

Special triangles are the isosceles, equilateral, and right triangles.

An **isosceles triangle** is a triangle that has two equal sides. Not only are two sides equal, but the angles opposite the equal sides, called base angles, are also equal.

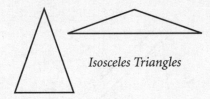

Isosceles Triangles

Equilateral triangles are triangles in which all three sides are equal. Because all the sides are equal, all the angles are also equal. All three angles in an equilateral triangle measure 60 degrees, regardless of the lengths of the sides.

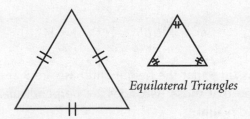

Equilateral Triangles

A **right triangle** is a triangle with a right angle. Every right triangle has exactly one right angle and two acute angles. The sides opposite the acute angles are called the **legs**. The side opposite the right angle is called the **hypotenuse**. In a right triangle, the right angle is always the largest angle, and the longest side is always opposite the largest angle, so the hypotenuse is always the longest side of a right triangle.

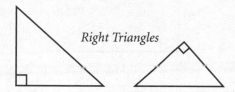

Right Triangles

Right Triangles

Right triangles are one of the most important shapes in geometry. Knowing when and how to use the Pythagorean theorem and special side-angle ratios will make questions involving these shapes easier to work with on Test Day.

Pythagorean Theorem

The Pythagorean theorem is as follows:

$$(\text{leg}_1)^2 + (\text{leg}_2)^2 = (\text{hypotenuse})^2 \text{ or } a^2 + b^2 = c^2$$

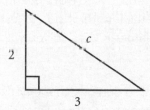

If one leg is 2 and the other leg is 3, then you can use the Pythagorean theorem to find the hypotenuse (c):

$$2^2 + 3^2 = c^2$$
$$c^2 = 4 + 9$$
$$c = \sqrt{13}$$

Pythagorean "Triples"

A Pythagorean triple is a right triangle where all three sides of the triangle are integers. When you recognize that a right triangle has two of the three sides in a Pythagorean triple, you can easily find the length of the third side. When using Pythagorean triples to find side lengths, it's important to remember that the third number in a Pythagorean triple represents the hypotenuse.

If a right triangle's leg-to-leg ratio is 3:4 or if the leg-to-hypotenuse ratio is either 3:5 or 4:5, then you know that it is a **3-4-5 triangle**. Pythagorean triples include the simplified ratio and multiples of it, so a 3-4-5 triangle can include triangles like this one:

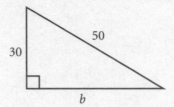

In this right triangle, the leg-to-hypotenuse ratio is 30:50, and this reduces down to 3:5, meaning that this is a 3:4:5 triangle. To find the length of side b, just figure out what multiple of 3-4-5 it is. The ratio 30:50 is ten times as large as 3:5, so you will need to multiply 4×10 to determine that $b = 40$.

If a right triangle's leg-to-leg ratio is 5:12 or if the leg-to-hypotenuse ratio is 5:13 or 12:13, then you know that it is a **5-12-13 triangle**. Look at the following example:

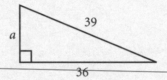

In this right triangle, the leg-to-hypotenuse ratio is 36:39, and this reduces down to 12:13, meaning that this is a 5:12:13 triangle. To find the length of side a, just figure out what multiple of 5-12-13 it is. The ratio 36:39 is three times as large as 12:13, so you will need to multiply 5×3 to determine that b is equal to 15.

There are infinite Pythagorean triples, so don't try to memorize them all. Instead, make sure you're comfortable using the two most common ratios shown here: 3-4-5 and 5-12-13 triangles. Remember, you can still use the Pythagorean theorem on Pythagorean triples if you don't remember them. Using a memorized Pythagorean triple will save you time compared to using the Pythagorean theorem, but both strategies will work for these types of triangles.

Side-Angle Ratios

Side-angle ratios will help you figure out special right triangle side lengths, similar to Pythagorean triples. Unlike Pythagorean triples, using side-angle ratios only requires you to know one of the three side lengths. This means that when a question provides a right triangle and only one side length, you should look for one of these two side-angle ratios.

The sides of a 30-60-90 triangle are in a ratio of $x:x\sqrt{3}:2x$. This relationship means that for 30-60-90 triangles, you can use one side length and this ratio to determine the other two side lengths. If the hypotenuse is 6, then the shorter leg is half that, or 3, and then the longer leg, p, is equal to the short leg times $\sqrt{3}$, or $3\sqrt{3}$.

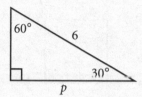

The sides of a 45-45-90 triangle are in a ratio of $x:x:x\sqrt{2}$. Just like you can for 30-60-90 triangles, this means that you can use one side length and this ratio to determine the other two side lengths. If one leg is 3, then the other leg is also 3, and the hypotenuse, q, is equal to a leg multiplied by $\sqrt{2}$, or $3\sqrt{2}$.

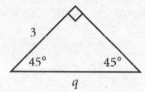

QUADRILATERALS

The **perimeter** of a polygon is the sum of the lengths of its sides. The perimeter of the quadrilateral in the figure above is $5 + 8 + 3 + 7 = 23$.

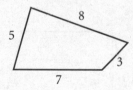

A **rectangle** is a parallelogram containing four right angles. Opposite sides are equal. In the previous figure, ℓ = length and w = width.

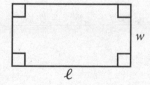

The formula for the perimeter of a rectangle is $p = 2\ell + 2w$

The formula for the area of a rectangle is $a = \ell w$

A **square** is a rectangle with four equal sides. In the previous diagram, $s =$ the length of a side.

The formula for the perimeter of a square is $p = 4s$

The formula for the area of a square is $a = s^2$

A **parallelogram** is a quadrilateral with two sets of parallel sides. Opposite sides are equal, as are opposite angles. In the previous diagram, $h =$ height and $b =$ base.

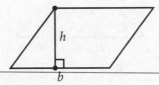

The formula for the area of a parallelogram is $a = bh$

A **trapezoid** is a quadrilateral with one pair of parallel sides. In the previous diagram, $h =$ height, $b_1 =$ base 1, and $b_2 =$ base 2.

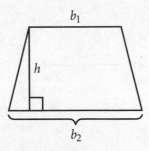

The formula for the area of a trapezoid is $a = \frac{1}{2}(b_1 + b_2)(h)$

If two polygons are similar, then corresponding angles are equal and corresponding sides are proportional.

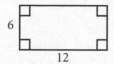

The two rectangles above are similar because all the angles are right angles, and each side of the larger rectangle is $1\frac{1}{2}$ times the corresponding side of the smaller.

CIRCLES

A **circle** is a figure on which each point is an equal distance from its center. In the diagram, O is the center of the circle.

The **radius** of a circle is the straight-line distance from its center to any point on the circle. All radii of one circle have equal lengths. In the previous figure, OA is a radius of circle O.

A **chord** is a line segment that connects any two points on a circle. Segments AB and AC are both chords. The largest chord that may be drawn in a circle will be a diameter of that circle.

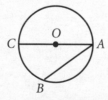

A **diameter** of a circle is a chord that passes through the circle's center. All diameters are the same length and are equal to twice the radius. In the figure above, AC is a diameter of circle O.

The **circumference** of a circle is the distance around it. It is equal to πd, or $2\pi r$. In this example, the circumference is equal to πd, which is equal to 6π.

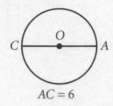

$AC = 6$

The **area** of a circle equals π times the square of the radius, or πr^2. In this example, since AC is the diameter, you can determine that the radius $\frac{6}{2}$, which is equal to 3, and the area is equal to πr^2, which is equal to $\pi(3^2)$, or 9π.

WHAT'S π?

The symbol pi, represented by the Greek letter π, is an infinite and nonrepeating decimal, but all you need to remember is that it's approximately 3.14.

PRACTICE QUESTIONS

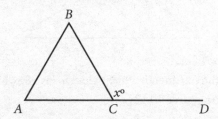

1. In the figure above, segments *AB*, *BC*, *CD*, and *AC* are all equal. What is the value of *x*?

    (A) 30

    (B) 45

    (C) 60

    (D) 90

    (E) 120

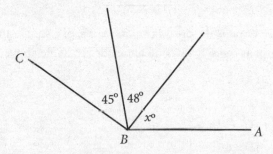

2. If the measure of angle *ABC* is 145°, what is the value of *x*?

    (A) 39

    (B) 45

    (C) 52

    (D) 55

    (E) 62

3. If the perimeter of a square is 32 meters, what is the area of the square, in square meters?

    (A) 16

    (B) 32

    (C) 48

    (D) 56

    (E) 64

4. In triangle *XYZ*, the measure of angle *Y* is twice the measure of angle *X*, and the measure of angle *Z* is three times the measure of angle *X*. What is the degree measure of angle *Y*?

    (A) 15

    (B) 30

    (C) 45

    (D) 60

    (E) 90

5. The perimeter of triangle *ABC* is 24. If $AB = 9$ and $BC = 7$, then $AC =$

    (A) 6

    (B) 8

    (C) 10

    (D) 15

    (E) 17

6. If the perimeter of an equilateral triangle is 150, what is the length of one of its sides?

    (A) 35

    (B) 40

    (C) 50

    (D) 75

    (E) 100

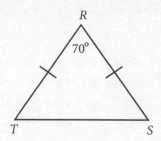

7. In triangle *RST*, if *RS = RT*, what is the degree measure of angle *S*?

(A) 40

(B) 55

(C) 70

(D) 110

(E) It cannot be determined from the information given.

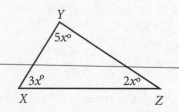

8. In triangle *XYZ*, what is the degree measure of angle *YXZ*?

(A) 18

(B) 36

(C) 54

(D) 72

(E) 90

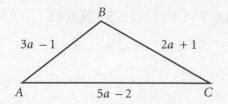

9. If the perimeter of triangle *ABC* is 18, what is the length of *AC*?

(A) 2

(B) 4

(C) 5

(D) 6

(E) 8

10. What is the area, in square units, of a square that has the same perimeter as the rectangle above?

(A) 25

(B) 36

(C) 49

(D) 64

(E) 81

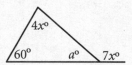

11. What is the value of *a* in the figure above?

(A) 20

(B) 40

(C) 60

(D) 80

(E) 140

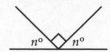

12. In the figure above, what is the value of *n*?

(A) 30

(B) 60

(C) 45

(D) 90

(E) 135

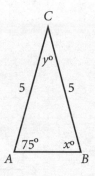

13. In the figure above, what is the value of $x - y$?

(A) 30

(B) 45

(C) 75

(D) 105

(E) 150

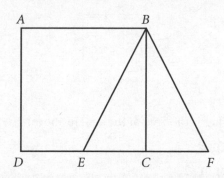

14. A square and a triangle are drawn together as shown above. The perimeter of the square is 64 and $DC = EF$. What is the area of triangle *BEF*?

(A) 32

(B) 64

(C) 128

(D) 256

(E) It cannot be determined from the information given.

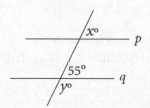

15. If line *p* is parallel to line *q*, what is the value of $x + y$?

(A) 90

(B) 110

(C) 125

(D) 180

(E) 250

$2\sqrt{2}$

16. What is the area of the square above?

    (A) 4

    (B) $4\sqrt{2}$

    (C) 8

    (D) 16

    (E) 24

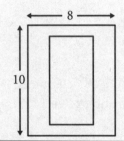

17. What is the area of the frame in the figure above if the inside picture has a length of 8 and a width of 4?

    (A) 4

    (B) 8

    (C) 16

    (D) 24

    (E) 48

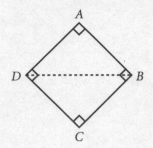

18. In the figure above, $ABCD$ is a square, and the area of triangle ABD is 8. What is the area of square $ABCD$?

    (A) 2

    (B) 4

    (C) 8

    (D) 16

    (E) 64

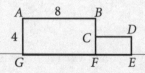

Note: Figure not drawn to scale.

19. In the figure above, $ABFG$ and $CDEF$ are rectangles, CD bisects BF, and EF has a length of 2. What is the area of the entire figure?

    (A) 4

    (B) 16

    (C) 32

    (D) 36

    (E) 72

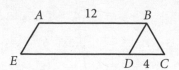

20. In the figure above, *ABDE* is a parallelogram, and *BCD* is an equilateral triangle. What is the perimeter of *ABCE*?

    (A) 12
    (B) 16
    (C) 24
    (D) 32
    (E) 36

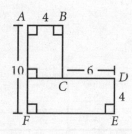

21. In the figure above, what is the perimeter of *ABCDEF*?

    (A) 14
    (B) 24
    (C) 28
    (D) 38
    (E) 40

22. If the shaded regions are 4 rectangles, what is the area of the unshaded region?

    (A) 9
    (B) 12
    (C) 16
    (D) 19
    (E) 20

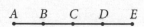

Note: Figure not drawn to scale.

23. In the figure above, *AB* is twice the length of *BC*, *BC = CD*, and *DE* is triple the length of *CD*. If *AE* = 49, what is the length of *BD*?

    (A) 14
    (B) 21
    (C) 28
    (D) 30
    (E) 35

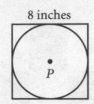

8 inches

24. In the figure above, circle P is inscribed in a square with sides of 8 inches. What is the area of the circle?

(A) 4π square inches

(B) 16 square inches

(C) 8π square inches

(D) 16π square inches

(E) 32π square inches

25. What is the radius of a circle whose circumference is 36π?

(A) 3

(B) 6

(C) 8

(D) 18

(E) 36

26. If the perimeter of the square is 36, what is the circumference of the circle?

(A) 6π

(B) 9π

(C) 12π

(D) 15π

(E) 18π

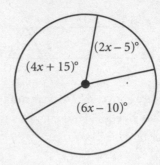

27. In the figure above, what is the value of x?

(A) 15

(B) 30

(C) 55

(D) 70

(E) 135

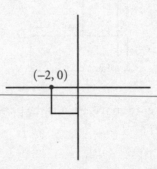

(−2, 0)

28. In the figure above, a square is graphed on the coordinate plane. If the coordinates of one corner are $(-2, 0)$, what is the area of the square?

(A) $\frac{1}{4}$

(B) 1

(C) 2

(D) 4

(E) 16

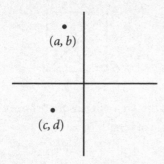

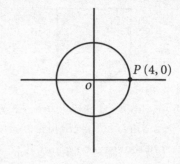

29. Points (a, b) and (c, d) are graphed in the coordinate plane as shown above. Which of the following statements MUST be true?

    (A) $bd > ac$

    (B) $c > ad$

    (C) $b > acd$

    (D) $bc > ad$

    (E) A relationship cannot be determined from the information given.

30. What is the distance from the point $(0, 6)$ to the point $(0, 8)$ in a standard coordinate plane?

    (A) 2

    (B) 7

    (C) 10

    (D) 12

    (E) 14

31. Circle O above has its center at the origin. If point P lies on circle O, what is the area of circle O?

    (A) 4π

    (B) 8π

    (C) 10π

    (D) 12π

    (E) 16π

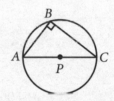

32. In the figure above, right triangle ABC is inscribed in circle P, with AC passing through center P. If $AB = 6$ and $BC = 8$, what is the area of the circle?

    (A) 10π

    (B) 14π

    (C) 25π

    (D) 49π

    (E) 100π

33. In the figure above, a circle is inscribed within a square. If the area of the circle is 25π, what is the perimeter of the shaded region?

(A) $40 + 5\pi$

(B) $40 + 10\pi$

(C) $100 + 10\pi$

(D) $100 + 25\pi$

(E) $40 + 50\pi$

34. What is the slope of the line that contains points $(3, -5)$ and $(-1, 7)$?

(A) -3

(B) $-\dfrac{1}{3}$

(C) $-\dfrac{1}{4}$

(D) $\dfrac{1}{3}$

(E) 3

35. If the circumference of a circle is 16π, what is its area?

(A) 8π

(B) 16π

(C) 32π

(D) 64π

(E) 256π

36. What is the area of the square above with diagonals of length 6?

(A) 9

(B) 12

(C) $9\sqrt{2}$

(D) 15

(E) 18

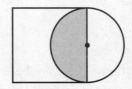

37. A square and a circle are drawn as shown above. The area of the square is 64. What is the area of the shaded region?

(A) 4π

(B) 8π

(C) 16π

(D) 32π

(E) It cannot be determined from the information given.

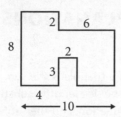

38. What is the area of the polygon above if each corner of the polygon is a right angle?

(A) 40

(B) 62

(C) 68

(D) 74

(E) 80

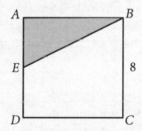

39. *ABCD* is a square. If *E* is the midpoint of *AD*, what is the area of the shaded region?

(A) 8

(B) 12

(C) 16

(D) 24

(E) 32

40. Circle *A* has radius $r + 1$. Circle *B* has radius $r + 2$. What is the positive difference between the circumference of circle *B* and the circumference of circle *A*?

(A) 1

(B) 2π

(C) $2\pi + 3$

(D) $2\pi r + 3$

(E) $2\pi(2r + 3)$

41. Erica has 8 squares of felt, each with an area of 16. For a certain craft project, she cuts the largest circle possible from each square of felt. What is the combined area of the excess felt left over after cutting out all the circles?

(A) $4(4 - \pi)$

(B) $8(4 - \pi)$

(C) $8(\pi - 2)$

(D) $32(4 - \pi)$

(E) $8(16 - \pi)$

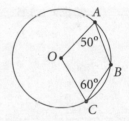

42. In the figure above, points *A*, *B*, and *C* lie on the circumference of the circle centered at *O*. If $\angle OAB$ measures 50° and $\angle BCO$ measures 60°, what is the degree measure of $\angle AOC$?

(A) 110

(B) 125

(C) 140

(D) 250

(E) It cannot be determined from the information given.

PRACTICE QUESTIONS ANSWERS AND EXPLANATIONS

1. E

Because $AB = BC = AC$, triangle ABC is equilateral. Therefore, all of its angles are 60°. Because angle BCD, or x, is supplementary to angle BCA, a 60° angle, the value of x is $180 - 60$, or 120. Answer choice (E) is correct.

2. C

Since the degree measure of angle ABC is 145, you can create the following equation:

$$45 + 48 + x = 145$$
$$93 + x = 145$$
$$x = 52$$

This matches answer choice (C).

3. E

A square has four equal sides, so its perimeter is equal to $4s$, where s is the length of a side of the square. Its perimeter is 32, so its side length is $32 \div 4 = 8$. The area of a square is equal to s^2, so the area of the square is 8^2, or 64. Answer choice (E) is correct.

4. D

In any triangle, the measures of the three interior angles sum to 180°, so $X + Y + Z = 180$. Because the measure of angle Y is twice the measure of angle X, $Y = 2X$. Similarly, $Z = 3X$, so you have the following equation:

$$X + 2X + 3X = 180$$
$$6X = 180$$
$$X = 30$$

Because $Y = 2X$, the degree measure of angle Y is $2 \times 30 = 60$. Answer choice (D) is correct.

5. B

The perimeter of a triangle is the sum of the lengths of its sides. Add up the side lengths, substituting the known values into the equation, and then solve for AC:

$$AB + BC + AC = 24$$
$$9 + 7 + AC = 24$$
$$16 + AC = 24$$
$$AC = 8$$

Answer choice (B) is correct.

6. C

In an equilateral triangle, all three sides have equal length. The perimeter of a triangle is equal to the sum of the lengths of its three sides. Because all three sides are equal, each side must be $\frac{1}{3}$ of 150, or 50. This matches answer choice (C).

7. B

Because RS and RT are equal, the angles opposite them must be equal. Therefore, angle T = angle S. Since the three angles of a triangle sum to 180, you can set up an equation and solve:

$$70 + S + T = 180$$
$$70 + S + S = 180$$
$$70 + 2S = 180$$
$$2S = 110$$
$$S = 55$$

Answer choice (B) is correct.

8. C

The three interior angles of a triangle add up to 180 degrees. Set up an equation and solve for x:

$$2x + 3x + 5x = 180$$
$$10x = 180$$
$$x = 18$$

Angle YXZ has a degree measure of $3x = 3(18) = 54$. Answer choice (C) is correct.

9. E

The perimeter of triangle *ABC* is 18, so $AB + BC + AC = 18$. Substituting the algebraic expressions given for the length of each side, you get:

$$(3a - 1) + (2a + 1) + (5a - 2) = 18$$
$$10a - 2 = 18$$
$$10a = 20$$
$$a = 2$$

The length of *AC* is given as $5a - 2$, so $AC = 5(2) - 2 = 8$. Answer choice (E) is correct.

10. C

The perimeter of a rectangle is $2(\ell + w)$, where ℓ represents its length and w its width. The perimeter of this rectangle is $2(9 + 5) = 28$. A square has four equal sides, so a square with a perimeter of 28 has sides of length 7. The area of a square is equal to the length of a side squared, so the area of a square with a perimeter of 28 is 7^2, or 49. This matches answer choice (C).

11. B

An exterior angle of a triangle equals the sum of the two remote interior angles. Set up an equation and solve for *x*:

$$7x = 4x + 60$$
$$3x - 60$$
$$x = 20$$

So the angle marked $7x°$ has a degree measure of $7(20) = 140$. The angle marked $a°$ is supplementary to this angle, so its measure is $180 - 140 = 40$. Answer choice (B) is correct.

12. C

A straight angle contains $180°$, so all of the angles must sum to 180. One of these angles is right, so its measure is $90°$. Set up an equation and solve for *n*:

$$n + 90 + n = 180$$
$$2n + 90 = 180$$
$$2n = 90$$
$$n = 45$$

Answer choice (C) is correct.

13. B

Because $AC = CB$, the angles opposite these sides are equal as well. So angle *CAB* = angle *CBA*, and $x = 75$. The three interior angles of a triangle sum to 180 degrees, so $2(75) + y = 180$ and $y = 30$. The question asks for the value of $x - y$, or $75 - 30 = 45$. This matches answer choice (B).

14. C

The area of a triangle is equal to $\frac{1}{2}bh$. In triangle *BEF*, the height is *BC* and the base is *EF*. The square's perimeter is 64, so each of its sides is $\frac{1}{4}$ of 64, or 16. Therefore, $BC = 16$. The question also states that $DC = EF$, so $EF = 16$ as well. Plugging this in to the formula, the area of triangle *BEF* is $\frac{1}{2}(16 \times 16) = 128$. Answer choice (C) is correct.

15. D

When parallel lines are intersected by a transversal, all acute angles formed are equal, and all acute angles are supplementary to all obtuse angles. So in this diagram, the obtuse angle measuring $y°$ is supplementary to the acute angle measuring $x°$, so $x + y = 180$. Answer choice (D) is correct.

16. C

The area of a square is equal to the square of one of its sides. In this case, the square has a side length of $2\sqrt{2}$, so its area is $\left(2\sqrt{2}\right)^2$, or $2 \times 2 \times \sqrt{2} \times \sqrt{2}$, or $4 \times 2 = 8$. This matches choice (C).

17. E

To find the area of the frame, find the area of the frame and picture combined (the outer rectangle) and subtract from it the area of the picture alone (the inner rectangle). The outer rectangle has an area of $10 \times 8 = 80$, and the inner rectangle has an area of $8 \times 4 = 32$. Thus, the area of the frame is $80 - 32 = 48$. Answer choice (E) is correct.

18. D

Diagonal *BD* divides square *ABCD* into two identical triangles. If the area of triangle *ABD* is 8, the area of the square must be twice this, or 16. This matches answer choice (D).

19. D

The area of the entire figure is equal to the area of rectangle *ABFG* plus the area of rectangle *CDEF*. The area of *ABFG* is 8 × 4 = 32. So the area of the entire figure must be greater than 32. You can eliminate choices A, B, and C. Because *BF* has length 4, and *C* bisects *BF*, *CF* has length 2. The question states that *EF* has length 2, so *CDEF* is actually a square, and its area is 2^2, or 4. So the area of the entire figure is 32 + 4 = 36. Answer choice (D) is correct.

20. E

The perimeter of *ABCE* is equal to *AB* + *BC* + *CD* + *DE* + *EA*. Because triangle *BCD* is equilateral, *BC* = *CD* = *BD* = 4. Because *ABDE* is a parallelogram, *AB* = *DE* = 12 and *BD* = *EA* = 4. Therefore, the perimeter of *ABCE* is 12 + 4 + 4 + 12 + 4 = 36. Choice (E) is correct.

21. E

To find the perimeter, simply add the six sides of the L-shaped figure. Four of them are labeled, and you can use these to figure out the remaining two.

The length of side *EF* must be equal to the sum of sides *AB* and *CD*, so *EF* = 4 + 6 = 10.

The length of side *BC* is equal to the difference between sides *AF* and *DE*, so *BC* = 10 − 4 = 6.

Therefore, the perimeter is 10 + 10 + 4 + 6 + 6 + 4 = 40. Choice (E) is correct.

22. A

Each of the shaded rectangles has a side of length 3 opposite the side contributing to the interior unshaded region. So the interior region, a square, has an area of 3^2, or 9. Answer choice (A) is correct.

23. A

Let *BC* = x. *AB* has twice the length of *BC*, so it is 2x. You know *BC* = *CD*, so *CD* = x. *DE* is three times the length of *CD*, or 3x. Since *AE* = 49, you can set up an equation and solve for x:

$$49 = 2x + x + x + 3x$$
$$49 = 7x$$
$$7 = x$$

BD is composed of segments *BC* and *CD*, so its length is 7 + 7 = 14. Answer choice (A) is correct.

24. D

Since circle *P* is inscribed within the square, you know that its diameter is equal in length to a side of the square. The circle's diameter is 8, so its radius is half this, or 4. Area of a circle = πr^2, where *r* is the radius, so the area of circle *P* is $\pi(4)^2 = 16\pi$ square inches. This matches answer choice (D).

25. D

Circumference of a circle can be found using the equation $C = 2\pi r$, where *r* is the radius of the circle. So a circle with a circumference of 36π has a radius of $\frac{36\pi}{2\pi} = 18$. Answer choice (D) is correct.

26. B

The perimeter of the square is 36, and because all four sides are equal, one side has length 9. Since the circle is inscribed in the square, its diameter is equal in length to a side of the square, or 9. Circumference is πd, where *d* represents the diameter, so the circumference of the circle is 9π. This matches answer choice (B).

27. B

You know a circle contains 360°, so set up an equation to find *x*:

$$(4x + 15) + (2x - 5) + (6x - 10) = 360$$
$$4x + 2x + 6x + 15 - 5 - 10 = 360$$
$$12x = 360$$
$$x = 30$$

Answer choice (B) is correct.

28. D

The area of a square is equal to the square of the length of one of its sides. Because one vertex (corner) of the square lies on the origin at (0, 0) and another vertex lies on the point (−2, 0), the length of a side of the square is the distance from the origin to the point (−2, 0). This can be found by calculating the absolute value of the difference between the *x*-coordinates of the points, namely $|-2 - 0| = |-2| = 2$. Therefore, the area of the square is $2^2 = 4$. Answer choice (D) is correct.

29. C

While there's no way to determine the numerical values of a, b, c, or d, from their positions on the coordinate plane, you do know that a is negative, b is positive, c is negative, and d is negative. Bearing in mind that a negative times a negative is a positive, consider each answer choice. Choice (C) is indeed true: b, which is positive, is greater than the product acd, which is negative.

30. A

The points $(0, 6)$ and $(0, 8)$ have the same x-coordinate. That means that the segment that connects them is parallel to the y-axis. Therefore, all you have to do to determine the distance is subtract the y-coordinate and find the absolute value of the difference. You have $|8 - 6| = 2$, so the distance between the points is 2. Answer choice (A) is correct.

31. E

OP is the radius of the circle. Because O has coordinates $(0, 0)$, the length of OP is $|4 - 0| = |4| = 4$. The area of a circle is πr^2, where r is the radius, so the area of circle O is $\pi(4)^2 = 16\pi$. This matches answer choice (E).

32. C

Right triangle ABC has legs of 6 and 8, so the legs are in a ratio of 3:4, and the triangle is a multiple of the 3-4-5 right triangle. Since $3 \times 2 = 6$ and $4 \times 2 = 8$, you can double the hypotenuse ratio of 5 to find the hypotenuse of triangle ABC equals 10. Notice that the hypotenuse is also the diameter of the circle. To find the area of the circle, you need its radius. Radius is half the diameter, so the radius of circle P is 5. The area of a circle is πr^2, where r is the radius, so the area of circle P is $\pi(5)^2 = 25\pi$. Answer choice (C) is correct.

33. B

The area of a circle is πr^2, where r is the radius, and because the area of the circle is 25π, its radius is 5. Circumference is equal to $2\pi r$, or $2\pi(5) = 10\pi$. Only choices B and C contain 10π, so you can eliminate choices A, D, and E.

Since the circle is inscribed within the square, its diameter is equal to the side length of the square. The diameter of the circle is $2r$, or 10, so a side of the square is 10 and its perimeter is $4(10) = 40$.

Therefore, the perimeter of the shaded region is $40 + 10\pi$. Answer choice (B) is correct.

34. A

The slope of a line can be found using the formula $m = \dfrac{y_2 - y_1}{x_2 - x_1}$, where m is the slope, and (x_1, y_1) and (x_2, y_2) represent two points on the line. Substitute the given coordinates into the formula (it doesn't matter which you designate as point 1 or point 2; just be consistent):

$$\begin{aligned} \text{slope} &= \frac{y_2 - y_1}{x_2 - x_1} \\ &= \frac{7 - (-5)}{-1 - 3} \\ &= \frac{12}{-4} \\ &= -3 \end{aligned}$$

Answer choice (A) is correct.

35. D

The circumference of a circle is $2\pi r$, where r is the radius, so a circle whose circumference is 16π has a radius of $\dfrac{16\pi}{2\pi} = 8$. The area of a circle is πr^2, so in this case the area is $\pi(8)^2 = 64\pi$. Answer choice (D) is correct.

36. E

Since all sides of a square are equal, the diagonal of the square is also the hypotenuse of an isosceles right triangle. Use this information to determine the length of a side of the square, marked s in the figure. The ratio of the sides in such a triangle is $x:x:x\sqrt{2}$. Because $x\sqrt{2}$ represents the hypotenuse, which is equal to 6, solve the equation $x\sqrt{2} = 6$. Divide by $\sqrt{2}$ to get $x = \dfrac{6}{\sqrt{2}}$. So the length of a side of the square is $\dfrac{6}{\sqrt{2}}$. The area of a square is therefore $\left(\dfrac{6}{\sqrt{2}}\right)^2 = \dfrac{36}{2} = 18$. Answer choice (E) is correct.

37. B

The shaded region represents one-half the area of the circle. Find the length of the radius to determine this area. Notice that the diameter of the circle is equal to a side of the square. Because the area of the square is 64, it has a side length of 8 ($8^2 = 64$). So the diameter of the circle is 8, and its radius is 4. The area of the circle is πr^2, or $\pi(4)^2 = 16\pi$. This isn't the answer though; the shaded region is only half the circle, so its area is 8π. Answer choice (B) is correct.

38. B

Think of the figure as three smaller rectangles. Sketch in lines to make three rectangles:

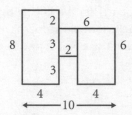

Now, find the area of the all three rectangles. The left rectangle has an area of $8 \times 4 = 32$ square units. The middle rectangle has an area of $3 \times 2 = 6$ square units. The third rectangle has an area of $4 \times 6 = 24$ square units. Adding these rectangles together will give you the area of the entire figure: $32 + 6 + 24 = 62$ square units. Answer choice (B) is correct.

39. C

Because *ABCD* is a square, all four sides have the same length, and the corners meet at right angles. The area you're looking for is that of a triangle, and because all corners of the square are right angles, angle *EAB* is a right angle, which makes triangle *EAB* a right triangle. The area of a right triangle is $\frac{1}{2}(\text{leg}_1)(\text{leg}_2)$. The diagram shows that *BC* has length 8, so $AB = AD = 8$. Point *E* is the midpoint of *AD*, so *AE* is 4. Now that you have the lengths of both legs, you can substitute into the formula:

$$\frac{1}{2}(AB)(AE) = \frac{1}{2}(8)(4) = 16$$

Answer choice (C) is correct.

40. B

The circumference of a circle is equal to $2\pi r$, where r is the radius. The circumference of circle *A* is $2\pi(r + 1) = 2\pi r + 2\pi$. The circumference of circle *B* is $2\pi(r + 2) = 2\pi r + 4\pi$. Finally, take the positive difference between the two circumferences:

$$2\pi r + 4\pi - (2\pi r + 2\pi)$$
$$2\pi r + 4\pi - 2\pi r - 2\pi$$
$$4\pi - 2\pi$$
$$2\pi$$

Answer choice (B) is correct.

41. D

A square with area 16 has sides of length 4. Therefore, the largest circle that could possibly be cut from such a square would have a diameter of 4.

Such a circle would have a radius of 2, making its area $\pi(2)^2 = 4\pi$. So the amount of felt left after cutting such a circle from one of the squares of felt would be $16 - 4\pi$, or $4(4 - \pi)$. There are 8 such squares, so the total area of the leftover felt is $8 \times 4(4 - \pi) = 32(4 - \pi)$. Answer choice (D) is correct.

42. C

The key to solving this problem is to draw in *OB*:

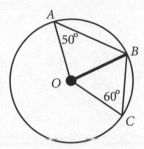

Because *OA*, *OB*, and *OC* are all radii of the same circle, triangle *AOB* and triangle *BOC* are both isosceles triangles. Each therefore has equal base angles:

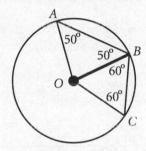

Using the fact that the three interior angles of a triangle add up to 180°, you can figure out that the vertex angles measure 80° and 60° as shown:

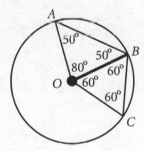

Angle *AOC* measures 80 + 60 = 140. Answer choice (C) is correct.

CHAPTER 15

Data Analysis and Probability

CHAPTER OBJECTIVES

With practice, this chapter will help you:

1. Construct equations involving ratios, proportions, and percents

2. Interpret data sets

3. Apply the distance-rate-time relationship

4. Describe and apply concepts of probability

DATA ANALYSIS

On the SSAT and ISEE, Data Analysis and Probability questions test your ability to create and answer questions using data, select and use statistical measures, and calculate and interpret probabilities. This section will go over these important concepts and give you a chance to practice questions dealing with these subjects.

To excel at data analysis, you must recognize the many ways that charts communicate information. The most common types of charts and graphs include pie charts, line graphs, bar graphs, and pictographs.

EXPERT TIP

Before working on Data Analysis questions, briefly study the chart and determine what it represents and what patterns appear in the data.

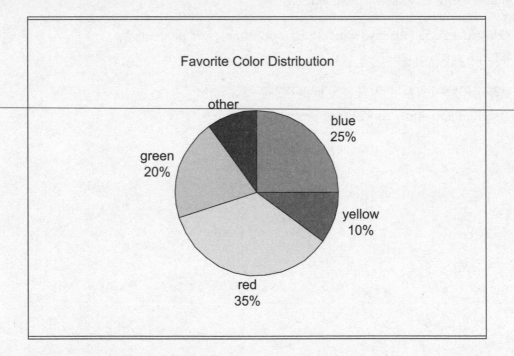

Favorite Color Distribution

(A) What conclusions can you draw from the circle graph?

_____

_____

_____

(B) What's missing from the circle graph?

_____

_____

_____

(C) If 200 people were surveyed, how many more people picked red than picked yellow as their favorite color?

STATISTICAL MEASURES

Sometimes, data analysis on the SSAT or ISEE will include statistical measures. The most commonly tested statistical measures on these two exams are average (mean), median, and mode. Use the numbers 15, 18, 15, 32, and 20 to practice calculating the following statistical measures:

The **average**, or arithmetic mean, of a group of terms is the sum of the terms divided by the number of terms. This relationship is often written using a three-part formula:

$$\text{average} = \frac{\text{sum of terms}}{\text{number of terms}}$$

The average of 15, 18, 15, 32, and 20 is 20:

$$\text{average} = \frac{15 + 18 + 15 + 32 + 20}{5} = \frac{100}{5} = 20$$

The **median** is the value of the middle term, with the terms arranged in increasing or decreasing order.

To find the median of the terms 15, 18, 15, 32, and 20, start by putting the terms in order: 15, 15, 18, 20, 32. Then, identify the middle term. Since there are five terms, the middle term is 18. If there is an even number of terms in a data set, the median is the average of the two middle terms with the terms arranged in order.

The **mode** is the value of the term that occurs most.

Of the terms 15, 18, 15, 32, and 20, the number 15 occurs twice, so it is the mode. If every number occurs only once, there is no mode. If more than one number occurs the most, then all numbers that occur the most would be the modes.

PERCENTS

The key to solving most fractions and percents word problems is to identify the part and the whole. Usually you'll find the **part** associated with the verb *is/are* and the **whole** associated with the word *of*. In the sentence "Half of the boys are soccer players," the whole is the boys ("*of* the boys"), and the part is the soccer players ("*are* soccer players").

Whether you need to find the part, the whole, or the percent, there is one particularly helpful three-part formula:

$$\text{percent (decimal)} = \frac{\text{part}}{\text{whole}}$$

Note that the percent is represented as a decimal in this formula. It can be rewritten in other ways:

$$\text{whole} = \frac{\text{part}}{\text{percent (decimal)}}$$

$$\textbf{part} = \textbf{percent (decimal)} \times \textbf{whole}$$

Look at some examples:

1. What is 12% of 25?

Setup an equation using the formula and solve:

$$0.12 = \frac{\text{part}}{25}$$

$$\text{part} = 0.12 \times 25$$

$$\text{part} = 3$$

2. 15 is 3% of what number?

Setup an equation using the formula and solve:

$$0.03 = \frac{15}{\text{whole}}$$

$$\frac{15}{0.03} = \frac{0.03 \times \text{whole}}{0.03}$$

$$500 = \text{whole}$$

3. 45 is what percent of 9?

Setup an equation using the formula and solve:

$$\text{percent (decimal)} = \frac{45}{9}$$

$$= 5$$

But wait, you're not done yet. To convert a whole number to a percent, do the same thing you would do a decimal number: move the decimal place two places to the right. To finish up and get to your answer, multiply:

$$5 \times 100\% = 500\%$$

To increase or decrease a number by a given percent, **add or subtract that percent of the original number to/from 100% and add multiply that percent by the number**.

To increase 25 by 60%, first add 60% to 100%:

$$60\% + 100\% = 160\%$$

Then, find 160% of the original number, 25:

$$1.6 \times 25 = 40$$

To decrease 200 by 22%, subtract the 22% from 100%:

$$100\% - 22\% = 78\%$$

Then, find 78% of the original number, 200:

$$0.78 \times 200 = 0.78 \times 2 \times 100$$
$$= 1.56 \times 100$$
$$= 156$$

To find the **original whole before a percent increase or decrease**, it is helpful to set up a different three-part equation:

$$\text{percent change} = \frac{\text{new amount} - \text{old amount}}{\text{original whole}}$$

If the question stem states that there is a 10% decrease in the price of a movie and the new price of one movie ticket is \$4.50, then you can use the percent change formula to determine the original price (whole):

$$10\% \text{ decrease} = \frac{\text{new} - \text{old}}{\text{old}}$$

$$-10\% = \frac{\$4.50 - \text{old}}{\text{old}}$$

$$-10\% \times \text{old} = \$4.50 - \text{old}$$

$$-0.1\,\text{old} = \$4.50 - 1\,\text{old}$$

$$-0.1\,\text{old} + 1\,\text{old} = \$4.50$$

$$0.9\,\text{old} = \$4.50$$

$$\text{old} = \$4.50 \div \frac{9}{10}$$

$$= \$4.50 \times \frac{10}{9}$$

$$= \$\frac{45.0}{9}$$

$$= \$5.00$$

Although using the percent change formula backward can be time consuming, knowing how to use the formula flexibly will help you work more efficiently on Test Day. Try another example:

If 70% of k is 14, what is 15% of $4k$?

Setup an equation using the formula and solve:

$$\text{percent (decimal)} = \frac{\text{part}}{\text{whole}}$$

$$0.7 = \frac{14}{k}$$

$$0.7k = 14$$

$$k = 14 \div \frac{7}{10}$$

$$= 14 \times \frac{10}{7}$$

$$= 20$$

To calculate patterns related to the the combined effect of multiple percent increases and/or decreases, start with 100 and see what happens.

A price went up 20% one year, and the new price went up 10% the next year. What was the combined percent increase?

Setup an equation using the formula and solve:

First increase: 20% + 100% = 120% of the original price

If the original price is $100, the second price would be about $120.

Second increase: 10% + 100% = 110% of the second price

If the second price is $120, then 110% would be $12 + $120 = $132.

Percent Increase $= \dfrac{132 - 100}{100} = \dfrac{32}{100} = 32\%$ increase

COMMON PERCENT EQUIVALENCIES

Familiarity with the relationships among percents, decimals, and fractions can save you time on Test Day. Don't worry about memorizing the following chart. Simply use it to refresh your recollection of relationships you already know (e.g., $50\% = 0.50 = \frac{1}{2}$) and to familiarize yourself with some that you might not already know.

To change a fraction or a decimal to a percent, multiply by 100 (move the decimal two points to the right) and add a % sign. To change a percent to a decimal, divide by 100 (move the decimal two points to the left) and drop the % sign.

You can change a decimal into a fraction by thinking about place value and writing the decimal as a fraction of its number of tenths, hundredths, thousandths, etc. ($0.05 = 5$ hundredths $= \frac{5}{100}$). To change a fraction into a decimal, use your knowledge of common fraction equivalences and/or reverse the decimal-to-fraction process by creating an equivalent fraction that has 10, 100, 1000, or another multiple of 10 in the denominator. You can then write the numerator in decimal form by thinking about place value.

EXPERT TIP

The more confidently and flexibly you can move between fractions, decimals, and percents, the easier it will be to make SSAT or ISEE math calculations without a calculator, which will save valuable time.

Fraction	Decimal	Percent
$\frac{1}{20}$	0.05	5%
$\frac{1}{10}$	0.10	10%
$\frac{1}{8}$	0.125	12.5%
$\frac{1}{6}$	$0.16\overline{6}$	$16\frac{2}{3}$%
$\frac{1}{5}$	0.20	20%
$\frac{1}{4}$	0.25	25%
$\frac{1}{3}$	$0.33\overline{3}$	$33\frac{1}{3}$%
$\frac{3}{8}$	0.375	37.5%
$\frac{2}{5}$	0.40	40%
$\frac{1}{2}$	0.50	50%
$\frac{3}{5}$	0.60	60%
$\frac{2}{3}$	$0.66\overline{6}$	$66\frac{2}{3}$%
$\frac{3}{4}$	0.75	75%
$\frac{4}{5}$	0.80	80%
$\frac{5}{6}$	$0.83\overline{3}$	$83\frac{1}{3}$%
$\frac{7}{8}$	0.875	87.5%

EXPERT TIP

A handy shortcut: x% of $y = y$% of x.

RATIOS, PROPORTIONS, AND RATES

Ratios can be expressed in three forms. The most basic form is *a* to *b*. If you have 15 dogs and 5 cats, the ratio of dogs to cats is 15 to 5, and the ratio of cats to dogs is 5 to 15. In other words, for every 15 dogs, there are 5 cats, and for every 5 cats, there are 15 dogs.

Another ratio form is $\frac{a}{b}$. If you have 15 dogs and 5 cats, the ratio of dogs to cats is $\frac{15}{5}$ and the ratio of cats to dogs is $\frac{5}{15}$. Like any other fraction, these ratios can be simplified: $\frac{15}{5}$ can be simplified to $\frac{3}{1}$, and $\frac{5}{15}$ can be simplified to $\frac{1}{3}$. In other words, for every 3 dogs, there is 1 cat, and for every 1 cat, there are 3 dogs.

The final ratio form is ***a:b***. The ratio of dogs to cats is 15:5 or 3:1. The ratio of cats to dogs is 5:15 or 1:3.

Always pay close attention to which ratios are specified in the question. Remember that the ratio of dogs to cats is different from the ratio of cats to dogs.

A **proportion** is two ratios (in fraction form) set equal to each other. Proportions are an efficient way to solve certain problems, but you must exercise caution when setting them up. Watching the units of each piece of the proportion will help you with this. To solve a proportion, cross-multiply:

$$\frac{x}{5} = \frac{3}{4}$$

$$4x = 5(3)$$

$$x = \frac{15}{4}$$

$$= 3.75$$

A **rate** is any "something per something"—days per week, miles per hour, dollars per gallon, etc. Pay close attention to the units of measurement, because often the rate is given in one measurement in the question and a different measurement in the answer choices. This means you need to convert the rate to the other measurement before you can identify the correct answer.

EXPERT TIP

Be sure to get comfortable with the DIRT equation before Test Day: **Distance Is Rate times Time** ($d = rt$). You can use a manipulation of this equation to solve most rate questions.

PROBABILITY

Probability measures the likelihood of an event taking place. It can be expressed as a fraction ("The probability of snow tomorrow is $\frac{1}{2}$"), a decimal ("There is a 0.5 chance of snow tomorrow"), or a percent ("The probability of snow tomorrow is 50%"). ISEE Math questions will require more in-depth knowledge of probability than SSAT Math questions, but you should become comfortable with the three-part probability formula no matter which test you're taking.

To compute a probability, divide the number of desired outcomes by the number of possible outcomes:

$$\text{probability} = \frac{\text{number of desired outcomes}}{\text{number of possible outcomes}}$$

Try this example:

If you have 12 shirts in a drawer and 9 of them are white, what is the probability of picking a white shirt at random?

When picking a shirt in this situation, there are 12 possible outcomes, 1 for each shirt. Of these 12, 9 of them are white, so there are 9 desired outcomes. Therefore, the probability of picking a white shirt at random is $\frac{9}{12} = \frac{3}{4}$. The probability can also be expressed as 0.75 or 75%.

A **probability of 0** means that the event has no chance of happening. A **probability of 1** means that the event will always happen.

> **EXPERT TIP**
>
> Probability is a part-to-whole ratio and can therefore never be greater than 1.

Thus, probability is just another ratio, specifically a part-to-whole ratio. How many parts desired? How many total parts? Finding the probability that something *won't* happen is simply a matter of taking the other piece of the pie.

If the probability of picking a white shirt is $\frac{3}{4}$, the probability of not picking a white shirt is $\frac{1}{4}$, or 1 minus the probability that it will happen. These two events are called **complementary events**.

To find the probability that **two separate events** will both occur, *multiply* the probabilities. For example, the probability of rolling a die and getting a 2 is $\frac{1}{6}$, and the probability of rolling a die and getting an even number is $\frac{3}{6} = \frac{1}{2}$. These two rolls are separate events: the outcome of one roll does not affect the outcome of the other roll. Therefore, if you want to find the probability that you can roll a die twice and get a 2 the first time and an even number the second time, the probability is $\frac{1}{6} \times \frac{1}{2} = \frac{1}{12}$.

PRACTICE QUESTIONS

1. A bag contains 8 white, 4 red, 7 green, and 5 blue marbles. Eight marbles are withdrawn randomly. How many of the withdrawn marbles were white if the chance of drawing a white marble is now $\frac{1}{4}$?

   (A) 0
   (B) 3
   (C) 4
   (D) 5
   (E) 6

2. A museum records 16 visitors to an exhibit on Monday, 21 on Tuesday, 20 on Wednesday, 17 on Thursday, 19 on Friday, 21 on Saturday, and 17 on Sunday. What is the median number of visitors for the week?

   (A) 18.5
   (B) 18.75
   (C) 19
   (D) 19.5
   (E) 19.75

3. If the average of five consecutive odd numbers is 11, then the largest number is

   (A) 17
   (B) 15
   (C) 13
   (D) 11
   (E) 9

4. n is an odd integer and $10 < n < 19$. What is the mean of all possible values of n?

   (A) 13
   (B) 13.5
   (C) 14
   (D) 14.5
   (E) 15.5

5. Jon works 4.5 hours a day, 3 days each week after school. He is paid $7.25 per hour. How much is his weekly pay (rounded to the next highest cent)?

   (A) $13.50
   (B) $21.75
   (C) $32.63
   (D) $54
   (E) $97.88

6. Zim buys a calculator that is marked 30% off. If he pays $35, what was the original price?

   (A) $24.50
   (B) $45.50
   (C) $47
   (D) $50
   (E) $62.50

7. If 35% of x is 7, what is x% of 35?

   (A) 7
   (B) 20
   (C) 28
   (D) 35
   (E) 42

8. If Matthew scored an average of 15 points per basketball game and played 20 games in one season, how many points did he score in the season?

   (A) 15
   (B) 35
   (C) 210
   (D) 300

9. Adam runs for 15 minutes at 12 miles per hour. How far does he run?

   (A) $\frac{1}{3}$ mile

   (B) 3 miles

   (C) 9 miles

   (D) 180 miles

10. A motorist travels 120 miles at a rate of 60 miles per hour. If he returns the same distance at a rate of 40 miles per hour, what is the average speed for the entire trip, in miles per hour?

    (A) 50

    (B) 48

    (C) 45

    (D) 35

11. A car travels 60 kilometers in one hour before a piston breaks, then travels at 30 kilometers per hour for the remaining 60 kilometers to its destination. What is its average speed in kilometers per hour for the entire trip?

    (A) 20

    (B) 40

    (C) 45

    (D) 50

12. The ratio of 8th graders to 7th graders in chorus is 5:3. If there are a total of 24 people in chorus, how many 7th graders are there?

    (A) 12

    (B) 11

    (C) 10

    (D) 9

    (E) 8

13. In a game, 20 small squares of paper are numbered 1 through 20. If Egan randomly selects 1 piece of paper, what is the probability that he will select a multiple of 4?

    (A) $\frac{1}{20}$

    (B) $\frac{1}{16}$

    (C) $\frac{3}{20}$

    (D) $\frac{1}{5}$

    (E) $\frac{1}{4}$

14. Jordan owns a small car dealership. The numbers of different types of vehicles on his car lot are given in the table that follows. What fraction of the vehicles on Jordan's lot are NOT luxury vehicles?

Vehicle Type	Number on Lot
Subcompact	64
Compact	30
Midsize	61
Full-size	58
Luxury	35
SUV	44
Truck	28
Total	**320**

    (A) $\frac{17}{160}$

    (B) $\frac{7}{64}$

    (C) $\frac{59}{80}$

    (D) $\frac{57}{64}$

    (E) $\frac{143}{160}$

15. What value of x solves the following proportion?

$$\frac{2}{9} = \frac{x}{15}$$

(A) $2\frac{2}{5}$

(B) 3

(C) $3\frac{1}{3}$

(D) $4\frac{1}{3}$

(E) $5\frac{1}{2}$

16. If 250% of a number is 480, what is 20% of the number?

(A) 19.2

(B) 38.4

(C) 96

(D) 192

(E) 200

17. Remy scored 150, 195, and 160 in 3 bowling games. What should she score on her next bowling game if she wants to have an average score of exactly 175 for the 4 games?

(A) 205

(B) 195

(C) 185

(D) 175

(E) 165

18. A jar contains 8 red markers, 14 blue markers, 11 yellow markers, and 6 green markers. If a marker is selected at random, what is the probability that it will be green?

(A) $\frac{2}{39}$

(B) $\frac{2}{13}$

(C) $\frac{8}{39}$

(D) $\frac{3}{13}$

(E) $\frac{11}{39}$

19. A scientist measured all of the trees in an area that was once a waste dump and is now being returned to nature. The scientist made the histogram that follows to show the heights of the trees.

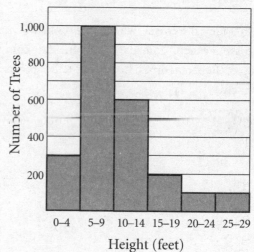

Tree Heights in Renewal Area

According to the data, how many trees did the scientist measure?

(A) 1,000

(B) 2,200

(C) 2,300

(D) 22,000

(E) 23,000

20. The line plot below represents the amount of water carried by all of the campers on a backpacking trip, in gallons.

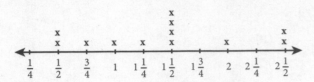

Water Record

Which of the following statements must be true?

(A) $\frac{3}{4}$

(B) $\frac{5}{6}$

(C) $1\frac{1}{12}$

(D) $1\frac{5}{12}$

(E) $1\frac{1}{2}$

21. In 3 fair coin tosses, what is the probability of tossing exactly 2 heads? (Note: In a fair coin toss, the 2 outcomes, heads and tails, are equally likely.)

(A) $\frac{1}{8}$

(B) $\frac{3}{8}$

(C) $\frac{1}{2}$

(D) $\frac{2}{3}$

(E) $\frac{7}{8}$

22. Crowville has a population of 4,500. If 15% of the residents are moving away, how many people will remain?

(A) 225

(B) 450

(C) 675

(D) 3825

(E) 4050

23. The line graphed below shows the predicted amount of ice cream sold at a certain store. Which of the following is the closest estimate of this store's predicted rate of ice cream sales, in gallons per day?

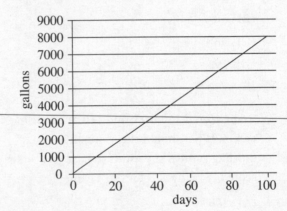

(A) 60

(B) 72

(C) 80

(D) 88

(E) 100

PRACTICE QUESTIONS ANSWERS AND EXPLANATIONS

1. C

By adding the 8 white, 4 red, 7 green, and 5 blue marbles, you get a total of 24 marbles. After 8 are withdrawn, 16 remain in the bag. If the chance of drawing a white marble is now $\frac{1}{4}$, then 4 white marbles remain in the bag. Originally, there were 8 white marbles, and now there are 4, so $8 - 4 = 4$ white marbles must have been drawn out. Choice (C) is correct.

2. C

The numbers for the week are 16, 21, 20, 17, 19, 21, 17. Listing them in ascending order, you have 16, 17, 17, 19, 20, 21, 21. There is an odd number of numbers, so the median is the number in the middle of the set: 19. Choice (C) is correct.

3. B

The average of an odd number of consecutive numbers is equal to the middle term. Because 11 is the average of these five consecutive odd numbers, 11 is the third and middle term. So the five numbers are 7, 9, 11, 13, and 15. The largest number is 15. Choice (B) is correct.

4. C

The mean (or average) is the sum of the terms divided by the number of terms. The numbers included are 11, 13, 15, and 17. Note that 19 is not in the set, because n is less than 19. The average is $\frac{11+13+15+17}{4} = \frac{56}{4} = 14$. The average is an even number although the numbers in the set are all odd. Choice (C) is correct.

5. E

Multiply the number of hours per day times the number of days times the rate per hour: $4.5 \times 3 \times 7.25 = 97.875$, which rounds to $97.88. Choice (E) is correct.

6. D

Say the original price is x dollars. The price paid is 70 percent of the original price (100% minus 30%). So, $0.7x = 35$; $70x = 3,500$; $x = 50$. Choice (D) is correct.

7. A

This question is a snap if you remember that a% of $b = b$% of a. In this case, 35% of $x = x$% of 35, so x% of 35 is 7, choice (A).

If you didn't remember that a% of $b = b$% of a, you could also have solved the statement that 35% of x is 7 for x and then found x% of 35:

Use the formula percent $\times$ whole = part:

$$\frac{35}{100}x = 7$$
$$35x = 700$$
$$x = 20$$

So x% of 35 is 20% of 35, which is 7, choice (A).

8. D

Use the average formula to figure out Matthew's total points scored:

$$\text{average} = \frac{\text{sum of terms}}{\text{number of terms}}$$

The average is 15 points per game and Matthew played 20 games, so plug in those values and solve for the sum of the terms—the total number of points scored in all games:

$$15 = \frac{\text{sum of terms}}{20}$$
$$15 \times 20 = \text{sum of terms}$$
$$300 = \text{sum of terms}$$

Matthew scored 300 points. Choice (D) is correct.

9. B

Because your rate is in hours, first convert the time in minutes to hours. Then substitute the value in to the rate formula and solve for distance.

Start by converting the minutes into hours:

$15 \text{ minutes} \times \frac{1\text{ hour}}{60\text{ min}} = \frac{1}{4}$ hour.

Then, use the DIRT formula to find the distance: distance = 12 miles per hour $\times \frac{1}{4}$ hour = 3 miles. Choice (B) is correct.

10. B

During the first part of the trip, the motorist traveled at 60 miles per hour for 120 miles. This took him $\frac{120 \text{ miles}}{60 \text{ mph}} = 2$ hours.

On the way back, he traveled the same distance at 40 miles per hour, so it took him $\frac{120 \text{ miles}}{40 \text{ mph}} = 3$ hours.

Total distance: 120 miles + 120 miles = 240 miles

Total time: 2 hours + 3 hours = 5 hours

Therefore, his average speed was $\frac{240 \text{ miles}}{5 \text{ hours}} = 48$ miles per hour, which matches choice (B). Be suspicious of choice A, which is the average of the two speeds, not the average of the entire trip.

11. B

Before the piston broke, the car took one hour to travel 60 kilometers. Afterwards, it traveled another 60 kilometers at a speed of 30 kilometers per hour, so it took 2 hours to travel the second 60 kilometers.

Total distance: 60 km + 60 km = 120 km

Total time: 1 hr + 2 hr = 3 hr

Therefore, the average speed was $\frac{120 \text{ km}}{3 \text{ hr}} = \frac{40 \text{ km}}{\text{hr}}$, which matches choice (B). Choice C might be tempting, but be careful; 45 kilometers per hour is the average of the two speeds, not the car's average speed for the entire trip.

12. D

Always be alert to exactly what a ratio is telling you. Is it 7th graders to 8th graders or 8th graders to 7th graders? And are you looking for one of these quantities or a total of some sort?

Because the ratio of 8th graders to 7th graders is 5:3, the ratio of 7th graders to committee members is 3:(5 + 3), or 3:8. There are a total of 24 people, so $\frac{3}{8} = \frac{s}{24}$, where s is the number of 7th graders in chorus. Cross-multiply to solve the proportion:

$$\frac{3}{8} = \frac{s}{24}$$
$$8s = 24 \times 3$$
$$s = \frac{72}{8}$$
$$= 9$$

This means choice (D) is correct. If working through the proportion doesn't go well, notice that all the answer choices are whole numbers, meaning this question can also be solved by Backsolving.

13. E

The probability that an event will occur is given by the following formula:

$$\text{probability} = \frac{\text{number of desired outcomes}}{\text{number of possible outcomes}}$$

Here, the number of possible outcomes is 20. To find the number of desired outcomes (multiples of 4), make a list: 4, 8, 12, 16, 20. There are five desired outcomes, so the probability of randomly selecting a multiple of 4 is $\frac{5}{20} = \frac{1}{4}$. Choice (E) is correct.

14. D

Make sure you read all the data in the table. The bottom row gives you the total number of vehicles on the lot, so you don't have to add up all the numbers. To save time, rather than adding the numbers of vehicles that are NOT luxury, you can subtract the number that ARE luxury from the total to find that 285 out of 320, or $\frac{285}{320}$ of the vehicles are not luxury. To simplify the fraction, divide the numerator and denominator by 5. The result is $\frac{57}{64}$, which is choice (D).

15. C

Cross-multiply to solve the proportion. Be careful when converting the improper fractions into mixed fractions.

$$\frac{2}{9} = \frac{x}{15}$$
$$9x = 15 \times 2$$
$$x = \frac{30}{9} = \frac{10}{3} = 3\frac{1}{3}$$

Choice (C) is correct.

16. B

Write an equation by translating from English to math: The word *of* translates to *times*. Let *n* be the original number and write 250% as $2.5 = \frac{10}{4}$:

$$\frac{10}{4}\, n = 480$$

$$n = \frac{480}{\frac{10}{4}}$$

$$= 480 \times \frac{4}{10}$$

$$= 48 \times 4$$

$$= 192$$

Now, find 20% of $n = 192$ by multiplying by $0.20 = 2 \times 0.10 = 2 \times \frac{1}{10}$. The result is $2 \times \frac{1}{10} \times 192 = 2 \times 19.2 = 38.4$, which matches choice (B).

17. B

The average of a set of terms is the sum of the terms divided by the number of terms. You can either set up an equation involving the missing score or try plugging each of the possible scores into the question stem to see which one works. Backsolving is often a great way to solve questions about averages, especially ones that give you the average and ask for a missing number. Without a calculator, however, sometimes the calculations can be too time consuming. Always consider your own arithmetic skills and the most efficient path to the answer when it comes to calculating values as large as these.

To answer the question algebraically, call the missing score *x* and set up the average equation:

$$\frac{150 + 195 + 160 + x}{4} = 175$$

$$505 + x = 700$$

$$x = 195$$

If you Backsolve, remember to start with the middle number:

Choice C: $\frac{150 + 195 + 160 + \boxed{185}}{4} = \frac{690}{4} = 172.5$

Too low? Try the next-largest number:

Choice (B): $\frac{150 + 195 + 160 + \boxed{195}}{4} = \frac{700}{4} = 175$

Choice (B) is correct.

18. B

The probability that an event will occur is given by this formula:

$$\text{probability} = \frac{\text{number of desired outcomes}}{\text{number of possible outcomes}}$$

In this question, a desired outcome is getting a green marker while a possible outcome is simply getting any marker. There are $8 + 14 + 11 + 6 = 39$ total markers in the jar. Of these, 6 are green, so the probability of getting a green marker is $\frac{6}{39}$, which simplifies to $\frac{2}{13}$. This matches choice (B).

19. C

Read the graph and axis labels carefully. The heights of the bars represent the number of trees in the various height ranges. This means the scientist measured $300 + 1,000 + 600 + 200 + 100 + 100 = 2,300$ trees. Choice (C) is correct.

20. B

Start by finding the total amount of water. To make the calculations easier, add halves together and do the same for quarters. The total amount is:

$$\frac{1}{2} + \frac{1}{2} + 1\frac{1}{2} + 1\frac{1}{2} + 1\frac{1}{2} + 1\frac{1}{2} + 2\frac{1}{2} + 2\frac{1}{2}$$

$$+ \frac{3}{4} + \frac{1}{4} + 1 + 1 + 2 = 17 \text{ gallons}$$

Now divide by the number of campers, which you can find by counting the Xs in the plot: There are 12, so each camper should receive $\frac{17}{12} = 1\frac{5}{12}$ gallons of water each, which is choice (B).

21. B

To find the probability of getting exactly 2 heads, use the probability formula:

$$\text{probability} = \frac{\text{number of desired outcomes}}{\text{number of possible outcomes}}$$

You can toss exactly 2 heads in three different three ways: THH, HTH or HHT. There are three other ways the coin tosses can turn out: all heads (HHH), one head (HTT, THT, or TTH), and no heads (TTT). There are 3 ways to get exactly two heads out of 8 total possible coin flips, so the probability is $\frac{3}{8}$. This means choice (B) is correct.

22. D

Make sure you answer the question that is asked. You are asked about the number of people who will *remain*. To calculate this, multiply the original amount by 0.10 to get $4{,}500 \times (0.10) = 450$ and then half that amount to determine 0.05 of $4{,}500 = 225$. Finally, subtract these two numbers from $4{,}500$: $4{,}500 - 450 - 225 = 3825$, which is choice (D).

23. C

Avoid simple errors on graph questions by drawing horizontal and vertical lines from the axes to the point of interest on a graphed line. To find the most accurate estimate of the rate, look for a point on the graphed line that aligns with tick marks on both axes and will be easy to divide without a calculator. The line passes through a point at approximately 8,000 gallons and 100 days, so the per day rate is:

$$\frac{8{,}000 \text{ gallons}}{100 \text{ days}} = 80 \text{ gallons per day}$$

This matches choice (C).

PART 4

Learning Resources

CHAPTER 16

Study Planning

KAPLAN METHODS CHEAT SHEET FOR THE SSAT

3-Step Method for Analogies

1. Build a bridge

2. Plug in the answer choices

3. Adjust your bridge if necessary

3-Step Method for Synonyms

1. Define the stem word

2. Find the answer choice that best fits your definition

3. If no choice fits, think of other definitions for the stem word and go through the choices again

4-Step Method for Reading Comprehension

1. Read the passage and take notes

2. Decode the question stem

3. Research the details

4. Predict the answer and check the choices

3-Step Method for Math

1. Read through the question and decide when to answer it

2. Answer the question by:

   a. Using math skills

   b. Backsolving

   c. Picking Numbers

   d. Guessing strategically

3. Check that you answered the question

4-Step Method for Writing

1. Prompt (brainstorm the topic)

2. Plan your response

3. Produce your writing

4. Proofread

Test Day Strategies

- Answer the easy questions first. On the second pass, answer the more difficult questions.

- Guess when you can eliminate at least one incorrect answer choice. Leave it blank when you cannot.

- No calculators, rulers, or dictionaries.

- Schools will read the Writing Sample, so take it seriously.

- Bring multiple #2 pencils and erasers.

SSAT Test Format

SSAT Upper and Middle Levels		
Section	Questions	Time Allowed
Writing Sample	1 prompt	25 minutes
Break		5 minutes
Quantitative (Math)	25 questions	30 minutes
Reading	40 questions	40 minutes
Break		10 minutes
Verbal	60 questions	30 minutes
Quantitative (Math)	25 questions	30 minutes
Experimental*	16 questions	15 minutes
Total	**167 questions**	**3 hours, 5 minutes**

*Of the 167 items including the writing sample, only 150 questions are scored.

KAPLAN METHODS CHEAT SHEET FOR THE ISEE

4-Step Method for Writing

1. Prompt (brainstorm the topic)
2. Plan your response
3. Produce your writing
4. Proofread

4-Step Method for Reading Comprehension

1. Read the passage and take notes
2. Decode the question stem
3. Research the details
4. Predict the answer and check the choices

3-Step Method for Synonyms

1. Define the stem word
2. Find the answer choice that best fits your definition
3. If no choice fits, think of other definitions for the stem word and go through the choices again

4-Step Method for Sentence Completions

1. Read the sentence, marking clues
2. Predict the answer
3. Find the fit
4. Plug in your selection

3-Step Method for Math

1. Read through the question and decide when to answer it
2. Answer the question by:
   a. Using math skills
   b. Backsolving
   c. Picking Numbers
   d. Guessing strategically
3. Check that you answered the question

Strategies for Quantitative Comparisons

- Compare piece by piece
- Make one column look like the other
- Do the same thing to both columns
- Pick numbers
- Avoid Quantitative Comparison distractors

Test Day Strategies

- Answer the easy questions first. On the second pass, answer the more difficult questions.
- There is no guessing penalty. Never leave a question blank.
- No calculators, rulers, or dictionaries.
- Schools will read the writing sample, so take it seriously.
- Bring multiple #2 pencils and erasers and a black or blue ink pen (erasable permitted).

ISEE Test Format

ISEE Middle and Upper Levels	
Section	**Questions (Time Allowed)**
Verbal Reasoning	40 questions (20 minutes)
Quantitative Reasoning	37 questions (35 minutes)
Break (5–10 minutes)	
Reading Comprehension	36 questions (35 minutes)
Mathematics Achievement	47 questions (40 minutes)
Break (5–10 minutes)	
Essay*	1 writing prompt (30 minutes)
Total Time	**2 hours, 50 minutes–3 hours**
*The essay will neither be scored nor included with your home report, but it will be sent to the schools to which you are applying.	

YOUR STUDY SCHEDULE

Take the time now to plan out your anticipated study schedule leading up to Test Day.

General SSAT/ISEE Study Tips:

- If you have 2–3 months to study, you should plan to study about 1–2 hours a day, exactly 6 days a week. If you have less or more time than that, you will want to study more each day or spread out your prep by spending only 30–60 minutes studying each day. Always take at least one day completely off of test prep to avoid burning out.

- Your top priority each week will depend on the topics you plan to study during that specific week. In general, your studying should include both reviewing the instructional information at the beginning of each chapter and completing and reviewing practice questions from the end of most chapters.

- Review every problem thoroughly, regardless if you got it correct or incorrect.

- After you finish answering and reviewing the practice questions in a chapter, don't stop! Use Chapters 18–21 to continue practicing the concepts you started in Parts 1, 2, and 3.

How to Make a Study Schedule (do this weekly):

- Open an online calendar or a calendar app, or grab a paper calendar if you prefer!

- Write in all of your non-test prep commitments first: school, sports, extracurricular activities, any scheduled outings with friends, etc.

- Select your "break day" (i.e., the day you take completely off from studying test prep).

- Finally, in the other six days, write in blocks of SSAT/ISEE study time. Take a short break every 30–60 minutes, and don't work more than 2 hours at a stretch without an extended (30+ minute) break.

Check out this sample study schedule:

	Sun 19	Mon 20	Tue 21
6am			
7am		School 7:30am – 3:30pm	School 7:30am – 3:30pm
8am			
9am			
10am			
11am			
12pm	Homework 12 – 2pm		
1pm			
2pm			
3pm	SSAT Studying 2:30 – 3:30pm		Practice 3:30 – 5:30pm
4pm	Volunteering 4 – 6pm	SSAT Studying 4 – 5pm	
5pm			
6pm		dinner 5:30 – 6:30pm	dinner 6 – 7pm
7pm	dinner 6:30 – 7:30pm	Homework 7 – 8pm	SSAT Studying 7:30 – 8:30pm
8pm			
9pm			Homework 9 – 10pm
10pm			

TEST REVIEW

Your Kaplan Practice Test results not only tell you how well you did, but also tell you what to do before your next test. Use these pages to review your results carefully and determine a study plan.

ISEE: _____ Practice Test 1 _____ / _____ Practice Test 2 _____

- Verbal _____ / _____

- Quantitative Reasoning _____ / _____

- Reading Comprehension _____ / _____

- Mathematics Achivement _____ / _____

SSAT: _____ Practice Test 1 _____ / _____ Practice Test 2 _____

- Quantitative (Math): _____ / _____

- Reading: _____ / _____

- Verbal: _____ / _____

- Quantitative (Math): _____ / _____

Verbal Reasoning

1. On which question type did you perform the best?

2. Which question type needed the most improvement?

3. How can you improve? (Circle all that apply.)

   - Learn and practice Kaplan Methods and Strategies.

   - Improve vocabulary knowledge.

   - Budget time.

   - Practice more questions.

   - Eliminate choices before guessing.

   - Use word charge, word roots, or context.

Quantitative/Mathematics

1. In which three SmartPoint categories did you perform the best?

2. Which three categories need the most improvement?

3. How can you improve? (Circle all that apply.)

   - Learn and practice Kaplan Methods and Strategies.

   - Improve math knowledge.

   - Backsolve or Pick Numbers.

   - Budget time.

   - Identify topics tested.

   - Eliminate choices before guessing.

Reading Comprehension

1. In which three SmartPoint categories did you perform the best?

2. Which three categories need the most improvement?

3. How can you improve? (Circle all that apply.)

   - Learn and practice Kaplan Methods and Strategies.

   - Budget time.

   - Practice more questions.

   - Eliminate choices before guessing.

   - Read actively.

   - Rephrase questions and choices in your own words.

   - Make predictions.

Essay

1. Did you apply the Kaplan 4-Step Method for Writing? ❑ Yes ❑ No

2. Did you answer the assignment question? ❑ Yes ❑ No

   If so, where? _____

3. Does your writing response have an introduction/beginning? ❑ Yes ❑ No

4. Does your writing response have a conclusion/end? ❑ Yes ❑ No

5. Did you provide a relevant example(s)/clear plot, strong details, and logical structure? ❑ Yes ❑ No

   If so, what examples did you provide? _____

   _____

   _____

6. Are your examples well developed? ❑ Yes ❑ No

7. Does the writing response have any errors? ❑ Yes ❑ No

   If so, what are they? _____

   _____

   _____

8. Overall, do you think this is a good writing response? ❑ Yes ❑ No

   Why or why not? _____

   _____

   _____

TRACKING YOUR PROGRESS: SSAT

As you prepare for your upcoming Test Day, keep in mind that practice makes progress. The best way to asses how far you've come is to compare your performance over time. After you have completed the appropriate practice test in this book, you can correct it using the answer keys provided. Guidelines for calculating your scaled scores can be found in Chapter 25.

Follow these steps to keep track of your practice test scores using the following charts.

1. Tally up your correct, incorrect, and omitted answers. Add 1 point per correct answer and subtract $\frac{1}{4}$ point per incorrect answer.

2. Chart the percentages for each section.

3. Take notes on individual SmartPoint categories.

4. Focus in on question types and content topics you still need to improve.

SSAT Practice Test 1

Date _____

Scaled Scores

Quantitative (Math) _____

Reading _____

Verbal _____

	# Correct	# Incorrect	# Omitted	Raw Score
Quantitative (Math)				
Reading				
Verbal				

SSAT Practice Test 2

Date _____

Scaled Scores

Quantitative (Math) _____

Reading _____

Verbal _____

	# Correct	# Incorrect	# Omitted	Raw Score
Quantitative (Math)				
Reading				
Verbal				

	Official SSAT Upper or Middle Level Practice Test Date _____ **Scaled Scores** Quantitative (Math) _____ Reading _____ Verbal _____			
	# Correct	**# Incorrect**	**# Omitted**	**Raw Score**
Quantitative (Math)				
Reading				
Verbal				

Question Review Tracker			
Page and Question #	**Category**	**Correct?**	**Why or why not?**

TRACKING YOUR PROGRESS: ISEE

As you prepare for your upcoming Test Day, keep in mind that practice makes progress! The best way to asses how far you've come is to compare your performance over time. After you have completed the appropriate practice test in this book, you can correct it using the answer keys provided. Guidelines for calculating your scaled scores can be found in Chapter 28.

Follow these steps to keep track of your practice test scores using the following charts.

1. Tally up your correct and omitted/incorrect answers.

2. Chart the percentages for each section.

3. Take notes on individual SmartPoint categories.

4. Focus in on question types and content topics you still need to improve.

	ISEE Practice Test 1 Date _____ **Scaled Scores** Verbal Reasoning _____ Quantitative Reasoning _____ Reading Comprehension _____ Mathematics Achievement _____	
	# Correct	**Raw Score**
Verbal Reasoning		
Quantitative Reasoning		
Reading Comprehension		
Mathematics Achievement		

	ISEE Practice Test 2	
	Date _____	
	Scaled Scores	
	Verbal Reasoning	_____
	Quantitative Reasoning	_____
	Reading Comprehension	_____
	Mathematics Achievement	_____
	# Correct	**Raw Score**
Verbal Reasoning		
Quantitative Reasoning		
Reading Comprehension		
Mathematics Achievement		

	Official ISEE Upper Level Practice Test	
	Date _____	
	Scaled Scores	
	Verbal Reasoning	_____
	Quantitative Reasoning	_____
	Reading Comprehension	_____
	Mathematics Achievement	_____
	# Correct	**Raw Score**
Verbal Reasoning		
Quantitative Reasoning		
Reading Comprehension		
Mathematics Achievement		

		Official ISEE Middle Level Practice Test	
	Date _____		
	Scaled Scores		
	Verbal Reasoning	_____	
	Quantitative Reasoning	_____	
	Reading Comprehension	_____	
	Mathematics Achievement	_____	
	# Correct	**Raw Score**	
Verbal Reasoning			
Quantitative Reasoning			
Reading Comprehension			
Mathematics Achievement			

Question Review Tracker			
Page and Question #	**Category**	**Correct?**	**Why or why not?**

CHAPTER 17

Managing Your Stress

CHAPTER OBJECTIVES

With practice, this chapter will help you:

1. Describe specific steps for managing your stress during the weeks before Test Day

2. Explain the characteristics of an effective study plan for the final weeks leading up to Test Day

MANAGING YOUR STRESS

Is it starting to feel as though your whole life is a buildup to the SSAT or ISEE? You really want to go to a certain school, and you know your parents want you to as well. You have worried about the test for months and spent at least a few hours in solid preparation for it. As the test gets closer, you may find your anxiety is on the rise. Don't worry. After the preparation you've received from this book, you're in good shape for the test.

To calm any pretest jitters you may have, this chapter leads you through a sane itinerary for the last week.

THE WEEK BEFORE THE TEST

- Focus your remaining practice time on the areas of the test in which you usually score the highest.

- Determine *exactly* how you're going to approach each section and question type.

- Sit down and do practice problems or complete extra drills you might have skipped the first time through.

- Practice waking up early and eating breakfast so that you'll be alert in the morning on Test Day.

THE DAYS JUST BEFORE THE TEST

- The best test takers do less and less as the test approaches. Taper off your study schedule and take it easy. Give yourself time off, especially the evening before the exam. By that time, if you've studied well, everything you need to know is firmly stored in your memory bank.

- Positive self-talk can be extremely liberating and invigorating, especially as the test looms closer. Tell yourself things such as "I will do well" rather than "I hope things go well" and "I can" rather than "I cannot." Replace any negative thoughts with affirming statements that boost your self-esteem.

- Get everything you'll need together sooner rather than later. Have everything (including choice of clothing) laid out in advance. Most importantly, make sure you know where the test will be held and the easiest, quickest way to get there. You'll have great peace of mind by knowing that all the little details—gas in the car, directions, etc.—are set before the day of the test.

- Go to the test site a few days in advance, especially if you are going somewhere new.

- Forgo any practice on the day before the test. It's in your best interest to marshal your physical and psychological resources for 24 hours or so. The best athletes spend their remaining hours before a performance trusting in their training and preparing themselves for the event. Keep the upcoming test out of your thoughts; instead, do something relaxing, like going to a movie, taking a pleasant hike, or just relaxing. Don't eat junk food or tons of sugar; instead, try to eat a healthy meal, just like you would before a physical event. Finally, be sure to get plenty of rest the night before—but don't go to bed too early. It's hard to fall asleep earlier than you're used to, and you don't want to lie there worrying about the test.

THE NIGHT BEFORE THE TEST

Don't study. Get together the following items:

- Your admission/registration ticket

- Photo ID

- A watch (choose one that is easy to read, but don't pick a fitness tracker or a smart watch!)

- Slightly dull #2 pencils (so they fill in the ovals faster) with erasers

- (ISEE only) two black or blue ballpoint pens (erasable allowed)

- Pencil sharpener

- Erasers

- Clothes you'll wear (Dress in layers! The climate at the test location may vary, as may your body temperature. Make sure you can warm up or cool down easily.)

- Snacks (easy to open or partially unwrapped)

- Money (for possible vending machines)

- Packet of tissues and a bottle of water (for breaks)

Relax the night before the test. No studying! Read a good book, take a bubble bath, watch TV. Get a good night's sleep. Go to bed at a reasonable hour and leave yourself extra time in the morning.

> **EXPERT TIP**
>
> A Kaplan instructor who won big on Jeopardy!™ noticed something unusual in the green room before the show: the contestants who were quiet and "within themselves" were the ones who did great on the show. Alternatively, the contestants who didn't perform as well were those who were cramming facts and talking a lot before the show. Learn from their mistakes; spend your final hours before the test getting sleep, meditating, and generally relaxing.

THE MORNING OF THE TEST

Eat breakfast. Make it something substantial and nutritious, but don't deviate too much from your everyday pattern. If you don't normally eat much for breakfast, keep it light. If you're used to a full meal, make sure you give yourself enough time to enjoy it.

Be sure to get there early. Leave enough time to allow for transportation delays, forgotten items, and any other snag that could slow you down.

Dress in layers so that you can adjust to the temperature of the test room. While you're waiting for the test to start, read something to warm up your brain.

> **EXPERT TIP**
>
> The night before the test, do NOT:
>
> - memorize the dictionary
> - stay up all night watching movies
> - try a new food trend
> - apply to clown school
> - start making flashcards

DURING THE TEST

Don't be shaken. If you find your confidence slipping, remind yourself how well you've prepared: you know the structure of the test, you know the instructions, and you've studied for every question type.

The biggest stress monster will be the test itself. Fear not; there are methods of quelling your stress during the test:

- Keep moving forward, and don't get bogged down in a difficult question. You don't have to get everything correct to achieve a fine score, so don't linger out of desperation on a question that is going nowhere even after you've spent considerable time on it. The best test takers skip difficult material temporarily in search of the easier stuff. They mark the ones that require extra time and thought.

- Don't be thrown if other test takers seem to be working more busily and furiously than you are. Don't mistake other people's sheer activity as a sign of progress and higher scores. You're ready for this test!

- **Keep breathing!** Weak test takers tend to share one major trait: they don't breathe properly as the test proceeds. They might hold their breath without realizing it or breathe erratically. Improper breathing hurts confidence and accuracy. Just as importantly, it interferes with clear thinking.

> **EXPERT TIP**
>
> If you find yourself needing a moment, close your eyes and breathe deeply for 5–10 seconds. It's better to take a moment to breathe than to keep moving forward while frustrated, nervous, or experiencing any other negative emotions.

Some quick exercises during the test—especially if concentration is wandering or energy is waning—can help. Try this:

- Put your palms together and press intensely for a few seconds. Concentrate on the tension you feel through your palms, wrists, forearms, and up into your biceps and shoulders. Then, quickly release the pressure. Feel the difference as you let go. Focus on the warm relaxation that floods through the muscles.

Here's another exercise that will relieve tension in both your neck and eye muscles:

- Slowly rotate your head from side to side, turning your head and eyes to look as far back over each shoulder as you can. Feel the muscles stretch on one side of your neck as they contract on the other. Repeat five times in each direction.

Now you're ready to return to the task.

With what you've just learned here, you're armed and ready to do battle with the test. This book and your studies will give you the information you'll need to answer the questions. It's all firmly planted in your mind. You also know how to deal with any excess tension that might come along, both when you're studying for and taking the exam. You've experienced everything you need to tame your test anxiety and stress. You're going to get a great score.

If something does go really wrong, don't panic. If the test booklet is defective—two pages are stuck together or the ink has run—stay calm and raise your hand to tell the proctor that you need a new book. If you accidentally misgrid your answer page or put the answers in the incorrect section, don't panic! The proctor might be able to arrange for you to regrid your test after it's over, when it won't cost you any time. Raise your hand, and explain your situation. It's better to ask than to assume the worst.

AFTER THE TEST

Once the test is over, put it out of your mind. Start thinking about more interesting things. You might walk out of the test thinking that you blew it, but you probably didn't. In general, people tend to remember the questions that stumped them, not the questions that they knew.

Celebrate the hard work you've put into your prep so far, and commit to further prep if needed. Mark on your calendar the date scores will come back, and be sure to record your progress in Chapter 25 or 28.

CHAPTER 18

Verbal Wrap-Up

CHAPTER OBJECTIVES

With practice, this chapter will help you:

1. Explain the steps of the Kaplan 3-Step Method for Synonyms

2. Explain the steps of the 4-Step Method for Sentence Completions (ISEE) or the Kaplan 3-Step Method for Analogy Questions (SSAT)

3. Explain the steps of the Kaplan 4-Step Method for Reading Comprehension and its role in answering Reading questions accurately and efficiently

4. Identify Reading Comprehension concepts and strategies in need of further practice or review

VERBAL WRAP-UP STRATEGY REVIEW

Use this chapter to reflect on your progress. Review previous chapters for more details on how to approach individual sections of the test.

1. How does the test maker make Verbal questions more difficult?

_____

_____

_____

2. What should you remember about pacing on the Verbal sections?

_____

_____

_____

3. What are some Kaplan Verbal methods and strategies you can rely on?

_____

_____

_____

4. How and when should you guess?

_____

_____

_____

REMEMBER

Your goal is to get as many points as possible. To accomplish this, you need to use all of your vocabulary knowledge, reading skills, and the Kaplan methods and strategies.

ANSWERS AND EXPLANATIONS

1. The test makers make Verbal questions more difficult by requiring more inferences or using complicated vocabulary.

2. It's important to keep moving. On the SSAT Reading section, you have about 4.5–5 minutes per passage and question set, and on the SSAT Verbal section, you have about 30 seconds per question. Meanwhile, on the ISEE, you have about 30 seconds per Verbal Reasoning question and about 6 minutes per passage and questions set in the Reading section. The SSAT and ISEE math sections are similar in style and difficulty. On the ISEE, you have less than 1 minute per math question. Unlike the SSAT, the first math section of the ISEE—Quantitative Reasoning—is different from the second math section—Mathematics Achievement. The Quantitative Reasoning section has Word Problems requiring only one or two steps and Quantitative Comparisons requiring comparisons of two side-by-side expressions. The Mathematics Achievement section has lengthier word problems that will require multiple steps.

3. **Kaplan 3-Step Method for Analogies**

   Step 1. Build a bridge

   Step 2. Plug in the answer choices

   Step 3. Adjust your bridge if necessary

   Kaplan 4-Step Method for Sentence Completions

   Step 1. Read the sentence, marking clues

   Step 2. Predict the answer

   Step 3. Find the fit

   Step 4. Plug in your selection

   Kaplan 4-Step Method for Reading Comprehension

   Step 1. Read the passage and take notes

   Step 2. Decode the question stem

   Step 3. Research the details

   Step 4. Predict the answer and check the choices

4. When you should guess depends on which exam you're taking. If you're taking the ISEE, you should guess whenever you can't pick one specific answer. If you're taking the SSAT, however, you should only guess if you can eliminate at least one answer choice.

SYNONYMS

1. The Kaplan 3-Step Method for Synonyms:

Step 1. _____

Step 2. _____

Step 3. _____

2. When do you need to use Step 3? _____

_____

Answers and Explanations

1. The Kaplan 3-Step Method for Synonyms:

Step 1. Define the stem word

Step 2. Find the answer choice that best fits your definition

Step 3. If no choice fits, think of other definitions for the stem word and go through the choices again

2. You should use Step 3 when none of the answer choices match the definition you chose.

SENTENCE COMPLETIONS

Remember, Sentence Completions appear only on the ISEE.

1. The Kaplan 4-Step Method for Sentence Completions:

Step 1. _____

Step 2. _____

Step 3. _____

Step 4. _____

Why is Step 4 important? _____

REMEMBER
Eliminate incorrect answer choices using vocabulary you do know.

Answers and Explanations

1. The Kaplan 4-Step Method for Sentence Completions:

    Step 1. Read the sentence, marking clues

    Step 2. Predict the answer

    Step 3. Find the fit

    Step 4. Plug in your selection

2. Step 4 is important because sometimes an answer can seem correct in isolation but not fit back into the sentence or passage as a whole.

ANALOGIES

1. The Kaplan Method for Analogies:

    Step 1. _____

    Step 2. _____

    Step 3. _____

2. Why is Step 3 important? _____

> **EXPERT TIP**
>
> There are classic bridges to help you on Test Day. Learning as many different bridge types as possible before Test Day will help you think flexibly about how two words are related.

Answers and Explanations

1. The Kaplan 3-Step Method for Analogies:

    Step 1. Build a bridge

    Step 2. Plug in the answer choices

    Step 3. Adjust your bridge if necessary

2. Step 3 is important because sometimes your bridge will fit more than one of the answer choices.

READING COMPREHENSION

Rember, you should use this chapter to reflect on your progress. Review previous chapters for more details on how to approach the Reading section of the test.

1. The Kaplan 4-Step Method for Reading Comprehension:

Step 1. _____

Step 2. _____

Step 3. _____

Step 4. _____

2. What are the question types you will see in the Reading Comprehension section?

_____

_____

3. What types of incorrect answers can you expect to see?

_____

_____

4. What types of passages can you expect to see?

_____

_____

Answers and Explanations

1. The Kaplan 4-Step Method for Reading Comprehension

   Step 1. Read the passage and take notes

   Step 2. Decode the question stem

   Step 3. Research the details

   Step 4. Predict the answer and check the choices

2. The Reading section includes six different question types for each exam: Main Idea, Supporting Ideas, Inference, Vocab-in-Context, Tone/Style/Figurative Language, Organization/Logic (ISEE only), and Author's Purpose and Arguments (SSAT only).

3. The Reading section includes some common incorrect answer choices. Some incorrect answer choices are extreme. They state that things are *always* or *never* true, or they go way beyond what's stated in the passage. Other incorrect answer choices are misused details. These are ideas that are discussed in the passage but don't actually answer the question. When it comes to Vocab-in-Context questions, be on the lookout for the "regular" definition of words. The exam is almost always asking you for a lesser known usage of the vocabulary word they've highlighted.

4. The SSAT and ISEE exams include predictable Reading passage types, including narrative, informational, and instructional passages. On the ISEE, these passages will be pretty uniform in length and have numbering for every line. On the SSAT, these passages can vary in length and have numbering every five lines.

PRACTICE QUESTIONS

Use the Kaplan Method for Synonyms to answer the following questions.

1. BENIGN:

    (A) gentle

    (B) malicious

    (C) starved

    (D) hesitant

2. METICULOUSLY:

    (A) seriously

    (B) persistently

    (C) carefully

    (D) instantaneously

3. ANGUISH:

    (A) fury

    (B) suffering

    (C) elation

    (D) reprieve

Use the Kaplan Method for Sentence Completions on these questions.

4. Known for their devotion to their masters, dogs were often used as symbols of ------- in medieval and Renaissance painting.

    (A) treachery

    (B) prosperity

    (C) loyalty

    (D) antiquity

5. Most bats are ------- creatures; they rest in caves and other dark places during the daylight hours and venture forth at night to find food.

    (A) nocturnal

    (B) predatory

    (C) sluggish

    (D) stubborn

6. Although she earned praise for her striking murals, the artist felt that her sculpture merited greater -------.

    (A) viewing

    (B) development

    (C) acclaim

    (D) contempt

EXPERT TIP

Use word charge to figure out if you need a positive or negative word in the blank.

Use the Kaplan Method for Analogies on these questions.

EXPERT TIP

Identifying a bridge as strong or weak will help you in your analysis.

7. Fish is to school as

   (A) cow is to cattle

   (B) crop is to farm

   (C) gaggle is to geese

   (D) lion is to pride

   (E) general is to army

9. Anomalous is to standard as

   (A) rude is to kind

   (B) demonstrative is to impassive

   (C) profound is to brief

   (D) taxing is to exhausting

   (E) stoic is to urbane

8. Liquid is to gas as condensation is to

   (A) precipitation

   (B) evaporation

   (C) sublimation

   (D) freezing

   (E) crystallization

EXPERT TIP

Think about where you've heard or read a word before to try to eliminate answer choices.

Use the Kaplan Method for Reading Comprehension to read the passage and answer the questions.

This is an ISEE-style passage.

1   During the 1950s, many writers feared that
2 advertisers would eventually develop the ability to
3 manipulate and even dictate our desires and behavior.
4 The sociologist Vance Packard sounded this alarm in
5 his book *The Hidden Persuaders*, which revealed to
6 the public for the first time the techniques for
7 "consumer exploitation" that the advertising industry
8 had developed. Packard warned that if the advertising
9 industry was not brought under control, it would
10 eventually run people's lives. As it turned out,
11 Packard's dire predictions underestimated the public's
12 ability to critically evaluate advertising messages. As
13 advertising techniques became more sophisticated,
14 consumers became harder to persuade. As a result,
15 today's advertisers are forced to continually update
16 their methods in order to remain one step ahead of
17 the public.

> **EXPERT TIP**
>
> Avoid answer choices that are too broad or too narrow in scope.

10. With which of the following statements would the author most likely agree?

    (A) People will believe anything they hear.

    (B) Science can achieve the impossible.

    (C) Consumers are easily fooled.

    (D) People can think for themselves.

11. In line 9, the word "critically" most nearly means

    (A) negatively.

    (B) sarcastically.

    (C) rationally.

    (D) crucially.

12. According to the passage, Vance Packard's book *The Hidden Persuaders* contained all the following EXCEPT

    (A) bleak predictions about the future.

    (B) the warning that consumers would become increasingly sophisticated.

    (C) a call for industry control of the advertising industry.

    (D) an argument that people's decisions would eventually be determined by advertisers.

> **EXPERT TIP**
>
> Avoid answer choices that contradict or distort the passage.

PRACTICE QUESTIONS ANSWERS AND EXPLANATIONS

1. A

Benign comes from the root "bene," which means "good." So something benign is "good" in some way. Choice (A), gentle, matches this prediction. Choice B, malicious, is ill-intentioned, which is the exact opposite of what you need. Choices C, starved, and D, hesitant, are words that generally have a negative connotation, which doesn't match the meaning of benign.

2. C

A meticulous person does things carefully. Choice (C) is a great match for meticulously. Someone who is careful may also be serious (choice A) or persistent (choice B), but these words do not have overlapping meanings. Choice D is not a good match; someone who is careful is unlikely to do things instantaneously.

3. B

Anguish is a negative feeling. Choice A, fury, is likely to evoke negative feelings, but its direct meaning is extreme anger. Choice C, elation, is feeling exceptionally happy. Choice D, reprieve, is a break. Neither of these will work. Only answer choice (B), suffering, matches.

4. C

Dogs were known for showing devotion to their masters. Devotion is another word for loyalty, so choice (C) is correct. Dogs who are treacherous would not be known for devotion, so choice A is incorrect. Devotion is also an illogical match for prosperity (choice B) or antiquity (choice D).

5. A

Bats rest during daylight hours and go out at night. This is the definition of a nocturnal creature, so answer choice (A) is correct. Nothing in the sentence would support the idea that bats are predatory (choice B), sluggish (choice C), or stubborn (choice D).

6. C

The word "although" indicates a contrast relationship between what the artist believes and the reality. The artist earned praise, but she felt her sculpture deserved more praise. The correct answer represents this praise. Answer choice (C), acclaim, is correct. Views do not necessarily result in greater praise, so choice A isn't strong enough to match the clues in the sentence. If the artist felt her sculpture merited greater praise, she probably wouldn't also say that it needed development, so choice B is incorrect. Contempt, choice D, is negative, so the artist definitely wouldn't want her sculpture to receive more of that.

7. D

Choice (D) is correct. This is a strong Part/Whole Bridge here. A *fish* is one part of many in a *school*, and a *lion* is one part of many in a *pride*.

8. B

Choice (B) is the correct answer choice. This is an Association Bridge. By definition, a *liquid* transitions to *gas* when heated. By definition, *condensation* transitions to *evaporation* when heated.

9. B

Choice (B) is the correct answer choice. This is an Antonym Bridge. By definition, something that is *anomalous* is *not standard*. By definition, something that is *demonstrative* is *not impassive*.

10. D

Choice (D) is correct. The author describes Packard's warning but ultimately asserts the ability of the consumer to think critically about advertisements.

Choices A and C are the opposite; the passage argues against each one. Choice B is extreme and out of scope; nothing in the passage states what science can or cannot achieve.

11. C

Choice (C) is correct. The word "critically" is used to describe the way the public evaluates ads. Today's advertisers are having to work harder to keep up with the public, so the public must be doing a good job accurately interpreting these ads.

Choices A, B, and D are not supported by the passage. Nothing suggests that people now evaluate ads "negatively," "sarcastically," or "crucially."

12. B

Choice (B) is correct. According to lines 6–7, "Packard's dire predictions underestimated the public's ability to critically evaluate advertising messages." This supports the idea that his book did not include a warning that the public would become more sophisticated.

Choice A is in the passage on lines 1–2. Choices C and D are in the passage on lines 6–8.

CHAPTER 19

Verbal Reference

PUNCTUATION REVIEW

Commas

1. Use commas to separate items in a series.

If more than two items are listed in a series, they should be separated by commas. The final comma—the one that precedes the word "and"—may be omitted. An omitted final comma would not be considered an error on the SSAT or ISEE.

> Example: My recipe for buttermilk biscuits includes flour, baking soda, salt, shortening, and buttermilk.

> Example: My recipe for buttermilk biscuits includes flour, baking soda, salt, shortening and buttermilk.

Be watchful for commas placed before the first element of a series or after the last element.

> INCORRECT: My recipe for chocolate cake includes, flour, baking soda, sugar, eggs, milk and chocolate.

> INCORRECT: Flour, baking soda, sugar, eggs, milk and chocolate, are the ingredients in my chocolate cake.

2. Use commas to separate two or more adjectives before a noun.

> Example: I can't believe you sat through that long, dull movie three times in a row.

It is incorrect to place a comma after the last adjective in a series.

> INCORRECT: The manatee is a blubbery, bewhiskered, creature.

3. Use commas to set off parenthetical clauses and phrases.

If a phrase or clause is not necessary to the main idea expressed by a sentence, it should be set off by commas.

> Example: Phillip, who never had any formal chef's training, bakes excellent cheesecake.

The main idea here is that Phillip bakes an excellent cheesecake. The intervening clause merely serves to further describe Phillip; it should therefore be enclosed in commas.

4. Use commas after introductory phrases.

> Example: Having watered his petunias every day during the drought, Harold was disappointed when his garden was destroyed by aphids.

> Example: After the banquet, Harold and Melissa went dancing.

5. Use commas to separate independent clauses.

Use a comma before a conjunction (*and*, *but*, *nor*, *yet*, etc.) that connects two independent clauses.

> Example: Marta is good at basketball, but she's better at soccer.

Semicolons

Like commas, semicolons can be used to separate independent clauses. As noted previously, two related independent clauses that are connected by a conjunction such as *and*, *but*, *nor*, or *yet* should be punctuated by a comma. If the words *and*, *but*, *nor*, or *yet* aren't used, the clauses should be separated by a semicolon.

> Example: Whooping cranes are an endangered species; there are only 50 of them alive today.

> Example: Whooping cranes are an endangered species, and they are unlikely to survive if we continue to pollute their habitat.

Semicolons may also be used between independent clauses connected by words like *therefore*, *nevertheless*, and *moreover*. Remember, if you can use a period on the SSAT or ISEE, you can use a semicolon! For more on this topic, see the section on "Sentence Structure."

Colons

In standard written English, the colon is used only as a means of signaling that what follows is a list, definition, explanation, or restatement of what has gone before. A word or phrase such as *like the following*, *as follows*, *namely*, or *this* is often used along with the colon to make it clear that a list, summary, or explanation is coming up.

Example: This is what I found in her refrigerator: a moldy lime and a jar of peanut butter.

Example: Your instructions are as follows: read the passage carefully, answer the questions, and turn over your answer sheet.

Dashes

The dash has two uses. One is to indicate an abrupt break in thought.

Example: The alligator, unlike the crocodile, will usually not attack humans—unless, that is, she feels that her young are in danger.

The dash can also be used to set off a parenthetical expression from the rest of the sentence.

Example: At 32° Fahrenheit—which is zero on the Celsius scale—water will freeze.

Apostrophes

The apostrophe has two distinct functions. It is used with contracted verb forms to indicate that one or more letters have been eliminated:

Example: The **boy's** an expert at chess. (The boy is an expert at chess.)

Example: The **boy's** left for the day. (The boy has left for the day.)

The apostrophe is also used to indicate the possessive form of a noun.

Example: The **boy's** face was covered with mosquito bites after a day in the swamp.

GRAMMAR REVIEW

Subject-Verb Agreement

The form of a verb must match, or agree with, its subject in two ways: person and number.

1. Agreement of Person

When you talk about "person," you're talking about whether the subject and verb of a sentence show that the author is making a statement about himself (first person), the person he is speaking to (second person), or some other person, place, or thing (third person).

First-person subjects: I, we.

Example: **I am** going to Paris. **We are** going to Rome.

Second-person subject: you.

Example: **Are you** sure you weren't imagining that flying saucer?

Third-person subjects: he, she, they, it, *and names of people, places, and things.*

Example: **He is driving** me crazy.

2. Agreement of Number

When you talk about number, you're talking about whether the subject and verb show that one thing is being discussed (singular) or that more than one thing is being discussed (plural).

HINT: Subjects and verbs must agree in number.

INCORRECT: The **children catches** the school bus every morning.

CORRECT: The **children catch** the school bus every morning.

Be especially careful of subject-verb agreement when the subject and verb are separated by a long string of words.

INCORRECT: **Wild animals** in jungles all over the world **is endangered.**

CORRECT: **Wild animals** in jungles all over the world **are endangered.**

Pronouns

A **pronoun** is a word that is used in place of a noun. The **antecedent** of a pronoun is the word to which the pronoun refers.

Example: <u>Mary</u> [ANTECEDENT] was late for work because <u>she</u> [PRONOUN] forgot to set the alarm.

Occasionally, an antecedent will appear in a sentence *after* the pronoun.

Example: Because <u>he</u> [PRONOUN] sneezes so often, <u>Arthur</u> [ANTECEDENT] always thinks <u>he</u> [PRONOUN] might have the flu.

1. Pronouns and Agreement

In clear, grammatical writing, a pronoun must clearly refer to, and agree with, its antecedent.

NUMBER AND PERSON

	Singular	**Plural**
First Person	I, me	we, us
	my, mine	our, ours
Second Person	you	you
	your, yours	your, yours
Third Person	he, him	they, them
	she, her	
	it	
	one	
	his	their, theirs
	her, hers	
	its	
	one's	

Number Agreement

Pronouns must agree in number with their antecedents. A singular pronoun should stand in for a singular antecedent. A plural pronoun should stand in for a plural antecedent.

> INCORRECT: The bank turned Harry down when he applied for a loan because **their** credit department discovered that he didn't have a job.

What does the plural possessive *their* refer to? The singular noun *bank*. The singular possessive *its* is what is needed here.

> CORRECT: The bank turned Harry down for a loan because **its** credit department discovered that he didn't have a job.

Person Agreement

Pronouns must agree with their antecedents in person, too. A first-person pronoun should stand in for a first-person antecedent, and so on. One more thing to remember about which pronoun to use with which antecedent: never use the relative pronouns *that* or *which* to refer to a human being. Instead, use *who* or *whom*.

> INCORRECT: The woman **that** is standing at the piano is my sister.

> CORRECT: The woman **who** is standing at the piano is my sister.

2. Pronouns and Case

A more subtle type of pronoun problem is one in which the pronoun is in the incorrect case. Look at the following chart:

CASE

	Subjective	Objective
First Person	I	me
	we	us
Second Person	you	you
Third Person	he	him
	she	her
	it	it
	they	them
	one	one
Relative Pronouns	who	whom
	that	that
	which	which

When to Use Subjective Case Pronouns

Use the subjective case for the subject of a sentence.

> Example: **She** is falling asleep.

> INCORRECT: Nancy, Claire, and **me** are going to the ballet.

> CORRECT: Nancy, Claire, and **I** are going to the ballet.

Use the subjective case after a linking verb like *to be*.

> Example: It is **I.**

Use the subjective case in comparisons between the subject of verbs that are not stated but understood.

> Example: Gary is taller than **they** (are).

When to Use Objective Case Pronouns

Use the objective case for the object of a verb.

> Example: I called **her.**

Use the objective case for the object of a preposition.

   Example: I laughed at **him**.

Use the objective case after infinitives and gerunds.

   Example: Asking **him** to go was a big mistake.

   Example: To give **him** the scare of his life, we all jumped out of his closet.

Use the objective case in comparisons between objects of verbs that are not stated but understood.

   Example: She calls you more than (she calls) **me**.

3. Who and Whom

Another thing you'll need to know is when to use the relative pronoun *who* (subjective case) and when to use the relative pronoun *whom* (objective case: *whom* goes with *him* and *them*). The following method is very helpful when you're deciding which one to use.

   Example: Sylvester, (*who* or *whom*?) is afraid of the dark, sleeps with a Donald Duck night-light on.

Look only at the relative pronoun in its clause. Ignore the rest of the sentence.

   (Who or whom?) is afraid of the dark.

Turn the clause into a question. Ask yourself:

   Who or whom is afraid of the dark?

Answer the question with an ordinary personal pronoun.

   He is.

If you've answered the question with a subjective case pronoun (as you have here), you need the subjective case *who* in the relative clause.

   Sylvester, **who** is afraid of the dark, sleeps with a Donald Duck night-light on.

If you answer the question with an objective case pronoun, you need the objective case *whom* in the relative clause.

   HINT: Try answering the question with *he* or *him*. *Who* goes with *he* (subjective case), and *whom* goes with *him* (objective case).

Sentence Structure

A **sentence** is a group of words that can stand alone because it expresses a complete thought. To express a complete thought, it must contain a subject, about which something is said, and a verb, which says something about the subject.

Example: Dogs bark.

Example: The explorers slept in yak-hide tents.

Example: Looking out of the window, John saw a flying saucer.

Every sentence consists of at least one clause. Many sentences contain more than one clause (and phrases, too).

A **clause** is a group of words that contains a subject and a verb. "Dogs bark," "The explorers slept in a yak-hide tent," and "John saw a flying saucer" are all clauses.

A **phrase** is a group of words that does not have both a subject and a verb. "Looking out of the window" is a phrase.

1. Sentence Fragments

A **sentence fragment** is a group of words that seems to be a sentence but that is *grammatically* incomplete because it lacks a subject or a verb or that is *logically* incomplete because other elements necessary for it to express a complete thought are missing.

INCORRECT: Eggs and fresh vegetables on sale at the farmers' market.

This is not a complete sentence because there's no verb to say something about the subject, *eggs and fresh vegetables*.

INCORRECT: Because Richard likes hippopotamuses.

Even though this contains a subject (Richard) and a verb (likes), it's not a complete sentence because it doesn't express a complete thought. You don't know what's true "*because* Richard likes hippopotamuses."

INCORRECT: Martha dreams about dinosaurs although.

This isn't a complete sentence because it doesn't express a complete thought. What makes Martha's dreaming about dinosaurs in need of qualification or explanation?

2. Run-On Sentences

Just as unacceptable as an incomplete sentence is a "too-complete" sentence: a run-on sentence.

A **run-on sentence** is actually two complete sentences stuck together either with just a comma or with no punctuation at all.

INCORRECT: The children had been playing in the park, they were covered with mud.

INCORRECT: The children had been playing in the park they were covered with mud.

There are a number of ways to fix this kind of problem. They all involve a punctuation mark or a connecting word that can properly connect two clauses.

Join the clauses with a semicolon.

CORRECT: The children had been playing in the park; they were covered with mud.

Join the clauses with a coordinating conjunction (*and, but, for, nor, or, so, yet*) and a comma.

CORRECT: The children had been playing in the park, and they were covered with mud.

Join the clauses with a subordinating conjunction (*after, although, if, since, while*).

CORRECT: Because the children had been playing in the park, they were covered with mud.

OR

CORRECT: The children were covered with mud because they had been playing in the park.

And, of course, the two halves of a run-on sentence can be written as two separate, complete sentences.

CORRECT: The children had been playing in the park. They were covered with mud.

Verbs

English has six tenses, and each has a simple form and a progressive form.

	Simple	**Progressive**
Present	I work	I am working
Past	I worked	I was working
Future	I will work	I will be working
Present Perfect	I have worked	I have been working
Past Perfect	I had worked	I had been working
Future Perfect	I will have worked	I will have been working

1. Using the Present Tense

Use the present tense to describe a state or action occurring in the present time.

> Example: I **am** a student.

> Example: They **are studying** the Holy Roman Empire.

Use the present tense to describe habitual action.

> Example: They **eat** at Joe's Diner every night.

> Example: My father never **drinks** coffee.

Use the present tense to describe things that are always true.

> Example: The earth **is** round.

> Example: Grass **is** green.

2. Using the Past Tense

Use the simple past tense to describe an event or state that took place at a specific time in the past and is now over and done with.

> Example: Norman **broke** his toe when he tripped over his son's tricycle.

3. Using the Future Tense

Use the future tense for actions expected in the future.

> Example: I **will call** you on Wednesday.

Future actions are often expressed with the expression *to be going to.*

> Example: I **am going to move** to another apartment soon.

4. Using the Present Perfect Tense

Use the present perfect tense for actions and states that started in the past and continue up to and into the present time.

> Example: I **have been living** here for the last two years.

Use the present perfect for actions and states that happened a number of times in the past and may happen again in the future.

> Example: I **have heard** that song several times on the radio.

Use the present perfect for something that happened at an unspecified time in the past.

> Example: Anna **has seen** that movie already.

5. Using the Past Perfect Tense

The past perfect tense is used to represent past actions or states that were completed before other past actions or states. The more recent past event is expressed in the simple past, and the earlier past event is expressed in the past perfect.

> Example: When I turned my computer on this morning, I realized that I **had exited** the program yesterday without saving my work.

6. Using the Future Perfect Tense

Use the future perfect tense for a future state or event that will take place before another future event.

> Example: By the end of the week, I **will have worked** four hours of overtime.

7. Using the Proper Past Participle Form

If you use the present, past, or future perfect tense, make sure that you use the past participle and not the simple past tense.

> INCORRECT: I have **swam** in that pool every day this week.

> CORRECT: I have **swum** in that pool every day this week.

Irregular verbs have two different forms for simple past and past participle tenses. The following are some of the most common irregular verbs.

IRREGULAR VERBS

Infinitive	Simple Past	Past Participle
arise	arose	arisen
become	became	become
begin	began	begun
blow	blew	blown
break	broke	broken
come	came	come
do	did	done
draw	drew	drawn
drink	drank	drunk
drive	drove	driven
eat	ate	eaten
fall	fell	fallen
fly	flew	flown
freeze	froze	frozen
give	gave	given
grow	grew	grown
know	knew	known
ride	rode	ridden
rise	rose	risen
run	ran	run
see	saw	seen
shake	shook	shaken
shrink	shrank	shrunk
sing	sang	sung
speak	spoke	spoken
take	took	taken
throw	threw	thrown

Adjectives and Adverbs

An **adjective** modifies, or describes, a noun or pronoun.

Example: A woman in a **white** dress stood next to the **old** tree.

Example: The boat, **leaky** and **dirty**, hadn't been used in years.

An adverb modifies a verb, an adjective, or another adverb. Most, but not all, adverbs end in *-ly*. (Don't forget that some **adjectives**—*friendly, lovely*—also end in *-ly*.)

Example: The interviewer looked *approvingly* at the *neatly* dressed applicant.

Parallel Structure

Matching constructions must be expressed in parallel form. Make sure that when a sentence contains a **list** or makes a **comparison**, the items being listed or compared exhibit parallel structure.

1. Items in a List

INCORRECT: I love **running**, **jumping rope**, and **to play** basketball.

INCORRECT: I love **to run**, **jump rope**, and **to play** basketball.

CORRECT: I love **to run**, **jump rope**, and **play** basketball.

CORRECT: I love **to run**, **to jump rope**, and **to play** basketball.

CORRECT: I love **running**, **jumping rope**, and **playing** basketball.

2. Items in a Comparison

Comparisons must do more than just exhibit parallel structure. Most faulty comparisons relate to the notion that you can't compare apples and oranges. You don't merely want comparisons to be grammatically similar; they must be logically similar as well.

INCORRECT: **To visualize** success is not the same as **achieving** it.

CORRECT: **To visualize** success is not the same as **to achieve** it.

CORRECT: **Visualizing** success is not the same as **achieving** it.

INCORRECT: **The rules of chess** are more complex than **checkers**.

CORRECT: **The rules of chess** are more complex than **those of checkers**.

CORRECT: **Chess** is more complex than **checkers**.

STYLE REVIEW

Pronouns and Reference

When referencing pronouns and their antecedents, you say that pronouns refer to or refer back to their antecedents. This book notes earlier that pronouns must agree in person and number with their antecedents. However, a different kind of pronoun error exists when a pronoun either doesn't refer to any antecedent at all or doesn't refer clearly to one, and only one, antecedent.

Sometimes an incorrectly used pronoun has no antecedent:

> WEAK: Joe doesn't like what **they play** on this radio station.

Who are *they*? We can't tell, because there is no antecedent for *they*.

> CORRECT: Joe doesn't like what **the radio hosts play** on this radio station.

Don't use pronouns without antecedents when doing so makes a sentence unclear. Sometimes a pronoun seems to have an antecedent until you look closely and see that the word that appears to be the antecedent is not a noun, but an adjective, a possessive form, or a verb. The antecedent of a pronoun must be a noun.

> INCORRECT: When you are painting, make sure you don't get **it** on the floor.

> CORRECT: When you are painting, make sure you don't get **paint** on the floor.

Other examples of pronoun reference problems:

> INCORRECT: I've always been interested in astronomy and finally have decided to become **one**.

> CORRECT: I've always been interested in astronomy and finally have decided to become an **astronomer**.

Don't use pronouns with remote references. A pronoun that is too far away from what it refers to is said to have a **remote antecedent**.

> INCORRECT: Jane quit smoking and, as a result, temporarily put on a lot of weight. **It** was very bad for her health.

> CORRECT: Jane quit smoking because **it** was very bad for her health, and, as a result, she temporarily gained a lot of weight.

Don't use pronouns with faulty broad reference. A pronoun with broad reference is one that refers to a whole idea instead of to a single noun.

> INCORRECT: He built a fence to stop people from looking into his backyard. **That's** not easy.

> CORRECT: He built a fence to stop people from looking into his backyard. **The fence was not easy to build**.

Redundancy

Words or phrases are **redundant** when they have basically the same meaning as something already stated in the sentence. Don't use two phrases when one is sufficient.

> INCORRECT: The school was **established and founded** in 1906.

> CORRECT: The school was **established** in 1906.

Relevance

Everything in the sentence should serve to get across the point in question. Something unrelated to that point should be cut.

> LESS RELEVANT: No one can say for sure just how successful the new law will be in the fight against crime (just as no one can be sure whether he or she will ever be a victim of a crime).

> MORE RELEVANT: No one can say for sure just how successful the new law will be in the fight against crime.

Verbosity

Sometimes having extra words in a sentence results in a style problem.

> WORDY: The supply of **musical instruments that are antique** is limited, so they become more valuable each year.

> MORE CONCISE: The supply of **antique musical instruments** is limited, so they become more valuable each year.

> WORDY: We **were in agreement with each other** that Max was an unsuspecting old fool.

> MORE CONCISE: We **agreed** that Max was an unsuspecting old fool.

Commonly Misused Words

accept/except

Don't confuse the two. To *accept* means to receive or agree to something, whereas *except* is usually a preposition meaning excluding, although it can also mean to leave out.

INCORRECT: Can you **except** my apology?

CORRECT: Can you **accept** my apology?

affect/effect

These are easy to confuse. To *affect* means to have an *effect* on something. When the word is being used as a verb, the proper word to use is almost always *affect*; when it's being used as a noun, the proper word to use is almost always *effect*. (It should be noted that *effect* can also be a verb, meaning to bring about or cause to happen.)

INCORRECT: His affectations **effected** me to no good **affect**.

CORRECT: His affectations **affected** me to no good **effect**.

among/between

In most cases, you should use *between* for two items and *among* for more than two.

Example: The competition **between** Anne and Michael has grown more intense.

Example: He is always at his best **among** strangers.

When it comes to these two words, use common sense. Sometimes *among* just doesn't make sense.

Example: Plant the trees in the area **between** the road, the wall, and the fence.

amount/number

Amount should be used to refer to an uncountable quantity. *Number* should refer to a countable quantity.

Example: The **amount** of food he threw away would feed a substantial **number** of people.

as/like

Like is a preposition; it takes a noun object. *As*, when functioning as a conjunction, introduces a subordinate clause. Remember, a clause is a part of a sentence containing a subject and verb.

Example: He sings **like** an angel.

Example: He sings **as** an angel sings.

as...as...

The idiom is *as...as...*, **not** *as...than...*

> INCORRECT: That suit is **as** expensive **than** this one.

> CORRECT: That suit is **as** expensive **as** this one.

fewer/less

Use *fewer* for nouns you can count; use *less* before nouns that are singular and uncountable.

> Example: There are **less** apples on this tree than there were last year.

> Example: He has **fewer** than 10 items in the self-checkout lane.

its/it's

Many people confuse *its* and *it's*. *Its* is possessive; *it's* is a contraction of *it is or it has*.

> Example: The cat licked **its** paws.

> Example: **It's** raining cats and dogs.

neither...nor...

The correlative conjunction is *neither...nor...*, **not** *neither...or...*

> Example. He is **neither** strong **nor** flexible.

Avoid the redundancy caused by using *nor* following a negative.

> INCORRECT: Alice's departure was **not** noticed by Debby **nor** Sue.

> CORRECT: Alice's departure was **not** noticed by Debby **or** Sue.

their/they're/there

Many people confuse *their, they're,* and *there. Their* is possessive; *they're* is a contraction of *they are.*

> Example: The girls rode **their** bikes home.

> Example: **They're** training for the big race.

There has two uses: it can indicate place and it can be used as an expletive—a word that doesn't do anything in a sentence except delay the subject.

> Example: Put the book over **there**.

> Example: **There** will be 15 runners competing for the prize.

Idioms

Some phrases are incorrect simply because that's just not the way we say it in English. This is especially true of preposition-verb word combinations.

> INCORRECT: The fashion police **frown at** wearing hats adorned with flowers.

> CORRECT: The fashion police **frown upon** wearing hats adorned with flowers.

The first sentence is only incorrect because *frowns at* is not the correct idiomatic expression. There's no way to infer the correct idiom, so try to memorize the most common idiomatic phrases. If you can't think of another time you've heard that phrase, either guess (ISEE) or leave the question blank (SSAT).

Common Idioms

accuse *of*	discriminate *against*
apologize *for*	distinguish *from*
arrive *at*	dream *about/of*
associate *with*	forbid *to*
attribute *to*	frown *upon*
believe *in*	object *to*
believe *to be*	prohibit *from*
continue *to*	substitute *for*
contrast *with*	target *at*
credit *with*	use *as*
decide *to*	view *as*
define *as*	worry *about*
different *from*	

VOCABULARY REFERENCE

Root List

Root	Meaning	Examples
A, AN	not, without	amoral, atrophy, asymmetrical, anarchy, anesthetic, anonymity, anomaly, annul
AB, A	from, away, apart	abnegate, abortive, abrogate, abscond, absolve, abstemious, abstruse, avert, aversion, abnormal, abdicate, aberration, abhor, abject, abjure, ablution
AC, ACR	sharp, sour	acid, acerbic, exacerbate, acute, acuity, acumen, acrid, acrimony
AD, A	to, toward	adhere, adjacent, adjunct, admonish, adroit, adumbrate, advent, abeyance, abet, accede, accretion, acquiesce, affluent, aggrandize, aggregate, alleviate, alliteration, allude, allure, ascribe, aspersion, aspire, assail, assonance, attest
ALI, ALTR	another	alias, alienate, inalienable, altruism
AM, AMI	love	amorous, amicable, amiable, amity
AMBI, AMPHI	both	ambiguous, ambivalent, ambidextrous, amphibious
AMBL, AMBUL	walk	amble, ambulatory, perambulator, somnambulist
ANIM	mind, spirit, breath	animal, animosity, unanimous, magnanimous
ANN, ENN	year	annual, annuity, superannuated, biennial, perennial
ANTE, ANT	before	antecedent, antediluvian, antebellum, antepenultimate, anterior, antiquity, antiquated, anticipate
ANTHROP	human	anthropology, anthropomorphic, misanthrope, philanthropy
ANTI, ANT	against, opposite	antidote, antipathy, antithesis, antacid, antagonist, antonym
AUD	hear	audio, audience, audition, auditory, audible
AUTO	self	autobiography, autocrat, autonomous
BELLI, BELL	war	belligerent, bellicose, antebellum, rebellion

(Continued)

Root	Meaning	Examples
BENE, BEN	good	benevolent, benefactor, beneficent, benign
BI	two	bicycle, bisect, bilateral, bilingual, biped
BIBLIO	book	Bible, bibliography, bibliophile
BIO	life	biography, biology, amphibious, symbiotic, macrobiotics
BURS	money, purse	reimburse, disburse, bursar
CAD, CAS, CID	happen, fall	accident, cadence, cascade, deciduous
CAP, CIP	head	captain, decapitate, capitulate, precipitous, precipitate, recapitulate
CAP, CAPT, CEPT, CIP	take, hold, seize	capable, capacious, captivate, deception, intercept, precept, inception, anticipate, emancipate, incipient, percipient
CARN	flesh	carnal, carnage, carnival, carnivorous, incarnate, incarnadine
CED, CESS	yield, go	cede, precede, accede, recede, antecedent, intercede, secede, cession, cease, cessation, incessant
CHROM	color	chrome, chromatic, monochrome
CHRON	time	chronology, chronic, anachronism
CIDE	murder	suicide, homicide, regicide, patricide
CIRCUM	around	circumference, circumlocution, circumnavigate, circumscribe, circumspect, circumvent
CLIN, CLIV	slope	incline, declivity, proclivity
CLUD, CLUS, CLAUS, CLOIS	shut, close	conclude, reclusive, claustrophobia, cloister, preclude, occlude
CO, COM, CON	with, together	coeducation, coagulate, coalesce, coerce, cogent, collateral, colloquial, colloquy, commensurate, commodious, compassion, compatriot, complacent, compliant, complicity, compunction, concerto, conciliatory, concord, concur, condone, conflagration, congeal, congenial, congenital, conglomerate, conjure, conjugal, conscientious, consecrate, consensus, consonant, constrained, contentious, contrite, contusion, convalescence, convene, convivial, convoke, convoluted, congress

(Continued)

Root	Meaning	Examples
COGN, GNO	know	recognize, cognition, cognizance, incognito, diagnosis, agnostic, prognosis, gnostic, ignorant
CONTRA	against	controversy, incontrovertible, contravene, contradict
CORP	body	corpse, corporeal, corpulence
COSMO, COSM	world	cosmopolitan, cosmos, microcosm, macrocosm
CRAC, CRAT	rule, power	democracy, bureaucracy, theocracy, autocrat, aristocrat, technocrat
CRED	trust, believe	incredible, credulous, credence
CRESC, CRET	grow	crescent, crescendo, accretion
CULP	blame, fault	culprit, culpable, inculpate, exculpate
CURR, CURS	run	current, concur, cursory, precursor, incursion
DE	down, out, apart	depart, debase, debilitate, declivity, decry, deface, defamatory, defunct, delegate, demarcation, demean, demur, deplete, deplore, depravity, deprecate, deride, derivative, desist, detest
DEC	ten, tenth	decade, decimal, decathlon, decimate
DEMO, DEM	people	democrat, demographics, demagogue, epidemic, pandemic, endemic
DI, DIURN	day	diary, diurnal, quotidian
DIA	across	diagonal, diatribe, diaphanous
DIC, DICT	speak	diction, interdict, predict, abdicate, indict, verdict, dictum
DIS, DIF, DI	not, apart, away	disaffected, disband, disbar, disburse, discern, discordant, discredit, discursive, disheveled, disparage, disparate, dispassionate, dispirit, dissemble, disseminate, dissension, dissipate, dissonant, dissuade, distend, differentiate, diffidence, diffuse, digress, divert
DOC, DOCT	teach	doctrine, docile, doctrinaire
DOL	pain	condolence, doleful, dolorous, indolent
DUC, DUCT	lead	seduce, induce, conduct, viaduct, induct
EGO	self	ego, egoist, egocentric

(Continued)

Root	Meaning	Examples
EN, EM	in, into	enter, entice, encumber, endemic, ensconce, enthrall, entreat, embellish, embezzle, embroil, empathy
ERR	wander	erratic, aberration, errant
EU	well, good	eulogy, euphemism, euphony, euphoria, eurythmics, euthanasia
EX, E	out, out of	exit, exacerbate, excerpt, excommunicate, exculpate, execrable, exhume, exonerate, exorbitant, exorcise, expatriate, expedient, expiate, expunge, expurgate, extenuate, extort, extremity, extricate, extrinsic, exult, evoke, evict, evince, elicit, egress, egregious
FAC, FIC, FECT, FY, FEA	make, do	factory, facility, benefactor, malefactor, fiction, fictive, beneficent, affect, confection, refectory, magnify, unify, rectify, vilify, feasible
FAL, FALS	deceive	false, infallible, fallacious
FERV	boil	fervent, fervid, effervescent
FID	faith, trust	confident, diffidence, perfidious, fidelity
FLU, FLUX	flow	fluent, flux, affluent, confluence, effluvia, superfluous
FORE	before	forecast, foreboding, forestall
FRAG, FRAC	break	fragment, fracture, diffract, fractious, refract
FUS	pour	profuse, infusion, effusive, diffuse
GEN	birth, class, kin	generation, congenital, homogeneous, heterogeneous, ingenious, engender, progenitor, progeny
GRAD, GRESS	step	graduate, gradual, retrograde, centigrade, degrade, gradation, gradient, progress, congress, digress, transgress, ingress, egress
GRAPH, GRAM	writing	biography, bibliography, epigraph, grammar, epigram
GRAT	pleasing	grateful, gratitude, gratis, ingrate, congratulate, gratuitous, gratuity
GRAV, GRIEV	heavy	grave, gravity, aggravate, grieve, aggrieve, grievous
GREG	crowd, flock	segregate, gregarious, egregious, congregate, aggregate

(Continued)

Root	Meaning	Examples
HABIT, HIBIT	have, hold	habit, inhibit, cohabit, habitat
HAP	by chance	happen, haphazard, hapless, mishap
HELIO, HELI	sun	heliocentric, helium, heliotrope, aphelion, perihelion
HETERO	other	heterosexual, heterogeneous, heterodox
HOL	whole	holocaust, catholic, holistic
HOMO	same	homosexual, homogenize, homogeneous, homonym
HOMO	man	*Homo sapiens*, homicide, bonhomie
HYDR	water	hydrant, hydrate, dehydration
HYPER	too much, excess	hyperactive, hyperbole, hyperventilate
HYPO	too little, under	hypodermic, hypothermia, hypochondria, hypothesis, hypothetical
IN, IG, IL, IM, IR	not	incorrigible, indefatigable, indelible, indubitable, inept, inert, inexorable, insatiable, insentient, insolvent, insomnia, interminable, intractable, incessant, inextricable, infallible, infamy, innumerable, inoperable, insipid, intemperate, intrepid, inviolable, ignorant, ignominious, ignoble, illicit, illimitable, immaculate, immutable, impasse, impeccable, impecunious, impertinent, implacable, impotent, impregnable, improvident, impassioned, impervious, irregular
IN, IL, IM, IR	in, on, into	invade, inaugurate, incandescent, incarcerate, incense, indenture, induct, ingratiate, introvert, incarnate, inception, incisive, infer, infusion, ingress, innate, inquest, inscribe, insinuate, inter, illustrate, imbue, immerse, implicate, irrigate, irritate
INTER	between, among	intercede, intercept, interdiction, interject, interlocutor, interloper, intermediary, intermittent, interpolate, interpose, interregnum, interrogate, intersect, intervene
INTRA, INTR	within	intrastate, intravenous, intramural, intrinsic
IT, ITER	between, among	transit, itinerant, reiterate, transitory
JECT, JET	throw	eject, interject, abject, trajectory, jettison
JOUR	day	journal, adjourn, sojourn

(Continued)

Root	Meaning	Examples
JUD	judge	judge, judicious, prejudice, adjudicate
JUNCT, JUG	join	junction, adjunct, injunction, conjugal, subjugate
JUR	swear, law	jury, abjure, adjure, conjure, perjure, jurisprudence
LAT	side	lateral, collateral, unilateral, bilateral, quadrilateral
LAV, LAU, LU	wash	lavatory, laundry, ablution, antediluvian
LEG, LEC, LEX	read, speak	legible, lecture, lexicon
LEV	light	elevate, levitate, levity, alleviate
LIBER	free	liberty, liberal, libertarian, libertine
LIG, LECT	choose, gather	eligible, elect, select
LIG, LI, LY	bind	ligament, oblige, religion, liable, liaison, lien, ally
LING, LANG	tongue	lingo, language, linguistics, bilingual
LITER	letter	literate, alliteration, literal
LITH	stone	monolith, lithograph, megalith
LOQU, LOC, LOG	speech, thought	eloquent, loquacious, colloquial, colloquy, soliloquy, circumlocution, interlocutor, monologue, dialogue, eulogy, philology, neologism
LUC, LUM	light	lucid, illuminate, elucidate, pellucid, translucent
LUD, LUS	play	ludicrous, allude, delusion, allusion, illusory
MACRO	great	macrocosm, macrobiotics
MAG, MAJ, MAS, MAX	great	magnify, magnanimous, magnate, magnitude majesty, master, maximum
MAL	bad	malady, maladroit, malevolent, malodorous
MAN	hand	manual, manuscript, emancipate, manifest
MAR	sea	submarine, marine, maritime
MATER, MATR	mother	maternal, matron, matrilineal
MEDI	middle	intermediary, medieval, mediate
MEGA	great	megaphone, megalomania, megaton, megalith
MEMOR, MEMEN	remember	memory, memento, memorabilia, memoir

(Continued)

Root	Meaning	Examples
METER, METR, MENS	measure	meter, thermometer, perimeter, metronome, commensurate
MICRO	small	microscope, microorganism, microcosm, microbe
MIS	wrong, bad, hate	misunderstand, misanthrope, misapprehension, misconstrue, misnomer, mishap
MIT, MISS	send	transmit, emit, missive
MOLL	soft	mollify, emollient, mollusk
MON, MONIT	warn	admonish, monitor, premonition
MONO	one	monologue, monotonous, monogamy, monolith, monochrome
MOR	custom, manner	moral, mores, morose
MOR, MORT	dead	morbid, moribund, mortal, amortize
MORPH	shape	amorphous, anthropomorphic, metamorphosis, morphology
MOV, MOT, MOB, MOM	move	remove, motion, mobile, momentum, momentous
MUT	change	mutate, mutability, immutable, commute
NAT, NASC	born	native, nativity, natal, neonate, innate, cognate, nascent, renascent, renaissance
NAU, NAV	ship, sailor	nautical, nauseous, navy, circumnavigate
NEG	not, deny	negative, abnegate, renege
NEO	new	neoclassical, neophyte, neologism, neonate
NIHIL	none, nothing	annihilation, nihilism
NOM, NYM	name	nominate, nomenclature, nominal, cognomen, misnomer, ignominious, antonym, homonym, pseudonym, synonym, anonymity
NOX, NIC, NEC, NOC	harm	obnoxious, noxious, pernicious, internecine, innocuous
NOV	new	novelty, innovation, novitiate
NUMER	number	numeral, numerous, innumerable, enumerate
OB	against	obstruct, obdurate, obfuscate, obnoxious, obsequious, obstinate, obstreperous, obtrusive
OMNI	all	omnipresent, omnipotent, omniscient, omnivorous

(Continued)

Root	Meaning	Examples
ONER	burden	onerous, onus, exonerate
OPER	work	operate, cooperate, inoperable
PAC	peace	pacify, pacifist, pacific
PALP	feel	palpable, palpitation
PAN	all	panorama, panacea, panegyric, pandemic, panoply
PATER, PATR	father	paternal, paternity, patriot, compatriot, expatriate, patrimony, patricide, patrician
PATH, PASS	feel, suffer	sympathy, antipathy, empathy, apathy, pathos, impassioned
PEC	money	pecuniary, impecunious, peculation
PED, POD	foot	pedestrian, pediment, expedient, biped, quadruped, tripod
PEL, PULS	drive	compel, compelling, expel, propel, compulsion
PEN	almost	peninsula, penultimate, penumbra
PEND, PENS	hang	pendant, pendulous, compendium, suspense, propensity
PER	through, by, for, throughout	perambulator, percipient, perfunctory, permeable, perspicacious, pertinacious, perturbation, perusal, perennial, peregrinate
PER	against, destruction	perfidious, pernicious, perjure
PERI	around	perimeter, periphery, perihelion, peripatetic
PET	seek, go toward	petition, impetus, impetuous, petulant, centripetal
PHIL	love	philosopher, philanderer, philanthropy, bibliophile, philology
PHOB	fear	phobia, claustrophobia, xenophobia
PHON	sound	phonograph, megaphone, euphony, phonetics, phonics
PLAC	calm, please	placate, implacable, placid, complacent
PON, POS	put, place	postpone, proponent, exponent, preposition, posit, interpose, juxtaposition, depose
PORT	carry	portable, deportment, rapport
POT	drink	potion, potable

(Continued)

Root	Meaning	Examples
POT	power	potential, potent, impotent, potentate, omnipotence
PRE	before	precede, precipitate, preclude, precocious, precursor, predilection, predisposition, preponderance, prepossessing, presage, prescient, prejudice, predict, premonition, preposition
PRIM, PRI	first	prime, primary, primal, primeval, primordial, pristine
PRO	ahead, forth	proceed, proclivity, procrastinator, profane, profuse, progenitor, progeny, prognosis, prologue, promontory, propel, proponent, propose, proscribe, protestation, provoke
PROTO	first	prototype, protagonist, protocol
PROX, PROP	near	approximate, proximity, propinquity
PSEUDO	false	pseudoscientific, pseudonym
PYR	fire	pyre, pyrotechnics, pyromania
QUAD, QUAR, QUAT	four	quadrilateral, quadrant, quadruped, quarter, quarantine, quaternary
QUES, QUER, QUIS, QUIR	question	quest, inquest, query, querulous, inquisitive, inquiry
QUIE	quiet	disquiet, acquiesce, quiescent, requiem
QUINT, QUIN	five	quintuplets, quintessence
RADI, RAMI	branch	radius, radiate, radiant, eradicate, ramification
RECT, REG	straight, rule	rectangle, rectitude, rectify, regular
REG	king, rule	regal, regent, interregnum
RETRO	backward	retrospective, retroactive, retrograde
RID, RIS	laugh	ridiculous, deride, derision
ROG	ask	interrogate, derogatory, abrogate, arrogate, arrogant
RUD	rough, crude	rude, rudimentary
RUPT	break	disrupt, interrupt, rupture, erupt
SACR, SANCT	holy	sacred, sacrilege, consecrate, sanctify, sanction, sacrosanct

(Continued)

Root	Meaning	Examples
SCRIB, SCRIPT, SCRIV	write	scribe, ascribe, circumscribe, inscribe, proscribe, script, manuscript, scrivener
SE	apart, away	separate, segregate, secede, sedition
SEC, SECT, SEG	cut	sector, dissect, bisect, intersect, segment, secant
SED, SID	sit	sedate, sedentary, supersede, reside, residence, assiduous, insidious
SEM	seed, sow	seminar, seminal, disseminate
SEN	old	senior, senile, senescent
SENT, SENS	feel, think	sentiment, sentient, nonsense, assent, consensus, sensual
SEQU, SECU	follow	sequence, sequel, subsequent, obsequious, obsequy, non sequitur, consecutive
SIM, SEM	similar, same	similar, verisimilitude, semblance, dissemble
SIGN	mark, sign	signal, designation, assignation
SIN	curve	sine curve, sinuous, insinuate
SOL	sun	solar, parasol, solarium, solstice
SOL	alone	solo, solitude, soliloquy, solipsism
SOMN	sleep	insomnia, somnolent, somnambulist
SON	sound	sonic, consonance, dissonance, assonance, sonorous, resonate
SOPH	wisdom	philosopher, sophistry, sophisticated, sophomoric
SPEC, SPIC	see, look	spectator, circumspect, retrospective, perspective, perspicacious
SPER	hope	prosper, prosperous, despair, desperate
SPERS, SPAR	scatter	disperse, aspersion, sparse, disparate
SPIR	breathe	respire, inspire, spiritual, aspire, transpire
STRICT, STRING	bind	strict, stricture, constrict, stringent, astringent
STRUCT, STRU	build	structure, obstruct, construe
SUB	under	subconscious, subjugate, subliminal, subpoena, subsequent, subterranean, subvert
SUMM	highest	summit, summary, consummate

(Continued)

Root	Meaning	Examples
SUPER, SUR	above	supervise, supercilious, supersede, superannuated, superfluous, insurmountable, surfeit
SURGE, SURRECT	rise	surge, resurgent, insurgent, insurrection
SYN, SYM	together	synthesis, sympathy, synonym, syncopation, synopsis, symposium, symbiosis
TACIT, TIC	silent	tacit, taciturn, reticent
TACT, TAG, TANG	touch	tact, tactile, contagious, tangent, tangential, tangible
TEN, TIN, TAIN	hold, twist	detention, tenable, tenacious, pertinacious, retinue, retain
TEND, TENS, TENT	stretch	intend, distend, tension, tensile, ostensible, contentious
TERM	end	terminal, terminus, terminate, interminable
TERR	earth, land	terrain, terrestrial, extraterrestrial, subterranean
TEST	witness	testify, attest, testimonial, testament, detest, protestation
THE	god	atheist, theology, apotheosis, theocracy
THERM	heat	thermometer, thermal, thermonuclear, hypothermia
TIM	fear, frightened	timid, intimidate, timorous
TOP	place	topic, topography, utopia
TORP	stiff, numb	torpedo, torpid, torpor
TORT	twist	distort, extort, tortuous
TOX	poison	toxic, toxin, intoxication
TRACT	draw	tractor, intractable, protract
TRANS	across, over, through, beyond	transport, transgress, transient, transitory, translucent, transmutation, transpire, intransigent
TREM, TREP	shake	tremble, tremor, tremulous, trepidation, intrepid
TURB	shake	disturb, turbulent, perturbation
UMBR	shadow	umbrella, umbrage, adumbrate, penumbra
UNI, UN	one	unify, unilateral, unanimous

(Continued)

Root	Meaning	Examples
URB	city	urban, suburban, urbane
VAC	empty	vacant, evacuate, vacuous
VAL, VAIL	value, strength	valid, valor, ambivalent, convalescence, avail, prevail, countervail
VEN, VENT	come	convene, contravene, intervene, venue, convention, circumvent, advent, adventitious
VER	true	verify, verity, verisimilitude, veracious, aver, verdict
VERB	word	verbal, verbose, verbiage, verbatim
VERT, VERS	turn	avert, convert, revert, incontrovertible, divert, subvert, versatile, aversion
VICT, VINC	conquer	victory, conviction, evict, evince, invincible
VID, VIS	see	evident, vision, visage, supervise
VIL	base, mean	vile, vilify, revile
VIV, VIT	life	vivid, convivial, vivacious, vital
VOC, VOK, VOW	call, voice	vocal, equivocate, vociferous, convoke, evoke, invoke, avow
VOL	wish	voluntary, malevolent, benevolent, volition
VOLV, VOLUT	turn, roll	revolve, evolve, convoluted
VOR	eat	devour, carnivorous, omnivorous, voracious

VOCABULARY LIST

Word	Definition, Context, Synonyms
ABHOR	to hate, to view with repugnance, to detest *After repeated failure to learn the Pythagorean theorem, Susan began to* abhor *geometry.* Synonyms: **hate, loathe, abominate**
ABSURD	ridiculously unreasonable, lacking logic *Ironing one's underwear is* absurd. Synonyms: **ridiculous, ludicrous, preposterous, bizarre**
ACCLAIM	(n) praise, enthusiastic approval *The artist won international* acclaim; *critics and viewers all over the world were intrigued by the works.* Synonyms: **praise, approval** (v) to approve, to welcome with applause and praise *The critic was eager to* acclaim *the actress for her performance.* Synonyms: **cheer, applaud, praise, honor**
ACUTE	sharp in some way (as in an acute angle) or sharp in intellect; crucial *There is an* acute *shortage of food, which will ultimately result in a famine if something is not done soon to increase the food supply.* Synonyms: **perceptive, sharp, keen, shrewd, crucial**
ADJUNCT	something or someone associated with another but in a defendant or secondary position *An* adjunct *professor is one not given the same full-time status as other faculty members.* Synonyms: **additional, supporting, assisting, accessory**
ADMONISH	to scold (sometimes in a good natured way); to urge to duty, remind; to advise against something *My mother began to* admonish *me about my poor grades.* Synonyms: **warn, caution, scold**
AFFABLE	pleasantly easy to get along with; friendly and warm *He was an* affable *host and made us feel right at home.* Synonyms: **agreeable, amiable**
AGHAST	overcome by surprise, disgust, or amazement; seized with terror; shocked *The investigator was* aghast *at the horrible conditions in the nursing home.* Synonyms: **astounded, dismayed, appalled, astonished, shocked**
ALLEVIATE	to make easier to bear, lessen *This medicine will help to* alleviate *the pain.* Synonyms: **relieve, allay, assuage, ease, decrease, lessen, mitigate**
ALOOF	distant in relations with other people *The newcomer remained* aloof *from all our activities and therefore made no new friends.* Synonyms: **detached, cool, blase, remote**

(Continued)

Word	Definition, Context, Synonyms
ALTRUISTIC	concerned for the welfare of others *The altruistic woman gave out money to all who seemed needy.* Synonyms: **benevolent, charitable, compassionate, humane**
AMEND	to improve; to alter; to add to or subtract from by formal procedure *Congress will amend the bill so that the president will sign it.* Synonyms: **alter, improve, repair, mend, make better, ameliorate**
AMORPHOUS	lacking a specific shape *In the movie* The Blob, *the creature was an amorphous one that was constantly changing shape.* Synonyms: **shapeless, vague**
ANIMOSITY	feeling of ill will, intense dislike for someone or something *The deep-rooted animosity between them made it difficult for the brothers to work together.* Synonyms: **ill will, ill feeling, bitterness, rancor, acrimony**
ANNIHILATE	to destroy completely *The first troops to land on the beach during the invasion were annihilated by the powerful artillery of the enemy.* Synonyms: **destroy, devastate, demolish**
ARDENT	characterized by passion or desire *After a 25-game losing streak, even the Mets' most ardent fans realized the team wouldn't finish first.* Synonyms: **passionate, enthusiastic, fervent**
ARTICULATE	(adj) well-spoken, lucidly presented *Joe's articulate argument was so persuasive that we all agreed with him.* Synonyms: **eloquent, glib** (v) to pronounce clearly *The great actor articulated every word so clearly that it was easy to understand him.* Synonym: **enunciate**
ARTIFICE	(1) trickery, clever ruse *Ralph's use of rubber masks proved to be a brilliant artifice.* Synonyms: **stratagem, trick, ploy, deception, ruse, maneuver** (2) ability to create or imagine *Many question the meaningfulness of Jamie's science fiction novel, but its fantastic images and ingenious plot cannot fail to impress with its sheer artifice.* Synonyms: **creativity, inventiveness, innovation, resourcefulness, imagination, ingenuity**
ASCERTAIN	to find out or discover by examination *Try though he did, the archaeologist couldn't ascertain the correct age of the Piltdown man's skeleton.* Synonyms: **determine, discover, unearth, find out**

(Continued)

Word	Definition, Context, Synonyms
ASTUTE	shrewd and perceptive; able to understand clearly and quickly *The novelist Judy Blume is an* astute *judge of human character.* Synonyms: **keen, discerning, penetrating, incisive, perceptive, crafty, foxy, wily, shrewd**
ATROCITY	horrible act *During the Indian bid for freedom from British colonial rule, a British officer committed the* atrocity *of slaughtering a large congregation of peaceful Indian demonstrators.* Synonyms: **horror, barbarity, outrage**
AUDACITY	boldness or daring, especially with disregard for personal safety *He had the* audacity *to insult the president to his face.* Synonyms: **boldness, daring, impudence**
BANAL	boringly predictable *A boring conversation is likely to be full of* banal *statements like "Have a nice day."* Synonyms: **boring, dull, bland, insipid**
BEGUILE	to delude, deceive by trickery *Beguiled by the supernatural songs of the Sirens, Odysseus wanted to abandon all his men and forget his family.* Synonyms: **charm, allure, bewitch, captivate**
BELLIGERENCE	aggressive hostility *A soldier can be shocked by the* belligerence *of his enemy.* Synonyms: **aggressiveness, combativeness**
BENEFACTOR	someone giving financial or general assistance *A wealthy alumnus who gives $5 million to his old college would be considered a great* benefactor. Synonyms: **patron, backer, donor**
BENEVOLENCE	inclination to do good deeds *The* benevolence *of the generous donor was recognized by a plaque.* Synonym: **largess**
BEWILDERED	completely confused or puzzled, perplexed *I was* bewildered *by the complex algebra problem.* Synonyms: **confused, puzzled, perplexed**
BIAS	(n) prejudice, particular tendency *Racial* bias *in employment is illegal in the United States.* Synonym: **partiality** (v) to cause prejudice in (a person); to influence unfairly *The article is not accurate and may* bias *some readers.* Synonyms: **influence, sway, distort, skew**
BLISS	supreme happiness, utter joy or contentment; heaven, paradise *For lovers of ice cream, this new flavor is absolute* bliss. Synonyms: **joy, delight, ecstasy**

(Continued)

Word	Definition, Context, Synonyms
BOISTEROUS	loud and unrestrained *The boisterous party made so much noise last night that I got no sleep.* Synonyms: **loud, noisy, raucous**
BOUNTY	generosity in giving; reward *The police offered a bounty for the capture of the criminal.* Synonyms: **abundance, cornucopia, reward, loot**
BRAVADO	showy and pretentious display of courage *The coward's bravado quickly vanished when his captors threatened to hit him; he began to whine for mercy.* Synonyms: **bluster, bombast, swagger**
BREVITY	state of being brief, of not lasting a long time *The brevity of your visit to my home implied that you did not enjoy my family's company.* Synonyms: **shortness, fleetness, swiftness**
CACHE	hiding place for treasures, etc.; anything in such a hiding place *The secret panel hid a cache of jewels.* Synonym: **stash**
CAJOLE	to wheedle, persuade with promises or flattery, coax *The spoiled girl could cajole her father into buying her anything.* Synonyms: **coax, wheedle**
CANDOR	frankness and sincerity; fairness *The candor of his confession impressed his parents, and they gave him a light punishment as a result.* Synonyms: **honesty, sincerity**
CAPRICE	sudden, unpredictable change *With the caprice of an irrational man, he often went from rage to laughter.* Synonyms: **impulse, whim, fancy**
CELESTIAL	relating to the heavens *Venus is a celestial body sometimes visible from Earth.* Synonyms: **heavenly, divine, spiritual**
CENSOR	to remove material from books, plays, magazines, etc., for moral, political, or religious reasons *After they censored the "dirty" parts out of the book, all that was left was the dedication and half of the cover.* Synonyms: **suppress, delete**
CHASM	gorge or deep canyon *If you look down from the top floor of a New York City skyscraper, it seems as though you're looking into a deep chasm.* Synonyms: **ravine, canyon, abyss**

(Continued)

Word	Definition, Context, Synonyms
CHRONIC	continuing over a long period of time, long-standing *Joshua suffered from chronic tiredness; most days he slept straight through geometry class.* Synonyms: **continuous, constant, persistent, confirmed, settled**
COARSE	rough or loose in texture or speech *My feet felt smooth after walking though the rough, coarse sand of the beach.* Synonyms: **rough, scratchy, prickly, rude, impolite, uncivil**
COLLISION	crash, clash, or conflict *The collision of the two cars made a terrible sound and tied up traffic for hours.* Synonyms: **crash, clash, impact**
COMPASSION	deep feeling of pity or sympathy for others *The jury decided that the cold-hearted killer felt no compassion for his victims.* Synonyms: **pity, sympathy, mercy**
COMPEL	to force someone or something to act *Even torture couldn't compel the spy to reveal his secrets.* Synonyms: **force, coerce, goad, motivate**
COMPETENT	having enough skill for some purpose; adequate but not exceptional *He was not the most qualified candidate, but at least he was competent.* Synonyms: **qualified, capable, fit**
CONCISE	brief and compact *Barry gave a concise speech: he said everything he needed to and was finished in five minutes.* Synonyms: **brief, terse, succinct, compact**
CONDONE	to pardon, to forgive, or to overlook *"We cannot condone your behavior," said Ben's parents after he missed his curfew. "You are grounded for two weeks."* Synonyms: **pardon, excuse, forgive, absolve, overlook, accept, tolerate, allow, permit, suffer, endure, bear, stomach**
CONTEMPLATION	thoughtful observation *When the philosopher studied complicated issues, he often became so lost in contemplation that he forgot to eat or sleep.* Synonyms: **thought, deliberation, meditation, reflection**
CONTEND	to fight or struggle against; to debate *Some people contend that no boxer past or present would have been able to keep up with Muhammad Ali for boxing's World Heavyweight Championship.* Synonyms: **combat, compete, argue, assert**
CONVENE	to assemble or meet *The members of the board convene at least once a week.* Synonyms: **gather, assemble, meet**
CONVENTIONAL	established or approved by general usage *Conventional wisdom today says that a good job requires a college education.* Synonyms: **customary, well-established, habitual**

(Continued)

Word	Definition, Context, Synonyms
COPIOUS	abundant, large in number or quantity, plentiful *The hostess had prepared* copious *amounts of food.* Synonyms: **abundant, plentiful, profuse**
COUNTENANCE	(n) face or facial expression, or the general appearance or behavior of something or someone *Jeremy felt quite unsettled about the new Music Appreciation instructor; she seemed to have an evil* countenance. Synonyms: **face, aspect, appearance, bearing, demeanor, air, visage** (v) to approve or support *When Dorothy and Irene started their nightly pillow fight, the babysitter warned them, "I will not* countenance *such behavior."* Synonyms: **sanction, approve, endorse, bless, favor, encourage, condone**
COURIER	person who carries messages, news, or information *The* courier *will deliver the document.* Synonyms: **messenger, runner, carrier**
DAWDLE	to waste time with idle lingering *If you* dawdle *on your way to school, you'll be late.* Synonyms: **delay, linger, dally**
DEARTH	scarcity, lack *The* dearth *of supplies in our city made it difficult to hold out for long against the attack of the aliens.* Synonyms: **shortage, lack, scarcity**
DEBRIS	charred or spoiled remains of something that has been destroyed *Scavengers searched for valuables amid the* debris. Synonyms: **trash, rubbish, wreckage, remains**
DECEIVE	to delude or mislead *A liar often will try to* deceive *you by not telling the truth.* Synonyms: **mislead, delude, trick, dupe, lie**
DECLAMATION	exercise in speech giving; attack or protest *The candidate made a* declamation *against the new tax law.* Synonyms: **long speech, harangue**
DEFICIENT	defective, insufficient, or inadequate *Failing to study will make you* deficient *in your readiness for the test.* Synonyms: **inadequate, defective, insufficient, failing, lacking**
DEJECTED	depressed, sad *He was too ambitious to become* dejected *by a temporary setback.* Synonyms: **saddened, depressed, discouraged, disheartened**
DELUDE	to deceive, to mislead *After three hours of pouring rain, we stopped* deluding *ourselves that the picnic could go on.* Synonyms: **deceive, dupe, hoax, trick**

(Continued)

Word	Definition, Context, Synonyms
DEPLORE	to regard as deeply regrettable and hateful *"I simply deplore your table manners," she told him, as he stuck his head into the bowl to lick the last of the oatmeal.* Synonyms: **regret, lament, bemoan, bewail, mourn, denounce, condemn, protest, oppose, despise, loathe, abominate**
DESOLATION	condition of being deserted and destroyed *The terrible flood, which destroyed all the buildings and caused everyone to flee, left only desolation in its path.* Synonyms: **barrenness, desertion, bleakness**
DESPICABLE	deserving contempt *Stealing from poor people is despicable. In fact, stealing from anyone is despicable.* Synonyms: **hateful, contemptible, base, mean, vile, detestable, depraved**
DESPONDENT	in a state of depression *Mrs. Baker was despondent after her husband's death.* Synonyms: **depressed, morose, gloomy, sad, brooding, desolate, forlorn, woeful, mournful, dejected**
DESTITUTE	bereft (of something), without or left without (something); poor *Destitute of friends, Charlotte wandered the streets alone.* Synonyms: **bereft, devoid, lacking; poor, impoverished**
DEVOTEE	someone passionately devoted *The opera devotee didn't mind standing in line for hours to get a ticket.* Synonyms: **enthusiast, fan, admirer**
DEVOUT	deeply religious *Priests and nuns are known to be devout people.* Synonyms: **pious, religious, reverent**
DIMINISH	to become or to make smaller in size, number, or degree *He was once such a beautiful actor, but now his beauty has greatly diminished. As has his bank account.* Synonyms: **decrease, lessen, dwindle, shrink, contract, decline, subside, wane, fade, recede, weaken, moderate**
DIN	loud, confused noise *The din in the cafeteria made conversation difficult.* Synonyms: **noise, uproar, clamor**
DIPLOMATIC	tactful; skilled in the art of conducting negotiations and other relations between nations *Our host had a very diplomatic nature, which enabled her to bring together people who disagreed strongly on many points.* Synonyms: **polite, tactful**
DISCLAIM	to deny ownership of or association with *Francine's statement was so silly that she later disclaimed it, pretending that it had been made by someone who looked exactly like her.* Synonyms: **repudiate, reject, disown, disavow, renounce**

(Continued)

Word	Definition, Context, Synonyms
DISCURSIVE	covering a wide area or digressing from a topic *The professor, who was known for his* discursive *speaking style, covered everything from armadillos to zebras in his zoology lecture.* Synonyms: **digressive, rambling**
DISMAL	causing gloom; cheerless *Our team made a* dismal *showing in the play-offs; we lost every game.* Synonyms: **miserable, dreary**
DISPUTE	(n) argument or quarrel *The* dispute *between the United States and the Soviet Union arose in part as a result of disagreement over the occupation of Berlin.* Synonyms: **argument, disagreement** (v) to argue or quarrel *There was no way to* dispute *the DNA evidence.* Synonyms: **argue, disagree with**
DISSEMINATE	to scatter or spread widely *The Internet* disseminates *information rapidly, so events get reported all over the world shortly after they happen.* Synonyms: **spread (an idea or a message), broadcast, disperse**
DIVERT	(1) to change the course of *Emergency crews tried to* divert *the flood waters by building a wall of sandbags across the road.* Synonyms: **deflect, reroute, turn, detour** (2) to draw someone's attention by amusing them *While their mother napped, Dad* diverted *the twins by playing hide-and-seek.* Synonyms: **amuse, entertain, distract**
DOGMATIC	asserting without proof; stating opinion as if it were fact in a definite and forceful manner *The* dogmatic *professor would not listen to the students' views; she did not allow debate in class.* Synonyms: **absolute, opinionated, dictatorial, authoritative, arrogant**
EBULLIENT	overflowing with fervor, enthusiasm, or excitement; high-spirited *The* ebullient *child exhausted the babysitter, who lacked the energy needed to keep up with her.* Synonyms: **bubbling, enthusiastic, exuberant**
ECCENTRIC	(n) person who differs from the accepted norms in an odd way *The old* eccentric *was given to burning hundred-dollar bills.* Synonyms: **freak, oddball, weirdo, nonconformist** (adj) deviating from accepted conduct *Her* eccentric *behavior began to worry her close friends.* Synonyms: **odd, unorthodox, unconventional, offbeat**
ECSTATIC	deliriously overjoyed *Mortimer was* ecstatic *when he learned of his 2400 SAT score.* Synonyms: **delighted, overjoyed, euphoric**

(Continued)

Word	Definition, Context, Synonyms
ELUSIVE	hard to find or express *The* elusive *nature of the platypus makes it difficult to spot them in the wild. Their ugliness makes it unpleasant.* Synonyms: **slippery, evasive**
EMBELLISH	to add detail, make more complicated *Sanjev's short story is too short: it needs to be* embellished *with more details about life among penguins.* Synonyms: **elaborate, expand, ornament**
EMINENT	distinguished, high in rank or station *They were amazed that such an* eminent *scholar could have made such an obvious error.* Synonyms: **prominent, well-known, famous, distinguished, noteworthy**
EMULATE	to imitate or copy *Hundreds of writers have* emulated *Stephen King, but the result is usually a poor imitation.* Synonyms: **imitate, simulate, copy, follow**
ENCOMPASS	to form a circle or a ring around *In New York City, Manhattan is an island, so it is completely* encompassed *by water.* Synonyms: **encircle, circumscribe**
ENDORSE	to approve, sustain, support *The principal refused to* endorse *the plan to put a video arcade in the cafeteria.* Synonyms: **accept, approve, authorize, accredit, encourage, advocate, favor, support**
ENIGMA	mystery or riddle *The source of the mysterious hole remained an* enigma. Synonyms: **mystery, riddle, puzzle**
ENTICE	to lure or attract by feeding desires *Millions of dollars couldn't* entice *Michael Jordan to play basketball in Europe.* Synonyms: **tempt, lure, attract**
ERA	period of time *The invention of the atomic bomb marked the beginning of a new* era *in warfare.* Synonyms: **period (of time), age, epoch**
ERUDITE	knowledgeable and learned *We were not surprised to read the praises of Mario's history of ancient Greece, for we had expected an* erudite *work from him.* Synonyms: **wise, learned, knowledgeable, informed**
ESSENTIAL	of the innermost nature of something; basic, fundamental; of great importance *Eating vegetables is* essential *to your well-being.* Synonyms: **basic, central, fundamental, important, crucial, necessary, urgent**

(Continued)

Word	Definition, Context, Synonyms
EXHIBIT	(v) to publicly present for inspection *The Car Exposition* exhibits *the latest model of sports cars.* Synonyms: **show, reveal, display** (n) an object or collection on public display *The* exhibits *at the Metropolitan Museum of Art include a Roman sarcophagus and an Egyptian temple.* Synonyms: **object, item, showpiece**
EXOTIC	of foreign origin or character; strange, exciting *The atmosphere of the restaurant was* exotic, *but the food was pedestrian.* Synonyms: **foreign, alien, unfamiliar**
EXPUNGE	to delete or omit completely *The censor wanted to* expunge *all parts of Joyce's* Ulysses *he thought were obscene.* Synonyms: **erase, obliterate, strike out**
EXTRICATE	to release from difficulty or an entanglement *The fly was unable to* extricate *itself from the flypaper.* Synonyms: **disengage, release, withdraw**
EXTROVERTED	outgoing or interested in people *An* extroverted *person wouldn't think twice about going to a party of strangers.* Synonyms: **outgoing, gregarious**
FANATIC	someone with excessive enthusiasm, especially in politics or religion *Unable to listen to differing opinions, the* fanatic *politician screamed at his opponent and ran out of the debate.* Synonym: **zealous**
FATAL	causing, or capable of causing, death or ruin *The race car driver suffered a* fatal *accident when his car hit a patch of oil on the roadway.* Synonyms: **lethal, deadly, killing, mortal, malignant**
FATIGUE	(v) to exhaust the strength of *The energetic baby* fatigued *me.* Synonyms: **tire out, weary, enervate** (n) weariness, tiredness from exertion *The recruits suffered from* fatigue *after the twenty-mile march.* Synonyms: **exhaustion, weariness**
FAUNA	animals of a given area *Darwin studied the* fauna *of the Galapagos Islands.* Synonyms: **animals, creatures, beasts**
FERVENT	showing great warmth, intensity, feeling, enthusiasm; hot, burning, glowing *I am a* fervent *admirer of that author's works; I think she is a genius.* Synonyms: **warm, eager, enthusiastic**

(Continued)

Word	Definition, Context, Synonyms
FICKLE	easily changeable, especially in emotions *She earned a reputation for being a* fickle *customer; she always changed her order at least twice.* Synonym: **inconstant**
FIDELITY	faithfulness to duties; truthfulness *A traitor is someone whose* fidelity *is questioned.* Synonyms: **loyalty, allegiance, faithfulness, devotion, truthfulness, accuracy**
FLAGRANT	outrageously glaring, noticeable, or evident; notorious, scandalous *His* flagrant *disregard for the rules has resulted in his dismissal from the job.* Synonyms: **obvious, glaring**
FLIPPANT	not serious, playful; irreverent *John was* flippant *to the teacher, so she sent him to the principal's office.* Synonyms: **frivolous, flip, playful**
FORETELL	to predict the future *Some prophets claim to* foretell *the future.* Synonyms: **forecast, prophesy, auger**
FORMIDABLE	able to inspire awe or wonder because of outstanding power, size, etc. *The steep face of rock we were directed to climb was indeed* formidable. Synonyms: **impressive, awe-inspiring, impregnable, invincible**
FRENZY	a spell of violent, wild behavior; temporary madness *As she watched her basketball team lose the game, Susan gradually worked herself into a* frenzy. Synonyms: **mania, hysteria, craze, furor, mania, turmoil**
FUTILE	ineffective, useless; unimportant *Our attempt to reach the shore before the storm was* futile; *the wind blew us back into the middle of the lake.* Synonyms: **useless, hopeless, pointless**
GERMINATE	to bud or sprout *Three weeks after planting, the seeds will* germinate. Synonyms: **sprout, grow**
GLEE	joy, pleasure, happiness *The child was filled with* glee *at the sight of so many presents.* Synonyms: **joy, elation**
GLIB	able to speak profusely; having a ready flow of words (It often implies lying or deceit.) *The politician was a* glib *speaker.* Synonyms: **flip, fluent, verbose, smooth, smug**
GREGARIOUS	fond of company *For the* gregarious *person, dormitory life is a pleasure.* Synonyms: **sociable, companionable, amiable, convivial**

(Continued)

Word	Definition, Context, Synonyms
GROVEL	to humble oneself, to beg *The dog* groveled *at his owner's feet.* Synonyms: **crawl, beg**
GRUESOME	grisly, horrible *The horror film was filled with* gruesome *scenes.* Synonyms: **frightful, shocking, ghastly**
HALLOWED	regarded as holy; sacred *The Constitution is a* hallowed *document in the United States.* Synonyms: **holy, sacred**
HARBINGER	omen, precursor, forerunner *The groundhog's appearance on February 2 is a* harbinger *of spring.* Synonyms: **precursor, forerunner, omen, messenger**
HASTY	done quickly (often too quickly); rushed, sloppy *Henry was too* hasty *in completing his research paper and forgot to put his name on it.* Synonyms: **rushed, sloppy, shoddy, careless**
HEED	(n) careful attention, notice, observation *Pay* heed *to his warnings about that place; he's been there enough times to know the dangers.* Synonym: **attention** (v) to listen to and obey *The naughty children did not* heed *their mothers rules.* Synonyms: **listen to, obey**
HETEROGENEOUS	not uniform; made up of different parts that remain separate (Its opposite is *homogeneous.*) *The United Nations is a* heterogeneous *body.* Synonyms: **mixed, unlike, diverse, dissimilar, various**
HORRID	something that causes horror or is at least pretty bad *The weather has been just* horrid; *we've had three storms in a week.* Synonyms: **dreadful, horrible, shocking**
IMMACULATE	spotless; free from error *After I cleaned my apartment for hours, it was finally* immaculate. Synonyms: **errorless, faultless, unblemished, impeccable**
IMMINENT	about to happen, on the verge of occurring *Joan was becoming nervous about her* imminent *wedding.* Synonyms: **impending, approaching, near**
IMPASSE	(1) road having no exit *A rock slide produced an* impasse, *so we could proceed no further on the road.* (2) a dilemma with no solution *The meeting was at an* impasse *because neither side was willing to compromise.* Synonyms: **deadlock, standoff, stalemate, standstill**

(Continued)

Word	Definition, Context, Synonyms
IMPERVIOUS	incapable of being penetrated; unable to be influenced *Superman is* impervious *to bullets.* Synonym: **impenetrable**
IMPLY	to suggest without stating directly *Although Jane did not state that she loved Mr. Rochester, it was clearly* implied *in her look.* Synonyms: **hint, suggest, intimate**
INADVERTENT	unintentional *I wrote my paper in such a hurry that I made many* inadvertent *errors.* Synonyms: **accidental, unintentional**
INCENTIVE	motivation or drive to do a particular task or to go in a given direction *His father's encouragement gave him the* Incentive *to try again.* Synonyms: **motive, inducement, stimulus**
INCREDULOUS	not believing *I was* incredulous *about Ismael's wild fishing story about "the one that got away."* Synonyms: **skeptical, disbelieving**
INERT	having no power to move or act; resisting motion or action *In the heat of the desert afternoon, lizards are* inert. Synonyms: **sluggish, passive, inactive, dormant, lethargic, lifeless**
INGENUITY	inventive skill or cleverness *Use your* ingenuity *to come up with a new solution to the problem.* Synonyms: **creativity, cleverness, inventiveness**
INHABIT	to reside or live in *Arboreal creatures, such as monkeys,* inhabit *the trees.* Synonyms: **live, occupy, reside, dwell, stay**
INNATE	present at birth *The plan was doomed from the start; there was an* innate *problem with it.* Synonyms: **natural, inborn, inherent, instinctive**
INSINUATION	devious hint or sly suggestion made to cause suspicion or doubts *During the last election, the* insinuation *that the congressman had taken kickbacks cost him thousands of votes.* Synonyms: **hint, suggestion, reference, implication**
INSOMNIA	inability to fall sleep *No matter how tired I am, I continue to suffer from* insomnia. Synonym: **sleeplessness**
INSURGENT	(n) rebel *When secrets were being leaked to the enemy, we realized we had an* insurgent *among our ranks.* Synonyms: **rebel, mole** (adj) rising in revolt, starting a revolution *The* insurgent *crew staged a mutiny and threw the captain overboard.* Synonyms: **rebellious, mutinous**

(Continued)

Word	Definition, Context, Synonyms
IRATE	full of anger, wrathful, incensed *He was* irate *at being wrongly accused of the crime.* Synonyms: **angry, indignant, infuriated, enraged**
JEER	(n) taunting remark *The* jeers *of the crowd were enough to make the performers run off stage crying.* Synonyms: **gibe, taunt** (v) to mock in an abusive way *My brother loved to* jeer *at me because he knew how much it hurt my feelings.* Synonyms: **ridicule, mock, scoff**
JUBILANT	feeling joy or happiness *We were* jubilant *after our victory in the state championships.* Synonyms: **exultant, gleeful, joyful, ecstatic**
JUDICIOUS	having wise judgment *The wise and distinguished judge was well-known for having a* judicious *temperament.* Synonyms: **wise, sage, sagacious**
KINETIC	relating to motion *A* kinetic *sculpture is one that moves.* Synonyms: **animated, energetic, spirited, moving**
LETHARGY	drowsiness, tiredness, inability to do anything much *A feeling of* lethargy *came over me, and I wanted nothing more than a nice long nap.* Synonyms: **sluggishness, fatigue**
MAGNANIMOUS	having a great or noble spirit; acting generously, patiently, or kindly *Although at first he seemed cold, Uncle Frank turned out to be a very* magnanimous *fellow.* Synonyms: **big-hearted, generous, noble, princely, forgiving, patient, tolerant, indulgent, ungrudging, unresentful**
MALLEABLE	able to be molded or shaped *Gold is so* malleable *that it can be beaten into a thin foil.* Synonyms: **soft, flexible, yielding**
MAR	to damage something and make it imperfect *Telephone poles* mar *the beauty of the countryside.* Synonyms: **deform, impair, spoil, disfigure, damage**
MEAGER	very small or insufficient *He rented an expensive apartment and dined at fine restaurants, but he earned a* meager *wage and soon ran out of money.* Synonyms: **slight, trifling, skimpy, puny, scant, inadequate, insufficient, insubstantial**
MEEK	humble and submissive *People who are too* meek *won't stand up for themselves.* Synonyms: **passive, unassertive, docile, compliant**

(Continued)

Word	Definition, Context, Synonyms
MELANCHOLY	very sad or depressing *The rainy weather made James feel* melancholy. Synonyms: **gloomy, mournful, somber**
MIMIC	imitate, copy (not always in a complimentary way) *Mary got in trouble for* mimicking *the teacher.* Synonyms: **mock, impersonate, simulate, counterfeit**
MOURN	feel sad for, regret *The family gathered to* mourn *for the dead.* Synonyms: **lament, grieve**
NEBULOUS	hazy, not well-defined *During the campaign, the candidate promised to fight crime. But when reporters asked for details, his plan was* nebulous—*he could not say whether he would hire more police or support longer jail sentences.* Synonyms: **hazy, cloudy, ill-defined, unclear, shapeless, vague, unspecific**
NIMBLE	quick and agile in movement or thought *A* nimble *athlete is a well-coordinated one.* Synonyms: **agile, active, quick, clever, cunning**
NOMAD	someone who has no permanent home and wanders *The Berbers are a tribe of* nomads *who travel from place to place searching for grassland for their herds.* Synonyms: **wanderer, vagrant**
OBSCURE	(adj) hard to see; unknown, uncertain *The references the author made were so* obscure, *I don't think half the readers knew what he was talking about.* Synonyms: **vague, unclear, dubious** (v) to hide or make difficult to find *Because he didn't want to go to jail, he tried to* obscure *the fact that he had been embezzling money for years.* Synonyms: **confuse, becloud**
OBSOLETE	no longer in use; discarded or outmoded *It's as* obsolete *as a telephone modem.* Synonyms: **outdated, passé, old-fashioned**
OBSTINATE	stubborn *Hal's mother tried to get him to eat his spinach, but he remained* obstinate. Synonyms: **mulish, dogged**
OBSTRUCT	to get in the way of, to block, to hamper *He removed his hat so as not to* obstruct *another's view of the stage.* Synonyms: **block, check, clog, impede**
OMINOUS	threatening, menacing, having the character of an evil omen *The sky filled with* ominous *dark clouds before the storm.* Synonym: **foreboding**

(Continued)

Word	Definition, Context, Synonyms
OPPORTUNE	appropriate to time or circumstances: timely, lucky *Dalbert's investment in plastics, made just before the demand for plastics began to rise, was* opportune. Synonyms: **timely, appropriate, lucky**
OSTENTATIOUS	pretentious and flashy *Some think Las Vegas, winner of multiple "world's largest" awards in a variety of areas, is really an* ostentatious *display of wealth and poor taste.* Synonyms: **conspicuous, flashy, flamboyant, showy**
PALATABLE	good tasting *Her cooking is quite* palatable. Synonyms: **savory, agreeable, appetizing, delicious, acceptable**
PARADOX	contradiction, something that doesn't fit; something that shouldn't be true because it seems to offend common sense, yet is true anyway *The* paradox *of government is that the person who most desires power is the person who least deserves it.* Synonym: **contradiction**
PASSIVE	not active; someone who lets things happen rather than himself taking action *Ned portrayed himself as the* passive *victim of external forces.* Synonym: **submissive**
PERSEVERE	to continue in some course of action despite setbacks and opposition *Although at first the problems looked difficult, Wendy* persevered *and found that she could answer almost all of them.* Synonyms: **continue, endure, persist**
PIOUS	religiously devout or moral *Saul, a* pious *man, walks to the synagogue on the Sabbath and prays daily.* Synonyms: **devout, religious, God-fearing, reverent, moral, upstanding, scrupulous**
PLAUSIBLE	seeming to be true *Joachim's excuse for lateness to class sounded* plausible *at the time, but I later learned that it had been a lie.* Synonyms: **credible, believable, likely, probable, conceivable**
POMPOUS	characterized by stiff, unnatural formality *Gerald began his speech to the class with a* pompous *quote from Julius Caesar.* Synonyms: **stuffy, stiff, affected, mannered, unnatural, pretentious, self-important, conceited**
PROFOUND	deep, wise, serious *Both the* Book of Ecclesiastes *and the* Tao Te Ching *contain* profound *observations about human life.* Synonyms: **wise, deep, sagacious**
PROLIFIC	producing great amounts; fertile *Stephen King, a* prolific *writer, seems to write new books as fast as they are published.* Synonyms: **productive, fertile**

(Continued)

Word	Definition, Context, Synonyms
PROPHESY	to predict the future using divine guidance *The ancient Greek oracles at Delphi were supposed to be able to* prophesy *the future.* Synonyms: **predict, foretell, forecast, auger**
QUELL	to quiet something raucous (often a rebellion); crush, defeat, conquer *The dictator dispatched troops to* quell *the rebellion.* Synonyms: **quash, overpower, overcome, quench, suppress**
QUENCH	to satisfy a need or desire *After coming in from the desert, Ezra needed gallons of water to* quench *his thirst.* Synonyms: **satisfy, extinguish, subdue, sate**
RANCOR	bad feeling, bitterness *Herbert was so filled with* rancor *that he could think of nothing but taking revenge on those who had humiliated him.* Synonyms: **animosity, resentment, hatred, malice, spite**
RANSACK	to search thoroughly and messily *Did the burglars* ransack *your entire house?* Synonyms: **plunder, pillage, search, loot, pilfer, steal**
RAVENOUS	(literally) wildly eager to eat *The homeless man had not had a bite of food in two days and was* ravenous. (figuratively) hungry for anything *The abandoned puppy was* ravenous *for affection and tenderness.* Synonyms: **hungry, famished, voracious, starved**
RAZE	to destroy (a building, city, etc.) utterly *The house had been* razed: *where once it had stood there was nothing but splinters and bricks.* Synonyms: **demolish, destroy, wreck, level, flatten**
RECLUSE	someone who lives far away from other people *Anthony left the city and lived as a* recluse *in the desert.* Synonyms: **hermit, loner**
REFRAIN	to stop or avoid doing something, quit *The librarian insisted that everyone* refrain *from making any noise.* Synonyms: **abstain, cease, desist**
REGAL	royal, splendid *Prince Charles was married with full* regal *ceremony.* Synonyms: **kingly, majestic**
REIGN	rule over, govern, dominate *The British monarch used to* reign *over the entire British Empire.* Synonyms: **rule, prevail**
REINFORCE	strengthen, add to *The purpose of the homework is to* reinforce *what's taught in class.* Synonym: **support**

(Continued)

Word	Definition, Context, Synonyms
RENOWNED	well-known, famous, celebrated *Having spent her whole childhood banging on things, Jane grew up to be a* renowned *drummer.* Synonyms: **famed, distinguished, notable**
REPUGNANT	something gross, repulsive, or revolting *Bill liked his macaroni and cheese with jelly, a combination that many of his friends found* repugnant. Synonyms: **distasteful, objectionable, offensive**
REVEL	celebrate noisily, have a party *The whole school got together to* revel *in the football team's victory.* Synonyms: **celebrate, indulge, enjoy**
SCARCE	rare, uncommon *Water is* scarce *in the Sahara Desert.* Synonyms: **sparse, infrequent**
SCRUPULOUS	(1) acting in accordance with a strict moral code *David could not have stolen Sheila's money; he was too* scrupulous. Synonyms: **moral, upstanding, virtuous, principled, ethical** (2) thorough in the performance of a task *Roger is a* scrupulous *editor who checks every word his reporters write.* Synonyms: **careful, conscientious, thorough, diligent**
SEETHE	to heave or bubble from great inner turmoil, as a volcano; to boil *Immediately after learning of Roger's gossip about me, I began to boil with anger, and by the time I reached his house, I was* seething. Synonyms: **boil, bubble, steam, foam, surge, heave, swell**
SHREWD	clever, keen-witted, cunning, sharp in practical affairs *He was a* shrewd *businessman and soon parlayed his meager savings into a fortune.* Synonyms: **clever, keen, astute, cunning, wily, sharp, discerning**
SINISTER	threatening, evil, menacing *His friendly manner concealed* sinister *designs.* Synonyms: **ominous, wicked**
SQUANDER	to waste (often money) on some worthless purchase or practice *While I have carefully saved money to buy the piano I have always wanted, my friend Sean has* squandered *his earnings on thousands of lottery tickets.* Synonyms: **waste, fritter away, consume, exhaust**
STAUNCH	steady, loyal *A dog is a* staunch *friend.* Synonyms: **firm, sturdy, stable, solid, established, substantial, steadfast, faithful, unfailing**
STEALTHY	sneaky, secret *The children made a* stealthy *raid on the refrigerator during the night.* Synonyms: **sneaky, furtive, clandestine**

(Continued)

Word	Definition, Context, Synonyms
SUAVE	smooth, graceful, and confident in speech and behavior (sometimes insincerely) *Nina was a* suave *young woman who knew exactly how to act in any situation.* Synonyms: **smooth, gracious, courtly, worldly, sophisticated, urbane, cosmopolitan, cultivated, cultured, refined**
SUBDUE	to bring under control; to decrease the intensity of (as in the adjective subdued) *The king's army attempted to* subdue *the rebellious peasants, who were threatening to storm the castle.* Synonyms: **control, vanquish, suppress, repress, master, overcome, tame**
SUCCUMB	to give in, to submit *Don't* succumb *to temptation.* Synonyms: **yield, surrender, give in, submit, die, expire**
SUFFICE	to be adequate or enough *"A light dinner should* suffice *for the average person," said the thin man, eating his lettuce sandwich.* Synonym: **satisfy**
SUPPRESS	crush, hold in, hide *The students could hardly* suppress *their excitement on the last day of school.* Synonyms: **quell, contain**
SURMISE	(v) to guess, to infer *From his torn pants and bloody nose I* surmised *that he had been in a fight.* (n) instance of surmising *My* surmise *was correct; he had been in a fight.* Synonyms: **guess, conjecture, speculate, hypothesize, infer**
SYNOPSIS	short summary, outline *Oren wrote a 1-page* synopsis *of a 55-page book.* Synonyms: **summary, outline**
TACITURN	quiet, tending not to speak *Lyle is a* taciturn *boy who plays by himself and rarely says a word.* Synonyms: **quiet, shy, reserved, guarded**
TACTFUL	acting with sensitivity to others' feelings *I sent Eva to explain our sudden departure to our rude hosts, for she is the most* tactful *person I know.* Synonyms: **diplomatic, discreet, judicious, sensitive, considerate, thoughtful, politic, delicate**
TANGIBLE	can be felt by touching; having actual substance *The storming of the castle didn't bring the soldiers* tangible *rewards, but it brought them great honor. They would have preferred the rewards.* Synonyms: **material, real, touchable, palpable, concrete, perceptible**
TENACIOUS	steadily pursuing a goal, unwilling to give up; stubborn *For years, against all odds, women* tenaciously *fought for the right to vote.* Synonyms: **persistent, persevering, untiring, tireless**

(Continued)

Word	Definition, Context, Synonyms
TEPID	(1) neither hot nor cold; lukewarm *Roxanne refused to take a bath in the* tepid *water, fearing that she would catch a cold.* Synonyms: **lukewarm, mild, temperate** (2) lacking character or spirit, bland *Neither liking nor disliking Finnegan's film, the critics gave it* tepid *reviews.* Synonyms: **unenthusiastic, halfhearted, indifferent**
TERMINATE	to stop, end *Amy and Zoe* terminated *their friendship and never spoke to each other again.* Synonyms: **cease, finish, conclude**
TERSE	concise, brief; using few words *Kate was noted for her* terse *replies, rarely going beyond "yes" or "no."* Synonyms: **concise, succinct, compact**
TREPIDATION	fear, apprehension *Mike approached the door of the principal's office with* trepidation. Synonyms: **fright, anxiety, trembling, hesitation**
TRITE	lacking originality, inspiration, and interest *Lindsay's graduation speech was the same* trite *nonsense we've heard a hundred times in the past.* Synonyms: **tired, banal, unoriginal, common, stale, stock**
TYRANNY	harsh exercise of absolute power *The students accused Ms. Morgenstern of* tyranny *when she assigned them seats instead of letting them choose their own.* Synonyms: **oppression, repression**
ULTIMATE	marking the highest point; cannot be improved upon; final *The new fashions from Paris are the* ultimate *in chic.* Synonyms: **maximum, remotest, final, conclusive, last, elemental, primary, fundamental**
UNANIMOUS	approved by everyone concerned *The student council voted* unanimously; *not one person opposed the plan.* Synonyms: **unchallenged, uncontested, unopposed, united, harmonious**
VACUOUS	silly, empty-headed, not serious *The book that Victor loved when he was 6 struck him as utterly* vacuous *when he was 20. But he still liked the pictures.* Synonyms: **shallow, vapid**
VAGUE	not clear or certain *It took us a while to find John's house because the directions were* vague. Synonyms: **nebulous, imprecise**
VEHEMENT	with deep feeling *Susanne responded to the accusation of cheating with a* vehement *denial.* Synonyms: **passionate, earnest, fervent**

(Continued)

Word	Definition, Context, Synonyms
VEX	to irritate to a great degree, to annoy *Your constant sniveling is beginning to* vex *me.* Synonyms: **tease, irritate, provoke, torment, pester, harass, bother, annoy**
VIVACIOUS	lively, full of spirit *Quiet and withdrawn at first, Joan became increasingly* vivacious. Synonyms: **animated, sprightly, spirited**
WANTONLY	without a reason *Instead of singling out appropriate targets for his anger, the crazed robot struck out* wantonly. Synonyms: **randomly, indiscriminately**
WRATH	extreme anger *He denounced the criminals in a speech filled with righteous* wrath. Synonyms: **ire, fury, rage**
WRETCHED	miserable, pathetic *Steve felt* wretched *when he failed the test.* Synonyms: **dejected, woebegone, forlorn**
ZEALOUS	enthusiastic, eager *Serge was a* zealous *supporter of the cause and never missed a rally.* Synonyms: **fervent, fervid, intense, passionate**

CHAPTER 20

Math Wrap-Up

CHAPTER OBJECTIVES

With practice, this chapter will help you:

1. Explain the steps of the Kaplan Method for Math and its role in answering Math questions accurately and efficiently

2. Identify Math concepts and strategies, including Backsolving and Picking Numbers, in need of further practice or review

MATH WRAP-UP STRATEGY REVIEW

Use this chapter to reflect on your progress. Review previous chapters for more details on how to approach individual sections of the test.

1. How does the test maker make math questions more difficult?

_____

_____

_____

2. What should you remember about pacing?

_____

_____

_____

3. The Kaplan Method for Math:

Step 1. _____

Step 2. _____

Step 3. _____

4. What are some Kaplan math strategies you can rely on?

_____

_____

_____

5. How and when should you guess?

_____

_____

_____

Answers and Explanations

1. The test makers make math questions more difficult by adding steps, using more complicated numbers or expressions, and testing more advanced concepts.

2. It's important to keep moving. On the SSAT, you have a little more than one minute per math question. The two separate math sections are similar in style and difficulty. On the ISEE, you have less than one minute per math question. Unlike the SSAT, the first math section of the ISEE—Quantitative Reasoning—is different from the second math section—Mathematics Achievement. The Quantitative Reasoning section has Word Problems requiring only one or two steps and Quantitative Comparisons requiring comparisons of two side-by-side expressions. The Mathematics Achievement section has lengthier word problems that will require multiple steps.

3. **The Kaplan Method for Math**

   1. Read through the question and decide whether to answer it now or later

   2. Answer the question by:

      a. Using math skills

      b. Backsolving

      c. Picking Numbers

      d. Guessing strategically

   3. Check that you answered the question

4. Picking Numbers and Backsolving are two strategies that will help you answer math questions. Picking Numbers is useful when there are variables, and Backsolving is useful when there are simple numbers in the answer choices.

5. If you take the SSAT, you should leave a question blank if you have no time left or no idea what to do. If you can start on a question and eliminate at least one answer choice, however, you should guess. If you take the ISEE, then you should never leave a question blank. Eliminate choices if you can, but always fill in an answer.

BACKSOLVING

Backsolving means using the answer choices to solve the question. Rather than following the textbook approach, you can simply substitute values from the answer choices to see which one fits the criteria of the question.

1. When can you Backsolve?

    _____

2. When can't you Backsolve?

    _____

3. What are some classic Backsolving situations?

    _____

    _____

Use Backsolving to answer the questions below.

4. A painter charges $12 an hour while his son charges $6 an hour. If the father and the son worked the same number of hours on a job, how many hours did each of them work if the combined charge for their labor was $108?

    (A) 6

    (B) 8

    (C) 9

    (D) 12

5. Murray has 12 lollipops and Dave has 24. How many lollipops must Dave give Murray if each are to have the same number?

    (A) 12

    (B) 10

    (C) 8

    (D) 6

    (E) 4

Answers and Explanations

1. You can Backsolve when there are straightforward numbers in the answer choices.

2. You cannot Backsolve when there are variables in the answer choices or the answer choices include complex numbers or expressions that would be difficult to plug in.

3. Backsolving is a great tool for when the final answer is a single digit integer. Even larger numbers can be good candidates for Backsolving if they fit into the question stem easily and finding the solution doesn't require lengthy or complex calculations.

4. The correct answer represents the hours each person worked. If you say that choice C is correct, then each person worked 9 hours. The painter would charge 9×11 dollars and his son would charge 9×6 dollars. If choice C is correct, this will sum to $108. You should know that $9 \times 6 = 54$, and because $12 = 2 \times 6$, 9×12 will be twice as large as 9×6, and choice C is going to be too large. At this point, you can also eliminate choice D. You can now test either choice (A) or choice B, but choice (A) will most likely include faster multiplication: $6 \times 12 + 6 \times 6 = 72 + 36 = 108$. Choice (A) is correct.

5. The correct answer will represent how many lollipops Dave must give Murray so that they both have the same number. Start with choice C: if Dave gives Murray 8 lollipops, Dave will have $24 - 8 = 16$ lollipops and Murray will have $12 + 8 = 20$ lollipops. These amounts are not equal, so choice C is incorrect. You may not be sure whether to go to B or D next. For this question, think about what happened: Dave gave Murray so many lollipops that now Murray has more than him. That means the option you chose was too large, so you can eliminate C, B, and A. Try choice (D) next: if Dave gives Murray 6 lollipops, Dave will have $24 - 6 = 18$ lollipops and Murray will have $12 + 6 = 18$ lollipops. These amounts are equal, so choice (D) is correct.

PICKING NUMBERS

Picking Numbers is a great way to make abstract problems more concrete. To Pick Numbers, choose a hypothetical value and plug it into the question to find the answer.

1. When can you Pick Numbers? _____

2. When can't you Pick Numbers? _____

3. What are some classic Picking Numbers situations?

_____

_____

Use Picking Numbers to answer the questions below.

4. If $m = 2n - 4$, then what does $m + 2$ equal?

   (A) $2n - 6$

   (B) $2n - 2$

   (C) $4n - 6$

   (D) It cannot be determined from the information given.

5. Each of the members of Hamilton High School's Drama Club may bring up to four guests to a party. What is the maximum number of members and guests who might attend the party if m represents the number of members?

   (A) $m + 4$

   (B) $4m$

   (C) $4m + 4$

   (D) $5m$

Answers and Explanations

1. You can Pick Numbers when there are variables in the question stem and answer choices. You can also Pick Numbers when there is an unknown value.

2. You cannot Pick Numbers if there are no unknown values. There may not be variables, but rates or unknown values are also an indication that Picking Numbers might be a useful strategy.

3. When a question is a good candidate for Picking Numbers, you'll often see variables in both the question stem and the answer choices. Picking Numbers can be especially useful on ISEE Quantitative Comparisons questions. Questions with percents can often benefit from choosing 100 to represent the whole; it's easy to find any percent of 100.

4. The question does not provide any rules regarding the value of m, so start by picking a number such as $m = 2$. The answer choices should be equivalent to $m + 2$, so when $m = 2$, the correct answer choice must equal $2 + 2 = 4$. Before you can check the answer choices, you must plug in the value for m to the equation including n: $2 - 2n - 4$, so $6 = 2n$ and $n = 3$. Now, you're ready to plug in the value of n to the answer choices:

   Choice A: $2n - 6 = 2(3) - 6 = 0$

   Choice (B): $2n - 2 = 2(3) - 2 = 4$

   Choice C: $4n - 6 = 4(3) - 6 = 6$

   Only choice (B) matches the value of the question stem when $m = 2$. Choice (B) is correct.

5. Pick a possible number of members for Hamilton High School's Drama Club, such as 10. If all 10 members bring 4 guests each, there will be 10 members and 40 guests for a total of 50 people altogether. Check the answer choices using the value $m = 10$:

   Choice A: $m + 4 = 10 + 4 = 14$

   Choice B: $4m = 4(10) = 40$

   Choice C: $4m + 4 = 4(10) + 4 = 44$

   Choice (D): $5m = 5(10) = 50$

   Choice (D) is correct.

PRACTICE QUESTIONS

1. A subway car passes 3 train stations every 10 minutes. At this rate, how many stations will it pass in one hour?

   (A) 12

   (B) 15

   (C) 18

   (D) 30

2. $\dfrac{a}{b} = \dfrac{16}{c}$

   If $a = 3$ and $b = 12$, what is the value of c?

   (A) $\dfrac{1}{4}$

   (B) 4

   (C) 36

   (D) 64

3. If $N = 12$, then $2N =$

   (A) 3

   (B) 6

   (C) 8

   (D) 24

4. To which of the following is 7.07 closest?

   (A) 71

   (B) 7.7

   (C) 7.6

   (D) 7

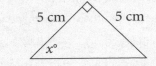

5. In the triangle in the figure above, what is the value of x?

   (A) 30

   (B) 40

   (C) 45

   (D) 60

6. If $x = 2y - 6$, then what is the value of $x + 3$?

   (A) $2y - 3$

   (B) $2y - 9$

   (C) $2x + 3$

   (D) $2y + 3$

7. In a class of 20 students, 8 received a grade of A on a math quiz. What percent of the students did not receive an A?

   (A) 12

   (B) 40

   (C) 60

   (D) 80

	Column A	Column B
8.	524	612
	308	220
	+993	+993

9.   John read 7 pages in 4 minutes.
       Kate read 10 pages in 5 minutes.

Column A	Column B
The average number of pages John read in one minute	The average number of pages Kate read in one minute

10.

The perimeter of the square is 16.

Column A	Column B
The diameter of the circle	4

PRACTICE QUIZ ANSWERS AND EXPLANATIONS

1. C

To determine the number of stations the subway car will pass in one hour, you can use straightforward math or Backsolving. To answer this question using straightforward math, set up a ratio:

$$\frac{3 \text{ stations}}{10 \text{ minutes}} = \frac{s \text{ stations}}{1 \text{ hour}}$$

$$\frac{3 \text{ stations}}{10 \text{ minutes}} = \frac{s \text{ stations}}{60 \text{ minutes}}$$

$$3(60) = 10s$$

$$180 = 10s$$

$$18 = s$$

Choice (C) is correct.

2. D

Plug in the values for a and b, and use either Backsolving or straightforward math to determine the value of c:

$$\frac{3}{12} = \frac{16}{c}$$

Start by simplifying $\frac{3}{12} = \frac{1}{4}$, then cross multiply. Because $c = 4(16)$ and $2(16) = 32$, you can eliminate choices A, B, and C, so answer choice (D) must be correct.

3. D

This is a simple substitution question. If $N = 12$, then $2N$ must equal $2 \times 12 = 24$. Choice (D) is correct.

4. D

Working with place value can be tricky. Write out all numbers to the hundredths place so you can easily compare them:

$$\text{Question stem} = 7.07$$
$$A = 7.70$$
$$C = 7.60$$
$$D = 7.00$$

The number 7.00 is only 0.07 less than 7.07, so choice (D) is correct.

5. C

You know that this is an isosceles triangle because two of the sides are 5 cm long and the other side is the hypotenuse. Because it is an isosceles triangle, the two interior angles of the triangle opposite the equal sides will have equal angle measures. The third angle is 90°, so the other two angles will be 45° each. Choice (C) is correct.

6. A

Substitute $2y - 6$ for x in the equation $x + 3$: $2y - 6 + 3 = 2y - 3$. This is a perfect match for answer choice (A).

7. C

There are 20 students in the class, and 8 of them received an A. Because $20 - 8 = 12$, there are 12 students who did not receive an A. To determine the percent, divide $12 \div 20 = \frac{6}{10} = 60\%$. Choice (C) is correct.

8. C

The third value in both columns is equal, so focus on the other two values in each column. Column A has $524 + 308 = 832$, while Column B has $612 + 220 - 832$. These two values are equivalent, so choice (C) is correct.

9. B

The average number of pages John read in one minute can be found by dividing 7 by 4. The average number of pages Kate can read in one minute can be found by dividing $10 \div 5$. John's average number of pages is equal to less than two, but Kate's average number of page is equal to exactly two. Kate's average number is greater, so Column B is greater than Column A. Choice (B) is correct.

10. A

Before you can answer this question, you must determine the dimensions of the square. The perimeter of the square is 16, so the side lengths must be the $4s = 16$, or $s = 4$. The diameter of the circle will be equal to the diagonal of the square. The diagonal of the square is the hypotenuse of a 45-45-90 triangle. For this question, the two identical side lengths of the triangle will be 4 and the hypotenuse will be $4\sqrt{2}$. Because 4 multiplied by the square root of 2 will be greater than the value of 4, Column A is greater than Column B. Choice (A) is correct.

CHAPTER 21

100 Essential Math Concepts

The math on the SSAT and ISEE covers a lot of ground—from arithmetic to algebra to geometry.

Don't let yourself be intimidated. We've highlighted the 100 most important concepts that you'll need and listed them in this chapter.

Use this list to remind yourself of the key concepts you'll need to know. Do four concepts a day, and you'll be ready within a month. If a concept continually causes you trouble, circle it and refer back to it as you try to do the questions.

You've probably been taught most of these concepts in school already, so this list is a great way to refresh your memory.

NUMBER PROPERTIES

1. Number Categories Signed

Integers are whole numbers; they include positive and negative numbers and zero, but not fractions or decimals.

A rational number is a number that can be expressed as a ratio of two integers. Irrational numbers are real numbers—they have locations on the number line—but they cannot be expressed precisely as a fraction or decimal. For the purposes of the SSAT and ISEE, the most important irrational numbers are $\sqrt{2}$, $\sqrt{3}$, and π.

2. Adding/Subtracting Signed Numbers

To add a positive and a negative, first ignore the signs and find the positive difference between the number parts. Then attach the sign of the original number with the larger number part. For example, to add 23 and -34, first ignore the minus sign and find the positive difference between 23 and 34—that's 11. Then, attach the sign of the number with the larger number part—in this case, it's the minus sign from the -34. So $23 + (-34) = -11$.

Make subtraction situations simpler by turning them into addition. For example, you can think of $-17 - (-21)$ as $-17 + (+21)$.

To add or subtract a string of positives and negatives, first turn everything into addition. Then, combine the positives and negatives so that the string is reduced to the sum of a single positive number and a single negative number.

3. Multiplying/Dividing Signed Numbers

To multiply and/or divide positives and negatives, treat the number parts as usual and attach a minus sign if there were originally an odd number of negatives. For example, to multiply -2, -3, and -5, first multiply the number parts: $2 \times 3 \times 5 = 30$. Then go back and note that there were three—an odd number—negatives, so the product is negative: $(-2) \times (-3) \times (-5) = -30$.

4. PEMDAS

When performing multiple operations, remember to perform them in the correct order: PEMDAS, which means Parentheses first, then Exponents, then Multiplication and Division (left to right), and lastly Addition and Subtraction (left to right). In the expression $9 - 2 \times (5 - 3)^2 + 6 \div 3$, begin with the parentheses: $(5 - 3) = 2$. Then do the exponent: $2^2 = 4$. You now have the following expression: $9 - 2 \times 4 + 6 \div 3$. Next, do the multiplication and division to get $9 - 8 + 2$, which equals 3. If you have difficulty remembering PEMDAS, use this sentence to recall it: Please Excuse My Dear Aunt Sally.

5. Counting Consecutive Integers

To count consecutive integers, subtract the smallest from the largest and add 1. To count the number of integers from 13 through 31, you first subtract: $31 - 13 = 18$. Next, add 1: $18 + 1 = 19$.

NUMBER OPERATIONS AND CONCEPTS

6. Exponential Growth

If r is the ratio between consecutive terms, a_1 is the first term, a_n is the nth term, and S_n is the sum of the first n terms, then $a_n = a_1 r^{n-1}$ and $S_n \dfrac{a_1 - a_1 r^n}{1 - r}$.

7. Union and Intersection of Sets

The things in a set are called elements or members. The union of Set A and Set B, sometimes expressed as $A \cup B$, is the set of elements that are in either or both of Set A and Set B. If Set $A = \{1, 2\}$ and Set $B = \{3, 4\}$, then $A \cup B = \{1, 2, 3, 4\}$. The intersection of Set A and Set B, sometimes expressed as $A \cap B$, is the set of elements common to both Set A and Set B. If Set $A = \{1, 2, 3\}$ and Set $B = \{3, 4, 5\}$, then $A \cap B = \{3\}$.

DIVISIBILITY

8. Factor/Multiple

The factors of integer n are the positive integers that divide into n with no remainder. The multiples of n are the integers that n divides into with no remainder. For example, 6 is a factor of 12, and 24 is a multiple of 12. Therefore, 12 is both a factor and a multiple of itself, since $12 \times 1 = 12$ and $12 \div 1 = 12$.

9. Prime Factorization

To find the prime factorization of an integer, continue factoring until all the factors are prime. For example, the factor of 36 is as follows: $36 = 4 \times 9 = 2 \times 2 \times 3 \times 3$.

10. Relative Primes

Relative primes are integers that have no common factor other than 1. To determine whether two integers are relative primes, break them both down to their prime factorizations. For example: $35 = 5 \times 7$ and $54 = 2 \times 3 \times 3 \times 3$. They have no prime factors in common, so 35 and 54 are relative primes.

11. Common Multiple

A common multiple is a number that is a multiple of two or more integers. You can always get a common multiple of two integers by multiplying them, but unless the two numbers are relative primes, the product will not be the *least* common multiple. For example, to find a common multiple for 12 and 15, you could just multiply: $12 \times 15 = 180$.

To find the least common multiple (LCM), check out the multiples of the larger integer until you find one that's also a multiple of the smaller integer. To find the LCM of 12 and 15, begin by taking the multiples of 15: 15 is not divisible by 12, neither is 30 or 45. But the next multiple of 15, 60, *is* divisible by 12, so it's the LCM.

12. Greatest Common Factor (GCF)

To find the greatest common factor, break down the integers into their prime factorizations and multiply all the prime factors they have in common. For example, $36 = 2 \times 2 \times 3 \times 3$ and $48 = 2 \times 2 \times 2 \times 2 \times 3$. These integers have a 2×2 and a 3 in common, so the GCF is $2 \times 2 \times 3 = 12$.

13. Even/Odd

To predict whether a sum, difference, or product will be even or odd, just take simple numbers such as 1 and 2 and see what happens. There are rules—"odd times even is even," for example—but there's no need to memorize them. What happens with one set of numbers generally happens with all similar sets.

14. Multiples of 2, 4, and 8

An integer is divisible by 2 (even) if the last digit is even. An integer is divisible by 4 if the last two digits form a multiple of 4. An integer is divisible by 8 if the last three digits form a multiple of 8. The last digit of 562 is 2, which is even, so 562 is a multiple of 2. The last two digits form 62, which is *not* divisible by 4, so 562 is not a multiple of 4. The integer 512, however, is divisible by 4 because the last two digits form 12, which is a multiple of 4. The integer 1,136 is divisible by 8 because the last 3 digits form 136, which is 8×17.

15. Multiples of 3 and 9

An integer is divisible by 3 if the sum of its digits is divisible by 3. An integer is divisible by 9 if the sum of its digits is divisible by 9. The sum of the digits in 957 is 21, which is divisible by 3 but not by 9, so 957 is divisible by 3 but not by 9.

16. Multiples of 5 and 10

An integer is divisible by 5 if the last digit is 5 or 0. An integer is divisible by 10 if the last digit is 0. The last digit of 665 is 5, so 665 is a multiple of 5 but *not* a multiple of 10.

17. Remainders

The remainder is the whole number left over after division. For example, 487 is 2 more than 485, which is a multiple of 5, so when 487 is divided by 5, the remainder is 2.

FRACTIONS AND DECIMALS

18. Reducing Fractions

To reduce a fraction to lowest terms, factor out and cancel all factors the numerator and denominator have in common:

$$\frac{28}{36} = \frac{4 \times 7}{4 \times 9} = \frac{7}{9}$$

19. Adding/Subtracting Fractions

To add or subtract fractions, first find a common denominator, then add or subtract the numerators:

$$\frac{2}{15} + \frac{3}{10} = \frac{4}{30} + \frac{9}{30} = \frac{4+9}{30} = \frac{13}{30}$$

20. Multiplying Fractions

To multiply fractions, multiply the numerators and multiply the denominators:

$$\frac{5}{7} \times \frac{3}{4} = \frac{5 \times 3}{7 \times 4} = \frac{15}{28}$$

21. Dividing Fractions

To divide fractions, invert the second one and multiply:

$$\frac{1}{2} \div \frac{3}{5} = \frac{1}{2} \times \frac{5}{3} = \frac{1 \times 5}{2 \times 3} = \frac{5}{6}$$

22. Mixed Numbers and Improper Fractions

To convert a mixed number to an improper fraction, multiply the whole number part by the denominator, then add the numerator. The result is the new numerator (over the same denominator). To convert $7\frac{1}{3}$, first multiply 7 by 3, then add 1, to get the new numerator of 22. Put that over the same denominator, 3, to get $\frac{22}{3}$.

To convert an improper fraction to a mixed number, divide the denominator into the numerator to get a whole number quotient with a remainder. The quotient becomes the whole number part of the mixed number, and the remainder becomes the new numerator—with the same denominator. For example, to convert $\frac{108}{5}$, first divide 5 into 108, which yields 21 with a remainder of 3. Therefore, $\frac{108}{5} = 21\frac{3}{5}$.

23. Reciprocal

To find the reciprocal of a fraction, switch the numerator and the denominator. The reciprocal of $\frac{3}{7}$ is $\frac{7}{3}$. The reciprocal of 5 is $\frac{1}{5}$. The product of reciprocals is 1.

24. Comparing Fractions

One way to compare fractions is to reexpress them with a common denominator. For example, $\frac{3}{4} = \frac{21}{28}$ and $\frac{5}{7} = \frac{20}{28}$. Now, $\frac{21}{28}$ is greater than $\frac{20}{28}$, so $\frac{3}{4}$ is greater than $\frac{5}{7}$. Another method is to convert them both to decimals. For example, $\frac{3}{4}$ converts to 0.75 , and $\frac{5}{7}$ converts to approximately 0.714.

25. Converting Fractions and Decimals

To convert a fraction to a decimal, divide the bottom into the top. To convert $\frac{5}{8}$, divide 8 into 5, yielding 0.625.

To convert a decimal to a fraction, set the decimal over 1 and multiply the numerator and denominator by 10 raised to the number of digits that are to the right of the decimal point.

To convert 0.625 to a fraction, you would multiply $\frac{0.625}{1}$ by $\frac{10^3}{10^3}$ (or $\frac{1,000}{1,000}$).

Then simplify: $\frac{625}{1,000} = \frac{5 \times 125}{8 \times 125} = \frac{5}{8}$.

26. Repeating Decimal

To find a particular digit in a repeating decimal, note the number of digits in the cluster that repeats. If there are two digits in that cluster, then every second digit is the same. If there are three digits in that cluster, then every third digit is the same. And so on.

For example, the decimal equivalent of $\frac{1}{27}$ is 0.037037037..., which is best written $0.\overline{037}$. There are three digits in the repeating cluster, so every 3rd digit is the same: 7. To find the 50th digit, look for the multiple of 3 just less than 50—that's 48. The 48th digit is 7, and with the 49th digit the pattern repeats with 0. The 50th digit is 3.

27. Identifying the Parts and the Whole

The key to solving most fraction and percent word problems is to identify the part and the whole. Usually you'll find the part associated with the verb *is/are* and the whole associated with the word *of*. In the sentence "Half of the boys are blonds," the whole is the boys (*of* the boys), and the part is the blonds (*are* blonds).

PERCENTS

28. Percent Formula

Whether you need to find the part, the whole, or the percent, use the same formula:

$$\text{part} = \text{percent} \times \text{whole}$$

Example: What is 12 percent of 25?
Setup: part = 0.12 × 25

Example: 15 is 3 percent of what number?
Setup: 15 = 0.03 × whole

Example: 45 is what percent of 9?
Setup: 45 = percent × 9

29. Percent Increase and Decrease

To increase a number by a percent, add the percent to 100 percent, convert to a decimal, and multiply. To increase 40 by 25 percent, add 25 percent to 100 percent, convert 125 percent to 1.25, and multiply by 40:

$$1.25 \times 40 = 50$$

30. Finding the Original Whole

To find the original whole before a percent increase or decrease, set up an equation. Think of the result of a 15 percent increase over x as $1.15x$.

Example: After a 5 percent increase, the population was 59,346. What was the population before the increase?

Setup: $1.05x = 59,346$

31. Combined Percent Increase and Decrease

To determine the combined effect of multiple percent increases and/or decreases, start with 100 and see what happens.

Example: A price went up 10 percent one year, and the new price went up 20 percent the next year. What was the combined percent increase?

Setup: First year: 100 + (10 percent of 100) = 110
           Second year: 110 + (20 percent of 110) = 132
           That's a combined 32 percent increase.

AVERAGES

32. Average Formula

To find the average of a set of numbers, add them and divide by the number of terms.

$$\text{average} = \frac{\text{sum of the terms}}{\text{number of terms}}$$

To find the average of the five numbers 12, 15, 23, 40, and 40, first add them: $12 + 15 + 23 + 40 + 40 = 130$. Then divide the sum by 5 (because there are 5 terms): $130 \div 5 = 26$.

33. Average of Evenly Spaced Numbers

To find the average of evenly spaced numbers, just average the smallest and the largest. The average of all the integers from 13 through 77 is the same as the average of 13 and 77:

$$\frac{13 + 77}{2} = \frac{90}{2} = 45$$

34. Using the Average to Find the Sum

$$\text{sum} = (\text{average}) \times (\text{number of terms})$$

If the average of 10 numbers is 50, then they add up to 10×50, or 500.

35. Finding the Missing Number

To find a missing number when you're given the average, use the sum. If the average of four numbers is 7, then the sum of those four numbers is 4×7, or 28. Suppose that three of the numbers are 3, 5, and 8. These three numbers add up to 16 of that 28, which leaves 12 for the fourth number.

36. Median and Mode

The median of a set of numbers is the value that falls in the middle of the ordered set. If you have five test scores, and they are 88, 86, 57, 94, and 73, you must first list the scores in increasing or decreasing order: 57, 73, 86, 88, 94.

The median is the middle number, or 86. If there is an even number of values in a set (six test scores, for instance), simply take the average of the two middle numbers.

The mode of a set of numbers is the value that appears most often. If your test scores were 88, 57, 68, 85, 99, 93, 93, 84, and 81, the mode of the scores would be 93 because it appears more often than any other score. If there is a tie for the most common value in a set, the set has more than one mode.

RATIOS, PROPORTIONS, AND RATES

37. Setting Up a Ratio

To find a ratio, put the number associated with the word *of* on top and the quantity associated with the word *to* on the bottom and reduce. The ratio *of* 20 oranges *to* 12 apples is $\frac{20}{12}$, which reduces to $\frac{5}{3}$.

38. Part-to-Part Ratios and Part-to-Whole Ratios

If the parts add up to the whole, a part-to-part ratio can be turned into two part-to-whole ratios by putting each number in the original ratio over the sum of the numbers. If the ratio of males to females is 1 to 2, then the males-to-people ratio is $\frac{1}{1+2} = \frac{1}{3}$ and the females-to-people ratio is $\frac{2}{1+2} = \frac{2}{3}$. In other words, $\frac{2}{3}$ of all the people are female.

39. Solving a Proportion

To solve a proportion, cross multiply:

$$\frac{x}{5} = \frac{3}{4}$$

$$4x = 3 \times 5$$

$$x = \frac{15}{4}$$

$$= 3.75$$

40. Rate

To solve a rate problem, use the units to keep things straight.

Example: If snow is falling at the rate of one foot every four hours, how many inches of snow will fall in seven hours?

Setup:

$$\frac{1\,\text{foot}}{4\,\text{hours}} = \frac{x\,\text{inches}}{7\,\text{hours}}$$

$$\frac{12\,\text{inches}}{4\,\text{hours}} = \frac{x\,\text{inches}}{7\,\text{hours}}$$

$$4x = 12 \times 7$$

$$x = 21$$

41. Average Rate

Average rate is *not* simply the average of the rates. Learn the following average formulas before Test Day:

$$\text{average } A \text{ per } B = \frac{\text{total } A}{\text{total } B}$$

$$\text{average speed} = \frac{\text{total distance}}{\text{total time}}$$

To find the average speed for 120 miles at 40 mph and 120 miles at 60 mph, don't just average the two speeds. First, figure out the total distance and the total time. The total distance is $120 + 120 = 240$ miles. The times are three hours for the first leg and two hours for the second leg, or five hours total. The average speed, then, is $\frac{240}{5} = 48$ miles per hour.

POSSIBILITIES AND PROBABILITY

42. Counting the Possibilities

The fundamental counting principle states that if there are *m* ways one event can happen and *n* ways a second event can happen, then there are *m* × *n* ways for the two events to happen. For example, with five shirts and seven pairs of pants to choose from, you can have 5 × 7 = 35 different outfits.

43. Probability

$$\text{probability} = \frac{\text{favorable outcomes}}{\text{total possible outcomes}}$$

For example, if you have 12 shirts in a drawer and 9 of them are white, the probability of picking a white shirt at random is $\frac{9}{12} = \frac{3}{4}$. This probability can also be expressed as 0.75 or 75%.

POWERS AND ROOTS

44. Multiplying and Dividing Powers

To multiply powers with the same base, add the exponents and keep the same base:

$$y^3 \times y^4 = y^{3+4} = y^7$$

To divide powers with the same base, subtract the exponents and keep the same base:

$$x^{13} \div x^8 = x^{13-8} = x^5$$

45. Raising Powers to Powers

To raise a power to a power, multiply the exponents:

$$(a^3)^4 = a^{3 \times 4} = a^{12}$$

46. Simplifying Square Roots

To simplify a square root, factor out the perfect squares under the radical, unsquare them, and put the result in front:

$$\sqrt{12} = \sqrt{4 \times 3} = \sqrt{4} \times \sqrt{3} = 2\sqrt{3}$$

47. Adding and Subtracting Roots

You can add or subtract radical expressions when the part under the radicals is the same:

$$2\sqrt{3} + 3\sqrt{3} = 5\sqrt{3}$$

Don't try to add or subtract when the radical parts are different. There's not much you can do with an expression such as the following:

$$3\sqrt{5} + 3\sqrt{7}$$

48. Multiplying and Dividing Roots

The product of square roots is equal to the square root of the product:

$$\sqrt{3} \times \sqrt{5} = \sqrt{3 \times 5} = \sqrt{15}$$

The quotient of square roots is equal to the square root of the quotient:

$$\frac{\sqrt{6}}{\sqrt{3}} = \sqrt{\frac{6}{3}} = \sqrt{2}$$

49. Negative Exponents and Rational Exponents

To find the value of a number raised to a negative exponent, simply rewrite the number, without the negative sign, as the bottom of a fraction with 1 as the numerator of the fraction: $3^{-2} = \frac{1}{3^2} = \frac{1}{9}$. If x is a positive number and a is a nonzero number, then $x^{\frac{1}{a}} = a\sqrt{x}$. So $4^{\frac{1}{2}} = 2\sqrt{4} = 2$. If p and q are integers, then $x^{\frac{p}{q}} = \sqrt[q]{x^p}$. So $4^{\frac{3}{2}} = \sqrt[2]{4^3} = \sqrt{64} = 8$.

ABSOLUTE VALUE

50. Determining Absolute Value

The absolute value of a number is the distance of the number from zero on the number line. Because absolute value is a distance, and distance cannot be negative, it is always positive. The absolute value of 7 is 7; this is expressed $|7| = 7$. Similarly, the absolute value of -7 is 7. $|-7| = 7$. Every positive number is the absolute value of two numbers: itself and its negative.

ALGEBRAIC EXPRESSIONS

51. Evaluating an Expression

To evaluate an algebraic expression, plug in the given values for the unknowns and calculate according to PEMDAS. To find the value of $x^2 + 5x - 6$ when $x = -2$, plug in -2 for x: $(-2)^2 + 5(-2) - 6 = -12$.

52. Adding and Subtracting Monomials

To combine like terms, keep the variable part unchanged while adding or subtracting the coefficients:

$$2a + 3a = (2 + 3)a = 5a$$

53. Adding and Subtracting Polynomials

To add or subtract polynomials, combine like terms:

$$(3x^2 + 5x - 7) - (x^2 + 12) =$$
$$3x^2 + 5x - 7 - x^2 - 12 =$$
$$(3x^2 - x^2) + 5x + (-7 - 12) = 2x^2 + 5x - 19$$

54. Multiplying Monomials

To multiply monomials, multiply the coefficients and the variables separately:

$$2a \times 3a = (2 \times 3)(a \times a) = 6a^2$$

55. Multiplying Binomials—FOIL

To multiply binomials, use FOIL. To multiply $(b + 3)$ by $(b + 4)$, first multiply the First terms: $b \times b = b^2$. Next, the Outer terms: $b \times 4 = 4b$. Then, the Inner terms: $3 \times b = 3b$. And finally, the Last terms: $3 \times 4 = 12$. Then add and combine like terms:

$$b^2 + 4b + 3b + 12 = b^2 + 7b + 12$$

56. Multiplying Other Polynomials

FOIL works only when you want to multiply two binomials. If you want to multiply polynomials with more than two terms, make sure you multiply each term in the first polynomial by each term in the second:

$$(x^2 + 3x + 4)(x + 5) =$$
$$x^2(x + 5) + 3x(x + 5) + 4(x + 5) =$$
$$x^3 + 5x^2 + 3x^2 + 15x + 4x + 20 =$$
$$x^3 + 8x^2 + 19x + 20$$

After multiplying two polynomials together, the number of terms in your expression before simplifying should equal the number of terms in one polynomial multiplied by the number of terms in the second. In the example, you should have $3 \times 2 = 6$ terms in the product before you simplify like terms.

FACTORING ALGEBRAIC EXPRESSIONS

57. Factoring Out a Common Divisor

A factor common to all terms of a polynomial can be factored out. All three terms in the polynomial $3x^3 + 12x^2 - 6x$ contain a factor of $3x$. Pulling out the common factor yields $3x(x^2 + 4x - 2)$.

58. Factoring the Difference of Squares

One of the test maker's favorite factorables is the difference of squares:

$$a^2 - b^2 = (a - b)(a + b)$$

The expression $x^2 - 9$, for example, factors to $(x - 3)(x + 3)$.

59. Factoring the Square of a Binomial

Recognize polynomials that are squares of binomials:

$$a^2 + 2ab + b^2 = (a + b)^2$$
$$a^2 - 2ab + b^2 = (a - b)^2$$

For example, $4x^2 + 12x + 9$ factors to $(2x + 3)^2$, and $n^2 - 10n + 25$ factors to $(n - 5)^2$.

60. Factoring Other Polynomials—FOIL in Reverse

To factor a quadratic expression, think about what binomials you could use FOIL on to get that quadratic expression. To factor $x^2 - 5x + 6$, think about what First terms will produce x^2, what Last terms will produce $+6$, and what Outer and Inner terms will produce $-5x$. Some common sense—and a little trial and error—will lead you to $(x - 2)(x - 3)$.

61. Simplifying an Algebraic Fraction

Simplifying an algebraic fraction is a lot like simplifying a numerical fraction. The general idea is to find factors common to the numerator and denominator and cancel them. Thus, simplifying an algebraic fraction begins with factoring.

For example, to simplify $\dfrac{x^2 - x - 12}{x^2 - 9}$, first factor the numerator and denominator:

$$\frac{x^2 - x - 12}{x^2 - 9} = \frac{(x - 4)(x + 3)}{(x - 3)(x + 3)}$$

Canceling $x + 3$ from the numerator and denominator leaves you with $\dfrac{x - 4}{x - 3}$.

SOLVING EQUATIONS

62. Solving a Linear Equation

To solve an equation, do whatever is necessary to both sides to isolate the variable. To solve the equation $5x - 12 = -2x + 9$, first get all the x terms on one side by adding $2x$ to both sides: $7x - 12 = 9$. Then add 12 to both sides: $7x = 21$. Then divide both sides by 7: $x = 3$.

63. Solving "in terms of"

To solve an equation for one variable in terms of another means to isolate the one variable on one side of the equation, leaving an expression containing the other variable on the other side of the equation. To solve the equation $3x - 10y = -5x + 6y$ for x in terms of y, isolate x:

$$3x - 10y = -5x + 6y$$
$$3x + 5x = 6y + 10y$$
$$8x = 16y$$
$$x = 2y$$

64. Translating from English into Algebra

To translate from English into algebra, look for the key words and systematically turn phrases into algebraic expressions and sentences into equations. Be careful about order, especially with subtraction.

Example: Celine and Remi play tennis. Last year, Celine won 3 more than twice the number of matches that Remi won. If Celine won 11 more matches than Remi, how many matches did Celine win?

Setup: You are given two sets of information. One way to solve this is to write a system of equations—one equation for each set of information. Use variables that relate well with what they represent. For example, use r to represent Remi's winning matches. Use c to represent Celine's winning matches. The phrase "Celine won 3 more than twice…Remi" can be written as:

$$c = 2r + 3$$

The phrase "Celine won 11 more matches than Remi" can be written as follows:

$$c = r + 11$$

65. Solving a Quadratic Equation

To solve a quadratic equation, put it in the "$ax^2 + bx + c = 0$" form, factor the left side (if you can), and set each factor equal to 0 separately to get the two solutions. To solve $x^2 + 12 = 7x$, first rewrite it as $x^2 - 7x + 12 = 0$. Then factor the left side:

$$(x - 3)(x - 4) = 0$$
$$x - 3 = 0 \text{ OR } x - 4 = 0$$
$$x = 3 \text{ OR } x = 4$$

66. Solving a System of Equations

You can solve for two variables only if you have two distinct equations. Two forms of the same equation will not be adequate. Combine the equations in such a way that one of the variables cancels out. To solve the two equations $4x + 3y = 8$ and $x + y = 3$, multiply both sides of the second equation by -3 to get $-3x - 3y = -9$. Now add the two equations; the $3y$ and the $-3y$ cancel out, leaving $x = -1$. Plug that back into either one of the original equations and you'll find that $y = 4$.

A second way to solve for two variables is to use substitution. This is especially useful if one of the variables has a coefficient of 1 or is already solved for. For example, to solve the two equations $5x + 2y = 12$ and $y = x - 1$, you can directly substitute from the second equation into the first one. This gives you $5x + 2(x - 1) = 12$, which becomes $5x + 2x - 2 = 12$. This is simplified to $7x = 14$, or $x = 2$. Now that you know x, you plug it back into the equations to find $y = 1$.

67. Solving an Inequality

To solve an inequality, do whatever is necessary to both sides to isolate the variable. Just remember that when you multiply or divide both sides by a negative number, you must reverse the sign. To solve $-5x + 7 < -3$, subtract 7 from both sides to get: $-5x < -10$. Now divide both sides by -5, remembering to reverse the sign, so you get $x > 2$.

68. Radical Equations

A radical equation contains at least one radical expression. Solve radical equations by using standard rules of algebra. If $5\sqrt{x} - 2 = 13$, then $5\sqrt{x} = 15$ and $\sqrt{x} = 3$. When an algebraic equation includes a square root on one side, you can square both sides to "get rid of" the radical. This means that $\left(\sqrt{x}\right)^2 = 3^2$, so $x = 9$.

FUNCTIONS

69. Function Notation and Evaluation

Standard function notation is written $f(x)$ and is read "f of 4." To evaluate a function $f(x)$ means to determine the value of the function at a given value of x. So, to evaluate the function $f(x) = 2x + 3$ for $f(4)$, replace x with 4 and simplify: $f(4) = 2(4) + 3 = 11$.

70. Direct and Inverse Variation

In direct variation, $y = kx$, where k is a nonzero constant. In direct variation, the variable y changes directly as x does. If a unit of Currency A is worth 2 units of Currency B, then $A = 2B$. If the number of units of B were to double, the number of units of A would double, and so on for halving, tripling, etc. In inverse variation, $xy = k$, where x and y are variables and k is a constant. A famous inverse relationship is $rate \times time = distance$, where distance is constant. Imagine having to cover a distance of 24 miles. If you were to travel at 12 miles per hour, you'd need two hours. But if you were to halve your rate, you would have to double your time. This is just another way of saying that rate and time vary inversely.

71. Domain and Range of a Function

The domain of a function is the set of values for which the function is defined. For example, the domain of $f(x) = \dfrac{1}{1-x^2}$ is all values of x except 1 and −1, because for those values the denominator has a value of 0 and is therefore undefined. The range of a function is the set of outputs or results of the function. For example, the range of $f(x) = x^2$ is all numbers greater than or equal to zero, because x^2 cannot be negative.

COORDINATE GEOMETRY

72. Finding the Distance between Two Points

To find the distance between points, use the Pythagorean theorem or special right triangles. The difference between the x-values is one leg and the difference between the y-values is the other. For example:

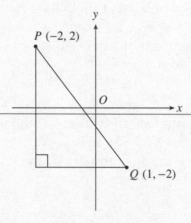

In the figure, PQ is the hypotenuse of a 3-4-5 triangle, so $PQ = 5$.

You can also use the distance formula:

$$d = \sqrt{(x_1 - x_2)^2 + (y_1 - y_2)^2}$$

To find the distance between $R(3, 6)$ and $S(5, -2)$ set up the following equation:

$$d = \sqrt{(3-5)^2 + [6-(-2)]^2}$$
$$= \sqrt{(-2)^2 + (8)^2}$$
$$= \sqrt{68}$$
$$= 2\sqrt{17}$$

73. Using Two Points to Find the Slope

$$\text{slope} = \frac{\text{change in } y}{\text{change in } x} \frac{\text{rise}}{\text{run}}$$

The slope of the line that contains the points $A(2, 3)$ and $B(0, -1)$ is:

$$\frac{y_A - y_B}{x_A - x_B} = \frac{3 - (-1)}{2 - 0} = \frac{4}{2}$$

74. Using an Equation to Find the Slope

To find the slope of a line from an equation, put the equation into the slope-intercept form:

$$y = mx + b$$

The slope is m. To find the slope of the equation $3x + 2y = 4$, isolate y on the left side of the equation:

$$3x + 2y = 4$$
$$2y = -3x + 4$$
$$y = -\frac{3}{2}x + 2$$

The slope is $-\frac{3}{2}$.

75. Using an Equation to Find an Intercept

To find the y-intercept, you can either put the equation into $y = mx + b$ (slope-intercept) form—in which case b is the y-intercept—or you can just plug $x = 0$ into the equation and solve for y. To find the x-intercept, plug $y = 0$ into the equation and solve for x.

LINES AND ANGLES

76. Intersecting Lines

When two lines intersect, adjacent angles are supplementary and vertical angles are equal.

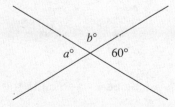

In the figure above, the angles marked $a°$ and $b°$ are adjacent and supplementary, so $a + b = 180$. Furthermore, the angles marked $a°$ and $60°$ are vertical and equal, so $a = 60$.

77. Parallel Lines and Transversals

A transversal across parallel lines forms four equal acute angles and four equal obtuse angles. If the transversal meets the lines at a right angle, then all eight angles are right angles.

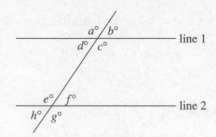

In the figure above, line 1 is parallel to line 2. Angles *a, c, e,* and *g* are obtuse, so they are all equal. Angles *b, d, f,* and *h* are acute, so they are all equal.

Furthermore, any of the acute angles is supplementary to any of the obtuse angles. Angles *a* and *h* are supplementary, as are *b* and *e, c* and *f,* and so on.

TRIANGLES—GENERAL

78. Interior and Exterior Angles of a Triangle

The three angles of any triangle add up to 180 degrees.

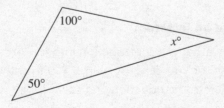

In the figure above, $x + 50 + 100 = 180$, so $x = 30$.

An exterior angle of a triangle is equal to the sum of the remote interior angles.

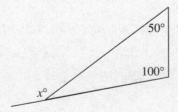

In the figure above, the exterior angle labeled $x°$ is equal to the sum of the remote angles:

$$x = 50 + 100 = 150$$

The three exterior angles of a triangle add up to 360 degrees.

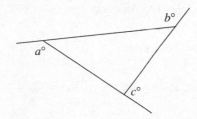

In the figure above, $a + b + c = 360$.

79. Similar Triangles

Similar triangles have the same shape: corresponding angles are equal and corresponding sides are proportional.

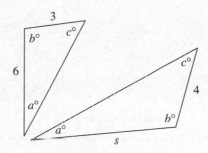

The triangles above are similar because they have the same angles. The 3 corresponds to the 4, and the 6 corresponds to the s, so you can solve for s:

$$\frac{3}{4} = \frac{6}{s}$$
$$3s = 24$$
$$s = 8$$

80. Area of a Triangle

The formula for the area of a triangle is as follows:

$$\text{area of triangle} = \frac{1}{2}(\text{base})(\text{height})$$

The height is the perpendicular distance between the side that's chosen as the base and the opposite vertex.

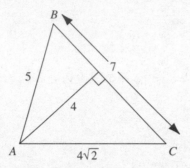

In the triangle above, 4 is the height when the 7 is considered the base.

$$\text{area} = \frac{1}{2}bh$$

$$= \frac{1}{2}(7)(4)$$

$$= 7(2)$$

$$= 14 \text{ units}^2$$

81. Triangle Inequality Theorem

The length of one side of a triangle must be greater than the difference and less than the sum of the lengths of the other two sides. For example, if it is given that the length of one side is 3 and the length of another side is 7, then you know that the length of the third side must be greater than $7 - 3 = 4$ and less than $7 + 3 = 10$.

82. Isosceles and Equilateral Triangles

An isosceles triangle is a triangle that has two equal sides. Not only are two sides equal, but the angles opposite the equal sides, called base angles, are also equal.

Equilateral triangles are triangles in which all three sides are equal. Since all the sides are equal, all the angles are also equal. All three angles in an equilateral triangle measure 60 degrees, regardless of the lengths of sides.

RIGHT TRIANGLES

83. Pythagorean Theorem

For all right triangles, the following is true:

$$(\text{leg}_1)^2 + (\text{leg}_2)^2 = (\text{hypotenuse})^2$$

$$a^2 + b^2 = c^2$$

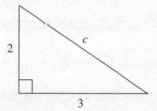

The hypotenuse, c, is the side opposite the right angle. The legs can be either a or b. If one leg is 2 and the other leg is 3, then you can find the length of the third leg:

$$2^2 + 3^2 = c^2$$

$$c^2 = 4 + 9$$

$$c = \sqrt{13}$$

84. The 3-4-5 Triangle

If a right triangle's leg-to-leg ratio is 3:4, or if the leg-to-hypotenuse ratio is 3:5 or 4:5, it's a 3-4-5 triangle and you don't need to use the Pythagorean theorem to find the third side. Just figure out what multiple of 3-4-5 each of the sides are.

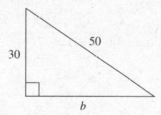

In the right triangle shown, one leg is 30 and the hypotenuse is 50. This is 10 times 3-4-5, so the other leg must be 40.

85. The 5-12-13 Triangle

If a right triangle's leg-to-leg ratio is 5:12, or if the leg-to-hypotenuse ratio is 5:13 or 12:13, then it's a 5-12-13 triangle and you don't need to use the Pythagorean theorem to find the third side. Just figure out what multiple of 5-12-13 each of the sides are.

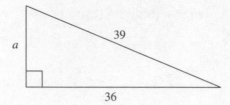

Here, one leg is 36 and the hypotenuse is 39. This is 3 times 5-12-13. The other leg must be 15.

86. The 30-60-90 Triangle

The sides of a 30-60-90 triangle are in a ratio of $x:x\sqrt{3}:2x$. You don't need the Pythagorean theorem.

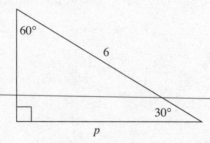

If the hypotenuse is 6, then the shorter leg is half that, or 3; and then the longer leg is equal to the short leg times $\sqrt{3}$, or $3\sqrt{3}$.

87. The 45-45-90 Triangle

The sides of a 45-45-90 triangle are in a ratio of $x:x:x\sqrt{2}$.

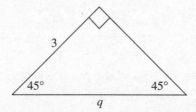

If one leg is 3, then the other leg is also 3, and the hypotenuse is equal to a leg times $\sqrt{2}$, or $3\sqrt{2}$.

OTHER POLYGONS

88. Characteristics of a Rectangle

A rectangle is a four-sided figure with four right angles. Opposite sides are equal. Diagonals are equal.

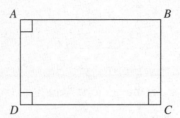

Quadrilateral *ABCD* above is shown to have three right angles. The fourth angle therefore also measures 90 degrees, and *ABCD* is a rectangle. The perimeter of a rectangle is equal to the sum of the lengths of the four sides, which is equivalent to 2(length + width).

$$\text{area of rectangle} = \text{length} \times \text{width}$$

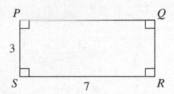

The area of a 7-by-3 rectangle is $7 \times 3 = 21$.

89. Characteristics of a Parallelogram

A parallelogram has two pairs of parallel sides. Opposite sides are equal. Opposite angles are equal. Consecutive angles add up to 180 degrees.

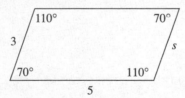

In the previous figure, *s* is the length of the side opposite the 3, so $s = 3$.

$$\text{area of parallelogram} = \text{base} \times \text{height}$$

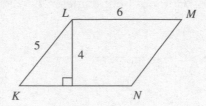

In parallelogram *KLMN* above, 4 is the height when *LM* or *KN* is used as the base, so base × height = $6 \times 4 = 24$.

90. Characteristics of a Square

A square is a rectangle with four equal sides.

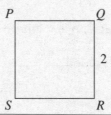

If *PQRS* is a square, all sides are the same length as *QR*. The perimeter of a square is equal to four times the length of one side.

$$\text{area of square} = (\text{side})^2$$

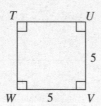

The square above, with sides of length 5, has an area of $5^2 = 25$.

91. Interior Angles of a Polygon

The sum of the measures of the interior angles of a polygon $= (n - 2) \times 180$, where *n* is the number of sides.

$$\text{sum of the angles} = (n - 2) \times 180$$

The eight angles of an octagon, for example, add up to $(8 - 2) \times 180 = 1{,}080$.

CIRCLES

92. Circumference of a Circle

Circumference $= 2\pi r$

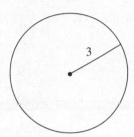

In the circle above, the radius is 3, and so the circumference is $2\pi(3) = 6\pi$.

93. Length of an Arc

An arc is a segment of the circumference. If n is the degree measure of the arc's central angle, then the formula is:

$$\text{Length of an Arc} = \left(\frac{n}{360}\right)(2\pi r)$$

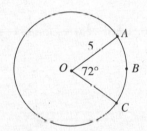

In the previous figure, the radius is 5 and the measure of the central angle is 72 degrees. The arc length is $\frac{72}{360}$, or $\frac{1}{5}$, of the circumference:

$$\frac{72}{360}(2\pi)(5) = \frac{1}{5}(10\pi) = 2\pi$$

94. Area of a Circle

area of a circle $= \pi r^2$

The area of the circle is $\pi(4)^2 = 16\pi$.

95. Area of a Sector

A sector is a section of the area of a circle. If *n* is the degree measure of the sector's central angle, then the formula is:

$$\text{area of a sector} = \left(\frac{n}{360}\right)(\pi r^2)$$

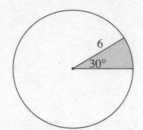

In the figure above, the radius is 6 and the measure of the sector's central angle is 30 degrees. The sector has $\frac{30}{360}$, or $\frac{1}{12}$, of the area of the circle:

$$\frac{30}{360}(\pi)(6^2) = \frac{1}{12}(36\pi) = 3\pi$$

96. Tangency

When a line is tangent to a circle, the radius of the circle is perpendicular to the line at the point of contact.

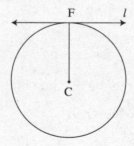

SOLIDS

97. Surface Area of a Rectangular Solid

The surface of a rectangular solid consists of three pairs of identical faces. To find the surface area, find the area of each face and add them up. If the length is *l*, the width is *w*, and the height is *h*, the formula is as follows:

$$\text{surface area} = 2lw + 2wh + 2lh$$

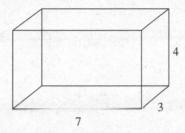

The surface area of the box above is:

$$2(7 \times 3) + 2(3 \times 4) + 2(7 \times 4) = 42 + 24 + 56$$

$$= 122$$

98. Volume of a Rectangular Solid

$$\text{volume of a rectangular solid} = lwh$$

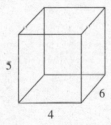

The volume of a 4-by-5-by-6 box is:

$$4 \times 5 \times 6 = 120$$

A cube is a rectangular solid with length, width, and height all equal. If *e* is the length of an edge of a cube, the volume formula is:

$$\text{volume of a cube} = e^3$$

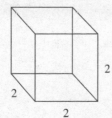

The volume of this cube is $2^3 = 8$.

99. Volume of a Cylinder

$$\text{volume of a cylinder} = \pi r^2 h$$

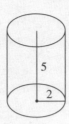

In the cylinder above, $r = 2$, $h = 5$, so use the formula to create an equation and determine the missing value:

$$\text{Volume} = \pi(2^2)(5) = 20\pi$$

100. Finding the Midpoint

The midpoint of two points on a line segment is the average of the x-coordinates of the endpoints and the average of the y-coordinates of the endpoints. If the endpoints are (x_1, y_1) and (x_2, y_2), the midpoint is $\left(\dfrac{x_1 + x_2}{2}, \dfrac{y_1 + y_2}{2}\right)$. The midpoint of $(3, 5)$ and $(9, 1)$ is $\left(\dfrac{3+9}{2}, \dfrac{5+1}{2}\right) = (6, 3)$.

CHAPTER 22

Writing Wrap-Up

CHAPTER OBJECTIVES

With practice, this chapter will help you:

1. Explain the steps of the Kaplan 4-Step Method for Writing and its role in writing an essay or writing sample effectively and efficiently

2. Identify Writing concepts and strategies in need of further practice or review

WRITING WRAP-UP STRATEGY REVIEW

As discussed in Chapter 9, writing a strong, descriptive essay or writing sample is a skill needed for admission to both private and independent schools. Although your essay is not scored, it is a great way for schools to see how you express yourself.

1. How does the test maker make the essay more difficult?

_____

_____

_____

2. What should you remember about pacing?

_____

_____

_____

3. The Kaplan 4-Step Method for Writing:

Step 1. _____

Step 2. _____

Step 3. _____

Step 4. _____

Answers and Explanations

1. The test makers make the essay more difficult by making the story prompts more creative and making the essay prompts more complex.

2. The step where you actually write your essay—Step 3—is not the only important step! Steps 1 and 2 should take up a substantial amount of time, and if you don't leave time for proofreading, it will reflect in your final product.

3. **The Kaplan 4-Step Method for Writing**

    Step 1. Prompt (brainstorm the topic)

    Step 2. Plan your response

    Step 3. Produce your writing

    Step 4. Proofread

PRACTICE

Use the checklist that follows to evaluate the writing sample below.

> Some people say that "no good deed goes unpunished." Do you agree or disagree with this statement?

People who believe this statement would apparently feel as many people in our society seem to, that they should not help their nieghbors. Instead, they would ignore people in trouble because they would be afraid that they would get in trouble themselves but I do not agree with this belief. Many times people who do good deeds do get rewarded. Sometimes a reward of money or recognition. Even when they don't, this hardly seems like a "punishment." After all, just feeling good about something you've done can be a reward unto itself.

Just recently, for example, there was a story on television about a "Good Samaritan" who ran into a buring building to rescue a child. Because his bravery, the child was saved from a certain death. As a reward this man got a lot of things. He was interviewed on the TV news, and a rich man who saw the news story gave the man a reward of $5,000. But this man had no way of knowing that any of this was going to happen when he saved the little girl, and I don't think he would have been sorry he'd done it. Even if the TV news people and the rich man never heard about it. For the rest of his life, he will have the good feeling, he saved a little girl's life.

In conclusion, while it may be true that some deeds don't get rewarded or cause trouble for the person who did them, I think most times good deeds are rewarded, not punished. Sometimes the reward is just a good feeling for the person who did the deed, but that's enough. I also think we would have a better society if fewer people believed in this statement that "No good deed goes unpunished."

Writing Sample Checklist

Does the writer answer the assignment question?   ❏ Yes   ❏ No

If so, where? _____

_____

_____

Does the writing sample have an introduction?   ❏ Yes   ❏ No

Does the writing sample have a conclusion?   ❏ Yes   ❏ No

Does the writer provide a relevant example or examples?   ❏ Yes   ❏ No

If so, what example(s) did she provide? _____

_____

_____

Is/are the writer's example(s) well developed?   ❏ Yes   ❏ No

Does the writing sample have any errors?   ❏ Yes   ❏ No

If so, what are they? _____

_____

_____

Overall, do you think this is a good writing sample?   ❏ Yes   ❏ No

Why or why not? _____

_____

_____

Answers and Explanations

Does the writer answer the assignment question? ☑ Yes ☐ No

If so, where?

In paragraph 1, the author states, "Many times people who do good deeds do get rewarded."

Does the writing sample have an introduction? ☑ Yes ☐ No

Does the writing sample have a conclusion? ☑ Yes ☐ No

Does the writer provide a relevant example or examples? ☑ Yes ☐ No

If so, what example(s) did she provide?

The example relates to someone being rewarded for a good deed. It would be a better example if it focused on an example without a good deed.

Is/are the writer's example(s) well developed? ☐ Yes ☑ No

Does the writing sample have any errors? ☑ Yes ☐ No

If so, what are they?

Multiple spelling errors (such as "nieghbor" and "buring building"), run-on sentences and sentence fragments, and misused or missing punctuation

Overall, do you think this is a strong writing sample? ☐ Yes ☑ No

Why or why not?

This essay is on the right track, but the author should have spent more time planning and proofreading to make sure it was on topic and well-planned.

Use what you've learned to continue practicing writing, answering the question posed by the prompt below. Use the blank space on the next page for your plan; write your actual writing sample on the following page.

You'll have 25 minutes for SSAT or 30 minutes for ISEE. Use these timing guidelines to help you budget your time.

DIRECTIONS: Read the following topic carefully. Take a few minutes to think about the topic and organize your thoughts before you begin writing. Be sure that your handwriting is legible and that you stay within the lines and margins.

Topic: Which book do you wish you could read again and why?

Assignment: Support your position with one or two specific examples from personal experience, the experience of others, current events, history, or literature.

Use this space to plan your writing sample.

DIRECTIONS: Read the following topic carefully. Take a few minutes to think about the topic and organize your thoughts before you begin writing. Be sure that your handwriting is legible and that you stay within the lines and margins.

> **Topic:** I peeked into the classroom and...

Use this space to plan your writing sample.

DIRECTIONS: Read the following topic carefully. Take a few minutes to think about the topic and organize your thoughts before you begin writing. Be sure that your handwriting is legible and that you stay within the lines and margins.

> Describe what you could consider a "team player." Explain why you consider this person and this person's qualities to be collaborative.

Use this space to plan your writing sample.

DIRECTIONS: Read the following topic carefully. Take a few minutes to think about the topic and organize your thoughts before you begin writing. Be sure that your handwriting is legible and that you stay within the lines and margins.

Write about a time when you made a mistake. Explain what you learned from this experience.

Use this space to plan your writing sample.

PART 5

SSAT Practice Tests and Explanations

SSAT TEST OVERVIEW

Total Time

Approximately three hours, including two breaks.

Questions

Aside from the essay, all questions are multiple-choice in format, with all answer choices labeled A, B, C, D, and E.

Content

The SSAT tests math, reading, writing, and verbal skills. There are two Math sections, one Verbal section, one Reading section, and one unscored Writing Sample.

Pacing

You are not expected to complete all items on the SSAT. This is particularly true if you are at the low end of the age range of test takers for your level. The best approach to pacing is to work as quickly as you can without losing accuracy. Further, if a question is giving you difficulty, circle it and move on. You can always come back to it later, but you shouldn't waste time on a question that is stumping you when you could be gaining valuable points elsewhere.

Guessing

You receive 1 point for each question answered correctly. For those questions you answer incorrectly, you lose $\frac{1}{4}$ point. As a result, guess *only* when you can do so strategically. In other words, don't guess wildly, but *do* guess if you can eliminate at least one answer choice as clearly incorrect.

CHAPTER 23

SSAT Upper/Middle Level Practice Test 1

HOW TO TAKE THIS PRACTICE TEST

Before taking this practice test, find a quiet room where you can work uninterrupted for two and a half hours. Make sure you have a comfortable desk and several #2 pencils.

Use the answer sheet provided to record your answers. You can cut it out or photocopy it.

Once you start this practice test, don't stop until you've finished. Remember: you can review any questions within a section, but you may not go backward or forward to any other sections.

You'll find answer explanations following the test. Scoring information is in Chapter 25.

If you are a Middle Level student, you should not expect to score as high as you would as an Upper Level student. No matter your score, you should focus on conducting in-depth reviews of all practice you complete, including this practice test.

Good luck.

SSAT Upper/Middle Level Practice Test 1
ANSWER SHEET

Remove (or photocopy) this answer sheet and use it to complete the practice test.

Start with number 1 for each section. If a section has fewer questions than answer spaces, leave the extra spaces blank.

SECTION 1

1. Ⓐ Ⓑ Ⓒ Ⓓ Ⓔ   6. Ⓐ Ⓑ Ⓒ Ⓓ Ⓔ   11. Ⓐ Ⓑ Ⓒ Ⓓ Ⓔ   16. Ⓐ Ⓑ Ⓒ Ⓓ Ⓔ   21. Ⓐ Ⓑ Ⓒ Ⓓ Ⓔ
2. Ⓐ Ⓑ Ⓒ Ⓓ Ⓔ   7. Ⓐ Ⓑ Ⓒ Ⓓ Ⓔ   12. Ⓐ Ⓑ Ⓒ Ⓓ Ⓔ   17. Ⓐ Ⓑ Ⓒ Ⓓ Ⓔ   22. Ⓐ Ⓑ Ⓒ Ⓓ Ⓔ
3. Ⓐ Ⓑ Ⓒ Ⓓ Ⓔ   8. Ⓐ Ⓑ Ⓒ Ⓓ Ⓔ   13. Ⓐ Ⓑ Ⓒ Ⓓ Ⓔ   18. Ⓐ Ⓑ Ⓒ Ⓓ Ⓔ   23. Ⓐ Ⓑ Ⓒ Ⓓ Ⓔ
4. Ⓐ Ⓑ Ⓒ Ⓓ Ⓔ   9. Ⓐ Ⓑ Ⓒ Ⓓ Ⓔ   14. Ⓐ Ⓑ Ⓒ Ⓓ Ⓔ   19. Ⓐ Ⓑ Ⓒ Ⓓ Ⓔ   24. Ⓐ Ⓑ Ⓒ Ⓓ Ⓔ
5. Ⓐ Ⓑ Ⓒ Ⓓ Ⓔ   10. Ⓐ Ⓑ Ⓒ Ⓓ Ⓔ   15. Ⓐ Ⓑ Ⓒ Ⓓ Ⓔ   20. Ⓐ Ⓑ Ⓒ Ⓓ Ⓔ   25. Ⓐ Ⓑ Ⓒ Ⓓ Ⓔ

correct in section 1

incorrect in section 1

SECTION 2

1. Ⓐ Ⓑ Ⓒ Ⓓ Ⓔ   9. Ⓐ Ⓑ Ⓒ Ⓓ Ⓔ   17. Ⓐ Ⓑ Ⓒ Ⓓ Ⓔ   25. Ⓐ Ⓑ Ⓒ Ⓓ Ⓔ   33. Ⓐ Ⓑ Ⓒ Ⓓ Ⓔ
2. Ⓐ Ⓑ Ⓒ Ⓓ Ⓔ   10. Ⓐ Ⓑ Ⓒ Ⓓ Ⓔ   18. Ⓐ Ⓑ Ⓒ Ⓓ Ⓔ   26. Ⓐ Ⓑ Ⓒ Ⓓ Ⓔ   34. Ⓐ Ⓑ Ⓒ Ⓓ Ⓔ
3. Ⓐ Ⓑ Ⓒ Ⓓ Ⓔ   11. Ⓐ Ⓑ Ⓒ Ⓓ Ⓔ   19. Ⓐ Ⓑ Ⓒ Ⓓ Ⓔ   27. Ⓐ Ⓑ Ⓒ Ⓓ Ⓔ   35. Ⓐ Ⓑ Ⓒ Ⓓ Ⓔ
4. Ⓐ Ⓑ Ⓒ Ⓓ Ⓔ   12. Ⓐ Ⓑ Ⓒ Ⓓ Ⓔ   20. Ⓐ Ⓑ Ⓒ Ⓓ Ⓔ   28. Ⓐ Ⓑ Ⓒ Ⓓ Ⓔ   36. Ⓐ Ⓑ Ⓒ Ⓓ Ⓔ
5. Ⓐ Ⓑ Ⓒ Ⓓ Ⓔ   13. Ⓐ Ⓑ Ⓒ Ⓓ Ⓔ   21. Ⓐ Ⓑ Ⓒ Ⓓ Ⓔ   29. Ⓐ Ⓑ Ⓒ Ⓓ Ⓔ   37. Ⓐ Ⓑ Ⓒ Ⓓ Ⓔ
6. Ⓐ Ⓑ Ⓒ Ⓓ Ⓔ   14. Ⓐ Ⓑ Ⓒ Ⓓ Ⓔ   22. Ⓐ Ⓑ Ⓒ Ⓓ Ⓔ   30. Ⓐ Ⓑ Ⓒ Ⓓ Ⓔ   38. Ⓐ Ⓑ Ⓒ Ⓓ Ⓔ
7. Ⓐ Ⓑ Ⓒ Ⓓ Ⓔ   15. Ⓐ Ⓑ Ⓒ Ⓓ Ⓔ   23. Ⓐ Ⓑ Ⓒ Ⓓ Ⓔ   31. Ⓐ Ⓑ Ⓒ Ⓓ Ⓔ   39. Ⓐ Ⓑ Ⓒ Ⓓ Ⓔ
8. Ⓐ Ⓑ Ⓒ Ⓓ Ⓔ   16. Ⓐ Ⓑ Ⓒ Ⓓ Ⓔ   24. Ⓐ Ⓑ Ⓒ Ⓓ Ⓔ   32. Ⓐ Ⓑ Ⓒ Ⓓ Ⓔ   40. Ⓐ Ⓑ Ⓒ Ⓓ Ⓔ

correct in section 2

incorrect in section 2

SECTION 3

1. Ⓐ Ⓑ Ⓒ Ⓓ Ⓔ   13. Ⓐ Ⓑ Ⓒ Ⓓ Ⓔ   25. Ⓐ Ⓑ Ⓒ Ⓓ Ⓔ   37. Ⓐ Ⓑ Ⓒ Ⓓ Ⓔ   49. Ⓐ Ⓑ Ⓒ Ⓓ Ⓔ
2. Ⓐ Ⓑ Ⓒ Ⓓ Ⓔ   14. Ⓐ Ⓑ Ⓒ Ⓓ Ⓔ   26. Ⓐ Ⓑ Ⓒ Ⓓ Ⓔ   38. Ⓐ Ⓑ Ⓒ Ⓓ Ⓔ   50. Ⓐ Ⓑ Ⓒ Ⓓ Ⓔ
3. Ⓐ Ⓑ Ⓒ Ⓓ Ⓔ   15. Ⓐ Ⓑ Ⓒ Ⓓ Ⓔ   27. Ⓐ Ⓑ Ⓒ Ⓓ Ⓔ   39. Ⓐ Ⓑ Ⓒ Ⓓ Ⓔ   51. Ⓐ Ⓑ Ⓒ Ⓓ Ⓔ
4. Ⓐ Ⓑ Ⓒ Ⓓ Ⓔ   16. Ⓐ Ⓑ Ⓒ Ⓓ Ⓔ   28. Ⓐ Ⓑ Ⓒ Ⓓ Ⓔ   40. Ⓐ Ⓑ Ⓒ Ⓓ Ⓔ   52. Ⓐ Ⓑ Ⓒ Ⓓ Ⓔ
5. Ⓐ Ⓑ Ⓒ Ⓓ Ⓔ   17. Ⓐ Ⓑ Ⓒ Ⓓ Ⓔ   29. Ⓐ Ⓑ Ⓒ Ⓓ Ⓔ   41. Ⓐ Ⓑ Ⓒ Ⓓ Ⓔ   53. Ⓐ Ⓑ Ⓒ Ⓓ Ⓔ
6. Ⓐ Ⓑ Ⓒ Ⓓ Ⓔ   18. Ⓐ Ⓑ Ⓒ Ⓓ Ⓔ   30. Ⓐ Ⓑ Ⓒ Ⓓ Ⓔ   42. Ⓐ Ⓑ Ⓒ Ⓓ Ⓔ   54. Ⓐ Ⓑ Ⓒ Ⓓ Ⓔ
7. Ⓐ Ⓑ Ⓒ Ⓓ Ⓔ   19. Ⓐ Ⓑ Ⓒ Ⓓ Ⓔ   31. Ⓐ Ⓑ Ⓒ Ⓓ Ⓔ   43. Ⓐ Ⓑ Ⓒ Ⓓ Ⓔ   55. Ⓐ Ⓑ Ⓒ Ⓓ Ⓔ
8. Ⓐ Ⓑ Ⓒ Ⓓ Ⓔ   20. Ⓐ Ⓑ Ⓒ Ⓓ Ⓔ   32. Ⓐ Ⓑ Ⓒ Ⓓ Ⓔ   44. Ⓐ Ⓑ Ⓒ Ⓓ Ⓔ   56. Ⓐ Ⓑ Ⓒ Ⓓ Ⓔ
9. Ⓐ Ⓑ Ⓒ Ⓓ Ⓔ   21. Ⓐ Ⓑ Ⓒ Ⓓ Ⓔ   33. Ⓐ Ⓑ Ⓒ Ⓓ Ⓔ   45. Ⓐ Ⓑ Ⓒ Ⓓ Ⓔ   57. Ⓐ Ⓑ Ⓒ Ⓓ Ⓔ
10. Ⓐ Ⓑ Ⓒ Ⓓ Ⓔ   22. Ⓐ Ⓑ Ⓒ Ⓓ Ⓔ   34. Ⓐ Ⓑ Ⓒ Ⓓ Ⓔ   46. Ⓐ Ⓑ Ⓒ Ⓓ Ⓔ   58. Ⓐ Ⓑ Ⓒ Ⓓ Ⓔ
11. Ⓐ Ⓑ Ⓒ Ⓓ Ⓔ   23. Ⓐ Ⓑ Ⓒ Ⓓ Ⓔ   35. Ⓐ Ⓑ Ⓒ Ⓓ Ⓔ   47. Ⓐ Ⓑ Ⓒ Ⓓ Ⓔ   59. Ⓐ Ⓑ Ⓒ Ⓓ Ⓔ
12. Ⓐ Ⓑ Ⓒ Ⓓ Ⓔ   24. Ⓐ Ⓑ Ⓒ Ⓓ Ⓔ   36. Ⓐ Ⓑ Ⓒ Ⓓ Ⓔ   48. Ⓐ Ⓑ Ⓒ Ⓓ Ⓔ   60. Ⓐ Ⓑ Ⓒ Ⓓ Ⓔ

correct in section 3

incorrect in section 3

SECTION 4

1. Ⓐ Ⓑ Ⓒ Ⓓ Ⓔ   6. Ⓐ Ⓑ Ⓒ Ⓓ Ⓔ   11. Ⓐ Ⓑ Ⓒ Ⓓ Ⓔ   16. Ⓐ Ⓑ Ⓒ Ⓓ Ⓔ   21. Ⓐ Ⓑ Ⓒ Ⓓ Ⓔ
2. Ⓐ Ⓑ Ⓒ Ⓓ Ⓔ   7. Ⓐ Ⓑ Ⓒ Ⓓ Ⓔ   12. Ⓐ Ⓑ Ⓒ Ⓓ Ⓔ   17. Ⓐ Ⓑ Ⓒ Ⓓ Ⓔ   22. Ⓐ Ⓑ Ⓒ Ⓓ Ⓔ
3. Ⓐ Ⓑ Ⓒ Ⓓ Ⓔ   8. Ⓐ Ⓑ Ⓒ Ⓓ Ⓔ   13. Ⓐ Ⓑ Ⓒ Ⓓ Ⓔ   18. Ⓐ Ⓑ Ⓒ Ⓓ Ⓔ   23. Ⓐ Ⓑ Ⓒ Ⓓ Ⓔ
4. Ⓐ Ⓑ Ⓒ Ⓓ Ⓔ   9. Ⓐ Ⓑ Ⓒ Ⓓ Ⓔ   14. Ⓐ Ⓑ Ⓒ Ⓓ Ⓔ   19. Ⓐ Ⓑ Ⓒ Ⓓ Ⓔ   24. Ⓐ Ⓑ Ⓒ Ⓓ Ⓔ
5. Ⓐ Ⓑ Ⓒ Ⓓ Ⓔ   10. Ⓐ Ⓑ Ⓒ Ⓓ Ⓔ   15. Ⓐ Ⓑ Ⓒ Ⓓ Ⓔ   20. Ⓐ Ⓑ Ⓒ Ⓓ Ⓔ   25. Ⓐ Ⓑ Ⓒ Ⓓ Ⓔ

correct in section 4

incorrect in section 4

The Writing Sample

Secondary schools will use an essay or story to get to know you better. Write about one of the two topics below. Choose the topic you find most interesting and bubble in the circle before you start writing.

(A) I opened the window and immediately…

(B) Technology makes the world smaller every day. Do you agree or disagree with this statement? Explain why you feel this way.

Notes

_____

_____

_____

_____

_____

_____

_____

_____

_____

_____

_____

_____

_____

Continue on next page.

SECTION 1
25 Questions

Each question has five suggested answers. Solve each question in your head or using the blank space at the right of the page. Then, examine the five choices and select the correct one.

<u>Note</u>: Figures in this section are as accurate as possible EXCEPT when it is stated that a figure is not drawn to scale.

Sample Question:

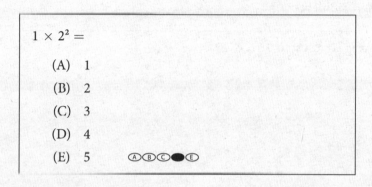

1. Each member of a club sold the same number of raffle tickets. If the club sold a total of 120 tickets, which of the following CANNOT be the number of tickets sold by each member?

    (A) 2

    (B) 8

    (C) 10

    (D) 12

    (E) 16

2. According to the graph, about how many students are art majors?

    (A) 200

    (B) 225

    (C) 280

    (D) 300

    (E) 360

MAJORS OF 900 STUDENTS

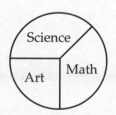

GO ON TO THE NEXT PAGE. ▶ ▶ ▶

3. Sean arrives home 14 minutes before midnight, and his sister gets home 25 minutes after him. When does Sean's sister arrive home?

    (A) 11 minutes before midnight

    (B) 11 minutes after midnight

    (C) 14 minutes after midnight

    (D) 25 minutes after midnight

    (E) 39 minutes after midnight

4. Which of the following is closest to 0.52×78?

    (A) $\frac{1}{5}$ of 70

    (B) $\frac{1}{5}$ of 80

    (C) $\frac{2}{5}$ of 70

    (D) $\frac{1}{2}$ of 70

    (E) $\frac{1}{2}$ of 80

5. The graph shows the amount of money Kiran, Arianna, and Dakota saved by the end of the summer.

    Arianna's summer savings are greater than Kiran's summer savings by how many dollars?

    (A) 3

    (B) 4

    (C) 150

    (D) 200

    (E) 300

SUMMER SAVINGS

$(\$) = \$50$

Kiran: $(\$)\ (\$)$

Arianna: $(\$)\ (\$)\ (\$)\ (\$)\ (\$)\ (\$)$

Dakota: $(\$)\ (\$)\ (\$)\ (\$)\ (\$)\ (\$)\ (\$)\ (\$)$

GO ON TO THE NEXT PAGE. ▶ ▶ ▶

6. How many students are in a class if 30 percent of the class is equal to 30 students?

   (A) 10

   (B) 90

   (C) 100

   (D) 900

   (E) It cannot be determined from the information given.

7. Each of the following is less than 2 EXCEPT

   (A) $\dfrac{15}{8}$

   (B) $\dfrac{45}{22}$

   (C) $\dfrac{99}{50}$

   (D) $\dfrac{180}{100}$

   (E) $\dfrac{701}{400}$

8. The sides and angles of triangles ABC, BDE, BCE, and CEF in the figure are all equal. Which of the following is the longest path from A to F?

   (A) $A - C - B - D - F$

   (B) $A - B - E - C - F$

   (C) $A - B - C - E - F$

   (D) $A - C - E - F$

   (E) $A - B - D - F$

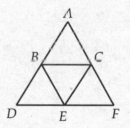

9. Which of the following is closest to 80.08?

   (A) 80

   (B) 80.01

   (C) 80.1

   (D) 81

   (E) 90

GO ON TO THE NEXT PAGE. ▶ ▶ ▶

10. If $\frac{1}{3}$ of a number is less than 12, then the number is always

    (A) less than 36

    (B) equal to 4

    (C) greater than 4

    (D) equal to 36

    (E) greater than 36

11. In a basketball game, Team A scored 39 points, and Team B scored more points than Team A. If Team B has 5 players, the average score of the players on Team B must have been at least how many points?

    (A) 1

    (B) 5

    (C) 6

    (D) 8

    (E) 12

12. In the triangle shown in the figure, what is the value of a?

    (A) 4

    (B) 6

    (C) 8

    (D) 9

    (E) It cannot be determined from the information given.

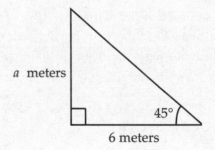

a meters

45°

6 meters

13. A man bought a piece of land for $40,000. Then, he spent $2 million to build a house on it. The cost of the house is how many times the cost of the land?

    (A) 5

    (B) 20

    (C) 50

    (D) 200

    (E) 500

GO ON TO THE NEXT PAGE. ▶ ▶ ▶

14. If $(x - y) + 2 = 6$ and y is less than 3, which of the following CANNOT be the value of x?

   (A) -3

   (B) 0

   (C) $1\frac{1}{2}$

   (D) 4

   (E) 8

15. In the figure, the distance from A to D is 55, and the distance from A to B is equal to the distance from C to D. If the distance from A to B is twice the distance from B to C, how far apart are B and D?

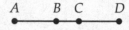

   (A) 11

   (B) 30

   (C) 33

   (D) 44

   (E) 45

16. A book is placed on a flat table surface, as shown in the figure. Which of the following best shows all of the points where the book touches the table?

   (A) ▢

   (B) ⬬

   (C) ▱

   (D) ○

   (E) ■

GO ON TO THE NEXT PAGE. ▶ ▶ ▶

17. Which of the following can be expressed as $(J + 2) \times 3$, where J is a whole number?

(A) 40

(B) 52

(C) 65

(D) 74

(E) 81

18. If $a - 7 = 3b + 4$, what does $a + 5$ equal?

(A) $b - 1$

(B) $4b - 1$

(C) $3b + 9$

(D) $3b + 16$

(E) It cannot be determined from the information given.

19. According to a census report for Country A, 21.5 out of every 100 families live in rural areas. Based on this report, how many of the 2 million families in Country A live in rural areas?

(A) 430,000

(B) 215,000

(C) 43,000

(D) 4,300

(E) 430

20. Bob is x years old, and Jerry is 7 years older. In terms of x, what was the sum of their ages, in years, 5 years ago?

(A) $2x + 3$

(B) $2x + 2$

(C) $2x - 3$

(D) $x - 3$

(E) $x - 10$

GO ON TO THE NEXT PAGE. ▶ ▶ ▶

21. A game show contestant answered exactly 20 percent of the questions correctly. Of the first 15 questions, he answered 4 correctly. If he answered only 1 of the remaining questions correctly, which of the following MUST be true?

    (A) There were a total of 20 questions.

    (B) He answered 10 percent of the remaining questions by guessing.

    (C) He didn't answer 9 of the remaining questions correctly.

    (D) He answered only 2 questions in a row correctly.

    (E) The questions got more difficult as the show went on.

22. If C is the product of consecutive integers A and B, then C must be

    (A) greater than $A + B$

    (B) a negative integer

    (C) a positive integer

    (D) an even integer

    (E) an odd integer

23. A 20 percent discount is offered on all sweaters at Store S. If a cotton sweater is on sale for $48.00 and a wool sweater is on sale for $64.00, what was the difference in price of the sweaters before the discount?

    (A) $16.00

    (B) $19.20

    (C) $20.00

    (D) $24.00

    (E) $32.00

GO ON TO THE NEXT PAGE. ▶ ▶ ▶

24. The maximum load that a railway car can carry is $17\frac{1}{3}$ tons of freight. If a train has 36 railway cars, and each of these carries $\frac{5}{9}$ of a ton less than its maximum load, how many tons of freight is the train carrying?

    (A) 604

    (B) $612\frac{7}{9}$

    (C) $640\frac{5}{9}$

    (D) 648

    (E) 660

---

25. $632 \div 5 =$

    (A) $\frac{60}{5} + \frac{32}{5}$

    (B) $\frac{600}{5} + 32$

    (C) $\frac{6}{5} + \frac{3}{5} + \frac{2}{5}$

    (D) $\frac{600}{5} \times \frac{30}{5} \times \frac{2}{5}$

    (E) $\frac{600}{5} + \frac{30}{5} + \frac{2}{5}$

IF YOU FINISH BEFORE TIME IS CALLED, YOU MAY CHECK YOUR WORK ON THIS SECTION ONLY. DO NOT TURN TO ANY OTHER SECTION IN THE TEST. **STOP**

SECTION 2
40 Questions

Read each passage and answer the related questions. For each question, use the passage to decide which one of the choices best answers the question.

Typical lemurs are primates with bodies similar to those of monkeys but with pointed muzzles and large eyes; most have long, bushy tails. Their fur is woolly and may be colored red, gray, brown, or black. The name of the lemur stems from the Latin *lemures*, the Roman name for vampire-like ghosts of the dead, which these large-eyed creatures were thought to resemble. Found only off the

Line 5 east coast of Africa on the island of Madagascar and neighboring islands, lemurs spend some time on the ground but most often are in the trees, building nests high in the branches. Besides leaves, lemurs eat eggs, fruit, insects, and small animals. They are active throughout the day and night and are reputed to be gentle, friendly creatures. Besides typical lemurs, the lemur family includes avahi, aye-aye, loris, and galogo. However, contrary to popular belief, the so-called flying lemur is not even

10 a primate, much less a true lemur; it is, in fact, a member of an altogether different order of mammals known as *Dermoptera*.

---

1. The style of the passage is most like that found in a

    (A) biology textbook

    (B) novel about Madagascar

    (C) zoologist's diary

    (D) tourist's guidebook

    (E) personal letter

2. Which of the following would be the best title for this passage?

    (A) The Lemur: Friend or Foe?

    (B) Madagascar's Loneliest Hunters

    (C) Facts about Lemurs

    (D) African Vampires

    (E) The Diet of the Lemur

3. According to the passage, all of the following are true about lemurs EXCEPT

    (A) they spend much of their time in trees

    (B) most have long, bushy tails

    (C) the flying lemur is not a true lemur

    (D) they eat only fruits and leaves

    (E) the body of the lemur resembles the body of the monkey

GO ON TO THE NEXT PAGE. ▶ ▶ ▶

4. The passage suggests that

   (A) the typical lemur is a member of an order of mammals known as *Dermoptera*

   (B) flying lemurs are only active during the night

   (C) the lemur is not an aggressive animal

   (D) lemurs spend most of their time on the ground

   (E) flying lemurs can only be found on Madagascar and neighboring islands

5. The author uses the phrase "so-called" (line 9) to show that

   (A) flying lemurs resemble typical lemurs

   (B) true lemurs are herbivores, but flying lemurs are carnivores

   (C) lemurs' large eyes mean that lemurs come out only at night

   (D) flying lemurs should not be classified with true lemurs

   (E) lemurs' pointed muzzles give them an excellent sense of smell

GO ON TO THE NEXT PAGE. ▶ ▶ ▶

Before a joint session of Congress in January 1918, President Woodrow Wilson outlined his plan for a post-World War I peace settlement. Known as the Fourteen Points, Wilson's plan is best remembered for its first point, which declared that international diplomacy should be conducted in the open and that quiet, unpublicized diplomacy should be made illegal. Wilson believed that public

Line 5 diplomacy would end the threat of war by preventing immoral national leaders from secretly plotting aggressive actions against others.

Although Wilson was a highly intelligent and well-meaning man, he lacked insight into the complexities of international politics. Contrary to Wilson's belief, war rarely results from the behind-the-scenes plotting of unscrupulous national leaders. Rather, war usually stems from unresolved

10 disagreements among nations—disagreements over territory, access to resources, and so forth. Even if quiet diplomacy could be eliminated, these disagreements would still remain, as would the threat of war.

6. The second paragraph of this passage is primarily about

(A) a post-World War I peace settlement

(B) diplomacy's role in international politics

(C) disagreements among nations

(D) the actual causes of war

(E) the first point in Wilson's Fourteen Points

7. The attitude of the writer toward the subject is

(A) calculating

(B) suspicious

(C) opinionated

(D) cheerful

(E) apologetic

8. The author would most likely agree that war between country A and country B would result from which of the following situations?

(A) a dispute over ownership of a piece of land bordering both countries

(B) an agreement by a leader in country A to tax imports from a third country

(C) the capture of a spy from country A in country B

(D) an unpublicized agreement by country A to sell weapons to country B

(E) a secret alliance made between country A and another country

9. Why does the author say that open diplomacy would not prevent war?

(A) Quiet diplomacy will always be a part of international relations.

(B) War breaks out because immoral rulers make decisions in secret.

(C) Open diplomacy is not a solution to the problems that lead to war.

(D) Disagreements over territory and resources rarely lead to conflict.

(E) International relations are too complex to be conducted in the public eye.

GO ON TO THE NEXT PAGE. ▶ ▶ ▶

10. Which of the following questions CANNOT be answered using information from the passage?

   (A) Does the author think the Fourteen Points was a good plan?

   (B) According to the author, why does war usually start?

   (C) Did Wilson support public diplomacy or concealed diplomacy?

   (D) Does the author feel he or she understands international politics better than Wilson did?

   (E) How does the author think the threat of war could be eliminated for good?

11. Which of the following is the author most likely to discuss next?

   (A) Wilson's domestic policies in the post–World War I period

   (B) the impact of import taxes on foreign trade relations

   (C) an example of a war that resulted from a territorial or resource dispute

   (D) the events leading up to World War I

   (E) other examples of Wilson's intelligence

GO ON TO THE NEXT PAGE. ▶ ▶ ▶

Live thy Life,
    Young and old,
Like yon oak,
    Bright in spring,
Line 5   Living gold;

Summer-rich
    Then: and then
Autumn-changed,
Soberer-hued
10   Gold again.

All his leaves
    Fall'n at length,
Look, he stands,
Trunk and bough,
15   Naked strength.

"The Oak," by Lord Alfred Tennyson

12. In this poem, the seasons represent different

(A) kinds of trees

(B) times of day

(C) stages of life

(D) styles of dress

(E) periods of history

13. In line 13, "he" refers to

(A) the poet

(B) life

(C) the oak

(D) autumn

(E) the reader

14. What does "Gold again" in line 10 signify?

(A) the arrival of autumn

(B) the richness of summer

(C) the increased wealth of the narrator

(D) the color of oak trees

(E) the revival of the past

15. During which season is the oak referred to as "Living gold" (line 5)?

(A) spring

(B) summer

(C) autumn

(D) winter

(E) This description does not relate to a season.

GO ON TO THE NEXT PAGE. ▶ ▶ ▶

16. With which of the following statements about life would the speaker be most likely to agree?

    (A) People should live every period of their lives to the fullest.

    (B) It is important to try to accomplish something during one's lifetime.

    (C) Life is too short to spend time doing unpleasant things.

    (D) The seasons are unpredictable.

    (E) Trees are an integral part of the enjoyment of life.

17. All of the following can describe the tone of the poem EXCEPT

    (A) optimistic

    (B) passionate

    (C) pompous

    (D) hopeful

    (E) thoughtful

GO ON TO THE NEXT PAGE. ▶ ▶ ▶

Tea is consumed by more people and in greater amounts than any other beverage in the world, with the exception of water. The tea plant, from whose leaves tea is made, is native to India, China, and Japan and was first cultivated for use by the Chinese in prehistoric times. The plant, which is characterized as an evergreen, can reach a height of about thirty feet but is usually pruned down to
Line 5 three or four feet for cultivation. It has dark green leaves and cream-colored, fragrant blossoms.

Cultivation of the tea plant requires a great deal of effort. The plant must grow in a warm, wet climate in a carefully protected, well-drained area. Its leaves must be picked by hand. (Cultivation in North America has been attempted, but was found to be impractical because of a shortage of cheap labor.) Today, the plant is cultivated in the lands to which it is native, as well as in Sri Lanka,
10 Indonesia, Taiwan, and South America.

Tea was probably first used as a vegetable relish and for medicinal purposes. In the 1400s Chinese and Japanese Buddhists developed a semireligious ceremony surrounding tea drinking. It was not until after 1700, however, that tea was first imported into Europe. Today, the United Kingdom imports more tea than does any other nation—almost one-third of the world's production. The
15 United States is also a large importer, but Americans have seemed to prefer coffee ever since the famous Boston Tea Party in 1773.

18. This passage is mainly about

(A) the tea plant

(B) the uses of the tea plant

(C) tea drinking throughout history

(D) the tea trade

(E) the cultivation of the tea plant

19. According to the passage, the tea plant

(A) was first cultivated in Japan in prehistoric times

(B) requires well-drained soil to grow properly

(C) is the largest import of the United Kingdom

(D) has odorless flowers

(E) is native to South America

20. Why is a large supply of cheap labor important for the cultivation of tea?

(A) Since the tea plant can reach a height of thirty feet, several workers are required to harvest each plant

(B) Since tea is exported all over the world, a lot of people are needed to handle the trade complications that arise.

(C) Since tea has been around since prehistoric times, many workers are employed to protect it and ensure that it doesn't die out.

(D) Since England and China are far away from each other, many workers are required to coordinate tea shipments and deliveries.

(E) Since the tea plant is handpicked, many laborers are needed at harvest time.

GO ON TO THE NEXT PAGE. ▶ ▶ ▶

21. The style in the passage is most like that found in a

    (A) newspaper article

    (B) passage in an encyclopedia

    (C) cookbook

    (D) journal entry

    (E) history textbook

22. Which of the following is the author most likely to discuss next?

    (A) the details and aftermath of the Boston Tea Party

    (B) other major imports of the United Kingdom and United States

    (C) current trends in tea consumption

    (D) other examples of plants that have a medicinal value

    (E) a description of what China was like in prehistoric times

23. The purpose of the second paragraph is to

    (A) describe the role of tea in religious ceremonies

    (B) explain why Americans prefer coffee

    (C) discuss historical uses of tea

    (D) describe the cultivation of tea

    (E) question the importance of tea

GO ON TO THE NEXT PAGE. ▶ ▶ ▶

There were moments of waiting. The youth thought of the village street at home before the arrival of the circus parade on a day in the spring. He remembered how he had stood, a small thrillful boy, prepared to follow the band in its faded chariot. He saw the yellow road, the lines of expectant people, and the sober houses. He particularly remembered an old fellow who used to sit upon a cracker box

Line 5   in front of the store and pretend to despise such exhibitions. A thousand details of color and form surged in his mind.

Someone cried, "Here they come!" There was rustling and muttering among the men.

They displayed a feverish desire to have every possible cartridge ready to their hands. The boxes were pulled around into various positions and adjusted with great care.

10   The tall soldier, having prepared his rifle, produced a red handkerchief of some kind. He was engaged in knitting it about his throat with exquisite attention to its position, when the cry was repeated up and down the line in a muffled roar of sound.

"Here they come! Here they come!" Gun locks clicked.

Across the smoke-infested fields came a brown swarm of running men who were giving shrill

15   yells. They came on, stooping and swinging their rifles at all angles. A flag, tilted forward, sped near the front.

24: In line 14, "swarm" most likely means

(A) army

(B) cloud

(C) concentrate

(D) flood

(E) increase

25. What is meant by the exclamation "Here they come!" in line 7?

(A) A band in a chariot is approaching.

(B) The circus is coming to town.

(C) The enemy soldiers are advancing.

(D) A group of men selling handkerchiefs is on its way.

(E) The youth's family is arriving to save him.

26. The mood of the passage undergoes a change from the first to the second paragraph that can best be described as a movement from

(A) anger to amusement

(B) reminiscence to anticipation

(C) informality to formality

(D) reluctance to fear

(E) respect to indifference

GO ON TO THE NEXT PAGE. ▶ ▶ ▶

27. In lines 7 and 13, the phrase "here they come!" is an example of

    (A) consonance

    (B) alliteration

    (C) onomatopoeia

    (D) synecdoche

    (E) repetition

28. In the first paragraph, the youth is primarily concerned with

    (A) reliving a fond childhood memory

    (B) describing a turning point in his life

    (C) preparing for the upcoming battle

    (D) planning his day at the circus

    (E) watching a soldier tie a handkerchief

GO ON TO THE NEXT PAGE. ▶ ▶ ▶

Acupuncture is a type of medical therapy that has been part of Chinese medicine since ancient times. It involves the insertion of thin, solid needles into specific sites on the body's surface. The belief is that the application of a needle at one particular point produces a specific response at a second point. It is based on the ancient Chinese philosophy that human beings are miniature
Line 5 versions of the universe and that the forces that control nature also control health. These forces are divided between two main principles called the yin and the yang, which have an opposite but complementary effect on each other. For example, one force keeps the body's temperature from rising too high, and the other keeps it from dropping too low. When they are in balance, the body maintains a constant, normal state. Disease occurs when these forces get out of balance.
10   Although acupuncture had been used in Western countries during many periods, it was not until the 1970s that it gained widespread interest, when it was determined that it could be used to control pain during surgery. The mechanism for its effectiveness is still a mystery, but it has become a very popular technique in many countries for the treatment of various diseases and medical problems.

29. The passage is written from the viewpoint of which of the following?

  (A) a researcher

  (B) a surgeon

  (C) a patient

  (D) an acupuncturist

  (E) a philosopher

30. This passage is primarily about

  (A) various diseases that are particularly common among the Chinese

  (B) the meaning and use of the yin and the yang

  (C) different types of medical therapies and their relative effectiveness

  (D) the historical and philosophical background of acupuncture

  (E) modern uses of acupuncture both in China and in Western countries

31. According to the passage, acupuncture is based on

  (A) the idea that the human body is a model of the universe and is therefore controlled by the forces of nature

  (B) a firm belief in the Chinese gods known as the yin and the yang

  (C) an ancient Chinese religious ceremony that involves the insertion of needles into the body

  (D) a philosophy of health and disease that originated in China but has been totally changed by Western countries

  (E) the ideas of an astronomer who was attempting to study the universe in ancient times

GO ON TO THE NEXT PAGE. ▶ ▶ ▶

32. According to the passage, the yin and the yang are principles that represent

    (A) high and low extremes of temperature

    (B) states of health and disease

    (C) similar treatments for different diseases

    (D) competing, balancing forces within the body

    (E) the ideas of comfort and pain

33. The author includes the example of the yin and the yang controlling the extremes of body temperature in order to

    (A) back up her claim that the forces within the body mirror the forces of the universe

    (B) clarify how these forces have a complementary effect on each other

    (C) provide proof that acupuncture is an effective medical therapy

    (D) suggest a possible explanation for why people sometimes run high fevers

    (E) highlight a feature of the body that acupuncture has not yet been shown to influence

34. The author's attitude in this passage could best be described as

    (A) critical

    (B) admiring

    (C) bitter

    (D) serene

    (E) neutral

GO ON TO THE NEXT PAGE. ▶ ▶ ▶

The painter Georgia O'Keeffe was born in Wisconsin in 1887, and grew up on her family's farm. At seventeen she left for Chicago and New York, but she never lost her bond with the land. Like most painters, O'Keeffe painted the things that were most important to her, and she became famous for her simplified paintings of nature. During a visit to New Mexico in 1929, O'Keeffe was moved by the
Line 5   desert's stark beauty, and she began to paint many of its images. From about 1930 until her death in 1986, her true home was in the western desert, and bleached bones, barren hills, and colorful flowers were her characteristic subjects.

O'Keeffe is widely considered to have been a pioneering American modernist painter. While most early modern American artists were strongly influenced by European art, O'Keeffe's position was
10   more independent.

Almost from the beginning, her work was more identifiably American—in its simplified and idealized treatment of color, light, space, and natural forms. Her paintings are generally considered "semiabstract," because, while they often depict recognizable images and objects, they don't present those images in a very detailed or realistic way. Rather, the colors and shapes in her paintings are
15   often so reduced and simplified that they begin to take on a life of their own, independent from the real-life objects they are taken from.

35. The author's tone in the passage can best be described as

(A) exuberant

(B) sympathetic

(C) respectful

(D) pleading

(E) condeming

36. O'Keeffe's relationship to nature is most similar to

(A) a photographer's relationship to a model

(B) a writer's relationship to a publisher

(C) a student's relationship to a part-time job

(D) a sculptor's relationship to an art dealer

(E) a carpenter's relationship to a hammer

37. Which of the following titles best describes the content of the passage?

(A) The Realistic Use of Color and Light

(B) Semiabstract Everyday Objects

(C) Nature's Everyday Scenes

(D) Georgia O'Keeffe and Semiabstract Paintings

(E) Modernist American Painters

38. According to the passage, O'Keeffe is considered an artistic pioneer because

(A) her work became influential in Europe

(B) she painted the American Southwest

(C) her paintings had a definite American style

(D) she painted things that were familiar to her

(E) her work was very abstract

GO ON TO THE NEXT PAGE. ▶ ▶ ▶

39. The passage's main point about O'Keeffe is that she

   (A) was the best painter of her generation

   (B) was a distinctive modern American painter

   (C) liked to paint only what was familiar to her

   (D) never developed fully enough as an abstract artist

   (E) used colors and shapes that are too reduced and simple

40. It can be inferred from the passage that modern European art of the time

   (A) did not depict images of the desert

   (B) was extremely abstract

   (C) did not portray natural shapes in a simple, idealistic manner

   (D) was not influenced by rural landscapes

   (E) approached colors in a semi-abstract manner

IF YOU FINISH BEFORE TIME IS CALLED, YOU MAY CHECK YOUR WORK ON THIS SECTION ONLY. DO NOT TURN TO ANY OTHER SECTION IN THE TEST.

SECTION 3
60 Questions

This section includes two question types: synonyms and analogies. There are directions and an example question for each type.

Synonyms

Each Synonym question consists of one word with five words or phrases as answer choices. Choose the one word or phrase that is most similar in meaning to the word in capital letters.

Sample Question:

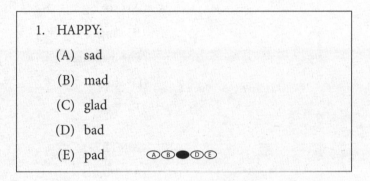

1. HAPPY:

   (A) sad

   (B) mad

   (C) glad

   (D) bad

   (E) pad

---

1. PLEAD:

   (A) strike

   (B) cry

   (C) tease

   (D) beg

   (E) try

2. PROWL:

   (A) growl

   (B) sneak

   (C) scrub

   (D) leave

   (E) fight

3. VESSEL:

   (A) blood

   (B) decoration

   (C) car

   (D) account

   (E) container

4. APPROVE:

   (A) command

   (B) ignore

   (C) pursue

   (D) commend

   (E) contemplate

GO ON TO THE NEXT PAGE. ▶ ▶ ▶

5. SEEP:

   (A) ooze

   (B) gurgle

   (C) liquefy

   (D) stick

   (E) fall

6. VEX:

   (A) scribble

   (B) locate

   (C) scream

   (D) play

   (E) irritate

7. DOZE:

   (A) graze

   (B) sleep

   (C) refresh

   (D) bore

   (E) ignore

8. WOVEN:

   (A) barricade

   (B) reap

   (C) intertwined

   (D) restriction

   (E) bounty

9. COARSE:

   (A) sifted

   (B) sticky

   (C) unpopular

   (D) difficult

   (E) rough

10. MEEK:

    (A) submissive

    (B) old

    (C) tiny

    (D) worried

    (E) quick

11. SATURATE:

    (A) soak

    (B) anger

    (C) measure

    (D) boil

    (E) pour

12. GENTEEL:

    (A) timid

    (B) loud

    (C) stupid

    (D) harmless

    (E) refined

13. WINSOME:

    (A) athletic

    (B) charming

    (C) critical

    (D) small

    (E) shy

14. REPROACH:

    (A) retreat

    (B) rebuke

    (C) insist

    (D) complain

    (E) whine

GO ON TO THE NEXT PAGE. ▶ ▶ ▶

15. DEMONSTRATE:

   (A) object

   (B) show

   (C) require

   (D) renew

   (E) imply

16. CAMOUFLAGE:

   (A) jewelry

   (B) outfit

   (C) disguise

   (D) outlook

   (E) helmet

17. AGHAST:

   (A) shocked

   (B) swollen

   (C) irritated

   (D) nasty

   (E) rude

18. RECOLLECT.

   (A) invent

   (B) remember

   (C) remove

   (D) discover

   (E) reject

19. INITIATE:

   (A) gather

   (B) try

   (C) start

   (D) command

   (E) celebrate

20. SUFFOCATE:

   (A) give instruction

   (B) pull out

   (C) make willing

   (D) surround completely

   (E) deprive of air

21. PREVAIL:

   (A) triumph

   (B) predict

   (C) entrust

   (D) cover

   (E) enlighten

22. PRANCE:

   (A) boast

   (B) lead

   (C) strut

   (D) pry

   (E) sing

23. PROFOUND:

   (A) stubborn

   (B) unfounded

   (C) perplexing

   (D) absurd

   (E) deep

24. LIMBER:

   (A) supple

   (B) wooden

   (C) skinny

   (D) sober

   (E) sociable

GO ON TO THE NEXT PAGE. ▶ ▶ ▶

25. TERMINATE:

   (A) extend

   (B) renew

   (C) finalize

   (D) sell

   (E) end

26. CONTEMPLATE:

   (A) ponder

   (B) reject

   (C) founder

   (D) dominate

   (E) deserve

27. CAPRICE:

   (A) idea

   (B) mistake

   (C) whim

   (D) decision

   (E) guess

28. ADAGE:

   (A) permission

   (B) disdain

   (C) humor

   (D) prevention

   (E) proverb

29. DIN:

   (A) outline

   (B) clamor

   (C) improvement

   (D) demonstration

   (E) pressure

30. EXPUNGE:

   (A) erase

   (B) handle

   (C) label

   (D) assault

   (E) keep

GO ON TO THE NEXT PAGE. ▶ ▶ ▶

Analogies

Each Analogy question asks you to determine the relationship between two words. Choose the answer choice that best completes the meaning of the sentence.

Sample Question:

> 1. Rain is to wet as
>
>   (A) sun is to dark
>
>   (B) cloud is to water
>
>   (C) cold is to ice
>
>   (D) sleep is to tired
>
>   (E) heat is to dry

Choice (E) is the best answer because heat causes things to be dry just like rain causes things to be wet. Of all the answer choices, (E) states a relationship that is most like the relationship between <u>rain</u> and <u>wet</u>.

---

31. Pilot is to airplane as

    (A) team is to players

    (B) horse is to cart

    (C) captain is to ship

    (D) passenger is to train

    (E) army is to country

32. Snake is to python as dog is to

    (A) terrier

    (B) canine

    (C) pet

    (D) mammal

    (E) quadruped

33. Mayor is to city as

    (A) governor is to state

    (B) member is to union

    (C) board is to district

    (D) secretary is to committee

    (E) citizen is to legislature

34. Paper is to novel as

    (A) person is to poll

    (B) paint is to brush

    (C) canvas is to portrait

    (D) back is to chair

    (E) color is to palette

35. Refined is to vulgar as

    (A) calm is to placid

    (B) submissive is to recalcitrant

    (C) happy is to ecstatic

    (D) helpful is to victorious

    (E) tranquil is to forgivable

36. Whip is to lash as

    (A) stick is to throw

    (B) shoe is to walk

    (C) saddle is to sit

    (D) food is to eat

    (E) club is to beat

GO ON TO THE NEXT PAGE. ▶ ▶ ▶

37. Migrate is to swan as

    (A) hibernate is to groundhog

    (B) pet is to dog

    (C) swim is to fish

    (D) sting is to bee

    (E) pounce is to cat

38. Weather is to meteorologist as vegetation is to

    (A) driver

    (B) artist

    (C) oceanographer

    (D) hunter

    (E) botanist

39. Track is to horse racing as

    (A) circus is to elephant

    (B) court is to tennis

    (C) net is to basketball

    (D) goal is to football

    (E) air is to bird

40. Director is to actor as coach is to

    (A) executive

    (B) player

    (C) chorus

    (D) airplane

    (E) officer

41. Dessert is to meal as

    (A) finale is to performance

    (B) lunch is to breakfast

    (C) fork is to spoon

    (D) plate is to table

    (E) ocean is to river

42. Confirm is to deny as

    (A) accept is to reject

    (B) assert is to proclaim

    (C) contend is to imply

    (D) pull is to tug

    (E) simplify is to organize

43. Hostile is to nemesis as

    (A) fortified is to stronghold

    (B) audible is to language

    (C) harmful is to sight

    (D) regiment is to ordered

    (E) disciplined is to recruit

44. Fidelity is to unfaithfulness as

    (A) loyalty is to honor

    (B) friendship is to gossip

    (C) honesty is to deceit

    (D) laziness is to slothfulness

    (E) intelligence is to unconcern

45. Widespread is to limited as

    (A) encompassed is to surrounded

    (B) enlarged is to big

    (C) broad is to narrow

    (D) unusual is to strange

    (E) provincial is to international

46. Saw is to carpenter as plow is to

    (A) banker

    (B) surveyor

    (C) farmer

    (D) physician

    (E) steelworker

GO ON TO THE NEXT PAGE. ▶ ▶ ▶

47. Racket is to tennis as glove is to

    (A) box

    (B) soccer

    (C) hockey

    (D) baseball

    (E) golf

48. Encourage is to demand as

    (A) insinuate is to hint

    (B) fire is to dismiss

    (C) suggest is to order

    (D) motivate is to undermine

    (E) condemn is to reprimand

49. Grin is to delight as

    (A) anxiety is to confusion

    (B) frown is to dismay

    (C) perspiration is to exhaustion

    (D) encouragement is to happiness

    (E) resignation is to uncertainty

50. Mysterious is to understandable as

    (A) unknown is to indefinable

    (B) doubtful is to incredulous

    (C) skillful is to swift

    (D) clouded is to warm

    (E) obscure is to clear

51. Injury is to heal as malfunction is to

    (A) repair

    (B) bandage

    (C) misinterpret

    (D) throw

    (E) disassemble

52. Jog is to sprint as trot is to

    (A) ramble

    (B) gallop

    (C) roam

    (D) saunter

    (E) soar

53. Bone is to body as

    (A) floor is to house

    (B) motor is to boat

    (C) driver is to car

    (D) knob is to door

    (E) beam is to building

54. Amorphous is to shape as odorless is to

    (A) appearance

    (B) weight

    (C) worth

    (D) scent

    (E) anger

55. Vain is to humility as

    (A) anxious is to boisterousness

    (B) cantankerous is to thoughtlessness

    (C) judicious is to leniency

    (D) authoritative is to discourse

    (E) extroverted is to shyness

56. Test is to study as

    (A) job is to apply

    (B) train is to practice

    (C) play is to rehearse

    (D) office is to employ

    (E) income is to work

GO ON TO THE NEXT PAGE. ▶ ▶ ▶

57. Smile is to frown as cheer is to

    (A) heckle

    (B) wince

    (C) laugh

    (D) extricate

    (E) leap

58. Banana is to peel as

    (A) egg is to crack

    (B) carrot is to uproot

    (C) apple is to core

    (D) bread is to slice

    (E) corn is to husk

59. Touch is to tactile as

    (A) sound is to noise

    (B) smell is to olfactory

    (C) mouth is to oral

    (D) eye is to visual

    (E) taste is to sense

60. Articulateness is to speech as

    (A) etiquette is to society

    (B) music is to note

    (C) ballet is to form

    (D) legibility is to handwriting

    (E) painting is to palette

IF YOU FINISH BEFORE TIME IS CALLED, YOU MAY CHECK YOUR WORK ON THIS SECTION ONLY. DO NOT TURN TO ANY OTHER SECTION IN THE TEST. **STOP**

SECTION 4
25 Questions

Each question has five suggested answers. Solve each question in your head or using the blank space at the right of the page. Then, examine the five choices and select the correct one.

<u>Note</u>: Figures in this section are as accurate as possible EXCEPT when it is stated that a figure is not drawn to scale.

Sample Question:

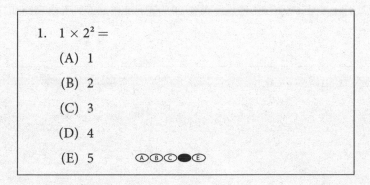

1. $1 \times 2^2 =$
    (A) 1
    (B) 2
    (C) 3
    (D) 4
    (E) 5   Ⓐ Ⓑ Ⓒ ● Ⓔ

---

1. The crown in the figure is made up of toothpicks that each have the same length. If each toothpick is 6 centimeters long, the base of the crown uses two toothpicks, and the three points use one toothpick on each side, what is the perimeter of the crown in meters?

    (A) 7
    (B) 12
    (C) 36
    (D) 42
    (E) 50

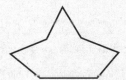

This figure not drawn to scale.

GO ON TO THE NEXT PAGE. ▶ ▶ ▶

2. Gary has a collection of 16 different movies, and his roommate Parth has a collection of 18 different movies. If Parth and Gary have 4 movies common to both collections, how many different movies do they have between them?

    (A) 18

    (B) 30

    (C) 34

    (D) 36

    (E) 38

3. If $\frac{1}{9}G = 18$, then $\frac{1}{3}G =$

    (A) 1

    (B) 9

    (C) 36

    (D) 54

    (E) 162

4. A model sailboat is floating on the water and attached to the dock using a 1 meter long string, as shown in the figure. If the string is tied to a post on the edge of the side of the dock, which of the following best shows the area of water on which the sailboat can float?

    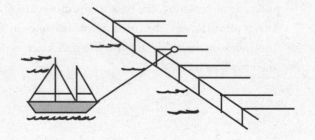

    (A)

    (B)

    (C)

    (D)

    (E)

GO ON TO THE NEXT PAGE. ▶ ▶ ▶

5. At a party, there are exactly 4 times as many adults as children. Which of the following could be the total number of people at this party?

   (A) 14

   (B) 16

   (C) 21

   (D) 25

   (E) 29

6. Using a pair of scissors, which of the following CANNOT be made from a 20 cm by 28 cm rectangular sheet of paper by one straight cut?

   (A) triangle

   (B) square

   (C) trapezoid

   (D) pentagon

   (E) hexagon

7. According to the graph, what was the average number of students taking the swimming class during the four months of March through June?

   (A) 50

   (B) 55

   (C) 60

   (D) 65

   (E) 70

NUMBER OF STUDENTS TAKING SWIMMING CLASS

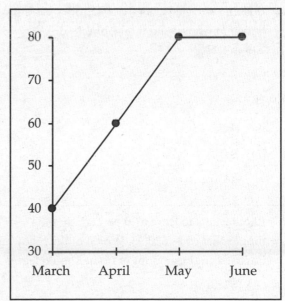

GO ON TO THE NEXT PAGE. ▶ ▶ ▶

Questions 8–9 are based on the following definition.

For all real numbers n and r, $n \clubsuit r = (n - 1) - \frac{n}{r}$.

EXAMPLE: $5 \clubsuit 3 = (5 - 1) - \frac{5}{3} = 4 - \frac{5}{3} = 2\frac{1}{3}$.

8. What is the value of $4 \clubsuit 2$?

    (A) 1

    (B) 2

    (C) 6

    (D) 8

    (E) 16

9. If $Q \clubsuit 2 = 4$, then $Q =$

    (A) 10

    (B) 8

    (C) 6

    (D) 4

    (E) 2

10. If Henry traveled at a rate of 45 miles per hour, how many hours did it take him to drive 225 miles?

    (A) 3

    (B) 4

    (C) $4\frac{1}{2}$

    (D) 5

    (E) $5\frac{1}{2}$

11. Raoul wants to leave a 20 percent tip for a dinner that costs \$20.95. Which of the following is closest to the amount of tip he should leave?

    (A) \$2.10

    (B) \$3.15

    (C) \$4.20

    (D) \$4.50

    (E) \$25.45

GO ON TO THE NEXT PAGE. ▶ ▶ ▶

12. Juan studied from 4:00 p.m. to 6:00 p.m. and finished one-third of his assignments. He is taking a break and wants to finish his homework by 10:30 p.m. If he plans to continue working at the same rate, what is the latest that he can return to his studies?

    (A) 6:30 p.m.

    (B) 7:00 p.m.

    (C) 7:30 p.m.

    (D) 8:00 p.m.

    (E) 8:30 p.m.

13. Mrs. Brown and her c children each ate four strawberries. What is the total number of strawberries they ate?

    (A) $c + 1$

    (B) $c + 4$

    (C) $4c$

    (D) $4c + 1$

    (E) $4c + 4$

14. $1\frac{1}{6} + \frac{2}{3} + 2\frac{3}{1} =$

    (A) 4.17

    (B) 4.25

    (C) 4.33

    (D) 4.50

    (E) 4.75

GO ON TO THE NEXT PAGE. ▶ ▶ ▶

15. Which figure can be drawn WITHOUT lifting the pencil or retracing?

    (A)

    (B)

    (C)

    (D)

    (E)

16. If 0.59 is about $\frac{N}{5}$, then N is closest to which of the following?

    (A) 0.3

    (B) 1

    (C) 2

    (D) 3

    (E) 30

17. If the largest of seven consecutive integers is 25, what is the average of the seven integers?

    (A) 24

    (B) 22

    (C) 21

    (D) 20

    (E) 16

18. The price of a bag of pretzels increased from $0.93 to $1.08. The increase in price is closest to what percent?

    (A) 1%

    (B) 14%

    (C) 15%

    (D) 16%

    (E) 20%

GO ON TO THE NEXT PAGE. ▶ ▶ ▶

$89.2 \overline{)7,236}$

19. The result of the above calculation is closest to which of the following?

(A) 8

(B) 9

(C) 80

(D) 90

(E) 800

20. What is the least number of square tiles with side 6 cm needed to cover a rectangular floor 72 cm long and 48 cm wide?

(A) 14

(B) 72

(C) 96

(D) 144

(E) 192

21. It takes Amari 5 minutes to type p pages. At this rate, how many minutes will it take him to type 20 pages?

(A) $\dfrac{p}{100}$

(B) $\dfrac{4}{p}$

(C) $\dfrac{100}{p}$

(D) $4p$

(E) $100p$

22. The width of a rectangular swimming pool is one-quarter of its length. If the length is 60 meters, what is the perimeter of the pool?

(A) 60 m

(B) 120 m

(C) 150 m

(D) 180 m

(E) 240 m

GO ON TO THE NEXT PAGE. ▶ ▶ ▶

23. The price of a dress at a clothing store decreases by 20 percent every month it is not sold. After 3 months, the current price of the unsold dress is approximately what percent of the original price?

    (A) 40%

    (B) 50%

    (C) 60%

    (D) 70%

    (E) 80%

24. If p is a positive integer and n is a negative integer, which of the following is greatest?

    (A) $\dfrac{p}{n}$

    (B) $\dfrac{n}{p}$

    (C) $\dfrac{1}{p-n}$

    (D) $\dfrac{1}{n-p}$

    (E) It cannot be determined from the information given.

25. At a party, $\dfrac{2}{3}$ of the guests drank only soda and $\dfrac{1}{4}$ of the guests drank only juice. If the remaining 5 guests had nothing to drink, then how many guests were at the party?

    (A) 60

    (B) 50

    (C) 45

    (D) 30

    (E) 25

IF YOU FINISH BEFORE TIME IS CALLED, YOU MAY CHECK YOUR WORK ON THIS SECTION ONLY. DO NOT TURN TO ANY OTHER SECTION IN THE TEST.

SECTION 5
16 Questions

This section includes two question types: synonyms and analogies. There are directions and an example question for each type.

Synonyms

Each Synonym question consists of one word with five words or phrases as answer choices. Choose the one word or phrase that is most similar in meaning to the word in capital letters.

Sample Question:

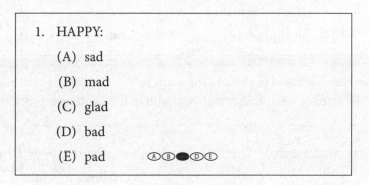

1. HAPPY:

(A) sad

(B) mad

(C) glad

(D) bad

(E) pad

---

1. KEEN:

   (A) sharp

   (B) nice

   (C) forgiving

   (D) dense

   (E) rotund

2. ADHERE:

   (A) connect

   (B) alter

   (C) stick

   (D) listen

   (E) complete

3. PROPEL:

   (A) intend

   (B) belie

   (C) fly

   (D) project

   (E) repel

GO ON TO THE NEXT PAGE. ▶ ▶ ▶

Analogies

Each Analogy question asks you to determine the relationship between two words. Choose the answer choice that best completes the meaning of the sentence.

Sample Question:

1. Rain is to wet as

    (A) sun is to dark

    (B) cloud is to water

    (C) cold is to ice

    (D) sleep is to tired

    (E) heat is to dry

Choice (E) is the best answer because heat causes things to be dry just like rain causes things to be wet. Of all the answer choices, (E) states a relationship that is most like the relationship between <u>rain</u> and <u>wet</u>.

---

4. Ruler is to measure as camera is to

    (A) piano

    (B) lung

    (C) soul

    (D) limb

    (E) photograph

5. Careful is to meticulous as

    (A) tired is to exhausted

    (B) alert is to asleep

    (C) concerned is to grateful

    (D) forgiving is to peaceful

    (E) fancy is to short

6. Caterpillar is to butterfly as

    (A) salmon is to fish

    (B) egg is to dinosaur

    (C) tadpole is to frog

    (D) nest is to chick

    (E) worm is to bait

GO ON TO THE NEXT PAGE. ▶ ▶ ▶

Read each passage and answer the related questions. For each question, use the passage to decide which one of the choices best answers the question.

> Being out of heart with government
> I took a broken root to fling
> Where the proud, wayward squirrel went,
> Taking delight that he could spring;
> *Line 5* And he, with that low whinnying sound
> That is like laughter, sprang again
> And so to the other tree at a bound.
> Nor the tame will, nor timid brain,
> Nor heavy knitting of the brow
> *10* Bred that fierce tooth and cleanly limb
> And threw him to laugh on the bough;
> No government appointed him.
>
> (From "An Appointment," *Responsibilities*, W.B. Yeats, 1914)

7. The author's attitude toward the government in this poem would best be described as

    (A) amused

    (B) disenchanted

    (C) furious

    (D) melancholy

    (E) neutral

8. Which of the following is NOT something the author admires about the squirrel?

    (A) his independence

    (B) his faith in systems of government

    (C) his ability to spring from tree to tree

    (D) his pride

    (E) his joyful spirit

9. The passage implies that the squirrel most resembles humans in

    (A) the timidity of his intellect

    (B) the sounds that he makes

    (C) the fierce expression on his face

    (D) his contempt for the world of politics

    (E) his concentration in moving from tree to tree

GO ON TO THE NEXT PAGE. ▶ ▶ ▶

10. The author most likely regards the squirrel's laugh as

    (A) a warning about the future

    (B) a reflection of his own happiness

    (C) a symbol of his freedom

    (D) a sign of friendliness toward the poet

    (E) an unexplained natural phenomenon

11. In line 9, the phrase "heavy knitting of the brow" most likely refers to

    (A) the movement toward political reform

    (B) the seriousness of government officials

    (C) the expression on the squirrel's face

    (D) the poet's attitude toward politicians

    (E) the beauty of the natural world

GO ON TO THE NEXT PAGE. ▶ ▶ ▶

Each question has five suggested answers. Solve each question in your head or using the blank space at the right of the page. Then, examine the five choices and select the correct one.

<u>Note</u>: Figures in this section are as accurate as possible EXCEPT when it is stated that a figure is not drawn to scale.

Sample Question:

$1 \times 2^2 =$

(A) 1

(B) 2

(C) 3

(D) 4

(E) 5   Ⓐ Ⓑ Ⓒ ● Ⓔ

12. Which of the following shapes can be folded to create a cube with no overlapping flaps?

(A)

(B)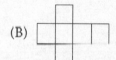

(C)

(D)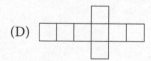

(E)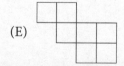

GO ON TO THE NEXT PAGE. ▶ ▶ ▶

13. Alice and Cindy are playing a board game. On Cindy's turn, she is 9 squares behind Alice. If Cindy rolls a 5 and a 6 and moves forward that number of spaces, she will be

    (A) 2 squares ahead of Alice

    (B) 2 squares behind Alice

    (C) 4 squares behind Alice

    (D) 5 squares ahead of Alice

    (E) 11 squares ahead of Alice

14. The map in the figure shows all the paths that connect *X* and *Y*, and all distances are expressed in miles. How many paths are there from *X* to *Y* measuring exactly seven miles?

    (A) 2

    (B) 3

    (C) 4

    (D) 5

    (E) 6

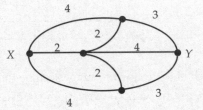

15. Which figure CANNOT be drawn without lifting the pencil or retracing?

(A)

(B)

(C)

(D)

(E)

16. A class of 25 girls and 15 boys built a haunted house for the Halloween carnival. If $\frac{1}{5}$ of the girls and $\frac{2}{3}$ of the boys participated, what fraction of the total class participated?

(A) $\frac{1}{5}$

(B) $\frac{3}{8}$

(C) $\frac{3}{7}$

(D) $\frac{3}{5}$

(E) $\frac{13}{15}$

IF YOU FINISH BEFORE TIME IS CALLED, YOU MAY CHECK YOUR WORK ON THIS SECTION ONLY. DO NOT TURN TO ANY OTHER SECTION IN THE TEST. STOP

ANSWER KEY

Section 1

1. E	6. C	11. D	16. E	21. C
2. B	7. B	12. B	17. E	22. D
3. B	8. A	13. C	18. D	23. C
4. E	9. C	14. E	19. A	24. A
5. D	10. A	15. C	20. C	25. E

Section 2

1. A	8. A	15. A	22. C	29. A	36. A
2. C	9. C	16. A	23. D	30. D	37. D
3. D	10. E	17. C	24. A	31. A	38. C
4. C	11. C	18. A	25. C	32. D	39. B
5. D	12. C	19. B	26. B	33. B	40. C
6. D	13. C	20. E	27. E	34. B	
7. C	14. A	21. B	28. A	35. C	

Section 3

1. D	11. A	21. A	31. C	41. A	51. A
2. B	12. E	22. C	32. A	42. A	52. B
3. E	13. B	23. E	33. A	43. A	53. E
4. D	14. B	24. A	34. C	44. C	54. D
5. A	15. B	25. E	35. B	45. C	55. E
6. E	16. C	26. A	36. E	46. C	56. C
7. B	17. A	27. C	37. A	47. A	57. A
8. C	18. B	28. E	38. E	48. C	58. E
9. E	19. C	29. B	39. B	49. B	59. B
10. A	20. E	30. A	40. B	50. E	60. D

Section 4

1. E	6. E	11. C	16. D	21. C
2. B	7. D	12. A	17. B	22. C
3. D	8. A	13. E	18. D	23. B
4. A	9. A	14. D	19. C	24. C
5. D	10. D	15. D	20. C	25. A

Section 5

1. A	5. A	9. B	13. A
2. C	6. C	10. C	14. C
3. D	7. B	11. B	15. E
4. E	8. B	12. B	16. B

ANSWERS AND EXPLANATIONS

The Writing Sample

Use the sample essay to help you review your own. Be sure to ask an adult who knows you to read your practice essay and give you feedback about how you did.

Prompt (A) Sample Response:

I opened the window and immediately felt the sting of the acidic air in my throat. I coughed and wheezed while the computerized voice droned "Unauthorized breech of airlock detected!" The window started to slide shut. As foul as the air in the city was, I fought for a few extra breaths.

I moved to the East Coast Megapolis from my parent's farm as part of the government's new Technological Training program. After our disastrous defeat in the War of 2137 resulted in an unbreathable atmosphere, the Senate decided that the youth of the country needed more training in science and technology. Forced enrollments at boarding schools were created, and four out of every ten teenagers between the ages of 14 and 18 were required to participate in the program. I was one of them.

"Idleness prohibited!" screeched the computer voice. I brought my focus back to the here and now. I looked back down at my book and read the title of the next chapter: Maximizing Productivity. Well, that's ironic, I thought.

My bunkmate Dave turned to me and sighed. "You know that they will tell us when the air is okay to breathe again. Stop letting that bad air in and finish studying so you can get started finding a solution. No wonder you always have trouble with your exams." I glared at him.

With a shudder, I thought about our upcoming test. There were so many people counting on us to fix everything that had gone wrong since the war. I ached for home and the simplicity of my former life. Since when were teenagers supposed to be responsible for fixing a problem the adults created and couldn't fix? I closed my book and got up. "I'm going for a walk," I announced and walked out of the room without waiting for a response.

Prompt (B) Sample Response:

With the internet and mobile phones, technology has made the world a smaller place. Now, it is extremely easy to find out what's going on in different parts of the world. My parents are from China, and my grandparents still live there. Whenever there's a news story about China on the TV or radio, my parents can simply call my grandparents to check on them. They don't have to rely on other sources for information; they're able to talk with my grandparents immediately and find out whatever they need to know immediately. Since we live in New York, mobile phones have really made the world seem smaller.

This fast, easy access to information is not limited to just news either. If I'm struggling with my math classes, I can watch lectures on YouTube. Wikipedia has detailed articles on these topics, which I can use to fill in gaps in my knowledge and locate sources to support my ideas. In the past, you could only learn about these topics if you attended an exclusive university or happened to live in a town with an outstanding public library. Now, there are in-depth courses available anytime to anyone with an internet connection.

Similarly, new apps like Instagram are continuing to make it easier to connect with others and share experiences. My parents told me when they first came to the US as students, it was expensive to call home. They had to keep their calls short, and there was no way to really show their family what life was like in the US. Now, with apps like Instagram and Snap, it's easy and free to take pictures and let everyone know right away exactly what you're doing and what different events look like. When my mom went to her friend's wedding in the US, she tried to explain it to her mom but it was hard for my grandmother to understand. Now, she just takes a photo and her mom immediately can see what's happening and ask questions about it.

Apps, the internet, mobile phones and other technology make the world smaller every day. We are truly fortunate to be living in this golden age of connection and freely available knowledge.

Section 1

1. E

You need an answer here that is not a factor of 120. In other words, a number that will not evenly divide into 120. Only choice (E), 16, is not a factor of 120.

2. B

Recall that all figures on the SSAT are drawn to scale unless stated otherwise. Extending the vertical line segment boundary of the art slice upward and extending the horizontal line segment boundary of the art slice to the right shows that the art slice is about 25% of the pie. Twenty-five percent, or $\frac{1}{4}$, of 900 (the total number of students) is 225 art students.

3. B

Sean's sister must arrive $25 - 14 = 11$ minutes after midnight because it takes 14 minutes to reach midnight and 11 more minutes to add up to 25 minutes.

4. E

The key here is to make what you are given look like the answer choices. No calculation is needed. Round off 0.52 to 0.5, or $\frac{1}{2}$ and round 78 to 80.

5. D

According to the graph, each bag of money equals $50. Arianna has 6 money bags, so she saved $6 \times \$50 = \$300$. Kiran has 2 money bags, so he saved $2 \times \$50 = \$100$. Arianna saved $200 more than Kiran, so choice (D) is correct.

6. C

Use a version of the percent formula: part = percent × whole. Plug in the numbers from the question stem: $30 = 30\% \times N$ (total number of students). You need to isolate the total number of students (N). Thirty percent $= \frac{30}{100}$, so the equation can be written as $30 = \frac{30}{100} \times N$. Now, multiply both sides of this equation by $\frac{100}{30}$; the N is by itself once $\frac{30}{100}$ and $\frac{100}{30}$ cancel out to 1. Multiplying $30 \times \frac{100}{30}$ gives a value of 100 for N. Choice (C) is correct.

7. B

Because of the word *except*, you need to determine which fraction *is not* less than 2, also known as the fraction that *is* greater than or equal to 2. In order to determine this, make all of the fractions improper and compare the numerators and denominators. The only fraction where the denominator can be divided by the numerator with a result of at least 2 is choice (B): $\frac{45}{22} = 2\frac{1}{22}$.

8. A

You are told all the sides are equal. Thus, you can set each segment equal to 1 and add before deciding which answer choice has the longest path:

Choice (A): $A - C - B - D - F -$
1 (A to C) + 1 (C to B) + 1 (B to D) +
2 (D to E and then E to F) = 5

Choice B: $A - B - E - C - F = 1 + 1 + 1 + 1 = 4$

Choice C: $A - B - C - E - F = 1 + 1 + 1 + 1 = 4$

Choice D: $A - C - E - F = 1 + 1 + 1 = 3$

Choice E: $A - B - D - F = 1 + 1 + 2 = 4$

The longest path is 5, so choice (A) is correct.

9. C

Quickly calculate the difference between 80.08 and each answer choice. Choice A, 80, is $80.08 - 80 = 0.08$ away from 80.08. Choice B, 80.01, is $80.08 - 80.01 = 0.07$ away from 80.08. Choice (C), 80.1, is $80.1 - 80.08 = 0.02$ away from 80.08. Choice D, 81, is 0.92 away from 80.08, and choice E, 90, is even farther away. The question asks for the choice closest to 80.08, so choice (C), 80.1, is correct.

10. A

Use N to represent "the number." Write an inequality using the information given. Remember, *of* means multiply, so your equation is $\frac{1}{3} \times N < 12$. You need to isolate N, your unknown value. Multiplying both sides by the reciprocal of $\frac{1}{3}$, which is 3, produces a result of $N < 12 \times 3$, and thus $N < 36$, which matches choice (A).

11. D

The minimum number of points Team B could have scored is 1 more than Team A, or 40. Use the average formula to plug in the given information:

$$average = \frac{sum\ of\ the\ terms}{number\ of\ terms}$$

$$= \frac{40\ points}{5\ players}$$

$$= 8\ points\ per\ player$$

Thus, the average score of the players on Team B must have been at least 8 points per player. Choice (D) is correct.

12. B

The sum of the three interior angles of any triangle is 180 degrees. The figure indicates that two of the angles have degree measures of 90 and 45. This means the third angle is $180 - 90 - 45 = 45$ and this is a 45–45–90 triangle. For all triangles, the sides opposite two equal angles must be equal, so $a = 6$, which matches choice (B).

13. C

Here, you need to divide 40,000 into 2,000,000: $\frac{2,000,000}{40,000}$. Simply cancel out four zeros from the bottom and four zeros from the top. You now have $\frac{200}{4}$, which equals 50. Choice (C) is correct.

14. E

The question states that y is less than 3, and you want to find the choice that x cannot equal, so solve the equation for x in terms of y and see if you can conclude something about x. The equation is $x - y + 2 = 6$. First, subtract 2 from both sides. Then, $x - y = 6 - 2$, or $x - y = 4$. Adding y to both sides, you get $x = y + 4$. Since y is less than 3, $y + 4$ must be less than 7. Because $x = y + 4$, x must be less than 7. Look for a choice that is not less than 7. Only choice (E), 8, is not less than 7. Because x cannot be 8, choice (E) is correct.

15. C

Think about the segments of $AD = 55$. The length of AB is 2 times the length of BC, so you can let $BC = x$ and let $AB = 2x$. You're told that $AB = CD$, so let $CD = 2x$ also. Now, use the total length of AD to find the value of x: $AD = AB + BC + CD = 2x + x + 2x = 5x = 55$. When $5x = 55$, $x = 11$, so the distance between $BD = BC + CD = x + 2x = 3x = 3 \times 11 = 33$. Choice (C) is correct.

16. E

The question asks for all the points. Choice A is tempting but incorrect because it only includes the rectangular boundary of the set of all the points that touch the table and does not include the points inside this rectangle that also touch the surface of the table. Only choice (E) indicates all of the points, not just the outline, and is correct.

17. E

The question is not asking for a value of J. Indeed, J could be any whole number. The question is asking for the answer choice that can be written in the form $(J + 2) \times 3$, where J is a whole number. Since 3 is a factor of $(J + 2) \times 3$, the choice you're looking for must be a multiple of 3. A whole number is a multiple of 3 if and only if the sum of its digits is a multiple of 3. After looking at the answer choices, you can determine that only the sum of the digits of choice (E), 81, is a multiple of 3. That is, the sum of the digits of 81 is $8 + 1 = 9$, which is a multiple of 3, so choice (E) is correct.

18. D

Using the information given, isolate a:
$a = 3b + 4 + 7 = 3b + 11$. Thus, $a = 3b + 11$.
Next add 5 to both sides of this equation:
$a + 5 = 3b + 11 + 5 = 3b + 16$. Choice (D) is correct.

19. A

They give us 21.5 out of 100, which is easily translated into 21.5%. Therefore, 21.5% of (multiplied by) 2,000,000 is $\frac{21.5}{100} \times 2,000,000$. Cancel out two zeros from the 100 in the denominator and from the 2,000,000 in the numerator to get $21.5 \times 20,000 = 430,000$. Choice (A) is correct.

20. C

Translate from English into math. Let Bob's current age $= x$, and let Jerry's current age $= x + 7$. To find their ages 5 years ago, subtract 5 years from each current age: 5 years ago, Bob was $x - 5$, and Jerry was $x + 7 - 5 = x + 2$. The sum of Bob and Jerry's ages 5 years ago was $x - 5 + x + 2 = 2x - 3$. Choice (C) is correct.

21. C

The contestant answered a total of 5 questions correctly. Using the percent formula, percent $\times$ whole = part, 20% $\times$ total number of questions = 5. Multiply both sides of the equation by $\frac{100}{20}$ (the reciprocal of 20%), and the total number of questions = 25. Eliminate choice A.

Next, look at the statement in choice B. You don't have any information about whether or not the contestant was guessing, so eliminate choice B.

Move on to choice (C). Now that you know the total number of questions, you can determine the number of remaining questions he answered correctly or incorrectly. There were 25 − 15 = 10 questions remaining, and he only answered 1 of these 10 questions correctly. This matches choice (C).

Choices D and E are incorrect because the question stem does not give you information about the order of the correct/incorrect questions or the question difficulty. It's possible the contestant was answering questions about an unknown topic.

22. D

This problem is perfect for the Picking Numbers strategy. Start by writing an equation: $C = A \times B$. Then, pick two consecutive numbers for A and B, such as 1 and 2. The product of 1 and 2 is 2, a positive, even number, so look for the answer choice that matches this. Choice A is out because $1 \times 2 = 2$, which is less than $1 + 2 = 3$. You can eliminate choices B and E because C can be positive or even. To determine whether the answer is positive or even, try out some negative numbers in the question stem. What if $A = 3$ and $B = -2$ or $A = -1$ and B = 3? Both of these examples could potentially give negative values, so you can eliminate choice C and select Choice (D) as correct.

23. C

Be careful here. The question asks for the difference before the discount. The sweaters were sold for 100% − 20% of their old price. Using the percent formula, part = percent $\times$ whole, you can determine that 48 = 80% $\times$ old price. Convert 80% to $\frac{80}{100}$ and multiply both sides by $\frac{100}{80}$. You now have $\frac{100}{80} \times 48 =$ old price. You can simplify this equation to $\frac{\overset{10}{\cancel{100}}}{\cancel{80}_{8}} \times 48 =$ old price

and then $\frac{10}{\cancel{8}_{1}} \times \cancel{48}^{6} =$ old price, which ultimately yields $60. Use the percent formula for the wool sweater, and you have the equation $64 = 80% $\times$ old price. When you do the math, you find that its original price was $80, so the difference is $80 − $60 = $20. Choice (C) is correct.

24. A

The maximum load that a car can carry is $17\frac{1}{3}$ tons. If each car carries the maximum load minus $\frac{5}{9}$ of a ton, then each car carries the following tons:

$$17\frac{1}{3} - \frac{5}{9} = \frac{52}{3} - \frac{5}{9} = \frac{52}{3} \times \frac{3}{3} - \frac{5}{9} = \frac{156 - 5}{9} = \frac{151}{9}$$

Next, multiply this amount carried in each car by 36 cars and you get $\frac{151}{9} \times 36$ tons. Cancel the 9 into the 36 and you get $151 \times 4 = 604$. Choice (A) is correct.

25. E

To divide a three-digit number by a single-digit number, break the number down by place value and divide each part. Choice D might be tempting, but 632 is the sum, not the product, of 600 + 30 + 2. Choice (E) is correct.

Section 2

Lemurs Passage

This fact-based passage introduces you to the lemur, a monkey-like animal that lives chiefly in Madagascar. You're given various information about lemurs: their physical characteristics, the origin of their name, where they're found, and so on.

1. A

The author's style is straightforward and informative, like the style of a biology textbook. A zoologist's diary would more likely be in the first-person ("June 20: Saw two lemurs in a jungle in southern Madagascar"), and a tourist's guidebook would go into less scientific detail and would place lemurs in a specific location ("Be sure to check out the lemurs in Avahi National Park"). Choice (A) is correct.

2. C

Summarize the passage in your own mind. You might have come up with something like "Things to Know about Lemurs." Choice (C) restates this idea and is therefore correct. Choices A, D, and E focus on details of the passage and are therefore incorrect. The passage doesn't mention whether lemurs hunt alone or in groups, so choice (B) is also incorrect.

3. D

You're looking for the detail that is *false*. The author states that lemurs eat "leaves…eggs, fruit, insects, and small animals" (line 6). Choice (D) must be incorrect because they eat fruits, leaves, and other items, such as eggs, insects, and small animals. Choice A is incorrect because the passage states in line 6 that lemurs are "most often…in the trees." Choice B is incorrect because line 2 states that lemurs have "long, bushy tails." Choice C is incorrect because the author explicitly states in lines 9–10 that the flying lemur is not a true lemur. Choice E is incorrect because line 2 states that "lemurs are primates with bodies similar to those of monkeys."

4. C

In line 8, the author states that lemurs "are reputed to be gentle, friendly creatures." If they're "gentle" and "friendly," you can infer that they're not very aggressive. Choice (C) is correct. Choice A is contradicted in the final sentence of the passage. Choices B and D are refuted when the author says that lemurs "are active throughout the day and night" (line 7) and "most often are in the trees" (line 6). You don't know enough about the flying lemur to infer that it can only be found in and around Madagascar, so choice E is also incorrect.

5. D

The author uses the phrase "so-called" to set up the comparison between flying lemurs and true lemurs. "Contrary to popular belief," the "so-called" lemurs are part of an entirely different order of mammals than true lemurs. Choice (D) is correct. Choices A and E are out of scope for this passage and are therefore incorrect. Choice B is incorrect because true lemurs are not herbivores; the passage states that "lemurs eat eggs…insects, and small animals" (line 7), and the diets of flying lemurs are not discussed. Choice C is incorrect because the passage says that lemurs "are active throughout the day" (line 7).

Woodrow Wilson Passage

This historical passage focuses on President Woodrow Wilson and his post-World War I peace settlement—specifically, on the Fourteen-Point Plan, which called for the abolition of secret diplomacy. Wilson considered open negotiations vital for peace, but in paragraph 2, the author disagrees, arguing that Wilson's view was too simplistic.

6. D

The first and second sentences of each paragraph usually reveal the paragraph's topic. In this case, it's the second sentence: Wilson was wrong—war stems not from secret deals by national leaders but from "unresolved disagreements among nations." Choice (D) is correct. Choices A and E summarize the topic of paragraph 1, not paragraph 2. Choice B is too general; the paragraph mainly discusses why one form of diplomacy usually fails to avert wars. Choice C is also too general because not all disagreements among nations lead to war.

7. C

The author states that Wilson called for an end to secret negotiations as a way to end war and then that Wilson was wrong—that "he lacked insight into the complexities of international politics" (line 7). Clearly, the author disagrees with Wilson. Choice (C) is correct. Choice A is tempting, given the author's "realpolitik" attitude, but she isn't being Machiavellian; she's simply stating why Wilson's idea was wrong. Choices B and D are too emotional, and choice E is incorrect because the author doesn't apologize for criticizing Wilson.

8. A

The scenario in choice (A) is the closest parallel to the author's thinking. As the next-to-last sentence of the passage puts it, "war usually stems from unresolved disagreements among nations…over territory…." Choice B's scenario is an economic trade agreement involving a third country—not very likely to lead to war. Choices C, D, and E involve secret deals or covert activity of the kind that Wilson—not the author—thought would lead to war.

9. C

Look at the last two sentences of the text. According to the author, open diplomacy can't solve the kinds of problems that lead to war. Choice (C) is correct. Choice A's assertion that quiet diplomacy will always be with us doesn't explain why open diplomacy won't prevent war. Choice B assumes that rulers will be immoral, but the author never asserts or supports this idea. The end of the passage directly contradicts choice D, and choice E is out of scope of the author's discussion.

10. E

To find the correct answer, try to answer each of the questions in the choices. Choice A is answered in lines 7–8; the author says Wilson's first point on diplomacy was wrong. Choice B is answered in lines 9–10; wars usually result from disagreements among nations. Choice C is answered in line 4; Wilson supported open (public) diplomacy. Choice D is answered in the second paragraph; the author says Wilson "lacked insight into the complexities of international politics" (line 7), and then the author proceeds to present his or her knowledge or international politics. Choice (E) is the answer because the passage does not tackle ways to eliminate the threat of war.

11. C

To imagine where the author might go next, retrace the steps of the argument: 1) Wilson offered a peace proposal that argued for open diplomacy, which he thought would end wars; 2) Wilson failed to grasp that secret diplomacy is not the cause of most wars, which occur because of unresolved disputes among nations over such things as territory and resources. Having disagreed with Wilson, it's most likely that the author will try to illustrate this last point by giving an example of a war that occurred because of a territorial or resource dispute. Choice (C) is correct. Choices A, D, and E suggest that the author will return to the subjects of President Wilson or World War I, but the text moves beyond Wilson to discuss the cause of war. Choice B brings up import taxes, a topic the author never discusses.

Poetry Passage

You are likely to see poetry on the SSAT. When you do, be alert for tone and the use of metaphor. Here, an oak tree is used as a metaphor—for living our lives as an oak tree does, in accordance with nature and the change of seasons. The first three lines of the poem generate its central metaphor: "Live thy life, Young and old, Like yon oak…" ("Yon" is short for "yonder," meaning "that oak over there.") In other words, "Live your life, at all ages, like that oak tree does."

12. C

You're asked to infer the poem's central metaphor. What do the seasons represent? The successive stages of life, choice (C): spring is youth, summer is maturity, autumn is middle age, and winter is old age. Choice A is too literal and choice B is too specific to fit this particular poem. Choices D and E are outside the scope of the passage; the poet never brings up styles of dress or periods of history.

13. C

Who is the "he" of line 13? The entire stanza provides clues: "he" has lost his leaves, "he" stands, "trunk and bough, naked strength." "He," then, is the oak tree. Choice (C) is correct. Choice D might be tempting, but the season of autumn does not have a trunk. Choices A, B, and E do not make sense in context.

14. A

The second stanza shows the oak tree in summer and in autumn; "gold again" refers to the seasonally changed color of the oak tree's leaves, so choice (A) is best here. Choices B, C, and E are pretty easily eliminated because they are out of scope. Choice D isn't correct because the arrival of autumn signals a change in foliage, and the "gold again" refers to the return of those leaf colors as opposed to the colors of one specific tree.

15. A

This is a Supporting Ideas question. The oak is referred to as "Living gold" in line 5 of the poem; the previous line says, "Bright in spring." Choice (A) is correct. Summer and autumn appear in later stanzas, and winter is not mentioned at all, so choices B, C, and D are incorrect. Choice E is incorrect because you can determine that this reference relates to spring.

16. A

This question basically asks for the statement that mirrors the poem's Main Idea, which is that you should be like the oak tree, living each season of your life as well as you can. Choice (A) restates this best. Choice B is incorrect because "something" can apparently be accomplished at any point in one's life; what about the other "seasons"? Choice C makes little sense given the context of the poem, and choice D contradicts the poem entirely. Choice E dispenses with the poem's central metaphor altogether: it's not that a good life includes the enjoyment of trees; it's that a good life is lived as a tree lives its life.

17. C

Think about how the poem would sound if you read it aloud. It would sound as if the poet were giving you advice on living life to the fullest. The poem is optimistic (seeking the best outcome), hopeful, and thoughtful, so you can eliminate choices A, D, and E. That leaves choice B, passionate (expressing intense feeling), and choice (C), pompous (arrogant). The poem does sound intense, so the tone of the poem would NOT be described as pompous. Choice (C) is correct.

Tea Passage

This passage is about tea—the plant and the history of its cultivation and uses. Paragraph 1 describes its universal appeal, its origin, and its description and look. Paragraph 2 describes the difficulties of cultivating tea and where the plant is currently grown. The final paragraph summarizes tea's history, from ancient times to today.

18. A

This passage is mainly about tea. All five choices mention tea, however, so narrow it down. This passage focuses mainly on the tea plant, so choice (A) is correct. Choices B, C, D, and E each touch on only one aspect of the passage.

19. B

In lines 6–7, the passage states that "the plant must grow in a warm, wet climate in a carefully protected, well-drained area." Choice (B) is correct. Choice A is incorrect because tea was first cultivated in China. Choice C distorts lines 13–14; the author states that the United Kingdom is the world's largest importer of tea, not that tea is the United Kingdom's largest import. Choice D is the opposite of the "fragrant blossoms" described in line 5. Choice E is incorrect because lines 2–3 state that the plant "is native to India, China, and Japan"—not South America.

20. E

The phrase "cheap labor" in the question stem is also found in paragraph 2, which states that, because tea leaves "must be picked by hand," cultivation in North America "was found to be impractical because of a shortage of cheap labor." In other words, tea cultivation requires a supply of cheap labor because the leaves must be handpicked. Choice (E) is correct. Choice A contradicts paragraph 1, which says that tea plants are "usually pruned down to three or four feet for cultivation." Choices B and C are never mentioned, and Choice D incorrectly reduces the world's cultivation and consumption of tea to two countries, England and China.

21. B

The author's style is informative, offering an encyclopedic summary of the cultivation and uses of tea. Choice (B) is correct. A newspaper article would have a more specific focus than simply the history of the tea plant, so choice A is incorrect. This isn't a recipe or a journal, so choices C and D are incorrect. Although choice E might be tempting, it is incorrect because the focus is on the tea plant itself, not its historical significance.

22. C

Because paragraph 3 summarizes the historic uses of tea, beginning with ancient times and ending with consumption today, it's likely that the author will continue to discuss current consumption trends. Choice (C) is correct. Choice A temptingly mentions the last detail in the passage, but the Boston Tea Party is only an aside, a lighthearted explanation of why consumption of tea in the United States today lags behind that of coffee. Choices B and E are incorrect because the passage is focused on the tea plant, and the author will not change the focus to a new subject for a subsequent paragraph. Although the medicinal benefits of tea are briefly mentioned in line 11, it's unlikely that the author will choose to focus an entire paragraph on this idea next, so choice D is incorrect.

23. D

Paragraph 2 describes the difficulties of cultivating tea and where it is currently cultivated. Choice (D) is correct. Choices A, B, and C are mentioned in paragraph 3, not paragraph 2. Choice E is out of scope; while the author does state that Americans seem to prefer coffee, she never directly questions the importance of tea.

Fiction Passage

This passage reflects the thoughts going through a soldier's mind in the final moments before battle. Notice how the two lines of dialogue toward the end of the passage increase the tension of the imminent attack. Be alert for shifts of tone and perspective and the use of metaphor.

24. A

Always go back to the passage to answer Vocab-in-Context questions. In the last paragraph, the author describes "a brown swarm of running men who were giving shrill yells." Choice (A), army, is the best fit to describe this group of men. Choices B, C, D, and E do not make sense in context.

25. C

The text jumps from one "scene" to another; the quoted exclamation breaks you away from the youth's daydream of the circus and into the reality of his current situation. A fellow soldier has shouted that the enemy is approaching, and you are jolted into the reality of the situation. Choice (C) is correct. Choices A and B incorrectly assume that the exclamation is part of the youth's memory, and choices D and E are completely unwarranted inferences.

26. B

As you have just seen in the previous question, the youth reminisces in paragraph 1. As you jump to the next paragraph and to the reality of the battle, the men prepare with anticipation. Choice (B) is correct. The first tone is neutral to positive, so choices A, C, and D are incorrect. While some might view the reality of the second paragraph with fear, there is not proof in the passage that the author or character view it that way, so choice E is incorrect.

27. E

The author repeats this phrase three times. Each time, it's used to emphasize the anticipation of what's coming next. Choice (E) is correct. Choice A is the repetition of consonant sounds and choice B is the repetition of vowel sounds, neither of which fits here. Choice C describes words that sound like their meaning, but "Here they come!" is definitely a phrase, not a sound. Choice D is incorrect because synecdoche is a figure of speech where a part represents a whole.

28. A

After the teaser in the opening sentence (moments of waiting for what?), the first paragraph details the youth's childhood memory of the circus in town. This matches choice (A). The circus's arrival couldn't be called a turning point in his life—it was simply a fond memory—so choice B is incorrect. Choice D is incorrect because the youth wasn't planning his day at the circus; he was simply enjoying the day as a spectator. Neither choice C nor E is discussed in the first paragraph, so both are incorrect as well.

Acupuncture Passage

This modified science passage discusses acupuncture, an ancient Chinese form of medical therapy. There's very little science in the passage. Instead, the author describes the thinking behind acupuncture and gives a brief history of its use in Western countries.

29. A

This passage is written in a neutral, informative tone, describing the thinking behind acupuncture and a brief history of its use. Choice (A) is correct. If this passage were written from the viewpoint of a surgeon, a patient, or an acupuncturist, the specific experience of that person would be discussed in depth. However, the passage only describes acupuncture from the perspective of an outsider, so choices B, C, and D are incorrect. Choice E might be tempting because the author mentions acupuncture's basis in philosophy, but it is incorrect because a philosopher would focus more on the positive and negative physical, mental, and emotional impact of acupuncture on humans than its general history.

30. D

The author describes what acupuncture involves, the ancient Chinese philosophy on which it's based, and how it recently spread to the West. The passage is primarily about the historical and philosophical background of acupuncture. Choice (D) is correct. Choice A is not mentioned, and choice B focuses too narrowly on the first paragraph. Choice C is too general, and choice E is incorrect because modern uses are only mentioned in the final paragraph.

31. A

Paragraph 1 states that acupuncture is based on the ancient Chinese belief that "human beings are miniature versions of the universe" and that the same forces control nature and health. Choice (A) is correct. Choice B is incorrect because yin and yang are not Chinese gods; they're principles. Choice C is incorrect because the passage never describes acupuncture as a religious act. Contrary to D, Western countries have not "totally changed" the Chinese philosophy of health and disease. They may have ignored it or failed to understand it, but they did not change it. Choice E is incorrect because the passage never mentions a specific early astronomer.

32. D

Paragraph 1 states that Yin and yang have "an opposite but complementary effect on each other.... When they are in balance, the body maintains a constant, normal [i.e., healthy] state." Choice (D) is correct. Choice A names an example of how the two principles operate, not what they represent. Choice B incorrectly states that one principle is healthy and the other unhealthy, but it's a balance of both that maintains health and an imbalance that results in sickness. Choice C mentions similar treatments for different diseases, but yin and yang represent opposite yet complementary forces. Choice E is incorrect because yin and yang represent opposite forces, not necessarily exclusively comfort and pain.

33. B

When yin and yang are in balance, the body is healthy, but when they're out of balance, disease occurs. These two forces work together, or complement, each other. Choice (B) is correct. The claim in choice A was made by ancient Chinese philosophy, and there is no actual proof in the passage for choice C. Choice D is the opposite; yin and yang are supposed to keep "the body's temperature from rising too high...[or] dropping too low." The author does not mention any part of the body that isn't influenced by acupuncture, so choice E is incorrect.

34. B

Are the author's points positive, negative, or neutral? The author sticks to pointing out what acupuncture is and how it has become a popular form of treatment. The author doesn't talk about the negative aspects, so the tone is positive. That rules out choices A, C, and E, leaving choices (B) and D: "admiring" and "serene." Next, think about how the passage would sound if you read it aloud. Does it sound as if the author holds acupuncture with high regard and respect (admiring), or does it sound calm and peaceful (serene)? Clearly, the author is excited about acupuncture and admires its effectiveness. Choice (B) is correct.

Georgia O'Keefe Passage

The final passage is about the American painter Georgia O'Keeffe—her life, her fame, and the subjects of her paintings. The opening sentence of paragraph 2 sums up the main point: O'Keeffe is "widely considered to have been a pioneering American modernist painter."

35. C

Choice (C) is supported by paragraph 2, which states that O'Keeffe was "more independent" than most other early modern American artists, who were "strongly influenced by European art." In addition, paragraph 3 describes how the colors and shapes in O'Keeffe's paintings were "so reduced and simplified that they [took] on a life of their own." Choice A is too strong for this passage. Choices B and D are out of scope of the information provided in the passage. Choice E is too strong in the opposite direction; the author is not trying to shame people into being more like someone else.

36. A

O'Keeffe was the artist, and nature was her favorite subject. Approach this question as you would an Analogy. The relationship of the artist to the subject is repeated in choice (A): the model is the photographer's subject. Similarly, nature is O'Keeffe's subject. Choice B inverts the relationship between the manager and managed. Choice C is incorrect because most students do not have a nature-focused outdoor job. Choice D is incorrect because it focuses on the relationship between the salesman and the purchaser, and choice E focuses on the functional relationship between a carpenter and his tool.

37. D

Only choice (D) connects O'Keeffe with the general style of her paintings. Choices A, B, C, and E are too general to describe the focus of this passage on George O'Keeffe.

38. C

According to paragraph 2, O'Keeffe was unlike her contemporary European painters because she was "considered to have been a pioneering American modernist painter…[whose] position was more independent." Paragraph 3 notes that her work was "identifiably American," which makes choice (C) correct. Choice A is incorrect because O'Keeffe's success in Europe

is not mentioned. Choices B and D are factually true, but they're not the reason why she's considered a pioneer. Choice E is incorrect because, as paragraph 3 notes, O'Keeffe's work was considered "semiabstract," not very abstract.

39. B

The main point is summed up in the opening sentence of paragraph 2. Choice (B) is correct. The author never claims that O'Keeffe was the best painter of her generation, choice A, or that she didn't develop a fully abstract style, choice D, or even that her colors and shapes were too simple, choice E. Choice C is plausible (though you never learn that O'Keeffe painted only familiar subjects), but it's not the main point.

40. C

You're told that European art strongly influenced most American artists of O'Keeffe's time. Unlike European art, however, paragraph 3 notes how O'Keeffe's paintings offered a "simplified and idealized treatment of color, light, space, and natural forms." Because European art was different from O'Keeffe's art, you can infer that it did not portray natural shapes in a simple, idealistic way, making choice (C) correct. No other answer choice can be inferred using the clues from the passage.

Section 3

Synonyms

1. D

To plead is to ask for something earnestly or desperately. This matches to beg, choice (D).

2. B

To prowl is to move around secretly, stealthily. This matches choice (B), sneak.

3. E

A vessel, such as a bowl or glass, is a container for holding something. This matches choice (E) exactly.

4. D

To approve means to judge something favorably. This matches choice (D).

5. A

To seep means to flow through little cracks. This matches choice (A), ooze.

6. E

To vex means to anger, or irritate. Choice (E) is correct.

7. B

To doze is to sleep lightly, which matches choice (B). You might doze because someone bores you, but the two words are not synonymous, so choice D is a distractor.

8. C

Something that is woven, such as a basket, is made by intertwining material. Choice (C) is correct.

9. E

Something coarse is harsh or rough. Choice (E) is correct.

10. A

Meek means mild mannered or submissive. Choice (A) is correct.

11. A

To saturate is to wet something thoroughly or soak it. You saturate a sponge in water, for example. Choice (A) is correct.

12. E

Genteel describes something elegant, aristocratic, or refined. Choice (E) is correct.

13. B

Winsome means pleasing or charming, such as a winsome smile. Choice (B) is correct.

14. B

To reproach means to express disapproval or disappointment in someone. Choice A, retreat, means to withdraw. Choice C is incorrect because you can insist on something without expressing disapproval or disappointment. Choices D and E are tempting, but you can complain or whine without expressing disapproval. Choice (B) is correct.

15. B

To demonstrate means to explain clearly or show. Choice (B) is correct.

16. C

A camouflage is a disguise or a concealment. Choice (C) is correct. An outfit may or may not be a camouflage, so choice B is a distractor.

17. A

Aghast is an adjective that means to be struck with amazement or horror. This matches choice (A), shocked.

18. B

To recollect means to remember. Choice (B) is correct.

19. C

To initiate means to begin or start. Choice (C) is correct.

20. E

To suffocate is to choke or deprive of air. Choice (E) is correct.

21. A

To prevail means to win, overcome, or triumph. Choice (A) is correct.

22. C

To prance is to walk in a cocky way or to strut. Choice A is a strong distractor; boasting is verbal, while prancing is physical. Choice (C) is correct.

23. E

Profound means deep-seated or intense. A parent has a profound love for his or her child. Choice (E) is correct.

24. A

Limber means flexible, lithe, nimble, or supple. Choice B, wooden, is a good antonym for limber, but that's the opposite of what you're looking for. Choice (A) is correct.

25. E

To terminate means to finish or bring to an end. Choice (E) is correct.

26. A

To contemplate means to think about or ponder. Choice (A) is correct.

27. C

A caprice is a sudden fancy or whim. Choice A is a tempting distractor, but not all ideas are whims or caprices. Choice (C) is correct.

28. E

An adage is a common saying or proverb. Choice (E) is correct.

29. B

A din is a loud, confused mixture of noises—in other words, a clamor. Choice (B) is correct.

30. A

To expunge is to get rid of or obliterate. This matches choice (A), erase.

Analogies

31. C

Choice (C) is correct. This is a Purpose Bridge. A pilot is used to direct a plane. A captain is used to direct a ship. Choice A might be tempting, but while a horse might direct a cart, its purpose is to pull the cart.

32. A

Choice (A) is correct. This is a Type/Kind Bridge. One type of snake is a python. One type of dog is a terrier. The relationships in the other answer choices are in the incorrect order as compared to the stem words. In other words, a python is in the snake family, but a dog is not the pet, mammal, or quadruped families. Quadruped, by the way, means four-legged.

33. A

Choice (A) is correct. This is a Association Bridge. A mayor is the highest official in a city. A governor is the highest official in a state. This easily eliminates choices B, C, and E. Choice D might be tempting, but a secretary is not usually the highest official on a committee—the chairperson is.

34. C

Choice (C) is correct. This is a Purpose Bridge. Paper is used as the material upon which a novel is written. Similarly, canvas is used as the material upon which a portrait is painted.

35. B

Choice (B) is correct. This is an Antonym Bridge. Refined is the opposite of vulgar. Submissive is the opposite of recalcitrant, which means stubbornly defiant. The words in choices A and C are synonyms, not opposites, and the word pairs in D and E have no obvious relationship to each other.

36. E

Choice (E) is correct. This is a Function Bridge. A whip is for lashing something. A club is for beating something. The other four answer choices do not fit this relationship.

37. A

Choice (A) is correct. This is a Association Bridge. In the winter, swans migrate, or travel seasonally. In the winter, groundhogs hibernate, or hide and sleep seasonally. Choices C, D, and E might be tempting, but these are not actions that the animals do seasonally.

38. E

Choice (E) Is correct. This is an Association Bridge. Flip the words: A meteorologist studies weather. Similarly, a botanist studies plants or vegetation.

39. B

Choice (B) is correct. This is a Purpose Bridge. A track is the surface for horse racing. A court is the surface for tennis.

40. B

Choice (B) is correct. This is an Association Bridge. A director tells an actor what to do, and a coach tells a player what to do.

41. A

Choice (A) is correct. This is a Part/Whole Bridge. Dessert is the last part of a meal. A finale is the last part of a performance. Lunch is eaten after breakfast, but it's a different meal, not part of the same one, so the relationship isn't the same.

42. A

Choice (A) is correct. This is an Antonym Bridge. Confirm is the opposite of deny. Accept is the opposite of reject. The words in the stem are opposites. Choice C might be tempting, but implying something is not the opposite of contending, or asserting, something; the opposite would be to deny it or not say anything at all.

43. A

Choice (A) is correct. This is an Association Bridge. This stem pair may be most manageable if you work from right to left and say that a nemesis is, by association, characterized as being hostile. A stronghold is characterized as being fortified, so choice A matches nicely. Language is not characterized as being audible, so choice B is incorrect. Choice D is tempting, but these words are in the reverse order: ordered is not characterized as being regiment, a regiment is characterized as being ordered.

44. C

Choice (C) is correct. This is an Antonym Bridge. Fidelity is the opposite of unfaithfulness. Honesty is the opposite of deceit.

45. C

Choice (C) is correct. This is a Lack Bridge. If something is widespread, it's not limited. If something is broad, it's not narrow.

46. C

Choice (C) is correct. This is a Individual-to-Object Bridge. A carpenter uses a saw. A farmer uses a plow. None of the other occupations listed here use a plow.

47. A

Choice (A) is correct. This is a Function Bridge. A racket is used to play tennis just as a glove is used to box.

48. C

Choice (C) is correct. This is a Degree Bridge. The second word is much stronger than the first. You can encourage or suggest that someone do something, and they may or may not do it. But if you demand or order them to do it, then they must. Choice E has the words in the incorrect order; condemn is stronger than reprimand, not the other way around.

49. B

Choice (B) is correct. This is an Association Bridge. A grin is a facial expression associated with delight. A frown is a facial expression associated with dismay (a mixture of fear and discouragement).

50. E

Choice (E) is correct. This is a Lack Bridge. Something mysterious is not understandable. Something obscure is not clear.

51. A

Choice (A) is correct. This is a Cause-and-Effect Bridge. When an injury heals, the body functions better. When a malfunction is repaired, the object functions better.

52. B

Choice (B) is correct. This is a Degree Bridge. A jog is a slow run; a sprint is a fast run. A trot is a slow run for a horse, while a gallop is a fast run.

53. E

Choice (E) is correct. This is a Part/Whole Bridge. A bone is one part of the structural system of the body—the system that holds it up. Similarly, a beam—a long piece of timber or steel—is one part of the structural system in the building that it holds up. Choice A may be tempting, but floors don't generally hold up other floors the way beams and bones hold up beams and bones.

54. D

Choice (D) is correct. This is a Lack Bridge. Something that is amorphous lacks shape. Something that is odorless lacks scent.

55. E

Choice (E) is correct. This is a Lack Bridge. Someone who is vain likely lacks humility, and someone who is extroverted likely lacks shyness.

56. C

Choice (C) is correct. This is a Purpose Bridge. You study to prepare for a test. You rehearse to prepare for a play. Choice A seems close, but the process of applying is not quite "preparation" for a job.

57. A

Choice (A) is correct. This is an Antonym Bridge. A smile is the opposite of a frown. A cheer is the opposite of a heckle. You cheer to signal your approval and heckle to indicate your disapproval of a sports team, for example.

58. E

Choice (E) is correct. This is a Word (specifically, noun-verb) Bridge. You peel the skin off a banana. You husk, or pull off the outer covering, of an ear of corn.

59. B

Choice (B) is correct. This is an Association Bridge. Tactile refers to anything perceptible through the sense of touch, just as olfactory refers to anything perceptible through the sense of smell. In order to be correct, choice D would have read "sight is to visual" and choice C would have to read "taste is to oral."

60. D

Choice (D) is correct. This is an Association Bridge. Articulateness is associated with speaking or writing clearly. Similarly, legibility is associated with clear, understandable handwriting.

Section 4

1. E

The perimeter of a polygon is the sum of the lengths of its sides. There are 2 toothpicks in the base, so the base is $6 + 6 = 12$ cm. Each point uses 2 toothpicks, so $3 \times (6 + 6) = 3 \times 12 = 36$ cm. Altogether, the perimeter of the crown is $12 + 36 = 50$ cm. Choice (E) is correct.

2. B

Gary and Parth have a total of $16 + 18 = 34$ movies put together. This number is equal to the number of movies that only Gary has plus the number of movies that only Parth has plus twice the number of movies eras that they both have in common. The number that they have in common was counted twice: once in the number of movies that Gary has and once in the number of movies that Parth has. Because the number of movies that they have in common should only be counted once, subtract the 4 they have in common from 34, and the result is 30 different movies. Choice (B) is correct.

3. D

You could solve for G by multiplying 18×9 and then dividing by 3, but without a calculator, it's probably not the most efficient path. Instead of jumping into calculations, compare the two equations you're given. In the second, G is divided by 3. In the first, G is divided by 9. This means the value of the $\frac{1}{3}$ G is three times as large as the value of $\frac{1}{9}$ G. Simply multiply 18×3 to find the correct answer, choice (D).

4. A

The boat can swing out and around as far as the line extends, or the wind can push it anywhere within this semicircle, so you need a shape that is shaded in. You might have been tempted by choice B, but if this were correct, the boat would float right through the dock! You want the choice indicating all the points within a semicircle shaded, which only matches choice (A).

5. D

The question stem gives you a part-to-part ratio but no whole, so you're looking for a multiple based on the ratio as opposed to the exact number. Let c represent the number of children and a represent the number of adults. The question states that the ratio of adults to children is 4 to 1, so for every 4 adults, there is one child. There cannot be a partial person, so the total number of people must be a multiple of 5. Multiples of 5 end in either 0 or 5, so only choice (D) can be correct.

6. E

Draw a figure. With a diagonal cut from corner to corner, triangles can be created. A square can be created by cutting to decrease the length 28 of the rectangle by 8 with a cut parallel to the sides of length 20. Cutting from a corner to an opposite side will create a trapezoid with two right angles. Finally, cutting from one side to a connecting side will result in a pentagon (five-sided figure). To create a hexagon, however, more than one straight cut would be needed. Choice (E) is correct.

7. D

Plug the data from the graph into the average formula: average $= \frac{\text{sum of terms}}{\text{number of terms}}$. You know there are four terms, but you need to find the sum of those terms. Based on the graph: March = 40, April = 60, May = 80, and June = 80. When you plug it in, the average is $\frac{40 + 60 + 80 + 80}{4} = \frac{260}{4} = 65$. Choice (D) is correct.

8. A

The value of n is 4, and the value of r is 2. Simply substitute these values into the equation that defines the symbol, but remember to follow the order of operations: $4 \clubsuit 2 = (4 - 1) - \frac{4}{2} = 3 - \frac{4}{2} = 3 - 2 = 1$.

Choice (A) is correct.

9. A

Here, you are given $n = Q$, $r = 2$, and $Q \clubsuit 2 = 4$. Even though you will work backward to find $Q (n)$, you will use the same equation and follow the same steps. First, plug in the values: $(Q - 1) - \frac{Q}{2} = 4$. Then, solve for Q. You can eliminate the denominator by multiplying both sides by 2: $2(Q - 1) - Q = 8$. Next, distribute the 2 through the parentheses: $2Q - 2 - Q = 8$. Finally, isolate the Q: $Q = 10$. Choice (A) is correct.

10. D

You might find the formula DIRT formula (Distance Is Rate × Time) easier to use than a proportion. Either will work, so use the one with which you're more comfortable.

$$225 \text{ miles} = 45 \text{ miles per hour} \times t \text{ hours}$$
$$225 = 45t$$
$$5 = t$$

or

$$\frac{45 \text{ miles}}{1 \text{ hour}} = \frac{225 \text{ miles}}{t \text{ hours}}$$
$$45t = 225$$
$$t = 5$$

Choice (D) is correct.

11. C

Use a variation of the percent formula: part = percent × whole. Raoul wants to leave a 20% tip on a dinner that costs $20.95, so plug in these values: tip $= 0.2 \times 20.95$. When solving percent or decimal questions without a calculator, it's often easy to start with finding 10% or 0.10 of it. Ten percent of 20.95 is about 2.10, so multiply this by 2 to find 20%: $2.10 \times 2 = \$4.20$. Choice (C) is correct.

12. A

This word problem looks complex, so take it one step at a time. Start by figuring out how many more hours Juan will need to work. Because he finished one-third in two hours, he has two-thirds to finish and will need about four hours. In order to finish by 10:30 p.m., Juan should start 4 hours earlier, at 6:30 p.m. Choice (A) is correct.

13. E

Mrs. Brown ate four strawberries and each c child ate four strawberries. Don't be distracted by choice C, which only accounts for the number of strawberries the children ate. Choice (E) is correct.

14. D

When adding mixed numbers and fractions, you can first add the whole numbers and the fractions separately. Solving $1 + 2 = 3$ is easy, but adding the fractions will require finding common denominators first. The least common multiple of 6, 3, and 4 is 12, so rewrite all three fractions with a denominator of 12: $\frac{4}{24} + \frac{16}{24} + \frac{18}{24}$. Now, you can easily add the numerators to determine the sum: $\frac{38}{24} = 1\frac{12}{24} = 1\frac{1}{2}$. Your final step is to combine the whole number sum and the fraction sum to find the final answer: $3 + 1\frac{1}{2} = 4\frac{1}{2}$. Unfortunately, the answers are given in decmial form, so convert $4\frac{1}{2}$ to 4.5. Choice (D) is correct.

15. D

You might recall a rule for these unique questions that ask about drawing figures in one fluid motion without lifting the pencil: in any given figure, if exactly zero or two points have an odd number of intersecting line segments and/or curves, it can be drawn without lifting the pencil or retracing. Choices A, B, C, and E all have four points at which three line segments intersect. Four points is too many, no matter how many lines intersect. Only choice (D), the correct answer, has exactly zero or two points that have an odd number (in this case, three) of intersecting lines.

16. D

The clue word "about" implies the need for rounding. For this question, round 0.59 to 0.6. Write an equation using this new value and solve for N: $0.6 = \frac{N}{5}$. Multiply both sides by 5 to get $N = 3$. Be careful placing the decimal point. Choice (D) is correct.

17. B

The consecutive integers must be 19, 20, 21, 22, 23, 24, and 25. The average of an odd number of equally spaced numbers is always the middle one. Consecutive integers are an instance of equally spaced numbers. If you don't know these tricks, simply use the average formula to add the integers and divide by 7. Choice (B) is correct.

18. D

The percent increase can be found using the percent change formula:

$$\frac{\text{new price} - \text{old price}}{\text{old price}} \times 100\%$$

The percent increase is as follows:

$$\text{percent change} = \frac{1.08 - 0.93}{0.93} \times 100\%$$

$$= \frac{0.15}{0.93} \times 100\%$$

$$= \frac{15}{93} \times 100\%$$

$$\approx \frac{15}{90} \times 100\%$$

$$\approx \frac{1}{6} \times 100\%$$

$$\approx 17\%$$

Choice (D) is correct.

19. C

To answer this question without a calculator, round both the divisor and the dividend to simplify the calculation: $90\overline{)7,200}$. This is much easier to think about. If you rewrite this as a fraction, $\frac{7,200}{90}$, you'll notice that this is equivalent to $\frac{7,200}{90}$, and think about the multiplication fact $8 \times 9 = 72$ to determine that $7,236 \div 89.2$ is approximately 80. Choice (C) is correct.

20. C

The area of the floor is found by multiplying 72×48. Dividing this result by the area of a single tile, which is 6×6, gives you the number of tiles needed. Rather than trying to multiply 72×48 without a calculator, set up a fraction and simplify: $\frac{72 \times 48}{6 \times 6}$. Both 72 and 48 are divisible by 6, so the denominator simplifies to 1 and you're left with $12 \times 8 = 96$. Choice (C) is correct.

21. C

Set up a ratio here: p pages is to 5 minutes as 20 pages is to how many minutes? Call m the number of minutes it will take to type 20 pages. Therefore, $\frac{p}{5} = \frac{20}{m}$. Cross multiplying, you get $mp = 100$. Finally, isolate the m by dividing each side by p: $m = \frac{100}{p}$, choice (C).

22. C

The length of the pool is 60 meters, and the width is one-fourth of that: $\frac{1}{4} \times 60 = 15$ meters. The perimeter is the sum of the lengths of all the sides: $60 + 60 + 15 + 15 = 150$ meters. Choice (C) is correct.

23. B

Remember, it can be helpful to pick 100 when dealing with percent problems. If the dress was $100 the first month, the second month it costs 80% of 100, or $80, and the third month it costs 80% of 80, which is $64. After 3 months, it costs 80% of $64, which is about $51. So, after 3 months, the cost is about 50% of the original price. Choice (B) is correct.

24. C

Picking Numbers is your best option here. Make sure you choose a positive integer for p and a negative integer for n: $p = 4$ and $n = -2$.

Choice A: $\dfrac{4}{-2} = -2$

Choice B: $\dfrac{-2}{4} = -\dfrac{1}{2}$

Choice (C): $\dfrac{1}{4 - (-2)} = \dfrac{1}{6}$

Choice D: $\dfrac{1}{(-2) - 4} = -\dfrac{1}{6}$

The greatest value is easily spotted as it's the only positive one. Choice (C) is the correct choice. This question can also be solved by realizing that for any positive integer p and any negative integer n, choices A, B, and D will all be negative.

25. A

Backsolving is a great way to get around setting up a complicated algebra equation. Start in the middle:

Choice C: $\dfrac{2}{3}(45) + \dfrac{1}{4}(45) + 5 =$

$$30 + 11\dfrac{1}{4} + 5 = 46\dfrac{1}{4}$$

A fractional number of people can't attend a party, you can eliminate choice C. It's okay if you aren't sure whether to eliminate the smaller or larger answer choices. When that happens, just pick one and keep working:

Choice B: $\dfrac{2}{3}(50) + \dfrac{1}{4}(50) + 5 =$

$$33\dfrac{1}{3} + 12\dfrac{1}{2} + 5 = 50\dfrac{5}{6}$$

It still didn't work, but you're getting closer to having the answer choice match the result (46.25 is 1.25 away from 45, but 50.87 is only 0.87 away from 50). This means you're going in the correct direction and choice (A) is probably correct, but check it, just in case:

Choice (A): $\dfrac{2}{3}(60) + \dfrac{1}{4}(60) + 5 =$

$$40 + 15 + 5 = 60$$

That works perfectly. Choice (A) is correct.

Section 5

1. A

To be keen is to be very smart, and sharp can mean this. Choice (A) is correct.

2. C

If you adhere to a decision, you stay with it or stick to it. Adhesive tape is sticky tape—it adheres. Choice (C) is correct.

3. D

To propel something is to thrust it forward or to project it. A strong wind can propel a ship through the water. Note that "project" is used as a verb here, not as a noun. Your answer must always be the same word form as that of the stem word. Choice (D) is correct.

4. E

Choice (E) is correct. This is a Function Bridge. A ruler is a tool used to measure something, just as a camera is a tool used to photograph something.

5. A

Choice (A) is correct. This is a Degree Bridge. To be meticulous is to be extremely careful. Similarly, to be exhausted is to be extremely tired. Choice B is the opposite of this relationship; to be alert is to be awake and aware, not asleep.

6. C

Choice (C) is correct. This is a Cause-and-Effect Bridge. A caterpillar is an animal that turns into a butterfly. A tadpole is an animal that turns into a frog.

7. B

The phrase "being out of heart with the government" in the first line should make you think of a person being "out of heart" with another person. This makes it sound like they used to think fondly about that person but no longer do. Choice (B), disenchanted, means disappointed or disillusioned, which is a good description for someone whose feelings have gone from positive to neutral or negative. Choice (B) is correct. Choice A, "amused," is the opposite of how the author would feel if they were disappointed with someone or something. "Furious" and "melancholy," choices C and D, are too strong to be correct. Choice E is a distortion; if the author felt "neutral," he most likely wouldn't have flung a broken root.

8. B

It's clear from the first line that the poet dislikes government. Choice (B) is correct. Choices C (lines 6–7), D (line 3), and E (lines 4–6) are all taken directly from the poem. Choice A is also something the author admires, but you have to infer that the poet likes the squirrel's independence from the overall description of the squirrel and its movement.

9. B

The author describes the squirrel's whinnying as "laughter" in lines 6 and 11. Choice (B) is correct. Choices A, C, D, and E are all out of scope; none of them are described by the author.

10. C

The squirrel's laughter is an expression, in the poet's eyes, of its freedom. The squirrel is "wayward" (line 3), moving from tree to tree "at a bound" (line 7). The statement "no government appointed him" in the third line implies that he is not bound to any responsibilities. Choice (C) correct. Choice A is a distortion; there is nothing menacing about the squirrel's noises. Choices B, D, and E are out of scope; the author never mentions the squirrel's ability to self-reflect or its friendliness to the author, and the sound isn't presented as an unusual or unexplained natural phenomenon.

11. B

"Heavy knitting of the brow" is an expression a serious government official would have, not a squirrel. The author focuses on the lightheartedness of the squirrel, and an independent, joyful creature would not have a heavy knitted brow. Choice (B) is correct. Choices A and E are out of scope; the political reformation movement and the beauty of the natural world are not mentioned. Choice C is opposite; the poet is describing the politicians' faces, not the squirrel's face. Choice D is a distortion; the poet isn't describing his own face, but those of the politicians he dislikes.

12. B

Remember, a cube has six faces. Because you're asked which shape can be folded into a cube with no overlapping flaps, the answer must contain exactly six faces. The only choice that does so is choice (B). Choices A and C have five faces, choice D has eight faces, and choice E has seven faces.

13. A

When solving Arithmetic word problems, be sure that you are performing the correct operation. Cindy's roll is $5 + 6 = 11$. Subtract Alice's 9-square lead and Cindy will be $11 - 9 = 2$ squares ahead of Alice. Choice (A) is correct.

14. C

Work systematically, checking one route at a time and keeping careful track of each path. There is a total of 4 paths from X to Y with a total length 7, as shown in the following figures:

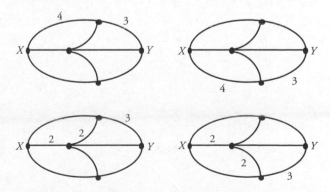

Choice (C) is correct.

15. E

Here is the rule for whether you can retrace a figure without having to lift your pencil: if exactly zero or two points have an odd number of intersecting line segments/curves, the figure can be drawn without lifting your pencil. So, if a figure has three points where an odd number of line segments intersect, you WOULD have to lift your pencil to retrace it. Don't be distracted by the number of points a figure has with an even number of intersecting line segments; that is irrelevant.

Count the number of line segments that meet at each point of intersection in each answer choice and record each point that has an odd number of intersections. If you find exactly zero or two points that meet this condition, the diagram can be drawn without lifting your pencil. The only figure that doesn't fit this criteria in these five answer choices is choice (E). There are six points of intersection, four of which have an odd number of intersecting segments. This does not meet the criteria of only zero or two points.

16. B

There are 25 girls and 15 boys in the class, a total of $25 + 15 = 40$ students. One-fifth of the girls, or $\frac{25}{5} = 5$ girls, and two-thirds of the boys, or $\frac{2}{3} \times 15 = 10$ boys, ran the haunted house. Add these together to determine that a total of $5 + 10 = 15$ students participated. The class has 40 students in all, so the fraction of the class that participated is $\frac{15}{40} = \frac{3}{8}$. Choice (B) is correct.

SSAT UPPER/MIDDLE LEVEL PRACTICE TEST 1: ASSESS YOUR STRENGTHS

Use the following tables to determine which topics and chapters you need to review most. If you need help with your essay, be sure to review Chapter 9: The Essay and Chapter 22: Writing Wrap-Up.

Topic	Question
Math	Section 2, questions 1–25 Section 5, questions 1–25
Reading Comprehension	Section 3, questions 1–40
Verbal: Synonyms	Section 4, questions 1–30
Verbal: Analogies	Section 4, questions 31–60

Topic	Number of Questions on Test	Number Correct	If You Struggled with these Questions, Study...
Math	50		Chapters 10–15 and Chapters 0–21
Reading Comprehension	40		Chapters 8 and 18–19
Verbal: Synonyms	30		Chapter 7 and Chapters 18–19
Verbal: Analogies	30		Chapter 2 and Chapters 18–19

CHAPTER 24

SSAT Upper/ Middle Level Practice Test 2

HOW TO TAKE THIS PRACTICE TEST

Before taking this practice test, find a quiet room where you can work uninterrupted for two and a half hours. Make sure you have a comfortable desk and several #2 pencils.

Use the answer sheet provided to record your answers. (You can cut it out or photocopy it.)

Once you start this practice test, don't stop until you've finished. Remember—you can review any questions within a section, but you may not go backward or forward a section.

You'll find answer explanations following the test. Scoring information can be found in Chapter 19.

If you are a Middle Level student, you should not expect to score as high as you would as an Upper Level student. No matter your score, you should focus on conducting in-depth reviews of all practice you complete, including this practice test.

Good luck.

SSAT Upper/Middle Level Practice Test 2
ANSWER SHEET

Remove (or photocopy) this answer sheet and use it to complete the practice test.

Start with number 1 for each section. If a section has fewer questions than answer spaces, leave the extra spaces blank.

SECTION 1

1. Ⓐ Ⓑ Ⓒ Ⓓ Ⓔ	6. Ⓐ Ⓑ Ⓒ Ⓓ Ⓔ	11. Ⓐ Ⓑ Ⓒ Ⓓ Ⓔ	16. Ⓐ Ⓑ Ⓒ Ⓓ Ⓔ	21. Ⓐ Ⓑ Ⓒ Ⓓ Ⓔ
2. Ⓐ Ⓑ Ⓒ Ⓓ Ⓔ	7. Ⓐ Ⓑ Ⓒ Ⓓ Ⓔ	12. Ⓐ Ⓑ Ⓒ Ⓓ Ⓔ	17. Ⓐ Ⓑ Ⓒ Ⓓ Ⓔ	22. Ⓐ Ⓑ Ⓒ Ⓓ Ⓔ
3. Ⓐ Ⓑ Ⓒ Ⓓ Ⓔ	8. Ⓐ Ⓑ Ⓒ Ⓓ Ⓔ	13. Ⓐ Ⓑ Ⓒ Ⓓ Ⓔ	18. Ⓐ Ⓑ Ⓒ Ⓓ Ⓔ	23. Ⓐ Ⓑ Ⓒ Ⓓ Ⓔ
4. Ⓐ Ⓑ Ⓒ Ⓓ Ⓔ	9. Ⓐ Ⓑ Ⓒ Ⓓ Ⓔ	14. Ⓐ Ⓑ Ⓒ Ⓓ Ⓔ	19. Ⓐ Ⓑ Ⓒ Ⓓ Ⓔ	24. Ⓐ Ⓑ Ⓒ Ⓓ Ⓔ
5. Ⓐ Ⓑ Ⓒ Ⓓ Ⓔ	10. Ⓐ Ⓑ Ⓒ Ⓓ Ⓔ	15. Ⓐ Ⓑ Ⓒ Ⓓ Ⓔ	20. Ⓐ Ⓑ Ⓒ Ⓓ Ⓔ	25. Ⓐ Ⓑ Ⓒ Ⓓ Ⓔ

correct in section 1

incorrect in section 1

SECTION 2

1. Ⓐ Ⓑ Ⓒ Ⓓ Ⓔ	9. Ⓐ Ⓑ Ⓒ Ⓓ Ⓔ	17. Ⓐ Ⓑ Ⓒ Ⓓ Ⓔ	25. Ⓐ Ⓑ Ⓒ Ⓓ Ⓔ	33. Ⓐ Ⓑ Ⓒ Ⓓ Ⓔ
2. Ⓐ Ⓑ Ⓒ Ⓓ Ⓔ	10. Ⓐ Ⓑ Ⓒ Ⓓ Ⓔ	18. Ⓐ Ⓑ Ⓒ Ⓓ Ⓔ	26. Ⓐ Ⓑ Ⓒ Ⓓ Ⓔ	34. Ⓐ Ⓑ Ⓒ Ⓓ Ⓔ
3. Ⓐ Ⓑ Ⓒ Ⓓ Ⓔ	11. Ⓐ Ⓑ Ⓒ Ⓓ Ⓔ	19. Ⓐ Ⓑ Ⓒ Ⓓ Ⓔ	27. Ⓐ Ⓑ Ⓒ Ⓓ Ⓔ	35. Ⓐ Ⓑ Ⓒ Ⓓ Ⓔ
4. Ⓐ Ⓑ Ⓒ Ⓓ Ⓔ	12. Ⓐ Ⓑ Ⓒ Ⓓ Ⓔ	20. Ⓐ Ⓑ Ⓒ Ⓓ Ⓔ	28. Ⓐ Ⓑ Ⓒ Ⓓ Ⓔ	36. Ⓐ Ⓑ Ⓒ Ⓓ Ⓔ
5. Ⓐ Ⓑ Ⓒ Ⓓ Ⓔ	13. Ⓐ Ⓑ Ⓒ Ⓓ Ⓔ	21. Ⓐ Ⓑ Ⓒ Ⓓ Ⓔ	29. Ⓐ Ⓑ Ⓒ Ⓓ Ⓔ	37. Ⓐ Ⓑ Ⓒ Ⓓ Ⓔ
6. Ⓐ Ⓑ Ⓒ Ⓓ Ⓔ	14. Ⓐ Ⓑ Ⓒ Ⓓ Ⓔ	22. Ⓐ Ⓑ Ⓒ Ⓓ Ⓔ	30. Ⓐ Ⓑ Ⓒ Ⓓ Ⓔ	38. Ⓐ Ⓑ Ⓒ Ⓓ Ⓔ
7. Ⓐ Ⓑ Ⓒ Ⓓ Ⓔ	15. Ⓐ Ⓑ Ⓒ Ⓓ Ⓔ	23. Ⓐ Ⓑ Ⓒ Ⓓ Ⓔ	31. Ⓐ Ⓑ Ⓒ Ⓓ Ⓔ	39. Ⓐ Ⓑ Ⓒ Ⓓ Ⓔ
8. Ⓐ Ⓑ Ⓒ Ⓓ Ⓔ	16. Ⓐ Ⓑ Ⓒ Ⓓ Ⓔ	24. Ⓐ Ⓑ Ⓒ Ⓓ Ⓔ	32. Ⓐ Ⓑ Ⓒ Ⓓ Ⓔ	40. Ⓐ Ⓑ Ⓒ Ⓓ Ⓔ

correct in section 2

incorrect in section 2

SECTION 3

1. Ⓐ Ⓑ Ⓒ Ⓓ Ⓔ	13. Ⓐ Ⓑ Ⓒ Ⓓ Ⓔ	25. Ⓐ Ⓑ Ⓒ Ⓓ Ⓔ	37. Ⓐ Ⓑ Ⓒ Ⓓ Ⓔ	49. Ⓐ Ⓑ Ⓒ Ⓓ Ⓔ
2. Ⓐ Ⓑ Ⓒ Ⓓ Ⓔ	14. Ⓐ Ⓑ Ⓒ Ⓓ Ⓔ	26. Ⓐ Ⓑ Ⓒ Ⓓ Ⓔ	38. Ⓐ Ⓑ Ⓒ Ⓓ Ⓔ	50. Ⓐ Ⓑ Ⓒ Ⓓ Ⓔ
3. Ⓐ Ⓑ Ⓒ Ⓓ Ⓔ	15. Ⓐ Ⓑ Ⓒ Ⓓ Ⓔ	27. Ⓐ Ⓑ Ⓒ Ⓓ Ⓔ	39. Ⓐ Ⓑ Ⓒ Ⓓ Ⓔ	51. Ⓐ Ⓑ Ⓒ Ⓓ Ⓔ
4. Ⓐ Ⓑ Ⓒ Ⓓ Ⓔ	16. Ⓐ Ⓑ Ⓒ Ⓓ Ⓔ	28. Ⓐ Ⓑ Ⓒ Ⓓ Ⓔ	40. Ⓐ Ⓑ Ⓒ Ⓓ Ⓔ	52. Ⓐ Ⓑ Ⓒ Ⓓ Ⓔ
5. Ⓐ Ⓑ Ⓒ Ⓓ Ⓔ	17. Ⓐ Ⓑ Ⓒ Ⓓ Ⓔ	29. Ⓐ Ⓑ Ⓒ Ⓓ Ⓔ	41. Ⓐ Ⓑ Ⓒ Ⓓ Ⓔ	53. Ⓐ Ⓑ Ⓒ Ⓓ Ⓔ
6. Ⓐ Ⓑ Ⓒ Ⓓ Ⓔ	18. Ⓐ Ⓑ Ⓒ Ⓓ Ⓔ	30. Ⓐ Ⓑ Ⓒ Ⓓ Ⓔ	42. Ⓐ Ⓑ Ⓒ Ⓓ Ⓔ	54. Ⓐ Ⓑ Ⓒ Ⓓ Ⓔ
7. Ⓐ Ⓑ Ⓒ Ⓓ Ⓔ	19. Ⓐ Ⓑ Ⓒ Ⓓ Ⓔ	31. Ⓐ Ⓑ Ⓒ Ⓓ Ⓔ	43. Ⓐ Ⓑ Ⓒ Ⓓ Ⓔ	55. Ⓐ Ⓑ Ⓒ Ⓓ Ⓔ
8. Ⓐ Ⓑ Ⓒ Ⓓ Ⓔ	20. Ⓐ Ⓑ Ⓒ Ⓓ Ⓔ	32. Ⓐ Ⓑ Ⓒ Ⓓ Ⓔ	44. Ⓐ Ⓑ Ⓒ Ⓓ Ⓔ	56. Ⓐ Ⓑ Ⓒ Ⓓ Ⓔ
9. Ⓐ Ⓑ Ⓒ Ⓓ Ⓔ	21. Ⓐ Ⓑ Ⓒ Ⓓ Ⓔ	33. Ⓐ Ⓑ Ⓒ Ⓓ Ⓔ	45. Ⓐ Ⓑ Ⓒ Ⓓ Ⓔ	57. Ⓐ Ⓑ Ⓒ Ⓓ Ⓔ
10. Ⓐ Ⓑ Ⓒ Ⓓ Ⓔ	22. Ⓐ Ⓑ Ⓒ Ⓓ Ⓔ	34. Ⓐ Ⓑ Ⓒ Ⓓ Ⓔ	46. Ⓐ Ⓑ Ⓒ Ⓓ Ⓔ	58. Ⓐ Ⓑ Ⓒ Ⓓ Ⓔ
11. Ⓐ Ⓑ Ⓒ Ⓓ Ⓔ	23. Ⓐ Ⓑ Ⓒ Ⓓ Ⓔ	35. Ⓐ Ⓑ Ⓒ Ⓓ Ⓔ	47. Ⓐ Ⓑ Ⓒ Ⓓ Ⓔ	59. Ⓐ Ⓑ Ⓒ Ⓓ Ⓔ
12. Ⓐ Ⓑ Ⓒ Ⓓ Ⓔ	24. Ⓐ Ⓑ Ⓒ Ⓓ Ⓔ	36. Ⓐ Ⓑ Ⓒ Ⓓ Ⓔ	48. Ⓐ Ⓑ Ⓒ Ⓓ Ⓔ	60. Ⓐ Ⓑ Ⓒ Ⓓ Ⓔ

correct in section 3

incorrect in section 3

SECTION 4

1. Ⓐ Ⓑ Ⓒ Ⓓ Ⓔ	6. Ⓐ Ⓑ Ⓒ Ⓓ Ⓔ	11. Ⓐ Ⓑ Ⓒ Ⓓ Ⓔ	16. Ⓐ Ⓑ Ⓒ Ⓓ Ⓔ	21. Ⓐ Ⓑ Ⓒ Ⓓ Ⓔ
2. Ⓐ Ⓑ Ⓒ Ⓓ Ⓔ	7. Ⓐ Ⓑ Ⓒ Ⓓ Ⓔ	12. Ⓐ Ⓑ Ⓒ Ⓓ Ⓔ	17. Ⓐ Ⓑ Ⓒ Ⓓ Ⓔ	22. Ⓐ Ⓑ Ⓒ Ⓓ Ⓔ
3. Ⓐ Ⓑ Ⓒ Ⓓ Ⓔ	8. Ⓐ Ⓑ Ⓒ Ⓓ Ⓔ	13. Ⓐ Ⓑ Ⓒ Ⓓ Ⓔ	18. Ⓐ Ⓑ Ⓒ Ⓓ Ⓔ	23. Ⓐ Ⓑ Ⓒ Ⓓ Ⓔ
4. Ⓐ Ⓑ Ⓒ Ⓓ Ⓔ	9. Ⓐ Ⓑ Ⓒ Ⓓ Ⓔ	14. Ⓐ Ⓑ Ⓒ Ⓓ Ⓔ	19. Ⓐ Ⓑ Ⓒ Ⓓ Ⓔ	24. Ⓐ Ⓑ Ⓒ Ⓓ Ⓔ
5. Ⓐ Ⓑ Ⓒ Ⓓ Ⓔ	10. Ⓐ Ⓑ Ⓒ Ⓓ Ⓔ	15. Ⓐ Ⓑ Ⓒ Ⓓ Ⓔ	20. Ⓐ Ⓑ Ⓒ Ⓓ Ⓔ	25. Ⓐ Ⓑ Ⓒ Ⓓ Ⓔ

correct in section 4

incorrect in section 4

Writing Sample

Secondary schools will use an essay or story to get to know you better. Write about one of the two topics below. Choose the topic you find most interesting and bubble in the circle before you start writing.

(A) I had thirty minutes to complete the mission.

(B) What is your favorite academic subject? Explain why you feel this way.

Notes

_____

_____

_____

_____

_____

_____

_____

_____

_____

_____

_____

_____

_____

_____

(Continued)

_____

_____

_____

_____

_____

_____

_____

_____

_____

_____

_____

_____

_____

_____

_____

_____

_____

_____

STOP. IF THERE IS TIME, YOU MAY CHECK YOUR WORK IN THIS SECTION ONLY.   **STOP**

SECTION 1
25 Questions

Each question has five suggested answers. Solve each question using the blank space at the right of the page. Then, examine the five choices and select the correct one.

<u>Note</u>: Figures in this section are as accurate as possible EXCEPT when it is stated that a figure is not drawn to scale.

Sample Question:

> 1. $1 \times 2^2 =$
>
>   (A) 1
>   (B) 2
>   (C) 3
>   (D) 4
>   (E) 5   Ⓐ Ⓑ Ⓒ ● Ⓔ

---

1. The polygon in the figure has a perimeter of 30. If each side of the polygon is the same length, what is the length of one side?

    (A) 3
    (B) 4
    (C) 5
    (D) 6
    (E) 7

USE THIS SPACE FOR FIGURING

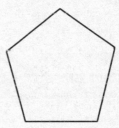

---

2. The Sweet Shop sold peppermint candy to 25 customers and caramel candy to 17 customers. If 4 of these customers bought both types of candy, how many bought only caramel candy?

    (A) 29
    (B) 25
    (C) 21
    (D) 17
    (E) 13

GO ON TO THE NEXT PAGE. ▶ ▶ ▶

3. In a new bag of 24 balls, there is an equal number of balls of each color. Which of the following CANNOT be the number of different colors in the bag?

(A) 2

(B) 3

(C) 4

(D) 5

(E) 6

USE THIS SPACE FOR FIGURING

4. $\left(-\frac{1}{4}\right)^3 =$

(A) $-\frac{1}{64}$

(B) $-\frac{1}{4}$

(C) $-\frac{1}{2}$

(D) $\frac{1}{2}$

(E) $\frac{1}{4}$

5. According to the graph, Susan spent about how many hours watching movies?

(A) 2

(B) 3

(C) 4

(D) 6

(E) 9

HOW SUSAN SPENT 12 HOURS WATCHING TV

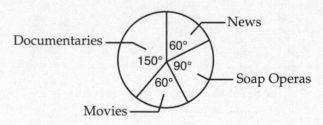

6. If $\frac{1}{2}R = 16$, then $\frac{3}{4}R =$

(A) 24

(B) 20

(C) 16

(D) 12

(E) 8

GO ON TO THE NEXT PAGE. ▶ ▶ ▶

7. Which of the following is closest to $\frac{1}{4}$ of 59?

    (A) 0.26×50

    (B) 0.41×50

    (C) 0.26×60

    (D) 0.41×60

    (E) 41×60

USE THIS SPACE FOR FIGURING

8. According to the graph, what were the average sales of Company M from 1993 to 1997?

    (A) $250,000

    (B) $260,000

    (C) $265,000

    (D) $270,000

    (E) $275,000

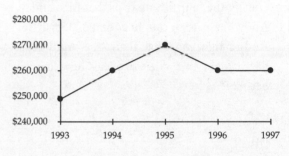

SALES OF COMPANY M: 1993–1997

Questions 9–10 are based on the following definition.

For all real numbers u and v, $u \phi v = u - \left(1 - \frac{1}{v}\right)$.

Example: $3 \phi 2 = 3 - \left(1 - \frac{1}{2}\right) = 3 - \frac{1}{2} = 2\frac{1}{2}$

9. Which of the following is equal to $5 \phi 5$?

    (A) 0

    (B) 1

    (C) $4\frac{1}{5}$

    (D) $4\frac{4}{5}$

    (E) 25

10. If $a \phi 3 = 4\frac{1}{3}$, then $a =$

    (A) $\frac{2}{3}$

    (B) 3

    (C) 4

    (D) $4\frac{2}{3}$

    (E) 5

GO ON TO THE NEXT PAGE. ▶ ▶ ▶

11. Twenty percent of 64 is equal to 5 percent of what number?

    (A) 16

    (B) 20

    (C) 64

    (D) 128

    (E) 256

USE THIS SPACE FOR FIGURING

12. During the four fishing trips that Rico and Andy made, Rich caught a total of 35 fish. If Andy caught more fish than Rico, Andy must have caught an average of a least how many fish per trip?

    (A) $8\frac{3}{4}$

    (B) 9

    (C) 36

    (D) 140

    (E) 144

13. Jeff, Todd, and Lee were hired by their father to work on the yard, and each was paid at the same hourly rate. Jeff worked 4 hours, Todd worked 6 hours, and Lee worked 8 hours. If the 3 boys together earned $108, how much did Lee earn?

    (A) $32

    (B) $48

    (C) $60

    (D) $64

    (E) $80

GO ON TO THE NEXT PAGE. ▶ ▶ ▶

14. Johnny picked apples from 9:00 a.m. to 11:30 a.m. and gathered 200 apples. He wants to pick a total of at least 600 apples before 7:15 p.m. If he plans to pick apples at the same rate, what is the latest time that he can start picking apples again?

    (A) 1:15 p.m.

    (B) 1:45 p.m.

    (C) 2.15 p.m.

    (D) 2:45 p.m.

    (E) 3:15 p.m.

USE THIS SPACE FOR FIGURING

15. If 0.88 equals $8W$, what is the value of W?

    (A) 0.11

    (B) 0.9

    (C) 1.1

    (D) 9

    (E) 11

16. In the triangle shown, what is the value of r?

    (A) 50

    (B) 60

    (C) 70

    (D) 80

    (E) It cannot be determined from the information given.

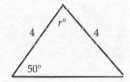

GO ON TO THE NEXT PAGE. ▶ ▶ ▶

17. In 2016, the number one company on the
    Fortune 500 list earned about $485 billion
    in net revenue. In 1995, that same company
    earned about $83 billion in net revenue. How
    many times greater was the company's income
    in 2016 than it was in 1995?

    (A) 10

    (B) 6

    (C) 5

    (D) 2

    (E) $\frac{1}{6}$

USE THIS SPACE FOR FIGURING

18. Which of the following can be expressed as
    $(5 \times R) + 2$ when R is a whole number?

    (A) 25

    (B) 33

    (C) 47

    (D) 56

    (E) 68

19. Which of the following can be drawn without
    lifting the pencil or retracing?

    (A)

    (B)

    (C)

    (D)

    (E)

GO ON TO THE NEXT PAGE. ▶ ▶ ▶

20. If the population of Country X increased by 10 percent each year over a two-year period, what was the total percent increase in the population over the entire period?

   (A) 2%

   (B) 10%

   (C) 11%

   (D) 20%

   (E) 21%

21. If $z = y + 2$, what does $2z + 1$ equal?

   (A) $y + 3$

   (B) $2y + 3$

   (C) $2y + 5$

   (D) $2y + 6$

   (E) It cannot be determined from the information given.

22. If x is greater than 0 but less than 1, and y is greater than x, which of the following is the LEAST?

   (A) $\dfrac{y}{x}$

   (B) $\dfrac{x}{y}$

   (C) xy

   (D) $\dfrac{1}{x - y}$

   (E) It cannot be determined from the information given.

GO ON TO THE NEXT PAGE. ▶ ▶ ▶

23. In a restaurant, there are x tables that can each seat 6 people, and there are y tables that can each seat 5 people. What is the maximum number of people that can be seated?

    (A) $5x + 6y$

    (B) $6x + 5y$

    (C) $11x + 11y$

    (D) $11xy$

    (E) $30xy$

USE THIS SPACE FOR FIGURING

24. Mrs. Smith bought 3 square pieces of fabric. A side of the largest piece is 3 times as long as a side of the middle one, and a side of the middle one is 3 times as long as a side of the smallest one. The area of the largest piece is how many times the area of the smallest piece?

    (A) 112

    (B) 81

    (C) 27

    (D) 9

    (E) 3

25. Mr. Dali's car uses $\frac{3}{4}$ gallons of gas each time he drives to work. If his gas tank holds exactly 9 gallons of gas, how many tanks of gas does he need to make 18 trips to work?

    (A) $1\frac{1}{2}$

    (B) $2\frac{1}{2}$

    (C) 4

    (D) 6

    (E) 9

IF YOU FINISH BEFORE TIME IS CALLED, YOU MAY CHECK YOUR WORK ON THIS SECTION ONLY. DO NOT TURN TO ANY OTHER SECTION IN THE TEST. STOP

SECTION 2
40 Questions

Read each passage and answer the related questions. For each question, use the passage to decide which one of the choices best answers the question.

Scott Joplin composed approximately 60 works during his lifetime, including 41 piano pieces called "rags," many songs and marches, and an opera entitled *Treemonisha*. His most significant creative contribution was to the development of ragtime, a type of instrumental music marked by its distinctive, choppy rhythm. Joplin's rhythmic diversity was very important to the development of
Line 5 ragtime as a genre, a unique musical form. In 1899, his "Maple Leaf Rag" became the most popular piano rag of the time and he was dubbed the "King of Ragtime." Despite all of those accomplishments, he was not considered a serious composer during his lifetime. It was not until 59 years after his death that he was properly recognized: In 1976, he was awarded the Pulitzer Prize for music, at last receiving the praise he deserved.

---

1. The term "rag," as it is used in the passage, refers to

   (A) a specific piece of operatic music

   (B) a genre of dance music

   (C) a piece of piano music known for its unique rhythm

   (D) a kind of instrumental music played by marching bands

   (E) a style of songs invented by Joplin

2. This passage deals primarily with

   (A) the fact that Joplin was not taken seriously during his lifetime

   (B) the history and development of ragtime music

   (C) the diversity of styles in which Joplin composed

   (D) how Joplin came to win the Pulitzer Prize

   (E) Joplin's contributions to and accomplishments in the world of music

3. In line 4, the word "choppy" is an example of

   (A) synecdoche

   (B) imagery

   (C) anaphora

   (D) onomatopoeia

   (E) irony

4. When discussing Scott Joplin, the author's tone in this passage could best be described as

   (A) indifferent

   (B) amused

   (C) envious

   (D) resentful

   (E) appreciative

GO ON TO THE NEXT PAGE. ▶ ▶ ▶

5. It can be inferred from the passage that a genre is

    (A) a particular type of ragtime music

    (B) a distinct category or style

    (C) a term that Joplin coined when he created ragtime

    (D) a rhythmic style characteristic of Joplin's period

    (E) an early form of "rag"

6. From this passage, it can be inferred that

    (A) although people liked Joplin's work, they did not appreciate its value while he was alive

    (B) Joplin died a destitute musician

    (C) ragtime wouldn't have existed had Joplin not written "Maple Leaf Rag"

    (D) all of Joplin's piano pieces were rags

    (E) Joplin played a lot of venues to popularize ragtime

GO ON TO THE NEXT PAGE. ▶ ▶ ▶

Thousands of species of birds exist today, and nearly every species has its own special courtship procedures and "identification checks." Identification checks are important, because if birds of different species mate, any offspring will usually be sterile or badly adapted to their surroundings.

Plumage often plays a key role in both identification and courtship. In breeding season, male
Line 5 birds often acquire distinctive plumage that they use to attract females who will, in turn, only respond to males with the correct markings. In some species, the females are more brightly colored, and the courtship roles are reversed. Distinctive behavioral changes can also be important aspects of courtship and breeding activity. Aggressiveness between males, and sometimes between females, is quite common. Some birds, like whooping cranes and trumpeter swans, perform wonderfully
10 elaborate courtship dances in which both sexes are enthusiastic participants.

Bird sounds are often a very central part of identification and courtship behavior between individuals in a given species. When a female migrates in the spring to her breeding region, she often encounters numerous birds of different species. By its singing, the male of a species both identifies itself and communicates to females of that species that it is in breeding condition. This information allows a
15 female to predict a male's response to her approach. Later, after mating has taken place, the note patterns of a particular male's song enable a nesting female to continue to identify her own partner.

7. The author implies that a bird engages in identification and courtship procedures mainly in order to

    (A) find a better nesting spot

    (B) find the most colorful partner it can

    (C) attract a mate of its own species

    (D) increase its control over its nesting partner

    (E) try to dominate the bird population of a given area

8. When discussing bird courtship, the author's tone in the passage could best be described as

    (A) hostile

    (B) humorous

    (C) solemn

    (D) objective

    (E) personal

9. The author uses the whooping crane as an example of a bird that

    (A) seldom participates in courtship procedures

    (B) acquires a distinctive breeding plumage

    (C) behaves in an unusual and noteworthy way during courtship

    (D) reverses the normal male and female courtship roles

    (E) displays unusual aggressiveness while courting

10. According to the passage, mating by birds of different species

    (A) is quite common

    (B) produces more sturdy offspring

    (C) may help to establish a permanent new species

    (D) does not usually result in healthy offspring

    (E) has never happened

GO ON TO THE NEXT PAGE. ▶ ▶ ▶

11. The passage is primarily about

    (A) causes of aggression between male birds

    (B) several courtship and identification methods used by birds

    (C) the breeding season of birds

    (D) the role of bird sounds in courtship identification

    (E) why birds migrate to particular breeding regions

12. This passage most likely comes from

    (A) a website on identifying birds

    (B) a book on birds and mating

    (C) a personal letter from a bird-watcher

    (D) a novel about breeding birds

    (E) a news article on endangered birds

GO ON TO THE NEXT PAGE. ▶ ▶ ▶

More than 1,500 Native American languages have thus far been discovered by linguists. Edward Sapir, a pioneer in the field of Native American linguistics, grouped these languages into six "families" more than three-quarters of a century ago.

Ever since that time, the classification of Native American languages has been a source of
Line 5   controversy. A small group of linguists has recently argued that all Native American languages fit into three linguistic families. These scholars believe that similarities and differences among words and sounds leave no doubt about the validity of their classification scheme. The vast majority of linguists, however, reject both the methods and conclusions of these scholars, arguing that linguistic science has not yet advanced far enough to be able to group Native American languages into a few
10   families. According to these scholars, Native American languages have diverged to such an extent over the centuries that it may never be possible to group them in distinct language families.

13. This passage is primarily about

    (A) the classification of Native American languages

    (B) the six families of Native American languages

    (C) scholars' views about language

    (D) the similarities and differences between words of Native American languages

    (E) linguistic debates about how to group languages

14. The scholars who believe that Native American languages can be classified into three families apparently believe that

    (A) these languages have diverged significantly over the last 75 years

    (B) languages can be classified according to the degree of similarities and differences between words

    (C) linguistic science has not advanced far enough to safely classify languages so narrowly

    (D) languages are all related by their common origins

    (E) distinct language families have their own peculiar grammatical rules

15. The style of the passage is most like that found in a

    (A) personal letter written by a linguistics student

    (B) textbook about linguistics

    (C) novel about Native American tribes

    (D) diary of a linguist

    (E) biography of Edward Sapir

16. It can be inferred that the classification of Native American languages has been a source of controversy because

    (A) scholars do not agree on the method for classifying languages

    (B) languages have split in several directions

    (C) linguistics is a very new field

    (D) there is not enough known about Native American vocabulary

    (E) Native Americans dislike such classifications

GO ON TO THE NEXT PAGE. ▶ ▶ ▶

17. Which of the following questions is answered by the passage?

    (A) Did Edward Sapir study languages other than Native American languages?

    (B) How many languages are in a typical linguistic family?

    (C) How many Native American languages are yet to discovered?

    (D) In what ways have Native American languages changed over time?

    (E) Into how many families did Edward Sapir classify Native American languages?

18. As used in the passage, "extent" (line 10) most nearly means

    (A) limit

    (B) language

    (C) range

    (D) time

    (E) duration

GO ON TO THE NEXT PAGE. ▶ ▶ ▶

"Hope" is the thing with feathers
That perches in the soul,
And sings the tune without the words
And never stops at all,

Line 5 And sweetest in the gale is heard;
And sore must be the storm
That could abash[1] the little bird
That kept so many warm.

I've heard it in the chillest land,
10 And on the strangest sea;
Yet, never, in extremity,
It asked a crumb of me.

[1]discourage
"Hope," by Emily Dickinson

---

19. In this poem, hope is compared to

   (A) a gale

   (B) a sea

   (C) a storm

   (D) a bird

   (E) a song

20. What is the poet saying in the last stanza of the poem?

   (A) It is terrible to imagine a world without hope, and we must therefore do everything possible to preserve our hopes.

   (B) The bird continues to sing through all conditions.

   (C) Hope can be found anywhere and never asks anything in return for its loyalty.

   (D) The bird is very hungry because it is constantly singing and never takes any time to eat.

   (E) The potential for hope is always present, but it takes a great effort to make it a reality.

21. The lines "the little bird / That kept so many warm" in the second stanza refer to the fact that

   (A) the feathers of birds have traditionally provided protection against the cold

   (B) hope has comforted a great many people over the years

   (C) the bird provided protection before it was destroyed in a storm

   (D) hope has often proven useless in the face of real problems

   (E) hope is a good last resort when faced with a difficult situation

GO ON TO THE NEXT PAGE. ▶ ▶ ▶

22. The attitude of the speaker in this poem can best be described as

    (A) angry

    (B) unconcerned

    (C) respectful

    (D) nervous

    (E) grateful

23. The term "sore" (line 6) most nearly means

    (A) hurt

    (B) angry

    (C) severe

    (D) kind

    (E) wet

GO ON TO THE NEXT PAGE. ▶ ▶ ▶

Although recycling has taken place in various forms for some time, today we are being asked to regard recycling as not only an important, but even a necessary measure.

Recycling, in its broadest sense, refers to the remaking of waste products and other used materials for practical purposes. For example, an old soda bottle can be returned, washed, and used as a bottle
Line 5 again, or it can be ground down and its glass can be employed for another useful purpose. Since fixing up old things is often cheaper than making brand new ones, this saves money. More importantly, it saves resources and reduces the amount of waste produced.

Businesses have been performing large-scale recycling for some time, based primarily on the goal of saving money. However, the amount of residential waste, that is, the waste produced at home, has
10 been steadily increasing, and the role of the individual in the recycling campaign has been seriously underemphasized. Although it is true that we, as individuals, cannot reduce the overall amount of waste significantly or save large amounts of money and resources on our own, taken collectively, we can have an important impact. Our increased efforts toward recycling can have a dramatic effect on the future availability of resources and the condition of the environment. It is our duty to ourselves
15 and to our fellow human beings to pitch in and help protect what remains of it.

24. This passage is written from the viewpoint of which of the following?

(A) A homeowner

(B) A recycling plant owner

(C) The mayor of a town

(D) An environmental activist

(E) A middle school student

25. The author would most likely agree that

(A) recycling is a good idea for big businesses but, on an individual level, it makes very little difference

(B) although businesses recycle to save money, individuals are motivated to recycle by a desire to serve the general good of society

(C) recycling is extremely important and everyone has a responsibility to contribute to the overall effort to preserve our environment

(D) although our natural resources are limited, we only live once and we shouldn't concentrate on conservation to such a degree that it interferes with our enjoyment of life

(E) recycling is a very expensive process and should be left to the owners of big businesses

GO ON TO THE NEXT PAGE. ▶ ▶ ▶

26. All of the following are examples of recycling EXCEPT

    (A) turning old newspapers into cardboard

    (B) melting down scraps of metal and recasting them

    (C) washing out empty soda bottles and using them as vases

    (D) selling a piece of jewelry and using the money to buy a car

    (E) crushing old cans and reusing the aluminum to make new ones

27. The author's attitude about recycling may best be described as

    (A) insistent

    (B) relaxed

    (C) formal

    (D) amused

    (E) disinterested

28. Which of the following is the author most likely to discuss next?

    (A) the current problem of toxic waste disposal

    (B) the negative aspects of recycling and the many problems that can develop when it is done too much

    (C) different ways that an old bottle can be either reused or remade into an entirely different object

    (D) other important differences between the way businesses and residences are run

    (E) examples of ways in which people can recycle their own waste and help out on an individual basis

29. What can be said about the author based on lines 8–9?

    (A) She is only interested in the economic aspects of recycling.

    (B) She believes that businesses are motivated to recycle primarily for monetary gain.

    (C) She knows little about the possible financial savings of recycling.

    (D) She is more concerned with the environmental benefits of recycling than the economic rewards.

    (E) She values recycling even though it results in the production of greater amounts of waste.

GO ON TO THE NEXT PAGE. ▶ ▶ ▶

Most of us who live in relatively mild climates rarely view bad weather as more than an inconvenience, but in certain, less fortunate parts of the world, a change in weather can have disastrous consequences for an entire society. Weather fluctuations along the northwest coast of South America, for instance, can periodically have a dramatic effect on the area's fishing villages. Under normal
Line 5 circumstances, the cold, steadily flowing waters of the Humboldt Current bring nutrients up from the sea floor along the coast, providing a dependable food supply for fish and squid. For centuries, the fishing villages have depended on this rich ocean harvest for food and trade. Occasionally, however, global weather patterns cause the current to fail, setting off a deadly chain reaction. Without nutrients, the fish and squid die, depriving the villagers of their livelihood. This destructive weather
10 phenomenon, called "El Niño" (The Boy Child) because it occurs at Christmastime, has sometimes forced entire villages to disband and move elsewhere to avoid starvation.

30. According to the passage, the Humboldt Current flows

   (A) only at Christmastime
   (B) without fail
   (C) east to west
   (D) along the northwest coast of South America
   (E) through warm water

31. This passage is mainly about

   (A) how the economy of South American villages depends exclusively on fishing
   (B) the importance of fish and squid in the food chain
   (C) the advantages of living in a mild climate
   (D) the undependable nature of the Humboldt Current
   (E) how changes in weather patterns can have a dramatic effect on the way people live

32. According to the passage, all of the following are true EXCEPT

   (A) the actions of the Humboldt Current help provide nutrients for fish and squid
   (B) the Humboldt Current affects the survival of fishing on the northwest coast of South America
   (C) the warm waters of the Humboldt Current affect the climate of nearby land masses
   (D) the failure of the Humboldt Current can set off a deadly chain reaction
   (E) the Humboldt Current sometimes fails as a result of global weather patterns

33. Which of the following would be the best title for this passage?

   (A) An Example of Weather's Social Impact
   (B) Fishing Villages of South America
   (C) El Niño: A Christmas Occurrence
   (D) Fish and Squid: A Rich Ocean Harvest
   (E) The Impact of Fishing on Coastal Villages

GO ON TO THE NEXT PAGE. ▶ ▶ ▶

34. The author's attitude toward the villagers along the northwest coast of South America can best be described as

    (A) sympathetic

    (B) unconcerned

    (C) condescending

    (D) angry

    (E) emotional

35. It is most reasonable to infer from the passage that

    (A) the Humboldt Current feeds all fishing villages

    (B) a chain reaction can cause species extinction

    (C) earthquakes cause village migration

    (D) weather fluctuations impact regions differently

    (E) normal rainfall causes massive water damage

GO ON TO THE NEXT PAGE. ▶ ▶ ▶

World War II left much of Western Europe deeply scarred in many ways. Economically, it was devastated. In early 1948, as the Cold War developed between the United States and the Soviet Union and political tensions rose, U.S. policymakers decided that substantial financial assistance would be required to maintain a state of political stability. This conclusion led Secretary of State
Line 5   George C. Marshall to announce a proposal: European countries were advised to draw up a unified plan for reconstruction, to be funded by the United States.
This European Recovery Program, also known as the Marshall Plan, provided economic and technical assistance to 16 countries. Between 1948 and 1952, participating countries received a combined total of 12 billion dollars in U.S. aid. In the end, the program was seen as a great success; it
10   revived the economies of Western Europe and set them on a course for future growth.

36. Which of the following would be the best title for this passage?

(A) The Aftermath of World War II

(B) The Marshall Plan: A Program for European Reconstruction

(C) The Economic Destruction of Europe

(D) George C. Marshall: The Man behind the Plan

(E) Western European Recovery

37. The tone of the author toward the Marshall Plan is

(A) objective

(B) excited

(C) insistent

(D) anxious

(E) unfavorable

38. The author's use of which of the following words is an example of personification?

(A) scarred

(B) devastated

(C) developed

(D) stability

(E) funded

39. The passage suggests that the driving force behind the Marshall Plan was

(A) a formal request for aid by European leaders

(B) fear of economic repercussions for the U.S. economy

(C) George C. Marshall's desire to improve his political career and public image

(D) a joint U.S.–Soviet agreement to assist the countries of Western Europe

(E) the increase in tension between the United States and the Soviet Union

40. Which of the following would the author be most likely to discuss next?

(A) developments in the Cold War during and after the years of the Marshall Plan

(B) the events leading up to Western Europe's economic collapse

(C) the detailed effects of the Marshall Plan on specific countries

(D) other successful economic recovery programs employed throughout history

(E) how George C. Marshall became the U.S. Secretary of State

IF YOU FINISH BEFORE TIME IS CALLED, YOU MAY CHECK YOUR WORK ON THIS SECTION ONLY. DO NOT TURN TO ANY OTHER SECTION IN THE TEST. **STOP**

SECTION 3
60 Questions

This section includes two question types: synonyms and analogies. There are directions and an example question for each type.

Synonyms

Each Synonym question consists of one word with five words or phrases as answer choices. Choose the one word or phrase that is most similar in meaning to the word in capital letters.

Sample Question:

1. HAPPY:

   (A) sad

   (B) mad

   (C) glad

   (D) bad

   (E) pad   Ⓐ Ⓑ ● Ⓓ Ⓔ

---

1. HARSH:

   (A) cold

   (B) angry

   (C) poor

   (D) useless

   (E) severe

2. INDICATE:

   (A) meet with

   (B) look at

   (C) help with

   (D) point out

   (E) search for

3. BLEAK:

   (A) unknown

   (B) quiet

   (C) cheerless

   (D) trembling

   (E) timid

4. SECURE:

   (A) unseen

   (B) aware

   (C) secret

   (D) safe

   (E) knotty

GO ON TO THE NEXT PAGE. ▶ ▶ ▶

5. ALIEN:

   (A) strange

   (B) futile

   (C) valuable

   (D) brutal

   (E) unclear

6. CHRONIC:

   (A) persistent

   (B) difficult

   (C) doubtful

   (D) legal

   (E) elaborate

7. QUENCH:

   (A) complete

   (B) compare

   (C) demean

   (D) satisfy

   (E) withdraw

8. INTENSE:

   (A) frozen

   (B) extreme

   (C) long

   (D) limited

   (E) essential

9. RANSACK:

   (A) search thoroughly

   (B) act quickly

   (C) cover completely

   (D) make secure

   (E) denounce publicly

10. SUMMIT:

    (A) plateau

    (B) landscape

    (C) slope

    (D) island

    (E) peak

11. TUMULT:

    (A) annoyance

    (B) commotion

    (C) insignificance

    (D) disagreement

    (E) blockage

12. MIMIC:

    (A) surrender

    (B) imitate

    (C) cure

    (D) limit

    (E) analyze

13. ANTIDOTE:

    (A) fantasy

    (B) remedy

    (C) substitute

    (D) award

    (E) decoration

14. SOLITARY:

    (A) mindful

    (B) careless

    (C) friendly

    (D) alone

    (E) troubled

GO ON TO THE NEXT PAGE. ▶ ▶ ▶

15. CAMOUFLAGE:

    (A) obstacle

    (B) range

    (C) emergency

    (D) disguise

    (E) amount

16. EXPEL:

    (A) finish off

    (B) teach

    (C) question

    (D) scold

    (E) cast out

17. LUNGE:

    (A) pursue

    (B) turn

    (C) thrust

    (D) restore

    (E) startle

18. BREVITY:

    (A) ambition

    (B) consistency

    (C) conflict

    (D) imagination

    (E) shortness

19. MARVEL:

    (A) discard

    (B) usurp

    (C) confuse

    (D) point

    (E) wonder

20. CANDOR:

    (A) majesty

    (B) daring

    (C) honesty

    (D) perception

    (E) fatigue

21. CONVENE:

    (A) clarify

    (B) serve

    (C) assemble

    (D) elect

    (E) dignify

22. CATASTROPHE:

    (A) illusion

    (B) disaster

    (C) indication

    (D) warning

    (E) estimate

23. GREGARIOUS:

    (A) sloppy

    (B) sociable

    (C) happy

    (D) intelligent

    (E) talented

24. DEXTERITY:

    (A) secrecy

    (B) equality

    (C) reserve

    (D) nimbleness

    (E) determination

GO ON TO THE NEXT PAGE. ▶ ▶ ▶

25. IMMINENT:

    (A) intense

    (B) impressive

    (C) proper

    (D) observable

    (E) forthcoming

26. ANIMOSITY:

    (A) doubt

    (B) hatred

    (C) sadness

    (D) illness

    (E) guilt

27. AMEND:

    (A) create

    (B) address

    (C) observe

    (D) exclude

    (E) improve

28. DESPONDENT:

    (A) depressed

    (B) unintended

    (C) artificial

    (D) literary

    (E) unconcerned

29. UNFLINCHING:

    (A) uncommitted

    (B) distinct

    (C) uncompromising

    (D) transitory

    (E) invalid

30. REPUDIATE:

    (A) renounce

    (B) impede

    (C) provoke

    (D) divert

    (E) submit

GO ON TO THE NEXT PAGE. ▶ ▶ ▶

Analogies

Each Analogy question asks you to determine the relationship between two words. Choose the answer choice that best completes the meaning of the sentence.

Sample Question:

> 1. Rain is to wet as
>
>   (A) sun is to dark
>
>   (B) cloud is to water
>
>   (C) cold is to ice
>
>   (D) sleep is to tired
>
>   (E) heat is to dry   Ⓐ Ⓑ Ⓒ Ⓓ ●

Choice (E) is the best answer because heat causes things to be dry just like rain causes things to be wet. Of all the answer choices, (E) states a relationship that is most like the relationship between <u>rain</u> and <u>wet</u>.

---

31. Sun is to solar as

(A) earth is to terrestrial

(B) pond is to marine

(C) ground is to subterranean

(D) tower is to architectural

(E) planet is to lunar

32. Botany is to plants as meteorology is to

(A) weather

(B) flora

(C) health

(D) language

(E) style

33. Hammer is to nail as

(A) axe is to wood

(B) lathe is to molding

(C) chisel is to marble

(D) nut is to bolt

(E) screwdriver is to screw

34. Joke is to laughter as spark is to

(A) wildfire

(B) bright

(C) dry

(D) dangerous

(E) success

35. Human is to primate as

(A) kangaroo is to vegetarian

(B) snake is to reptile

(C) disease is to bacterium

(D) bird is to amphibian

(E) dog is to pet

36. Tremor is to earthquake as

(A) eye is to hurricane

(B) desert is to sandstorm

(C) faucet is to deluge

(D) wind is to tornado

(E) flood is to lake

GO ON TO THE NEXT PAGE. ▶ ▶ ▶

37. Amusing is to uproarious as

    (A) silly is to serious

    (B) dead is to immortal

    (C) interesting is to mesmerizing

    (D) humorous is to dull

    (E) worthless is to valuable

38. Fickle is to steadfast as tempestuous is to

    (A) worth

    (B) open

    (C) inspiration

    (D) peace

    (E) ire

39. School is to fish as

    (A) fin is to shark

    (B) library is to student

    (C) flock is to bird

    (D) leg is to frog

    (E) college is to mascot

40. Cartographer is to map as chef is to

    (A) flower

    (B) silverware

    (C) table

    (D) meal

    (E) ingredient

41. Throne is to monarch as

    (A) miter is to pope

    (B) bench is to judge

    (C) lobby is to doorman

    (D) armchair is to general

    (E) ship is to captain

42. Canal is to river as

    (A) boat is to driftwood

    (B) puddle is to lake

    (C) hammer is to mallet

    (D) mine is to cavern

    (E) telephone is to computer

43. Milk is to sour as bread is to

    (A) bent

    (B) stale

    (C) folded

    (D) baked

    (E) hot

44. Ore is to mine as

    (A) apple is to peel

    (B) water is to purify

    (C) batter is to stir

    (D) grain is to plant

    (E) oil is to drill

45. Weight is to scale as

    (A) distance is to speedometer

    (B) number is to slide rule

    (C) length is to thermometer

    (D) reading is to gauge

    (E) altitude is to altimeter

46. Porcupine is to quill as

    (A) bat is to wing

    (B) horse is to tail

    (C) skunk is to odor

    (D) oyster is to pearl

    (E) tiger is to stripe

GO ON TO THE NEXT PAGE. ▶ ▶ ▶

47. Jar is to contain as pillar is to
    (A) stand
    (B) ascend
    (C) prepare
    (D) support
    (E) swing

48. Irrigate is to dry as
    (A) soften is to uneven
    (B) smooth is to coarse
    (C) purify is to distasteful
    (D) depend is to supportive
    (E) ferment is to salty

49. Electricity is to wire as
    (A) sound is to radio
    (B) water is to aqueduct
    (C) music is to instrument
    (D) light is to bulb
    (E) river is to bank

50. Contempt is to sneer as
    (A) shame is to shrug
    (B) anger is to laugh
    (C) enjoyment is to groan
    (D) agreement is to grimace
    (E) displeasure is to frown

51. Building is to foundation as plant is to
    (A) seed
    (B) stem
    (C) primer
    (D) floor
    (E) root

52. Nose is to olfactory as ear is to
    (A) beautiful
    (B) edible
    (C) auditory
    (D) raspy
    (E) allergic

53. Irk is to soothing as support is to
    (A) conciliating
    (B) elevating
    (C) undermining
    (D) annoying
    (E) vilifying

54. Illegible is to read as
    (A) invisible is to see
    (B) illegal is to act
    (C) broken is to fix
    (D) irreparable is to break
    (E) intense is to strain

55. Tact is to diplomat as
    (A) parsimony is to philanthropist
    (B) agility is to gymnast
    (C) vulnerability is to victim
    (D) training is to physician
    (E) bias is to judge

56. Ravenous is to hunger as
    (A) pliable is to obstinacy
    (B) agitated is to placidity
    (C) concerned is to apathy
    (D) smart is to tenacity
    (E) furious is to indignation

GO ON TO THE NEXT PAGE. ▶ ▶ ▶

57. Amplify is to sound as bolster is to

   (A) touch

   (B) courage

   (C) insomnia

   (D) light

   (E) silence

58. Auditorium is to lecture as

   (A) theater is to concert

   (B) attic is to storage

   (C) temple is to religion

   (D) cafeteria is to food

   (E) target is to arrow

59. Philanthropic is to benevolence as

   (A) smooth is to surface

   (B) ostentatious is to reserve

   (C) miserly is to stinginess

   (D) devout is to malice

   (E) realistic is to plan

60. Spurious is to authenticity as

   (A) lavish is to expense

   (B) abject is to subjectivity

   (C) affluent is to character

   (D) laughable is to seriousness

   (E) totalitarian is to completeness

IF YOU FINISH BEFORE TIME IS CALLED, YOU MAY CHECK YOUR WORK ON THIS SECTION ONLY. DO NOT TURN TO ANY OTHER SECTION IN THE TEST. **STOP**

SECTION 4
25 Questions

Each question has five suggested answers. Solve each question in your head or using the blank space at the right of the page. Then, examine the five choices and select the correct one.

<u>Note</u>: Figures in this section are as accurate as possible EXCEPT when it is stated that a figure is not drawn to scale.

Sample Question:

1. $1 \times 2^2 =$

(A) 1

(B) 2

(C) 3

(D) 4

(E) 5   Ⓐ Ⓑ Ⓒ ● Ⓔ

---

1. Justine bought a comic book at $5 above the cover price. A year later, she sold the book for $9 less than she paid. At what price did Justine sell the book?

(A) $14 below the cover price

(B) $4 below the cover price

(C) The cover price

(D) $4 above the cover price

(E) $14 above the cover price

USE THIS SPACE FOR FIGURING

---

2. How many fewer boxes of cereal were sold in February than in March?

(A) 2

(B) 3

(C) 20

(D) 40

(E) 60

Questions 2–3 are based on the graph.

CEREAL SALES AT STORE X

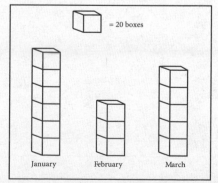

GO ON TO THE NEXT PAGE. ▶ ▶ ▶

3. The number of boxes sold in January was how many times the number of boxes sold in February?

   (A) 2

   (B) $2\frac{1}{2}$

   (C) 3

   (D) 40

   (E) 60

4. The Pirates had 4 times as many losses as it had ties this season. If they won none of their games, which could be the total number of games they played?

   (A) 12

   (B) 15

   (C) 18

   (D) 21

   (E) 26

5. The figure contains rectangles and a triangle. How many different rectangles are there?

   (A) 5

   (B) 7

   (C) 9

   (D) 10

   (E) 12

   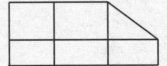

6. Which of the following is NOT less than $\frac{1}{4}$?

   (A) $\frac{2}{9}$

   (B) $\frac{3}{14}$

   (C) $\frac{14}{64}$

   (D) $\frac{19}{70}$

   (E) $\frac{27}{125}$

GO ON TO THE NEXT PAGE. ▶ ▶ ▶

7. In the figure, the sides of triangles *ABC* and *FGH* and squares *BCFE* and *CDGF* are all equal in length. Which of the following is the longest path from *A* to *H*?

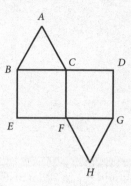

(A) *A – B – C – F – H*

(B) *A – B – E – F – H*

(C) *A – C – D – G – H*

(D) *A – B – E – G – H*

(E) *A – C – F – G – H*

8. If $5\frac{1}{3} \times (14 - x) = 0$, then what does x equal?

(A) 0

(B) 1

(C) $5\frac{1}{3}$

(D) 14

(E) It cannot be determined from the information given.

9. Which of the following is closest to 1.18?

(A) 12

(B) 2.2

(C) 1.9

(D) 1.1

(E) 1

10. If k is greater than 15, then $\frac{1}{3}$ of k must always be

(A) less than 5

(B) equal to 5

(C) greater than 5

(D) equal to 45

(E) less than 45

GO ON TO THE NEXT PAGE. ▶ ▶ ▶

11. Of the following, 35 percent of $38.95 is closest to

    (A) $15.00

    (B) $14.00

    (C) $12.00

    (D) $8.00

    (E) $4.00

---

12. If a factory could make 600 nails every 3 minutes, how long would it take to make 27,000 nails?

    (A) 45 minutes

    (B) 1 hour

    (C) 1 hour, 45 minutes

    (D) 2 hours, 15 minutes

    (E) 3 hours, 15 minutes

---

13. Sally has x dollars and receives $100 for her birthday. She then buys a bicycle that costs $125. How many dollars does Sally have remaining?

    (A) $x + 125$

    (B) $x + 100$

    (C) $x + 25$

    (D) $x - 25$

    (E) $x - 100$

---

14. If $\frac{A + B}{3} = 4$ and A is greater than 1, which of the following could NOT be the value of B?

    (A) -3

    (B) 0

    (C) 1

    (D) 2

    (E) 12

GO ON TO THE NEXT PAGE. ▶ ▶ ▶

15. The average of five numbers is 10. If two of the five numbers are removed, the average of the remaining three numbers is 9. What is the sum of the two numbers that were removed?

    (A) 17

    (B) 18

    (C) 21

    (D) 22

    (E) 23

16. The bottom of the shopping bag shown in the figure is placed flat on a table. Except for the handles, this shopping bag is constructed with rectangular pieces of paper. Which of the following diagrams best represents all the points where the shopping bag touches the table?

    (A)

    (B)

    (C)

    (D)

    (E)

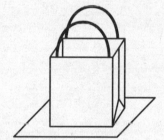

17. The number of students in a certain school is expected to increase from 1,086 students in 2015 to 1,448 students in 2016. What is the expected increase to the nearest percent?

    (A) 20%

    (B) 33%

    (C) 37%

    (D) 40%

    (E) 45%

GO ON TO THE NEXT PAGE. ▶ ▶ ▶

18. In the figure, the distance between W and Y is three times the distance between W and X, and the distance between X and Z is twice the distance between X and Y. If the distance from W to X is 2, how far apart are W and Z?

W   X   Y   Z

   (A) 10

   (B) 8

   (C) 6

   (D) 4

   (E) 2

19. A fence surrounds a rectangular field whose length is 3 times its width. If 240 meters of the fence is used to surround the field, what is the width of the field?

   (A) 30 m

   (B) 40 m

   (C) 60 m

   (D) 80 m

   (E) 90 m

20. Ms. Kirschner receives $50 for every $900 she collects from stock sales. How much does she receive if she collects $18,000 from stock sales?

   (A) $100

   (B) $180

   (C) $1,000

   (D) $1,200

   (E) $1,800

GO ON TO THE NEXT PAGE. ▶ ▶ ▶

21. What is the greatest number of rectangles 4 centimeters wide and 6 centimeters long that can be cut from a square piece of paper with a side of 24 centimeters?

    (A) 2

    (B) 10

    (C) 24

    (D) 36

    (E) 48

22. R is the sum of consecutive integers S and T. If S and T are negative, which of the following is ALWAYS true?

    (A) $R = -4$

    (B) $R = -1$

    (C) R is less than either S or T.

    (D) R is greater than either S or T.

    (E) $R + S + T$ is positive.

23. If 70 percent of k is 10, what is 35 percent of $2k$?

    (A) 7

    (B) 10

    (C) 17

    (D) 35

    (E) 70

24. If the average of seven consecutive whole numbers is 31, what is the smallest number?

    (A) 34

    (B) 31

    (C) 29

    (D) 28

    (E) 27

GO ON TO THE NEXT PAGE. ▶ ▶ ▶

25. Pedro and Beatriz each received a raise of 20 percent. If Pedro now earns $9.60 per hour and Beatriz now earns $10.80 per hour, how much more did Beatriz earn per hour than Pedro before their raises?

(A) $1.00

(B) $1.20

(C) $2.80

(D) $8.00

(E) $9.00

IF YOU FINISH BEFORE TIME IS CALLED, YOU MAY CHECK YOUR WORK ON THIS SECTION ONLY. DO NOT TURN TO ANY OTHER SECTION IN THE TEST.

588   Part 5: SSAT Practice Tests and Explanations

This section includes two question types: synonyms and analogies. There are directions and an example question for each type.

Synonyms

Each Synonym question consists of one word with five words or phrases as answer choices. Choose the one word or phrase that is most similar in meaning to the word in capital letters.

Sample Question:

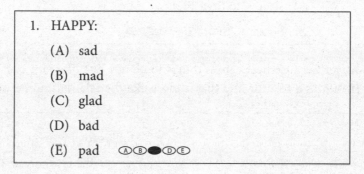

1. HAPPY:

    (A) sad

    (B) mad

    (C) glad

    (D) bad

    (E) pad

1. INDUSTRY:

    (A) element

    (B) accusation

    (C) diligence

    (D) phobia

    (E) warehouse

2. IMMINENT:

    (A) impenetrable

    (B) impossible

    (C) immature

    (D) implicated

    (E) impending

3. ADAGE:

    (A) permission

    (B) disdain

    (C) humor

    (D) prevention

    (E) proverb

GO ON TO THE NEXT PAGE. ▶ ▶ ▶

Analogies

Each Analogy question asks you to determine the relationship between two words. Choose the answer choice that best completes the meaning of the sentence.

Sample Question:

1. Rain is to wet as

    (A) sun is to dark

    (B) cloud is to water

    (C) cold is to ice

    (D) sleep is to tired

    (E) heat is to dry

Choice (E) is the best answer because heat causes things to be dry just like rain causes things to be wet. Of all the answer choices, (E) states a relationship that is most like the relationship between <u>rain</u> and <u>wet</u>.

---

4. Levee is to river as

    (A) sail is to boat

    (B) bridge is to truck

    (C) train is to track

    (D) path is to forest

    (E) shoulder is to road

5. Fan is to air as heart is to

    (A) power

    (B) blood

    (C) heat

    (D) lung

    (E) wind

6. Quill is to porcupine as

    (A) needle is to thread

    (B) wing is to duck

    (C) pouch is to kangaroo

    (D) scent is to skunk

    (E) tail is to pig

GO ON TO THE NEXT PAGE. ▶ ▶ ▶

Read each passage and answer the related questions. For each question, use the passage to decide which one of the choices best answers the question.

Animals that use coloring to safeguard themselves from predators are said to have "protective coloration." One common type of protective coloration is called cryptic resemblance, in which an animal adapts in color, shape, and behavior in order to blend into its environment. The camouflage of the pale green tree frog is a good example of cryptic resemblance. The tree frog blends so

Line 5 perfectly into its surroundings that, when it sits motionless, it is all but invisible against a background of leaves.

Many animals change their protective pigmentation with the seasons. The caribou sheds its brown coat in winter, replacing it with white fur. The stoat, a member of the weasel family, is known as the ermine in winter, when its brown fur changes to the white fur prized by royalty. The

10 chameleon, even more versatile, changes color in just a few minutes to match whatever surface it happens to be lying on or clinging to. Some animals use protective coloration not for camouflage but to stand out against their surroundings. The skunk's brilliant white stripe is meant to be seen, as a warning to predators to avoid the animal's stink. Similarly, the hedgehog uses its "salt and pepper" look to loudly announce its identity, since it depends on its evil stench and unpleasant texture to

15 make it unpalatable to the predators around it.

7. The author uses the caribou and the stoat as examples of animals that

(A) change their color according to the time of year

(B) are protected by disruptive coloring

(C) possess valuable white fur

(D) have prominent markings to warn predators

(E) protect themselves by constantly changing their coloring

8. This passage deals primarily with

(A) how animals blend into their surroundings

(B) several types of protective coloration

(C) a contrast between the tree frog, the zebra, the caribou, and the skunk

(D) a description of predators in the animal kingdom

(E) the difference between cryptic resemblance and disruptive coloring

9. The feature of the chameleon discussed in this passage is its ability to

(A) camouflage itself despite frequent changes in location

(B) cling to surfaces that are hidden from attackers

(C) adapt easily to seasonal changes

(D) use disruptive coloring to confuse predators

(E) change the colors of surfaces it is resting on

GO ON TO THE NEXT PAGE. ▶ ▶ ▶

10. It can be inferred that which of the following animals employs cryptic resemblance?

    (A) the hedgehog

    (B) the tiger

    (C) the chameleon

    (D) the giraffe

    (E) the skunk

11. The passage suggests that the hedgehog is different from the chameleon primarily in that

    (A) it changes its skin color less frequently

    (B) it makes its presence known to potential predators

    (C) it has fewer predators to avoid

    (D) its predators find it unpleasant to eat

    (E) its skin is almost devoid of color

GO ON TO THE NEXT PAGE. ▶ ▶ ▶

Each question has five suggested answers. Solve each question in your head or using the blank space at the right of the page. Then, examine the five choices and select the correct one.

<u>Note</u>: Figures in this section are as accurate as possible EXCEPT when it is stated that a figure is not drawn to scale.

Sample Question:

1. $1 \times 2^2 =$

    (A) 1

    (B) 2

    (C) 3

    (D) 4

    (E) 5   Ⓐ Ⓑ Ⓒ ● Ⓔ

12. The figure shown is a photograph of part of the ocean. At the center of this photograph is a small boat with an audio transmitter. The transmitter has a range of 15 meters in any direction. If the part of the ocean in the photograph is 60 meters long and 60 meters wide, which of the following best shows the size and shape of the transmitter's range?

USE THIS SPACE FOR FIGURING

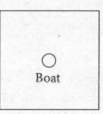

(A)

(B)

(C)

(D)

(E)

GO ON TO THE NEXT PAGE. ▶ ▶ ▶

13. $200 - 7\frac{1}{10} =$

   (A) $192\frac{9}{10}$

   (B) $193\frac{1}{10}$

   (C) $193\frac{9}{10}$

   (D) $194\frac{7}{10}$

   (E) 195

14. The width of a rectangle is one-third of its length. If the length is 12, what is its perimeter?

   (A) 3

   (B) 4

   (C) 16

   (D) 24

   (E) 32

15. In the figure, the days with thunderstorms make up what fraction of the days in this forecast?

   (A) $\frac{1}{6}$

   (B) $\frac{1}{5}$

   (C) $\frac{1}{4}$

   (D) $\frac{1}{3}$

   (E) $\frac{1}{2}$

SIX-DAY WEATHER FORECAST

Mon.	Tues.	Wed.	Thurs.	Fri.	Sat.
☀	☀	⚡	☀	⚡	☀

☀ clear

⚡ thunderstorms

GO ON TO THE NEXT PAGE. ▶ ▶ ▶

16. According to the graph, how many chocolate ice cream cones were sold?

(A) 25

(B) 30

(C) 50

(D) 75

(E) 100

USE THIS SPACE FOR FIGURING

Flavors of 300
Ice Cream Cones Served

IF YOU FINISH BEFORE TIME IS CALLED, YOU MAY CHECK YOUR WORK ON THIS SECTION ONLY. DO NOT TURN TO ANY OTHER SECTION IN THE TEST.

Chapter 24: SSAT Upper/Middle Level Practice Test 2   595

ANSWER KEY

Section 1

1. D	6. A	11. E	16. D	21. C
2. E	7. C	12. B	17. B	22. D
3. D	8. B	13. B	18. C	23. B
4. A	9. C	14. C	19. C	24. B
5. A	10. E	15. A	20. E	25. A

Section 2

1. C	8. D	15. B	22. E	29. B	36. B
2. E	9. C	16. A	23. C	30. D	37. A
3. B	10. D	17. E	24. D	31. E	38. A
4. E	11. B	18. C	25. C	32. C	39. E
5. B	12. B	19. D	26. D	33. A	40. C
6. A	13. A	20. C	27. A	34. A	
7. C	14. B	21. B	28. E	35. D	

Section 3

1. E	11. B	21. C	31. A	41. B	51. E
2. D	12. B	22. B	32. A	42. D	52. C
3. C	13. B	23. B	33. E	43. B	53. C
4. D	14. D	24. D	34. A	44. E	54. A
5. A	15. D	25. E	35. B	45. E	55. B
6. A	16. E	26. B	36. D	46. C	56. E
7. D	17. C	27. E	37. C	47. D	57. B
8. B	18. E	28. A	38. D	48. B	58. A
9. A	19. E	29. C	39. C	49. B	59. C
10. E	20. C	30. A	40. D	50. E	60. D

Section 4

1.	B	6.	D	11.	B	16.	B	21.	C
2.	D	7.	D	12.	D	17.	B	22.	C
3.	A	8.	D	13.	D	18.	A	23.	B
4.	B	9.	D	14.	E	19.	A	24.	D
5.	E	10.	C	15.	E	20.	C	25.	A

Section 5

1.	C	5.	B	9.	A	13.	A
2.	E	6.	D	10.	C	14.	E
3.	E	7.	A	11.	B	15.	D
4.	E	8.	B	12.	B	16.	D

ANSWERS AND EXPLANATIONS

The Writing Sample

Use the sample essay to help you review your own. Be sure to ask an adult who knows you to read your practice essay and give you feedback about how you did.

Prompt (A) Sample Response:

I had thirty minutes to complete the mission. The teacher and the rest of the class were at lunch, so I had just enough time to sneak in to the classroom, search for the drawing, and get back in line before I was missed. As I stood in the hallway looking vigilantly for stray hall monitors, I tried to think about how I got into this mess in the first place.

I have a problem. Most of the time, I can easily focus and stay on track in class. When my mind starts to drift, however, I suddenly look down and notice a paper full of drawings. I have to be careful not to drift off with a test or assignment in front of me, and normally, I'm able to erase any mistakes before they're seen. Today, however, I made a grave mistake.

This morning during second period, I found myself once again unable to concentrate on the lecture by my teacher, Mr. Millowick. So, by the time he was halfway through explaining square roots, I had a paper full of dragons. As usual, I flipped to a new page and tried to refocus. When it came time for us to turn in our homework from last night, my friend came over to ask to borrow a pencil. The bell rang as I handed it to her, so I quickly grabbed my homework and put it on Mr. Millowick's desk before chasing after my friend.

As I unwrapped my lunch, a thought hit me—my homework wasn't in my binder, it was in my backpack. A flood of terror swept over me as I pictured Mr. Millowick giving me a 0 for homework and showing my dragons to all of the other teachers after school that day. I quickly asked to use the restroom and turned the corner as quickly as possible.

I was in luck. No teachers, no hall monitors; a quick peek through the window showed a quiet, empty classroom. I snuck carefully into the room and shifted through the stack of homework papers. There it was! "You're coming with me," I whispered, shoving the drawing into my pocket. I took one last look around the room. Nobody had seen me. All I had to do now was make it back before anyone noticed where I'd gone.

Prompt (B) Sample Response:

History is my favorite subject. I love reading about other times and thinking what it must be like to have lived then. When we studied the American Revolution, I remembered my family's visit to Colonial Williamsburg, where I imagined I was making candles, bringing water in from the well, and cooking over the open fire just as women did in those times. I imagined what it must have been like to live during a war without TV or radio to know what was happening. I thought about how frightening it must have been to hear a knock on the door, and not know if it was an American or a British soldier.

Imagining myself in the same position as people in the historical situations we study helps me to appreciate their courage and contributions. The founders of our country faced death if captured by the British. Anyone who helped American soldiers could be imprisoned. When I imagine myself in that colonial cabin, under those historical conditions, I stand in awe of what the founders did to let us live as an independent nation today.

My visit to the Gettysburg battleground was similarly moving. From the road, it just looks like a big open field. It doesn't seem very impressive at all. As you wander through the battlefield, though, something changes. About 150 years ago, America was torn apart by civil war. As that reality dawned on me, I began to think how terrible it would be to see brother pitted against brother, or father against son. The enormous loss of life at Gettysburg is a grim reminder that war should be a last, desperate resort for all nations.

Studying history helps me to better understand what is happening in the world today. When I hear about revolutions in other countries, I think of our American Revolution. Our revolution brought us freedom and independence from control by another country. When I hear about civil wars and uprisings, I think of the horrors of Gettysburg. Although the media tends to emphasize how different nations are, I think that every decent citizen in every country is working for the same things.

Section 1

1. D

With a perimeter of 30 and 5 sides of equal length, the length of one side is $\frac{30}{5}$, or 6. Choice (D) is correct.

2. E

There were a total of 17 customers who bought caramel candy. Subtract the 4 customers who bought both, and you are left with the 13 customers who bought only caramel. Choice (E) is correct.

3. D

There can only be whole balls in the bag, so the number of colors in the bag must be a factor of 24. This means that the correct answer will NOT be a factor of 24. Choice (D) is correct because 24 does not end in 0 or 5 and is not divisible by 5.

4. A

Be sure to follow the order of operations. First, parentheses. There is a negative one-fourth being taken to the third power. Since the third power is odd, the result will be a negative number, and you can eliminate choices A and B. Cubing a number is the same as multiplying it by itself three times: $\left(-\frac{1}{4}\right) \times \left(-\frac{1}{4}\right) \times \left(-\frac{1}{4}\right)$. To multiply fractions, multiply the numerators and the denominators straight across: $-\frac{1 \times 1 \times 1}{4 \times 4 \times 4} = -\frac{1}{64}$. Choice (A) is correct.

5. A

Rotating all the way around a circle equals 360 degrees. Movies take up 60 degrees of that 360 degrees, which is equal to one-sixth of the pie chart. Susan spent about one-sixth of 12 hours, or 2 hours, watching movies. Choice (A) is correct.

6. A

To solve for R, multiply both sides of the equation by 2; hence, $R = 32$. Plug 32 for R into the expression $\frac{3}{4}R$, and you find that $\frac{3}{4}R = \frac{3}{4} \times 32 = 24$. Choice (A) is correct.

7. C

The fraction $\frac{1}{4}$ has a decimal value of 0.25; this means you can rule out Choices B, D, and E. If you round 59 to the nearest ten, you end up with 0.25 × 60; indeed, 59 is much closer to 60 than to 50, so choice (C) is correct.

8. B

There is no calculation necessary on this problem. Three of the five points lie on the horizontal $260,000 line, and the only other two points are the identical distance above and below the line. Thus, $260,000 is the correct answer. Choice (B) is correct.

9. C

These questions look complicated but can be answered quickly and easily. Simply plug in $u = 5$ and $v = 5$:

$5\phi5 = 5 - \left(1 - \frac{1}{5}\right) = 5 - \frac{4}{5} = 4\frac{1}{5}$. Choice (C) is correct.

10. E

Answer this question using the same process as the first one in this set. This time, however, you will need to do a little more algebra. When $u = a$, $v = 3$, and $a\phi3 = 4\frac{1}{3}$, you have $a - \left(1 - \frac{1}{3}\right) = 4\frac{1}{3}$. Solve to find $a = 5$. Choice (E) is correct.

11. E

Call the unknown number x and translate the information in the question into math. Remember that *of* means "times." Translate twenty percent of 64 into $\frac{20}{100}(64)$ and 5 percent of what number into $\frac{5}{100}x$. Finally, set these two expressions equal to each other and solve for x:

$$\frac{20}{100} \times 64 = \frac{5}{100} \times x$$

$$\frac{1}{5} \times 64 = \frac{1}{20} \times x$$

$$20 \times \frac{1}{5} \times 64 = 20 \times \frac{1}{20} \times x$$

$$4 \times 64 = x$$

$$x = 256$$

Choice (E) is correct.

12. B

The minimum number of fish Andy could have caught was 36, or 1 more than Rico caught. Use the average formula, average $= \frac{\text{sum of the terms}}{\text{number of terms}}$. The sum of the terms is 36, and the number of terms (fishing trips) is 4. Andy must have caught an average of at least $\frac{36}{4} = 9$ fish per trip. Choice (B) is correct.

13. B

You need to set up an equation here. You know all the boys earned the same amount per hour and that they worked $4 + 6 + 8 = 18$ hours altogether, the hourly rate is $108 \div 18 = \$6$ per hour. Lee worked 8 hours, so he earned $8 \times \$6 = \$48$. Choice (B) is correct.

14. C

Johnny has already picked 200 apples in 2.5 hours. He must pick an additional $600 - 200 = 400$ apples. Call the number of additional hours that Johnny must spend picking apples h. To find h, set up a ratio and solve for x: $\dfrac{200 \text{ apples}}{2.5 \text{ hours}} = \dfrac{400 \text{ apples}}{h \text{ hours}}$. Because the numerator of the fraction on the right is equal to twice the numerator of the fraction on the left, the denominator of the fraction on the right must also be equal to twice the denominator of the fraction on the left. This means that $h = 2 \times 2.5 = 5$. Johnny must work an additional 5 hours, so the latest time that he can begin picking apples again is 5 hours earlier than 7:15 p.m., or 2:15 p.m. Choice (C) is correct.

15. A

Translate the English into math and set up an equation: $8W = 0.88$. Isolate the W by dividing each side by 8: $W = \dfrac{0.88}{8} = 0.11$. Choice (A) is correct.

16. D

The diagram shows that the legs of two sides of the triangle are equal. This means the triangle is an isosceles triangle and the angles opposite the equal sides must be equal. The left base angle is 50 degrees, so the right base angle must also be 50 degrees. There are 180 degrees in a triangle, so we can find r by subtracting $180 - 50 - 50 = 80$ degrees. Choice (D) is correct.

17. B

To determine how many times greater the 2016 income was than the 1995 income, divide the 2016 income by the 1995 income. This gives you the fraction $\dfrac{485 \text{ billion}}{83 \text{ billion}}$. Round this fraction to $\dfrac{480}{80}$ billion to make it easier to divide without a calculator: $\dfrac{480}{80} = 6$. This means the company's income was about 6 times greater in 2016 than in 1995. Choice (B) is correct.

18. C

The correct answer choice, once 2 is subtracted from it, must be a multiple of 5. A number is a multiple of 5 only if its ones digit is a 5 or a 0. Only choice (C) can have 2 subtracted from it and be a multiple of 5. Choice (C) is correct.

19. C

Recall Kaplan's tip for these types of question: a figure can be drawn without lifting the pencil or retracing if there are exactly 0 or 2 points where an odd number of lines intersect. Choice (C) has zero points where an odd number of lines intersect; all of the intersection points have four lines. Choice (C) is correct.

20. E

Pick 100 as the initial population of Country X. The increase for the first year was $\dfrac{10}{100}$ of $100 = 10$, and the total at the end of the first year was $100\% + 10\% = 100 + 10$ people. The increase for the second year was $\dfrac{10}{100}$ of $110 = 11$, so the total at the end of the second year was $110 + 11 = 121$ people. The population increased from 100 to 121 over the two-year period, so the increase in the population was $\dfrac{121 - 100}{100} \times 100\% = \dfrac{21}{100} \times 100\% = 21\%$. Choice (E) is correct.

21. C

The value of z is given to you in terms of y; you need to multiply this value by 2 and add 1:

$$2z + 1 = 2(y + 2) + 1$$
$$= 2y + 4 + 1$$
$$= 2y + 5$$

Choice (C) is correct.

22. D

Picking Numbers for *x* and *y* is a foolproof method for solving this problem. Pick a positive fraction for *x* that is less than 1, such as $\frac{1}{2}$. Then, pick a positive value for *y* that is greater than *x*, which in this case means that the *y* that you pick must also be greater than $\frac{1}{2}$. Remember, the question says that *y* is greater than *x*, and the numbers you pick must always be consistent with the question stem. Try picking 1 for *y*:

Choice A: $\dfrac{\frac{1}{1}}{\frac{1}{2}} = 1 \times 2 = 2$

Choice B: $\dfrac{\frac{1}{2}}{\frac{1}{1}} = \frac{1}{2}$

Choice C: $\frac{1}{2} \times 2 = 1$

Choice (D): $\dfrac{1}{\frac{1}{2} - 1} = \dfrac{1}{-\frac{1}{2}} = 1 \times -2 = -2$

With these values, it's clear that choice (D) is correct. Upon further examining choice (D), note that the denominator, $x - y$, has a larger positive number *y* subtracted from a smaller positive number *x*. This means that $x - y$ will always be negative and $\frac{1}{x-y}$ will also always be negative.

23. B

If 6 people can sit at each of *x* tables and 5 people can sit at each of *y* tables, then the maximum number of people that may be seated is $6x + 5y$. This matches choice (B).

24. B

Draw 3 squares: big, bigger, and biggest. Let the side of the middle fabric piece be 9. The side of the largest fabric piece must be three times this, or 27. Likewise, the side of the smallest square piece must be 3. Each side of the largest square is 3 times larger than the side of the smallest square, so the area of the largest piece will be $3 \times 3 = 9$ times larger than the area of the smallest square. The smallest square piece has an area of $3 \times 3 = 9$ square units, so the largest square piece has an area of $9 \times 9 = 81$ square units. Choice (B) is correct.

25. A

Begin by determining how many gallons of gas it takes to make the 18 trips: $\frac{3}{4}$ gallons per trip $\times$ 18 trips = 13.5 gallons. If there are 9 gallons in one tank, Mr. Dali will need $\frac{13.5}{9} = 1.5$ tanks of gas. Choice (A) is correct.

Section 2

Scott Joplin Passage

First up is a brief history passage about Scott Joplin, a composer best known for his ragtime music. Don't try to absorb all the details, even in a brief passage like this. Just get a feel for the Big Idea, which is that Joplin was instrumental in developing the ragtime genre but wasn't recognized as a serious composer until almost 60 years after his death.

1.   C

Lines 1–2 note that Joplin composed 41 piano pieces known as "rags," and this is the only time the word is used in the passage. Choice (C), then, must be correct. Choice E is tempting, but the genre or style of songs Joplin invented is described as "ragtime," not "rag." Choice A's "operatic" is incorrect; Joplin's *Treemonisha* was his only opera. Choices B and D are incorrect because ragtime is never described as "dance" music or as being played by "marching bands."

2.   E

Only choice (E) has the proper scope here. Choices A and B focus too narrowly on details. It was Joplin's "rhythmic diversity" (line 4), not his stylistic diversity, choice C, that distinguished his composing. The passage doesn't say how Joplin finally won the Pulitzer, so choice D is incorrect.

3.   B

The word "choppy" in line 4 is meant to emphasize the jerky nature of Joplin's music, similar to how a chef might chop vegetables. This is an example of imagery. Choice (B) is correct. Choice A is incorrect because synecdoche is when a part is used to represent a whole (or vice versa), and this doesn't appropriately describe the rhythm of Joplin's music. Choice C is incorrect because anaphora is related to the repetition of words, which isn't happening here. Choice D is incorrect because onomatopoeia describes words that are named by how they sound, such as buzz or sizzle. Choice E is incorrect because irony is the contrast between what's stated or assumed and what actually happens.

4. E

In lines 2–3, the author discusses Joplin's "significant creative contribution" to music, his great popularity, and "the praise he deserved" and "at last" received. Thus, choice (E) best sums up the author's tone toward Joplin. Choices A, C, and D are all negative, which doesn't fit the passage. Choice B isn't negative, but it implies something humorous and the author is more focused on Joplin's accomplishments than his antics.

5. B

Line 5 states that Joplin was instrumental in developing ragtime "as a genre, a unique musical form." Therefore, choice (B) is the correct inference: a genre is a distinct category or style. While ragtime is an example of a musical genre, a genre is not an example of a particular type of ragtime, choice A. There's no evidence that Joplin coined the term *genre,* choice C. Choices D and E are incorrect because the word *genre* can be used in many different circumstances, not just Joplin's period or as an early form of "rag."

6. A

Line 7 states that "he was not considered a serious composer during his lifetime," even though his "Maple Leaf Rag" was "the most popular piano rag of the time" (lines 5–6). That says his work was liked but people didn't appreciate it as serious music. The last sentence says he wasn't celebrated until 59 years after he died. Choice (A) is correct. Choice B is out of scope of the passage; the author never discusses Joplin's circumstances when he died. Choice C is incorrect because line 3 says he made a "contribution" to ragtime; he didn't invent it. Choices D and E are extreme; you don't know that all of his piano pieces were rags or the exact process Joplin took to popularize ragtime.

Bird Courtship Passage

Next up is a science passage about the courtship procedures and "identification checks" used by birds during courtship and mating. Paragraph 1 introduces the topic, paragraph 2 details the roles of plumage and aggressive behavior, and paragraph 3 discusses the role of sounds in the birds' courting and mating rituals.

7. C

This Inference question is answered in the opening paragraph. The author states that the bird's identification and courtship procedures are important "because if birds of different species mate, any offspring" will be sterile and have a low chance for survival. Thus, the procedures are important because they help a bird find a mate of its own species Choice (C) is correct. Choice B focuses too narrowly on a detail from paragraph 2.

8. D

The author does describe the various behaviors of the birds, including their aggressiveness and friendliness, throughout the passage using a neutral, impartial tone. This matches choice (D). Choices A, B, and C might be tempting if you're thinking about the behavior of the bird, but none of these choices describe the author's tone when describing courtship. Choice E would be a better fit if the author focused on one particular set of birds or used language that made them more like humans. However, this isn't the case, so choice E is incorrect.

9. C

This Supporting Ideas question focuses on the last sentence of paragraph 2. There you learn that whooping cranes "perform wonderfully elaborate courtship dances." This means the whooping crane is an example of a bird that behaves in an unusual, noteworthy way during courtship. Choice (C) is correct. Choices B, D, and E incorrectly mention other details from paragraph 2— plumage, reversed roles, and aggressiveness.

10. D

The answer here is taken from the last sentence of paragraph 1. If birds of different species mate, "any offspring will usually be sterile or badly adapted to their surroundings." This point is restated in choice (D). Choice B is the opposite of the correct choice. Choice A, the frequency of interspecies mating, is not mentioned in the passage, but it must happen occasionally, contrary to choice E, or the author wouldn't warn against its dangers. The idea of a new species evolving, choice C, is not discussed.

11. B

This time the Main Idea question comes near the end of the set. The first paragraph tells you that the passage is about the various courtship behaviors and "identification checks" used by birds, which makes choice (B) correct. Choices A and E raise issues not debated in the passage. Choices C and D focus too narrowly on details.

12. B

Think about where you would most likely find this passage. The passage discusses how birds of the same species identify one another in order to mate, not how you would identify birds, so choice (B) is correct. Choices A and E are incorrect because the passage does not talk about identifying birds or endangered birds. Choices C and D are incorrect because the passage contains nothing personal or fictional, just facts.

Native American Passage

This passage is about the 1,500 Native American languages that have been discovered by linguists. The Main Idea here is simple: a pioneering linguist originally divided these 1,500 languages into six main groups, and while a recent group of scholars thinks they can all be divided into three broader groups, other scholars disagree with this new theory.

13. A

This passage focuses on Native American languages, so you can eliminate choices C and E. Choice B leaves out the recent debate over the revised classification of Native American languages into three groups. Choice D focuses too narrowly on a detail from paragraph 2. Only choice (A) describes the focus on classification and is therefore correct.

14. B

According to paragraph 2, scholars believe Native American languages can be classified into only three families because of "similarities and differences among words and sounds." Choice (B) is correct. Choice A distorts a detail from paragraph 1. Choice C is the argument of those who think Native American languages can't be classified into three families. Choice D is too broad, and Choice E is out of scope for the passage.

15. B

Where would you be likely to come upon this passage? In a discussion of Native American languages or a linguistics textbook. Choice (B) is correct. Choices A, C, and D are incorrect because there's nothing either personal or fictional in the text; it's just a series of factual statements. While Sapir pioneered the field of Native American linguistics, the passage doesn't contain any significant biographical information about his life, so choice E is incorrect.

16. A

Why is classifying Native American languages controversial? As noted in paragraph 2, those who group them into three families have "no doubt about the validity" of their theory. However, "the vast majority of linguists" argue that "linguistic science has not yet advanced far enough" to group 1,500 languages into only three families. So the controversy exists because scholars do not yet agree on how to classify languages. Choice (A) is correct. Choice B is a point argued by linguists who think Native American languages might never be properly grouped into families, but it's not the source of the controversy. You don't know when the field of linguistics was founded, but even though, as paragraph 2 points out, it hasn't "advanced far enough," it is not a "very new" field, so choice C is incorrect. There is no evidence for choices D and E.

17. E

Paragraph 1 states that Sapir classified Native American languages into six families. Choice (E) is correct. None of the other questions is answered in the passage.

18. C

Look at the last sentence in which "extent" appears. The author says the languages have "diverged" so much that it would be impossible to classify them into three linguistic families. Therefore, the answer needs to mean something close to "wide." Choice (C) is correct. Choice A is the opposite of something wide open. Choices B and D change the scope by referring to a new idea, and choice E doesn't specifically address the divergence of the different languages.

Poetry Passage

This is a famous poem by Emily Dickinson. The first stanza creates a metaphor of hope as a bird that lives inside us and never stops singing. The second stanza says that the bird of hope sings even in bad weather (i.e., bad times). In the final stanza, the poet claims that, while she has heard the bird of hope singing in distant places, "It never asked a crumb of me."

19. D

Hope is "the thing with feathers" in stanza 1 and "the little bird" in stanza 2. Choice (D) is correct. Choices A, B, and C are trials and dangers that the bird/hope faces, while choice E is what the bird sings.

20. C

Paraphrase the final stanza: "I've heard the bird of hope in far-off places, and it never asked me for anything." This points to choice (C) as correct. Choice A is incorrect because the poem says nothing about a world without hope or about preserving hope at all costs. Choice B summarizes the second stanza, not the third. Choice D takes the poem literally to the point of absurdity; the "crumb" line doesn't mean that the bird is always hungry, but rather that it gives its song of hope freely. Finally, choice E is incorrect because, according to the poet, hope is always present; no great effort is required to make it so.

21. B

Remember you're dealing with metaphor. This poem isn't about a bird; it's comparing hope to a bird that never stops singing. The statement that it "kept so many warm" means that hope has given comfort to a lot of people. Choice (B) is correct. Choices A and C take the poem literally. Choice D is pessimistic where the poet is optimistic about hope, and choice E implies that hope *only* works in the worst of situations. However, the poet is saying that hope is helpful *even* in the worst of situations.

22. E

The poet likens hope to a bird that, thankfully, is always there to help people, never asking anything in return. Her tone is one of gratitude. Choice (E) correct. Choice C is the closest, but "respectful" is too formal/distancing to fit here. Hope in this poem isn't a great person or awesome display of nature; it's a little bird "that perches in the soul." Choices A, B, and D do not reflect the positive tone of the poem.

23. C

Figure out what the poet is saying in the lines "sore" appears in. The poet is saying only the worst of storms could discourage the bird. The only choice that comes close to meaning "worst" is "severe." Choice (C) is correct. Choice A is the most literal definition of the word and doesn't make sense in context. Choice B conveys the correct idea, but there isn't enough support for a word as extreme as "angry." Choice D is the opposite of a storm that would discourage a bird, and choice E is too literal to fit within this context.

Recycling Passage

The next passage is about recycling, the remaking of waste products and materials for practical purposes. You learn that recycling is now considered a necessity, that it saves money and resources and reduces waste. The author focuses on residential recycling—what private citizens can do to reduce waste.

24. D

The passage is written from the perspective of an individual who believes strongly in the benefits of recycling and wants others to do more. This describes an environmental activist, choice (D). A homeowner, a mayor, and a student are all capable of holding this belief, but the passage does not include support for any of these answers, so choices A, C, and E are incorrect. Choice B may be tempting, but the passage's focus on residential recycling is contrary to what a recycling plant owner would likely write.

25. C

The author believes you should be motivated by the greater good to do more to recycle. This is supported by the author's statement in paragraph 3 that "our increased efforts toward recycling can have a dramatic effect on the future availability of resources and the condition of the environment." Choice (C) is correct. Choice A is easily eliminated: the author notes in paragraph 3 that the individual's role in recycling "has been seriously under emphasized." The first half of choice B is correct (businesses do recycle to save money), but the second half is incorrect (the author doesn't think individuals are motivated to recycle by a sense of the greater good), so choice B is incorrect. Choice D says people shouldn't recycle, which the author would certainly disagree with, and choice E claims that recycling is only the responsibility of businesses, which goes against the thrust of paragraph 2.

26. D

You're looking for the choice that is not an example of recycling, which the author defines in lines 3–4 as "the remaking of waste products and other used materials for practical purposes." Using this definition, choices A, B, and E are easily crossed off as examples of recycling. Choice C involves a second use for empty soda bottles, as does the author's example in lines 4–5. This leaves choice (D): selling jewelry to buy a car is not recycling because the jewelry is not a waste product that's being remade. Choice (D) is correct.

27. A

In the first paragraph, the author argues that recycling is "important…even…necessary" and in the final paragraph that "it is our duty to ourselves and to our fellow human beings." These and similar signals throughout the passage reveal the author's tone as insistent, choice (A). By the same token, choices B, D, and E are easy to eliminate. Choice C may be tempting since the author tells you that the future of humanity is at stake, but choice (A) remains the best choice because, more than being formal, the author is trying to motivate you to do something (recycle).

28. E

Paragraph 3 argues that individuals can and must learn to recycle their waste products. You can predict, then, that the author will go on to suggest one or more ways in which individuals can pitch in to help the recycling effort, a point restated in choice (E). There's no evidence to support choices A and B, and choice C incorrectly suggests the author will return to a detail from the previous paragraph. Choice D doesn't even mention recycling.

29. B

In lines 8–9, the author states that businesses recycle "based primarily on the goal of saving money." You can infer that the author believes that businesses recycle primarily for financial gain. Choice (B) is correct. Choice A is incorrect because the economics of recycling are of greatest interest to businesses, not to the author. Similarly, it cannot be inferred from these lines that the author's knowledge of the financial aspects of recycling is limited, so choice C is incorrect. While choice D is probably true, it can't be inferred from lines 8–9. Finally, choice E is incorrect because the author never discusses the amount of waste produced when recycling.

El Niño Passage

The passage begins with a statement that, although bad weather is usually only an "inconvenience" for us, it can have "disastrous consequences" for communities in other parts of the world. The remainder of the passage describes an example of this disastrous bad weather: El Niño, a change in the Humboldt Current (an ocean current) that disrupts marine life and can thereby threaten villagers on the northwest coast of South America with starvation.

30. D

The Humboldt Current flows off the northwest coast of South America, making choice (D) correct. Each of the other choices contradicts the passage. El Niño occurs only at Christmastime, but the Humboldt Current flows all year long, so choice A is incorrect. The Humboldt Current does fail when El Niño occurs, so choice B is incorrect. The passage does not state the directional flow of the Humboldt Current so you cannot eliminate choice C, but it does state that it is a cold-water current, not a hot-water current, which eliminates choice E.

31. E

The bulk of the passage concerns what happens when the Humboldt Current fails, which makes choice D very tempting, but the Main Idea of the passage is really stated in the first sentence, which notes that changes in weather patterns can dramatically affect the way people live, making choice (E) correct here. Remember, the Humboldt Current and El Niño information is there only to back up this claim by the author. Choices A, B, and C focus on details.

32. C

Here you're looking for the one choice that isn't true. Only choice (C) is not confirmed in the passage. The Humboldt Current carries cold water, not warm; the passage also never states that the current affects "the climate of nearby land masses." Choices A, B, D, and E are all listed in the passage.

33. A

This passage is not about El Niño. El Niño is discussed in order to prove the author's larger point: bad weather can harm communities. This means that choice (A) is correct and choice C is incorrect. Choices B, D, and E are all too specific to cover topics in this passage.

34. A

You are told that bad weather can have a "dramatic effect" (line 4) on these villages, "depriving the villagers of their livelihood" (line 9). The author's attitude toward the villagers, then, is—what? Not condescending, choice C, angry, choice D, or emotional, choice E. Though the author doesn't express undue alarm, you wouldn't say she was simply unconcerned about the villagers, as choice B puts it. No, the author's attitude is best described as sympathetic. The villagers occasionally have this awful problem, and the author expresses concern about it. Choice (A) is correct.

35. D

To answer open-ended Inference questions like this, go through the answer choices one at a time, eliminating incorrect choices based on the passage. Choice A is a distortion; in line 7, the author mentions the dependable supply of food provided by the Humboldt Current, but saying that this current feeds ALL villages goes too far. Choice B is also a distortion; the author states that a chain reaction would be deadly, but species extinction is not discussed. Choice C is out of scope; the author never discusses earthquakes. Choice (D) is correct; in the first sentence, the author states that "in certain, less fortunate parts of the world, a change in weather can have disastrous consequences for an entire society," and line 3 states that this passage is focused on how weather fluctuations impact the coast of South America. Choice E is also out of scope; the impact of normal weather events is not discussed in this passage.

Marshall Plan Passage

This passage is a history passage about the Marshall Plan, an American scheme to help rebuild Europe after World War II. Paragraph 1 sets the scene, explaining that the United States believed that Europe's economic devastation needed to be cured in order to keep it from falling under the domination of the Soviet Union. Paragraph 2 explains that in 1948, U.S. Secretary of State George Marshall instituted the Marshall Plan, which distributed $12 billion among 16 different European countries over the next four years.

36. B

The answer will probably mention the Marshall Plan and how it helped Europe. Choice (B) fits this bill nicely. Choices A and E are way too broad. Choice C describes what happened during World War II that made the Marshall Plan so necessary but says nothing about the Plan itself. Choice D suggests that the passage is about Marshall himself, when the author actually tells you nothing more than Marshall's name and job—Secretary of State.

37. A

The author's tone is not noticeably positive, choice B, or negative, choice E. It betrays no personal feelings, such as insistence, choice C, or anxiety, choice D. Instead, it's objective, so choice (A) is correct.

38. A

Personification is the process of giving non-human animals or objects human-like traits. A scar is most commonly known as the mark left on skin when it is damaged in some way. The author is describing how WWII, an event, damaged Europe, a continent, using a word typically reserved for human injuries. Choice (A) is correct. The words in choices B, C, D, and E are all general words that do not have specific human-like connotations.

39. E

What was the driving force behind the Marshall Plan? Early in paragraph 1, you learn that post-World War II Western Europe was economically devastated and that when tensions between the United States and the Soviet Union escalated, U.S. policymakers felt "substantial financial assistance" (line 3) was needed in Western Europe "to maintain a state of political stability" (line 4). This points to choice (E). None of the other choices draws a correct inference from the passage.

40. C

The first paragraph describes the postwar economic and political problems that the Marshall Plan was intended to solve, and paragraph 2 describes, in general terms, how much money was distributed and how well the plan worked. You can infer, then, that the author will go on to talk about specifics—how the Plan's money was put to work in some or all of the 16 participating countries. This matches choice (C). Choice A incorrectly sees the Cold War, not the Marshall Plan, as the focus of the passage. Choice B goes back in time, to events before the Marshall Plan was ever dreamed up. Other economic recovery plans are never mentioned, so choice D is incorrect, and choice E is also unwarranted.

Section 3

Synonyms

1. E

Harsh means rough or overly demanding. This is a good match for severe. Choice (E) is correct. Be careful not to be tempted by choice B; one can be angry without being harsh.

2. D

Indicate means to show or state, which is similar to point out. Choice (D) is correct.

3. C

Bleak means desolate and barren. This matches cheerless, choice (C).

4. D

Secure means free from danger. This is a good match for safer, so choice (D) is correct.

5. A

Alien means foreign or strange. This is a perfect match for choice (A).

6. A

Chronic means frequently occurring or habitual. This matches persistent, choice (A).

7. D

To quench a thirst means to satisfy it, choice (D).

8. B

Intense means extreme, which is a perfect match for choice (B). Frozen might sound intense to you, but don't think associatively; look for the word that's closest in meaning to the stem word.

9. A

When thieves ransack an apartment, they turn it upside down looking for things to steal. In other words, to ransack is to search thoroughly, choice (A).

10. E

The summit is the top of something, as in the summit of a mountain peak, which makes choice (E) correct.

11. B

A tumult is a loud noise or an uproar. This matches commotion, choice (B).

12. B

To mimic means to copy. Choice (B), imitate, is correct.

13. B

An antidote is a cure. Remedy, choice (B), is a clear match.

14. D

Solitary is the state of being alone, a perfect match for choice (D).

15. D

To camouflage means to hide. This matches choice (D), disguise.

16. E

To expel means to drive out or reject. This matches cast out, choice (E).

17. C

To lunge is to make a sudden forward stride or to leap. A lunge—especially with a weapon—can also be called a thrust, choice (C). To pursue, choice A, means to chase. A pursuit might begin with a lunge, but lunge and pursue are not synonyms. In similar fashion, a lunge may startle someone, choice E, but lunge and startle are not synonyms, either.

18. E

Brevity is the quality of being brief. A short duration, shortness, matches, so choice (E) is correct.

19. E

To marvel is to feel surprise or amazed curiosity. This matches wonder, choice (E).

20. C

Candor is truthfulness. This matches honesty, choice (C). To be daring is to be bold but not necessarily honest, so choice B is a distractor.

21. C

To convene is to meet. That matches assemble, choice (C). The closest distractors, choices B and D, are actions associated with meetings that are convened, but serve and elect are not synonyms for convene.

22. B

A catastrophe is a great misfortune or a terrible occurrence. This matches disaster, choice (B).

23. B

Gregarious means talkative or outgoing. This matches sociable, choice (B).

24. D

Dexterity is mental or physical skill and quickness. The best synonym here is nimbleness, choice (D).

25. E

To say that something is imminent means that it's about to happen. Another word for this is forthcoming, choice (E).

26. B

Animosity is hostility, ill will, or resentment. The best synonym here is hatred, choice (B).

27. E

To amend means to change or alter. This matches improve, choice (E).

28. A

Someone who feels despondent is very sad. Another word for this is depressed, choice (A).

29. C

Unflinching means not flinching or shrinking back from something; it's the quality of being steadfast. The best synonym here is uncompromising, choice (C).

30. A

To repudiate means to cast off, disown, or refuse to have anything to do with. The choice with the closest meaning to repudiate is renounce, choice (A). Choice B is a strong distractor, but to impede is to slow or interfere with someone's progress, and slowing down has a different meaning than refusing.

Analogies

31. A

Choice (A) is correct. This is a Definition Bridge. Anything having to do with the sun is solar. In the same way, anything having to do with the earth is terrestrial. Marine refers to a sea or an ocean, not to a pond. Subterranean refers to what is below the ground, not to the ground itself. Choice E is tempting, but lunar refers to anything having to do with the moon, not planets.

32. A

Choice (A) is correct. This is an Association Bridge. Botany is the study of plants. Similarly, meteorology is the study of weather. Choice B is tempting, but flora is the generic word for plant life or vegetation, not the study of either.

33. E

Choice (E) is correct. This is a Purpose Bridge. You use a hammer to *put in* a nail. In the same way, you use a screwdriver to *put in* a screw.

34. A

Choice (A) is correct. This is a Cause-and-Effect Bridge. A joke causes laughter. A spark causes wildfire.

35. B

Choice (B) is correct. This is a Type/Kind Bridge. A primate is an order of mammals that includes monkeys, apes, and humans. So a human is one type of primate, just as a snake is one type of reptile. Choice E is tempting; a dog is a type of pet, but pet and primate do not have similar enough meanings for this to be a strong fit.

36. D

Choice (D) is correct. This is a Degree Bridge. A tremor is a quivering motion of the earth, and a powerful tremor is called an earthquake. In the same way, wind is a motion of the air, and a tornado is classified by the level of its powerful winds. In choice A, an eye is a part of a hurricane; a hurricane is not a powerful level of its eye. In choice E, a powerful flood would be called a tsunami, not a lake.

37. C

Choice (C) is correct. This is a Definition Bridge. Something tremendously amusing is uproarious; similarly, something tremendously interesting is hypnotic, fascinating, or mesmerizing.

38. D

Choice (D) is correct. This is an Antonym Bridge. Being fickle, or inconstant, is the opposite of steadfastness. In the same way, being tempestuous, or stormy, is the opposite of peacefulness. Ire, choice E, means anger, which is closer to being a synonym than a antonym.

39. C

Choice (C) is correct. This is a Whole/Part Bridge. A school is made up of individual fish, and a flock is made up of individual birds.

40. D

Choice (D) is correct. This is a Function Bridge. A cartographer creates maps, just as a chef creates meals.

41. B

Choice (B) is correct. This is a Association Bridge. A throne is the official chair for a monarch, just as a bench is the official chair for a judge. A miter is the headdress worn by bishops. While an armchair is a place to sit, it isn't the name of an official chair for a general.

42. D

Choice (D) is correct. This is a Degree Bridge. A canal is a man-made river, just as a mine is a man-made cavern.

43. B

Choice (B) is correct. This is an Association Bridge. When milk goes bad, it gets sour; when bread goes bad, it gets stale.

44. E

Choice (E) is correct. This is a Word (noun-verb) Bridge. Ore is mined to bring it up out of the earth, just as oil is drilled to bring it up out of the earth, (E). Grain, choice D, is not planted to bring it up out of the earth, it's harvested.

45. E

Choice (E) is correct. This is a Purpose Bridge. A scale is used to measure weight, just as an altimeter is used to measure altitude. Don't be distracted by choice A; speed, not distance, is measured on a speedometer. A slide rule is used to calculate, not measure, so choice B doesn't fit.

46. C

Choice (C) is correct. This is a Purpose Bridge. A porcupine uses quills to protect itself. In a similar fashion, a skunk uses its odor to protect itself.

47. D

Choice (D) is correct. This is a Function Bridge. The purpose of a jar is to contain, just as the purpose of a pillar is to support.

48. B

Choice (B) is correct. This is a Association Bridge. Irrigate means to flush with liquid. When you irrigate something that is dry, you're trying to make it less dry. When you smooth something that is coarse, you're trying to make it less coarse. Although purifying something might make it less distasteful, the purpose of purifying is to remove the impurities, so choice C does not fit.

49. B

Choice (B) is correct. This is an Association Bridge. Electricity flows through a wire, just as water flows through an aqueduct. Sound is broadcast from a radio, which is a different method of delivery, so choice A does not fit. Choice E is too literal to fit the analogy of the first word pair.

50. E

Choice (E) is correct. This is a Function Bridge. A sneer is used to express contempt. A frown is used to express displeasure.

51. E

Choice (E) is correct. This is a Whole/Part Bridge. The base of a building, the whole, is its foundation, the part. The plant will represent the whole, so the correct answer choice represents the base part of a plant: its root.

52. C

Choice (C) is correct. This is a Purpose Bridge. Olfactory refers to having to do with the sense of smell, and a nose is used to smell. Auditory refers to having to do with a sense of hearing, and an ear is used to hear.

53. C

Choice (C) is correct. This is an Antonym Bridge. Irk means to annoy, disgust, or irritate, so something that irks is definitely not soothing. In the same way, support would not be undermining, or damaging. Choice D seems to fit, as well, but it is possible for support to be annoying, so this would not create a strong relationship between word pairs.

54. A

Choice (A) is correct. This is a Lack Bridge. Something illegible cannot be read, just as something invisible cannot be seen. Something broken is not by definition impossible to fix so choice C does not work.

55. B

Choice (B) is correct. This is an Association Bridge. Tact is sensitivity, or the ability to do or say the correct thing with people. Tact is a useful quality for a diplomat. In the same way, agility is a useful quality for a gymnast.

56. E

Choice (E) is correct. This is a Degree Bridge. Ravenous means extremely hungry. Furious means extremely angry, or indignant. None of the other choices has a first word that's an extreme version of the second word. Don't be distracted by choice D. Someone can be smart, tenacious, both, or neither; the two words do not exist on a spectrum of related ideas.

57. B

Choice (B) is correct. This is a Word (verb-noun) Bridge. To amplify sound is to make it stronger or louder. To bolster something means to strengthen it, and courage is the only option here that can be bolstered.

58. A

Choice (A) is correct. This is a Purpose Bridge. An auditorium is a good location for a lecture. A theater is a good location for a concert. While an attic might be used for storage, choice B, and cafeterias are good locations for food, choice D, these two choices do not focus on the location of an event.

59. C

Choice (C) is correct. This is an Association Bridge. Philanthropic means generous or giving, and benevolence can be described as the quality of generosity. An easier way to say this is, "A philanthropic act is evidence of benevolence." In the same way, a miserly act is evidence of stinginess. Choice B, ostentatious, means showy or extravagant, which is unlikely to be evidence of reserve.

60. D

Choice (D) is correct. This is a Lack Bridge. Spurious is simply a fancy word meaning fake, so something spurious lacks authenticity. Similarly, something laughable lacks seriousness.

Section 4

1. B

Begin with $5 + cover price − $9 and simplify it: cover price − $4 means that it is sold for $4 below the cover price. Choice (B) is correct.

2. D

Note here that each cube = 20 boxes. February has two cubes less than March, so $2(20) = 40$ boxes less. Choice (D) is correct.

3. A

In January, 6 cubes were sold, and in February, 3 cubes were sold. In January, the number of boxes sold was $\frac{6}{3} = 2$ times the number of boxes sold in February. It is not necessary to perform the calculation using the fact that 20 boxes are represented by each cube because this question is only asking you to compare the two months. Choice (A) is correct.

4. B

Let $t =$ the number of ties for the Pirates; keep in mind that x is an integer here. Thus, the Pirates had $4t$ losses. Adding the losses and ties (there were no wins), the number of games the team played was $t + 4t = 5t$. Because the number of ties, t, is an integer, the correct answer choice must be a multiple of 5. Choice (B) is correct.

5. E

In order to make the discussion simpler, the five rectangles that are in the figure to begin with have been labeled.

Systematically count the different rectangles in the figure. There are 5 rectangles in the figure to begin with, which we will call basic rectangles. There are 5 rectangles made up of the basic rectangles: A, B, C, D, and E. There are 5 rectangles made up of 2 basic rectangles: A and B, C and D, D and E, A and C, and B and D. There is 1 rectangle made up of 3 basic rectangles: C, D, and E. Finally, there is 1 rectangle made up of 4 basic rectangles: A, B, C, and D. There are no other rectangles that can be made up of basic rectangles, so there are a total of $5 + 5 + 1 + 1 = 12$ different rectangles in the figure. Choice (E) is correct.

6. D

You are looking for the fraction that is NOT less than $\frac{1}{4}$, so the correct answer will be a fraction that is greater than or equal to $\frac{1}{4}$. Use multiples of 4 to find close, if not exact, equivalents for the denominators:

Choice A: $\frac{2}{9} < \frac{2}{8}$

Choice B: $\frac{3}{14} = \frac{6}{28} < \frac{1}{4}$

Choice C: $\frac{16}{64} \approx \frac{1}{4} = 0.25$

Choice (D): $\frac{1}{(-2) - 4} = -\frac{1}{6}$

Choice E: $\frac{1}{(-2) - 4} = -\frac{1}{6}$

Choice (D) is correct.

7. D

You are told all the sides are equal. Thus, you can set each segment equal to 1 and add before deciding which answer choice has the longest path:

Choice A: $A - B - C - F - H = 1$ (A to B) $+ 1$ (B to C) $+ 1$ (C to F) $+ 1$ (F to H) $= 4$

Choice B: $A - B - E - F - H = 1 + 1 + 1 + 1 = 4$

Choice C: $A - C - D - G - H = 1 + 1 + 1 + 1 = 4$

Choice (D): $A - B - F - G - H = 1 + 1 + 2 + 1 = 5$

Choice E: $A - C - F - G - H = 1 + 1 + 1 + 1 = 4$

The longest path is 5, so choice (D) is correct.

8. D

No lengthy calculation is needed here. In order for a product of numbers to equal 0, at least one of the numbers must equal zero. Because $5\frac{1}{3}$ is not 0, the other factor, $14 - x$, must be equal to 0. So $14 - x = 0$, which means $x = 14$. Choice (D) is correct.

9. D

Since 1.18 has 2 places after the decimal point, you should write each answer choice with 2 places after the decimal point:

Choice A: 12.00 is more than 10 away from 1.18

Choice B: 2.20 is more than 1 away from 1.18

Choice C: 1.90 is more than 0.70 away from 1.18

Choice (D):   1.10 is more than 0.08 away from 1.18

Choice E: 1.00 is more than 0.10 away from 1.18

Choice (D) is correct.

10. C

Write out the given inequality: $k > 15$. Next, multiply both sides by $\frac{1}{3}$ (or divide both sides by 3). You now have $\frac{1}{3}k > \frac{1}{3}(15)$, which simplifies to $\frac{1}{3}k > 5$. Choice (C) is correct.

11. B

Round $38.95 to $40.00. Now, you have $\frac{35}{100} \times 40 = ?$ Canceling yields $\frac{7}{20} \times 40 = 14$. Choice (B) is correct.

12. D

Let m be the number of minutes. Set up a ratio:

$$\frac{600}{3} = \frac{27,000}{m}$$

$$\frac{200}{1} = \frac{27,000}{m}$$

$$200m = 27,000$$

Divide both sides by 100 to make the next step easier:

$$2m = 270$$

$$m = 135$$

Put this into the time format of hours and minutes by dividing 135 minutes by 60 minutes per hour, and you have $2\frac{1}{4}$ hours, which is 2 hours and 15 minutes. Choice (D) is correct.

13. D

Translate what is stated in the question step-by-step. To begin with, Sally has x dollars. After she receives 100 dollars, she has $x + 100$ dollars. She spends 125 dollars, so she has $(x + 100) - 125$ dollars left. Now simplify $(x + 100) - 125$: $(x + 100) - 125 = x + 100 - 125 = x - 25$. Sally has $x - 25$ dollars left, so choice (D) is correct.

14. E

Begin by multiplying both sides by 3 to eliminate the denominator and get $A + B = 12$. If A is greater than 1 and B is 12, then $A + B = 1 + 12 = 13$. Because $A + B$ should equal 12, B could NOT equal 12. Choice (E) is correct.

15. E

Use the average formula: $\text{average} = \frac{\text{sum of the terms}}{\text{number of terms}}$. Call s the sum of all 5 numbers: $\frac{s}{5} = 10$, so $s = 50$. Call r the sum of the 3 remaining numbers: $\frac{r}{3} = 9$, so $r = 27$. To find the two numbers that were removed, subtract the sum of the remaining numbers from the sum of all 5 numbers: $s - r = 50 - 27 = 23$. Choice (E) is correct.

16. B

The bottom surface of the bag is a rectangle, and the bag will touch all points inside the rectangle, so choice (B) is correct. Choice A is a strong distractor; the bottom of the bag is a rectangle, so the bag will touch everywhere within the rectangle, not just the edges.

17. B

The formula for percent increase is

$$\text{percent change} = \frac{\text{new value} - \text{old value}}{\text{old value}} \times 100\%.$$ Plug in the new and old values and solve:

$$\text{percent change} = \frac{1,448 - 1,086}{1,086} \times 100\%$$

$$= \frac{362}{1,086} \times 100\%$$

$$= \frac{1}{3} \times 100\%$$

$$= 33\frac{1}{3}\%$$

Choice (B) is correct.

18. A

Add information from the question stem to the drawing. Add the distance from W to X. Then, mark $WY = 3 \times 2 = 6$. Because $WY = 6$ and $WX = 2$, $XY = 6 - 2 = 4$. The question states that XZ is two times XY, so $XZ = 2 \times 4 = 8$. Finally, add the lengths together to find $WZ = 10$ (the exact lengths you combine is up to you). Choice (A) is correct.

19. A

Draw a rectangle. Label its width, w, and its length, $3w$. The perimeter is 240, so write the equation $p = l + w + l + w$ and plug in what you know: $3w + w + 3w + w = 240$, so $8w = 240$ and $w = 30$. Choice (A) is correct.

20. C

The phrase "for every" indicates a ratio is needed. Call the amount she receives from the $18,000 collection x. Set up your ratio: $\frac{50}{900} = \frac{x}{18,000}$. After simplifying the fraction on the left, you have $\frac{1}{18} = \frac{x}{18,000}$. Cross multiply to get $18x = 18,000$. Solve for x by dividing each side by 18, and $x = 1,000$. Choice (C) is correct.

21. C

You need to find out how many 4 cm × 6 cm rectangles fit into a square with sides of 24 cm. Use the area formula to divide the total area by the area of one square:

$$a = l \times w: \frac{\overset{6}{\cancel{24}} \times \overset{4}{\cancel{24}}}{\underset{1}{\cancel{4}} \times \underset{1}{\cancel{6}}}$$

$$= \frac{24}{1}$$

$$= 24$$

Choice (C) is correct.

22. C

Pick numbers to make abstract questions like this more concrete. Let $S = -2$ and $T = -3$. This gives you $R = -5$. Using this value for R, look through your choices. Only choice (C) fits and must therefore be correct.

23. B

Start by translating English into math:

70 percent of k is 10 → $0.7k = 10$

35 percent of $2k$ is the answer → $0.35(2k)$ = the answer

When you simplify the second equation, you get $0.7k$ = the answer. The question tells you that $0.7k = 10$, so "the answer" is equal to 10. Choice (B) is correct.

24. D

This type of math question is common at the end of the SSAT Math section. Answer it quickly and easily by thinking about the meaning of the word consecutive: in a row. If you have an odd number of consecutive numbers, the middle number is the average. If the middle number is 31, count backward to find the smallest number:

__, __, __, 31, __, __, __

28, 29, 30, 31, __, __, __

Choice (D) is correct.

25. A

First, figure out Pedro's original wage: his original wage plus 20% of his original wage is equal to $9.60. Convert this into an equation and solve:

$$P + 0.20P = 9.60$$

$$1.2P = 9.60$$

$$P = 8$$

Set up a similar equation for Beatriz and solve:

$$B + 0.20B = 10.80$$

$$1.2B = 10.80$$

$$B = 9$$

Before you select an answer, make sure you check that you addressed the question. This question asks you to figure out how much more Beatriz earned than Pedro before their raises, so subtract: $9 − $8 = $1. Choice (A) is correct.

Section 5

1. C

Industry is commonly thought of as manufacturing, but it also means hard work, or diligence. A person who possesses great industry is a person who is very diligent. Choice (C) is correct.

2. E

An imminent event is just about to happen—It is impending. For centuries, people have believed that the end of the world is imminent. Choice (E) is correct.

3. E

An adage is a common saying or proverb. Choice (E) is correct.

4. E

Choice (E) is correct. This is an Association Bridge. A levee is a border of a river, just as a shoulder is a border of a road. Choice D is a strong distractor; a path may be on the border of a forest, but it doesn't have to be.

5. B

Choice (B) is correct. This is a Purpose Bridge. A fan circulates air, and a heart circulates blood.

6. D

Choice (D) Is correct. This is an Association Bridge. A quill is used by a porcupine as a means of defense, just as scent is used by a skunk as a means of defense. Choices B, C, and E are strong distractors because they all reference animals and their parts. However, ducks use wings as a means of flying, kangaroos use pouches as a means to care for their young, and pig tails are not known to have any specific function.

7. A

Go back to paragraph 2, where the author mentions animals and protective coloring. The caribou and the stoat are examples of animals that change their color with the change of seasons, so choice (A) is correct. Choices B and D are the opposite of what's stated about the caribou and the stoat; both replace their brown fur with white fur in the winter, which helps them blend into snow better. Choice C is a misused detail; the passage does state that white stoat fur is valuable, but the stoat's valuable fur isn't why the author mentions both animals in this paragraph. Choice E is a distortion; both the caribou and the stoat change their coloring for the entire season. The author only mentions the chameleon as an animal capable of changing color constantly.

8. B

The first sentence in the passage states that some animals use protective coloration "to safeguard themselves." The rest of the passage describes various types of protective coloration. Choice (B) is correct. Choice A is a distortion; while the ways some animals blend into their surroundings are mentioned, not all of the animals the author discusses are focused on blending in. Choice C is a distortion; while these animals are all mentioned, they're used as examples, not discussed as the main idea. Choice D is out of scope; predators are only mentioned in relation to animals who have protective coloration. Choice E is out of scope because the author never explicitly discusses disruptive coloration, let alone compare it to cryptic resemblance.

9. A

In paragraph 2, the author mentions the chameleon as an example of an animal that can change colors rapidly to match whatever surface it happens to be on. Choice (A) is correct. Choice B is out of scope; the chameleon's ability to cling to surfaces is never discussed. Choice C is out of scope; the author doesn't discuss how easily the chameleon can adapt to changing seasons. Choice D is out of scope; disruptive coloring is never mentioned. Choice E is the opposite of what's stated in the passage; the chameleon changes its own colors, not the colors of the surface it's on.

10. C

Cryptic resemblance is the process by which an animal adapts in color, shape, and behavior in order to blend into its environment. The chameleon blends into its environment by changing its color to match the surface it stands on. Choice (C) is correct. Choices A and E are misused details because, while both are examples of animals with protective coloration, neither the hedgehog or the skunk is trying to blend in. Choices B and D are both out of scope; the author never discusses the coloration of giraffes or tigers.

11. B

The hedgehog, unlike the chameleon, "loudly announce[s] its identity" (line 14) to predators, so choice (B) is correct. Choice A is a distortion; the hedgehog is unable to change its skin color at all. Choice C is out of scope; the number of predators for each of these animals is never discussed. Choice D is a distortion; this is true about the hedgehog, but the author never discusses the chameleon's predators. Choice E is the opposite of what's stated in line 13; the hedgehog actually has a distinct "'salt and pepper' look."

12. B

When a problem asks you to describe the size and shape of something, draw it in your test booklet to help you see it better. Because the transmitter can transmit 15 meters in any direction, its range must be a circle with a radius of 15 meters and all of the points inside. Eliminate choices C and D because these show a rectangular range. To decide between choices A, (B), and E, think about the scale of the photograph. The square portion of the ocean in the photograph is 60 meters long and 60 meters wide. A circle whose radius is 15 has a diameter of 30. Thirty is half of 60, so the transmitter's range is a circle that's half the width of the square. Choice (B) is correct.

13. A

Always express the answer to an Arithmetic problem in the same format as the answer choices. Converting fractions to decimals or vice versa at the last minute can be confusing, especially since you do not have a calculator. To solve this problem using your math skills, rewrite the numbers as improper fractions, subtract them, and express your answer as a mixed number:

$$7\frac{1}{10} = \frac{2,000}{10} - \frac{71}{10} = \frac{1,929}{10} = 192\frac{9}{10}$$

Choice (A) is correct. This method works, but it is not the fastest way to solve the problem. You can also realize that a number a little more than 7 subtracted from 200 will give a number a little greater than 192; it will be 192 with a fraction after it. This leaves choice (A) as the only possible choice.

There's a third way you can tackle this question: Back-solving. Try adding the answer choices to $7\frac{1}{10}$ to find an answer choice that equals 200. Start with choice C.

$$\text{Choice C: } 193\frac{9}{10} + 7\frac{1}{10} = 201$$

This is too large, so eliminate D and E and try choice B.

$$\text{Choice B: } 193\frac{1}{10} + 7\frac{1}{10} = 200\frac{2}{10}$$

This is still too large, so choice (A) is correct.

If you want to confirm choice (A), plug it in: $192\frac{9}{10} + 7\frac{1}{10} = 200$. This is exactly what you wanted.

14. E

The perimeter of a rectangle is equal to $2(l + w)$, where l and w represent the length and width, respectively. The length of the rectangle is 12, but you need to find its width in order to find the perimeter. You're told that the width of the rectangle is one-third of its length, so translate this English into math and solve: $\frac{12}{3} = 4$, so the width is 4. Plug $l = 12$ and $w = 4$ into the formula: $P = 2(l + w) = 2(12 + 4) = 2(16) = 32$. Choice (E) is correct.

15. D

When setting up a fraction, remember that the numerator is the part and the denominator is the whole. There are 6 days in this forecast, and 2 of them will have thunderstorms. Therefore, $\frac{2}{6} = \frac{1}{3}$ of the days in this forecast will have thunderstorms. Choice (D) is correct.

16. D

According to the graph, the slice labeled chocolate represents $\frac{1}{4}$ of the entire pie. Because a total of 300 cones were sold, $\frac{1}{4} \times 300 = 75$ chocolate cones were sold. Choice (D) is correct.

SSAT UPPER/MIDDLE LEVEL PRACTICE TEST 2: ASSESS YOUR STRENGTHS

Use the following tables to determine which topics and chapters you need to review most. If you need help with your essay, be sure to review Chapter 9: The Essay and Chapter 22: Writing Wrap-Up.

Topic	Question
Math	Section 2, questions 1–25 Section 5, questions 1–25
Reading Comprehension	Section 3, questions 1–40
Verbal: Synonyms	Section 4, questions 1–30
Verbal: Analogies	Section 4, questions 31–60

Topic	Number of Questions on Test	Number Correct	If you struggled with these questions, study...
Math	50		Chapters 10–15 and Chapters 20–21
Reading Comprehension	40		Chapters 8 and 18–19
Verbal: Synonyms	30		Chapter 7 and Chapters 18–19
Verbal: Analogies	30		Chapter 2 and Chapters 18–19

CHAPTER 25

Scoring Your SSAT Practice Test

Your SSAT score is calculated by using a formula that cannot be directly applied to your practice tests. Therefore, it is impossible to provide a completely accurate score for your practice tests. Nevertheless, you'll understandably want to get an idea of how well you have performed.

Follow the steps described below to obtain a rough approximation of what your score on the actual SSAT might be. First, add up the number of questions you got correct and the number of questions you got incorrect. Questions left blank are worth zero points. Then, do the math based on the following:

	Verbal (60 questions total)	(Quantitative) Math (50 questions total)	Reading Comprehension (40 questions total)
+1 point for each correct answer	_____	_____	_____
$-\frac{1}{4}$ point for each incorrect answer	_____	_____	_____
TOTAL:	_____	_____	_____

This is called your **raw score**. Next, take your raw score and look at the following charts, which *approximate* a conversion to a **scaled score**. A scaled score takes into account the range in difficulty level of the various editions of the test.

Again, while the following scores are close approximations, they do not reflect the official scores and percentiles used on the SSAT. Among other contributing factors, your actual test score will take into account the group of students to whom you will be compared to on your test administration.

UPPER LEVEL SCORES

Upper Level scores are based on a scale of 500–800. Use the approximate score conversions below to gauge how well you have done on your practice tests.

Remember, if you are a Middle Level student, you should not expect to score as high as you would as an Upper Level student. No matter your score, you should focus on conducting in-depth reviews of all practice you complete, including this practice test.

Verbal Scaled Score

Raw Score	Approximate Score	Raw Score	Approximate Score
60	800	27	677
59	800	26	672
58	800	25	667
57	800	24	661
56	800	23	656
55	800	22	651
54	799	21	646
53	797	20	641
52	795	19	635
51	793	18	630
50	791	17	625
49	787	16	620
48	782	15	615
47	777	14	610
46	772	13	604
45	767	12	598
44	761	11	592
43	756	10	586
42	751	9	580
41	746	8	574
40	741	7	568
39	737	6	562
38	732	5	556
37	727	4	549
36	722	3	543
35	717	2	537
34	712	1	531
33	707	0	525
32	702	−1	520
31	697	−2	516
30	692	−3	511
29	687	−4	506
28	682	−5	501

Quantitative Scaled Score

Raw Score	Approximate Score	Raw Score	Approximate Score
50	800	22	677
49	798	21	672
48	796	20	667
47	794	19	661
46	792	18	656
45	790	17	651
44	785	16	645
43	780	15	640
42	774	14	634
41	769	13	628
40	764	12	622
39	760	11	616
38	755	10	610
37	750	9	603
36	745	8	596
35	740	7	590
34	735	6	584
33	731	5	578
32	726	4	571
31	721	3	565
30	716	2	558
29	711	1	551
28	706	0	544
27	701	−1	540
26	696	−2	535
25	692	−3	530
24	687	−4	525
23	682	−5	521

Reading Scaled Score

Raw Score	Approximate Score	Raw Score	Approximate Score
40	800	17	628
39	757	16	623
38	754	15	619
37	751	14	613
36	748	13	606
35	745	12	599
34	739	11	593
33	732	10	586
32	725	9	579
31	718	8	572
30	711	7	565
29	705	6	559
28	699	5	553
27	693	4	546
26	687	3	540
25	681	2	534
24	673	1	528
23	665	0	522
22	657	−1	519
21	649	−2	515
20	641	−3	511
19	636	−4	507
18	632	−5	503

PART 6

ISEE Practice Tests and Explanations

ISEE TEST OVERVIEW

Total Time

Approximately 3 hours, including two breaks.

Questions

Aside from the essay, all questions are multiple-choice format, with all answer choices labeled A–D.

Content

The ISEE tests math, reading, and verbal skills. There are two scored math sections, one scored reading comprehension section, one scored verbal section, and one unscored essay.

Pacing

You are not expected to complete all items on the ISEE. This is particularly true if you are at the low end of the age range of test takers for your level. The best approach to pacing is to work as quickly as you can without losing accuracy. Further, if a question is giving you difficulty, circle it and move on. You can always come back to it later, but you shouldn't waste time on a question that is stumping you when you could be gaining valuable points elsewhere.

Guessing

There is no guessing penalty on the ISEE. You receive 1 point for each question that you answer correctly. You don't lose any points for questions left blank or for questions answered incorrectly. As a result, it's always to your advantage to guess on questions you don't know. However, it's better to answer questions correctly, so only guess if you try to answer the question and can't figure it out or if you are running out of time.

CHAPTER 26

ISEE Upper/Middle Level Practice Test 1

HOW TO TAKE THIS PRACTICE TEST

Before taking this practice test, find a quiet room where you can work uninterrupted for three hours. Make sure you have a comfortable desk and several #2 pencils.

Use the answer sheet provided to record your answers. You can cut it out or photocopy it.

Once you start this practice test, don't stop until you have finished. Remember: you can review any questions within a section, but you may not go backward or forward to any other sections.

You'll find answer explanations following the test. Scoring information is in Chapter 28.

If you are a Middle Level student, you should not expect to score as high as you would as an Upper Level student. No matter your score, you should focus on conducting in-depth reviews of all practice you complete, including this practice test.

Good luck.

ISEE Upper/Middle Level Practice Test 1
ANSWER SHEET

Remove (or photocopy) the answer sheet and use it to complete the practice test.

Start with number 1 for each section. If a section has fewer questions than answer spaces, leave the extra spaces blank.

SECTION 1

1. Ⓐ Ⓑ Ⓒ Ⓓ	9. Ⓐ Ⓑ Ⓒ Ⓓ	17. Ⓐ Ⓑ Ⓒ Ⓓ	25. Ⓐ Ⓑ Ⓒ Ⓓ	33. Ⓐ Ⓑ Ⓒ Ⓓ
2. Ⓐ Ⓑ Ⓒ Ⓓ	10. Ⓐ Ⓑ Ⓒ Ⓓ	18. Ⓐ Ⓑ Ⓒ Ⓓ	26. Ⓐ Ⓑ Ⓒ Ⓓ	34. Ⓐ Ⓑ Ⓒ Ⓓ
3. Ⓐ Ⓑ Ⓒ Ⓓ	11. Ⓐ Ⓑ Ⓒ Ⓓ	19. Ⓐ Ⓑ Ⓒ Ⓓ	27. Ⓐ Ⓑ Ⓒ Ⓓ	35. Ⓐ Ⓑ Ⓒ Ⓓ
4. Ⓐ Ⓑ Ⓒ Ⓓ	12. Ⓐ Ⓑ Ⓒ Ⓓ	20. Ⓐ Ⓑ Ⓒ Ⓓ	28. Ⓐ Ⓑ Ⓒ Ⓓ	36. Ⓐ Ⓑ Ⓒ Ⓓ
5. Ⓐ Ⓑ Ⓒ Ⓓ	13. Ⓐ Ⓑ Ⓒ Ⓓ	21. Ⓐ Ⓑ Ⓒ Ⓓ	29. Ⓐ Ⓑ Ⓒ Ⓓ	37. Ⓐ Ⓑ Ⓒ Ⓓ
6. Ⓐ Ⓑ Ⓒ Ⓓ	14. Ⓐ Ⓑ Ⓒ Ⓓ	22. Ⓐ Ⓑ Ⓒ Ⓓ	30. Ⓐ Ⓑ Ⓒ Ⓓ	38. Ⓐ Ⓑ Ⓒ Ⓓ
7. Ⓐ Ⓑ Ⓒ Ⓓ	15. Ⓐ Ⓑ Ⓒ Ⓓ	23. Ⓐ Ⓑ Ⓒ Ⓓ	31. Ⓐ Ⓑ Ⓒ Ⓓ	39. Ⓐ Ⓑ Ⓒ Ⓓ
8. Ⓐ Ⓑ Ⓒ Ⓓ	16. Ⓐ Ⓑ Ⓒ Ⓓ	24. Ⓐ Ⓑ Ⓒ Ⓓ	32. Ⓐ Ⓑ Ⓒ Ⓓ	40. Ⓐ Ⓑ Ⓒ Ⓓ

correct in section 1

incorrect in section 1

SECTION 2

1. Ⓐ Ⓑ Ⓒ Ⓓ	9. Ⓐ Ⓑ Ⓒ Ⓓ	17. Ⓐ Ⓑ Ⓒ Ⓓ	25. Ⓐ Ⓑ Ⓒ Ⓓ	33. Ⓐ Ⓑ Ⓒ Ⓓ
2. Ⓐ Ⓑ Ⓒ Ⓓ	10. Ⓐ Ⓑ Ⓒ Ⓓ	18. Ⓐ Ⓑ Ⓒ Ⓓ	26. Ⓐ Ⓑ Ⓒ Ⓓ	34. Ⓐ Ⓑ Ⓒ Ⓓ
3. Ⓐ Ⓑ Ⓒ Ⓓ	11. Ⓐ Ⓑ Ⓒ Ⓓ	19. Ⓐ Ⓑ Ⓒ Ⓓ	27. Ⓐ Ⓑ Ⓒ Ⓓ	35. Ⓐ Ⓑ Ⓒ Ⓓ
4. Ⓐ Ⓑ Ⓒ Ⓓ	12. Ⓐ Ⓑ Ⓒ Ⓓ	20. Ⓐ Ⓑ Ⓒ Ⓓ	28. Ⓐ Ⓑ Ⓒ Ⓓ	36. Ⓐ Ⓑ Ⓒ Ⓓ
5. Ⓐ Ⓑ Ⓒ Ⓓ	13. Ⓐ Ⓑ Ⓒ Ⓓ	21. Ⓐ Ⓑ Ⓒ Ⓓ	29. Ⓐ Ⓑ Ⓒ Ⓓ	37. Ⓐ Ⓑ Ⓒ Ⓓ
6. Ⓐ Ⓑ Ⓒ Ⓓ	14. Ⓐ Ⓑ Ⓒ Ⓓ	22. Ⓐ Ⓑ Ⓒ Ⓓ	30. Ⓐ Ⓑ Ⓒ Ⓓ	38. Ⓐ Ⓑ Ⓒ Ⓓ
7. Ⓐ Ⓑ Ⓒ Ⓓ	15. Ⓐ Ⓑ Ⓒ Ⓓ	23. Ⓐ Ⓑ Ⓒ Ⓓ	31. Ⓐ Ⓑ Ⓒ Ⓓ	39. Ⓐ Ⓑ Ⓒ Ⓓ
8. Ⓐ Ⓑ Ⓒ Ⓓ	16. Ⓐ Ⓑ Ⓒ Ⓓ	24. Ⓐ Ⓑ Ⓒ Ⓓ	32. Ⓐ Ⓑ Ⓒ Ⓓ	40. Ⓐ Ⓑ Ⓒ Ⓓ

correct in section 2

incorrect in section 2

SECTION 3

1. Ⓐ Ⓑ Ⓒ Ⓓ	9. Ⓐ Ⓑ Ⓒ Ⓓ	17. Ⓐ Ⓑ Ⓒ Ⓓ	25. Ⓐ Ⓑ Ⓒ Ⓓ	33. Ⓐ Ⓑ Ⓒ Ⓓ
2. Ⓐ Ⓑ Ⓒ Ⓓ	10. Ⓐ Ⓑ Ⓒ Ⓓ	18. Ⓐ Ⓑ Ⓒ Ⓓ	26. Ⓐ Ⓑ Ⓒ Ⓓ	34. Ⓐ Ⓑ Ⓒ Ⓓ
3. Ⓐ Ⓑ Ⓒ Ⓓ	11. Ⓐ Ⓑ Ⓒ Ⓓ	19. Ⓐ Ⓑ Ⓒ Ⓓ	27. Ⓐ Ⓑ Ⓒ Ⓓ	35. Ⓐ Ⓑ Ⓒ Ⓓ
4. Ⓐ Ⓑ Ⓒ Ⓓ	12. Ⓐ Ⓑ Ⓒ Ⓓ	20. Ⓐ Ⓑ Ⓒ Ⓓ	28. Ⓐ Ⓑ Ⓒ Ⓓ	36. Ⓐ Ⓑ Ⓒ Ⓓ
5. Ⓐ Ⓑ Ⓒ Ⓓ	13. Ⓐ Ⓑ Ⓒ Ⓓ	21. Ⓐ Ⓑ Ⓒ Ⓓ	29. Ⓐ Ⓑ Ⓒ Ⓓ	37. Ⓐ Ⓑ Ⓒ Ⓓ
6. Ⓐ Ⓑ Ⓒ Ⓓ	14. Ⓐ Ⓑ Ⓒ Ⓓ	22. Ⓐ Ⓑ Ⓒ Ⓓ	30. Ⓐ Ⓑ Ⓒ Ⓓ	38. Ⓐ Ⓑ Ⓒ Ⓓ
7. Ⓐ Ⓑ Ⓒ Ⓓ	15. Ⓐ Ⓑ Ⓒ Ⓓ	23. Ⓐ Ⓑ Ⓒ Ⓓ	31. Ⓐ Ⓑ Ⓒ Ⓓ	39. Ⓐ Ⓑ Ⓒ Ⓓ
8. Ⓐ Ⓑ Ⓒ Ⓓ	16. Ⓐ Ⓑ Ⓒ Ⓓ	24. Ⓐ Ⓑ Ⓒ Ⓓ	32. Ⓐ Ⓑ Ⓒ Ⓓ	40. Ⓐ Ⓑ Ⓒ Ⓓ

correct in section 3

incorrect in section 3

SECTION 4

1. Ⓐ Ⓑ Ⓒ Ⓓ	11. Ⓐ Ⓑ Ⓒ Ⓓ	21. Ⓐ Ⓑ Ⓒ Ⓓ	31. Ⓐ Ⓑ Ⓒ Ⓓ	41. Ⓐ Ⓑ Ⓒ Ⓓ
2. Ⓐ Ⓑ Ⓒ Ⓓ	12. Ⓐ Ⓑ Ⓒ Ⓓ	22. Ⓐ Ⓑ Ⓒ Ⓓ	32. Ⓐ Ⓑ Ⓒ Ⓓ	42. Ⓐ Ⓑ Ⓒ Ⓓ
3. Ⓐ Ⓑ Ⓒ Ⓓ	13. Ⓐ Ⓑ Ⓒ Ⓓ	23. Ⓐ Ⓑ Ⓒ Ⓓ	33. Ⓐ Ⓑ Ⓒ Ⓓ	43. Ⓐ Ⓑ Ⓒ Ⓓ
4. Ⓐ Ⓑ Ⓒ Ⓓ	14. Ⓐ Ⓑ Ⓒ Ⓓ	24. Ⓐ Ⓑ Ⓒ Ⓓ	34. Ⓐ Ⓑ Ⓒ Ⓓ	44. Ⓐ Ⓑ Ⓒ Ⓓ
5. Ⓐ Ⓑ Ⓒ Ⓓ	15. Ⓐ Ⓑ Ⓒ Ⓓ	25. Ⓐ Ⓑ Ⓒ Ⓓ	35. Ⓐ Ⓑ Ⓒ Ⓓ	45. Ⓐ Ⓑ Ⓒ Ⓓ
6. Ⓐ Ⓑ Ⓒ Ⓓ	16. Ⓐ Ⓑ Ⓒ Ⓓ	26. Ⓐ Ⓑ Ⓒ Ⓓ	36. Ⓐ Ⓑ Ⓒ Ⓓ	46. Ⓐ Ⓑ Ⓒ Ⓓ
7. Ⓐ Ⓑ Ⓒ Ⓓ	17. Ⓐ Ⓑ Ⓒ Ⓓ	27. Ⓐ Ⓑ Ⓒ Ⓓ	37. Ⓐ Ⓑ Ⓒ Ⓓ	47. Ⓐ Ⓑ Ⓒ Ⓓ
8. Ⓐ Ⓑ Ⓒ Ⓓ	18. Ⓐ Ⓑ Ⓒ Ⓓ	28. Ⓐ Ⓑ Ⓒ Ⓓ	38. Ⓐ Ⓑ Ⓒ Ⓓ	48. Ⓐ Ⓑ Ⓒ Ⓓ
9. Ⓐ Ⓑ Ⓒ Ⓓ	19. Ⓐ Ⓑ Ⓒ Ⓓ	29. Ⓐ Ⓑ Ⓒ Ⓓ	39. Ⓐ Ⓑ Ⓒ Ⓓ	49. Ⓐ Ⓑ Ⓒ Ⓓ
10. Ⓐ Ⓑ Ⓒ Ⓓ	20. Ⓐ Ⓑ Ⓒ Ⓓ	30. Ⓐ Ⓑ Ⓒ Ⓓ	40. Ⓐ Ⓑ Ⓒ Ⓓ	50. Ⓐ Ⓑ Ⓒ Ⓓ

correct in section 4

incorrect in section 4

Section 1

Verbal Reasoning

Time—20 Minutes

40 Questions

The Verbal Reasoning section includes two different question types split into two different parts. When you finish Part One, move on to Part Two. You may write on the test. For each answer you choose, fill in the corresponding bubble on your answer grid.

Part One—Synonyms

Part One questions consist of one word in capital letters followed by four words or phrases. Choose the answer choice that is most similar in meaning to the word in capital letters.

Part Two—Sentence Completions

Part Two questions consist of one sentence with either one or two blanks. One blank means that one word is missing. Two blanks mean that two words are missing. Each sentence has four answer choices. Choose the word or phrase that best completes the meaning of the sentence.

STOP. DO NOT GO ON UNTIL TOLD TO DO SO.　STOP

PART ONE: SYNONYMS

Choose the word that is the closest in meaning to the word in capital letters.

1. SPONTANEOUS:

   (A) impulsive

   (B) excitable

   (C) ingenious

   (D) dazzling

2. APPARITION:

   (A) clothing

   (B) ghost

   (C) guard

   (D) wall

3. BENEVOLENT:

   (A) disobedient

   (B) charitable

   (C) sensitive

   (D) widespread

4. LAMENT:

   (A) support

   (B) decline

   (C) solidify

   (D) grieve

5. REIMBURSE:

   (A) punish

   (B) divert

   (C) compensate

   (D) recollect

6. DECEIT:

   (A) civility

   (B) trickery

   (C) rudeness

   (D) despair

7. DESPONDENT:

   (A) heightened

   (B) annoyed

   (C) relaxed

   (D) depressed

8. SATIATE:

   (A) prolong

   (B) elongate

   (C) seal

   (D) satisfy

9. ADAMANT:

   (A) thin

   (B) enlarged

   (C) admiring

   (D) stubborn

10. PIETY:

   (A) rarity

   (B) smell

   (C) faith

   (D) meal

GO ON TO THE NEXT PAGE. ▶ ▶ ▶

11. LAUD:

    (A) touch

    (B) praise

    (C) insult

    (D) hear

12. AVERT:

    (A) vindicate

    (B) prevent

    (C) explain

    (D) dislike

13. HAUGHTINESS:

    (A) heat

    (B) height

    (C) opulence

    (D) arrogance

14. APPREHENSION:

    (A) appreciation

    (B) worry

    (C) aggravation

    (D) elevation

15. WARINESS:

    (A) extremity

    (B) caution

    (C) superiority

    (D) mobility

16. SCARCE:

    (A) delicious

    (B) afraid

    (C) thin

    (D) rare

17. PERCEPTIVE:

    (A) confused

    (B) round

    (C) observant

    (D) imbued

18. VERIFY:

    (A) complete

    (B) prove

    (C) violate

    (D) consume

19. CANDOR:

    (A) odor

    (B) honesty

    (C) ability

    (D) wealth

20. ABHOR:

    (A) despise

    (B) horrify

    (C) avoid

    (D) deny

GO ON TO THE NEXT PAGE. ▶ ▶ ▶

PART TWO: SENTENCE COMPLETIONS

Select the word or word pair that best completes the sentence.

21. The ------- writer was on her 12th novel.

    (A) myopic

    (B) prolific

    (C) nefarious

    (D) elusive

22. The advent of the computer chip made Armando's job -------.

    (A) exuberant

    (B) eminent

    (C) belligerent

    (D) obsolete

23. All efforts to save the nature preserve proved -------.

    (A) inextricable

    (B) insular

    (C) glib

    (D) futile

24. In spite of her ------- work, Priyanka did not receive a promotion.

    (A) tardy

    (B) industrious

    (C) irate

    (D) occasional

25. After the military government banned the opposing political party, its members continued to meet in ------- groups.

    (A) clandestine

    (B) amicable

    (C) sanctioned

    (D) elaborate

26. Sheri showed genuine ------- when she was caught: she cried and promised never to hurt anyone again.

    (A) remorse

    (B) melodrama

    (C) wit

    (D) enthusiasm

27. Highly influenced by Frank Lloyd Wright's principles of design, the architect E. Fay Jones has built homes reputed to equal—even -------—Wright's successes at building in harmony with natural surroundings.

    (A) echo

    (B) question

    (C) reconstruct

    (D) surpass

28. The captain demonstrated her ------- for the crew by bellowing her commands in a harsh voice.

    (A) admiration

    (B) contempt

    (C) reverence

    (D) affinity

GO ON TO THE NEXT PAGE. ▶ ▶ ▶

29. Caleb never failed to charm listeners with his ------- stories.

    (A) lethargic

    (B) wan

    (C) insufferable

    (D) engaging

30. Trumpets, including Pacific conch-shell trumpets, African ivory trumpets, orchestral valve trumpets, and tubas, comprise one of the most ------- categories of wind instruments.

    (A) excessive

    (B) discordant

    (C) coherent

    (D) diverse

31. The powerful forest fire, which ------- the mountains of Indonesia, was the most severe ------- disaster the region has ever experienced.

    (A) destroyed . . . inflammable

    (B) devastated . . . environmental

    (C) singed . . . intangible

    (D) burned . . . scientific

32. At one time, historians spoke of ancient Greece as though its cultural and scientific achievements were wholly -------, whereas it is now generally recognized that at least some Greek science and culture was -------.

    (A) primitive . . . simple

    (B) original . . . derivative

    (C) mistaken . . . dubious

    (D) successful . . . significant

33. Rahul danced with such ------- that no one could ------- his talent any longer.

    (A) speed . . . ascertain

    (B) grace . . . affirm

    (C) agility . . . question

    (D) melancholy . . . deny

34. Once a ------- propagated only by science fiction movies, the possibility of life on Mars has recently become more -------.

    (A) wish . . . doubtful

    (B) myth . . . plausible

    (C) story . . . impossible

    (D) hypothesis . . . empty

35. Screaming and laughing, the students were ------- by their ------- experience on the white-water raft.

    (A) amused . . . tepid

    (B) irritated . . . continued

    (C) exhilarated . . . first

    (D) frightened . . . secure

36. Many writers of the 20th century were influenced by Hemingway's ------- writing style and consequently discontinued the ------- language characteristic of the 19th-century novel.

    (A) sparse . . . verbose

    (B) dull . . . insipid

    (C) peaceful . . . descriptive

    (D) complete . . . florid

GO ON TO THE NEXT PAGE. ▶ ▶ ▶

37. The ------- journey ------- us all; even my dog sat down to take a rest.

    (A) panoramic . . . exhausted

    (B) tortuous . . . invigorated

    (C) strenuous . . . fatigued

    (D) arduous . . . rejuvenated

38. That Chinese pieces of silk dating over 1,500 years old have been found in Egypt is ------- because the landscape between these two countries includes both arid deserts and several ------- mountain ranges.

    (A) known . . . required

    (B) impressive . . . reduced

    (C) predictable . . . steep

    (D) incredible . . . massive

39. Once a(n) ------- gathering, the Greek festival has, in recent times, become highly -------.

    (A) urban . . . contemporary

    (B) religious . . . commercialized

    (C) mournful . . . gloomy

    (D) parallel . . . transformed

40. The volunteer association ------- people with a wide range of ------- to staff their offices.

    (A) recruited . . . attributes

    (B) fired . . . skills

    (C) rejected . . . experiences

    (D) hired . . . tendencies

STOP. IF THERE IS TIME, YOU MAY CHECK YOUR WORK IN THIS SECTION ONLY. STOP

Section 2

Quantitative Reasoning

Time—35 Minutes

37 Questions

The Quantitative Reasoning section includes two different question types split into two different parts. When you finish Part One, move on to Part Two. For each answer you choose, fill in the corresponding bubble on your answer grid.

Any figures that accompany the questions in this section may be assumed to be drawn as accurately as possible EXCEPT when it is stated that a particular figure is not drawn to scale. Letters such as x, y, and n stand for real numbers.

Part One—Word Problems

Part One questions consist of a word problem with four answer choices. You may write on the test, but you might be able to solve many of these questions using mental math. Choose the best answer choice.

Part Two—Quantitative Comparisons

Part Two questions are quantitative comparisons between the values of Column A and Column B. Using the information given in each question, compare the values of Column A and Column B. Then, choose one of these four answer choices:

(A) The value of Column A is greater.

(B) The value of Column B is greater.

(C) The two values are equal.

(D) The values in the two columns cannot be compared using the information provided.

STOP. DO NOT GO ON UNTIL TOLD TO DO SO.   STOP

PART ONE: WORD PROBLEMS

Choose the best answer out of the four choices.

1. Ayanna has 50 cents and Tyrel has $4.60. If Tyrel gives Ayanna 75 cents, how much money will Ayanna have?

    (A) $1.00

    (B) $1.25

    (C) $1.50

    (D) $5.50

2. In triangle XYZ, the measure of angle Y is twice the measure of angle X, and the measure of angle Z is three times the measure of angle X. What is the degree measure of angle Y?

    (A) 15

    (B) 30

    (C) 45

    (D) 60

3. If $3a + 6a = 36$, what is the value of a?

    (A) 1

    (B) 2

    (C) 3

    (D) 4

4. If a six-sided pencil with a trademark on one of its sides is rolled on a table, what is the probability that the side with the trademark is not touching the surface of the table when the pencil stops?

    (A) $\frac{5}{6}$

    (B) $\frac{2}{3}$

    (C) $\frac{1}{3}$

    (D) $\frac{1}{6}$

5. If a jet travels at a constant rate of 270 miles per hour, approximately how many hours will it take to reach its destination 3,300 miles away?

    (A) 12.22

    (B) 15.38

    (C) 18.91

    (D) 23.68

6. If $a + 2 > 5$ and $a - 4 < 1$, which of the following is a possible value for a?

    (A) 2

    (B) 3

    (C) 4

    (D) 5

7. If two radii of a circle combine to form a diameter, what is the measure of the angle?

    (A) 90 degrees

    (B) 120 degrees

    (C) 180 degrees

    (D) 240 degrees

8. If two fair coins are tossed simultaneously, what is the probability that two tails are thrown?

    (A) 1

    (B) $\frac{1}{2}$

    (C) $\frac{1}{4}$

    (D) $\frac{1}{8}$

GO ON TO THE NEXT PAGE. ▶ ▶ ▶

9. In a class, 70 percent of the students are right-handed, and the rest are left-handed. If 70 percent of the left-handed students have brown eyes, then left-handed students with brown eyes make up what percent of the entire class?

    (A) 14%

    (B) 21%

    (C) 30%

    (D) 49%

10. Each of the n students in a class may invite up to 3 guests to an awards ceremony. What is the maximum number of students and guests who might attend the awards ceremony?

    (A) $n + 3$

    (B) $3n$

    (C) $3n + 4$

    (D) $4n$

11. If $r = 8$, then what is the value of $(r + 4)^2$?

    (A) 24

    (B) 64

    (C) 80

    (D) 144

12. The average weight of Omari, Fernando, and Izyan is 60 kilograms. If Omari and Fernando both weigh 50 kilograms, how much, in kilograms, does Izyan weigh?

    (A) 50

    (B) 60

    (C) 70

    (D) 80

13. A farmer pays $58 for 6 new chickens. How many eggs must the farmer sell at 16 cents apiece in order to pay for the chickens?

    (A) 360

    (B) 361

    (C) 362

    (D) 363

14. If $2x + 4 = 26$, then what is the value of $x + 4$?

    (A) 9

    (B) 11

    (C) 13

    (D) 15

15. Sophia shoveled snow for $2\frac{1}{3}$ hours in the morning and then for another $1\frac{3}{4}$ hours in the afternoon. How many hours did she shovel in total?

    (A) $3\frac{4}{7}$

    (B) $3\frac{5}{6}$

    (C) $4\frac{1}{12}$

    (D) 7

16. How many integers are there from 1,960 to 1,980, inclusive?

    (A) 10

    (B) 20

    (C) 21

    (D) 30

GO ON TO THE NEXT PAGE. ▶ ▶ ▶

17. If $n* = 2n + 4$, what is the value of $10*$?

    (A) 14

    (B) 24

    (C) 40

    (D) 44

18. Triangle *ABC* and triangle *CED* are both equilateral triangles.

    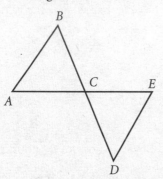

    What is the measure in degrees of $\angle BCE$?

    (A) 60

    (B) 90

    (C) 120

    (D) 180

19. Talia baked 42 biscuits for her 12 guests. If 6 biscuits remain uneaten, what is the average number of biscuits that the guests ate?

    (A) 2

    (B) 3

    (C) 4

    (D) 6

20. What is the greatest number of squares with sides of 2 centimeters that can be cut from a square with an area of 36 square centimeters?

    (A) 4

    (B) 9

    (C) 18

    (D) 36

GO ON TO THE NEXT PAGE. ▶ ▶ ▶

PART TWO: QUANTITATIVE COMPARISONS

Using the information in the question, compare the value of Column A to the value of Column B. All questions in Part Two have these answer choices:

(A)   The value of Column A is greater.

(B)   The value of Column B is greater.

(C)   The two values are equal.

(D)   The values in the two columns cannot be compared using the information provided.

	Column A	Column B
21.	$1{,}000 - 3.45002$	$1{,}000 - 3.45601$

The ages of the 5 members of a certain family are 8, 12, 16, 20, and 24.

	Column A	Column B
22.	The average (arithmetic mean) age of the 5 family members	16

$$3x - 12 = 3x - 6x$$

	Column A	Column B
23.	$x + 2$	2

	Column A	Column B
24.	Area of a triangle with a base of 6 and a height of 10	Area of a triangle with a base of 12 and a height of 5

	Column A	Column B
25.	$2(2x + 1)$	$4x + 4$

	Column A	Column B
26.	The average of 106, 117, 123, and 195	The average of 110, 118, 124, and 196

A video game sells for $60.

	Column A	Column B
27.	The price of the video game after a 10% discount	$50

	Column A	Column B
28.	$\dfrac{4}{5} \times \dfrac{15}{45} \times \dfrac{3}{16}$	0.05

$$d < 0$$

	Column A	Column B
29.	$3d - 2$	$-2d - 2$

$$\frac{8}{9} > x > \frac{1}{2}$$

	Column A	Column B
30.	x	$\dfrac{2}{3}$

$$x < 0$$

	Column A	Column B
31.	$2x$	$(2x)(1x)$

	Column A	Column B
32.	Perimeter of an octagon with sides of equal length	8

GO ON TO THE NEXT PAGE. ▶ ▶ ▶

	Column A	Column B
33.	n	n^2

	Column A	Column B
34.	98% of 51	51% of 98

Set A: {6, 13, 4, 22, 7, 9, 0, 11}

	Column A	Column B
35.	The mean of the set	The median of the set

	Column A	Column B
36.	The number of degrees in one angle of a regular hexagon	The number of degrees in one angle of a regular pentagon

	Column A	Column B
37.	The probability of flipping tails and then heads	The probability of randomly choosing a diamond out of a deck of cards

STOP. IF THERE IS TIME, YOU MAY CHECK YOUR WORK IN THIS SECTION ONLY.

Section 3

Reading Comprehension

Time—35 Minutes

36 Questions

This section includes six reading passages. Each passage has six questions that can be answered using information stated or implied in the passage. You may write on the test.

Questions 1–6

1   Edward Stratemeyer is most often recognized
2 as the creator of the Hardy Boys, Nancy Drew,
3 and the Bobbsey Twins. These stories were
4 popular when they were published and
5 influential for generations. However,
6 Stratemeyer did not gain enormous commercial
7 success through luck alone. His books, in which
8 young amateur detectives had fantastic
9 adventures and always saved the day, had a
10 particular appeal in the time they were written.
11 They continue to appeal to young readers, with
12 new sequels of some series being published as
13 recently as 2017.
14   Stratemeyer was born in New Jersey in 1862.
15 When he was a boy, the harsh economics of an
16 industrializing America quickly forced children
17 to become adults. As factories were built across
18 the country, the owners looked for the cheapest
19 way to run them: child workers. Many families
20 in the U.S. were poor, and children often
21 dropped out of school to make money for their
22 families.
23   By 1900, however, 28 states had passed laws
24 regulating child labor, and by 1938, the Fair
25 Labor Standards Act made schooling
26 compulsory until the age of sixteen. These
27 changes helped prolong childhood for many

28 children, creating a new stage of life:
29 adolescence.
30   Young Americans, with more free time than
31 the working youth of the previous century,
32 looked to fiction and fantasy for adventure.
33 Stratemeyer, writing under a variety of
34 pseudonyms from 1876 to 1930, responded to
35 the changing needs of his readers with a slew of
36 heroic super-teens. By the time he died, he had
37 published 168 books and dozens of short stories,
38 dime novels, and magazine stories.
39   As a writer, Stratemeyer had more ideas for
40 stories than time to write them, so he created a
41 new writing method involving many different
42 people that would become the Stratemeyer
43 Syndicate. The Syndicate allowed Stratemeyer
44 the chance to outline his ideas and have
45 ghostwriters complete the stories. Stratemeyer
46 and his assistant would then review the stories
47 to ensure that they fit within the series as a
48 whole before sending them to be revised or published.
49   After Stratemeyer's death, his daughters
50 continued to run the Syndicate together for
51 many years. Although the Stratemeyer Syndicate
52 no longer exists, Stratemeyer's books continue to
53 appeal to adolescents looking for adventure.

GO ON TO THE NEXT PAGE. ▶ ▶ ▶

1. The passage primarily serves to explain

    (A) the universal appeal of Stratemeyer's characters.

    (B) the benefits of mandatory schooling for teenagers.

    (C) the underlying reason for a writer's popularity.

    (D) the economic boom created by child labor laws.

2. The passage suggests that the appeal of Stratemeyer's fictional heroes lay partly in the fact that

    (A) they worked long hours in industrial jobs.

    (B) their activities were not restricted by fictional parents.

    (C) they were the same age as his readers.

    (D) they were based on young people Stratemeyer actually knew.

3. According to the passage, children under sixteen during the 1930s

    (A) led lives of fun and adventure.

    (B) were better off financially than ever before.

    (C) began to lose interest in Stratemeyer's books.

    (D) were legally required to attend school.

4. According to the passage, Stratemeyer wrote his books

    (A) in a single thirty-year span.

    (B) using a series of pseudonyms.

    (C) to pay off family debts.

    (D) without ever gaining commercial success.

5. In line 28, "stage" most nearly means

    (A) period.

    (B) platform.

    (C) era.

    (D) produce.

6. The author's attitude toward Stratemeyer can best be described as

    (A) surprised.

    (B) tired.

    (C) admiring.

    (D) scornful.

GO ON TO THE NEXT PAGE. ▶ ▶ ▶

Questions 7–12

1 A ventriloquist's "dummy" is the wooden
2 figure that a ventriloquist uses to create the
3 illusion of "throwing" his or her voice. Although
4 ventriloquism began as a religious practice, it
5 became established as a performance art in the
6 1800s. When the art was first developing,
7 ventriloquists often focused on "throwing" their
8 voices to make them seem as though they were
9 coming from a different location. In 1886,
10 however, Fred Russell introduced his dummy,
11 "Coster Joe," and engaged in a conversation with
12 him. Russell's act was so influential to the art of
13 ventriloquism that he is now referred to as the
14 father of ventriloquism.
15   On the outside, the first dummies, such as the
16 one used by Russell, looked very much like many
17 used today. Ventriloquist dummies typically
18 have the same exaggerated mouth and limited
19 range of movement. On the inside, however,
20 these dummies can vary greatly. Some of the
21 original wooden figures were a curious fusion of
22 engineering feats and sculpture. Underneath the
23 wig, the back of the dummy's head opens up,
24 revealing tangled innards of metal and wire,
25 screws, and levers.

26   Over time, these dummies have become more
27 complex. Some of the most mechanically
28 complex dummies were made by the McElroy
29 brothers, who together created one hundred
30 different figures in the ten years prior to the
31 Second World War. The mechanical brains of
32 the McElroy dummies were assembled from
33 some 300 different springs, pieces of metal,
34 typewriter keys, and bicycle spokes—a
35 synergistic effort comparable to the work of the
36 Wright Brothers. At one point, the McElroy
37 dummies were even compared to renowned
38 quality of Stradivarius instruments.
39   Modern dummies are often made of many
40 different materials and range in size, from only
41 about a foot tall to as tall as a human. These
42 modern dummies can be quite complex, but the
43 dummies created and used by those like Russell
44 and the McElroy brothers helped ensure the
45 success of the art of ventriloquism. Though
46 modern dummies may look or feel different,
47 they continue to engage in conversations with
48 their ventriloquists whenever it is time to
49 perform.

GO ON TO THE NEXT PAGE. ▶ ▶ ▶

7. The primary purpose of the passage is to

(A) compare the achievements of two different families of inventors.

(B) relate the history of the ventriloquist's art.

(C) compare the ventriloquists' dummies of the 19th century with those produced today.

(D) describe the complex craftsmanship behind early ventriloquists' dummies.

8. It can be inferred from the passage that the varied outward appearance of ventriloquists' dummies

(A) is meant to seem as lifelike as possible.

(B) has not changed their roles in ventriloquists' acts.

(C) depends on what mechanical devices are inside them.

(D) changed after the work of the McElroy brothers.

9. The passage suggests that the most complex dummies are

(A) created using scientific and artistic craftsmanship.

(B) able to fool the most discerning observer.

(C) those with the widest range of movement.

(D) those made since the end of the Second World War.

10. The author probably argues that the McElroy brothers' dummies were "a synergistic effort" (lines 34–35) because

(A) the McElroys were related to the Wright Brothers.

(B) the McElroys borrowed design concepts from other inventors.

(C) the McElroys worked together on the design.

(D) their dummies required so much energy to operate.

11. The author's attitude toward the McElroy brothers can best be described as

(A) skeptical.

(B) puzzled.

(C) elated.

(D) appreciative.

12. All the following questions can be answered by the passage EXCEPT:

(A) How does a ventriloquist throw his or her voice?

(B) What is a dummy?

(C) How did the McElroy brothers' dummies differ from others?

(D) Did the McElroy brothers start making dummies before or after the war?

GO ON TO THE NEXT PAGE. ▶ ▶ ▶

Questions 13–18

1   The Romantic period in England was a major
2 force for change in the 18th and 19th centuries.
3 The Romantic poets in 19th-century
4 Britain prided themselves on their rejection of
5 many of the traditional practices of English
6 poetry. In addition to the belief in spontaneity,
7 the Romantic movement focused on the
8 difficulty of transforming human emotions into
9 art, including poetry.
10   William Wordsworth, one of the leaders of
11 the Romantic movement, wished to avoid what
12 he considered the emotional insincerity and
13 affectation characteristic of much earlier poetry.
14 Instead, he attempted to achieve spontaneity and
15 naturalness of expression in his verse. According
16 to Wordsworth, a poet should be "a man
17 speaking to men" rather than a detached
18 observer delivering pronouncements from an
19 ivory tower.
20   John Keats, Wordsworth's younger
21 contemporary, brought a similar attitude to his

22 poetry. Keats tried to make even the structure of
23 his sentences seem unpremeditated. "If poetry,"
24 he claimed, "comes not as naturally as the leaves
25 to a tree, it had better not come at all."
26 Unfortunately, his poetry was not well-received
27 during his lifetime, and it was not until after his
28 death that his writing reached the peak of its
29 influence. In addition, his letters that were
30 published more than 20 years after his death
31 were initially considered unimportant; almost a
32 century later, T.S. Eliot remarked on their
33 importance to the poetry community.
34   English Romantic poetry included many
35 different themes, but Romantic poets are often
36 remembered for writing about nature. However,
37 many of these poets wrote about a range of
38 themes, including imagination, melancholy, and
39 the world of ancient Greece.

GO ON TO THE NEXT PAGE. ▶ ▶ ▶

13. The passage is primarily concerned with

    (A) describing an artistic movement.

    (B) detailing the achievements of William Wordsworth.

    (C) criticizing traditional English poetry.

    (D) providing information about John Keats.

14. In line 5, "traditional" most nearly means

    (A) conservative.

    (B) formal.

    (C) boring.

    (D) standard.

15. It is implied by the passage that

    (A) Romantic poets were better than their predecessors.

    (B) Keats imitated Wordsworth's poetry.

    (C) Keats is considered a Romantic poet.

    (D) Keats only wrote poetry about nature.

16. By the statement in lines 16–17 that a poet should be "a man speaking to men," Wordsworth probably meant that poetry should

    (A) be written in the form of a dialogue.

    (B) always be read aloud to an audience.

    (C) not be written by women.

    (D) have the directness and spontaneity of real speech.

17. All of the following are true about Wordsworth and Keats EXCEPT

    (A) both were Romantic poets.

    (B) both wrote with a naturalness of expression.

    (C) both liked poetry that was told from an angle of a detached observer.

    (D) both wanted to stray from traditional English poetry.

18. Based on the passage, in which of these aspects of poetry did Keats strive to reflect spontaneity?

    (A) the use of emotional language

    (B) the syntax of his sentences

    (C) the subject matter of his poems

    (D) the specific word use

GO ON TO THE NEXT PAGE. ▶ ▶ ▶

Questions 19–24

1   The Neanderthal was an early human that
2   flourished throughout Europe and western Asia
3   over 40,000 years ago. Scientists are still making
4   discoveries and learning new information about
5   this extinct group of humans that descended
6   from a common ancestor about 400,000 years
7   ago. Although Neanderthals lived a long time
8   ago, they are believed to be the first primate
9   species to create symbolic objects and bury their
10 dead, sophisticated behaviors in any animal
11 species.
12   Physically, Neanderthals differed from
13 modern humans in many important ways. They
14 had massive limb bones and a barrel chest, but
15 they were shorter than most humans today.
16 Their faces were large in the middle, and their
17 noses were much larger than modern human's.
18 They had thick brow ridges, a receding forehead,
19 and a bun-like bulge on the back of the skull, and
20 on average, Neanderthal brains and skulls were
21 slightly larger, matching their larger body size.

22   Yet, despite Neanderthals' reputation for low
23 intelligence and their larger brain, there is
24 nothing that clearly distinguishes a
25 Neanderthal's brain from that of modern
26 humans. Combining enormous physical
27 strength with manifest intelligence,
28 Neanderthals appeared to be supremely well
29 adapted to survival. They are known for having
30 used a wide variety of tools, controlled fire, and
31 built shelters, and they were skilled hunters, with
32 evidence showing that they ate big land animals
33 and a variety of marine animals.
34   Nevertheless, around 40,000 years ago,
35 Neanderthals vanished from the face of the
36 earth. The question of what became of the
37 Neanderthals still baffles paleontologists and is
38 perhaps the most talked-about issue in human
39 origins research today.

GO ON TO THE NEXT PAGE. ▶ ▶ ▶

19. The primary purpose of this passage is to

(A) inform the reader about the Neanderthals' physical and mental characteristics.

(B) describe the history of the Neanderthals.

(C) explain the Neanderthals' fate.

(D) refute the theory that Neanderthals had low intelligence.

20. It can be inferred from the passage that most Neanderthals probably had

(A) strong arms.

(B) wide-set eyes.

(C) bowed legs.

(D) narrow feet.

21. According to the passage, Neanderthals lived

(A) in caves and mud dwellings.

(B) by hunting in packs.

(C) in Europe and Asia.

(D) on all the continents.

22. In line 37, "battles" most nearly means

(A) angers.

(B) intrigues.

(C) annoys.

(D) confuses.

23. The passage suggests that modern humans tend to think of Neanderthals as

(A) peaceful.

(B) skilled artists.

(C) farmers.

(D) unintelligent.

24. According to the passage, one question paleontologists are still trying to solve is:

(A) What constituted the basic Neanderthal diet?

(B) What were the Neanderthals' migratory patterns?

(C) Why did the Neanderthal species become extinct?

(D) Where did the Neanderthals originally come from?

GO ON TO THE NEXT PAGE. ▶ ▶ ▶

Questions 25–30

1   Researchers have identified two phenomena
2   that in previous literature were confounded
3   under one category: nightmares. Traditionally, a
4   nightmare is any moment of fear that is
5   experienced at night. However, these researchers
6   have proved that there are both nightmares and
7   night terrors. On the one hand, there is the true
8   nightmare, which is an actual, detailed dream.
9   On the other hand, there is the "night terror,"
10   from which the sleeper, often a child, suddenly
11   awakes in great fright with no memory of a
12   dream, often screaming and sometimes going off
13   in a sleepwalking trance.
14   Nightmares most often occur during rapid
15   eye movement, or REM, sleep. This unique
16   phase of sleep is defined by random movement
17   of the eyes, relaxed muscles, and vivid dreams.
18   After a nightmare, the person dreaming can
19   retell the dream with detail, and these details can
20   make it difficult to fall back asleep.

21   Someone who is experiencing a night terror
22   wakes up suddenly with no memory of a dream.
23   Those experiencing night terrors are often
24   confused, unaware of their surroundings, and
25   unable to communicate, and usually go right
26   back to sleep. In the morning, they often won't
27   remember what happened.
28   Night terrors, which share some
29   commonalities with nightmares, can appear
30   horrifying to anxious parents, but they are
31   seldom of serious consequence. Outside of
32   taking commonsense precautions—such as
33   making sure a sleepwalker does not go to bed
34   near an open window or on a balcony—there is
35   nothing much to do about them. A child's night
36   terrors can be reduced somewhat with a
37   consistent sleep schedule and by avoiding
38   excessive fatigue. Excessive concern or
39   medication should usually be avoided.

GO ON TO THE NEXT PAGE. ▶ ▶ ▶

25. In line 2, "confounded" most nearly means

(A) entitled.

(B) confused.

(C) written.

(D) underappreciated.

26. The passage suggests that, until recently, sleep researchers

(A) knew very little about the nature of dreams.

(B) studied only adult sleeping habits, not those of children.

(C) did not differentiate between nightmares and night terrors.

(D) prescribed medication for children suffering from night terrors.

27. According to the passage, a nightmare is a

(A) full-fledged dream.

(B) dream fragment.

(C) hallucination.

(D) trancelike state.

28. The passage implies that parents of children who experience night terrors

(A) tend to dismiss them as inconsequential.

(B) also suffered night terrors when they were children.

(C) find their occurrence nearly as frightening as the children themselves do.

(D) should consult a doctor as soon as possible.

29. Which of the following questions is NOT answered in the passage?

(A) What is the difference between nightmares and night terrors?

(B) What are some precautions parents can take to ensure the safety of children who experience night terrors?

(C) Does a child who is frightened upon waking from a night terror remember dreaming?

(D) Why does a consistent sleep schedule reduce the incidence of night terrors?

30. According to the passage, how are night terrors different from nightmares?

(A) One is remembered by the sleeper, and the other is not.

(B) One happens when the person is asleep, and the other does not.

(C) One will bring harm to the sleeper, and the other will not.

(D) One requires hospitalization, while the other does not.

GO ON TO THE NEXT PAGE. ▶ ▶ ▶

Questions 31–36

1   In the sport of orienteering, competitors use a
2   map and compass to navigate their way cross
3   country along an unfamiliar course. The history
4   of orienteering began in the late 1800s in Sweden
5   as military training. At the end of World War I,
6   the man who would become the father of
7   orienteering organized a large-scale
8   orienteering meet in Stockholm, Sweden. As
9   compasses became more reliable, the sport
10   gained popularity, and by the mid-1900s,
11   orienteering had spread as far as the United
12   States.
13   At first glance, orienteering is a
14   straightforward sport: there is a list of places to
15   go, and the task is to visit each one, in order, as
16   quickly as you can. The novice quickly finds,
17   however, that the most important question in
18   orienteering is not compass bearing but choice
19   of route. There are almost always several
20   different ways to get from one point to another,

21   and the beeline on a direct compass bearing over
22   a mountain is seldom the best choice.
23   Indeed, veteran orienteers tend to disdain
24   beelining over obstacles as a crude approach;
25   instead, they aspire to intellectual finesse. If
26   climbing 20 feet in elevation requires the time
27   and energy it would take to travel 250 feet on
28   level ground—the sort of quick calculation
29   orienteers are always making—then it may be
30   better to follow a prominent contour along one
31   flank of the mountain or even to stick to the
32   safety of a trail looping around the base. For
33   those who prefer to enjoy exploring without a
34   deadline, there are orienteering courses that can
35   be enjoyed at whatever pace or difficulty. As
36   navigation tools become cheaper and more
37   accessible, it is likely that people will continue to
38   enjoy orienteering as either a competitive or
39   noncompetitive sport—or both!

GO ON TO THE NEXT PAGE. ▶ ▶ ▶

31. The passage suggests that a hiker with a map and compass is NOT orienteering if she

   (A) climbs more than one mountain per route.

   (B) travels over a known, familiar route.

   (C) takes more than one route per day.

   (D) follows a direct path over an obstacle.

32. According to the passage, an orienteer places greatest importance on

   (A) maintaining a single compass bearing.

   (B) avoiding hazardous terrain.

   (C) overcoming obstacles as fast as possible.

   (D) choosing the best route available.

33. It can be inferred from the passage that most orienteers would consider a competitor who climbs a mountain in order to take the most direct route to be

   (A) gaining a major advantage.

   (B) lacking sophistication.

   (C) breaking the rules.

   (D) endangering other competitors.

34. The passage suggests that one skill orienteers require is the ability to

   (A) run while carrying a backpack.

   (B) swim long distances.

   (C) set up a campsite.

   (D) make rapid calculations.

35. In line 25, "finesse" most nearly means

   (A) skill.

   (B) movement.

   (C) inefficiency.

   (D) devotion.

36. Which of the following best describes the author's attitude toward the subject?

   (A) respect

   (B) disdain

   (C) indifference

   (D) appreciation

STOP. IF THERE IS TIME, YOU MAY CHECK YOUR WORK IN THIS SECTION ONLY. STOP

Section 4

Mathematics Achievement

Time—40 Minutes

47 Questions

Each question has four answer choices. Read each question and choose the best answer. You may write on your test.

1. A bag contains only blue and red marbles. If there are three blue marbles for every red marble, what fraction of all the marbles is red?

   (A) $\frac{1}{4}$

   (B) $\frac{1}{3}$

   (C) $\frac{1}{2}$

   (D) $\frac{3}{4}$

Questions 2–3 refer to the graph.

The graph shows the distribution of shirt sizes sold by Ace T-Shirt Company in September.

SEPTEMBER SALES FOR ACE T-SHIRT CO.

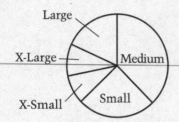

September Sales
for Ace T-Shirt Co.

Total Sales: 1,200 shirts

2. Approximately how many medium-sized shirts were sold?

   (A) 300

   (B) 400

   (C) 500

   (D) 600

3. If each shirt sells for $5.95, approximately how much was spent on small-sized shirts?

   (A) $300

   (B) $900

   (C) $1,800

   (D) $3,600

4. Five percent of the guests at a Halloween party were dressed as witches. If there were 8 witches at the party, how many guests were at the party?

   (A) 40

   (B) 80

   (C) 160

   (D) 200

GO ON TO THE NEXT PAGE. ▶ ▶ ▶

Questions 5–6 refer to the following definition.

For all real numbers a and b,

$a@b = (a \times b) - (a + b)$.

5. $9@8 =$

   (A) 55

   (B) 71

   (C) 72

   (D) 73

6. If $10@N = -1$, then what is the value of N?

   (A) 0

   (B) 1

   (C) 9

   (D) 11

7. The perimeter of a rectangle is 32. If its length is three times as long as its width, what is its width?

   (A) 4

   (B) 6

   (C) 8

   (D) 12

8. Aurica averaged 168 in the first three games she bowled. What must she score in her fourth game in order to raise her average 5 points?

   (A) 158

   (B) 163

   (C) 178

   (D) 188

9. Which of the following equations could NEVER be true?

   (A) $N \times 0 = N$

   (B) $1 \times N = N$

   (C) $N \times N = N$

   (D) $N - 1 = N$

10. If X is the set of numbers greater than 6, and Y is the set of numbers less than 11, how many whole numbers exist that are in both sets?

    (A) 4

    (B) 5

    (C) 6

    (D) Infinitely many

11. Warren has 30% more money than Eduardo has. If Eduardo has $65, how much money does Warren have?

    (A) $45.50

    (B) $50.00

    (C) $80.00

    (D) $84.50

12. If $12 + P = 20 - 2 \times 3$, then what is the value of P?

    (A) 2

    (B) 14

    (C) 36

    (D) 42

GO ON TO THE NEXT PAGE. ▶ ▶ ▶

13. If m is greater than n, and n is greater than 4, which of the following is LEAST?

   (A) $\dfrac{1}{4m}$

   (B) $\dfrac{1}{4n}$

   (C) $\dfrac{1}{4+m}$

   (D) $\dfrac{1}{4+n}$

14. At a party, $\dfrac{1}{3}$ of the guests drank only water, and $\dfrac{2}{5}$ of the guests drank only juice. If the remaining 16 guests had nothing to drink, then how many guests were at the party?

   (A) 30

   (B) 45

   (C) 50

   (D) 60

15. What are all the values of x for which $(x-2)(x+5)=0$?

   (A) -5

   (B) -2

   (C) 2 and -5

   (D) -2 and -5

16. What is the value of $\dfrac{1}{9}+\dfrac{7}{12}+\dfrac{5}{6}$?

   (A) $\dfrac{9}{13}$

   (B) $1\dfrac{19}{36}$

   (C) $1\dfrac{2}{3}$

   (D) 2

17. Which of the following is closest to 15%?

   (A) $\dfrac{1}{7}$

   (B) $\dfrac{1}{5}$

   (C) $\dfrac{1}{4}$

   (D) $\dfrac{1}{3}$

18. When the sum of a set of numbers is divided by the average of these numbers, the result is j. What does j represent?

   (A) Half of the sum of the numbers in the set

   (B) The average of the numbers in the set

   (C) Half of the average of the numbers in the set

   (D) The quantity of numbers in the set

19. If $a=3$ and $b=4$, what is the value of $a^2+2ab+b^2$?

   (A) 14

   (B) 24

   (C) 49

   (D) 144

20. How many distinct prime factors are there of 726?

   (A) 2

   (B) 3

   (C) 4

   (D) 5

GO ON TO THE NEXT PAGE. ▶ ▶ ▶

21. On Monday, the temperatures of four different cities were 55° F, −18° F, 25° F, and −15° F. What was the average (arithmetic mean) temperature on Monday for these four cities?

    (A) 11.75° F

    (B) 12° F

    (C) 20° F

    (D) 47° F

22. What is $\frac{1}{4}$ of 0.72?

    (A) 0.018

    (B) 0.18

    (C) 1.8

    (D) 18

23. In a certain garage, 3 out of every 10 vehicles are trucks. If there are 180 vehicles at the garage, how many of them are trucks?

    (A) 27

    (B) 45

    (C) 54

    (D) 60

24. Andres is x years old, and Percy is three times as old as Andres. What was the sum of their ages, in years, five years ago?

    (A) $x - 5$

    (B) $2x + 2$

    (C) $3x - 10$

    (D) $4x - 10$

25. If the perimeter of an equilateral hexagon is 42, what is the sum of the lengths of two sides?

    (A) 6

    (B) 7

    (C) 12

    (D) 14

26. Which of the following is a possible value of z if $2(z - 3) > 6$ and $z + 4 < 15$?

    (A) 3

    (B) 6

    (C) 7

    (D) 11

27. Daniela has y cards from a trading card game. She gives 5 cards to each of three different friends and, in return, receives 2 cards from each friend. How many cards does Daniela have after the exchange?

    (A) $y - 9$

    (B) $y - 5$

    (C) $y + 3$

    (D) $y + 5$

28. If the average of 6 numbers is 9, what is the sum of those numbers?

    (A) 15

    (B) 30

    (C) 54

    (D) 96

GO ON TO THE NEXT PAGE. ▶ ▶ ▶

29. Four side measures of the complex figure are shown in the diagram.

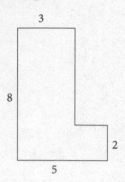

What is the total area of the figure?

(A) 10

(B) 24

(C) 28

(D) 45

30. How many distinct prime factors are there of 48?

(A) 1

(B) 2

(C) 3

(D) 4

31. Four angle measures are shown in the diagram.

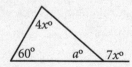

What is the value of a?

(A) 20

(B) 40

(C) 60

(D) 80

32. If $2x + 4 = 26$, then what is the value of $x + 4$?

(A) 9

(B) 11

(C) 13

(D) 15

33. If $x + y$ equals an odd number and $x + z$ equals an even number, which of the following statements could NOT be true?

(A) x is even and y is odd.

(B) y is even and z is odd.

(C) x and z are even and y is odd.

(D) x and y are even and z is odd.

34. If $\frac{1}{2} > x > 0$ and $\frac{1}{3} > x > \frac{1}{10}$, which of the following is a possible value for x?

(A) $\frac{2}{3}$

(B) 0.47

(C) $\frac{1}{5}$

(D) $\frac{1}{20}$

35. Makayla began reading from the beginning of page 42 of a book and stopped at the end of page 83. How many pages did she read?

(A) 40

(B) 41

(C) 42

(D) 43

GO ON TO THE NEXT PAGE. ▶ ▶ ▶

36. Three angle measures of a triangle are shown in the diagram.

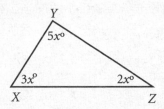

What is the degree measure of angle *YXZ*?

(A) 18

(B) 36

(C) 54

(D) 72

37. What is the difference between 30% of 400 and 15% of 400?

(A) 30

(B) 60

(C) 150

(D) 200

38. Three angle measures of a triangle are shown in the diagram.

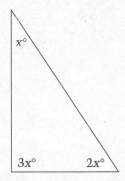

What is the value of *x*?

(A) 20

(B) 30

(C) 45

(D) 90

Questions 39–40 refer to the following definition.

For all real numbers q and r, let $q \mathbin{//} r = (qr) - (q - r)$.

39. What is the value of 8 // 2?

(A) 6

(B) 8

(C) 10

(D) 16

40. If $P // 3 = 11$, then what is the value of *P*?

(A) 3

(B) 4

(C) 6

(D) 7

41. Three points are labeled on the line segment below.

$$A \qquad B \qquad C$$

If $AB = 8$ and $AC = 14$, how far is the midpoint of AB from the midpoint of BC?

(A) 3

(B) 4

(C) 7

(D) 8

42. What is the slope of the line that contains points $(3, -5)$ and $(-1, 7)$?

(A) -3

(B) $-\dfrac{1}{3}$

(C) $-\dfrac{1}{4}$

(D) $\dfrac{1}{3}$

GO ON TO THE NEXT PAGE. ▶ ▶ ▶

43. If one-fourth of a number is 3, what is one-third of the same number?

   (A) 3

   (B) 4

   (C) 6

   (D) 12

44. Isaiah's family is painting several rooms. If 2 gallons of paint can cover 725 square feet of surface, how many gallons will they need to cover 2,175 square feet of surface?

   (A) 3

   (B) 4

   (C) 6

   (D) 8

45. If $r = 8$, then what is the value of $(r + 4)^2$?

   (A) 24

   (B) 64

   (C) 80

   (D) 144

46. At which of the following times is the smaller angle formed by the minute hand and the hour hand of a clock less than 90 degrees?

   (A) 1:30

   (B) 3:00

   (C) 4:30

   (D) 6:00

47. Four equations are shown.

$$2{,}955 \times A = 35{,}460$$
$$11{,}820 \times B = 35{,}460$$
$$3{,}940 \times C = 35{,}460$$
$$7{,}092 \times D = 35{,}460$$

   If each of the equations is correctly solved, which of the following has the greatest value?

   (A) A

   (B) B

   (C) C

   (D) D

STOP. IF THERE IS TIME, YOU MAY CHECK YOUR WORK IN THIS SECTION ONLY. **STOP**

Section 5

Essay

Time—30 Minutes

1 Question

The ISEE Essay is a 30-minute section during which you will plan and write an essay on a given topic. **Writing on another topic is not acceptable.**

The essay gives you a chance to show how well you can write. Express your thoughts as clearly as possible. What you write is not as important as how well you write, but you need to write enough for a reader to understand your point.

You will probably write more than one paragraph. Be aware that a copy of your essay is sent to schools along with your test results. Write only in the lined pages of the answer sheet. You may print or use cursive, but be sure that your writing can be read by someone who is not familiar with your handwriting.

The next page includes space for notes and other essay plans. Give yourself enough time to write a final draft in your answer sheet. On Test Day, you must copy the topic onto your answer sheet, on page 3, in the space provided. This allows schools to know which topic you were provided.

Remember to write only the final draft on pages 3 and 4 of your answer sheet and in blue or black pen. Again, you may print or use cursive. Only pages 3 and 4 will be sent to the schools when you take the official ISEE.

STOP. DO NOT GO ON UNTIL TOLD TO DO SO. STOP

Prompt: Technology makes the world smaller every day. Do you agree or disagree with this statement? Explain why you feel this way.

Notes

_____

_____

_____

_____

_____

_____

_____

_____

_____

_____

_____

_____

_____

_____

_____

_____

STOP. IF THERE IS TIME, YOU MAY CHECK YOUR WORK IN THIS SECTION ONLY. **STOP**

ANSWER KEY

Section 1—Verbal Reasoning

1. A	8. D	15. B	22. D	29. D	36. A
2. B	9. D	16. D	23. D	30. D	37. C
3. B	10. C	17. C	24. B	31. B	38. D
4. D	11. B	18. B	25. A	32. B	39. B
5. C	12. B	19. B	26. A	33. C	40. A
6. B	13. D	20. A	27. D	34. B	
7. D	14. B	21. B	28. B	35. C	

Section 2—Quantitative Reasoning

1. B	8. C	15. C	22. C	29. A	36. A
2. D	9. B	16. C	23. A	30. D	37. C
3. D	10. D	17. B	24. C	31. B	
4. A	11. D	18. C	25. B	32. D	
5. D	12. D	19. B	26. B	33. D	
6. C	13. D	20. B	27. A	34. C	
7. C	14. D	21. A	28. C	35. A	

Section 3—Reading Comprehension

1. C	7. D	13. A	19. A	25. B	31. B
2. C	8. B	14. D	20. A	26. C	32. D
3. D	9. A	15. C	21. C	27. A	33. B
4. B	10. C	16. D	22. C	28. C	34. D
5. A	11. D	17. C	23. D	29. D	35. A
6. C	12. A	18. B	24. C	30. A	36. A

Section 4—Mathematics Achievement

1. A	9. D	17. A	25. D	33. D	41. C
2. B	10. A	18. D	26. C	34. C	42. A
3. C	11. D	19. C	27. A	35. C	43. B
4. C	12. A	20. B	28. C	36. C	44. C
5. A	13. A	21. B	29. C	37. B	45. D
6. B	14. D	22. B	30. B	38. B	46. C
7. A	15. C	23. C	31. B	39. C	47. A
8. D	16. B	24. D	32. D	40. B	

ANSWERS AND EXPLANATIONS

Section 1—Verbal Reasoning

Part One: Synonyms

1. A
If a person is "spontaneous," they act suddenly upon feeling an impulse to do something. This best matches with answer choice (A), "impulsive," which means to be swayed by impulses.

2. B
An "apparition" is a supernatural being, with matches perfectly with answer choice (B), "ghost."

3. B
You can remember the meaning of the word "benevolent" by knowing that the root 'bene-' means good. Someone who does good works is considered "charitable," answer choice (B).

4. D
To "lament" means to feel sorrow for. If someone is feeling sorrow after a loss, they are grieving, making answer choice (D) correct.

5. C
To "reimburse" someone is to pay him back. Reimburse has a similar meaning to "compensate," which means to pay someone for something. Answer choice (C) is correct.

6. B
If someone practices "deceit," they are deceiving others in order to mislead them. This definition is most similar to answer choice (B), "trickery," meaning to trick or deceive.

7. D
Someone who is "despondent" feels hopeless, just like someone who feels "depressed." Answer choice (D) is correct.

8. D
If you are very hungry and then eat a large meal, you can say that your appetite has been satiated, as you are now full. This is most similar to the word "satisfied," answer choice (D).

9. D
"Adamant" people are convinced that they are correct. Another word for someone who is convinced he or she is correct no matter what is answer choice (D), "stubborn." Watch out for answer choice C, "admiring." Just because a word looks similar doesn't mean that it has a similar meaning.

10. C
To have "piety" is to be devout in faith, which matches answer choice (C). You can remember the definition of piety by thinking of the word pious, which has a similar meaning.

11. B
To "laud" is to praise, which matches answer choice (B). An easy way to remember the definition of laud is that it is part of the word applaud. Applauding is what you do when you want to show appreciation for someone's work.

12. B
"Avert" has two primary meanings: to turn away or to ward off. The second meaning most closely matches answer choice (B), "prevent."

13. D
A person who is haughty is overly proud, just like someone who is arrogant, so answer choice (D) is correct.

14. B
If someone is apprehensive, she anticipates that something negative will happen in the future. This person also worries about the future. Answer choice (B) is correct. Watch out for answer choice A; this is another example of words that look similar but do not have similar meanings.

15. B

Someone who is wary is on the lookout for danger. This person is also cautious, which makes answer choice (B) correct.

16. D

If an item is "scarce," there is not much of it to go around. The answer choice that has a similar meaning is choice (D), "rare."

17. C

To be "perceptive" is to have insight and see things that others may not. Someone who is "observant" is alert or watchful. Answer choice (C) is correct.

18. B

To "verify" is to make sure something is correct, which is the same as proving it is correct. Answer choice (B) is correct.

19. B

Speaking with "candor" is speaking openly and sincerely. Part of candor is also being honest, which makes answer choice (B) correct.

20. A

"Abhor" is a strongly negative word meaning to loathe or dislike something. This has a similar meaning to "despise," which means to feel disgust or contempt for something. Answer choice (A) is correct.

Part Two: Sentence Completions

21. B

Context clues are essential to figuring out which answer choice will correctly complete this sentence. The clue in this sentence is that the author has written 12 books. The correct answer will describe the fact that the author has written a large number of books. This matches answer choice (B). Answer choices A, C, and D do not fit with the context of this sentence.

22. D

In this sentence, there is a cause-and-effect relationship between the advent (or introduction) of the computer chip and something happening to Armando's job. This new technology has made his job outdated, or not as useful as it was in the past. This matches answer choice (D), "obsolete." Answer choices A, B, and C would not be used to describe a job, so they are incorrect in this context.

23. D

There are not many clues in this sentence to make a solid prediction, but the key word here is "proved." Using the meaning of that word, you can assume that there were many efforts, but they did not prove successful. Answer choice A, "inextricable," looks tempting, as it means incapable of being disentangled (think of extricating yourself from something), but it doesn't make sense here. Answer choice (D), "futile," means being ineffective, making it the correct answer choice.

24. B

The phrase "in spite of" indicates a contrast or paradox: even though Priyanka worked hard, she did not get the promotion. This prediction matches the correct answer, choice (B), "industrious." The other answer choices would not be reasons that Priyanka should get a promotion, making them incorrect in the context of this sentence.

25. A

Here you have a political party that is banned yet continues to meet. Since this group shouldn't be meeting, you can assume that they are meeting in secret so that the government doesn't know they are doing so. The only answer choice that matches this prediction is choice (A), "clandestine." Answer choice C, "sanctioned," meaning approved or with permission, is the opposite of the meaning that fits the context of this sentence.

26. A

The second part of this sentence (after the semicolon) is a clue about how Sheri was feeling about being caught. She felt guilty about her actions and promised to not hurt anyone again. This prediction matches answer choice (A), "remorse." If you missed the word "genuine" before the blank, you may have been tempted by answer choice B, "melodrama." However, melodrama means to act in an exaggerated way, which does not fit with being genuine.

27. D

The key phrase in this sentence is "to equal—even [blank]—Wright's successes." The architect not only equaled Wright's successes, he exceeded them. Answer choice (D), "surpass," matches this prediction exactly.

28. B

The captain is speaking harshly to her crew, which we can assume is because she dislikes them. The only answer choice with a negative meaning is answer choice (B), "contempt," making it the correct one.

29. D

The biggest clue in this sentence is that Caleb is charming when he tells his stories. This means that his stories are interesting and neither boring nor sad. Answer choice (D), "engaging," is the only one with a positive tone to reflect Caleb's charming storytelling.

30. D

There are many different types of trumpets mentioned as part of the same category of wind instruments. The group has a lot of variety within it. Answer choice (D), "diverse," fits this prediction. Even though answer choice B, "discordant," may be tempting, it is not the correct answer because there is nothing in the sentence to indicate that the variety within this instrument group is a negative thing.

31. B

When answering Sentence Completions with two blanks, start with the easier blank first. In this sentence, the second blank is the easier of the two because there is only one answer choice that fits the context of the sentence. Based on the details that this is a forest fire in the mountains, a prediction for the second blank is *natural*. A powerful forest fire would logically devastate an area, so answer choice (B) the correct answer. Answer choice A contains a trap: "inflammable." While the mountains are able to be set on fire, the disaster is not, making answer choice A incorrect.

32. B

In this sentence, the clue word "whereas" tells you this is a contrast question. The correct answer will have a contrast between the two blanks. Only answer choice (B) has two words that have contrasting meanings, making it the correct answer.

33. C

This question is difficult if you try to predict the blanks separately. In this case, use the clues given to find a pair of words that matches the relationship described. Rahul must be a talented dancer if those who see him can't deny his abilities. These predictions match answer choice (C), "agility . . . question." Although answer choice D's second word does match the prediction, the first word, "melancholy," gives the impression that the dancing is sad in nature. Sad or somber dancing would not make others believe in Rahul's dancing abilities.

34. B

In this sentence, there is a contrast between what was once only possible in movies and what is now a real possibility. For the second blank, a strong prediction would be *possible*. The correct answer, choice (B), has the word "plausible" for the second blank, which means believable or credible, matching with the prediction. The first word in this answer choice, "myth," also fits within the contrast in this sentence. None of the other answer choices have a contrast relationship.

35. C

If you have ever been on a roller coaster, you can relate to the feeling described in this sentence. The clues "screaming and laughing" let you know that the students are having a good time, but they are also a little scared. This matches the first word for answer choice (C), "exhilarated," which means invigorated. It makes sense that if the students were equal parts excited and scared this was their "first experience on the . . . raft." Together, these clues make answer choice (C) the correct answer.

36. A

Based on the keyword, "consequently," there is a contrast between the writing style of Hemingway in the 20th century and that of a 19th-century novel. This means that you are looking for two words that have a contrasting relationship. The only answer choice that has this type of relationship is choice (A). Sparse means "not dense," while verbose means "wordy."

37. C

According to this sentence, even the dog had to rest during this journey. You can assume that the journey was difficult, which eliminates answer choice A. After a difficult journey, one would feel extremely tired, or "fatigued." It makes sense that fatigue would happen after a strenuous journey, which makes the correct answer choice (C). Both answer choices B and D have words for the second blank that are the opposite of the desired definition.

38. D

Finding the correct answer for this sentence is easiest by starting with the second blank. Mountain ranges are by definition large, which matches "massive" from answer choice (D). It is amazing that silk from China was found in Egypt thousands of miles away. This also fits with the first word in answer choice (D), "incredible." Although "steep" could be used to describe mountain ranges, it is definitely not predictable that Chinese silk would be found in Egypt. This makes answer choice C incorrect.

39. B

This sentence describes contrasting characteristics for the Greek festival. Therefore, the correct answer will have two words that also are contrasting. The only answer choice with this relationship between the blanks is answer choice (B), making it the correct answer.

40. A

Although at first there may not be obvious clues in this sentence, you can conclude that the volunteer association is in the process of staffing its offices. This means that the association is likely *hiring*, or "recruiting," people to work for them. For the second blank, a strong prediction would be *characteristics*. Both predictions match the words in answer choice (A). Although "hired" from answer choice D makes sense within the context of this sentence, "tendencies" is not the correct word to match the idea that workers at the volunteer office should have specific skills.

Section 2—Quantitative Reasoning

Part One: Word Problems

1. B

Ayanna originally has $0.50 and is given $0.75 by Tyrel. To get the total, simply add the two amounts together to get answer choice (B), $1.25.

2. D

In any triangle, the measures of the three interior angles sum to 180°, so $X + Y + Z = 180$. Because the measure of angle Y is twice the measure of angle X, $Y = 2X$. Similarly, $Z = 3X$. So $X + 2X + 3X = 180$, $6X = 180$, and $X = 30$. Because $Y = 2X$, the degree measure of angle Y is $2 \times 30 = 60$. Answer choice (D) is correct.

3. D

The first step is to combine the like terms on the left side of the equation. If $3a + 6a = 36$, then $9a = 36$. Divide by 9 on both sides to get $a = 4$. Answer choice (D) is correct.

4. A

The probability of an event happening is the ratio of the number of desired outcomes to the number of possible outcomes:

$$\text{probability} = \frac{\text{number of desirable outcomes}}{\text{number of total possible outcomes}}$$

One side of the pencil has the trademark on it, and the other five sides are blank. When any one of the five blank sides is touching the surface of the table, the marked side cannot be touching the table. So there are five different ways for the pencil to lie on the table without the marked side touching the surface. The total number of possible sides for the pencil to lie on is six. The probability that the trademark will not be touching the surface of the table when the pencil stops rolling is $\frac{5}{6}$, choice (A).

5. D

If distance equals rate times time, then time equals distance divided by rate. Here, the distance is 3,300 miles and the rate is 270 miles per hour, so divide: $3,300 \div 270 = \frac{3,300}{270} \approx 12.22$. Answer choice (D) is correct.

6. C

To solve this problem, you first need to determine the limits of possible values for a:

$$a + 2 > 5$$
$$a > 3$$
$$a - 4 < 1$$
$$a < 5$$

So a is between 3 and 5. The only value from the answer choices that fits in the limits is answer choice (C), 4.

7. C

The easiest way to visualize this problem is to draw a quick diagram in your scratch area. If the two radii form a diameter, they form a straight line. A straight line is equal to 180 degrees, or answer choice (C).

8. C

To find the probability of something occurring, use the probability formula:

$$\text{probability} = \frac{\text{number of desirable outcomes}}{\text{number of total possible outcomes}}$$

If a coin is tossed once, the probability of getting tails is $\frac{1}{2}$. If a coin is tossed twice, the probability of flipping tails both times is determined by multiplying the two individual probabilities together: $\frac{1}{2} \times \frac{1}{2} = \frac{1}{4}$. Answer choice (C) is correct.

9. B

If 70 percent of the students are right-handed and the rest are left-handed, then $100 - 70 = 30$ percent are left-handed. Of that 30 percent, 70 percent have brown eyes. Seventy percent of 30 percent is $(0.70)(0.30) = 0.21$, or 21 percent, which is answer choice (B).

10. D

If every one of the n students invited 3 guests, that would be a total of $3n$ guests. So, n students plus $3n$ guests adds up to $n + 3n = 4n$ attendees. Answer choice (D) is correct.

11. D

To find the correct answer, substitute 8 for r and solve:

$$(8 + 4)^2 = 12^2$$
$$= 144$$

Answer choice (D) is correct.

12. D

Start by using the average formula to determine the total weight:

$$\text{average} = \frac{\text{sum of the terms}}{\text{number of the terms}}$$

$$60 = \frac{\text{total weight}}{3}$$

$$60 \times 3 = \text{total weight}$$

$$180 = \text{total weight}$$

Omari and Fernando each weigh 50 kilograms, so $50 + 50 + $ Izyan's weight $= 180$ kilograms. Therefore, Izyan must weigh 80 kilograms, which is answer choice (D).

13. D

The eggs cost 16 cents apiece. You need to figure out how many eggs can make up for the cost of 6 new chickens, or $58. In other words, how many times does 16 cents divide into $58? Set this problem up as you would any division problem, paying attention to decimal places.

$$0.16 \overline{)58.00}$$

$$362.5$$

$$16 \overline{)5800.0}$$

Since the farmer cannot sell half of an egg, he must sell 363 eggs in order to pay for the chickens, which is answer choice (D).

14. D

The first step is to solve for x:

$$2x + 4 = 26$$
$$2x = 22$$
$$x = 11$$

If $x = 11$, then $x + 4 = 15$, which is answer choice (D).

15. C

Sophia shoveled for a total of $2\frac{1}{3} + 1\frac{3}{4}$ hours. To add, first convert to improper fractions: $\frac{7}{3} + \frac{7}{4}$. Then find a common denominator: $\frac{28}{12} + \frac{21}{12} = \frac{49}{12}$. Lastly, convert to a mixed number: $4\frac{1}{12}$. Sophia shoveled snow for $4\frac{1}{12}$ hours in total, answer choice (C).

16. C

To find the number of integers in an inclusive range, subtract the first integer from the last integer, and then add 1: $1{,}980 - 1{,}960 = 20$; $20 + 1 = 21$, answer choice (C).

17. B

To find the value of 10*, use the definition of n* given in the question and plug in 10 for n. $10* = 2(10) + 4 = 20 + 4 = 24$, which is answer choice (B).

18. C

If triangle ABC is equilateral, then each angle is equal to 60 degrees. You know that $\angle BCA$ and $\angle BCE$ are supplementary, which means they equal 180 degrees, so set up an equation:

$$\angle BCA + \angle BCE = 180$$
$$60 + \angle BCE = 180$$
$$120 = \angle BCE$$

This matches answer choice (C).

19. B

If 6 biscuits remain, $42 - 6 = 36$ were eaten by the 12 guests. Now, use the average formula to find the number of biscuits eaten by guests:

$$\text{average} = \frac{\text{sum of the terms}}{\text{number of the terms}}$$
$$\frac{36}{12} = 3.$$

This makes the correct answer choice (B).

20. B

A square with an area of 36 square centimeters has sides of length 6 centimeters. Thus, each side of the large square gets cut into thirds, and the whole large square gets divided into $3 \times 3 = 9$ smaller squares:

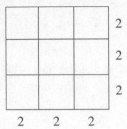

This matches answer choice (B).

Part Two: Quantitative Comparisons

21. A

Remember to use strategic thinking to solve Quantitative Comparisons as efficiently as possible. You don't need to figure out the exact numbers for each column because in both cases, you're subtracting some number from 1,000. Because you're subtracting more from 1,000 in Column B, the resulting number in Column A will be larger than that of Column B. This means that the correct answer is choice (A).

22. C

The strategic test taker remembers that the average of a group of consecutive integers is equal to the middle value:

$$\text{average} = \frac{\text{sum of terms}}{\text{number of terms}}$$
$$\text{average age} = \frac{8 + 12 + 16 + 20 + 24}{5}$$
$$= \frac{80}{5}$$
$$= 16$$

The ages of the family are consecutive multiples of 4, so their average is the middle value, or 16. Either way, the correct answer is choice (C).

23. A

The first step to solving this one is to simplify the equation at the top of the question:

$$3x - 12 = 3x - 6x$$
$$3x - 12 = -3x$$
$$-12 = -6x$$
$$2 = x$$

If $x = 2$, then $x + 2 = 4$. Therefore, Column A is bigger, making answer choice (A) correct.

24. C

To find the area of a triangle, use the formula $\frac{1}{2}$(base) (height) $= A$. For Column A, this is $\frac{1}{2}(6)(10) = 30$. In Column B, this is $\frac{1}{2}(12)(5) = 30$. The columns are equal, so answer choice (C) is correct.

25. B

Multiplying through Column A gives you $4x + 2$. Compare piece by piece: while you may not know the value of $4x$, it will be the same in both columns. Looking at the second piece in each column, 4 is greater than 2, so the correct answer is choice (B).

26. B

Find the average for each set of numbers separately and then compare the values. For Column A, $\frac{106 + 117 + 123 + 195}{4} = 135.25$. For Column B, $\frac{110 + 118 + 124 + 196}{4} = 137$. Because the value for Column B is larger than the one for Column A, the correct answer choice is choice (B).

27. A

Ten percent of $60 is $6, so the sale price for the video game is $60 − $6 = $54. This is greater than $50 in Column B, so the correct answer is choice (A).

28. C

The first step to solving this question is to simplify the expression under Column A. The middle fraction, $\frac{15}{45}$, simplifies to $\frac{1}{3}$ because both the numerator and denominator can be divided by 15. From $\frac{4}{5} \times \frac{1}{3} \times \frac{3}{16}$, cancel out the 3 in the denominator of the second fraction and in the numerator of the third fraction. Then, factor out a 4 from the the numerator of the first fraction and the denominator of the third fraction. Finally, determine the product of the two fractions and convert to a decimal (because Column B is in decimal form): $\frac{1}{5} \times \frac{1}{4} = \frac{1}{20} = 0.05$. By doing this, you will see that both columns equal 0.05, making the correct answer choice (C).

29. A

Picking Numbers is a great way to solve Algebra questions that involve variables. Be sure to select numbers that are easy to work with and fit the information in the question stem. For this question, select an easy negative integer to work with, like -1. Substitute -1 for d in each of the columns to find the correct answer:

Column A: $3(-1) - 1 = -3 - 1 = -4$

Column B: $-2(-1) - 2 = 0$

Because Column A is larger than Column B, answer choice (A) is correct.

30. D

You're given that x is between $\frac{8}{9}$ and $\frac{1}{2}$, and you're asked to compare x to $\frac{2}{3}$. The fraction $\frac{2}{3}$ is between $\frac{8}{9}$ and $\frac{1}{2}$, but so are lots of other fractions. Some are less than $\frac{2}{3}$, and others are greater than $\frac{2}{3}$. Column A could be greater than, equal to, or less than Column B, so the answer is choice (D).

31. B

The strategic test taker will notice that this question can be solved with little actual math. You are told that x is negative. Before you start plugging in values for x, examine the expression under Column B: $(2x)(1x)$. If you multiplied these x's together, whatever the value, the result would be positive. The value under Column A, however, would remain negative. Because a positive is always greater than a negative, the correct answer is choice (B).

32. D

Don't be fooled by the number 8 under Column B. Column A asks you to find the perimeter of an octagon with sides of equal length. The problem is, you don't know what those lengths are. One side could equal 1, in which case the answer would be (C). One side could be 2, in which case the answer would be (A). You already have two possibilities, which tells you that the correct answer must be choice (D).

33. D

Because there are only variables in each column, this is a perfect question to use the Picking Numbers strategy. If $n = 1$, then Column A is 1 and Column B is 1^2, or 1, so the columns are equal. But if $n = 2$, then Column A is 2 and Column B is 2^2, or 4, so Column B is greater. Because there is more than one possible relationship between the columns, answer choice (D) is correct.

34. C

This question could seem tricky at first glance, but if you remember the rule that "A% of B is equal to B% of A," this one is a breeze. In this case, 98% of 51 is $0.98 \times 51 = 49.98$, and 51% of 98 is $0.51 \times 98 = 49.98$. This means that the columns are equal, so answer choice (C) is correct.

35. A

The mean of the set can be found by adding all the numbers in the set and then dividing by the number of terms.

$$\text{average} = (6 + 13 + 4 + 22 + 7 + 9 + 0 + 11) \div 8$$
$$= 72 \div 8$$
$$= 9$$

To find the median of the set, first put the terms in order: 0, 4, 6, 7, 9, 11, 13, 22. Because this set has an even number of terms, take the average of the middle two numbers of the set: $(7 + 9) \div 2 = 8$. Because 9 is greater than 8, answer choice (A) is correct.

36. A

To find the number of degrees in a regular polygon, use the formula $180 (n - 2)$, where $n =$ the number of sides. For Column A, the number of sides in a hexagon is 6, so the total number of degrees in a pentagon is $180 (6 - 2) = 180 (4) = 720$. Because regular means that all angles in the polygon are equal, one angle in the hexagon measures $720 \div 5 = 144$ degrees. For Column B, the number of sides in a pentagon is 5, so the total number of degrees in a pentagon is $180 (5 - 2) = 180 (3) = 540$. One angle in the regular pentagon is equal to $540 \div 5 = 108$. Because Column A is larger, the correct answer is choice (A).

37. C

To find the probability of something occurring, use the formula: $\text{probability} = \dfrac{\text{number of desirable outcomes}}{\text{number of total possible outcomes}}$. If a coin is tossed once, the probability of getting either heads or tails is $\dfrac{1}{2}$. If a coin is tossed twice, the probability of flipping first tails and then heads is determined by multiplying the two individual probabilities together: $\dfrac{1}{2} \times \dfrac{1}{2} = \dfrac{1}{4}$. There are 13 diamond cards in a deck of 52 cards. This means that the probability of randomly selecting a diamond is $\dfrac{13}{52}$, which reduces to $\dfrac{1}{4}$. The two columns are equal, which means that choice (C) is the correct answer.

Section 3—Reading Comprehension

Edward Stratemeyer Passage

This passage is about Edward Stratemeyer, a writer who created those fictional teen heroes and heroines the Hardy Boys, Nancy Drew, and the Bobbsey Twins. The author gives some biographical information about Stratemeyer, but the passage's main thrust is that he was so successful because his career coincided with the growth of a new population segment—adolescents. Labor laws passed early in the 20th century required children to stay in school until the age of 16, which gave them more free time than they'd ever had before. Wanting adventure, they read Stratemeyer's books.

1. C

This question is a Main Idea question, which you can determine from the reference to the entire passage and the phrase "primarily serves to." For Main Idea questions, first summarize the passage in your own words, and then find which answer choice most closely matches your prediction. This passage is mainly about the different factors that led to Stratemeyer's books gaining popularity among teenagers. This matches answer choice (C).

2. C

The second sentence describes the adventurous young heroes of Stratemeyer's books as having particular appeal and the final sentence notes that Stratemeyer satisfied his readers' needs with a "slew of heroic super-teens." Since Stratemeyer's readers were mostly teenagers, you can infer that his fictional heroes appealed to them because of their similar ages, which matches answer choice (C). Answer choices A, B, and D are not mentioned in the passage.

3. D

The passage states that, by 1930, adolescence had come of age because labor laws required children to be in school until the age of sixteen. This makes answer choice (D) correct. Answer choice C could be a trap if you don't remember that this is a Supporting Ideas question, which means that the answer is directly stated in the passage. The year 1930 is described as the end of the heyday of Stratemeyer's career, but that doesn't necessarily mean his reading audience started to drop; it may just as well mean he stopped writing so many books.

4. B

The phrase "according to the passage" signals that this is a Supporting Ideas question. In the final sentence of the passage, the author states that Stratemeyer was "… writing under a variety of pseudonyms," which matches answer choice (B). Watch out for answer choice D: the passage states that Stratemeyer didn't get commercial success by luck alone, but he was successful.

5. A

For this Vocab-in-Context question, go back to the referenced line and predict your own word or phrase to fit where "stage" is. In lines 26–29, the author states, "These changes [created] a new stage of life: adolescence." The author is describing how children who once had to drop out of school and work in factories were now staying in school and having free time, which they could use to read for fun, before they become adults. Predict that adolescence is a part of growing up, between being a young child and an adult. Another word for this is period, a length of time. This matches answer choice (A).

6. C

Questions about the author's attitude are generally asking about the tone of the passage. Are the author's points positive, negative, or neutral? The author uses phrases such as "did not gain enormous commercial success through luck alone" and "responded to the needs of his readers with a slew of heroic super-teens." Those show that the author had a positive attitude, and that rules out answer choices B and D. Next, think about how the passage would sound if you read it aloud. Does it sound as if the author didn't think Stratemeyer would be successful, or does it sound as if the author respected Stratemeyer's work? Answer choice (C) is correct.

Dummies Passage

This passage is about ventriloquists' dummies. The author tells you when dummies were first developed and that although early dummies looked, on the outside, much like those of today, they were in fact a complicated mixture of "engineering feats and sculpture" on the inside. The passage goes on to describe the inside of early dummy heads, especially the dummies made by the McElroy brothers. Their creations are said to have rivaled those of the Wright Brothers—inventors of the airplane—in complexity.

7. D

Throughout this passage, the author gives many details about how ventriloquists' dummies are made and some historical facts about prominent artists who made them. This matches the correct answer, choice (D). Answer choice A is incorrect because the passage does not focus on two different families, only one. Answer choice B is too broad, because this passage mainly focuses on technical details about the dummies, not the art form more generally. Answer choice C is incorrect because the author does not describe the dummy today as compared to the original models.

8. B

The word "inferred" in the question stem is a clue that this is an Inference question. The author discusses the outward appearance of the dummies in both the second and fourth paragraphs. Although their outward appearance has changed over time, the function of the dummies themselves has NOT changed. When they were first created, they were used to help ventriloquists have a conversation instead of simply throwing their voices. The author concludes by stating that modern dummies continue to serve this purpose, even if they look different. You can infer that the outward appearance "has not changed their roles in ventriloquists' acts," which is answer choice (B).

9. A

This is an Inference question, as indicated by the word "suggests." The correct answer, choice (A), restates the main idea of paragraphs 2 and 3: the interiors of the best dummies "were a curious fusion of engineering feats and sculpture"—that is, a mix of science and art. With their exaggerated features, even the best-made dummies aren't meant to fool the observer, answer choice B; instead, it's the "throwing" of the ventriloquist's voice that does the fooling. Answer choice C distorts the point, in paragraph 4, that dummies from all eras have similar range of movement. Finally, the McElroy brothers' dummies, arguably the best ever made, were constructed before World War II, not after, making answer choice D incorrect.

10. C

A "synergistic effort" describes two things working together so that the effect of the whole is more than the effect of the parts working separately. You know that the McElroy brothers worked together on their puppets, making choice (C) the correct answer. There's no evidence for answer choice A in the passage, and answer choices B and D are never mentioned.

11. D

The author clearly admires the work of the McElroy brothers, so answer choices A and B are easily eliminated. Answer choice C, elated, means extremely happy, which doesn't fit within the dry, expository passage. Answer choice (D) remains as the correct answer with its positive (but not overly positive) connotation.

12. A

This question is difficult to predict, so eliminate answer choices that are not discussed in the passage. Answer choice B is answered in lines 1–3. Answer choice C is in lines 27–28, with answer choice D answered shortly after in lines 29–31. Answer choice (A) is not addressed in the passage, so it is therefore correct.

Romantic Passage

This passage is about the Romantic poets, a group of writers in 19th-century England who "prided themselves on their rejection of" earlier English poetry. In other words, the Romantic poets tried to write differently than their predecessors. In support of this thesis, you're told about how two major Romantic poets, Wordsworth and Keats, rejected pre-Romantic poems as insincere and affected and tried to write more spontaneous-seeming poems.

13. A

The correct answer is choice (A): the passage describes the Romantic movement in British poetry, an artistic movement. Answer choices B and D are equally incorrect, as each focuses on only one Romantic poet. While answer choice C describes how the Romantics felt about earlier English poetry (they were critical of it), it doesn't sum up the passage, which also describes the kind of poetry the Romantics themselves tried to write.

14. D

The word "traditional" is used here to describe earlier British poetry. The Romantics rebelled against what they saw as the usual or standard practices of earlier poets, so (D) is correct. A, B, and C are all fairly plausible in other contexts, but they don't have the equivalent meaning of "traditional" in this sentence.

15. C

This Inference question is difficult to predict, so eliminate answer choices that do not include information that can be inferred from the passage. The correct answer, choice (C), can be inferred from lines 20–21, in which Keats is described as "Wordsworth's younger contemporary." Since Wordsworth was a Romantic poet, it makes sense that Keats would be, too. Although answer choice A may be tempting, all you know from the passage is that the specific techniques for Romantic poetry were different than the poetry of their predecessors, not that Romantic poetry was of higher quality.

16. D

To figure out the correct answer, read the sentence starting in line 14. In that sentence, the author states that Wordsworth "attempted to achieve spontaneity and naturalness of expression" in his poems. This matches answer choice (D). Answer choices A, B, and C all interpret Wordsworth's statement too literally. Wordsworth meant that poetry should seem like spontaneous speech, not that it should actually be written in dialogue form, or always read aloud, or only be written by men.

17. C

This is another question that will require you to eliminate answer choices until you are left with the correct answer. For this question, you will eliminate any answer choices that have support in the passage. Answer choice A can be found in lines 10–11 and 20–22. Answer choice B is in line 15 and lines 22–23. Answer choice D is in lines 4–6. Answer choice (C) is contradicted in lines 15–19, making it the correct one.

18. B

In lines 22–23, the author states that "Keats tried to make even the structure of his sentences seem unpremeditated." This best matches answer choice (B), which refers to the syntax of his poetry. Answer choice A would apply to the poetry of Keats's predecessors, making it an incorrect answer choice. Neither answer choice C nor D is directly stated in the passage.

Neanderthal Passage

This passage is about the Neanderthal, an early human who lived in Europe and Asia until about 35,000 years ago. The passage puts forth two ideas: first, that Neanderthals were physically very different from modern humans, and second, that despite their reputation to the contrary, Neanderthals were probably quite intelligent. The passage concludes with a teaser: the disappearance of this capable creature mystifies and fascinates scientists and is "perhaps the most talked-about issue in human origins research today."

19. A

When answering Main Idea questions, focus on the big picture and what the main idea of the entire passage is. For this passage, the author gives lots of details about Neanderthals with respect to their physical appearance, as well as their intellectual capabilities. This best matches answer choice (A). Although there are some historical details about the Neanderthal in this passage, those details are not the focus of this passage, which makes answer choice B incorrect. The author states that we do not know what happened to the Neanderthals to cause their disappearance, so answer choice C is not correct. Finally, this is not a persuasive passage, so answer choice D does not make sense.

20. A

All four choices are physical attributes of the Neanderthal. In the author's description of Neanderthals (paragraph 2), "massive limb bones" are the first item on the list. A "limb" is an arm or a leg, so you can infer from this that most Neanderthals had strong arms, answer choice (A). You can't infer, however, that their legs were bowed because "bowed" implies shape, not size. The set of Neanderthal eyes and the breadth of their feet are never mentioned. Answer choice (A) is correct.

21. C

This Supporting Ideas question requires you to know which answer choice is directly stated in the passage. The opening sentence states that Neanderthals lived "throughout Europe and western Asia," which makes answer choice (C) correct. The passage never mentions what kind of dwellings they lived in, how they hunted, or whether they lived on all the continents. This makes answer choices A, B, and D out of scope and incorrect.

22. C

Because this is a Vocab-in-Context question, go back to the passage and form a prediction for the word in the context of the sentence. According to the sentence, scientists still have a question about what happened to the Neanderthals, which best matches answer choice (D). Both answer choices A and C could be true, but do not fit with the context of this particular sentence.

23. D

To answer this question most efficiently, look for where "modern humans" are mentioned in the passage. Modern humans are first mentioned in the second paragraph when the author is describing the physical appearance of Neanderthals. Then, at the beginning of paragraph 3, the author writes that "despite Neanderthals' reputation for low intelligence . . . there is nothing that clearly distinguishes a Neanderthal's brain from that of modern humans." The first part of this sentence signifies that enough humans believe this about Neanderthals for them to have this reputation. This matches answer choice (D). The other answer choices are not mentioned in the passage.

24. C

The word "question" appears only once in the passage, in the final sentence. You know from the previous sentence that Neanderthals vanished or died out around 40,000 years ago. However, it is unknown what actually happened to them. Therefore, answer choice (C) is correct. The questions in the other answer choices are not found in the passage.

Night Terrors

This is a passage about two psychological phenomena: first, nightmares, and second, something called night terrors. In the latter, the sleeper, usually a child, wakes up in great fright with no memory of having dreamed. The passage begins with the statement that, while nightmares and night terrors used to be confused with each other, researchers now know they are two different phenomena. The rest of the passage focuses on night terrors, noting that they're not really dangerous and that parents should use common sense, taking precautions and not worrying unduly.

25. B

Two phenomena, long "confounded" under one heading, are now known to be separate things. The word in question, then, should mean confused, or mixed up, answer choice (B). None of the other words means anything remotely similar to "confounded."

26. C

The correct answer, choice (C), restates the first sentence of the passage. None of the other choices are suggested by information in the passage, not even answer choice D, which is a distorted echo of the passage's final sentence. The author says that children suffering from night terrors should usually not be medicated. This is a far cry from saying that sleep researchers used to prescribe medication for such children but have recently stopped.

27. A

The correct answer for this question will be directly stated in the passage. Line 8 says that a nightmare "is an actual, detailed dream." Answer choice (A) correctly restates this fact. No mention is made of dream fragments, hallucinations, or trances.

28. C

According to the passage, parents of children with night terrors themselves sometimes find their child's experience "horrifying" and that a child suffering from night terrors can make a parent "anxious." You can infer, then, that the parents find night terrors nearly as frightening as the children do, so answer choice (C) is correct. Choice A is the opposite of what the author says. Answer choice B is out of scope, since the passage never suggests that these parents also suffered night terrors when they were children. The last sentence of the passage implies, if anything, that a doctor usually should not be consulted at all, rather than as soon as possible.

29. D

The difference between nightmares and night terrors is defined in paragraph 1. The question in Choice B is answered in the final paragraph. Paragraph 3 notes that the child waking from a night terror does not remember dreaming, which means that answer choice C is incorrect This leaves answer choice (D) as correct, and indeed, the author merely advises a sleep schedule, never explaining why a sleep schedule helps reduce night terrors.

30. A

To help answer this question, pay attention to the phrases "on the one hand" (line 7) and "on the other" (line 9). The contrast in those lines aligns closely with answer choice (A), which is the correct one. Answer choice B is incorrect because both nightmares and night terrors occur when someone is asleep. Answer choices C and D are not mentioned in the passage.

Orienteering Passage

This passage is about the sport of orienteering, in which competitors make their way across unfamiliar terrain using only a map and a compass. The author focuses on the notion that the most important element of orienteering is choosing a good route. Why? Because the shortest route from point A to point B is rarely the fastest or easiest way.

31. B

What defines orienteering, if not having a compass and a map? Orienteers have to "navigate their way cross-country along an unfamiliar course." Therefore, a hiker with a map and compass is NOT orienteering if she travels over a known, familiar route, so answer choice (B) is correct. Answer choices A and C propose rules that are never mentioned in the passage. Answer choice D describes an orienteer who takes the "crude" approach.

32. D

The author states in lines 17–19 that, "the most important question in orienteering is not compass bearing but choice of route," which eliminates answer choice A and makes answer choice (D) correct. While it is no doubt important to avoid hazardous terrain and to overcome obstacles quickly, the passage places the highest priority on the choice of route.

33. B

The competitor in question climbs a mountain to take the most direct route, but line 22 states that this is "seldom the best" and that orienteers "tend to disdain" (line 23) competitors who do so as crude and lacking intellectual finesse, or sophistication. This best matches answer choice (B). Answer choice A is incorrect because the competitor's beeline approach will probably put him at a disadvantage in terms of both time and energy. The beeline approach may be stupid, but the author never says it's against the rules, answer choice C, or that it can endanger other competitors, answer choice D.

34. D

The passage never mentions the activities in answer choices A, B, or C (running or backpacks, swimming, or setting up campsites). Answer choice (D) is the only answer left and is the correct one. In fact, lines 28–29 note that orienteers "are always making" quick calculations of the times and distances involved in various possible routes.

35. A

To get to the correct answer, first look at the sentence "finesse" appears in. The author contrasts "intellectual finesse" with "beelining over obstacles," which means orienteers would rather use their minds before acting, so you know the answer's not answer choice B, "movement." Answer choice C is incorrect, too, because "intellectual inefficiency" doesn't make sense based on what you know about orienteering. That leaves "skill" (ability) and "devotion" (dedication). Answer choice (A) fits with the meaning of the sentence and is therefore correct.

36. A

Questions about the author's attitude are generally asking about the tone of the passage. To answer these types of questions most effectively, consider if the author's points are positive, negative, or neutral. The passage mentioned orienteers' "intellectual finesse" and the "quick calculation (they) are always making." That rules out answer choices B and C because they have a negative tone. Between the two choices left, answer choice (A) makes the most sense because the author clearly thinks highly of orienteers, but she isn't necessarily grateful for what they do.

Section 4—Mathematics Achievement

1. A

If there are 3 blue marbles for every red marble, 1 out of every 4 marbles is red. Therefore, red marbles represent $\frac{1}{4}$ of all the marbles. Answer choice (A) is correct.

2. B

Looking at the pie chart, you can see that the slice that represents medium shirts represents about $\frac{1}{3}$ of the pie. The entire pie represents 1,200 shirts, so $\frac{1}{3}$ represents 400 shirts, answer choice (B).

3. C

The slice that represents small shirts represents about $\frac{1}{4}$ of the pie. Since the whole pie is 1,200 shirts, there were 300 small shirts sold. Each shirt sold for $5.95. The question asks approximately how much was spent on the small shirts, so estimate the price of a shirt to be $6 to make the calculation easier. The choices are pretty far apart, so it's okay to do this. $300 \times \$6 = \$1,800$, so answer choice (C) is correct.

4. C

According to the question, 5 percent of the guests at the party are witches. You also know that there are 8 witches at the party. Set up an equation to find the total number of people (x) at the party:

$$5 \text{ percent of } x = 8 \text{ people}$$

$$\frac{5}{100}x = 8$$

$$\frac{1}{20}x = 8$$

$$x = 8(20)$$

$$x = 160$$

There are 160 total guests at the party, which matches answer choice (C).

5. A

Plug the given values into the formula to solve: $9@8 = (9 \times 8) - (9 + 8) = 72 - 17 = 55$. Answer choice (A) is correct.

6. B

Plug into the formula and solve for N:

$$10@N = -1$$

$$(10 \times N) - (10 + N) = -1$$

$$10N - 10 - N = -1$$

$$9N - 10 = -1$$

$$9N = 9$$

$$N = 1$$

The correct answer is choice (B).

7. A

Let $w =$ the width of the rectangle. Its length is three times its width, or $3w$. Perimeter is equal to $2(l + w)$, where l and w represent length and width, respectively. The perimeter is 32, so $2(l + w) = 32$. Plug in $3w$ for l: $2(3w + w) = 32$; $8w = 32$; $w = 4$. The correct answer is choice (A).

8. D

Because $\text{average} = \frac{\text{sum of terms}}{\text{number of terms}}$, $\text{average} \times \text{number of terms} = \text{sum of terms}$. If Aurica averaged 168 in her first three games, that means she scored a total of $3 \times 168 = 504$ points. With her last game, Aurica needs to score enough to raise her average by 5 points, bringing the sum to $168 + 5 = 173$. This means that she needs to score a total of $173 \times 4 = 692$ for all four games. Since she scored 504 in the first three games, she'll need to score $692 - 504 = 188$ in her last game. Answer choice (D) is correct.

9. D

Evaluate each statement. If you can come up with even one value for N that makes the statement true, eliminate it:

Choice A: If $N = 0$, $0 \times 0 = 0$, so the statement is true—eliminate.

Choice B: If $N = 1$, $1 \times 1 = 1$, so the statement is true—eliminate.

Choice C: If $N = 1$, $1 \times 1 = 1$, so the statement is true—eliminate.

Choice (D): $N - 1 = N$, so $N = N + 1$. There is no value of N for which adding 1 to it will result in a sum of N, so this statement can never be true.

Answer choice (D) is correct.

10. A

The strategic test taker will notice that this question is simply asking how many whole numbers are there between 6 and 11. There are 4 distinct whole numbers in that set, making answer choice (A) correct.

11. D

If Warren has $65, Eduardo has $65 + 30%($65) = $65 + $19.50 = $84.50. Answer choice (D) is correct.

12. A

To solve for P, move all other values to the other side of the equals sign:

$$12 + P = 20 - 2 \times 3$$
$$12 + P = 20 - 6$$
$$12 + P = 14$$
$$P = 2$$

Answer choice (A) is correct.

13. A

The four fractions you're comparing all have the same numerator (1), and they all have positive denominators, so the fraction with the least value must be the one with the greatest denominator. You know m is greater than n, so $4m$ is greater than $4n$, and $4 + m$ is greater than $4 + n$. That eliminates answer choices B and D. Because $m > 4$, $4m > 4 + m$. Thus, answer choice (A) has the greatest denominator and therefore the least value.

14. D

The $\frac{1}{3}$ who drank water only and the $\frac{2}{5}$ who drank juice only account for $\frac{1}{3} + \frac{2}{5} = \frac{5}{15} + \frac{6}{15} = \frac{11}{15}$ of the guests. The 16 who drank nothing therefore account for the other $\frac{4}{15}$.

So you want to find out what number multiplied by $\frac{4}{15}$ will give you 16: $\frac{4}{15}x = 16$; $x = 16 \times \frac{15}{4} = 4 \times 15 = 60$. Answer choice (D) is correct.

15. C

The expression $(x - 2)(x + 5)$ will equal 0 when either quantity $(x - 2)$ or $(x + 5)$ is equal to 0. To find out what the value of x is in either case, set each quantity equal to 0 and solve. This equation is true when $x = 2$ or $x = -5$, which is answer choice (C).

16. B

To solve this problem, you need to find a common denominator. In this case, the lowest common denominator is 36:

$$\frac{1}{9} + \frac{7}{12} + \frac{5}{6} = \frac{4}{36} + \frac{21}{36} + \frac{30}{36}$$
$$= \frac{55}{36}$$
$$= 1\frac{19}{36}$$

Answer choice (B) is correct.

17. A

Fifteen percent is equal to $\frac{15}{100}$, or 0.15. Convert each choice to a decimal to see which comes closest to 0.15.

Choice (A): $\frac{1}{7} = 0.142$

Choice B: $\frac{1}{5} = 0.2$

Choice C: $\frac{1}{4} = 0.25$

Choice D: $\frac{1}{3} = 0.03\overline{3}$

Of the choices, 0.142 is closest to 0.15, so answer choice (A) is correct.

18. D

Translating complicated word problems into written equations can help you figure out where to get started. Solve for j using the average formula:

$$\text{average} = \frac{\text{sum of terms}}{\text{number of terms}}$$

Now, rearrange this equation so the "average of terms" is in the denominator of the fraction, to match the information in the question:

$$\frac{\text{sum of terms}}{\text{average of terms}} = \text{number of terms} = j$$

Answer choice (D) is correct.

19. C

Plug $a = 3$ and $b = 4$ into the expression:

$$a^2 + 2ab + b^2 = 3^2 + 2(3)(4) + 4^2$$
$$= 9 + 24 + 16$$
$$= 49$$

Answer choice (C) is correct.

20. B

Break 726 down to its prime factorization by factoring out any prime factors you see one at a time:

$$726 = 2 \times 363$$
$$= 2 \times 3 \times 121$$
$$= 2 \times 3 \times 11 \times 11$$

There are 3 distinct prime factors: 2, 3, and 11. Answer choice (B) is correct.

21. B

You know average $= \dfrac{\text{sum of terms}}{\text{number of terms}}$, so set up an equation to find the average temperature on Monday:

$$\text{average} = \frac{55 + (-18) + 25 + (-15)}{4}$$
$$= \frac{80 + (-33)}{4}$$
$$= 11\frac{3}{4} = 11.75°$$

Answer choice (B) is correct.

22. B

The easiest way to solve this problem is to convert $\dfrac{1}{4}$ to a decimal, 0.25, and then multiply. Again, make sure that you remember to count your decimal places.

$$(0.72) \times (0.25) = 0.18$$

Answer choice (B) is correct

23. C

Let $t =$ the number of trucks and set up a proportion:

$$\frac{3}{10} = \frac{t}{180}$$
$$(3)(180) = 10t$$
$$540 = 10t$$
$$54 = t$$

The correct answer is answer choice (C).

24. D

Today, Andres is x years old and Percy is $3x$ years old. Five years ago, Andres was $x - 5$ years old and Percy was $3x - 5$, so the sum of their ages was $(x - 5) + (3x - 5) = 4x - 10$. This matches answer choice (D).

25. D

The key to solving this problem is to take in the information one piece at a time. You're told that you have an equilateral hexagon. *Equilateral* means that all sides are equal. A hexagon has 6 sides. If you divide 6 into 42, you have the measure of one side: 7. So, two sides would total 14. Answer choice (D) is correct.

26. C

Simplify each inequality:

$$2(z - 3) > 6 \qquad\qquad z + 4 < 15$$
$$2z - 6 > 6 \qquad\qquad z < 15 - 4$$
$$2z > 6 + 6 \qquad\qquad z < 11$$
$$2z > 12$$
$$z > 6$$

Because z must be a solution for both inequalities, z is between 6 and 11. The only answer choice that qualifies is answer choice (C), 7.

27. A

Daniela starts with y cards. Giving away 5 to each of 3 friends means giving away $3 \times 5 = 15$, leaving her with $y - 15$. Receiving 2 from each of 3 friends means receiving $3 \times 2 = 6$, leaving her with $y - 15 + 6 = y - 9$. Choice (A) is correct.

28. C

Use the average formula:

$$\text{average} = \frac{\text{sum of the items}}{\text{number of items}}$$
$$9 = \frac{\text{sum}}{6}$$
$$\text{sum} = 9 \times 6 = 54$$

Answer choice (C) is correct.

29. C

The easiest way to solve this problem is to break the diagram on the right into two rectangles. Then solve for each area and add them together.

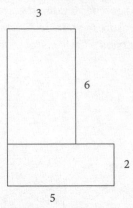

The area of the rectangle on top is $3 \times 6 = 18$. The area of the rectangle on bottom is $5 \times 2 = 10$. The total area is $18 + 10 = 28$. Answer choice (C) is correct.

30. B

First, you need to break down 48 into its prime factors. Then, you can determine how many *distinct* ones there are.

$$48 = 2 \times 24$$
$$= 2 \times 2 \times 12$$
$$= 2 \times 2 \times 2 \times 6$$
$$= 2 \times 2 \times 2 \times 2 \times 3$$

There are only two distinct prime factors for 48: 2 and 3. Answer choice (B) is correct.

31. B

An exterior angle of a triangle equals the sum of the two remote interior angles. So $7x = 4x + 60$, $3x = 60$, and $x = 20$. So the angle marked $7x°$ has a degree measure of $7(20) = 140$. The angle marked $a°$ is supplementary to this angle, so its measure is $180 - 140 = 40$. Answer choice (B) is correct.

32. D

To solve this equation, we first need to find the value of x:

$$2x + 4 = 26$$
$$2x = 22, \text{ so } x = 11$$

Therefore, $11 + 4 = 15$. Answer choice (D) is correct.

33. D

To efficiently tackle this problem, use the Picking Numbers strategy. If $x + y$ is an odd number, x could be 2 and y could be 3. If $x + z$ is even, and $x = 2$, z could be 4. With these numbers, answer choices A and C could be true, so those can be eliminated. Since you first picked an even number for x, try $x = 3$ for the next round of Picking Numbers. If $x = 3$, y could equal 2 to satisfy the scenario. Since $x = 3$, z could also equal 1 to make $x + z$ even. Based on these new numbers, you can eliminate answer choice B, making answer choice (D) the correct one.

34. C

Consider each answer choice. Answer choice A gives you the value $\frac{2}{3}$, but you know that x must be smaller than $\frac{1}{2}$, and because $\frac{2}{3}$ is not, you can eliminate it. Answer choice B proposes 0.47, but x must be smaller than $\frac{1}{3}$, and 0.47 is not, so eliminate choice B. Answer choice (C) gives you $\frac{1}{5}$, which is smaller than $\frac{1}{3}$ but larger than $\frac{1}{10}$—it fits the given criteria. Since there can only be one correct answer, there is no reason to check the last answer choice, but if you do, you'll find that choice D is incorrect because $\frac{1}{20}$ is less than $\frac{1}{10}$, and x cannot be less than $\frac{1}{10}$. Answer choice (C) is correct.

35. C

The strategic test taker will realize that this question is really asking for the inclusive range from $42 - 83$. The range is inclusive because Makayla read all of pages 42 and 83. To find the number of integers in an inclusive range, subtract the smaller integer from the larger and then add 1: $83 - 42 = 41 + 1 = 42$. Answer choice (C) is correct.

36. C

The three interior angles of a triangle add up to 180 degrees:

$$2x + 3x + 5x = 180$$
$$10x = 180$$
$$x = 18$$

Because angle YXZ has a degree measure of $3x$, you must multiply x by 3 to determine the angle measure: $3 \times 18 = 54$. Answer choice (C) is correct.

37. B

You could figure out 30% of 400, then figure out 15% of 400, and then find their difference, but that will take precious extra time on Test Day. The difference between 30% of a number and 15% of that same number is 30% − 15% = 15% of that number. Therefore, 15% of 400 is 60, so choice (B) is correct.

38. B

Just like any triangle, the three interior angles have to add up to 180°, so set up an equation:

$$x + 2x + 3x = 180$$
$$6x = 180$$
$$x = 30$$

Answer choice (B) is correct.

39. C

Plug $q = 8$ and $r = 2$ into the definition:

$$q \,//\, r = (qr) - (q - r)$$
$$8 \,//\, 2 = (8 \times 2) - (8 - 2)$$
$$= 16 - 6 = 10$$

Answer choice (C) is correct.

40. B

Plug $q = P$ and $r = 3$ into the definition:

$$q \,//\, r = (qr) - (q - r)$$
$$P \,//\, 3 = (P \times 3) - (P - 3)$$
$$= 3P - P + 3$$
$$= 2P + 3$$

The question stem tells you that this definition equals 11, so just do the math:

$$2P + 3 = 11$$
$$2P = 8$$
$$P = 4$$

Answer choice (B) is correct.

41. C

Looking at the figure, you can see that $AB + BC = AC$. Therefore, $8 + BC = 14$, so $BC = 6$.

The midpoint of AB divides it into two segments of length 4, and the midpoint of BC divides it into two segments of length 3. Therefore, the distance between their midpoints is $4 + 3 = 7$. Answer choice (C) is correct.

42. A

Slope of a line is defined by the formula $\frac{y_2 - y_1}{x_2 - x_1}$, where (x_1, y_1) and (x_2, y_2) represent two points on the line. Substitute the given coordinates into the formula (it doesn't matter which you designate as point 1 or point 2; just be consistent):

$$\text{slope} = \frac{y_2 - y_1}{x_2 - x_1} = \frac{7 - (-5)}{-1 - 3}$$
$$= \frac{12}{-4}$$
$$= -3$$

Choice (A) is correct.

43. B

To solve this question, translate the problem into algebra and solve:

$$\frac{1}{4}x = 3$$
$$x = 12$$
$$\frac{1}{3}(12) = 4$$

Answer choice (B) is correct.

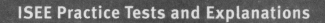

44. C

The question states that it takes Isaiah 2 gallons of paint to cover 725 square feet. If you are looking for how many gallons of paint it takes to cover 2,175 square feet, it is most efficient to set up a proportion:

$$\frac{2 \text{ gallons}}{725 \text{ sq. ft.}} = \frac{x \text{ gallons}}{2,175 \text{ sq. ft.}}$$

$$725x = 2 \times 2,175$$

$$725x = 4,350$$

$$x = \frac{4,350}{725} = 6 \text{ gallons}$$

It will take 6 gallons of paint to cover 2,175 square feet of surface, so answer choice (C) is correct.

45. D

To solve this question, substitute 8 for r in the equation: $(8 + 4)^2 = (12)^2 = 12 \times 12 = 144$. Answer choice (D) is correct.

46. C

The easiest way to solve this is to quickly sketch out the different times on a clock face and see which one is smaller than a right angle.

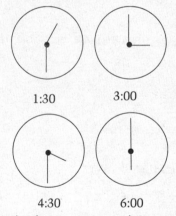

1:30   3:00

4:30   6:00

The only time that forms an acute angle is answer choice (C).

47. A

It is possible to solve for each of the four variables, but you want to be efficient on Test Day. Note that each of the equations is equal to 35,460. Therefore, the largest variable will be the one with the smallest coefficient because it takes fewer of a larger number to come up with the same product. Looking at the equations, you see that because 2,955 is the smallest coefficient, answer choice (A) must have the greatest value and is, therefore, the correct answer.

Section 5—Essay

Use the sample essay to help you review your own. Be sure to ask an adult who knows you to read your practice essay and give you feedback about how you did.

With the internet and mobile phones, technology has made the world a smaller place. Now, it is extremely easy to find out what's going on in different parts of the world. My parents are from China, and my grandparents still live there. Whenever there's a news story about China on the TV or radio, my parents can simply call my grandparents to check on them. They don't have to rely on other sources for information; they're able to talk with my grandparents immediately and find out whatever they need to know immediately. Since we live in New York, mobile phones have really made the world seem smaller.

This fast, easy access to information is not limited to just news either. If I'm struggling with my math classes, I can watch lectures on YouTube. Wikipedia has detailed articles on these topics, which I can use to fill in gaps in my knowledge and locate sources to support my ideas. In the past, you could only learn about these topics if you attended an exclusive university or happened to live in a town with an outstanding public library. Now, there are in-depth courses available anytime to anyone with an internet connection.

Similarly, new apps like Instagram are continuing to make it easier to connect with others and share experiences. My parents told me when they first came to the US as students, it was expensive to call home. They had to keep their calls short, and there was no way to really show their family what life was like in the US. Now, with apps like Instagram and Snap, it's easy and free to take pictures and let everyone know right away exactly what you're doing and what different events look like. When my mom went to her friend's wedding in the US, she tried to explain it to her mom but it was hard for my grandmother to understand. Now, she just takes a photo and her mom immediately can see what's happening and ask questions about it.

Apps, the internet, mobile phones and other technology make the world smaller every day. We are truly fortunate to be living in this golden age of connection and freely available knowledge.

ISEE UPPER/MIDDLE LEVEL PRACTICE TEST 1: ASSESS YOUR STRENGTHS

Use the following tables to determine which topics and chapters you need to review most. If you need help with your essay, be sure to review Chapter 9: The Essay and Chapter 22: Writing Wrap-Up.

Topic	Question
Verbal: Synonyms	Section 1, questions 1–20
Verbal: Sentence Completions	Section 1, questions 21–40
Quantitative Reasoning: Word Problems	Section 2, questions 1–20
Quantitative Reasoning: Quantitative Comparisons	Section 2, questions 21–37
Reading Comprehension	Section 3, questions 1–36
Mathematics Achievement	Section 4, questions 1–47

Topic	Number of Questions on Test	Number Correct	If You Struggled with These Questions, Study...
Verbal: Synonyms	20		Chapter 7 and Chapters 18–19
Verbal: Sentence Completions	20		Chapter 4 and Chapters 18–19
Quantitative Reasoning: Word Problems	20		Chapters 10–15 and Chapters 20–21
Quantitative Reasoning: Quantitative Comparisons	17		Chapter 5 and Chapters 20–21
Reading Comprehension	36		Chapter 8 and Chapters 18–19
Mathematics Achievement	47		Chapters 10–15 and Chapters 20–21

CHAPTER 27

ISEE Upper/Middle Level Practice Test 2

HOW TO TAKE THIS PRACTICE TEST

Before taking this practice test, find a quiet room where you can work uninterrupted for three hours. Make sure you have a comfortable desk and several #2 pencils.

Use the answer sheet provided to record your answers. (You can cut it out or photocopy it.)

Once you start this practice test, don't stop until you have finished. Remember—you can review any questions within a section, but you may not go backward or forward a section.

You'll find answer explanations following the test.

Good luck.

ISEE Upper/Middle Level Practice Test 2
ANSWER SHEET

Remove (or photocopy) the answer sheet and use it to complete the practice test.

Start with number 1 for each section. If a section has fewer questions than answer spaces, leave the extra spaces blank.

SECTION 1

1. Ⓐ Ⓑ Ⓒ Ⓓ	9. Ⓐ Ⓑ Ⓒ Ⓓ	17. Ⓐ Ⓑ Ⓒ Ⓓ	25. Ⓐ Ⓑ Ⓒ Ⓓ	33. Ⓐ Ⓑ Ⓒ Ⓓ
2. Ⓐ Ⓑ Ⓒ Ⓓ	10. Ⓐ Ⓑ Ⓒ Ⓓ	18. Ⓐ Ⓑ Ⓒ Ⓓ	26. Ⓐ Ⓑ Ⓒ Ⓓ	34. Ⓐ Ⓑ Ⓒ Ⓓ
3. Ⓐ Ⓑ Ⓒ Ⓓ	11. Ⓐ Ⓑ Ⓒ Ⓓ	19. Ⓐ Ⓑ Ⓒ Ⓓ	27. Ⓐ Ⓑ Ⓒ Ⓓ	35. Ⓐ Ⓑ Ⓒ Ⓓ
4. Ⓐ Ⓑ Ⓒ Ⓓ	12. Ⓐ Ⓑ Ⓒ Ⓓ	20. Ⓐ Ⓑ Ⓒ Ⓓ	28. Ⓐ Ⓑ Ⓒ Ⓓ	36. Ⓐ Ⓑ Ⓒ Ⓓ
5. Ⓐ Ⓑ Ⓒ Ⓓ	13. Ⓐ Ⓑ Ⓒ Ⓓ	21. Ⓐ Ⓑ Ⓒ Ⓓ	29. Ⓐ Ⓑ Ⓒ Ⓓ	37. Ⓐ Ⓑ Ⓒ Ⓓ
6. Ⓐ Ⓑ Ⓒ Ⓓ	14. Ⓐ Ⓑ Ⓒ Ⓓ	22. Ⓐ Ⓑ Ⓒ Ⓓ	30. Ⓐ Ⓑ Ⓒ Ⓓ	38. Ⓐ Ⓑ Ⓒ Ⓓ
7. Ⓐ Ⓑ Ⓒ Ⓓ	15. Ⓐ Ⓑ Ⓒ Ⓓ	23. Ⓐ Ⓑ Ⓒ Ⓓ	31. Ⓐ Ⓑ Ⓒ Ⓓ	39. Ⓐ Ⓑ Ⓒ Ⓓ
8. Ⓐ Ⓑ Ⓒ Ⓓ	16. Ⓐ Ⓑ Ⓒ Ⓓ	24. Ⓐ Ⓑ Ⓒ Ⓓ	32. Ⓐ Ⓑ Ⓒ Ⓓ	40. Ⓐ Ⓑ Ⓒ Ⓓ

correct in section 1

incorrect in section 1

SECTION 2

1. Ⓐ Ⓑ Ⓒ Ⓓ	9. Ⓐ Ⓑ Ⓒ Ⓓ	17. Ⓐ Ⓑ Ⓒ Ⓓ	25. Ⓐ Ⓑ Ⓒ Ⓓ	33. Ⓐ Ⓑ Ⓒ Ⓓ
2. Ⓐ Ⓑ Ⓒ Ⓓ	10. Ⓐ Ⓑ Ⓒ Ⓓ	18. Ⓐ Ⓑ Ⓒ Ⓓ	26. Ⓐ Ⓑ Ⓒ Ⓓ	34. Ⓐ Ⓑ Ⓒ Ⓓ
3. Ⓐ Ⓑ Ⓒ Ⓓ	11. Ⓐ Ⓑ Ⓒ Ⓓ	19. Ⓐ Ⓑ Ⓒ Ⓓ	27. Ⓐ Ⓑ Ⓒ Ⓓ	35. Ⓐ Ⓑ Ⓒ Ⓓ
4. Ⓐ Ⓑ Ⓒ Ⓓ	12. Ⓐ Ⓑ Ⓒ Ⓓ	20. Ⓐ Ⓑ Ⓒ Ⓓ	28. Ⓐ Ⓑ Ⓒ Ⓓ	36. Ⓐ Ⓑ Ⓒ Ⓓ
5. Ⓐ Ⓑ Ⓒ Ⓓ	13. Ⓐ Ⓑ Ⓒ Ⓓ	21. Ⓐ Ⓑ Ⓒ Ⓓ	29. Ⓐ Ⓑ Ⓒ Ⓓ	37. Ⓐ Ⓑ Ⓒ Ⓓ
6. Ⓐ Ⓑ Ⓒ Ⓓ	14. Ⓐ Ⓑ Ⓒ Ⓓ	22. Ⓐ Ⓑ Ⓒ Ⓓ	30. Ⓐ Ⓑ Ⓒ Ⓓ	38. Ⓐ Ⓑ Ⓒ Ⓓ
7. Ⓐ Ⓑ Ⓒ Ⓓ	15. Ⓐ Ⓑ Ⓒ Ⓓ	23. Ⓐ Ⓑ Ⓒ Ⓓ	31. Ⓐ Ⓑ Ⓒ Ⓓ	39. Ⓐ Ⓑ Ⓒ Ⓓ
8. Ⓐ Ⓑ Ⓒ Ⓓ	16. Ⓐ Ⓑ Ⓒ Ⓓ	24. Ⓐ Ⓑ Ⓒ Ⓓ	32. Ⓐ Ⓑ Ⓒ Ⓓ	40. Ⓐ Ⓑ Ⓒ Ⓓ

correct in section 2

incorrect in section 2

SECTION 3

1. Ⓐ Ⓑ Ⓒ Ⓓ	9. Ⓐ Ⓑ Ⓒ Ⓓ	17. Ⓐ Ⓑ Ⓒ Ⓓ	25. Ⓐ Ⓑ Ⓒ Ⓓ	33. Ⓐ Ⓑ Ⓒ Ⓓ
2. Ⓐ Ⓑ Ⓒ Ⓓ	10. Ⓐ Ⓑ Ⓒ Ⓓ	18. Ⓐ Ⓑ Ⓒ Ⓓ	26. Ⓐ Ⓑ Ⓒ Ⓓ	34. Ⓐ Ⓑ Ⓒ Ⓓ
3. Ⓐ Ⓑ Ⓒ Ⓓ	11. Ⓐ Ⓑ Ⓒ Ⓓ	19. Ⓐ Ⓑ Ⓒ Ⓓ	27. Ⓐ Ⓑ Ⓒ Ⓓ	35. Ⓐ Ⓑ Ⓒ Ⓓ
4. Ⓐ Ⓑ Ⓒ Ⓓ	12. Ⓐ Ⓑ Ⓒ Ⓓ	20. Ⓐ Ⓑ Ⓒ Ⓓ	28. Ⓐ Ⓑ Ⓒ Ⓓ	36. Ⓐ Ⓑ Ⓒ Ⓓ
5. Ⓐ Ⓑ Ⓒ Ⓓ	13. Ⓐ Ⓑ Ⓒ Ⓓ	21. Ⓐ Ⓑ Ⓒ Ⓓ	29. Ⓐ Ⓑ Ⓒ Ⓓ	37. Ⓐ Ⓑ Ⓒ Ⓓ
6. Ⓐ Ⓑ Ⓒ Ⓓ	14. Ⓐ Ⓑ Ⓒ Ⓓ	22. Ⓐ Ⓑ Ⓒ Ⓓ	30. Ⓐ Ⓑ Ⓒ Ⓓ	38. Ⓐ Ⓑ Ⓒ Ⓓ
7. Ⓐ Ⓑ Ⓒ Ⓓ	15. Ⓐ Ⓑ Ⓒ Ⓓ	23. Ⓐ Ⓑ Ⓒ Ⓓ	31. Ⓐ Ⓑ Ⓒ Ⓓ	39. Ⓐ Ⓑ Ⓒ Ⓓ
8. Ⓐ Ⓑ Ⓒ Ⓓ	16. Ⓐ Ⓑ Ⓒ Ⓓ	24. Ⓐ Ⓑ Ⓒ Ⓓ	32. Ⓐ Ⓑ Ⓒ Ⓓ	40. Ⓐ Ⓑ Ⓒ Ⓓ

correct in section 3

incorrect in section 3

SECTION 4

1. Ⓐ Ⓑ Ⓒ Ⓓ	11. Ⓐ Ⓑ Ⓒ Ⓓ	21. Ⓐ Ⓑ Ⓒ Ⓓ	31. Ⓐ Ⓑ Ⓒ Ⓓ	41. Ⓐ Ⓑ Ⓒ Ⓓ
2. Ⓐ Ⓑ Ⓒ Ⓓ	12. Ⓐ Ⓑ Ⓒ Ⓓ	22. Ⓐ Ⓑ Ⓒ Ⓓ	32. Ⓐ Ⓑ Ⓒ Ⓓ	42. Ⓐ Ⓑ Ⓒ Ⓓ
3. Ⓐ Ⓑ Ⓒ Ⓓ	13. Ⓐ Ⓑ Ⓒ Ⓓ	23. Ⓐ Ⓑ Ⓒ Ⓓ	33. Ⓐ Ⓑ Ⓒ Ⓓ	43. Ⓐ Ⓑ Ⓒ Ⓓ
4. Ⓐ Ⓑ Ⓒ Ⓓ	14. Ⓐ Ⓑ Ⓒ Ⓓ	24. Ⓐ Ⓑ Ⓒ Ⓓ	34. Ⓐ Ⓑ Ⓒ Ⓓ	44. Ⓐ Ⓑ Ⓒ Ⓓ
5. Ⓐ Ⓑ Ⓒ Ⓓ	15. Ⓐ Ⓑ Ⓒ Ⓓ	25. Ⓐ Ⓑ Ⓒ Ⓓ	35. Ⓐ Ⓑ Ⓒ Ⓓ	45. Ⓐ Ⓑ Ⓒ Ⓓ
6. Ⓐ Ⓑ Ⓒ Ⓓ	16. Ⓐ Ⓑ Ⓒ Ⓓ	26. Ⓐ Ⓑ Ⓒ Ⓓ	36. Ⓐ Ⓑ Ⓒ Ⓓ	46. Ⓐ Ⓑ Ⓒ Ⓓ
7. Ⓐ Ⓑ Ⓒ Ⓓ	17. Ⓐ Ⓑ Ⓒ Ⓓ	27. Ⓐ Ⓑ Ⓒ Ⓓ	37. Ⓐ Ⓑ Ⓒ Ⓓ	47. Ⓐ Ⓑ Ⓒ Ⓓ
8. Ⓐ Ⓑ Ⓒ Ⓓ	18. Ⓐ Ⓑ Ⓒ Ⓓ	28. Ⓐ Ⓑ Ⓒ Ⓓ	38. Ⓐ Ⓑ Ⓒ Ⓓ	48. Ⓐ Ⓑ Ⓒ Ⓓ
9. Ⓐ Ⓑ Ⓒ Ⓓ	19. Ⓐ Ⓑ Ⓒ Ⓓ	29. Ⓐ Ⓑ Ⓒ Ⓓ	39. Ⓐ Ⓑ Ⓒ Ⓓ	49. Ⓐ Ⓑ Ⓒ Ⓓ
10. Ⓐ Ⓑ Ⓒ Ⓓ	20. Ⓐ Ⓑ Ⓒ Ⓓ	30. Ⓐ Ⓑ Ⓒ Ⓓ	40. Ⓐ Ⓑ Ⓒ Ⓓ	50. Ⓐ Ⓑ Ⓒ Ⓓ

correct in section 4

incorrect in section 4

Section 1

Verbal Reasoning

Time—20 Minutes

40 Questions

The Verbal Reasoning section includes two different question types split into two different parts. When you finish Part One, move on to Part Two. You may write on the test. For each answer you choose, fill in the corresponding bubble on your answer grid.

Part One—Synonyms

Part One questions consist of one word in capital letters followed by four words or phrases. Choose the answer choice that is most most similar in meaning to the word in capital letters.

Part Two—Sentence Completions

Part Two questions consist of one sentence with either one or two blanks. One blank means that one word is missing. Two blanks means that two words are missing. Each sentence has four answer choices. Choose the word or phrase that best completes the meaning of the sentence.

STOP. DO NOT GO ON UNTIL TOLD TO DO SO.   STOP

PART ONE: SYNONYMS

Choose the word that is the closest in meaning to the word in capital letters.

1. EXCESS:

   (A) exit

   (B) surplus

   (C) disorder

   (D) end

2. ASTOUND:

   (A) stun

   (B) laugh

   (C) suspend

   (D) scold

3. MASSIVE:

   (A) high

   (B) inferior

   (C) huge

   (D) ancient

4. BLEAK:

   (A) charming

   (B) warm

   (C) drowsy

   (D) dreary

5. AMORAL:

   (A) unethical

   (B) lovable

   (C) transparent

   (D) imaginary

6. HARDY:

   (A) healthy

   (B) mysterious

   (C) firm

   (D) obese

7. METAMORPHOSIS:

   (A) change

   (B) compliment

   (C) rejection

   (D) meeting

8. NEUTRAL:

   (A) inventive

   (B) foreign

   (C) unbiased

   (D) detailed

9. TOLERANT:

   (A) open-minded

   (B) friendly

   (C) grave

   (D) ambitious

10. VIGOROUS:

   (A) robust

   (B) hungry

   (C) destructive

   (D) lovely

GO ON TO THE NEXT PAGE. ▶ ▶ ▶

11. DIN:

(A) departure

(B) clamor

(C) code

(D) supper

12. HALLOWED:

(A) carved

(B) distinguished

(C) empty

(D) sacred

13. OFFEND:

(A) divulge

(B) betray

(C) soothe

(D) insult

14. WAN:

(A) short

(B) pale

(C) foreign

(D) insincere

15. ARID:

(A) light

(B) clean

(C) worried

(D) dry

16. DECEIVE:

(A) trick

(B) empty

(C) dye

(D) view

17. FICTION:

(A) presumption

(B) growth

(C) falsehood

(D) wound

18. DOCILE:

(A) old

(B) tame

(C) active

(D) rare

19. LYRICAL:

(A) mythical

(B) bright

(C) musical

(D) wet

20. DESECRATE:

(A) defend

(B) deny

(C) describe

(D) defile

GO ON TO THE NEXT PAGE. ▶ ▶ ▶

PART TWO: SENTENCE COMPLETIONS

Select the word or word pair that best completes the sentence.

21. The company employed many unproductive employees who had a(n) ------- approach to their work.

    (A) creative

    (B) discontented

    (C) independent

    (D) lackadaisical

22. Except for periods where they function as "loners," wolves are generally ------- animals, living in packs.

    (A) carnivorous

    (B) fearsome

    (C) social

    (D) wild

23. The ballet dancers performed with a grace and a(n) ------- that left the audience breathless.

    (A) hilarity

    (B) ineptitude

    (C) elegance

    (D) reserve

24. The puppy was ------- to discipline and whined when reprimanded by its new owner.

    (A) anxious

    (B) unaccustomed

    (C) jovial

    (D) used

25. Liam has a(n) ------- personality and is very uncomfortable in social situations.

    (A) jolly

    (B) introverted

    (C) outgoing

    (D) gregarious

26. Although Jayla was an interior decorator, her home was ------- decorated.

    (A) sufficiently

    (B) impressively

    (C) modestly

    (D) amply

27. Raccoons are -------: they come out at night to look for food and sleep during the day.

    (A) nocturnal

    (B) friendly

    (C) precocious

    (D) monolithic

28. Mason not only respected his grandfather, but he also ------- his grandfather.

    (A) feared

    (B) retired

    (C) resembled

    (D) revered

GO ON TO THE NEXT PAGE. ▶ ▶ ▶

29. At first the empty house seemed frightening with all its cobwebs and creaking shutters, but we soon realized that it was quite -------.

    (A) benign

    (B) deceptive

    (C) affluent

    (D) obliterated

30. Though underfunded, the school made the best of its ------- resources.

    (A) meager

    (B) emphatic

    (C) acrid

    (D) belittled

31. Beneath the calm surface of the ocean, marine creatures ------- continually for food.

    (A) qualified

    (B) survived

    (C) contested

    (D) gathered

32. The soap opera regularly dwells on the ------- aspects of life; just last week two characters died.

    (A) morbid

    (B) presumptuous

    (C) exciting

    (D) expensive

33. The candidate changed his positions on so many issues that people began to think he was -------.

    (A) reliable

    (B) dependent

    (C) aloof

    (D) flighty

34. The sky jumper was ------- to survive after his parachute operated -------.

    (A) unable…perfectly

    (B) anxious…instinctively

    (C) surprised…adequately

    (D) fortunate…improperly

35. Despite his ------- beginnings as the son of a minor tribal chieftain, the warrior became one of the greatest ------- in Asia.

    (A) humble…rulers

    (B) luxurious…leaders

    (C) innocent…monarchs

    (D) regal…kings

36. Normally -------, Charlotte lacked her usual ------- when I called her and invited her to a movie.

    (A) absurd…severity

    (B) scornful…predilection

    (C) amiable…enthusiasm

    (D) distraught…cheeriness

37. Weighing more than 70 tons, brachiosaurus was a(n) ------- creature, yet its brain was quite -------.

    (A) intelligent…enormous

    (B) gargantuan…small

    (C) minute…tiny

    (D) prodigious…extant

GO ON TO THE NEXT PAGE. ▶ ▶ ▶

38. I did not set out to ------- my classmate; I meant well, but my words came across as -------.

    (A) irk...affable

    (B) offend...gauche

    (C) ostracize...sincere

    (D) impress...confused

39. Relying on every conceivable gimmick and stereotype, the latest Hollywood movie is not only ------- but also -------.

    (A) dull...ambivalent

    (B) predictable...absurd

    (C) complete...erudite

    (D) boring...enlightening

40. The ------- nature of the platypus makes it difficult to spot, even in the ------- space of a zoological exhibit.

    (A) elusive...confined

    (B) crafty...massive

    (C) playful...structured

    (D) slothful...open

STOP. IF THERE IS TIME, YOU MAY CHECK YOUR WORK IN THIS SECTION ONLY. **STOP**

Section 2

Quantitative Reasoning

Time—35 Minutes

37 Questions

The Quantitative Reasoning section includes two different question types split into two different parts. When you finish Part One, move on to Part Two. For each answer you choose, fill in the corresponding bubble on your answer grid.

Any figures that accompany the questions in this section may be assumed to be drawn as accurately as possible EXCEPT when it is stated that a particular figure is not drawn to scale. Letters such as x, y, and n stand for real numbers.

Part One—Word Problems

Part One questions consist of a word problem with four answer choices. You may write on the test, but you might be able to solve many of these questions using mental math. Choose the best answer choice.

Part Two—Quantitative Comparisons

Part Two questions are quantitative comparisons between the values of of Column A and Column B. Using the information given in each question, compare the values of Column A and Column B. Then, choose one of these four answer choices:

(A) The value of Column A is greater.

(B) The value of Column B is greater.

(C) The two values are equal.

(D) The values in the two columns cannot be compared using the information provided.

STOP. DO NOT GO ON UNTIL TOLD TO DO SO.   STOP

PART ONE: WORD PROBLEMS

Choose the best answer out of the four choices.

1. Damian is twice as old as Noah. If Damian is x years old, how many years old is Noah, in terms of x?

   (A) $0.5x$

   (B) $2x$

   (C) $x + 2$

   (D) $x - 2$

2. Raquel spent $\frac{1}{2}$ of her day at work and $\frac{2}{3}$ of her time at work in meetings. What fraction of her entire day did Raquel spend in meetings?

   (A) $\frac{1}{6}$

   (B) $\frac{1}{5}$

   (C) $\frac{1}{3}$

   (D) $\frac{1}{2}$

3. A certain machine caps 5 bottles every 2 seconds. At this rate, how many bottles will be capped in 1 minute?

   (A) 75

   (B) 150

   (C) 225

   (D) 300

4. The measure of two sides and two angles of a triangle are shown in the diagram.

   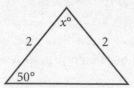

   What is the value of x?

   (A) 50

   (B) 60

   (C) 80

   (D) 100

5. The price of a stock doubled from Monday to Tuesday. What is the percent increase in the price of the stock from Monday to Tuesday?

   (A) 50%

   (B) 100%

   (C) 150%

   (D) 200%

6. On the first test, Peyton scored 7 percentage points above the passing grade. On the second test, he scored 12 percentage points lower than he did on his first test. His score on the second test was how many points below or above the passing grade?

   (A) 19 percentage points below

   (B) 12 percentage points below

   (C) 5 percentage points below

   (D) 2 percentage points above

GO ON TO THE NEXT PAGE. ▶ ▶ ▶

7. In a certain library there are 3 fiction books for every 8 nonfiction books. If the library has 600 nonfiction books, how many books does it have?

   (A) 2,200

   (B) 1,400

   (C) 825

   (D) 800

8. A photocopier makes copies at a constant rate of 15 copies per minute. A certain copy job requires 600 copies. What fraction of the job will the machine finish in 5 minutes?

   (A) $\dfrac{1}{200}$

   (B) $\dfrac{1}{40}$

   (C) $\dfrac{1}{8}$

   (D) $\dfrac{1}{5}$

9. If Julia needs to drive 328 miles in 4 hours, at what rate of speed must she drive?

   (A) 92 miles per hour

   (B) 82 miles per hour

   (C) 72 miles per hour

   (D) 67 miles per hour

10. When Mr. Fernandez arrived at the grocery store, there were 8 cases of soda on the shelf. One case contained 11 cans of soda, and each of the others contained 6. If Mr. Fernandez bought all 8 cases, how many cans of soda did he purchase at this store?

    (A) 53

    (B) 54

    (C) 57

    (D) 59

11. Four points are labeled on a line segment below.

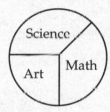

   The distance from B to C is twice the distance from A to B, and the distance from C to D is equal to half the distance from A to C. If the distance from B to C is 12, what is the distance from A to D?

   (A) 18

   (B) 24

   (C) 27

   (D) 32

12. The graph shows the distribution of majors chosen by 900 different students.

   MAJORS OF 900 STUDENTS

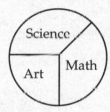

   About how many students are art majors?

   (A) 200

   (B) 225

   (C) 280

   (D) 300

GO ON TO THE NEXT PAGE. ▶ ▶ ▶

13. One angle measure is labeled in the diagram below.

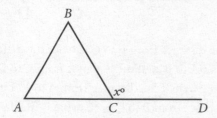

Segments *AB*, *BC*, *CD*, and *AC* are all equal. What is the value of *x*?

(A) 45

(B) 60

(C) 90

(D) 120

14. If the largest of seven consecutive integers is 25, what is the average of the seven integers?

(A) 24

(B) 22

(C) 21

(D) 20

15. If the value of *x* is an integer and $x < 2$, then $3x + 6$ could NOT be which of the following values?

(A) 12

(B) 9

(C) 6

(D) 3

16. One angle measure of the triangle is shown in the diagram.

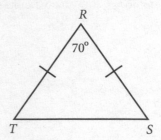

In $\triangle RST$, if $\angle S + \angle T = 110°$, what is the degree measure of $\angle S$?

(A) 40

(B) 55

(C) 70

(D) 110

17. If the average of 8, 3, 12, 11, and *x* is 0, then what is the value of *x*?

(A) 34

(B) 8.5

(C) 0

(D) −34

18. If $\frac{x}{3} = \frac{y}{6} = 3$, what is the value of $x + y$?

(A) 27

(B) 21

(C) 18

(D) 9

GO ON TO THE NEXT PAGE. ▶ ▶ ▶

19. Line p is parallel to line q in the diagram.

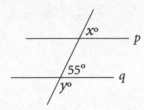

What is the value of x?

(A) 45

(B) 55

(C) 60

(D) 90

20. Chloe is playing a strategy game in which she needs to roll an even number twice in a row to win. If she is rolling a six-sided die, what is the probability that she will roll an even number on the next two rolls of the die?

(A) 90

(B) 110

(C) 125

(D) 180

GO ON TO THE NEXT PAGE. ▶ ▶ ▶

PART TWO: QUANTITATIVE COMPARISONS

Using the information in the question, compare the value of Column A to the value of Column B. All questions in Part Two have these answer choices:

(A)   The value of Column A is greater.

(B)   The value of Column B is greater.

(C)   The two values are equal.

(D)   The values in the two columns cannot be compared using the information provided.

	Column A	Column B
21.	$3 + 4$	3×4

	Column A	Column B
22.	$\frac{1}{4}$ of 12,948	25% of 12,948

$$10M + 2 = 32$$

	Column A	Column B
23.	3	M

	Column A	Column B
24.	$\frac{1}{4}$	$0.2569 - 0.007$

	Column A	Column B
25.	$9.9999 - 2$	$0.99999 + 7$

$$x > 0$$
$$y > 0$$

	Column A	Column B
26.	$x + 1$	y

	Column A	Column B
27.	The number of 32-cent stamps that can be purchased with $5	The number of 29-cent stamps that can be purchased with $5

$$\frac{5}{7} \text{ of } x \text{ is } 35.$$

	Column A	Column B
28.	x	48

	Column A	Column B
29.	$\frac{1}{2} + \frac{3}{4} + \frac{7}{8}$	$\frac{2}{5} + \frac{3}{4} + \frac{7}{9}$

	Column A	Column B
30.	5% of $(3 + 4)$	4% of (3×4)

	Column A	Column B
31.	The number of prime factors of 21	3

Set A: {5, 9, 11, 14, 26}

	Column A	Column B
32.	The average of the numbers in Set A	The average of the numbers in Set A if two distinct numbers are added to the set

$$AC = BD$$

A———B———C———D

	Column A	Column B
33.	AB	BC

GO ON TO THE NEXT PAGE. ▶ ▶ ▶

$$2x - 6 = 2x + 3x$$

Column A	Column B
x^2	4

34.

A fruit bowl has 4 apples, 6 kiwis, and 2 clementines in it.

Column A	Column B
The probability of randomly picking 2 apples in a row (without putting any fruit back)	4

35.

	Column A	Column B
36.	Average of midterm grades: {86, 96, 72, 80, 66}	Average of final exam grades: {100, 93, 88, 70, 99}

$$a > b > c > d$$

	Column A	Column B
37.	$a^2 + c$	$b^2 + d$

STOP. IF THERE IS TIME, YOU MAY CHECK YOUR WORK IN THIS SECTION ONLY. **STOP**

Section 3

Reading Comprehension

Time—35 Minutes

36 Questions

This section includes six reading passages. Each passage has six questions that can be answered using information stated or implied in the passage. You may write on the test.

Questions 1–6

1   The plague, or Black Death, struck Europe in a
2   series of outbreaks in the 13th and 14th centuries,
3   killing an estimated one-third of the continent's
4   population. This plague was one of the deadliest in
5   human history, and scientists have determined that
6   one specific pathogen is responsible for killing
7   millions of people.
8   The Black Death wrought enormous changes in
9   European society, some of which, ironically, were
10 beneficial. Reform in the medical profession, which
11 had mostly failed to relieve the suffering, was one
12 of the most immediate benefits. A great many
13 doctors died or simply ran away during the plague.
14 Those that survived learned more about ways to
15 care for those who are sick and dying.

16   By the mid-1300s, many universities were lacking
17 professors of medicine and surgery. Into this void
18 rushed people with new ideas. In addition, ordinary
19 people began acquiring medical guides and taking
20 command of their own health, demanding that those
21 with advanced knowledge share this with others.
22 Gradually, more medical texts began to appear in
23 everyday languages rather than in Latin, making
24 medical knowledge more accessible. In the years since,
25 scientists have continued using the knowledge they
26 gained during the Black Death to improve the lives of
27 humans all over the world.

GO ON TO THE NEXT PAGE. ▶ ▶ ▶

1. The passage focuses primarily on

    (A) the enormous loss of life caused by the plague.

    (B) the lack of qualified doctors during the plague.

    (C) one positive result of a catastrophic event.

    (D) the translation of medical texts into everyday language.

2. In line 8, "wrought" most nearly means

    (A) caused.

    (B) needed.

    (C) accelerated.

    (D) offered.

3. The passage suggests that, prior to the plague outbreaks, European medicine was

    (A) hampered by a shortage of doctors.

    (B) available only to university students.

    (C) in need of sweeping changes.

    (D) practiced mainly in Latin-speaking countries.

4. It can be inferred from the passage that after the 1300s, medical texts

    (A) included information on how to cure the plague.

    (B) were more easily available to the general population.

    (C) were no longer written in Latin.

    (D) were not written by university professors.

5. Which of the following best describes the tone of the article?

    (A) Mournful

    (B) Sarcastic

    (C) Favorable

    (D) Sensible

6. All of the following are outcomes of the plague EXCEPT

    (A) medical information was made more accessible to people.

    (B) people started learning Latin to understand the medical texts.

    (C) people with new ideas on medicine started teaching medicine and surgery.

    (D) a lot of people died from the plague.

GO ON TO THE NEXT PAGE. ▶ ▶ ▶

Questions 7–12

1   The heyday of the log cabin occurred between 1780
2 and 1850, when a great number of settlers forged
3 westward. These cabins were built using logs, chips,
4 and mud. Although the exact origin is uncertain, the
5 first log buildings were most likely built in Europe over
6 5,000 years ago.
7   While early cabins were primitive, with dirt floors
8 and sod roofs, later settlers built fine two-story,
9 log-hewn farmhouses with rooms for entertaining.
10 The original log cabins were not built to last for many
11 years, focusing instead on providing shelter to meet an
12 immediate need. These temporary homes would
13 eventually be replaced by larger, more permanent
14 houses, so settlers did not worry about the durability
15 of their original log cabins.

16   By the 1840s, the log cabin began fading out. Factors
17 contributing to its decline included sawmills, nails, and
18 the rising popularity of the Greek Revival-style house,
19 with its democratic roots in ancient Greece and its
20 templed front facing the street. Trains brought
21 hardware, manufactured goods, and an end to
22 geographic isolation. Climate and the proximity of the
23 local forest no longer set architectural limits. In
24 hundreds of towns, log homes were gradually sheathed
25 with clapboard or brick or, in many instances, were
26 simply burned. Logs continued to house livestock, but
27 after the 1850s, fewer and fewer people chose to live in
28 log houses.

GO ON TO THE NEXT PAGE. ▶ ▶ ▶

7. The passage suggests that the origins of the Greek Revival style

   (A) arose out of a general desire to replace log cabins.

   (B) widely influenced contemporary Greek architects.

   (C) were popular with devoutly religious Americans.

   (D) appealed to democratic-minded Americans.

8. In line 3, "forged" most nearly means

   (A) fled.

   (B) wandered.

   (C) moved.

   (D) returned.

9. It can be inferred from the passage that, unlike Greek Revival homes, log cabins

   (A) did not always face the street.

   (B) lacked indoor plumbing.

   (C) could not have glass windows.

   (D) were built near lakes and rivers.

10. It can be inferred from the passage that a limiting factor in the construction of a settler's log cabin was often

    (A) the availability of nails.

    (B) the location of the nearest forest.

    (C) the opinions of other settlers.

    (D) the laws of the local government.

11. According to the passage, most log structures after 1850 were built

    (A) in wilderness areas.

    (B) in frontier towns.

    (C) as railroad depots.

    (D) to shelter animals.

12. Which of the following questions is NOT answered in the passage?

    (A) In their heyday, were log cabins common in the West?

    (B) When did log cabins finally disappear?

    (C) Why was the Greek Revival–style house popular?

    (D) How did log cabins in the 1780s differ from log cabins in the 1840s?

GO ON TO THE NEXT PAGE. ▶ ▶ ▶

Questions 13–18

1   Coyotes are one of the most primitive of living dogs.
2 According to the fossil record, a close relative of the
3 contemporary coyote existed here two to three million
4 years ago. It in turn seems to have descended from a
5 group of small canids that was widely dispersed
6 throughout the world and that also gave rise to the
7 jackals of Eurasia and Africa.

8   One to two million years ago, a division occurred
9 between the coyote and the wolf. Time passed, and
10 glaciers advanced and receded. Mammoths,
11 saber-toothed tigers, and dire wolves (canids with
12 enormous heads) came and went. Native horses left the
13 continent over land bridges, and others returned on
14 galleons. Some animals evolved to depend more on
15 hunting and meat eating, while other animals ate a mix
16 of both meat and plants.

17   There is some debate over the exact relationship
18 between the modern wolf and the modern coyote, but
19 most scientists agree that dogs are more closely related
20 to wolves than to coyotes. Although wolves are
21 considered specialized carnivores, coyotes do have
22 some dependencies on vegetable matter, and coyotes
23 tend to be smaller than most wolves (and dogs of a
24 similar size). Through it all, coyotes remained basically
25 the same—primitive in evolutionary terms but
26 marvelously flexible, always progressive and
27 innovative—riding out, adjusting to, and exploiting the
28 changes.

GO ON TO THE NEXT PAGE. ▶ ▶ ▶

13. The primary focus of the passage is on

(A) the ability of the coyote species to survive unchanged.

(B) the unfortunate extinction of many prehistoric life forms.

(C) the changing nature of animal life in prehistoric times.

(D) the evolutionary division between coyotes and wolves.

14. The passage suggests that modern dogs are

(A) direct descendants of dire wolves.

(B) native to North America but not to Eurasia.

(C) genetically related to coyotes.

(D) lacking in evolutionary flexibility.

15. According to the passage, a close relative of the coyote existed in North America

(A) ten million years ago.

(B) seven million years ago.

(C) five million years ago.

(D) two million years ago.

16. The author probably mentions mammoths and saber-toothed tigers in order to give examples of

(A) the coyote's more distant relatives.

(B) animals that did not leave North America by land bridge.

(C) species that the jackal hunted into extinction.

(D) species that failed to adapt as the coyote did.

17. When the passage states that "others returned on galleons" (lines 15–16), it most probably means that

(A) some species of horse became extinct, then others appeared.

(B) horses were reintroduced to North America when Europeans brought them by ship.

(C) some coyotes were introduced into Africa and Eurasia.

(D) prehistoric horses and dire wolves became extinct at roughly the same time.

18. All the following are true EXCEPT

(A) mammoths and dire wolves no longer exist.

(B) horses were in North America before the Europeans brought them here.

(C) coyotes are related to wolves.

(D) coyotes are not good at adapting to change.

GO ON TO THE NEXT PAGE. ▶ ▶ ▶

Questions 19–24

1　The word "chocolate" is a generic term used to
2　describe a variety of foods made from the seeds, or
3　beans, of the cacao tree. For a period of time, cacao
4　beans were considered valuable enough to use as
5　money. Though many modern historians believe that
6　chocolate has been around for over 2,000 years, recent
7　research indicates that it may be even older than that.

8　The Mayans are believed to have first discovered
9　cacao, but the first people known to have consumed
10　chocolate were the Aztecs, who used cacao seeds to
11　brew a bitter, aromatic drink. According to legend, this
12　drink was taught to them by the Aztec God of
13　Vegetation, Quetzacoatl. When the other gods realized
14　what Quetzacoatl had done, he was subsequently
15　banished from paradise. Because few Aztecs were
16　wealthy enough to afford chocolate, many of

17　Qutzacoatl's students likely paid others to keep the
18　secrets of their practice.

19　It was not until the Mexican expedition of Hernan
20　Cortes in 1519, however, that Europeans first learned of
21　cacao, and this discovery had a long-lasting impact on
22　the world. Cortes came to the New World primarily in
23　search of gold, but his interest was apparently also
24　piqued by the Aztecs' peculiar beverage, for when he
25　returned to Spain, his ship's cargo included three
26　chests of cacao beans. It was from these beans that
27　Europe experienced its first taste of what seemed a very
28　exotic beverage. The drink soon became popular
29　among those wealthy enough to afford it, and over the
30　next century cafes specializing in chocolate drinks
31　began to spring up throughout Europe.

GO ON TO THE NEXT PAGE. ▶ ▶ ▶

19. In line 1, "generic" most nearly means

    (A) scientific.

    (B) technical.

    (C) general.

    (D) obscure.

20. The passage suggests that chocolate foods can be

    (A) unhealthy if consumed in excessive quantities.

    (B) one of the staples of a society's diet.

    (C) made from part of the cacao tree.

    (D) made from ingredients other than the cacao tree.

21. It can be inferred from the passage that Cortes journeyed to Mexico mainly in order to

    (A) conquer the Aztecs.

    (B) increase his personal wealth.

    (C) claim new land for Spain.

    (D) gain personal glory.

22. The author implies in lines 22–31 that Cortes found the Aztecs' chocolate drink to be

    (A) sweet.

    (B) relaxing.

    (C) stimulating.

    (D) strange.

23. The passage suggests that most of the chocolate consumed by Europeans in the 1500s was

    (A) expensive.

    (B) candy.

    (C) made by Aztecs.

    (D) made by Cortes.

24. All of the following questions can be answered in the passage EXCEPT:

    (A) Did Cortes return to Europe with gold?

    (B) How did the Aztecs consume chocolate?

    (C) Were cacao beans well received in Europe?

    (D) Who were the first people to enjoy chocolate?

GO ON TO THE NEXT PAGE. ▶ ▶ ▶

Questions 25–30

1 It has been known for some time that wolves live
2 and hunt in hierarchically structured packs,
3 organized in a kind of "pecking order" similar
4 to that found in flocks of birds. This organization
5 allows wolves to hunt animals that they may not
6 otherwise be able to kill, such as moose. Wolf packs are
7 known to hunt as a team and to lead prey into
8 situations in which the rest of the team is waiting to
9 ambush the prey.
10 At the top of the hierarchy in any wolf pack are the
11 senior males, dominating all others in matters of
12 privilege and leadership. As many as three other
13 distinct subgroups may exist within a pack: mature
14 wolves with subordinate status in the hierarchy,
15 immature wolves that will not be treated as adults until
16 their second year, and outcast wolves rejected by the
17 rest of the pack. Wolves who have difficulty finding a
18 role within one of these three subgroups may branch
19 out on their own in an attempt to become a senior
20 male.
21 Each individual wolf, moreover, occupies a specific
22 position within these subgroups. These positions take
23 precedence over wolves of lower rank in the selection
24 of food, mates, and resting places. In addition, these
25 positions determine whether wolves hold a greater
26 share of the responsibility for protecting the pack from
27 strange wolves and other dangers.

GO ON TO THE NEXT PAGE. ▶ ▶ ▶

25. According to the passage, wolves and birds are similar in that they both

    (A) mate for life.

    (B) become adults at two years of age.

    (C) defer to senior females.

    (D) live in structured groups.

26. The passage suggests that our knowledge of the social hierarchies of wolves is

    (A) mostly theoretical.

    (B) not a recent discovery.

    (C) based on observations of individual wolves.

    (D) in need of long-range studies.

27. What is implied in the passage about outcast wolves?

    (A) They never share the pack's food.

    (B) They sometimes kill the pack's young.

    (C) Their status is lower than that of immature wolves.

    (D) They are incapable of protecting the pack from strange wolves.

28. According to the passage, the structure of a wolf pack is determined by each wolf's share of all of the following EXCEPT

    (A) food.

    (B) water.

    (C) resting place.

    (D) mate.

29. The author's attitude toward the subject may best be described as

    (A) admiring.

    (B) critical.

    (C) informative.

    (D) indifferent.

30. In line 14, "subordinate" most nearly means

    (A) top.

    (B) inferior.

    (C) short.

    (D) immature.

GO ON TO THE NEXT PAGE. ▶ ▶ ▶

Questions 31–36

1　　In 1916, James Van Der Zee opened a photography
2　studio in New York City's Harlem. It was the eve of
3　the Harlem Renaissance—the decade-long flowering
4　of art and culture that established Harlem as the most
5　artistically vigorous African American community in
6　the nation. Once the Harlem Renaissance began, Van
7　Der Zee photographed many different people,
8　including African American celebrities like Florence
9　Mills and Adam Clayton Powell Jr.
10　　For some 40 years, Van Der Zee captured the life
11　and spirit of that burgeoning community, producing
12　thousands of portraits, not only of notables but of
13　ordinary citizens—parents and children, brides and
14　grooms, church groups, and women's clubs. He then
15　enhanced these photographs using darkroom
16　techniques, known for occasionally sneaking images of
17　the dead onto an original photograph.

18　　Critics consider these images important today not
19　only for their record of Harlem life but for their
20　reflection of their subjects' keen sense of the
21　importance of their culture. Van Der Zee's carefully
22　staged photographs spotlighted his subjects' pride and
23　self-assurance. His unique vision recorded time, place,
24　and culture that might otherwise have slipped away,
25　even though others may not agree with his strategies
26　for doing this.

GO ON TO THE NEXT PAGE. ▶ ▶ ▶

31. This passage focuses primarily on

   (A) the cultural achievements of the Harlem Renaissance.

   (B) the history of African-American photography.

   (C) the creative influences that shaped one photographer's career.

   (D) the cultural record left by a Harlem photographer.

32. It can be inferred from the passage that Van Der Zee opened his studio

   (A) just before the Harlem Renaissance began.

   (B) in order to photograph African-American celebrities.

   (C) without having previous photographic experience.

   (D) with financial support from his community.

33. The passage most likely describes the subjects of Van Der Zee's photographs (lines 10–11) in order to

   (A) demonstrate the artist's flair for composition.

   (B) show that his work represented the whole community.

   (C) highlight the self-assurance of Harlem residents.

   (D) reflect upon the nature of photography.

34. The author's attitude toward Van Der Zee can best be described as

   (A) neutral.

   (B) condescending.

   (C) admiring.

   (D) generous.

35. Which of the following statements is NOT true?

   (A) Van Der Zee helped trigger the Harlem Renaissance.

   (B) If it weren't for Van Der Zee, a part of Harlem life would have been forgotten.

   (C) The Harlem Renaissance helped establish the neighborhood as an artistic community.

   (D) Van Der Zee captured the lives of a variety of people in Harlem.

36. In line 8, "burgeoning" most nearly means

   (A) beautiful.

   (B) barren.

   (C) quiet.

   (D) thriving.

STOP. IF THERE IS TIME, YOU MAY CHECK YOUR WORK IN THIS SECTION ONLY.

Section 4

Mathematics Achievement

Time—40 Minutes

47 Questions

Each question has four answer choices. Read each question and choose the best answer. You may write on your test.

STOP

1. How many seconds are there in $\frac{1}{20}$ of a minute?

   (A) 2

   (B) 3

   (C) 20

   (D) 30

2. What is the greatest number of squares, each measuring 2 centimeters by 2 centimeters, that can be cut from a rectangle with a length of 8 centimeters and a width of 6 centimeters?

   (A) 6

   (B) 8

   (C) 12

   (D) 48

3. A movie collection was divided among six people so that each received the same number of movies. Which of the following could be the number of movies in the collection?

   (A) 10

   (B) 15

   (C) 21

   (D) 24

4. If $\frac{1}{2} + \frac{1}{3} = \frac{M}{12}$, then what is the value of M?

   (A) 8

   (B) 9

   (C) 10

   (D) 11

5. If $N_¿ = N \times 10$, then what is the value of $30_¿ + 2_¿$?

   (A) 32

   (B) 302

   (C) 320

   (D) 3,200

6. The graph shows the number of students who took the swimming class each month from the months of March to June.

NUMBER OF STUDENTS TAKING
SWIMMING CLASS

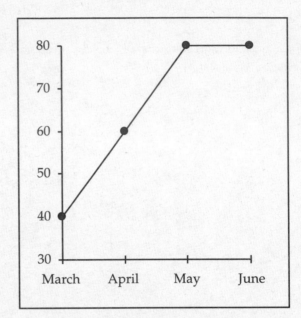

According to the graph, what is the the average number of students taking the swimming class during the four months?

   (A) 55

   (B) 65

   (C) 70

   (D) 80

7. What is twenty percent of 30?

   (A) 6

   (B) 8

   (C) 10

   (D) 12.5

GO ON TO THE NEXT PAGE. ▶ ▶ ▶

8. If $x = 4y + 3$, then what does $x - 5$ equal?

    (A) $4y - 8$

    (B) $4y - 2$

    (C) $4y + 5$

    (D) $5y - 8$

9. If n is an odd number, which of the following MUST be even?

    (A) $-2n - 1$

    (B) $2n + 1$

    (C) $2n - 1$

    (D) $4n$

10. The diagram is a complex figure composed of six squares.

    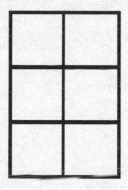

    How many rectangles are there in the figure?

    (A) 20

    (B) 18

    (C) 15

    (D) 12

11. If 45 is divided by the product of 3 and 5, what is the result?

    (A) 3

    (B) 5

    (C) 9

    (D) 15

12. If $a + b = 6$, then which expression is equal to b?

    (A) $b = a - 6$

    (B) $b = 6 - a$

    (C) $b = 6a$

    (D) $b = \dfrac{6}{a}$

13. In a basketball game, Team A scored 39 points, and Team B scored more points than Team A. If Team B has 5 players, the average score of the players on Team B must have been at least how many points?

    (A) 5

    (B) 6

    (C) 8

    (D) 12

14. What is the value of one and one-third minus five-sixths?

    (A) $\dfrac{1}{4}$

    (B) $\dfrac{1}{3}$

    (C) $\dfrac{1}{2}$

    (D) $\dfrac{3}{4}$

GO ON TO THE NEXT PAGE. ▶ ▶ ▶

15. The measures of two sides and one angle of a triangle are shown in the diagram.

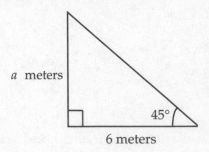

What is the value of *a*?

(A) 4

(B) 6

(C) 8

(D) 9

16. What is the value of $\dfrac{64}{2 \times 4}$?

(A) 8

(B) 24

(C) 42

(D) 128

17. What is the area of a triangle with a base of 4 inches and a height of 6 inches?

(A) 10

(B) 12

(C) 20

(D) 24

18. In a certain class, there are twice as many bus riders as walkers. If the total number of students in the class is 36, how many bus riders are there?

(A) 24

(B) 18

(C) 12

(D) 9

19. A museum records 16 visitors to an exhibit on Monday, 21 on Tuesday, 20 on Wednesday, 17 on Thursday, 19 on Friday, 21 on Saturday, and 17 on Sunday. What is the median number of visitors for the week?

(A) 18

(B) 18.71

(C) 19

(D) 19.5

20. If $\dfrac{1}{5}$ of a number is less than 20, what is the number?

(A) Less than 4

(B) Greater than 4

(C) Less than 100

(D) Greater than 100

21. If $Q + 7 - 8 + 3 = 23$, what is the value of Q?

(A) 19

(B) 20

(C) 21

(D) 22

22. If $a + 2 > 5$ and $a - 4 < 1$, which of the following is a possible value for a?

(A) 2

(B) 3

(C) 4

(D) 5

23. The expression $2 \times 4 \times 7 \times 9$ is equal to the product of 18 and what number?

(A) 8

(B) 14

(C) 28

(D) 36

GO ON TO THE NEXT PAGE. ▶ ▶ ▶

24. What is the value of $(65 \times 10^2) + (31 \times 10^3) + 12$?

    (A) 375,120

    (B) 37,512

    (C) 3,751.20

    (D) 375.12

25. If the product of integers a and b is 16, and a is greater than 4, then which of the following MUST be true?

    I. $b = 2$

    II. The sum of a and b is greater than zero

    III. a is greater than b

    (A) II only

    (B) III only

    (C) I and II only

    (D) II and III only

26. If $x = \sqrt{3}$, $y = 2$, and $z = \frac{1}{2}$, then what is the value of $x^2 - 5yz + y^2$?

    (A) 1

    (B) 2

    (C) 4

    (D) 8

27. If 9 is x percent of 90, what is 50 percent of x?

    (A) 5

    (B) 10

    (C) 15

    (D) 18

28. If 9 is added to the product of 12 and 4, what is the result?

    (A) 17

    (B) 25

    (C) 57

    (D) 84

29. A net is shown.

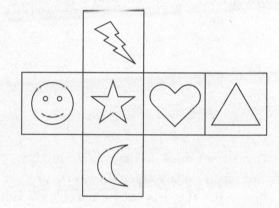

    Which figure is a possible cube for the net?

    (A)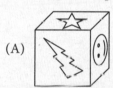

    (B)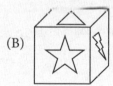

    (C)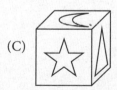

    (D)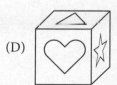

GO ON TO THE NEXT PAGE. ▶ ▶ ▶

30. If $\dfrac{700}{x} = 35$, then what is the value of x?

   (A) 2

   (B) 5

   (C) 20

   (D) 200

31. When an integer is multiplied by itself, it can end in all of the following EXCEPT what digit?

   (A) 1

   (B) 3

   (C) 5

   (D) 6

32. Diya has six more dollars than her brother. How many dollars would she have to give him so that they would have an equal amount of money?

   (A) 6

   (B) 4

   (C) 3

   (D) 2

33. If $\dfrac{28}{a} = \dfrac{48}{12}$, then what is the value of a?

   (A) 7

   (B) 8

   (C) 9

   (D) 10

34. The graph of points (a, b) and (c, d) is shown.

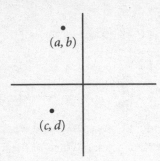

   Which of the following statements MUST be true?

   (A) $bd > ac$

   (B) $c > ad$

   (C) $b > acd$

   (D) $bc > ad$

35. What is the slope of a line that goes through the points $(-42, 10)$ and $(6, -8)$?

   (A) $-\dfrac{8}{3}$

   (B) $-\dfrac{3}{8}$

   (C) $\dfrac{3}{8}$

   (D) $\dfrac{8}{3}$

36. A six-story apartment building has x apartments on each of its lower 3 floors and y apartments on each of its upper 3 floors. If 3 people live in each apartment, how many people live in the building?

   (A) $3x + 3y$

   (B) $3x + 3y + 3$

   (C) $9x + 9y$

   (D) $3x + 3y + 18$

GO ON TO THE NEXT PAGE. ▶ ▶ ▶

37. If Selena is in school for 6 hours per day, 5 days per week, how many seconds does Selena spend in school in one week?

    (A) 1,108,000

    (B) 180,000

    (C) 108,000

    (D) 18,000

38. A grocer buys oranges at a price of four for $1 and then sells them in her store for 40 cents each. How many oranges must she sell to earn a profit of $3?

    (A) 2

    (B) 10

    (C) 15

    (D) 20

39. The average of a set of six numbers is 6. If 3 is subtracted from each of four of the numbers, what is the new average?

    (A) 1.5

    (B) 2

    (C) 3

    (D) 4

40. Sebastian finished $\frac{1}{3}$ of his homework assignment between 6:00 p.m. and 7:30 p.m. He needs to finish the assignment by 11:00 p.m. If he works at the same rate, what is the latest time that he can return to his homework?

    (A) 7:45 p.m.

    (B) 8:00 p.m.

    (C) 8:30 p.m.

    (D) 9:30 p.m.

41. Four points are labeled on the line segment below.

    The distance from A to D is 55, and the distance from A to B is equal to the distance from C to D. If the distance from A to B is twice the distance from B to C, how far apart are B and D?

    (A) 11

    (B) 30

    (C) 33

    (D) 44

42. Two supplementary angles have measurements of 3x and 7x, respectively. What is the measurement in degrees of the smaller angle of the pair?

    (A) 18

    (B) 54

    (C) 90

    (D) 126

Questions 43–44 refer to the graph.

The graph shows the amount of money Kiran, Arianna, and Dakota saved by the end of the summer.

SUMMER SAVINGS

43. Arianna's summer savings are greater than Kiran's summer savings by how many dollars?

    (A) 3

    (B) 4

    (C) 150

    (D) 200

GO ON TO THE NEXT PAGE. ▶ ▶ ▶

44. The amount of money saved by Dakota is how many times the amount of money saved by Kiran?

    (A) 4

    (B) 8

    (C) 100

    (D) 400

45. If 20 percent of J is 1,500, what is 15 percent of J?

    (A) 1,125

    (B) 3,000

    (C) 5,125

    (D) 6,000

46. If $x - y = 5$ and $4x + 6y = 20$, then what is the value of $x + y$?

    (A) 3

    (B) 4

    (C) 5

    (D) 6

47. A bag contains eight white, four red, seven green, and five blue marbles. Eight marbles are pulled out of the bag randomly. How many of the withdrawn marbles were white if the chance of drawing a white marble is now $\frac{1}{4}$?

    (A) 0

    (B) 3

    (C) 4

    (D) 5

STOP. IF THERE IS TIME, YOU MAY CHECK YOUR WORK IN THIS SECTION ONLY. **STOP**

Section 5

Essay

Time—30 Minutes

1 Question

The ISEE Essay is a 30-minute section during which you will plan and write an essay on a given topic. **Writing on another topic is not acceptable.**

The essay gives you a chance to show how well you can write. Express your thoughts as clearly as possible. What you write is not as important as how well you write, but you need to write enough for a reader to understand your point.

You will probably write more than one paragraph. Be aware that a copy of your essay is sent to schools along with your test results. Write only in the lined pages of the answer sheet. You may print or use cursive, but be sure that your writing can be read by someone who is not familiar with your handwriting.

The next page includes space for notes and other essay plans. Give yourself enough time to write a final draft in your answer sheet. On Test Day, you must copy the topic onto your answer sheet, on page 3, in the space provided. This allows schools to know which topic you were provided.

Remember to write only the final draft on pages 3 and 4 of your answer sheet and in blue or black pen. Again, you may print or use cursive. Only pages 3 and 4 will be sent to the schools when you take the official ISEE.

STOP. DO NOT GO ON UNTIL TOLD TO DO SO. | STOP

Prompt: What is your favorite academic subject? Explain why you feel this way.

Notes

_____

_____

_____

_____

_____

_____

_____

_____

_____

_____

_____

_____

_____

_____

_____

_____

_____

_____

_____

_____

STOP. IF THERE IS TIME, YOU MAY CHECK YOUR WORK IN THIS SECTION ONLY. **STOP**

ANSWER KEY

Section 1—Verbal Reasoning

1. B	8. C	15. D	22. C	29. A	36. C
2. A	9. A	16. A	23. C	30. A	37. B
3. C	10. A	17. C	24. B	31. C	38. B
4. D	11. B	18. B	25. B	32. A	39. B
5. A	12. D	19. C	26. C	33. D	40. A
6. A	13. D	20. D	27. A	34. D	
7. A	14. B	21. D	28. D	35. A	

Section 2—Quantitative Reasoning

1. A	8. C	15. D	22. C	29. A	36. B
2. C	9. C	16. B	23. C	30. B	37. D
3. B	10. A	17. A	24. A	31. B	
4. C	11. C	18. D	25. B	32. D	
5. B	12. B	19. B	26. D	33. D	
6. C	13. D	20. B	27. B	34. C	
7. C	14. C	21. B	28. A	35. C	

Section 3—Reading Comprehension

1. C	7. D	13. A	19. C	25. D	31. D
2. A	8. C	14. C	20. C	26. B	32. A
3. C	9. A	15. D	21. B	27. C	33. B
4. B	10. B	16. D	22. D	28. B	34. C
5. D	11. D	17. B	23. A	29. D	35. A
6. B	12. B	18. D	24. A	30. B	36. D

Section 4—Mathematics Achievement

1. B	9. D	17. B	25. D	33. A	41. C
2. B	10. C	18. D	26. B	34. C	42. B
3. D	11. A	19. C	27. A	35. C	43. D
4. C	12. B	20. C	28. C	36. C	44. A
5. C	13. C	21. C	29. A	37. B	45. A
6. B	14. C	22. C	30. C	38. D	46. C
7. A	15. B	23. C	31. B	39. D	47. C
8. B	16. A	24. C	32. C	40. B	

ANSWERS AND EXPLANATIONS

Section 1—Verbal Reasoning

Part One: Synonyms

1. B
If there is an "excess" of something, there is more quantity than is needed. This matches the meaning of "surplus," so answer choice (B) is correct.

2. A
To "astound" is to overwhelm with amazement or to surprise someone. Astound has a close meaning to "stun," answer choice (A), which means to astonish or amaze.

3. C
Something that is "massive" is very large or gigantic. Another word to describe something that is massive is "huge," answer choice (C). Even though tall things like mountains or buildings can be described as massive, don't be tempted by answer choice A, high.

4. D
A "bleak" scene is one that is desolate, cold, and not inviting. Often this term is used to describe something that creates a feeling of hopelessness. This word most closely matches the meaning of answer choice (D), "dreary."

5. A
The strategic test taker will remember that the prefix 'a–' at the beginning of a word can turn the original word into the opposite meaning. "Amoral" simply means without morals, which means that someone does not have moral standards. It makes sense that someone without those standards would also lack a sense of ethics, making answer choice (A) correct.

6. A
The word "hardy" means just what it looks like: to be strong and able to withstand the elements or physical fatigue. Something that is "healthy" would also have the ability to withstand things, making the correct answer (A). Watch out for answer choice C: even though hard and firm have similar meanings, hardy has a slight different connotation.

7. A
You may have heard the term "metamorphosis" in science class when studying how caterpillars turn into butterflies. During that process, the caterpillers go through many changes, so answer choice (A) is correct.

8. C
The word "neutral" can have different meanings depending on how it is used. No matter which meaning you think of, though, the basic characteristic of being neutral is to not take a side. This best matches with the word "unbiased," answer choice (C), meaning not preferring one side or the other.

9. A
A person who is "tolerant" is open to other people's opinions and does not judge others based on his or her own views. A tolerant person is therefore "open-minded," answer choice (A). Don't be trapped by answer choice B. Even though tolerant people may in general be friendly, that is not part of the definition of the word.

10. A
Someone who is "vigorous" is strong and very active. The word "robust," answer choice (A), most closely matches this definition because it means to be strong and healthy.

11. B

"Din" quite simply means a loud noise or racket. Of the answer choices listed, the closest one in meaning is "clamor," answer choice (B), which means a loud roar or outcry.

12. D

Although you may think of the word Halloween when you see "hallowed," the definition is actually holy, or "sacred," answer choice (D). Don't confuse the word hallowed for hollowed, which may lead you to accidentally choose either answer choice A or answer choice C, both of which are incorrect.

13. D

When you "offend" someone, you make them upset or resentful. To "insult," answer choice (D), is the closest answer choice in meaning, which means to treat with disrespect. Answer choices A and B are both actions that could cause someone to get offended, but neither matches the meaning of the word itself.

14. B

Someone who looks "wan" appears sick or weak. Often, people who are sick are also "pale" in complexion. Answer choice (B) is correct.

15. D

The word "arid" means extremely "dry," as in a desert's climate. This matches answer choice (D) exactly.

16. A

To "deceive" is to make another person believe something that is not true. Someone who deceives tricks people into believing falsehoods. The correct answer is choice (A).

17. C

You have likely heard the word "fiction" as it relates to literature. Use the fact that fiction is made up, or not true, to match this word with its synonym, "falsehood." Answer choice (C) is correct.

18. B

A "docile" animal is one that is calm and easily taught. This best matches answer choice (B), "tame." Although docile animals may be that way due to their advanced age, not all docile animals are by definition old.

19. C

When you see the word "lyrical," you may think of the word lyrics, which are the words to songs. Lyrical can also be a quality relating to music, or "musical." Answer choice (C) is correct.

20. D

To easily remember the definition of the word "desecrate," notice that the root part of the word is similar to *sacred*. Adding the prefix de- to that root creates the definition to take away something sacred. This best matches the word "defile," answer choice (D), which means to make unclean or impure.

Part Two: Sentence Completions

21. D

"Unproductive" is the clue here—it suggests that the company employs people who don't work hard. In other words, they have a "lackadaisical" approach to their work. Answer choice (D) is correct.

22. C

There is a contrast set up in this sentence between what wolves generally do and being "loners" during other times. To be social is to be the opposite of a loner. Answer choice (C) is correct.

23. C

The biggest hint for what the correct answer will be is "grace and…" This means that the word that fits in the blank has to be something related to grace. "Elegance," answer choice (C) is the closest in meaning to grace and, therefore, correct.

24. B

This sentence has a cause-and-effect relationship. The puppy whines after being disciplined, which you can assume means that it is not used to be reprimanded. This means that the puppy was "unaccustomed" to being disciplined, which matches answer choice (B).

25. B

In this sentence, you know that Liam is "very uncomfortable in social situations." Someone who is "introverted" has this reaction to social situations, making answer choice (B) correct. Answer choices A, C, and D have similar meanings that are the opposite of what is correct.

26. C

"Although" is a key contrast word to help you answer Sentence Completion questions. There is a contrast between the lavish homes Jayla designs and her own humble home. It's logical that her home is modest, which matches answer choice (C). Answer choices A and D could seem correct if you miss the contrast word at the beginning of the sentence, so be sure to read carefully.

27. A

The phrase "come out at night" indicate that raccoons are "nocturnal," which matches answer choice (A).

28. D

The phrase "not only" indicates that you are looking for a stronger version of the word "respected." Answer choice (D), "revered," fits that definition.

29. A

"At first" should have clued you in to the contrast here: the house seemed "frightening," but later proved "benign," or friendly. Answer choice (A) is correct.

30. A

If the school is "underfunded," it does not have much money. This fits with the definition of "meager," which is to have little resources. The correct answer is choice (A). Answer choice D, "belittled," does have 'little' within that word, but belittled actually means to disparage, which doesn't fit within the context of the sentence.

31. C

There is an implied contrast in this sentence between the "calm surface" of the ocean and what is happening with the animals below. A contrast to the calm of the surface would be *fighting* for food below. This matches with answer choice (C), "contested."

32. A

According to the sentence, two people died on the soap opera last week. Therefore, you need to find a word that describes that characteristic of the television show. Answer choice (A), "morbid," means a fascination with death and fits the sentence perfectly.

33. D

For this sentence, you are looking for a word that reflects the fact that "the candidate [often] changed his positions." The only answer choice that matches is choice (D), "flighty." Be careful not to choose answer choice A; "reliable" is the opposite of the desired word in this context.

34. D

There aren't many hints in this sentence to know which is the correct answer, so go with the choice that makes the most sense logically. Answer choice (D) is logical because the jumper would definitely be lucky, or "fortunate," if the chute didn't open properly, but he still survived.

35. A

The key word in this sentence is "despite" because it signals a contrast between the first and second parts of the sentence. If the warrior became great, he must have started life without much fame or prestige. This matches answer choice (A). The warrior had "humble beginnings" but was later a "great ruler."

36. C

The two clue words "normally" and "usual" suggest that both blanks mean more or less the same. Answer choice (C), "amiable...enthusiasm," works best here.

37. B

"Weighing more than 70 tons" leads you to predict a word like *large* or *gigantic* for the first blank. The word "yet" sets up a contrast for the second blank, so you want a word like small for the second blank. Only "gargantuan" and "prodigious" work for the first blank. Of these two options, only "small" works for the second blank, so answer choice (B) is correct.

38. B

When a Sentence Completion question has two blanks, start with whichever blank is easier to predict. In this case, the second part of the sentence has a clue: the person "meant well," but the words came across differently. A strong prediction would be that the words were *hurtful*. Answer choices A and C both have words for the second blank that are positive, while answer choice D doesn't make sense in context. The correct answer, choice (B), uses the word "gauche," which means tactless or lacking sensitivity, which fits perfectly with the meaning of this sentence.

39. B

The movie is described as "relying on gimmick[s] and stereotype[s]," so both blanks will contain words with negative connotations. The correct choice is answer choice (B) because being "predictable" and "absurd" are qualities that would result in a bad movie. Answer choice A may have been tempting, but a movie wouldn't likely be described as "ambivalent."

40. A

The easier blank to start with is the first one in this sentence. If the platypus is "difficult to spot," it must be *good at hiding*. You can also assume that the zoo exhibit is contained, like an aquarium. "Crafty" for the first blank (answer choice B) could make sense in context because it means skillful, but the second word, "massive," doesn't fit with the fact that although it should be easy to see the platypus, the animal is able to hide from people. The answer choice that matches both predictions is answer choice (A).

Section 2—Quantitative Reasoning

Part One: Word Problems

1. A

Damian's age is represented by x. Because Noah is twice as old as Damian, Damian is half as old as Noah, or $0.5x$. The correct answer is answer choice (A).

2. C

Raquel spent $\frac{1}{2}$ of her day at work and $\frac{2}{3}$ of that time in meetings. So the amount of time she spent in meetings was $\frac{1}{2} \times \frac{2}{3} = \frac{2}{6} = \frac{1}{3}$ of her day. The correct answer is choice (C).

3. B

The most efficient way to solve this problem is to set up a proportion. If $x =$ the number of bottles in 1 minute, you can set up the proportion below. Don't forget to convert 1 minute into 60 seconds since the other rate is given in bottles per second:

$$\frac{5}{2} = \frac{x}{60}$$
$$(5)(60) = 2x$$
$$300 = 2x$$
$$150 = x$$

Answer choice (B) is correct.

4. C

The triangle in the diagram is isosceles because it has two sides of length 2. Therefore, the angles opposite these sides are also equal, and the unidentified base angle must equal 50°. The interior angles of a triangle sum to 180°, so set up an equation:

$$50 + 50 + x = 180$$
$$100 + x = 180$$
$$x = 80$$

Answer choice (C) is correct.

5. B

This question is asking for the percent increase of this particular stock from Monday to Tuesday. Although you know the amount the stock increased, you don't actually have a price given. This is a perfect question to pick numbers. Assume the starting price of the stock is $100. If the stock price doubles, the new price is $200. This is an increase of $100 or 100%, which matches answer choice (B).

6. C

To answer this question, translate the word problem into variables. If the passing grade is x, Peyton received 7 points higher: $(x + 7)$. On the second test, he performed 12 points lower: $(x + 7) - 12 = x - 5$. This corresponds to answer choice (C).

7. C

Three fiction books for every 8 nonfiction books means that 8 out of $3 + 8$, or $\frac{8}{11}$, of all the books are nonfiction. The 600 nonfiction books are $\frac{8}{11}$ of the number you're looking for, so set up an equation:

$$\frac{8}{11}x = 600$$

$$x = 600 \times \frac{11}{8}$$

$$= \frac{6,600}{8}$$

$$= 825$$

Answer choice (C) is correct.

8. C

If the printer completes 15 copies per minute, then it completes 75 copies in 5 minutes: $15 \times 5 = 75$. The fraction of the total job that has been completed is $\frac{75}{600} = \frac{1}{8}$, answer choice (C).

9. C

Rate is equal to distance divided by time. So 328 miles divided by 4 hours is $\frac{328}{4} = 82$ miles per hour. Answer choice (C) is correct.

10. A

Mr. Fernandez bought 1 case with 11 cans and 7 cases with 6 cans each, so he bought $1 \times 11 + 7 \times 6$, or $11 + 42 = 53$ cans of soda. Answer choice (A) is correct.

11. C

Don't forget to fill in the figure with information from the question to help you solve this question most efficiently. $\overline{AB}$ is half the length of $\overline{BC}$, which is given as 12, so $AB = 6$ and $AC = 6 + 12 = 18$. $\overline{CD}$ is half the length of $\overline{AC}$, so $CD = 9$. Thus, $AD = AB + BC + CD = 6 + 12 + 9 = 27$. Answer choice (C) is correct.

12. B

Recall that all figures on the ISEE are always drawn to scale unless stated otherwise. Extending the vertical line segment boundary of the art slice upward and extending the horizontal line segment boundary of the art slice to the right shows that the art slice is about 25% of the pie. Twenty-five percent, or $\frac{1}{4}$, of 900 (the total number of students) is 225 art students. Answer choice (B) is correct.

13. D

If line segments AB, BC, and AC are equal, $\triangle ABC$ is an equilateral triangle. In an equilateral triangle, each interior angle measures 60 degrees. Therefore, $\angle ACB = 60°$ and $\angle BCD = 180° - 60° = 120°$. The correct answer is choice (D).

14. C

Consecutive integers are an instance of equally spaced numbers. In this case, because the largest integer is 25, the consecutive integers must be 19, 20, 21, 22, 23, 24, and 25. You can use the average formula to find the answer, or you can use the rule that the average of an odd number of equally spaced numbers is always the middle one. Since the average is 22, answer choice (C) is correct.

15. D

Picking Numbers works well on inequalities questions that involve variables. In this case, the largest possible integer value of x for $x < 2$ is $x = 1$. Plug that into the given expression: $3 \times 1 + 6 = 9$. The largest possible value of $3x + 6$ is 9, so choice (D) is the correct answer.

ISEE Practice Tests and Explanations

16. B

Because $RS = RT$, then $\angle S$ and $\angle T$ are also congruent. Because the sum of $\angle S$ and $\angle T$ is 110°, you know that $\angle S$ is one-half of 110°, or 55 degrees. Answer choice (B) is correct.

17. A

The average formula is $\text{average} = \dfrac{\text{sum of the terms}}{\text{number of the terms}}$. Because the average of 8, 3, 12, 11, and x is 0, you can write the equation $0 = \dfrac{8 + 3 + 12 + 11 + x}{5}$. Simplifying the numerator of the algebraic fraction on the right side, you can determine that $0 = \dfrac{34 + x}{5}$. After multiplying both sides by 5, you get $34 + x = 0$. Finally, subtract 34 from both sides to get $x = -34$. Answer choice (A) is correct.

18. D

To solve this question, attack each fraction separately. If $\dfrac{x}{3} = 3$, then $x = 9$. If $\dfrac{y}{6} = 3$, then $y = 18$. Finally, determine the value of $x + y$: $9 + 18 = 27$. Answer choice (D) is correct.

19. B

Because line p is parallel to line q, you know that corresponding angles are equal. This means that angle x is equal to 55 degrees. Answer choice (B) is correct.

20. B

To find the probability of two separate events, find the individual probabilities and then multiply those numbers together. There is a $\dfrac{3}{6}$ chance that Chloe will roll an even number. Simplify this fraction to $\dfrac{1}{2}$. The probability of rolling an even number twice is $\dfrac{1}{2} \times \dfrac{1}{2} = \dfrac{1}{4}$. Answer choice (B) is correct.

Part Two: Quantitative Comparisons

21. B

In Column A, $3 + 4 = 7$. In Column B, $3 \times 4 = 12$. Because Column B is greater, answer choice (B) is correct.

22. C

In Column A, you have $\dfrac{1}{4}$ of 12,948, and in Column B, you have 25% of 12,948. Because $\dfrac{1}{4} = 25\%$, the columns will be equal. Notice that you didn't need to do any calculation to solve this problem; in fact, calculating would waste time you could use to answer other questions. Answer choice (C) is correct.

23. C

You know $10M + 2 = 32$, so $10M = 30$ and $M = 3$. Therefore, the columns are equal. Answer choice (C) is correct.

24. A

Quantitative Comparison questions are easiest to answer when the components are in the same form, so they are easier to compare. In Column A, $\dfrac{1}{4} = 0.25$. In Column B, $0.2569 - 0.007 = 0.2499$, just less than 0.25 in Column A. Answer choice (A) is correct.

25. B

The value in Column A is 7.9999, and the value in Column B is 7.99999. Column A only shows four places to the right of the decimal place, so any other places are understood to be zeros. Therefore, Column A is actually 7.99990, so Column B is 0.00009 greater than Column A. Answer choice (B) is correct.

26. D

All you know about x and y is that both are positive. You don't know their relative values, and you don't know if x is greater than y or vice versa. Consequently, you can't determine if adding the number 1 to the value of x would make Column A greater, less than, or equal to the value under Column B. The answer here must therefore be answer choice (D).

27. B

This problem requires no math at all. You are given a certain amount of money: 5 dollars. Can you buy more expensive items (32-cent stamps) or more cheap items (29-cent stamps) with this amount of money? You can buy more of the cheaper items, so the answer must be answer choice (B).

28. A

Translate the expression into an equation: $\frac{5}{7}$ of x is 35

$$\frac{5}{7}x = 35$$

$$x = 35 \times \frac{7}{5}$$

$$x = 49$$

Because 49 is greater than 48, answer choice (A) is correct.

29. A

Remember to compare, not calculate; there is no reason to look for common denominators and do the math here. The $\frac{1}{2}$ in Column A is just slightly larger than the $\frac{2}{5}$ in Column B. Both columns contain $\frac{3}{4}$. The $\frac{7}{8}$ in Column A is also larger than the $\frac{7}{9}$ in Column B, so overall, whatever the total value, Column A is larger than Column B. This means that answer choice (A) is correct.

30. B

Find the value of each column:

$$5\% \text{ of } (3+4) = 5\% \text{ of } 7$$

$$= (0.05)(7)$$

$$= 0.35$$

$$4\% \text{ of } (3 \times 4) = 4\% \text{ of } 12$$

$$= (0.04)(12)$$

$$= 0.48$$

Because 0.48 is greater than 0.35, answer choice (B) is correct.

31. B

The factors of 21 are 1, 3, 7, and 21. Of these, only two are prime (3 and 7). Compare that to the value under Column B, 3, and the answer is choice (B).

32. D

The strategic test taker will notice right away that there's no information about the numbers added to the set in Column B. Although you could find the average of the given set of numbers, there's no need to here. Without knowing what numbers are added to the set, it's impossible to tell what affect those new numbers would have on the average. Answer choice (D) is correct.

33. D

It looks at first glance like B and C divide the segment into three equal pieces. However, you should check the mathematics of the situation to be sure. You're given that $AC = BD$:

What can you deduce from that? You can subtract the length of $\overline{BC}$ from both equal lengths, and you'll end up with another equality. $AB = CD$. But what about the length of $\overline{BC}$? Does it have to be the same as the lengths of $\overline{AB}$ and $\overline{CD}$? No. The diagram could be resketched like this:

Now you can see that it's possible for both $\overline{AC}$ and $\overline{BD}$ to be the same size and for $\overline{BC}$ to be longer than $\overline{AB}$. It's also possible for $\overline{BC}$ to be shorter than $\overline{AB}$:

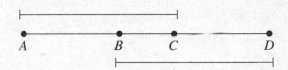

More than one relationship is possible, so the answer is choice (D).

34. C

Solve for x in the centered equation. First, subtract $2x$ from both sides. This will leave you with $-6 = 3x$. Divide both sides by 3. Now, $x = -2$. Plug in -2 for x to find the value of x^2 in Column A: $x^2 = (-2)^2 = 4$. The quantities in both columns are equal, so answer choice (C) is correct.

35. C

Remember when determining probability to figure out the individual probabilities first and then multiply them together. For Column A, the probability of picking an apple is $\frac{4}{12}$, or $\frac{1}{3}$. The probability of picking another apple (without putting the first one back in the bowl) is $\frac{3}{11}$. Finally, multiply the two probabilities together: $\frac{1}{3} \times \frac{3}{11} = \frac{3}{33} = \frac{1}{11}$. For Column B, the probability of selecting a kiwi is $\frac{6}{12}$ or $\frac{1}{2}$, and the probability of then

picking a clementine is $\frac{2}{11}$. Once again, multiply the probabilities together: $\frac{1}{2} \times \frac{2}{11} = \frac{2}{22} = \frac{1}{11}$. The two columns are equal, so answer choice (C) is correct.

36. B

At first glance, this question is pretty straightforward, because it asks you to find the average of each column. However, the strategic test taker will try to find a way to answer this (and every) question in the most efficient way possible. If you put the two sets of numbers in order, you will see that the final exam grades are all larger than the number in the same order of the midterm grade set. Column B will have the larger average, making answer choice (B) correct. If you do use the average formula, just add up the numbers and see which sum is bigger. Because both sets have 5 terms, the larger sum will equal the larger average.

37. D

Because the variables could be positive or negative, pick different kinds of numbers for the variables to see if different relationships between the columns are possible. Remember that the values you pick must be consistent with the centered information, which is that $a > b > c > d$.

If $a = 4$, $b = 3$, $c = 2$, and $d = 1$, then the value of Column A is $a^2 + c = 4^2 + 2 = 16 + 2 = 18$, and the value of Column B is $b^2 + d = 3^2 + 1 = 9 + 1 = 10$. Column A is greater, and if you pick only positive numbers, then it will always be true that $a^2 + c > b^2 + d$. Be careful not to fall for the trap here of automatically assuming that $a^2 + c$ is always greater than $b^2 + d$; be sure to try having some or all of the variables be negative.

Let $a = -1$, $b = -2$, $c = -3$, and $d = -4$; these values are consistent with the information relating all four variables. This time the value of Column A is $a^2 + c = (-1)^2 + (-3) = 1 - 3 = -2$, and the value of Column B is $b^2 + d = (-2)^2 + (-4) = 4 - 4 = 0$. So in this case, Column B is greater.

Since more than one relationship is possible, answer choice (D) is correct.

Section 3—Reading Comprehension

Plague Passage

This passage is about the plague, an epidemic that killed one-third of the people in Europe in the 13th and 14th centuries. The author says that, ironically, the plague brought about some beneficial changes in European society. One of these changes—the focal point of the passage—was in the medical profession. The plague created a shortage of doctors, allowing people with new ideas to enter the profession. In addition, having been failed by the old doctors with their Latin medical texts, ordinary people began clamoring for medical texts printed in everyday languages. These were eventually published, making medical knowledge more accessible to everyone.

1. C

This is a Main Idea question, so the correct answer will be something that describes the entire passage and not just one part of it. The passage starts with a brief description of what the plague was, but the rest of the passage focuses on the unanticipated future beneficial effects of a terrible situation. The answer choice that best matches this summary of the passage is answer choice (C). If you were looking for an answer with the word "plague" in it, you may have been tempted by answer choices A or B. However, those answer choices are too specific because they are only mentioned in passing and are not the main idea of the entire passage.

2. A

For this Vocab-in-Context question, use the context of the sentence to predict a word that would fit into the blank, and then find the answer choice that matches. The plague brought changes to society, which would best fit answer choice (A), "caused." Answer choice C is incorrect because the passage does not include information to indicate the rate at which these changes occurred.

3. C

The key work "suggests" in the question stem tells you that this is an Inference question. According to the passage, the medical profession "had mostly failed to relieve the suffering" during the plague. You can assume, then, that the reforms mentioned were necessary in order to improve the quality of medical care in Europe. This matches answer choice (C).

4. B

According to the passage, "…more medical texts began to appear in everyday languages rather than in Latin" (lines 21–22) after the plague. This made the texts "more accessible" (line 23). Answer choice (B) best fits with the information given in the final sentence of the passage. Answer choice C is a distortion; just because the texts were in other languages doesn't mean that they were not in Latin anymore.

5. D

To determine the tone of a passage, think about how the author presents the material. This is an informative passage, so answer choices A and B do not make sense here. The author seems to believe that the changes that happened during this time were practical and make sense, so answer choice (D) is correct.

6. B

Each of the answer choices has direct support in the passage except one. There is no mention of people learning Latin to understand the medical texts. In fact, the texts were translated to other languages so they were more accessible, so answer choice (B) does not fit with the information given and is therefore the correct answer.

Log Cabin Passage

The passage is about log cabins and the era of their greatest popularity (a period from 1780 to 1850). The author describes early simple cabins and grand later ones and then discusses the factors that led to a decline in the log cabin's popularity, factors such as the greater availability of hardware and building materials, the rising popularity of the Greek Revival style of house, and the spread of the railroads. The passage ends with a brief description of what happened to most log cabins as their heyday ended.

7. D

In line 10, the author describes the Greek Revival-style house as having "democratic roots in ancient Greece." People interested in this style of house would like also be interested in democracy. This matches answer choice (D).

8. C

Just like any other Vocab-in-Context question, predict your own word to go where "forged" is. Settlers went westward during this time period, which is the same meaning as answer choice (C), "moved."

9. A

Only a few specific details are given about Greek Revival-style homes. In line 20, one characteristic of these houses is that they have a "templed front facing the street." You can assume that log cabins did not have that characteristic, which makes answer choice (A) correct.

10. B

Around the time that log cabins were becoming less popular, trains were more prevalent and able to bring building materials to new locations. Also, the passage states that "the proximity of the local forest no longer set architectural limits" (lines 22–23). Therefore, you can assume that it previously mattered how close the local forest was. Answer choice (B) is correct.

11. D

For this Supporting Ideas question, determine which information is in the passage about log cabins after 1850. The passage states that log cabins were less popular during this time, but they were used to house livestock. The correct answer choice is choice (D).

12. B

For this question, eliminate any answer choice that is directly addressed in the passage. The only one that isn't answered is answer choice (B). Although you do know that the popularity of log cabins had diminished significantly, the cabins were still being used for livestock in the 1850s, with no further mention of what happened to log cabins after that point.

Coyotes Passage

The passage is about coyotes. The author's main focus is not on the behavioral habits of living coyotes, but rather on the evolution of the coyote as found in the fossil record. Both the coyote and the wolf, you learn, had a common ancestor living in North America as long as three million years ago. One or two million years ago, the coyote and the wolf became separate species. As time passed, other species such as the mammoth and the saber-toothed tiger lived and became extinct, but the coyote endured—basically the same primitive animal, but still marvelously adaptable to its environment.

13. A

As with any Main Idea question, think of the big picture to help answer this one. There are many details about the coyote throughout time, all to illustrate the fact that the species has largely remained the same. This matches answer choice (A).

14. C

There is only one place in the passage that mentions dogs today: the first sentence. Coyotes are a "primitive" of modern dogs, which means that dogs and coyotes must be related species. Answer choice (C) is correct. Answer choice A may be tempting, but you only know from the passage that dire wolves are a type of canid, not that they evolved directly into the dogs you know today.

15. D

To find the answer to this question, look for specific phrases from the question stem in the passage itself. In the second sentence, the author states "a close relative of the contemporary coyote existed here two to three million years ago." This is an exact match for answer choice (D).

16. D

The passage makes it clear that coyotes are unique because they were able to survive and adapt throughout time. Mammoths and saber-toothed tigers, on the other hand, "came and went" (line 12). The author gives these examples to show the contrast between coyotes and other animals from the past, so answer choice (D) is correct.

17. B

Even if you are not sure what the word "galleons" means, you can still answer this question effectively by looking for other clues in the passage. The passage states that native horses were left on land, but others came back to North America. You can eliminate answer choice C because this sentence is about horses, not coyotes. Answer choice A doesn't have support in the passage because there is no discussion of different types of horses. Answer choice D doesn't make sense because there are no specific times given for when the horse and dire wolf went extinct. This leaves answer choice (B), which fits with the fact that horses left and then came back later to the same area.

18. D

For this EXCEPT question, eliminate anything that has direct support in the passage. Answer choice (D) is the opposite of the main idea of the passage and is, therefore, correct.

Chocolate Passage

The passage is about chocolate, which comes from the seeds, or beans, of the cacao tree. You're told that chocolate was first known to have been consumed (in drink form) by the Aztec people of Mexico, that the Spanish explorer Cortes learned of chocolate in 1519 on his expedition among the Aztecs, and that he brought three chests of cacao beans back to Spain. Over the next century, the passage concludes, the chocolate drink became popular with the wealthy throughout Europe.

19. C

Line 1 contains a reference to chocolate as a "generic" term to describe different types of foods made from the cacao bean. A strong prediction for "generic" is broad or general, which matches answer choice (C) exactly.

20. C

Remember to only use information from the passage to answer Reading Comprehension questions. Although answer choice A is logical, the passage doesn't discuss this aspect of chocolate. The first sentence does state that chocolate is made from the seeds of the cacao tree, which makes answer choice (C) correct.

21. B

Based on information in the passage, Cortes came to Mexico in search of gold, but he became interested in the Aztecs' chocolate beverage. If he was interested in gold, he must have wanted to become more wealthy, which matches answer choice (B). Although some of the other answer choices may be true, only the desire for gold is specifically mentioned in the passage.

22. D

In line 24, the author describes the drink as "peculiar." This word most closely means strange, answer choice (D). Be careful not to get trapped by answer choice A. Although chocolate as you know it today is often sweet, the drink is described as "bitter" in line 11 of this passage.

23. A

The passage describes how chocolate became popular in Europe in the last sentence. The drink was popular "among those wealthy enough to afford it." Therefore, you can assume the drink was answer choice (A), "expensive."

24. A

As with other EXCEPT questions, elimination is the best strategy here. Although you know that Cortes returned to Spain with cacao beans, you have no idea what else was in his ship's cargo hold. Therefore, the correct answer is choice (A).

Wolves Passage

The passage is about the structured packs that wolves live in. These packs are described as hierarchies similar to the "pecking order" of birds. Senior male wolves are at the top of the hierarchy, followed by mature wolves, young or immature wolves, and outcast wolves. You learn that a wolf's place in the hierarchy determines its selection of "food, mates, and resting places" and how much responsibility each wolf is given in terms of protecting the pack from danger.

25. D

To find the answer to this question, look for where wolves and birds are both mentioned. The only place this happens is in the first sentence of the passage. Wolves hunt in "hierarchically structured packs" similar to what is found in bird flocks. Answer choice (D) is correct.

26. B

The first sentence of the passage states that the structure of wolf packs "has been known for some time." It can be inferred that these discoveries are not recent, so answer choice (B) is correct.

27. C

Outcast wolves are ones that have been rejected by the pack. Because these wolves have been rejected, they are at the lowest hierarchical level. Therefore, they are a lower status than immature wolves, so answer choice (C) is correct.

28. B

Line 24 gives the different things for which higher-ranking wolves have preference over lower-ranking ones. This list includes all but answer choice (B).

29. D

Overall, the tone is neutral, which best fits answer choice (D). The author does not seem to have an overly positive or negative opinion about this subject, so answer choices A and B are incorrect. A purpose can be informative, but it would not be common to describe the author's attitude in that way, also eliminating answer choice C.

30. B

Mature wolves have a lower status than senior males. "Lower" is closest in definition to answer choice (B), "inferior."

James Van Der Zee Passage

The sixth and last passage on this test is about James Van Der Zee, a photographer who worked in Harlem. You learn that Van Der Zee's career started in 1916, just before an African American cultural boom known as the Harlem Renaissance, and that, in a career spanning 40 years, he took thousands of photographs of Harlem residents. The passage states that these photographs—of celebrities and unknown citizens alike—are now considered an important cultural record of a proud community.

31. D

In Main Idea questions, not only do you have to watch out for answer choices that are too specific, but you also have to be sure that an answer choice isn't too broad. Both answer choices A and B are too broad because this passage focuses on a specific artist. The passage doesn't discuss James Van Der Zee's specific influences, but the passage does make clear that his influence was important because he captured the time and place effectively. Answer choice (D) is correct.

32. A

According to the passage, when James Van Der Zee opened his studio, "It was the eve of the Harlem Renaissance" (lines 2–3). This matches answer choice (A).

33. B

In the lines cited, the author mentions that Van Der Zee had ordinary people as his subjects. You can infer that the artist wanted to portray all people from his community, instead of only wealthy, or "important," people. Answer choice (B) is the correct answer.

34. C

Throughout the passage, the author is complimentary to Van Der Zee, even mentioning his "unique vision" (line 23). It is clear that the author admires this artist and his work, so answer choice (C) is correct.

35. A

In the passage, James Van Der Zee is credited with doing several things as part of the Harlem Renaissance. He is not, however, credited with starting the movement, so answer choice (A) is correct.

36. D

To help answer this question, read around the given line to see what other clues can help to define "burgeoning." In line 12, the author describes the community as "artistically vigorous." The community was metaphorically coming alive and becoming more active during this time, which matches answer choice (D).

Section 4—Mathematics Achievement

1. B

There are 60 seconds in a minute, so in $\frac{1}{20}$ of a minute there are $60 \times \frac{1}{20} = \frac{60}{20} = 3$ seconds. Answer choice (B) is correct.

2. B

Sketch yourself a diagram:

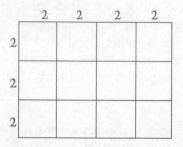

The 8-inch length can be divided into four 2-inch segments, and the 6-inch width can be divided into three 2-inch segments, which gives you a total of $4 \times 3 = 12$ squares. Answer choice (B) is correct.

3. D

If a movie collection can be evenly divided among 6 people, the number of movies must be a multiple of 6. Only 24 is a multiple of 6 ($6 \times 4 = 24$), so answer choice (D) is correct.

4. C

Remember that fractions have to have the same denominator to add them together. The first step is to make the denominator 12 for all the fractions, so the question is easiest to solve:

$$\frac{1}{2} + \frac{1}{3} = \frac{M}{12}$$
$$\frac{6}{12} + \frac{4}{12} = \frac{10}{12}$$

So $M = 10$, and answer choice (C) is correct.

5. C

To solve this question, follow the definition of the symbol and plug in the given numbers:

$$\text{If } N_i = N \times 10, \, 30_i + 2_i = 30 \times 10 + 2 \times 10$$
$$= 300 + 20$$
$$= 320$$

Answer choice (C) is correct.

6. B

You must note how many students were in the class each month. March $= 40$, April $= 60$, May $= 80$, and June $= 80$. Use the average formula: $\text{average} = \dfrac{\text{sum of terms}}{\text{number of terms}}$.

Here, the average is $\dfrac{40 + 60 + 80 + 80}{4} = \dfrac{260}{4} = 65$.

Answer choice (B) is correct.

7. A

The easiest way to solve this question is to first translate the percent into a fraction: $20\% = 0.20 = \dfrac{20}{100} = \dfrac{1}{5}$. $\dfrac{1}{5}(30) = 6$. Answer choice (A) is correct.

8. B

You may be tempted to try and solve for x or y in this question, but all of the answer choices still have y in them. If you subtract 5 from both sides, you will find what $x - 5$ equals:

$$x - 4y + 3$$
$$x - 5 = 4y + 3 - 5$$
$$= 4y - 2$$

Answer choice (B) is correct.

9. D

This is a perfect question to pick numbers for because there are variables in the question and the answer choices. You can choose any odd number and plug it in for n:

$$\text{If } n = 3$$
$$\text{Choice A: } -2(3) - 1 = -7$$
$$\text{Choice B: } 2(3) + 1 = 7$$
$$\text{Choice C: } 2(3) - 1 = 5$$
$$\text{Choice (D): } 4(3) = 12$$

Only answer choice (D) is even, so this is the correct answer.

10. C

Each of the six squares is a rectangle.

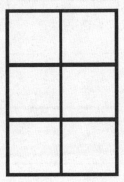

And these two:

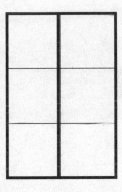

And this one:

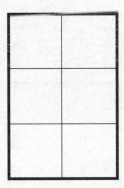

Plus, there are these two rectangles:

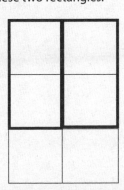

Plus this one:

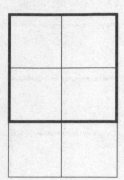

And there are also these 3:

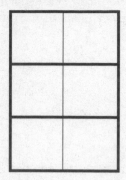

That's a total of $6 + 2 + 1 + 2 + 1 + 2 + 1 + 3 = 18$. Answer choice (C) is correct.

And lastly these two:

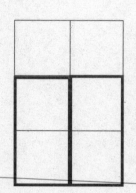

And this one:

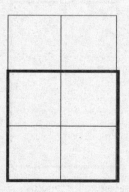

11.   A

This question is pretty straightforward if you carefully translate the words into math and then follow the order of operations:

$$\frac{45}{5 \times 3} = \frac{45}{15}$$
$$= 3$$

Answer choice (A) is correct.

12.   B

If $a + b = 6$, in order to solve for b, you need to move a to the right side of the equation by subtracting it from 6, so $b = 6 - a$. Choice (B) is correct.

13.   C

The question states that Team B scored more points that Team A. Team B must have scored at least 40 points. To find the average of points Team B scored, use the average formula with 40 for the minimum needed sum of points scored:

$$\text{average} = \frac{\text{sum of terms}}{\text{number of terms}}$$
$$= \frac{40}{5}$$
$$= 8$$

On average, each player on Team B needed to score 8 points to score more total points than Team A, so answer choice (C) is correct.

14. C

The first step for this question is to translate the words into math: $1\frac{1}{3} - \frac{5}{6}$. Then, convert the mixed number into an improper fraction: $1\frac{1}{3} - \frac{5}{6} = \frac{4}{3} - \frac{5}{6}$. Finally, make both fractions have a common denominator:

$$\frac{4}{3} - \frac{5}{6} = \frac{16}{12} - \frac{10}{12}$$
$$= \frac{6}{12}$$
$$= \frac{1}{2}$$

Answer choice (C) is correct.

15. B

The diagram shows that this is a right triangle, with one angle measuring 45 degrees. Because all angles in a triangle add up to 180 degrees, the remaining angle measures $180 - 90 - 45 = 45$ degrees. In an isosceles right triangle, the legs have equal length. This means that *a* equals 6 meters, so answer choice (B) is correct.

16. A

Remember to follow the order of operations to determine the value of this expression:

$$\frac{64}{2 \times 4} = \frac{64}{8} = 8$$

Answer choice (A) is correct.

17. B

Use the formula for the area of a triangle:

$$\text{Area} = \frac{1}{2}(\text{base})(\text{height})$$
$$= \frac{1}{2}(4)(6) = 12$$

Answer choice (B) is correct.

18. D

Let the number of walkers equal *x*. If there are twice the number of bus riders as walkers, you can represent bus riders as $2x$. Set up an equation to find the total number of students:

$$36 = 2x + x$$
$$36 = 3x$$
$$12 = x$$

The question is asking you to find the number of bus riders, and you know there are twice as many. Therefore, there are $2 \times 12 = 24$ bus riders, so answer choice (D) is correct.

19. C

The numbers for the week are 16, 21, 20, 17, 19, 21, 17. Listing them in ascending order, you have 16, 17, 17, 19, 20, 21, 21. There are an odd number of numbers, so the median is the number in the middle of the set: 19. Answer choice (C) is correct.

20. C

Translate this question into an inequality to solve most efficiently. If one-fifth of a number is less than 20, then you can set up an equation:

$$\frac{1}{5}x < 20$$
$$x < 20 \times \frac{5}{1}$$
$$x < 100$$

Answer choice (C) is correct.

21. C

To get to the correct answer, solve this question like you would any equation and combine the like terms as the first step:

$$Q + 7 - 8 + 3 = 23$$
$$Q + 2 = 23$$
$$Q = 21$$

Answer choice (C) is correct.

22. C

To solve this problem, you first need to determine the limits of possible values for a:

$$a + 2 > 5$$
$$a > 3$$
$$a - 4 < 1$$
$$a < 5$$

If a is between 3 and 5, the only answer choice that works is 4, so answer choice (C) is correct.

23. C

When solving a question like this, it is easy to do extra steps when you don't need to. Notice that two of the numbers actually multiply to equal 18. That means that you can group the expression like this: $2 \times 9 \times 4 \times 7 = 18 \times 28$. Answer choice (C) is the correct answer.

24. C

The first step for this problem is to simplify the amounts inside the parentheses:

$$(65 \times 10^2) + (31 \times 10^3) + 12 = (65 \times 100) +$$
$$(31 \times 1{,}000) + 12$$
$$= 6{,}500 + 31{,}000 + 12$$
$$= 37{,}512$$

Answer choice (C) is correct.

25. D

To efficiently answer this question, look at each statement individually to see if it is always true or if you can think of a time that the statement is not true. Because a is anything greater than 4, a can be 8 or 16, so b doesn't have to be 2; this eliminates statement I and answer choice C. However, you do know that b has to be positive because a is positive (it's greater than 4) and the product of a and b is positive (it's 16). Therefore, the sum of a and b is positive, and statement II is true, so you can eliminate answer choice B. Lastly, when $a = 8$, $b = 2$; when $a = 16$, $b = 1$. Thus, a is greater than b, and statement III is true. Answer choice (D) is correct.

26. B

This is another "plug-in" question. Remember, $5yz$ means $5 \times y \times z$. First, replace x, y, and z with the values given. Then, carry out the indicated operations using PEMDAS:

$$x^2 - 5yz + y^2 = \left(\sqrt{3}\right)^2 - 5 \times 2 \times \frac{1}{2} + 2^2$$
$$= 3 - 5 \times 2 \times \frac{1}{2} + 4$$
$$= 3 - 5 + 4$$
$$= -2 + 4$$
$$= 2$$

Answer choice (B) is correct.

27. A

If 9 is x percent of 90, then $9x = 90$, and $x = 10$. Because 50 percent of 10 is 5, answer choice (A) is correct.

28. C

The product of two numbers is the result of multiplying them together, so the product of 12 and 4 is $12 \times 4 = 48$. Adding 9 to 48 gives you 57, answer choice (C).

29. A

The star and the triangle must be on opposite sides of the triangle, so you must eliminate any answer choice with a cube showing a star and a triangle. Answer choices B, C, and D are all incorrect. Therefore, answer choice (A) has to be correct.

30. C

Manipulate the values in the equation to isolate x.

$$\frac{700}{x} = 35$$
$$700 = 35x$$
$$20 = x$$

Answer choice (C) is correct.

31. B

Picking Numbers is the best strategy to use with this question. If you multiply the first few numbers times themselves, you can eliminate three of the answer choices: $1^2 = 1$; $2^2 = 4$; $3^2 = 9$; $4^2 = 16$; $5^2 = 25$. All of the answer choices have been eliminated except for answer choice (B), so that must be the correct one.

32. C

You can use pick numbers to answer this question quickly on Test Day. Assume that Diya has $8 and her brother has 2 dollars. Together, they have $10. For them to equally divide the 10 dollars, Diya would have to give her brother 3 of her dollars so they both have 5 dollars. Answer choice (C) is correct.

33. A

Start by simplifying the fraction on the right side of the equation: $\frac{48}{12} = \frac{4}{1} = 4$, so $\frac{28}{a} = 4$. From there, solve the equation like you would any other one:

$$\frac{28}{a} = 4$$
$$28 = 4a$$
$$7 = a$$

Answer choice (A) is correct.

34. C

While there's no way to determine the numerical values of a, b, c, or d from their positions on the coordinate plane, you do know that a is negative, b is positive, c is negative, and d is negative. Bearing in mind that a negative times a negative is a positive, consider each answer choice. You know $b > acd$ is indeed true: b, which is positive, is greater than the product acd, which is negative. Answer choice (C) is correct.

35. C

To find the slope of a line when given two points, use the slope formula:

$$\text{slope} = \frac{y_2 - y_1}{x_2 - x_1}$$
$$= \frac{-8 - 10}{-42 - 6}$$
$$= \frac{-18}{-48}$$
$$= \frac{3}{8}$$

Answer choice (C) is correct.

36. C

If the apartment building has x apartments on the lower three floors, the total apartments on the lower floors is $3x$. Similarly, there are $3y$ apartments on the upper floors. If 3 people live in each apartments, $3 \times 3x + 3 \times 3y = 9x + 9y$ people live in the entire building, so answer choice (C) is correct.

37. B

If Selena is in school for 6 hours per day, five days a week, she is in school for 30 hours total each week. To find the number of seconds that are in 30 hours, first convert hours to minutes, and then minutes to seconds:

$$30 \text{ hours} \times \left(\frac{60 \text{ minutes}}{1 \text{ hour}}\right) = 1{,}800 \text{ minutes}$$
$$1{,}800 \text{ minutes} \times \left(\frac{60 \text{ seconds}}{1 \text{ minute}}\right) = 108{,}000 \text{ seconds}$$

Answer choice (B) is correct.

38. D

The grocer buys four oranges for $1, which means that she pays $0.25 per orange. If she sells them for $0.40, she makes a profit of $0.15 on each one. To figure out how many oranges she needs to sell to make $3, set up an equation:

$$0.15x = 3.00$$
$$x = 20$$

Answer choice (D) is correct.

39. D

If there is a set of six numbers and the average of that set is 6, the sum of those six numbers must be 36:

$$\text{average} = \frac{\text{sum of terms}}{\text{number of terms}}$$

$$6 = \frac{\text{sum of terms}}{6}$$

$$36 = \text{sum of terms}$$

If 3 is subtracted from four of the terms, a total of 12 is subtracted from the sum. With the new sum of 24, use the average formula to find the new average of the set:

$$\text{average} = \frac{\text{sum of terms}}{\text{number of terms}}$$

$$= \frac{24}{6}$$

$$= 4$$

Answer choice (D) is correct.

40. B

Sebastian finishes $\frac{1}{3}$ of his homework in 1.5 hours. This means that he will finish his whole assignment in three times this amount of time: $1.5 \times 3 = 4.5$ hours. He needs $4.5 - 1.5 = 3$ additional hours before 11:00 p.m. to complete the assignment, so he should start working no later than 8:00 p.m. Answer choice (B) is correct.

41. C

To tackle this question, start by filling in information on the figure. If $BC = x$, then $AB = 2x$. If $AB = 2x$, then $CD = 2x$. Now, find the total distance from A to D:

$$x + 2x + 2x = 55$$

$$5x = 55$$

$$x = 11$$

Segment BD is $11 + 22 = 33$ units long. Answer choice (C) is correct.

42. B

Supplementary angles by definition add up to 180 degrees. From there, set up an equation to solve for x:

$$180 = 3x + 7x$$

$$180 = 10x$$

$$18 = x$$

Be careful! The smaller angle is not just the measure of x. The total measure of the smaller angle is $3x$: $3 \times 18 = 54$ degrees. Answer choice (B) is correct.

43. D

According to the graph, each bag of money equals $50. Arianna has 6 money bags, so he saved $6 \times \$50 = \$300$. Kiran has 2 money bags, so he saved $2 \times \$50 = \$100$. Arianna saved $200 more than Kiran, so answer choice (D) is correct.

44. A

Dakota has 8 bags of money on the graph, so the total amount of money she saved was $8 \times \$50 = \$400$. Kiran saved $100, which means that Dakota saved 4 times more than Kiran, so answer choice (A) is correct.

45. A

If 20 percent of J is 1,500, then $0.20J = 1,500$ and $J = 7,500$. Multiply to determine the value of 15 percent of 7,500: $0.15 \times 7,500 = 1,125$. Answer choice (A) is correct.

46. C

You can tackle this question by either using combination or substitution. Be on the lookout for where combination is the quicker way to solve a system of equations question. Multiply the first equation by 6, so when you add it to the second equation, the y terms cancel out:

$$6(x - y) = 5(6)$$

$$6x - 6y = 30$$

Then, combine the two equations:

$$6x - 6y = 30$$
$$+(4x + 6y = 20)$$
$$\overline{10x = 50}$$
$$x = 5$$

If $x = 5$, then y must equal 0 because $x - y = 5$. To answer the question, find the sum: $x + y = 5$. Answer choice (C) is correct.

47. C

By adding the eight white, four red, seven green, and five blue, you have a total of 24 marbles. If eight are withdrawn, 16 remain in the bag. If the chance of drawing a white marble is now one-fourth, four white marbles remain in the bag, so 8 − 4 = 4 white marbles must have been drawn out. Answer choice (C) is correct.

Section 5—Essay

Use the follow sample essay to help review your own. Be sure to ask an adult who knows you to read your practice essay and give you feedback about how you did.

History is my favorite subject. I love reading about other times and thinking what it must be like to have lived then. When we studied the American Revolution, I remembered my family's visit to Colonial Williamsburg, where I imagined I was making candles, bringing water in from the well, and cooking over the open fire just as women did in those times. I imagined what it must have been like to live during a war without TV or radio to know what was happening. I thought about how frightening it must have been to hear a knock on the door, and not know if it was an American or a British soldier.

Imagining myself in the same position as people in the historical situations we study helps me to appreciate their courage and contributions. The founders of our country faced death if captured by the British. Anyone who helped American soldiers could be imprisoned. When I imagine myself in that colonial cabin, under those historical conditions, I stand in awe of what the founders did to let us live as an independent nation today.

My visit to the Gettysburg battleground was similarly moving. From the road, it just looks like a big open field. It doesn't seem very impressive at all. As you wander through the battlefield, though, something changes. About 150 years ago, America was torn apart by civil war. As that reality dawned on me, I began to think how terrible it would be to see brother pitted against brother, or father against son. The enormous loss of life at Gettysburg is a grim reminder that war should be a last, desperate resort for all nations.

Studying history helps me to better understand what is happening in the world today. When I hear about revolutions in other countries, I think of our American Revolution. Our revolution brought us freedom and independence from control by another country. When I hear about civil wars and uprisings, I think of the horrors of Gettysburg. Although the media tends to emphasize how different nations are, I think that every decent citizen in every country is working for the same things.

ISEE UPPER/MIDDLE LEVEL PRACTICE TEST 2: ASSESS YOUR STRENGTHS

Use the following tables to determine which topics and chapters you need to review most. If you need help with your essay, be sure to review Chapter 9: The Essay and Chapter 22: Writing Wrap-Up.

Topic	Question
Verbal: Synonyms	Section 1, questions 1–20
Verbal: Sentence Completions	Section 1, questions 21–40
Quantitative Reasoning: Word Problems	Section 2, questions 1–20
Quantitative Reasoning: Quantitative Comparisons	Section 2, questions 21–37
Reading Comprehension	Section 3, questions 1–36
Mathematics Achievement	Section 4, questions 1–47

Topic	Number of Questions on Test	Number Correct	If You Struggled with These Questions, Study...
Verbal: Synonyms	20		Chapter 7 and Chapters 18–19
Verbal: Sentence Completions	20		Chapter 4 and Chapters 18–19
Quantitative Reasoning: Word Problems	20		Chapters 10–15 and Chapters 20–21
Quantitative Reasoning: Quantitative Comparisons	17		Chapter 5 and Chapters 20–21
Reading Comprehension	36		Chapter 8 and Chapters 18–19
Mathematics Achievement	47		Chapters 10–15 and Chapters 20–21

CHAPTER 28

Scoring Your ISEE Practice Test

Your ISEE score is calculated by using a formula that cannot be directly applied to your practice tests. Therefore, it is impossible to provide a completely accurate score for your practice tests. Nevertheless, you'll understandably want to get an idea of how well you have performed.

Follow the steps described below to obtain a rough approximation of what your score on the actual ISEE might be. First, add up the number of questions you got correct. Questions that you answered incorrectly or left blank are worth zero points.

	Verbal Reasoning (40 questions total)	Quantitative Reasoning (37 questions total)	Reading Comprehension (36 questions total)	Mathematics Achievement (47 questions total)
Number of correct answers				

This is called your **raw score**. Next, take your raw score and look at the following charts, which *approximate* a conversion to a **scaled score**. A scaled score takes into account the range in difficulty level of the various editions of the test.

Again, while the following scores are close approximations, they do not reflect the official scores and percentiles used on the ISEE. Among other contributing factors, your actual test score will take into account the group of students to whom you will be compared to on your test administration.

UPPER LEVEL SCORES

Upper Level scores are based on a scale of 760–940 per section. Use the following approximate score conversions to gauge how well you have done on your practice tests.

Remember, if you are a Middle Level student, you should not expect to score as high as you would as an Upper Level student. No matter your score, you should focus on conducting in-depth reviews of all practice you complete, including this practice test.

Verbal Reasoning Scaled Score

Raw Score	Approximate Score	Raw Score	Approximate Score
35	925	17	873
34	922	16	870
33	919	15	867
32	917	14	864
31	914	13	861
30	911	12	859
29	908	11	856
28	905	10	853
27	902	9	850
26	899	8	847
25	896	7	843
24	893	6	841
23	890	5	838
22	888	4	835
21	885	3	832
20	882	2	829
19	879	1	826
18	876	0	823

Quantitative Reasoning Scaled Score

Raw Score	Approximate Score	Raw Score	Approximate Score
32	930	15	873
31	927	14	869
30	923	13	866
29	920	12	862
28	916	11	859
27	912	10	855
26	909	9	852
25	906	8	848
24	903	7	845
23	898	6	842
22	896	5	838
21	893	4	835
20	889	3	832
19	886	2	829
18	883	1	825
17	879	0	822
16	876		

Reading Comprehension Scaled Score

Raw Score	Approximate Score	Raw Score	Approximate Score
30	924	14	864
29	920	13	860
28	917	12	856
27	913	11	853
26	909	10	849
25	905	9	845
24	902	8	842
23	898	7	838
22	894	6	834
21	890	5	831
20	887	4	827
19	883	3	823
18	879	2	819
17	875	1	816
16	872	0	812
15	868		

Mathematics Scaled Score

Raw Score	Approximate Score	Raw Score	Approximate Score
42	935	20	876
41	932	19	873
40	930	18	870
39	927	17	868
38	924	16	865
37	922	15	862
36	919	14	860
35	916	13	857
34	913	12	854
33	911	11	852
32	908	10	849
31	905	9	846
30	903	8	843
29	900	7	841
28	897	6	838
27	895	5	835
26	892	4	833
25	889	3	830
24	887	2	827
23	884	1	824
22	881	0	822
21	878		